FOURTH EDITION

Collective Bargaining and Labor Relations

E. Edward Herman

University of Cincinnati

Prentice Hall, Upper Saddle River, New Jersey 07632

Vice President/Editorial Director: *James Boyd*
Editor-in-Chief: *Natalie Anderson*
Associate Editor: *Lisamarie Brassini*
Editorial Assistant: *Crissy Statuto*
Marketing Manager: *Stephanie Johnson*
Production Editor: *Judith Leale*
Managing Editor: *Dee Josephson*
Manufacturing Manager: *Vincent Scelta*
Manufacturing Supervisor: *Arnold Vila*
Manufacturing Buyer: *Diane Peirano*
Cover Design: *Bruce Kenselaar*

Library of Congress Cataloging-in-Publication Data
Herman, E. Edward
     Collective bargaining and labor relations / E. Edward Herman.—
   4th ed.
        p.   cm.
     Includes bibliographical references and index.
     ISBN 0-13-296963-7 (hardbound)
     1. Collective bargaining—United States.   2. Industrial relations—
   United States.   I. Title.
   HD6508.H43   1997
   331.89′0973—dc21   97-13897
                                                                    CIP

Prentice-Hall International (UK) Limited, London
Prentice-Hall of Australia Pty. Limited, Sydney
Prentice-Hall Canada, Inc., Toronto
Prentice-Hall Hispanoamericana, S.A., Mexico
Prentice-Hall of India Private Limited, New Delhi
Prentice-Hall of Japan, Inc., Tokyo
Simon & Schuster Asia Pte. Ltd., Singapore
Editora Prentice-Hall do Brasil, Ltda., Rio de Janeiro

Printed in the United States of America

10   9   8   7   6   5   4   3   2   1

Contents

Preface

The fourth edition of *Collective Bargaining and Labor Relations* has been significantly updated and revised. The book contains a number of totally new chapters and sections on some of the following topics: the current state of and future outlook for the labor movement; mutual gains bargaining; ethics; the role of computers in collective bargaining; and the report and recommendations of the Commission on the Future of Worker-Management Relations. The book reflects the major changes that have taken place in labor relations and collective bargaining in the last 5 years. At the same time, it retains much of the rich institutional detail that puts current developments into perspective.

The field of collective bargaining and labor relations is dynamic and thus in continuous transition. Substantial changes have taken place in our work environment since the earlier editions of this text. The workplace is in a state of rapid change and is becoming more complex and competitive. The magnitude of the transformation taking place is apparent from the following list of changes and developments contained in the recent report of the Commission on the Future of Worker Management Relations, the Dunlop report:

1. Globalization of the U.S. economy
2. Increased international competitiveness of U.S. companies
3. Changing work technology
4. A shift of employment from goods-producing to service-producing sectors
5. A change in the labor force occupational skill mix
6. The impact of deregulation
7. Reduced government expenditures for defense and for other programs
8. A large influx of women into the work force
9. An increased representation of minorities in the workforce
10. A changed aged structure in the work force
11. An increased number of immigrants from developing countries
12. High levels of unemployment for the less skilled
13. Increased insecurity about jobs, particularly because of downsizing in both the public and private sectors
14. Falling real compensation for male workers, accompanied by stagnant real hourly compensation for all workers
15. A widening earning gap between higher- and lower-paid and better- and less-educated workers
16. Stagnation in the earning gap between white and nonwhite workers
17. An increasing number of jobs that diverge from the model of a full-time position with a single employer

The aforementioned changes, as well as global political developments, new and proposed labor legislation, and revised interpretations and applications of existing laws have all had—and will continue to have—impact on labor relations and collective bargaining in the United States. This edition attempts to capture the effects of these and other developments on the status of labor relations and collective bargaining. The statistical material contained in this volume and the comprehensive bibliography have been updated. The bibliography includes a section on electronic resources such as CD/ROMs, list servers, and web sites covering labor topics. Also, the latest research findings on subjects covered here have been incorporated into this book.

MAJOR CONTENT CHANGES

Some of the major content changes and additions to the fourth edition are found in Chapters 2, 9, 12, 13, and 17. These changes are described in the following paragraphs.

Chapter 2 contains new material on the state of the labor movement as well as on trends and patterns in union membership. It includes the latest statistics, gathered in 1995 and released in 1996, on labor organization membership and on union affiliation by age, sex, race, Hispanic origin, occupation, and industry. The chapter evaluates the outlook for the labor movement in the 1990s and beyond. It also examines union responses to current challenges, union organizing strategies, and benefits of unionization. One section also reviews the August 1, 1995, change in leadership of the AFL-CIO.

The negotiation process is the theme of Chapter 9, which, in several new sections, addresses the following topics: mutual gains bargaining, principled and traditional negotiations, joint gains, and win-win agreements; criticisms of mutual gains bargaining; and the transformation of the traditional labor management system and its impact on mutual gains bargaining. A new appendix presents the Colosi model of the bargaining process.

Computers and the collective bargaining process are the subject of Chapter 12. The following sections are incorporated in this chapter: costing of labor agreements; caveats for computer users; the electronic meeting system; generation of options or brainstorming by computer; transaction processing, expert systems, and decision support systems; software for drafting of agreements; and various computer programs for collective bargaining.

Chapter 13 covers ethical and unethical conduct and the collective bargaining process. The chapter comprises the following sections: ethical behavior in negotiations; distributive and integrative tactics and strategies; trust and ethics; the Pre-Negotiation Ethics Workshop, a totally new concept; two requirements of ethics; and respect for individual rights.

The report, recommendations, and impact of the Commission on the Future of Worker-Management Relations, referred to as the Dunlop Commission, are the subject of the last chapter of the book. It covers the following topics: societal demands on the workplace, new forms of work organization, legal issues regarding workplace employee involvement and participation, the role of unions in society, alternative forms of dispute resolution, arbitration, and the future of the American work force.

PRODUCT DIFFERENTIATION AND ORGANIZATION OF THIS BOOK

In addition to the major content changes just outlined, the book also provides in-depth coverage of a number of areas that are either omitted or underemphasized in other texts. Specifically, the reader is directed to the following chapters: "Some Effects of the Law on

Unions and Management," Chapter 4; "Management and Union Security," Chapter 6; "Bargaining Structure," Chapter 7; "Preparation for Bargaining," Chapter 8; and "Costing of Labor Contracts," Chapter 11. The text also includes recent arbitration cases addressing current issues, as well as a new bargaining simulation.

The highlights of Chapters 2, 9, 12, 13, and 17 were reviewed in the previous section, which summarized some of the major content changes in this edition. The remaining chapters, the simulation, and the arbitration cases are briefly described in the following paragraphs.

Chapter 1 discusses the development and growth of the labor movement. It reviews the emergence of the first unions; examines different types of unions; and discusses the Knights of Labor, the development of the American Federation of Labor, the IWW, and the separation and reunification of the AFL-CIO.

Chapter 3 presents the legal context within which unions and management operate. An examination of the evolution of this framework begins with the period of opposition to unions, including the Conspiracy Doctrine, the injunction, and the Sherman and Clayton Anti-Trust Acts. Next the period of support for unions, including passage of the Norris-LaGuardia and Wagner Acts, is reviewed. The focus then shifts to the period of control, during which the Taft-Hartley and Landrum-Griffin Acts and the Health Care Amendments were enacted. This chapter also provides a review and a critique, and it describes attempts at reform of the current law.

Chapter 4 evaluates the effects of the law on representation election, outcomes, bargaining power, and the attitudes of the parties toward bargaining. It analyzes the effects of the law on union and management security. It examines the current legal status of primary strikes, lockouts, secondary boycotts, and picketing. The chapter also assesses the effects of the law on union organizing. Finally, it addresses the question of whether the law fosters "mature" bargaining.

Chapter 5 treats the organizational structures of unions and employers. It looks at the local, national, and international unions and at the structure of the AFL-CIO. It also examines democracy in unions and problems associated with it. In reviewing management organizational structure, it examines the environmental constraints within which employers operate and the internal dimensions of organizations, including different forms and styles of management. The chapter also evaluates the attitudes of small, intermediate, and large employers toward unions.

Chapter 6 addresses the nature, status, and various dimensions of union and management security. The first part explores the problems, rationale, and allocation of managerial prerogatives. It treats the topics of interest and ability in the making of managerial decisions. One section evaluates the concept of secure versus insecure management and its effect on collective bargaining. Finally, background factors and patterns and trends in management security are reviewed. The second part of the chapter, on union security, poses the question of how much and what kinds of security are necessary for the union to function effectively. The relationships among union function, union responsibilities, union security, and the state of labor relations are analyzed; various forms of union security are presented and analyzed.

The bargaining unit and the structure of collective bargaining are the focus of Chapter 7. Formal and informal bargaining units are defined and evaluated. Bargaining units prevalent in various industries are examined. The chapter reviews the influence of employers, unions, and the NLRB on the dimensions of bargaining units. The pros and cons of different bargaining structures are discussed from the perspectives of various stakeholders.

Chapter 8 addresses the subject of preparation for bargaining. It covers the following topics: the composition, size, and selection of teams of union and management negotiators; the preparation and value of bargaining and economic data; the role of bargaining books; the formulation of union and management proposals and demands; tactical preparations for bargaining; and development of negotiating procedures.

Chapter 10 provides a theoretical framework that complements the practical aspects of negotiation presented in previous chapters. A review of bargaining theory is followed by an extensive review of two theoretical works: the Walton and McKersie behavioral theory of labor negotiations and Alfred Kuhn's model on transactions and power. We apply the Kuhn model to the negotiation process to examine and evaluate the impact of strike threats on the thinking and behavior of negotiators at the bargaining table. In the author's view, one cannot comprehend the process of collective bargaining and the various social interactions that it embodies without a notion of the theoretical foundations of this process.

Chapter 11 covers contract costing, a subject that until recently was absent from almost all texts. The understanding of contract costing is important for both unions and management. The computer revolution and the increasing number of sophisticated, quantitatively trained specialists occupying managerial positions is conducive to the shifting of many labor relations decisions away from labor relations personnel to actuaries, accountants, economists, and finance experts, most of whom lack background in labor relations. To prevent such a shift in responsibilities, labor relations staffs need a thorough understanding of finance and costing. To be effective at the bargaining table, union negotiators must possess the quantitative expertise mandated by the advent of the computer.

Every provision of a contract can have cost implications. Part of the preparation process is to decide on costing approaches and methodology that can be utilized during bargaining. Chapter 11 examines issues related to the costing of labor contracts, including different components of the compensation package. One section analyzes and critically reviews various methods that can be applied for costing wage and benefit proposals. Concepts such as elasticity of demand, present value, and discounted cash flow formulae are discussed and their implications for costing examined. Readers desiring more detailed coverage of contract costing will find a costing appendix at the end of the chapter.

Chapter 14 reviews dispute resolution and regulation. It discusses the level and implications of strike activity in the United States. The trends in the magnitude of strikes are examined, along with the presence of strike substitutes and supplements. Recognizing that potential for a bargaining impasse exists in every negotiation, the chapter incorporates a section on various methods of impasse resolution. Specifically, it examines mediation, fact finding, interest and final offer arbitration, and alternative impasse resolution methods. It also evaluates public interest in impasse resolution. Other topics treated in this chapter are strike prohibitions, compulsory waiting periods, and emergency procedures.

Chapter 15 covers contract administration. It explores the meaning and nature of organizational government, examines the judicial process and organizational jurisprudence, and reviews the steps and functions of the grievance procedure. Substantial attention is devoted to the operation and implementation of the grievance procedure and of the grievance arbitration process. The chapter also reviews grievance procedures in nonunion settings as well as the linkage between grievance procedures and the performance of firms.

Collective bargaining in the public sector is the subject of Chapter 16. This chapter reviews the growth of collective bargaining in the public sector and factors responsible for that growth. It covers federal, state, and local legislation governing public employees. It also evaluates the structure and operation of administrative agencies, unfair labor practices, determination of bargaining units, elections, and certification procedures. Other subjects addressed are the process and scope of bargaining in the public sector, major unions in the public sector, the sovereignty doctrine, union security, and the right to strike.

The text contains a new, comprehensive collective bargaining simulation based on actual negotiations in the grocery supermarkets industry. The simulation contains background information on the company and the union, financial data, present contract terms, instructions for negotiations, work sheets, role profiles, and evaluation questionnaires. Simulation participants are referred to external data sources that can be of assistance in their negotiations. Simulation instructions are available to adopters of this book.

The simulation has been successfully tested on students with and without background in labor relations as well as on managers from large corporations, some of whom have had significant negotiation experience. The response from the various groups has been excellent; the participants have highly endorsed the simulation as a teaching tool. The simulation, as contrasted with some others on the market, is structured so that it is never out-of-date. The accompanying work sheets permit instructors and students to utilize the latest published statistical data for simulation purposes.

A computer disk using spreadsheets to cost out economic items in the simulation will be available to the adopters of the text. The spreadsheets are set up in Microsoft Excel and follow the format of the worksheets provided with the simulation. The software was designed to make calculations on the costing worksheets simple so that participants can concentrate on negotiating the contract rather than on arithmetic and computations. The simulation does not have to rely on a computer; it can utilize the enclosed worksheets instead.

Negotiations do not end when a settlement is reached and an agreement is signed. Collective bargaining is a continuous process consisting of contract negotiations, administration, interpretation, and—at times—arbitration. The latter part of this book includes recent arbitration cases that illustrate such current workplace issues as drug testing, alcoholism, discipline, just cause, and discharges. The arbitration awards for these cases are included in the *Instructor's Manual.*

Every author faces hard choices in deciding what to include. The advantages of intensive coverage of the areas presented here outweigh those of an encyclopedic volume with briefer coverage of more numerous topics. Most chapters of this text are self-contained, giving instructors the flexibility to use chapters in whatever sequence best meets their needs. The book is intended for both undergraduate and master's students in industrial relations, collective bargaining, and labor-management relations courses. Many of the chapters should also be useful for labor relations practitioners. The text is designed to be complete without supplements, although some instructors may want to provide their own selections of readings.

The book is dedicated to my parents, Alice and Paul, my wife Halina, my daughter Diane Jacqueline, my son Robert Joseph, and the co-author of the first edition of this book, Alfred Kuhn.

"He that flies from his own family has far to travel."

(Longe fuit, quisquis suos fugit.)

Petronius, Satyricon, Sec. 43

Acknowledgments

I would like to express my appreciation and acknowledge the contributions and ideas received from my colleagues at the University of Cincinnati: Professors Howard M. Leftwich, Philip K. Way, and Sourushe Zandvakili. I would also like to thank Professor and Head, Joseph C. Gallo for his support. I am grateful to the following individuals: Professor Michael Marmo for reviewing the manuscript and making useful suggestions; to Professor Steven H. Kropp for revisions of Chapter 16; to Professor Robert Faaborg for his contribution to the subject of ethical and unethical conduct in Collective Bargaining; to Mr. Thomas R. Colosi, Vice President for National Affairs of the American Arbitration Association; and to Ms. Lois Gant, graduate student, for providing the material for Appendix A in Chapter 9; to Messrs Thomas B. Murphy, Group Vice President of the Kroger Company, and Brad Tomich, Manager of Labor Relations, for their written comments on costing a collective bargaining agreement. I am appreciative of the assistance received from Messrs Ed Verst and Earl Ledford, attorneys in the regional office of the NLRB in Cincinnati.

I would like to thank Mr. Louis J. Manchise, Commissioner FMCS, for all his contributions and ideas, particularly to the Collective Bargaining Simulation. I would also like to acknowledge the contribution to the simulation of Mr. Victor Horn, Director of Human Resources and Labor Relations of the Kroger Company, and Mr. Lenny Wyatt, President of Local 1099 of the United Food and Commercial Workers International Union.

I would particularly like to express my thanks to Ronald L. Seeber for his contribution as coauthor of the second edition and to Joshua L. Schwarz for his contribution as coauthor of the third edition.

During my sabbatical from the University of Cincinnati, I was appointed as a visiting scholar at the Massachusetts Institute of Technology, (1990–91), and at Harvard University (1991). These appointments provided me with a unique opportunity to interact with colleagues and to attend various graduate classes, workshops and seminars both at M.I.T. and at Harvard. Some of the thoughts and ideas contained in these pages are the result of those interactions. My very special thanks go to Professors Thomas A. Kochan and Robert B. McKersie of M.I.T. for their stimulating classes and for their friendship, and to Professor David Kuechli of Harvard University for all of his help. I would also like to express my appreciation to Professor Roger Fisher of the Harvard Law School for permitting me to participate in his excellent workshop on negotiation.

I gratefully acknowledge the help of my graduate students who have contributed to the current edition of this book. I especially wish to thank the following graduate students: Andy Assaley, Michele Barregarye, Catherine Conniff, Cindi Cox, Pamela Esterkamp, Kimberly Hamlin, James Hess, Dimitrinia Ispiridonova, Christa Jannides, Sandra Jennings, Erik Karmol, Jane Linden, Kevin Luken, Sharon Maul, Michael Ongkiko, David Sorg. I am also indebted to all those students who contributed to previous editions of this text and provided me with valuable comments for its revision.

I gratefully acknowledge and thank Mr. Philip R. Dankert, Collection Development Librarian at Cornell University, for his excellent contribution in preparing the glossary and an extensive labor relations, labor law and collective bargaining bibliography, including a listing of electronic resources.

I would like to express my thanks to the following individuals at Prentice Hall: Natalie Anderson, Editor-in-Chief, Judy Leale, Production Editor, and Helen Guinn for securing the necessary permissions. Thanks also to the people at Impressions Book and Journal Services, Inc., and to Jean Tucker for her copyediting skills.

My heartfelt appreciation is extended to Mrs. Geri Kirchner, an outstanding secretary and a great human being; who flawlessly typed the multiple revisions of this manuscript. Thanks.

Finally, but not least, my wife, Halina, deserves a special gratitude for her understanding and moral support. The real cost of the book to us were all the weekends, holidays, and evenings during which we were not able to do things together.

CHAPTER 1

Development and Growth of the Labor Movement

After reading this chapter, you should be able to

■ Distinguish between job-oriented and class-oriented approaches to unionism.

■ Understand the reasons for the success of early craft unions and the failure of cooperatives.

■ Describe the philosophy of the AFL at the time it was founded.

■ Comprehend the role of the CIO in organizing industrial workers.

■ Explain the reasons for the merger of the AFL and the CIO.

THE LABOR MOVEMENT

The development, growth, and survival of an institution such as the labor movement depends on several conditions. First, there must be some initial and continuing urge to seek new modes of behavior. Second, experimentation with new methods must take place. Third, those particular experiments that show significant success must be continued and repeated, and the failures must be discontinued.

The Industrial Revolution created unsatisfactory consequences that lasted a long time, and the succeeding century or so witnessed many exploratory activities of American working people as they tried to find some "better way" to improve their wages and working conditions. The following discussion is not so much a history of the American labor movement as a selection, largely chronological, of the experiments and experiences from which American unions learned certain lessons. It is those lessons that have shaped the structure and behavior of the labor movement as we know it today. (The legal aspects of labor history will be treated in Chapter 3.)

THE BARGAINING APPROACH VERSUS THE OWNERSHIP APPROACH

Before the Industrial Revolution, nonagricultural production took place largely through a craft system, regulated by a guild in each major craft. Significantly, once people completed their apprenticeships and became journeyman workers, they owned their own tools and had considerable freedom to move to different shops or to set up shop for themselves.

After the Industrial Revolution, people had to work with machines, not tools. For all practical purposes, workers lost the freedom to own their tools or to become their own bosses.

Following this loss of ownership of the tools of production, workers saw two possible remedies to their plight. One was to accept the loss of ownership and seek to bargain better terms from the new owners—an alternative called the *bargaining approach.* The other was to seek to regain ownership of the tools—the *ownership approach.* Because individual workers had little or no bargaining power under the new industrial system, successful bargaining required collective action. Individual workers also lacked the financial resources to own the new machines; hence, ownership would also have to be established collectively. Either approach seemed to require collective action, and this necessity led workers to form unions.

Job Orientation versus Class Orientation

To the extent that workers think of their problems as specific to their own jobs, firms, or industries and seek solutions at that level, their thinking is said to be job oriented and their programs job-wide in scope. Other, global problems confront workers in many crafts and industries. All receive their incomes mainly from wages rather than from interest, rents, or dividends. Many know the fear of unemployment: Few jobs are wholly safe from technological change, plant relocation, or administrative shakeup. All workers take orders rather than give them. All know that displeasing the boss may have serious consequences. Most know the difficulties of trying to live on a modest income. Off-the-job differences between boss and workers are apparent in most industries. Although it is not possible to draw a precise line between them, workers do not doubt that two groups exist and that they live in different worlds.

To the extent that workers see their problems and the possible solutions as common to all workers but different from the problems of employers, workers are class oriented, and their programs are class-wide in scope. They also can then be said to display employee consciousness. Employees and unions can, of course, think simultaneously in terms of both job and class and pursue programs at both levels. The real question is this: Which dominates their thinking and commands their major efforts?

The distinction between job and class orientations is not peculiar to workers. Associations of doctors, lawyers, personnel managers, or teachers reflect a job orientation, as do trade associations. On the other hand, the United States Chamber of Commerce and the National Association of Manufacturers reflect a class orientation because they unite employers across occupations and industries in efforts to deal with problems of interest to all employers.

Four Groups of Reactions

The thinking and behavior of unions can be classified into four approaches: job-oriented bargaining, class-oriented bargaining, job-oriented ownership, and class-oriented ownership. Although these four categories do not encompass all types of behavior, they nevertheless provide a useful framework within which to view the various experiments of the labor movement during its first century or so, and they seem to provide a more workable set of categories than Commons' two-way distinction between job-conscious and class-conscious unions.[1]

Let us illustrate the terms. A union following the job-oriented bargaining approach will seek concessions for its members from their employers; it may also strive to improve the economic position of the industry or occupation. Workers following a class-oriented bargaining approach would tend to form a single, strongly centralized union through which all workers would deal simultaneously with all employers, at least on major issues. Class-oriented and job-oriented bargainers might also use political or other pressures to win concessions from private employers. Laws governing minimum wage, unemployment compensation, Social Security, pensions, occupational safety and health, and family leave illustrate the use of government as a means of extracting concessions from private employers for the benefit of all workers. There is also a class-oriented and job-oriented interest in laws that regulate collective bargaining because they affect bargaining power, and hence concessions, for many different unions. Class-oriented unions following the ownership approach may advocate public ownership of important industries and perhaps of all industry. In the last 10 years, the idea of employees having ownership interest in the firms for which they work has gained some acceptance. Stock options, a common element of executive compensation, are used more frequently to compensate nonmanagerial employees as well. Employee stock ownership plans (ESOPS) are now available to many employees.

Job-oriented workers may also follow the ownership approach. They might, for example, purchase the plant in which they work and operate it as a producer cooperative.

HISTORICAL DEVELOPMENT OF THE AMERICAN LABOR MOVEMENT

In Europe at the start of the Industrial Revolution, labor was plentiful, whereas land and capital were scarce. In America land was plentiful, whereas labor and capital were comparatively scarce. With land plentiful and agriculture unmechanized, dissatisfied American wage workers had more opportunity than their European counterparts to leave their jobs and carve out homesteads. Although the obstacles were often formidable, self-employment was a feasible alternative to wage employment to a greater degree and for a longer time in America than in Europe. Individual bargaining power was greater here, and the need for unions was less acute. Accordingly, unions did not originate as soon or with as much vigor as in Europe. And when they did get under way, they placed greater confidence in bargaining and less in ownership. However, the fact that American workers had not lived through the transition from the feudal to the industrial system did not seriously mitigate the impact of industrialization when it finally arrived.

The First Unions

Strikes and labor disturbances in America are considerably older than unions, dating back as far as 1636. The Company of Shoemakers was granted a charter by the Colony of the Massachusetts Bay in 1648, and the coopers were granted a charter at the same time, the former, at least, operating after the fashion of a guild rather than a union, with power to maintain quality but not to raise prices.[2] In New York, journeyman tailors struck successfully in 1768, and journeyman printers demanded and received a wage increase in 1778. Although many other such isolated actions are recorded, the first union (that is, a continuous association) was that of the shoemakers in Philadelphia, formed in 1792. In 1793 and 1794, respectively, the carpenters and shoemakers formed organizations in Boston. In 1794 the printers organized in New York, as did their counterparts in Philadelphia in 1802. During the next 15 years, unions of one or more of the trades already mentioned, plus those of bakers, tailors, and others, were formed in most important cities in the United States. Some succeeded in obtaining wage increases, some got work hours reduced to 10 a day, and some prevented their employers from hiring journeymen from other towns at cut rates. These early unions were all confined to skilled trades. As will be noted in Chapter 3, some interesting legal cases arose during this period, notably the Cordwainers' (shoemakers') case in 1806.

In 1806 the Industrial Revolution had not yet had any significant impact on the American scene, but a widening market did put pressure on wage rates. When most commodities were produced for local consumption and sold directly at the shop, the master could pay a fair wage and charge a price to cover it. But by this period, some goods merchants were purchasing in large volume from those employers who would sell at the lowest prices. The merchants then shipped the goods to distant points for sale. Producers were thus put into direct competition with other producers in distant places, and the producers were forced by the merchants to bid against one another. Employers were then under greater pressure to cut wages. Thus, extension of the market fed the workers' urge to form unions as a means of self-defense.

Although "the colonists did not establish many societies modeled on the English guilds . . . a number were organized and thrived."[3] Apparently, nowhere except in Scandinavia did a guild evolve into a trade union. As organizations reflecting the unity of work and ownership, the guilds died a natural death when work and ownership were separated. Unions and trade associations are the contemporary organizations that represent the now separated interests of workers and owners, respectively.

This first round of unionism in the United States lasted from about 1790 to 1815 and was local in scope. All traces of unions as collective bargaining agencies disappeared during the depression that followed the War of 1812, although a few survived as social and beneficial organizations. From this first round, American workers learned that job-oriented collective bargaining with an employer can produce immediate and significant gains. They learned at the same time that depression can be lethal, at least to a locally based union.

A Different Type of Union

The Declaration of Independence had stated that all men were created equal and that life, liberty, and the pursuit of happiness were inalienable rights. But an apparent discrepancy between these brave words and the facts of life had brought much discontent. By the late 1820s, this feeling came to a head in the election of Andrew Jackson and the ensuing "era of the common man." The thinking of the time was largely class-wide.

Working people then suffered many difficulties now long forgotten. They could be imprisoned for debt. They could rarely obtain education for themselves or their children. They were paid in a variety of currencies of changing and uncertain value. They often worked 14 to 16 hours a day, and they held a low priority among the ranks of creditors if an employer happened to go bankrupt while owing them wages. Problems of this kind could be approached only through politics, not through bargaining with employers. In consequence, a variety of working people's parties were formed; they achieved notable success during the 1820s and 1830s in bringing free public education, banking reform, mechanics' lien laws, the elimination of imprisonment for debt, and the political franchise for white males who did not own property.

A number of local, job-wide craft unions formed during this second round were able to improve the conditions of workers at their jobs, as had the unions of the first round. But above and beyond those unions were local or regional class-wide organizations that tried to encompass workers of various kinds. The broad class coverage of unions founded during this period was useful for attacking the particular problems of the moment. But the membership was too diverse to hold together once the aims were accomplished. Most of these "unions" disappeared in the early 1830s, primarily because they were unable to do much successful bargaining with employers. Their legacy was a conviction that class-based organizations can be effective in dealing with certain kinds of broad problems but that they are ineffective in the bread-and-butter issues of winning specific concessions from employers. With the exception of some limited ventures into the field of producer cooperatives, the ownership approach was largely absent during this period.

The Appearance of National Unions

Partly because of the inability of the class-based unions to deal satisfactorily with employers, a third wave of unions got under way in 1834, building upon and adding to the group of unions that had been started in the preceding years. These new bodies were organized on the same craft base as the first-round unions and grew rapidly to a total of about 300,000 members—a rather impressive number, considering the size of the population. Within two years, each major city displayed from a half dozen to more than 50 different craft unions. Many bargained successfully on wages and hours. Because the broadening of the market was now accentuated by the wide development of canals and railroads, the workers in a local union in one city often found their wages limited by the wages paid to similar workers in other cities. They therefore began combining into national craft unions to prevent competitive wage cutting. The National Trades Union was formed in New York in 1834. It was a notable achievement for its time, presaging much that was to happen later, even though the particular organization apparently lasted only two or three years. Despite their wide geographic scope, such national unions were job oriented in that they confined their attention to a single type of worker.

Some awareness of class-wide problems was reflected in the joining of unions of different crafts at the local level into a city central, currently known also as a central labor union or central labor council. In 1834 an attempt was made to form a federation of national unions to deal with broader problems, but the federation lasted only a few months. The local federations and the attempted national-level federation did not represent an abandonment of job-oriented unionism, however. The individual local and national unions retained their independence and strength; the federation activities supplemented rather than supplanted the individual unions.

The depression and panic of 1837 hit suddenly and lasted more than a decade. With this shock, virtually the entire labor movement collapsed—national, city central, and local. The disappearance of these unions was attributable to adverse surrounding conditions; their performance, while they lasted, was good. It became part of the record from which later leaders learned their lessons.

The Ownership Approach in Action

The psychological state induced by the depression, along with the scarcity of jobs to be bargained about and the active interest of a group of intellectuals, produced a strong wave of humanitarian schemes centering on the cooperative communities recommended by the Englishman Robert Owen or the Frenchman François Fourier. Although about 50 of these communities were founded, all were eventually abandoned. Poor financing and heavy fixed charges accounted for many failures. Lack of managerial ability, internal dissension, and lack of common sense helped dissolve others. The refusal of private business (which thought them subversive) to sell them materials hastened the collapse of several.

The ineffectiveness of bargaining during this depressed period led to another variation on the ownership theme. Starting in 1836 with a worker-owned shoe factory in Philadelphia, producer cooperatives multiplied during the 1840s and 1850s, especially after a wave of unsuccessful strikes in 1851 and 1852. These ventures lasted about as long as their half-brothers, the cooperative communities; most became insolvent, and those that were successful took in hired employees and gradually lost their cooperative identities. They succeeded mainly in sapping the energies and funds of the unions that sponsored them, leaving the unions ill prepared to bargain collectively when that task again presented itself.

At the same time another movement, not subject to the same defect, got well under way with the sponsorship of unions and other sympathizers. This was the consumer cooperative movement. Run in the interests of its customers, the consumer cooperative has the single-minded objective of producing at lowest cost, with no undue concern for the welfare of its employees. In fact, the employees of a cooperative might themselves organize to bargain collectively with its management. The Civil War largely destroyed the movement, and except for farm cooperatives, credit unions, and miscellaneous other cooperatives, this institution has not fulfilled its early promise in the United States, though agricultural cooperatives have been more successful than other types of cooperatives. In England and Scandinavia, however, cooperatives have become a potent economic force and are closely allied to the union movement. The experiences with both consumer and producer cooperatives are detailed by Perlman.[4]

In the past, even during periods of deep disillusionment over the prospects of collective bargaining, attempts to use the ownership approach were usually limited and individualistic. They involved only small groups banded together to make their way cooperatively in a free and uncontrolled economy. These groups assumed that the worker had the opportunity to improve his lot if only he would apply the proper method. Each group tried to improve the well-being of its own members within the existing system but did not work toward uprooting the system.

During the period from roughly 1830 to 1850, the major exceptions to this general tendency were embodied in the doctrines of Thomas Skidmore and George Henry Evans. Early in this period, Skidmore advocated the equal division of all wealth among all citizens, along with the provision that the wealth be passed on in equal shares to each succeeding generation. Skidmore's ideological successor Evans proposed merely the equal division of land. He later softened his program, asking only that government lands in the West be available free to small settlers, not gobbled up by wealthy speculators.

These two movements originated among intellectuals, not workers. They were not heavily espoused by unions, for the community at large registered strong disapproval of tampering with the ownership of property. However, most working people did support the move for homestead laws, which would permit them to acquire unsettled lands at little or no cost. The agrarian and homestead movement was the focal point of working-class efforts during much of the nineteenth century. Once again, we note how abundant land diluted the urge for unions.

All in all, experience up to this point indicated (1) the success of narrowly conceived craft unions bargaining with their employers over mundane affairs of daily existence; (2) the success of political action for class-wide objectives but the impermanence of an organization based primarily on such objectives and accepting a heterogeneous membership; (3) the failure of cooperative communities and cooperative enterprises from internal and apparently inherent weaknesses, as well as their high cost to unions; and (4) the strong objection from the community at large to schemes that threatened property rights. Experience also led to a general distrust among workers of intellectuals and all their works. As to "heroic" long-run goals, the prospective task of subduing the West was heroic enough to subvert the notion of remolding the whole society under workers' control long before that notion moved from the field of thought to effective action.

The Arrival of Permanent Unions and Federations

The Industrial Revolution in the United States may be dated roughly from 1840. By 1850 it was beginning to have real impact, with railroads, steel making, factories, and rapid growth of employees in manufacturing industries. By 1850 prosperity had returned, bringing with it improved prospects of gains through bargaining. Once again came a wave of new unions—the fourth—this time with stronger emphasis on national organizations. Collective bargaining became firmly established in a number of industries. Indeed, some of the unions established during the nineteenth century have operated continuously ever since.

Many unions were destroyed by the depression of 1857 and some others by the turbulent conditions of the early Civil War years. During the later years of the war, however, a high demand for labor combined with rapid inflation—in which real wages dropped by about a third—to produce a new drive for unionism. Again there appeared a multitude of locals, city centrals, and national unions, along with a quasi federation called the National Labor Union, which started in 1866 and lasted six years. By 1870 some 30 national unions were in existence. Most dated from the Civil War, but some had survived from the previous decade.

There is no need to trace the ups and downs of the labor movement during the next few decades. Industrialism was on the march. Big business was beginning to hit its stride. Workers were still confused and divided over how to protect their interests. Each era of prosperity brought renewed emphasis on bargaining, which produced tangible gains. Each depression brought renewed emphasis on ownership, which produced confusion and depleted treasuries. During the last decades of the nineteenth century, the Iron Molders alone, under W. H. Sylvis, established at least 10 cooperative foundries. Unions set up similar enterprises in a score of other fields. Like the cooperatives of the 1840s, these too failed, leaving the sponsoring unions disillusioned and penniless. Although a few unions (mainly in railroads, building, printing, and machining) held rather closely to straight collective bargaining, most unions wandered regularly into other activities. During the 1870s and thereafter, the goal of unionism was further confused by the introduction of a Marxist-socialist element that actively struggled for but never gained control of the American labor movement.

The Knights of Labor

Amid the confusion of the 1870s and 1880s, two attempts at federation, one temporary and one permanent, stand out. The Knights of Labor was formed in Philadelphia in 1869. It remained a small and secret organization for almost 15 years, until a combination of circumstances brought a rapid increase to about two-thirds of a million members. Under the leadership of Terrence V. Powderly, this organization accepted unskilled labor, the self-employed, and indeed virtually any gainfully employed people except gamblers, saloon keepers, bankers, and a few other groups. The Knights hoped to improve the lot of working people through legislation, land reform, banking reform, producers' cooperatives, and an attack on monopoly. It did not officially approve of strikes, although it did conduct some successful ones, notably a strike against the Wabash Railroad, a part of the financial empire of Jay Gould. Gould's capitulation in 1886 marked the high point of this organization.

In due time, it was discovered that so diffuse an organization could not concentrate adequately on the particular needs of any of its component groups. In fact, the needs of some conflicted directly with those of others. In addition, members of craft unions that had affiliated with the Knights were faced with dual loyalty and double expense. By 1887 the membership and influence of the Knights had started to decline.

The American Federation of Labor

Meanwhile, the craft unions had started a new organization, the American Federation of Labor. Growing out of an organization begun in 1881, the AFL was founded in 1886. It soon became and has since remained a significant American labor organization, now known as the AFL-CIO. The federation was molded by the personality and beliefs of Samuel Gompers, who remained president for all but one year until his death in 1924. Despite Gompers's opposition to the Knights of Labor and friction between the Knights and the AFL, the interaction between the two organizations probably contributed to the development of the AFL. Though Gompers was heavily steeped in and partially sympathetic toward socialism, he had been convinced by previous events that strong and permanent unions could exist in the United States only if they stuck to job-oriented bargaining. According to Gompers, the unit of union structure must be a group of people having closely similar interests, which meant to him that they must belong to the same craft. They must eschew ownership ideas because these notions attack the prevailing concept of property and can generate powerful public resistance. Unions must make contracts with employers and scrupulously abide by them, just as do suppliers of other employer needs. Although they must not hesitate to strike, unions must largely accept the world of business as it is and in turn be businesslike in dealing with employers. If the basic union is to have the desired homogeneous membership, the importance and independence of the individual unions must be preserved. The federation must remain a loose agency of coordination with little real power. Gompers put great emphasis on the autonomy of the separate national unions and on the strict preservation of their jurisdictional lines. Because the AFL was a loose and relatively weak federation, its importance lay not so much in its actions as in the philosophy it gave the union movement.

It was recognized that, because government could inhibit the ability of unions to exist, grow, and strike, unions must pay attention to politics. But this attention should be confined to supporting candidates who espoused labor's aims rather than taking the form of permanent attachment to a political party. Government help should not be sought in the economic sphere because such action would encourage government interference and culminate in the public control of unions. By attending mainly to strong unionization, not to politics, labor, it was felt, could bargain satisfactory conditions from private employers.

By the end of the nineteenth century, the frontier had closed, and the nation was rapidly becoming urbanized and industrialized. These circumstances cut off a progressively larger and larger portion of the population from any source of income except wages and finally brought the full impact of the Industrial Revolution to the United States. The accelerated growth of the AFL, from 250,000 members in 1897 to 1.6 million in 1904 and to more than 2 million in 1914, attests to the fact that many American workers felt the need for some protective device and accepted the trade union for this purpose. Membership, however, was still confined largely to the building trades, the railroads, and the coal mines. The miners included the only substantial group of unionized unskilled and semi-skilled labor in the nation.

During World War I, organized labor received official recognition, to which it had long aspired but had not been accustomed. A War Labor Board was established to settle union-management disputes that might interfere with the war effort. By this act the government openly accepted unions as the "official" agents for workers. Labor representatives were also included on several government boards dealing with manpower and mobilization. Organized labor acquired new status and dignity on the American scene.

Left-Wing Unionism

The job-oriented bargaining approach of Gompers was by no means unchallenged. Founded in 1876 on principles of Marxist socialism, the Socialist Labor Party in 1889 came under the strong leadership of Daniel de Leon, who undertook to bring the AFL back to its "true historic mission"—as the Marxists saw it—of socialism. The depression, unemployment, and strike defeats of 1893 and 1894 seemed to support the socialist arguments that job-oriented bargaining was useless and that class-oriented ownership should be tried. At the 1894 AFL convention, a resolution that the AFL go on record as favoring "collective ownership by the people of all the means of production and distribution" lost by political maneuvering rather than by lack of support. That same year, Gompers was defeated for the presidency by a western coal miner, the socialist John McBride. Gompers returned to office, by a narrow margin, in 1895.

The IWW

The settlers and miners of the early West were hard fisted and direct acting. The new-blown capitalists' dealings with labor were often ruthless and primitive. The mines, lumber camps, docks, and—in part—farms employed many unskilled workers, often in remote areas without family or community life, where "the company" was the whole of life. Such conditions commonly foster militance. Dissatisfied with the conservative methods of the AFL and its lack of interest in their problems, the Western Federation of Miners left it in 1897. By 1905, with the help of the Socialists, they had established a new federation. They called it the Industrial Workers of the World—more commonly known as the IWW, or "Wobblies." Under the colorful and militant leadership (although not the initial presidency) of "Big Bill" Haywood, the IWW very competently stirred up and capitalized upon discontent. The IWW succeeded in winning several important strikes. But after winning a strike, the union would bound off to some new trouble spot instead of staying to build a lasting union structure. Its behavior was so erratic, in fact, that within several years it was abandoned by both the Socialists and the Western Federation of Miners. In due time, the IWW turned more conservative than the AFL itself and lost all significance as a separate organization. (In 1953 the Bureau of Labor Statistics listed only 22 locals with a total membership of 16,500, and by 1961 the IWW was no longer listed—although one source reports some scattered outposts, based mainly on nostalgia.) A brief resurgent interest in IWW philosophy and organization was experienced in the late 1960s and early 1970s, particularly among young radicals on college campuses.

In 1991 the union left Chicago, its headquarters for 86 years, for San Francisco and big dreams of a renewed push toward the goal of embracing all the world's workers in "one big union." In 1994 the union moved its national headquarters to Ypsilanti, Michigan. The IWW charges $12 a year for dues and has no hierarchy: All policy decisions are made by referendum. Whereas many other unions have evolved over the years, the IWW's guiding philosophy has remained unchanged. It is based on the idea that all workers—regardless of race, sex, national origin, or craft—should be organized into "one big union" seeking not only short-term improvements in wages and working conditions but also the eventual overthrow of the "wage slave system." For now, however, it appears that capitalists have little to worry about. The IWW's platform of no-holds-barred unionism—a "world without bosses"—is one that almost no one seems to subscribe to anymore.

Although the IWW's vision seems more remote today than ever, Wobbly leaders claim that their militant message gains new relevance every time a traditional AFL-CIO union suffers a defeat or sells out its members' interests. Establishment unionists today view the Wobblies more as a historical relic than as a viable means of labor empowerment. But the IWW retains its high idealism.[5] It continues to publish its newspaper, the *Industrial Worker.* The April 1995 issue of that publication included an IWW Directory listing addresses of the union in Australia, Canada, and the United Kingdom as well as in various parts of the United States.

The Molly Maguires[6] represent still another union that surfaced during the nineteenth century. The anthracite miners of eastern Pennsylvania faced a highly intransigent and authoritarian group of coal companies, particularly the "captive" mines of the Reading Railroad Company under the presidency of Franklin Gowen. In the 1870s, the Mollies' technique for achieving justice for miners took the eminently direct form of murdering company officials. Their violence came to a head in the railroad strikes of 1877.

The so-called Haymarket Riot in Chicago in 1886 also drew much public attention. Seven policemen were killed by the explosion of a bomb toward the end of a rather dreary meeting, held in Haymarket Square in connection with the aftermath of a strike at the McCormick Reaper Works. Four anarchists were eventually hanged, and one committed suicide before the execution; unions received much extremely bad publicity from the incident—though in the opinion of many people then, and apparently of nearly all who study the incident now, no really admissible evidence was ever adduced at the trial concerning the actual identity of the bomb thrower.[7] The lesson learned from these developments was that any violence or radical ideology associated with unions or strikes will be magnified in the press and will greatly increase the difficulties and reduce the effectiveness of the labor movement. This lesson reinforced the conviction that straight bargaining unionism, with no touch of radicalism and free of violence, was the only way to command the public acceptance necessary for union survival in the United States.

EMPLOYER OPPOSITION

The rapid increase in union membership from 1897 to 1904 stimulated employers into an opposition movement that was probably as well organized as the labor movement itself and perhaps more single-minded in its purpose. Starting in 1903, the National Association of Manufacturers (NAM) vigorously promulgated what it called the "open shop" as the standard "American plan" for dealing with employees. Although an open shop, strictly defined, is open on equal terms to both union and nonunion employees, the open shop of the association was closed completely to union members. Policies similar to those of the NAM were adopted by the trade associations in several industries. These groups maintained employer strike funds to assist companies suffering from strikes and blacklists of union members to ensure that they would not be hired anywhere in the industry. Sometimes the groups brought pressure against firms in their industries if the firms appeared inclined to deal with unions.

A period of about 20 years, starting shortly after the turn of the century, was marked by intense antagonism and considerable violence in many areas, particularly in the mining industry. Many employers maintained substantial arsenals of weapons or acquired them when a strike seemed likely. They also employed company guards who were prepared to use the weapons. In addition, the employers often hired professional strikebreakers supplied by "detective" agencies, and they tended to call out the National Guard more or less automatically whenever a strike was called. A typical pattern was for the courts to respond with an injunction against the strike and for the governor to respond with the militia. The coal mines of West Virginia and Colorado and the copper mines of northern Michigan were the scenes of some bloody fights. Notable was the 1914 "Ludlow Massacre" in connection with the Rockefeller-owned Colorado Fuel and Iron Company installation at Ludlow, Colorado. A total of 50 people died over a 10-day period in what was virtually open warfare. A typical management reaction during this period was a flat refusal to deal with a union or even to acknowledge its existence.

However, by no means all employers of the period were opposed to unions. During the 1890s and early 1900s, widespread agreements between unions and employers were reached in the stove, glass container, and building trades and in the newspaper publishing, brass polishing, coal mining, pottery, overalls manufacturing, railroads, and Great Lakes shipping industries. Many of these agreements continued for decades. A notable experiment based on a cooperative attitude was undertaken by the National Civic Federation, founded in 1900 as a result of the turmoil of the 1890s. Its cardinal premise was that labor and capital are interdependent. The organization probably helped pave the way for the acceptance of unions.

Nevertheless, organized employer opposition probably accounted for the slower rate of union growth after 1904. Following an upsurge in union membership during World War I, employers used new devices to reinforce their opposition to unions. One was to eliminate the desire for unionization by treating their employees better. Another tactic was to "join" that part of the union movement that they could not "lick." Employee associations—so-called company unions—were formed, financed, and guided by employers.

The continued open-shop movement, the "personnel offensive," and company unions,[8] along with persistent charges of union radicalism and several court decisions, all had a depressing effect on union membership. Economic conditions also contributed to this result. The stability of the 1920s provided no burning issues around which to rally workers, and the severe unemployment of the early 1930s was more than unions could offer to cure. Gompers's leadership was inadequate during his later years, and that of William Green, elected as a compromise candidate in 1924 to replace Gompers, was hardly better. The AFL was decaying from its own lack of strength, and its conspicuous failure to attempt to organize the rapidly growing steel, automobile, rubber, and petroleum industries made its weakness even more apparent. The combination of events carried union membership steadily downward from a total of five million in 1920 to less than three million in 1933. Even the boom of the late 1920s had not brought the customary increase in membership. There was suspicion in informed circles that unionism was entering a permanent eclipse.

UNIONS TAKE ON THEIR PRESENT DIMENSION

The demise of unions that seemed imminent at the beginning of the depression of the 1930s obviously did not occur. Whereas previous depressions had diminished or destroyed union strength, this one brought sweeping changes in legislation and government attitudes. These changes, combined with events within labor itself, unleashed a burst of unprecedented union growth. Because of lessons learned during the preceding century, this wave of growth was largely unencumbered by excursions into producer or consumer cooperatives, class-wide unionism, or socialism. The movement concentrated instead on organizing for collective bargaining.

The Norris-LaGuardia Act of 1932, the National Industrial Recovery Act (NIRA) of 1933, and the Wagner Act of 1935 protected and encouraged union organization. These laws also created an atmosphere in which unions seemed respectable, even desirable, to government and to much of the public. Unions quickly took advantage of this new environment to recruit members, and workers responded avidly.

THE CIO AND A SPLIT LABOR MOVEMENT

During the early 1930s, a long-smoldering debate came to a head in the AFL over the extent of its organizing activity and the structure of union organization. The United Mine Workers under the redoubtable John L. Lewis, the Amalgamated Clothing Workers under Sidney Hillman, the International Ladies' Garment Workers under David Dubinsky, the Textile Workers under Emil Rieve, and several other AFL unions felt that the only feasible organization for mass production industries was the "industrial union," in which all types of workers within a given plant belong to the same union. In their view, the then largely unorganized major industries, such as the automobile, radio, rubber, and steel industries, should be unionized on that basis.

Members of the AFL hierarchy were not averse to having new unions in these fields or to having them organized initially on an industrial basis. But they insisted that the charters be so drawn that the machinists, carpenters, electricians, and the like would later be divided into the separate craft unions, which held long-established control of the AFL. This procedure was entirely unacceptable to the proponents of industrial unionism.

Furthermore, the AFL had never done much organizing as a federation because it had left such actions largely to its constituent unions. But the workers in the mass production industries were mainly semiskilled operatives, who did not fall within any of the skilled-craft categories and whom the craft unions were notably uninterested in organizing. In 1935, in an effort to get more action, the dissatisfied unions formed a Committee for Industrial Organization (CIO), under the initial chairmanship of John L. Lewis, to encourage and facilitate unionization of the mass production industries within the AFL. Such assistance seemed necessary because the greater ease of replacing unskilled employees and the militancy of the large employers in the mass production industries had long frustrated the employees' unaided efforts to unionize.

The action of the CIO group was interpreted by the AFL Executive Committee as dual unionism—the cardinal sin of splitting labor. After some maneuvering on both sides, the CIO was suspended from the AFL in 1936. Refusing to repent, it was expelled in 1938. The AFL and the CIO subsequently developed an intense rivalry, in which the AFL finally engaged in strong drives to organize some of the mass production fields before the CIO could get them. Although it thus gained considerable membership, the AFL did not foreclose the CIO's drive, which captured the industries most central to its concern.

Which force was the more important is impossible to tell, but, between them, the two forces—the new attitude of government toward organized labor and the organizational rivalry within the labor movement—produced a rapid increase in union membership. From a low of 0.9 million in 1900 and a figure of 3.6 million in 1934, it rose to almost 9 million by 1939 and to 17 million by 1955, the year of the AFL-CIO merger. Union membership peaked at about 22 million in the mid-1970s. The most recent status of union membership will be discussed in more detail in Chapter 2.

UNIONS COME TO STEEL AND AUTOS

The introduction of unions into two important industries presents an interesting contrast on both the union and management fronts. In the steel industry, the Amalgamated Association of Iron, Steel, and Tin Workers had tried for some 40 years before 1930 to represent the workers. It never gained a foothold in more than a small part of the industry. It engaged in several very bitter strikes, largely defensive and unsuccessful. As a result, very few among the steelworkers, who were of mixed national origins, were easily aroused by rosy promises.

Following the passage of the NIRA and the Wagner Act, steel companies tried to siphon off the pressure of the new union ferment by forming company unions. Knowing the history of the situation, the Steel Workers Organizing Committee (SWOC, subsequently the United Steelworkers of America) of the CIO pursued a cautious educational program designed to lure the company unions into the CIO. The campaign was widely successful. One of the early supporters of the SWOC was John L. Lewis of the United Mine Workers Union; he made a significant contribution toward the formation of SWOC. Acknowledging defeat in the same quiet way the union had gained its victory, Myron C. Taylor, chairman of the board of United States Steel Corporation, signed an agreement with SWOC. This agreement recognized the union as representing its members and granted a 40-hour week, time-and-a-half for overtime, and a 10-cents-an-hour increase in wages. Many small steel companies followed suit shortly. But Little Steel (the three or four firms next in size to United States Steel) fought to keep the union out and capitulated only after two or three years of bitter struggle. Except in Little Steel, the advent of unionism to the steel industry was marked by restraint, nonviolence, and relative goodwill on both sides.

In the automobile industry, much younger than steel as a mass production industry, workers were acutely conscious of many complaints. These included speedup of assembly lines, alternating seasons of overtime and layoff, and lack of seniority (each laid-off worker was rehired each year as a new employee). The auto workers were ripe for unionization, which was severely resisted by management. But the workers did not like the AFL's idea of dividing them into craft unions, and the craft unions themselves were reluctant to admit a group of semiskilled workers who might outvote the skilled. The auto workers' enthusiasm was not dampened by sobering memories of unsuccessful strikes.

In the automobile industry, both management and labor followed tactics different from those used in Big Steel. Moreover, the industry consisted mainly of three large and well-financed companies that had apparently resolved to avoid unionization at all costs. The stage was set for a bitter battle. Extravagant demands, mass picketing, and assorted violence and intimidation by workers resulted in the purchase of tear gas and armaments and the hiring by management of strikebreaking thugs and spies. The parent CIO alternatively rejoiced over the exuberant response to its organizing call and despaired over the unruly growth and behavior of the United Auto Workers (UAW), which elicited unfavorable public reaction. Some of the auto strikes were considered premature by the CIO, which nevertheless could not abandon them. The advent of unions in the automobile industry involved bitter fighting, starting in the main Chevrolet plant of General Motors in 1937, proceeding to the Chrysler Corporation, and ending with Ford in 1941.

Along the way, the UAW used numerous sit-down strikes. In plant after plant, the workers would put down their tools but not leave the workplace. The sit-down not only halted the work of the regular employees, it also kept possible strikebreakers from entering the plant to replace them. Although many sit-downs were short, others continued for long periods, as food and blankets were provided by sympathizers from outside. The strikers' success was bolstered by the fact that Governor Frank Murphy of Michigan was sympathetic to the labor movement and rejected requests to use the state's police powers to remove the strikers. Managements took a dim view of this situation, which to them constituted illegal trespass as well as strike action, a position later upheld in the courts.

Among the auto makers, Ford Motor Company was best equipped organizationally and technically to fight battles at this level. The famed Ford Service Department, headed by one Harry Bennett, was a sort of combination intelligence agency and goon squad, which also infiltrated its operatives into some officerships of the union. When UAW officers Walter Reuther and Richard Frankensteen recognized the relative weakness of the union, they concentrated their organizing attempts on propagandizing. Some of the company's efforts involved black workers, of whom the company imported many from the South. Blacks were recruited into the union to be used as strikebreakers, without knowing how they were being used. Henry Ford used his personal connections with black preachers to have them discourage blacks from joining the union. Bennett also utilized muscular "loyal" blacks as "guards," amply equipped with blackjacks and other weapons.

Union propaganda efforts were inhibited by local regulations prohibiting the distribution of leaflets. In the famous Battle of the Overpass, while trying to distribute literature, Reuther and Frankensteen were severely beaten by "indignant, loyal workers" who, as photographs revealed, were carrying handcuffs in their pockets.[9]

Meanwhile, both the CIO and the AFL were also organizing such fields as transportation, public utilities, nonferrous metals, chemicals, and petroleum. They were also recruiting white-collar and professional workers in both private industry and government. By the beginning of World War II, the great bulk of mining, manufacturing, and transportation firms were dealing with unions. Thus, in the eight years from 1933 to 1941, unionism was transformed from a sick and declining institution representing only a few industries to a vigorous one firmly established in nearly every major industry. By 1941 unions had signed up a large proportion of the workers who could be considered "readily organizable." From then until the mid-1950s, their growth was just about equal to the growth in the labor force. Thereafter it declined relative to the size of the labor force.

REUNIFICATION OF ORGANIZED LABOR

By the end of World War II, many of the differences that had led to the separation of the CIO from the AFL had either disappeared or diminished in importance. Both groups recognized the importance of both craft and industrial unions, and the AFL had acquired some industrial affiliates. It appeared that organizing, political affairs, education, research, and some other activities could be carried on more expeditiously by a single all-inclusive organization. Raiding, in which one union tries to take away another union's members, had been a frequent source of friction, both within and between the two federations. When Philip Murray, president of the CIO, and William Green, president of the AFL, died within two weeks of each other in late 1952, they were replaced by Walter Reuther and George Meany, both of whom felt strongly the need for a reunited labor movement. They shortly negotiated a workable no-raiding agreement between the two federations and achieved closer cooperation in other activities. By the spring of 1955 they were able to conclude a merger agreement; by summer they had forged a new constitution; and in December each federation held a convention in New York City and adopted the merger agreement. Thereupon the first convention of the merged AFL-CIO was convened, and it adopted the new constitution.

The years since the reunification of the AFL and the CIO can perhaps best be described as a holding operation. George Meany was made the first president of the AFL-CIO and remained president until he retired for health reasons in late 1979 at age 85; he died shortly thereafter. He was replaced by Lane Kirkland, long his second in command, who was 57 at the time. It is interesting to observe that, over the years, Kirkland represented labor on various boards and commissions; as a result he probably developed long-standing personal relationships with people at the top of the American corporate structure.[10]

During most of the postmerger period, the United Mineworkers and the Teamsters remained outside the federation. The Auto Workers joined them in independent status in 1968, to a substantial extent because of what the UAW viewed as the ultraconservative stance of the federation—particularly with respect to foreign policy—and because of the federation's past strong reluctance to work with representatives from labor organizations in the former communist and third-world blocs.

While president of the UAW, Walter Reuther had sought to give the American labor movement a substantially more aggressive stance than did George Meany and the AFL group in the federation, and particularly to work out a more flexible and imaginative relationship between the labor forces of various nations and the large multinational corporations. In 1969 Reuther had the UAW join with the Teamsters in an organization they called the Alliance for Labor Action (ALA), with the possible eventual aim of developing a rival and more liberal federation. The ALA lasted only until Reuther's premature death in the crash of a private plane in 1970. The UAW reaffiliated with the AFL-CIO on July 1, 1981.[11]

On October 24, 1987, by a unanimous vote of the 35-member executive council, the Teamsters—a 1.7-million-member Union—were permitted to reaffiliate with the AFL-CIO. This action came as the Justice Department prepared a suit alleging that the Teamsters were influenced by organized crime and sought to place the international union under the control of a court-appointed trustee.[12] The United Mine Workers' 100,000 members reaffiliated with the AFL-CIO in October of 1989 after 42 years of independent status. This development occurred during the lengthy and bitter Pittston coal strike.[13] The main structural change following the AFL-CIO merger brought a somewhat enhanced role for the Industrial Union Department and a series of mergers of member unions. Many of these mergers brought together formerly separate AFL and CIO unions covering the same fields. Some other mergers simply brought together related types of employees, without reference to their former federation. Mergers still continue elsewhere, mainly reflecting certain economies of scale. Other aspects of more recent developments will be discussed in connection with particular problems in Chapters 2 through 7, particularly on the state of the labor movement, on union structure, bargaining structure, legal problems, negotiations, and union and management security.

SUMMARY

The forces driving workers toward unions were strong enough to cause most of the growth in union membership long after the initial impact of the Industrial Revolution wore off. The aftermath of the Industrial Revolution engendered workers' urge for self-defense through organization. The local unions of the Jacksonian era, the Knights of Labor, and several other experiments not described in this text demonstrated that the class-wide union is ineffective in bargaining and has poor survival value in the United States. Political activities succeeded in a number of cases, but labor organizations based primarily on such activities disappeared. Although individual unions are involved in politics, most political activity now rests with the federation, the AFL-CIO.

Class-based ownership has never been tried in the United States, but movements in this direction generated intense opposition from the community and hardly any interest from workers. By contrast, the goal of getting "more" through bargaining is immediate and tangible.

Although traditional types of bargaining interactions between employers and unions are prevalent in many organizations, some transformation seems to be taking place, with more emphasis on labor-management cooperation and employee participation. These topics will be discussed later in this text, particularly in Chapter 17, covering the Dunlop Commission report, as well as in the section on mutual gains bargaining in Chapter 9.

Notes

1. In reading elsewhere on the subject of unions, the student will often encounter the terms *job conscious* and *class conscious.* Job consciousness is nearly equivalent to what we have termed the "job-oriented bargaining approach"; the term *class consciousness* may be equated with what we have termed the "class-oriented ownership approach." Although the serious student of labor should certainly be aware of the terms *job conscious* and *class conscious,* we have largely avoided them because they fail to distinguish between the scope of the group with which the worker identifies him- or herself and the kind of action he or she wishes to take to protect his or her interest. For example, the terms fail to cover adequately either class-wide bargaining ac-

tivities or job-oriented ownership proposals. John R. Commons et al., *History of Labour in the United States, Volume I,* Reprints of Economic Classics (New York: Augustus M. Kelley Publishers, original edition 1918). John R. Commons et al., *A Documentary History of American Industrial Society* (Cleveland: Arthur H. Clark, 1910).

The term *class conscious* carries a Marxist connotation, whereas *class oriented* and *class-wide* do not. In addition, the traditional terminology has been confused by some authors, who consider class consciousness to be a prerequisite of any labor union movement—a usage clearly inconsistent with the Marxist implications of the term. Later in this chapter, by referring to this prerequisite condition as *employee consciousness,* we have tried to deal with the prerequisite conditions for unions without clashing with existing terminology.

2. John R. Commons, "American Shoemakers, 1648–1895," from *Labor and Administration* (New York: Macmillan, 1913), reprinted in *Readings in Labor Economics and Labor Relations,* 3rd ed., ed. Richard L. Rowan (Homewood, IL: Irwin, 1976), pp. 88–100.

3. Philip Taft, *Organized Labor in American History* (New York: Harper & Row, 1964), p. 2.

4. Selig Perlman, *A History of Trade Unionism in the United States* (New York: Macmillan, 1922), pp. 31 ff.

5. *Chicago Tribune,* December 12, 1991, p. 29. *San Francisco Chronicle,* July 24, 1991, p. C1. *Industrial Worker* 92, no. 4 (April 1994).

6. Details on the "Mollies" can be found in Wayne G. Broehl, Jr., *The Molly Maguires* (Cambridge, MA: Harvard University Press, 1964). This volume has the rare distinction of being an academic work for which the author has been able to sell movie rights—as reported in *Monthly Labor Review* 88, no. 4 (April 1965), p. 449.

7. Almost all histories of the American labor movement include a discussion of the Haymarket Riot. A convenient recent one is Taft, op. cit., pp. 130–35.

8. These are to be distinguished from independent unions that cover only a single company but are not dominated by the employer.

9. In this connection, consult August Meier and Elliot Rudwich, *Black Detroit and the Rise of the UAW* (New York: Oxford University Press, 1979), especially pp. 39–40.

10. *The Nation,* January 19, 1980, pp. 37–38.

11. *Proceedings of the 14th Constitutional Convention of the AFL-CIO,* New York, 1981, p. 58.

12. Kenneth B. Noble, "Teamsters Gain a Readmittance to AFL-CIO," *New York Times,* October 25, 1987, p. 1.

13. Bureau of National Affairs, "Mine Workers–AFL-CIO Affiliation," *What's New in Collective Negotiations & Contracts* 1158 (October 19, 1989), pp. 1–2.

CHAPTER 2

The State of the Labor Movement

After reading this chapter, you should be able to

■ Identify several factors that may explain the decline in union membership.

■ Outline the changes in leadership of the AFL-CIO.

■ Discuss the differing priorities of former president Kirkland and current president Sweeney.

■ Discuss and review the benefits of union membership as perceived by employees.

■ Discuss methods through which unions can improve their organizing activities.

■ Identify differences in rates of unionization based on type of industry, job, race, and gender of employees.

TRENDS AND PATTERNS IN UNION MEMBERSHIP

Chapter 1 reviewed the main forces that gave rise to the labor movement and brought it to its present state. This chapter examines trends in the extent of union membership and evaluates the future role of organized labor in the economy. Although there is no single continuous source of reliable data on union membership, some important trends can be observed from an examination of the available information (see Table 2.1).[1] Union membership grew substantially from 1900 to the end of World War I. From 1920 to 1933, membership dropped. During the rest of the 1930s and through the end of World War II, the labor movement experienced rapid growth. Union membership as a percentage of the civilian labor force peaked in about the middle 1950s at roughly 27 percent. The absolute number of union members continued to grow until the mid-1970s; it should be noted, however, that union growth between the mid-1950s and the mid-1970s was slower than that of the labor force as a whole. Since then there has been a very significant decline in the unionized percentage of the civilian labor force (see Table 2.1).

Whereas Table 2.1 indicates the proportion of the *labor force* that is unionized, Table 2.2 provides information on the proportion of *total employed* who are union members or

	TABLE 2.1 U.S. Labor Organization Membership, Selected Years		
Year	Total Membership (in thousands)	Civilian Labor Force* (in thousands)	Unionized Percentage of Civilian Labor Force
1900	868	28,376	3.1
1920	5,048	41,340	12.2
1933	2,973	50,882	5.8
1939	8,763	55,218	15.7
1945	14,332	53,860	26.6
1953	16,940	63,015	26.9
1960	17,049	69,629	24.5
1970	19,381	82,715	23.4
1975	22,207	96,613	23.0
1980	20,968	104,719	20.0
1981	20,647	106,393	19.4
1982	19,763	110,204	17.9
1983	17,717	111,551	15.8
1984	17,340	113,544	15.3
1985	16,996	115,463	14.7
1986	16,975	117,834	14.4
1987	16,913	119,865	14.1
1988	17,002	121,669	14.0
1989	16,960	123,869	13.7
1990	16,740	124,787	13.4
1991	16,568	125,303	13.2
1992	16,390	126,982	12.9
1993	16,598	128,040	12.9
1994	16,748	131,056	12.8
1995	16,360	132,284	12.4

*Civilian labor force includes those 14 and over for 1900 to 1945 and 16 and over thereafter.

Source: The U.S. Bureau of the Census, *Historical Statistics of the United States, Colonial Times to 1970,* Bicentennial Edition, Part 2 (Washington, DC: U.S. Government Printing Office, 1975), series 952–969, p. 178. Data from 1900 to 1933 include Canadian membership. Data from 1939 to 1970 come from Ibid., series 946–951, p. 178. Data from 1975 to 1981 are from Leo Troy and Neil Sheflin, *U.S. Union Sourcebook First Edition, 1985* (West Orange, NJ: Industrial Relations Data and Information Services, 1985), Table 3.91. Data from 1982 to 1995 are from U.S. Bureau of Labor Statistics, *Employment and Earnings,* various volumes (January issues) (Washington, DC: U.S. Government Printing Office).

who have been represented by unions since 1983. Tables 2.1 and 2.2 indicate that union membership is significantly higher as a percentage of *total employed* than as a percentage of the *labor force,* which also includes the unemployed. The totals are even higher when the statistics include workers who are represented by unions but who are not union members (see Table 2.2). In 1995 union membership as a percentage of the civilian labor force was 12.4 (see Table 2.1); union membership as a percentage of total employed was 14.9 (see Table 2.2).

According to the U.S. Department of Labor, Bureau of Labor Statistics,[2] in 1995 union membership was 16.3 million, slightly lower than the 16.7 million a year earlier (see Table 2.1). As indicated in Table 2.3, in 1995, 14.9 percent of employed wage and

TABLE 2.2 Employed Union Members and Other Employees Represented by Unions as Percentage of Employed Labor Force

Year	Total Employed (in thousands)	Members of Unions		Represented by Unions	
		Total (in thousands)	Percentage of Employed	Total (in thousands)	Percentage of Employed
1983	88,290	17,717	20.1	20,532	23.3
1984	92,194	17,340	18.8	19,932	21.6
1985	94,521	16,996	18.0	19,358	20.5
1986	96,903	16,975	17.5	19,278	19.9
1987	99,303	16,913	17.0	19,051	19.2
1988	101,407	17,002	16.8	19,241	19.0
1989	103,480	16,960	16.4	19,198	18.6
1990	103,905	16,740	16.1	19,058	18.3
1991	102,786	16,568	16.1	18,734	18.2
1992	103,688	16,390	15.8	18,540	17.9
1993	105,067	16,598	15.8	18,646	17.7
1994	107,989	16,748	15.5	18,850	17.5
1995	110,038	16,360	14.9	18,346	16.7

Note: In the 1985 January issue of *Employment and Earnings,* a monthly publication, the Bureau of Labor Statistics of the U.S. Department of Labor introduced a new series on the extent of unionization among American workers. The series began with annual averages for the years 1983 and 1984. The series show the number of persons who belonged to unions as well as data on workers who, although not belonging to unions, were in jobs covered by union contracts. The data for this series is obtained through the Current Population Survey of about 60,000 households, which provides the basic information on the Nation's labor force.

Source: US Department of Labor, Bureau of Labor Statistics, *Employment and Earnings* (January issues), 1985–1996.

salary workers age 16 and older were members of labor unions or employee associations similar to unions. Slightly less than three-fifths of union members (9.4 million) were in the private nonagricultural sector; they constituted 10.4 percent of the employed. The balance of union members (6.9 million) were in federal, state, and local government; they represented 37.8 percent of employed workers (see Table 2.4).

In the private sector, manufacturing accounted for the largest number of union members—3.4 million—followed by transportation and public utilities, 1.8 million; services, 1.6 million; wholesale and retail trade, 1.4 million; construction, 908,000; finance, 139,000; mining, 84,000; and agriculture, 33,000 (see Table 2.4). The highest union representation in the private sector was in transportation and public utilities—27.3 percent—followed by construction, 17.7 percent; manufacturing, 17.6; and mining, 13.8 percent. The other private-sector industry categories had unionization rates ranging from 2 to 6 percent. Unionization rates in wholesale and retail trade and in the private service sector are very low, even though a significant percentage of total employment is concentrated in these sectors (see Table 2.4).

Among the major occupational groups, the highest proportion of union members, approximately 1 in 4, was among precision, production, craft, and repair employees as well as operators, fabricators, and laborers (see Table 2.4). In farming, forestry, and fishing, union membership was significantly lower—1 in 20. In the technical occupations,

TABLE 2.3 Union Affiliation of Employed Wage and Salary Workers by Demographic Characteristics and Full- or Part-Time Status, 1995

		Members of Unions		Represented by Unions	
	Total Employed (in thousands)	Total (in thousands)	Percentage of Employed	Total (in thousands)	Percentage of Employed
Sex and Age					
Total, 16 years and over	110,038	16,360	14.9	18,346	16.7
Men, 16 years and over	57,669	9,929	17.2	10,868	18.8
Women, 16 years and over	52,369	6,430	12.3	7,479	14.3
Race and Hispanic Origin					
White, 16 years and over	92,760	13,149	14.2	14,747	15.9
Black, 16 years and over	12,644	2,519	19.9	2,819	22.3
Hispanic, 16 years and over	10,401	1,357	13.0	1,535	14.8
Full- or Part-Time Status					
Full-time workers	89,282	14,790	16.6	16,531	18.5
Part-time workers	20,550	1,537	7.5	1,781	8.7

Source: U.S. Department of Labor, Bureau of Labor Statistics, *Employment and Earnings,* January 1996, p. 210.

sales, and administrative support group, it was approximately 1 in 10; among the managerial and professional specialty employees, it was 1 in 7.

Union representation was higher among men—17.2 percent—as contrasted with about 12.3 for women (see Table 2.3). The percentage of women in labor unions may increase in the future. According to the latest news release from the Institute for Women's Policy Research,[3] more women are joining labor unions. The proportion of union membership among blacks was 20 percent, and compared with just 14 percent among whites and 13 percent among Hispanics (see Table 2.3). About 16.6 percent of all full-time workers were union members, as contrasted with 7.5 percent for part-time workers.

In addition to the 16.4 million workers who were union members in 1995, about 2.0 million more were represented by unions though they were not union members. Many of them were government employees (see Tables 2.2, 2.3, and 2.4).

According to the Dunlop Report, the ethnic composition of the work force changed dramatically between 1954 and 1994. In 1954 about 10 percent of the work force was non-white; by 1994 the percentage had increased to 15.2 percent. This trend is expected to continue, as indicated by the projected labor force growth rates for the period 1992 through 2005: white, 1.1 percent; black, 1.7 percent; Asian, 4.7 percent; and Hispanic, 3.9 percent.[4]

Table 2.5 shows historic and projected employment trends by occupation for the period 1979 through 2005. The table indicates a significant shift toward white-collar jobs. Projections represented here may have significant implications for unions. Whereas the most job growth is expected in professional specialties (37.4 percent), service occupa-

TABLE 2.4 Union Affiliation of Employed Wage and Salary Workers by Occupation and Industry, 1995

	Total Employed (in thousands)	Members of Unions		Represented by Unions	
		Total (in thousands)	Percentage of Employed	Total (in thousands)	Percentage of Employed
Occupation					
Managerial and professional specialties	29,827	4,116	13.8	4,909	16.5
Technical, sales, and administrative support	33,842	3,364	9.9	3,883	11.5
Service occupations	15,648	2,112	13.5	2,356	15.1
Precision production, craft, and repair	11,563	2,692	23.3	2,866	24.8
Operators, fabricators, and laborers	17,304	3,983	23.0	4,229	24.4
Farming, forestry, and fishing	1,855	91	4.9	104	5.6
Industry					
Agricultural wage and salary workers	1,575	33	2.1	43	2.7
Private nonagricultural wage and salary workers	90,121	9,400	10.4	10,318	11.4
Mining	609	84	13.8	88	14.4
Construction	5,135	908	17.7	963	18.8
Manufacturing	19,520	3,440	17.6	3,657	18.7
Transportation and public utilities	6,573	1,792	27.3	1,911	29.1
Wholesale and retail trade	23,028	1,401	6.1	1,550	6.7
Finance, insurance, and real estate	6,745	139	2.1	173	2.6
Services	28,511	1,636	5.7	1,976	6.9
Government workers	18,342	6,926	37.8	7,985	43.5

Source: U.S. Department of Labor, Bureau of Labor Statistics, *Employment and Earnings,* January 1996, p. 212.

tions (33.4 percent), and marketing and sales (20.6 percent), the lowest growth is expected among operators, fabricators, and laborers (9.5 percent), traditionally strongly unionized sectors of the economy.

The industry structure of employment in the United States has changed significantly during the last four decades. There has been a major shift from goods-producing manufacturing to service-producing sectors. In 1950 manufacturing represented 34 percent of nonagricultural employment; this declined to 17 percent in 1993. In 1950, 59 percent of nonagricultural employees worked in the service-producing sector; by 1990 employment in this sector had increased to 77 percent.[5]

The Bureau of Labor Statistics (BLS) forecasts the creation of about 21 million new jobs in the U.S. economy between 1986 and 2000.[6] The BLS predicts that manufacturing will lose about 1.2 million production and semiskilled support services jobs during this period. Because unions traditionally have found strong support in manufacturing, this development is not welcome news for labor unions. According to the BLS,

TABLE 2.5   Actual and Projected Employment Trends by Occupation, 1979 to 2005

	Actual Percent Change, 1979–1992	Number Employed in Millions, 1992	Projected Percent Change, 1992–2005
All Occupations	19.0	121.1	21.8
Executive, administrative, and managerial	50.4	12.1	25.9
Professional specialty	43.0	16.6	37.4
Technicians and related support	57.6	4.3	32.2
Marketing and sales	30.7	13.0	20.6
Service occupations	24.6	19.4	33.4
Administrative support, clerical	15.0	22.3	13.7
Precision production, craft, repair	4.3	13.6	13.3
Operators, fabricators, laborers	10.3	16.3	9.5
Agriculture, forestry, fishing	5.2	3.5	3.4

Source: The Dunlop Report, *Fact-Finding Report,* Commission on the Future of Worker-Management Relations, U.S. Department of Labor and U.S. Department of Commerce (Washington DC, May 1994), p. 7.

wholesale and retail trade will generate 30 percent of the new employment; services, narrowly defined to encompass business, professional, personal, entertainment, and lodging activities, are projected to create half of the net new jobs. The balance of the new jobs will be generated in finance, insurance, real estate, construction, government, transportation, and utilities. These projected labor force trends present major organizational challenges for unions.

REASONS FOR THE DECLINE IN UNIONIZATION

Many studies have explored the reasons for the decline of unionization. The most frequently cited explanation is the "structural shift hypothesis." According to this view, the structure of employment has shifted from highly unionized to nonunionized industries.[7] In the opinion of Chaison and Rose,[8] this hypothesis explains only one-quarter to one-third of union decline in the United States. It also does not provide a satisfactory explanation for growth of unions among unorganized employees, primarily in the government sector. A review of various studies suggests to Chaison and Rose that public policy and employer opposition to unionism are two factors that significantly influence union growth in the United States.

During the last 20 years, there has been a very significant decrease in requests for union representation and certification elections among nonunion workers. This development contributes to the decline in union membership as a proportion of the growing labor force. In 1973 there were 480,303 valid votes cast in union representation elections; unions won 51.1 percent of these elections. Twenty years later, in 1993, only 180,009 valid votes were cast, with unions prevailing 50.4 percent of the time.[9]

One explanation for the decrease in requests for union representation is the expanded role of government in areas traditionally addressed by unions. Currently, laws and regulations cover occupational safety, pensions, and family leave; in the past, unions struggled with employers over these issues at the bargaining table. Workers may feel that they need unions less now than in the past because of the expanded role of government in protecting employees.

According to Kochan and Wever, the decline in membership experienced by the American labor movement can be attributed to the following factors: international competition, conservatism in the political arena, and "employer strategies that are beyond the reach of American union influence, and workers' perception of organized labor as an institution that can do little more than help them address some aspects of job dissatisfaction."[10] For unions to be effective and successful in the future, they would have to be more attuned "to employees' diverse job- and career-related interests, new bargaining strategies that emphasize training and human resource development, and labor involvement in management policy."[11] In the current environment, it may be very difficult for unions to achieve some of these objectives.

One reason advanced for unions' low rate of success in representational elections is strong employer resistance. There are two versions of the employer resistance strategy, sometimes referred to as *preventive labor relations*. The first requires fostering a good employer-employee relationship so workers will not want union representation. The second involves vigorous resistance to any union activity with actions ranging from delay of elections and negotiations through protracted litigation to illegal threats, harassment, and firings of union activists. Studies indicate that management resistance reduces the chance of a union election victory.[12] Some observers point to these facts as evidence that public policy reform is needed in the labor relations area if workers are to have uncoerced choice about union representation.[13]

Farber and Krueger's analysis of the decline in unionization in the United States and Canada utilized a demand-supply framework. They measured "total worker demand for unions as the sum of union members and nonunion members who say they would vote for a union if a hypothetical election were held at their workplace."[14] Utilizing this framework, the two scholars reject some researchers' arguments that industrial and demographic shifts account for the decline of unionization in the United States. In Farber and Krueger's view, only about one-quarter of the decline can be attributed to such shifts. They find a decrease in demand-side factors to be responsible for most of the decline since 1977. They report that "none of the decline seems to be due to changes in the relative supply of union jobs as measured by frustrated demand."[15] Their analysis implies that nonunion workers were more satisfied with their jobs in 1984 and 1992 than in 1977. They conclude that this higher satisfaction may be the reason for the decline in the demand for union representation. Another explanation they offer for the decrease in demand is a perception on the part of nonunion employees that the services supplied by unions are no longer valuable. This perception in turn could be due to ineffective marketing by unions of the value of union representation. Farber and Krueger suggest that, for a better understanding of the decline in unionization, the causes of the decrease in demand for unions and the increase in work satisfaction require further research.

Another explanation of the decline in numbers of new members may be a reduction in union organizing efforts. The union policy makers who decide to initiate recruitment drives have both pragmatic and ideological considerations. The pragmatic considerations may involve the following calculations, much like those of a business selling the service of representation: If we invest x thousands of dollars in an organizing drive in ABC Company, how many members can we get, and how much net revenue can we derive from them in dues, adjusted for the probability that the organizing effort may fail? Given the increasing percentage of representation elections that are lost, some unions have become more cautious in their expenditures on new recruitment. It is clear that union resources devoted to organizing have been insufficient to stem membership losses. The effect is cumulative: The smaller the number of new union members, the narrower the base from which to finance subsequent expansion drives.

The ideological dimension of each recruitment campaign was very important for many organizers during the nineteenth century. During the 1930s—particularly within the Committee for Industrial Organization (CIO), discussed in Chapter 1—the union movement was seen as a heroic agent of change and reform, helping to remove poverty and enhance the dignity of working life. The labor movement has been successful in bringing into the middle class large numbers of Americans who are now not very interested in joining unions.

The idealism and sacrifice of many union leaders released vast energy, which in turn attracted many new recruits into the union ranks. However, the bright glow of a reform movement dims once it is institutionalized and most of its daily work is done by hired hands. The dedication that spurs the founders of a movement rarely carries into the next generation, and the American labor movement is now a few generations beyond the 1930s. Besides, it has long been evident that some union leaders can be just as prone to favoritism and venality as anyone else. Like any other organization, a union develops vested interests that it strives to protect. Barring some unforeseen upheaval, it seems unlikely that the large, self-sacrificing dedication of the past will soon reappear. To both leaders and members, the appeal will have to be more pragmatic.

THE OUTLOOK FOR THE LABOR MOVEMENT IN THE 1990S AND BEYOND

Union growth depends on the willingness of the unorganized to join unions and of organized workers to stay in unions. One of the best articles on the subject, titled "Why Workers Join Unions," was written by E. Wight Bakke in 1945. He formulated the following hypothesis: "The worker reacts favorably to union membership in proportion to the strength of his belief that this step will reduce his frustrations and anxieties and will further his opportunities relevant to the achievement of his standards of successful living. He reacts unfavorably in proportion to the strength of his belief that this step will increase his frustrations and anxieties and will reduce his opportunities relevant to the achievement of such standards."[16]

The employment shifts of the last 20 years and the sophisticated level of antiunion activity among employers pose major challenges to the future of the labor movement. Organizing tactics and slogans appropriate during the 1930s may have relatively little appeal to today's work force. Some writers claim that union members today are better educated and informed and more affluent than their predecessors. Many own homes rather than rent and are more concerned with taxes and schools and with sending their kids to college than with union positions on equal rights amendments, social programs, international trade, and consumer protection legislation. They are critical of union leaders who advocate increases in social spending. Some promanagement spokespersons claim that "the leaders of organized labor are out of touch with their membership . . . [and that] union members today are more independent and less beholden to the unions for their economic survival . . . [and that] many union officials have difficulty relating to the new workforce."[17]

UNION RESPONSES TO CURRENT CHALLENGES

The variety of pressures and challenges that confront unions propel them toward mergers. On July 28, 1995, three of the biggest industrial unions in the United States announced a merger that will take five years to conclude. The unions are the steelworkers, the automobile workers, and the machinists. The total membership of these three unions is about 1.9 million. These organizations hope that a single merged union will have more resources to try to organize workers; the merger will also save organizing funds. These unions will no longer have to compete against one another in efforts to recruit new members within the same company. The three unions have great financial reserves—over $1 billion—which they will be able to use for strikes as well as for organizing. The merger seems to be a part of an irreversible trend that has been visible in the labor movement for years. What is different about this merger is its size.

This great merger follows two smaller mergers. In summer 1995, the steelworkers absorbed the United Rubber Workers of America. Early in 1995 two of America's major needletrade unions, the International Ladies Garment Workers Union (ILGWU), founded in 1900, and the Clothing and Textile Workers Union, founded in 1914, merged to form UNITE, the Union of Needletrades, Industrial, and Textile Employees. Both of these unions have rich histories of being in the forefront in the fight for the eight-hour day, the 40-hour week, and the elimination of sweatshops and child labor.

The ultimate objectives of all the mergers are to gain power and to recruit more members. Prolonged declines in membership and hostile political and corporate environments are the catalysts for mergers. Unions are trying to protect their futures, save financial resources, and improve their power and leverage in collective bargaining. Mergers seem to be one of the approaches toward attainment of these objectives.

Unions are responding to today's challenges through critical self-examination and reappraisal of their functions and roles. To assess and evaluate the issues facing labor unions and come up with some potential answers, the AFL-CIO Executive Council created the Committee on the Evolution of Work. The council issued a number of recommendations addressing such topics as new methods of advancing the interests of workers, increasing members' participation in their union, improving the labor movement's communication, improving organizing activity, and proposing structural changes to enhance the labor movement's overall effectiveness.[18]

One new approach being tried was the creation of a new category of union membership called associate membership.[19] Under this program, instead of providing representation in collective bargaining, unions provide access to group health, disability, and life insurance; reduced-interest-rate credit cards; and a variety of other services. Associate membership permits unions to establish and maintain contact with union-oriented workers employed in nonunion organizations.

Another avenue many unions are exploring is labor-management cooperation. It is based on joint committees comprising both unionized workers and management who meet to share ideas and resolve problems not directly addressed in traditional adversarial collective bargaining. Joint committees and quality circles are also being formed in some nonunion companies. It is possible that, just as company unions developed into legitimate bargaining representatives in the 1930s, some quality circles might also fuel a desire among employees for a greater voice in their working lives through unionization.

Consistent with the trend toward labor-management cooperation is the idea that negotiations need not be viewed as a win-lose proposition but rather can be seen as a win-win or mutual-gains bargaining (MGB) model. The theory and practical application of MGB has been studied by a number of researchers at the Harvard Negotiations Project, Program on Negotiations, and elsewhere.[20] In the last 10 years, some employers and unions were able to reach settlements by utilizing some of the MGB techniques. If the MGB concepts gain more acceptance from management and unions, perhaps this approach may lead to less friction and more cooperation between the parties. Mutual Gains Bargaining is discussed at greater length in Chapter 9, on the negotiation process.

CHANGE OF LEADERSHIP IN THE AFL-CIO

In 1995 the AFL-CIO became energized with the election of a group of new leaders who promised to shake up the labor federation. In May 1995, a coalition of 11 national unions, headed by John T. Sweeney, president of the 1.1 million–member Service Employees International Union, and Gerald McEntee, president of the American Federation of State, County and Municipal Employees, demanded the retirement of AFL-CIO president Lane Kirkland. According to Sweeney, labor unions "had become irrelevant to the lives of most American workers as well as to the vast majority of unorganized workers."[21] The leaders of the anti-Kirkland coalition expressed the view that the federation president "must be replaced if the federation is to deal with the challenges facing organized labor."[22] Kirkland, his critics charged, was old and tired and not up to the task and challenge of leading a "dying organization in need of new energy and bold ideas."[23]

Although Kirkland retained the support of Albert Shanker, president of the 850,000-member American Federation of Teachers, and of Lenore Miller, president of the Retail, Wholesale and Department Store union, Kirkland resigned when he realized that he did not have sufficient support to remain at the helm of the AFL-CIO.

Following Kirkland's resignation, the federation's Executive Council had to select an interim president who would serve until a permanent successor could be elected at the AFL-CIO convention in October 1995. The two candidates for the interim position were John Sweeney, who had been instrumental in forcing Lane Kirkland from office, and Thomas Donahue, who had served as secretary-treasurer under Kirkland. Donahue, who received Kirkland's endorsement, was elected as interim president on August 1, 1995.

Despite his defeat, Sweeney was not prepared to give up his fight for the permanent presidency of the federation. In the vote of the Executive Council, each member casts one vote regardless of the size of the union that he or she represents. However, during the AFL-CIO convention, held in October 1995, the vote of each national union was weighted according to the size of its membership. Sweeney had support from larger unions.

In the first contested presidential election since the federations' merger 40 years earlier, there were two candidates, Sweeney and Donahue. The two looked and sounded remarkably similar. Both were over 60; both were Irish-American Catholics who had risen from the ranks of the same Service Employees local union in New York City.[24]

Both candidates focused their campaigns on four themes, reflecting the needs to revitalize organizing; to increase labor's political effectiveness; to improve labor's public image; and to increase the involvement of women, younger workers, and minorities in the AFL-CIO. John Sweeney won the election, receiving 7.3 million votes to Thomas Donahue's 5.7 million.[25]

Even before his election, it was clear that Sweeney intended to solicit greater involvement of women, younger workers, and minorities in the activities of the federation. The new AFL-CIO president realized that the federation's leadership had to more closely mirror and resemble the composition of the rank-and-file membership. "Union ranks today are one-third female and one-fifth black"; *The New York Times* reported that "nearly all unions—and the federation itself—are still led by white men, who have spent years in the labor bureaucracy."[26]

Sweeney chose the relatively young Richard Trumka, the 45-year-old president of the United Mine Workers, as his running mate for secretary-treasurer. The third member of his slate was Linda Chavez-Thompson, a former illegal immigrant who had risen to the rank of vice-president of the American Federation of State, County and Municipal Employees. Ms. Chavez-Thompson was selected for the newly created position of executive vice president.

The convention delegates elected Sweeney, Trumka, and Chavez-Thompson. They also voted to expand the membership of the Executive Council by 18 members, of whom 10 were women or minorities. Through this action, the percentage of council members who were women or minorities increased from 17 percent to 27 percent.[27] The Executive Council includes the following new members: Joe Greene, an African-American, head of the American Federation of School Administration; Sumi Haru, an Asian-American, president of the Screen Actors Guild; and Arturo Rodriguez, a Hispanic, president of the United Farm Workers of America.[28]

Perhaps most important, the Donahue-Sweeney face-off led supporters of both men to conclude that organizing workers had to be the federation's top priority. During his short tenure as interim president of the AFL-CIO, Thomas Donahue probably realized that Lane Kirkland had been forced to resign because "he gave little more than lip service to aggressively organizing new workers."[29] On his election as interim president, Donahue declared that organizing was the federation's top priority. In his first weeks in office, he significantly increased the budget of the AFL-CIO organizing institute and pledged to "produce 1,500 new organizers for our unions, and to turn the organizing institute and its graduates into the greatest force for unionization since the New Deal."[30] And in his report to the AFL-CIO 21st Constitutional Convention, which several days later would reject his attempts to remain as president, Donahue declared that "the labor movement has a moral responsibility to offer every worker the opportunity to form a union."[31]

John Sweeney, in order to revitalize the labor movement, allocated $20 million "to organize new work places, especially the women, minorities and exploited immigrants."[32] To obtain one dollar of AFL-CIO funds, a local union must provide three dollars of its own funds. This approach, if successful, would provide unions with $80 million for rebuilding "labor's lost culture of organizing."[33] President Sweeney's efforts may result in some increases in union membership over the next few years.

Under Sweeney's leadership, the AFL-CIO embarked on a major organizing drive. On May 1, 1996, the federation opened a new chapter in organizing by starting the "Union Summer" program. The program was designed to recruit for the summer of 1996 many young workers and college students, who would work on union organizing and political initiatives.[34] The program enlisted nearly 1,500 college volunteers[35] "to work on campaigns organizing the new work force—women, people of color and recent immigrants."[36] The young activists worked with community coalitions as well as with union organizing drives. The new type of organizing campaigns involved newly formed and existing community organizations. Unions realized that they "must take a community-wide approach in organizing workers."[37]

Named to head the organizing department was Richard Bensinger, who adapted some of the tactics of the 1960s civil rights movement to labor organizing. A "Union Summer" organizing campaign, modeled after the "Freedom Summer" drive of 1964 to register African-American voters in the South, was carried out during the summer of 1996.[38] Drawing on the experience of the civil rights movement, Bensinger recruited liberal college students and combined their efforts with those of workers. Bensinger stated, "We want to know how a Barnard [college] student with a nose ring relates to a steelworker."[39] Bensinger, an advocate of civil disobedience, believes that federal law does not provide sufficient protection and redress to employees engaged in organizing campaigns. According to Bensinger, "When you take someone's job away," the person's civil rights are violated.[40]

Increased attention to politics is another major area of concern currently being addressed by the AFL-CIO. "We are at the point in America where the average worker has to take into consideration what the people in Congress are doing to their jobs," observed Gerald McEntee, president of the American Federation of State, County and Municipal Employees. He also stated, "Overtime pay, health care, and workplace safety—they are all on the table to be taken away from them."[41]

John Sweeney, the new AFL-CIO president, vowed in his campaign to make the labor movement relevant again in American politics.[42] Sweeney proposed a temporary assessment on each union member of 15 cents a month for one year to build a political war chest of $35 million. The newly generated funds would be used to target congressional districts in which anti-union Republicans were most vulnerable. The unions were also expected to provide at least 100 political organizers in each of the targeted districts. "In the last year plus, we have seen the worst assault in history on the American worker," said Steve Rosenthal, head of the AFL-CIO's political department.[43] Furthermore, he stated that "if there is to be any economic justice in America, a strong labor movement is essential."[44]

Finally, the Sweeney administration is committed to improving the image of organized labor and will try to buy media time and space in order to "convey the importance of unions to working people."[45] The success of the federation's agenda depends on a positive public image, AFL-CIO leaders believe. According to Denise Mitchell, John Sweeney's assistant for public affairs, "Unless we redefine our image . . . we won't be able to accomplish bargaining and political legislative victories."[46]

The structural changes in the federation and new initiatives in organizing, politics, and public relations appear to indicate a new level of militancy and activism that has not been demonstrated by organized labor in many years.

BENEFITS OF UNIONIZATION

Quite aside from any economic benefit of unionization, many employees have a personal need for someone to speak for them in dealing with their employers. First, some people are rather inarticulate. They feel that they lose arguments not because they are wrong but because they lack the necessary verbal skills. Second, thousands of public laws and regulations affect working life, not to mention rules made by management. Because management hires specialists to know all these things, employees often feel that they also need specialists to speak for them. Third, most worker grievances are really complaints that the boss has done something wrong. Yet the boss is the one to whom a complaint must normally go, and employees may fear that bosses will hold complaints against them. It is humiliating to accept a boss's conclusion that you are wrong just because you fear that your job will be jeopardized if you protest your supervisor's action. The union provides a representative who can present complaints impersonally. Moreover, almost every contractually negotiated grievance procedure provides for a neutral third party as the final decision maker. A union can also assure employees that they will not be disciplined for the mere act of protesting. These needs parallel those for legal representation and due process in other areas of life, and they exist whether or not a worker has any interest in collective bargaining over economic matters.

A union, especially if it is large, gives employees both the feeling and some of the reality of power. The union can take the employee's case right through to top management or outside through various agencies and up to the Supreme Court, if need be. Union presidents may consult with the president of the United States. They can be photographed at the White House. They can testify before congressional committees. Such things convey a vicarious sense of importance to members. In some places, such as coal towns, the union is an encompassing social institution, a way of life.

To some, the union also embodies a philosophy that rationalizes a way of life; just as the term *free enterprise* and the slogan "What's good for business is good for the country" help rationalize the pursuit of self-interest by business, *solidarity* and "More purchasing power for workers is good for the economy" do the same for the worker. Chambers of Commerce and a host of trade and other employer organizations publicize slogans for business; unions are the organizations that do so for workers. On both sides, the slogans and underlying rationales provide a sense of identity, of affiliation, and of worth in the larger scene. Though the magnitude of this effect varies greatly from person to person—and though most are probably not conscious of it—its role in holding people in the union movement is not insignificant. At a more pragmatic level, the many offices and posts within a union offer some people the possibility to achieve positions of relative prestige and power without having to leave the sphere of working-class life.

UNION ORGANIZING STRATEGIES

In the last five years, a number of books have addressed the future of unions, the low levels of unionization in the United States, and the steps that unions might take to increase their membership. Some of the ideas presented in these books are discussed in this section. Charles B. Craver, in his book *Can Unions Survive?*[47] suggests that, in order to reverse the trend of declining membership totals, unions should develop comprehensive strategies for organizing traditionally nonunion employees, particularly white-collar and service personnel. Historically, unions derived their strength from the blue-collar manufacturing sector—steel, rubber, and glass.[48] This sector has been shrinking in size because of demographic and structural changes in the economy.

Craver expresses some optimism regarding the future of unions. He states that "despite the disadvantageous industrial and global trends, there continues to be a need for worker representation. If American labor organizations can offer dissatisfied employees representational services that will enhance their employment situation . . . they should be able to generate sustained union growth."[49]

Although the American labor movement suffered major membership declines in the last 20 years, there are some positive signs on the horizon, one of which is a favorable public view of unions. According to recent polls, many Americans support the right of employees to unionize and also approve of unions in general.[50] In a 1988 Gallup Poll, 69 percent of Americans expressed the opinion that "labor unions are good for the nation as a whole."[51] Approval of labor unions is also expressed in the 1991 Fingerhut/Powers survey, which finds "60 percent of the public agreeing (and 23 percent disagreeing) that unions have basically been good for American working people."[52] In a 1991 Gallup Poll, 60 percent of the respondents approved of labor unions, and only 30 percent disapproved.[53] However, "a 1992 Harris Poll showed that general approval of unions does not necessarily translate into support of their stand on particular issues, such as on NAFTA."[54] The fact that the public at large is supportive of unions is very significant for the future of American unions.

Like Craver, Bronfenbrenner and Juravich recognize the significance of union organizing activities. In a 1994 working paper titled *Seeds of Resurgence,* they state that "no revival of . . . an American labor movement will be possible without massive new organizing. While it is important to stem the loss of unionized manufacturing jobs and do a better job of mobilizing current union members, these alone will not put the labor movement on the road to renewal."[55] The two researchers think that unions need new members not only to strengthen bargaining power and political power but also to refocus the labor movement's vision and purpose.

According to Bronfenbrenner and Juravich, unions can increase their organizing success by changing their organizing approaches. In their view, traditional campaigns, relying on gate leafletting, mass meetings, and mass mailings instead of on personal contact, are not very productive. They recommend aggressive, creative campaigns that rely on grass-roots and rank-and-file organizing committees. The main focus of each campaign should be person-to-person contact. They also point out that "units with a majority of women and people of color are much more likely to organize than units dominated by white men."[56] Such suggestions have been supported by the new AFL-CIO leadership, as discussed earlier in this chapter, and are currently being incorporated into the federation's organizing strategy.

TURNING THE TIDE

David Weil, in a 1994 book titled *Turning the Tide,*[57] suggests that the labor movement can turn the tide in its favor by developing creative and proactive strategies in response to changes taking place in our system. John T. Dunlop, in his foreword to this book, quoting Weil, states that "much of the responsibility for the future of labor rests squarely in the hands of present and future labor leaders, and on their ability to shape their policies, programs, and approaches to fit the needs of the workers they represent while adapting to the realities posed by the *external environment*. . . . Creating and implementing new and innovative strategies and structures for the next decade represents the most important and exciting challenge currently facing labor unions."[58]

Weil discusses five major forces that represent the external environment facing unions.[59] These are

1. the labor market, which includes the supply of and demand for labor as well as the characteristics of the work force.

2. technology, both hardware and software, as well as the organization of work.

3. social attitudes toward unions, including historic moves, beliefs, and public opinions.

4. economic and product market forces, including the macroeconomy, competition, employers' cost structures, and competitive strategies.

5. political and regulatory elements, such as legislation, regulating policies, and political actions. For unions representing government employees, the status of government revenues and expenditures needs to be considered.

These five forces within the external environment must be monitored closely for new developments because the outlook for unions is affected by and inextricably bound to these forces.

According to Weil,[60] unions' recent organizing success can be attributed to two factors: their ability to adjust to changes in the environment and their capacity to respond to the needs of dissatisfied workers. Weil cites the development of a tripartite bargaining structure by the Farm Labor Organizing Committee (FLOC) as an example of adjustment to the environment. In this case, the union recognized that it had to bargain not only with tomato and cucumber farmers but also with processors. The successful organizational campaign run by the Harvard Union of Clerical and Technical Workers (HUCTW) shows a union responding to the concerns of dissatisfied white collar and technical employees by involving the rank and file in one-on-one organizing effort.

During the last 15 years, unions were able to organize workers in such nontraditional sectors of the economy as clerical and health care. In 1980 unions represented only 14 percent of health care employees; by 1990 this total had risen to 20 percent.[61] Despite some organizing successes, unions still have far to travel to reach the pre-1980s membership levels (see Table 2.1).

In contrast with Craver and Weil, some scholars predict a dim future for unions. Leo Troy[62] of Rutgers University predicts that the extent of private-sector nonagricultural unionization will fall to 7 percent of employment by the year 2001, from 10.4 percent in

1995 (see Table 2.4). That development would coincide with the 7-percent figure of 100 years earlier. Some employers, like T. J. Rodgers, president of Cypress Semiconductor, have expressed the view that "unions were a reasonable response to bad working conditions way back when, but they are outdated now,"[63] a view undoubtedly shared by many employers in the United States. Some employers would agree with a Ritz Carlton official in San Francisco who stated that "if there is a union . . . management deserves it."[64] Not all employers view unions as a liability. Some managers, like John Turnipseed, a Southwest Airlines official, consider unions a positive force that "make[s] changes easier."[65]

In a 1996 book, Kochan, Katz, and McKersie[66] express the view that a reversal of the reduction in union membership will require not only labor law reforms and the diffusion of labor-management innovations but also the development by unions of new strategies for organizing employees in expanding industries and occupations. Kochan et al. hold that a reversal of the current trend "requires the most fundamental shift in values, strategies, policies and practices of all parties to industrial relations."[67]

Some authors suggest that, in the long run, the best union organizers may be overconfident managers who ignore the needs of their employees. Craver states that "as American executives decide that labor organizations are moribund entities that will become insignificant factors by the end of the current decade,"[68] they may abuse their authority. This in turn may create the necessary conditions for concerted employee activities conducive to union growth. The employees may conclude that they need a collective approach as a countervailing force to management power.

Kochan et al. do not subscribe to the expectations of researchers who conclude that unions will make a comeback because of the "stupidity of American management."[69] The assumption here is that as unions lose strength and represent a lesser threat to employers and as economic pressures intensify, "management commitment to innovative human resource practices will weaken."[70] According to Kochan et al., the primary motivation for improvements and innovations in human resource activities is not union avoidance but rather the need to enhance productivity and efficiency. Kochan et al. also question the assumption made by some that "if managerial commitment to human resource innovation diminishes, workers will automatically turn to unions as a response."[71] If unions are to rebound, they must do more than just wait for managerial incompetence in human resource practices. Labor movement leaders will have to "improve and modify their . . . organizing strategies for those . . . employees who can benefit from traditional . . . bargaining and expand the range . . . to meet the needs of those for whom the traditional package of union services is not well suited."[72] Some unions have started moving in this direction by offering labor market information, career counseling, and other services that may be required by professional, temporary, and part-time employees.

One organizing tool that has been helpful to unions since 1994 is the "union privilege program." The August 1994 *AFL-CIO News* refers to the program as a "prescription for growth" and a "boon for organizing."[73] The program includes some of the following benefits:

> Financial assistance for Union Member Mortgage participants who are unable to meet their monthly mortgage payment because of a prolonged strike, lockout or disability.
>> Strike-related "skip-payment" provisions in the Life Insurance, Loan and Union MasterCard programs.
>> "Open credit" on Health Needs Service prescription purchases made during union-sanctioned strikes lasting more than 30 days.[74]

In 1994 the Operating Engineers Local 501 in California signed on 2,000 new members.[75] Local 501 credits the appeal of the privilege program for its successful organizing drive.

SUMMARY

Many people have written organized labor's obituary prematurely. Mark Twain's famous quote, on his reappearance after a long absence, may be applied to unions: "Reports of my death have been greatly exaggerated."[76]

To overcome the setbacks of the last few decades, the union movement will most likely continue to develop a variety of new and innovative organizing tools and programs in order to expand its ranks and recruit new members.

Notes

1. When examining "union membership" data, one must be careful to note whether the figures include nonmembers who are covered by union contracts, members of employee associations, and Canadian membership. Union density statistics are frequently calculated with any of the previously mentioned membership figures divided by the total labor force, the civilian labor force, the nonagricultural labor force, wage and salary workers, or employed wage and salary workers.

2. *News,* United States Department of Labor, Bureau of Labor Statistics, USDL:95–40, February 8, 1995, pp. 1–2. See also *Employment and Earnings,* United States Department of Labor, Bureau of Labor Statistics (January 1995), pp. 214–17.

3. *Wall Street Journal,* July 26, 1994, p. 1.

4. The Dunlop Report, *Fact-Finding Report,* Commission on the Future of Worker-Management Relations (Washington, DC: U.S. Department of Labor and U.S. Department of Commerce, May 1994), p. 12.

5. Ibid., p. 6.

6. M. Ross Boyle, "Projections of Changing Labor Force Skill Mix through the Year 2000," *Economic Development Review* 8, no. 1 (Winter 1990), pp. 7–9.

7. Leo Troy, "Is the U.S. Unique in the Decline of Private Sector Unionism? *Journal of Labor Research* 6 (Spring 1990), pp. 111–43. William J. Moore and Robert J. Newman, "A Cross Section Analysis of Postwar Decline in American Trade Union Membership," *Journal of Labor Research* 4 (Spring 1988), pp. 111–25.

8. Gary N. Chaison and Joseph B. Rose, "The Macrodeterminants of Union Growth and Decline" in *The State of the Unions,* eds. George Strauss, Daniel G. Gallagher, and Jack Fiorito (Madison, WI: Industrial Relations Research Association, 1991), pp. 3–45.

9. Source: NLRB Annual Reports and Annual Election Reports.

10. Thomas A. Kochan and Kirsten R. Wever, "American Unions and the Future of Worker Representation" in *The State of the Unions,* pp. 363–86.

11. Ibid., p. 383.

12. Richard B. Freeman, "Why Unions Are Faring Poorly in NLRB Representation Elections" in *Challenges and Choices Facing American Labor,* ed. Thomas Kochan (Cambridge, MA: MIT Press, 1985), pp. 52–61.

13. For a discussion of the effect of public policy on union membership, see John F. Burton Jr. and Terry Thomason, "The Extent of Collective Bargaining in the Public Sector" in *Public Sector Bargaining,* 2nd ed., eds. B. Aaron, J. Najita, and J. Stern (Washington, DC: Bureau of National Affairs, 1988), pp. 1–51.

14. Henry S. Farber and Alan B. Krueger, "Union Membership in the United States: The Decline Continues" in *Employee Representation: Alternatives and Future Direction,* eds. B. Kaufman and M. Kleiner (Madison, WI: Industrial Relations Research Association, 1993), p. 130.

15. Ibid.

16. E. Wight Bakke, "Why Workers Join Unions," *Personnel* 22, no. 1 (July 1945), p. 37.

17. *Nation's Business,* April 1979, p. 32.

18. *The Changing Situation of Workers and Their Unions.* A Report by the AFL-CIO Committee on the Evolution of Work, Washington, DC, February 1985.

19. Paul Jarley and Jack Fiorito, "Associate Membership: Unionism or Consumerism?" *Industrial and Labor Relations Review* 43 (January 1990), pp. 209–24. Casey Ichniowski and Jeffrey S. Zax, "Today's Associations, Tomorrow's Unions," *Industrial and Labor Relations Review* 43 (January 1990), pp. 191–208.

20. See Roger Fisher and William Ury, with Bruce Patton, ed., *Getting to Yes: Negotiating Agreement without Giving In,* 2nd ed. (New York: Penguin Books, 1991); Roger Fisher and Scott Brown, *Getting Together: Building a Relationship That Gets to Yes* (Boston: Houghton Mifflin, 1988).

21. Associated Press story, *Cincinnati Enquirer,* May 23, 1995, p. B9.

22. Ibid.

23. *New York Times,* May 11, 1995, p. A17.

24. Michael Byrne, "Delegates Stand Up for Labor Movement," *AFL-CIO News,* Oct. 23, 1995, p. 1.

25. Robert L. Rose and Asra Q. Nomani, "Sweeney Wins Bitter Fight for President of AFL-CIO," *Wall Street Journal,* October 26, 1995, p. A2.

26. Peter T. Kilborn, "Delegates of Labor Gather, Battered but Now Buoyant," *New York Times,* October 22, 1995, p. 28.

27. *New York Times,* October 26, 1995, pp. A1, D25.

28. Ibid.

29. *New York Times,* October 22, 1995, p. 28.

30. Muriel H. Cooper, "Unions Face 'Moral Duty' to Organize," *AFL-CIO News,* October 23, 1995, p. 1.

31. Ibid.

32. *The Cincinnati Enquirer,* April 21, 1996, p. H5.

33. Ibid.

34. Internet, http://www.aflcio.org/summeranswers.html, 8/7/96.

35. *Wall Street Journal,* October 29, 1996, pp. B1, B5.

36. *AFL-CIO News* 6, no. 8 (May 6, 1996), pp. 1, 12.

37. Ibid. 41, no. 12 (July 1, 1996), pp. 1, 6.

38. G. Pascal Zachary, "Chief AFL-CIO Organizer to Try Civil Rights Tactics," *Wall Street Journal,* February 8, 1996, pp. B1, B12.

39. Robert L. Rose, "Love of Labor: Training the Newest Generation of AFL-CIO Organizers," *Wall Street Journal,* October 26, 1995, p. B1.

40. *Wall Street Journal,* February 8, 1996, pp. B1, B12.

41. *New York Times,* October 22, 1995, pp. 1, 28.

42. Glen Burkins, "AFL-CIO Sets Drive to Back Democrats," *Wall Street Journal,* February 22, 1996, p. A2.

43. Michael Byrne, "Unprecented Political Push Planned," *AFL-CIO News,* February 5, 1996, p. 4.

44. Ibid.

45. Michael Byrne, "Federation Prepares for Major Changes," *AFL-CIO News,* February 5, 1996, p. 12.

46. Ibid.

47. Charles B. Craver, *Can Unions Survive?* (New York: New York University Press, 1993), p. 59.

48. John T. Dunlop, "The Future of Labor-Management Relations" in *The Future of Labor Management Innovation in the United States,* eds. James A. Auerbach and Jerome J. Barrett (Washington, DC: National Planning Association 1993), p. 87.

49. Craver, op. cit., p. 157.

50. Dunlop Report, p. 63.
51. Ibid.
52. Ibid.
53. Gallup Poll, Survey No. G0222007, August 3, 1991, in David Weil, *Turning the Tide* (New York: Lexington Books, 1994), p. 270.
54. Dunlop Report, p. 63.
55. Kate Bronfenbrenner and Tom Juravich, *Seeds of Resurgence* (Washington, DC: Institute for the Study of Labor Organizations, The George Meany Center for Labor Studies, 1994), p. 2.
56. Ibid., p. 5.
57. David Weil, *Turning the Tide: Strategic Planning for Labor Unions.* Copyright © 1994 David Weil. First published by Lexington Books. All correspondence should be sent to Jossey-Bass Inc., Publishers, San Francisco. All rights reserved.
58. Ibid., pp. xi–xii, 256.
59. Ibid., p. 24.
60. Ibid.
61. See Arthur Shostok, *Robust Unionism: Innovations on the Labor Movement* (Ithaca, N.Y.: ILR Press, 1990), p. 64.
62. *Wall Street Journal,* August 30, 1994, p. 1.
63. Ibid.
64. Ibid.
65. Ibid.
66. Thomas A. Kochan, Harry C. Katz, and Robert B. McKersie, *Transformation of American Industrial Relations* (Ithaca, NY: ILR Press, 1996), pp. 250–53.
67. Ibid., p. 253.
68. Craver, op. cit., p. 157.
69. Kochan et al., op. cit., p. 249.
70. Ibid.
71. Ibid.
72. Ibid., p. 250.
73. *AFL-CIO News,* August 8, 1994, pp. 6–7.
74. Ibid.
75. Ibid.
76. "Are Unions Dead?" Symposium, *Business and Society Review,* Summer 1990, p. 4.

CHAPTER 3

Evolution of the Legal Framework for Private-Sector Collective Bargaining

After reading this chapter, you should be able to

- Understand the application of the conspiracy doctrine.

- Comprehend the use of injunctions in labor cases.

- Describe the application of the Clayton Act to union activities.

- Identify and explain the major provisions of the Wagner Act.

- Identify and explain the major provisions of the Taft-Hartley Act and of the Landrum-Griffin Act.

- Discuss and explain the reasons for the passage of the Wagner Act, the Taft-Hartley Act, and the Landrum-Griffin Act.

PUBLIC POLICY TOWARD UNIONS AND COLLECTIVE BARGAINING

There is little doubt, as we review labor history, that our laws and our public policy regarding unions and collective bargaining and the attitudes of those who implemented those laws have profoundly affected the development and present status of collective bargaining in the United States. It is the purpose of this chapter and the next to describe and evaluate public policy with respect to unions and collective bargaining.

Although we recognize that such divisions are somewhat arbitrary, for analytical purposes we will divide the development of public policy toward unions and labor-management relations into five periods: opposition to unions, transition toward acceptance, support, control, and transformation.

THE PERIOD OF OPPOSITION TO UNIONS

The Conspiracy Doctrine

Employer complaints against unions started coming into the courts long before any legislation had been passed on the subject. Nevertheless, judges felt obligated to make decisions, which they did on the basis of their consciences (or prejudices) and precedents borrowed from other subjects. Such common-law decisions constituted the whole of the legal attitude toward unions during most of the nineteenth century. During most of this period, because judges came mainly from the upper middle classes, they seemed to have little sympathy for workers who sought to better their lot by forming unions. Hence, with a virtually clear field to choose from, they selected precedents detrimental to unions, chief among which was the conspiracy doctrine.[1]

The essence of the doctrine is that what is legal for one person becomes an illegal conspiracy if several persons join together for the same purpose. The first case to which the criminal conspiracy doctrine was applied involved the Philadelphia Cordwainers in 1806: Union members were fined for "conspiring" to raise their wages. The doctrine was stated clearly in 1823 in the Hatters case, involving a strike aimed at getting an employer to discharge a man who was working for "knocked-down wages." The strikers were found guilty on the ground that

> journeymen confederating and refusing to work, unless for certain wages, may be indicted for conspiracy—for the offense consists in the conspiracy and not in the refusal: and all conspiracies are illegal though the subject matter of them may be lawful—The gist of the conspiracy is the unlawful confederation, and the act is complete when the confederacy is made, and any act done in pursuit of it is a constituent part of the offense.[2]

It would be an exaggeration to say that unions themselves were illegal and that their mere existence was prohibited. They were taken to court only for specific actions against employers or fellow workers, and only the union activity, not the union itself, was held to be illegal. But when one considers that the main reason for union existence is to bargain collectively; that it is the fact of collectivity, not the bargaining, that is illegal; and that "the act is complete when the confederacy is made," the distinction becomes almost meaningless.

The bias of this doctrine against unions is plain, for the same line of reasoning was conspicuously not applied in other areas. Capitalists were permitted to join together in the joint-stock company, the forerunner of the modern corporation. Voters and candidates for public office were allowed to "conspire" to get control of the government through political parties. "Conspiracy" to do many things was evident on all sides, but only with respect to unions did the common law find it illegal. As the defense attorney in the original Cordwainers' case put it,

> Dancing is very fashionable and a very pleasing recreation; though according to the principle of my learned friends, a country dance would be criminal, a cotillion unlawful, even a minuet a conspiracy; and nothing but a hornpipe or a solo would be stepped with impunity![3]

The attorney added that to seek help in putting out the fire in one's house would be a conspiracy, and the city could be destroyed "or those who put out the blaze must be consumed in the flames of the common law."[4]

In partial justification of the use of the conspiracy doctrine, it may be observed that the economy was still close enough to a handicraft system that workers' banding together to raise their wages closely resembled a monopoly agreement by craftsmen to fix the price of their product and was strongly at odds with the new laissez-faire philosophy of the age. As the Recorder's charge to the jury put it at the end of the trial in the first case, "A combination of workmen to raise their wages may be considered in a two fold point of view: one is to benefit themselves . . . the other is to injure those who do not join their society. The rule of law condemns both."[5]

In 1842 the conspiracy doctrine was considerably softened by a decision of Chief Justice Shaw of the Massachusetts Supreme Court. Judge Shaw ruled that the conspiracy could not be prosecuted unless either its aims or its methods were illegal in themselves. This decision stopped only temporarily the use of the conspiracy doctrine against unions, and there were more conspiracy cases during the second half of the century than during the first half.[6] This phenomenon was legally possible despite the Shaw decision because the decision had not come out of the United States Supreme Court, and judges in future cases therefore had just as much right to apply the older precedents as the newer one. As a result, the doctrine of conspiracy persisted as a partial basis of decisions until about 1930.

The Injunction

As noted in Chapter 1, by the 1880s unions had begun to take on much of their present form and philosophy. The AFL was under way and was doing effective bargaining in some trades. Although the Knights of Labor had folded, it was evident that labor was on the march, and employers were alert for an effective method to combat it. This they found in the labor injunction, first used in England in 1868 and first copied in this country sometime during the rail strikes of the 1870s.

The injunction is a legal device with many uses other than in labor disputes. It is an order issued by a judge at the request of one party, directing a second party to refrain from some specified act. Its most obvious use is to prevent irreparable damage, as to prevent me from cutting down a magnificent tree that you claim is on your side of the property line until a full investigation has determined who is right. In business and labor relations, "irreparable" tends to mean something that could not be made good by a money payment that is within the capacity of the offender to pay.

A full-fledged injunction evolves through three stages—a temporary restraining order, a temporary injunction, and a permanent injunction.[7] The first may be issued by a judge on the basis of an ex parte hearing—that is, with only one of the affected parties present. Within a few days, both parties have an opportunity to be heard, and either the complaint will be dismissed or a temporary injunction will be issued. If the parties cannot settle the dispute under the temporary injunction, the court may make it permanent and forbid forever the enjoined act. Because of the temporary nature of the strike, permanent antistrike injunctions are rarely seen in labor disputes; the temporary restraining order is usually sufficient.

Four aspects of the injunction make it a particularly effective weapon for employers and a particularly detrimental one for unions when used against strikes. First, the judge has full discretion in deciding whether to issue the restraining order—without having to hear the union's side at all. Because of the bias already described, judges often tended to enjoin strikes upon the slightest pretext when asked to do so by employers. The exercise of the bias was facilitated by a second factor—the enormous breadth of meaning given to the term *property* by the courts. The property that could be protected by an injunction came to include not only tangible goods and buildings but such intangibles as goodwill, right of access, and eventually the right to operate one's business without interference. Under such broad definitions, almost any strike was potentially enjoinable.

A third aspect of the injunction was the method of levying penalties. Unlike violation of a law, for which minimum and maximum penalties are often specified by the law itself, violation of an injunction constitutes contempt of court. The penalty is at the discretion of the judge who issued the order and whose temper is usually not improved by having his or her personal orders disobeyed.

Finally, the notion that an injunction preserves the status quo until a fuller determination of the situation can be made simply does not apply in a strike. A strike is by nature dynamic, and a strike enjoined is a strike being lost, particularly when it is an organizing strike called by an incipient union trying to get established in a plant. The stamp of illegality often had a further inhibiting effect on those who were not confirmed and fighting unionists.

The impact of the injunction during its heyday (roughly 1880 to 1932) cannot be appreciated unless it is put in the context of the times. In that period, there was no legal protection of the right to join a union, and employers could freely fire anyone who participated in a strike or demonstrated sympathy for the union. A lost strike often meant lost jobs for all participants. Hence, solidarity, as evidenced by an uncrossed picket line, was crucial.

The Sherman Act

In 1890 the courts received from Congress an important new basis for injunctions, the Sherman Antitrust Act. There is much controversy over whether Congress intended the statute to apply to unions, which are not explicitly mentioned therein. In 1908, however, in the case of *Loewe v. Lawler,* the Supreme Court ruled that the Sherman Act made "every contract, combination, or conspiracy in restraint of trade illegal," whether of business, farmers, or labor.[8] By 1928 unions had been prosecuted 83 times under the act, accounting for 18 percent of all the cases brought under the act.[9]

One of the most important cases on record, and one that indicated the need for some restriction on the use of the injunction, was that of the Pullman strike in 1894. During the winter of 1893 to 1894, the Pullman Palace Car Company, near Chicago, instituted a wage reduction. In March its employees joined the American Railway Union, a new industrial union under the presidency of Eugene V. Debs, designed to include all workers connected with railways. In May the Pullman workers went on strike. After trying unsuccessfully to get the Pullman Company to arbitrate, the American Railway Union voted to stop handling all Pullman cars on the railroads. The railroad companies continued to make up their trains with Pullman cars included, so the boycott of Pullman cars shortly became a railway strike.

Within a few days, the attorney general of the United States obtained from the Chicago circuit court an injunction based on the Sherman Act and on the obstruction of the mails. It enjoined the union, its officers, and "all other persons whomsoever" from "in any way or manner interfering with" the business of the railroads entering Chicago, carrying United States mail, or engaging in interstate commerce. It forbade "compelling or inducing or attempting to compel or induce by threats, intimidation, persuasion, or force of violence, any of the employees . . . to refuse or fail to perform any of their duties as employees."[10] Many other restrictions were added, but the simple substance was that no one was allowed to strike or in any way, directly or indirectly, to assist the strike. Debs and several other union leaders were later jailed for contempt. The strike was marked by considerable violence and the presence of federal troops sent in by President Cleveland. After about two weeks, the strike was broken and the violence was ended.

The Abortive Clayton Act

Apparently in order to restrain judges from their continued application of the Sherman Act against unions, the Clayton Act, which in 1914 amended the Sherman Act, included this provision:

> SECTION 6: That the labor of a human being is not a commodity. Nothing contained in the anti-trust laws shall be construed to forbid the existence and operation of labor, agri-

cultural, or horticultural organizations, or to forbid or restrain individual members of such organizations from lawfully carrying out the legitimate objects thereof; nor shall such organizations, or the members thereof, be held or construed to be illegal combinations or conspiracies in restraint of trade under the anti-trust laws.[11]

In its Section 20, the Clayton Act also restricted the use of injunctions by federal courts to cases where "necessary to prevent irreparable injury to property, or to the property right . . . for which there is no adequate remedy at law." In view of what subsequently occurred, it is worth quoting the last paragraph of Section 20 in full:

> And no such restraining order or injunction shall prohibit any person or persons, whether singly or in concert, from terminating any relation of employment, or from ceasing to perform any work or labor, or from recommending, advising, or persuading others by peaceful means so to do; or from attending at any place where any such person or persons may lawfully be, for the purpose of peacefully obtaining or communicating information, or from peacefully persuading any person to work or to abstain from working; or from ceasing to patronize or to employ any party to such dispute, or from recommending, advising, or persuading others by peaceful and lawful means so to do: from paying or giving to, or withholding from, any person engaged in such a dispute, any strike benefits or other moneys or things of value; or from peaceably assembling in a lawful manner, and for lawful purposes; or from doing any act or thing which might lawfully be done in the absence of such dispute by any party thereto: nor shall any of the acts specified in this paragraph be considered or held to be violations of any law of the United States.[12]

Sections 6 and 20 together seem to provide unequivocally that a union itself, a strike, or any peaceful activity to organize or assist a strike is not to be considered a conspiracy in restraint of trade under the antitrust laws and is not under any circumstance to be enjoined by a federal court, except to prevent damage that the union could not, by the payment of damages or otherwise, make good. The Clayton Act was widely hailed as the "Magna Carta of labor."

One would think from reading the Clayton Act that the use of injunctions in general and injunctions under the Sherman Act in particular would have come to an end in labor disputes, except for cases plainly involving irreparable injury to property. The reverse actually occurred.

The tortuous argument by which the Supreme Court negated the wording of the law went as follows. The Clayton Act (said the Court) covers only peaceful activities by unions. But (the Court added, in a clause of questionable accuracy) the courts had never prohibited peaceful activities. Hence, the Clayton Act did not change anything. Because the act did not change anything, the courts could continue to apply all the precedents previously developed. The upshot of the matter was that, whereas injunctions under the Sherman Act had theretofore been confined to secondary boycotts and sympathy strikes, after the Clayton Act they came to be applied to ordinary primary strikes. The only advantage of the Clayton Act to unions was that the union itself could not be condemned as a conspiracy in restraint of trade, a matter not seriously in question in any event.[13]

The case that seems to have held the greatest potential for completely thwarting the actions of organized labor was that of the *Hitchman Coal and Coke Company v. Mitchell*.[14] The case started in 1907, well before the passage of the Clayton Act, but was not decided by the Supreme Court until 1917. The employees of Hitchman Coal had been induced to sign yellow-dog contracts, agreeing that they would not join a union while employed there. The Supreme Court upheld the enforceability of such contracts and approved an injunction against all organizing activity on the ground that any organizing efforts constituted an inducement to breach the contract.[15] The decision constituted a massive potential for blocking unionization because under it an employer could make it illegal for anyone even to ask an employee to join a union.

Summary of the Period of Opposition

Only the more important federal cases have been described in this chapter. Injunctions by state and local courts in purely routine strikes were continuing with mounting frequency from 1880 to about 1935. The long experience with governmental intervention on the side of business and against unions engendered the labor movement's philosophy of *voluntarism.* This term refers to a belief that rights and obligations in labor-management relations should flow from collective bargaining, not government regulation.

THE TRANSITION TOWARD ACCEPTANCE

Before World War I, several states enacted legislation recognizing the right of employees to organize. But these laws were of little avail, and most were thrown out by the courts. An important example was a law passed in 1903 in Kansas outlawing the yellow-dog contract, which was overruled by the Supreme Court of the United States in 1915. The federal Erdman Act of 1898, dealing with the settlement of labor disputes on the railroads, prohibited yellow-dog contracts in that industry. In 1908 the Supreme Court ruled it unconstitutional as a violation of the Fifth Amendment.[16] Justice Holmes dissented, the basis of his reasoning (here as in a number of other cases) being that the court majority had assumed that the bargaining power of employers and individual workmen was equal and that this assumption was contrary to fact.

Some occurrences on the administrative front also presaged the development of a new policy. Late in World War I, the federal government established a War Labor Conference Board, consisting of five management, five labor, and two public representatives to plan for the handling of labor problems. This board recommended the creation of a National War Labor Board and certain guiding principles for labor relations. Among other principles the War Labor Conference Board included the following:

> Right to organize—1. The right of workers to organize in trade unions and to bargain collectively through chosen representatives is recognized and affirmed. This right shall not be denied, abridged, or interfered with by employers in any manner whatsoever.[17]

No provisions were established for enforcing the principle, and meanwhile the Supreme Court continued to deny it, as in the *Hitchman* and *Kansas* decisions. The shortage of labor, however, did give bargaining power to employees, and union membership grew apace during the war period.

The National War Labor Board was set up to handle labor disputes. The mere fact that union leaders could appear before such a government board as recognized representatives of organized employees was in itself a marked advance. From 1917 to 1920, the railroads were operated by the government. Under its policy of strict nondiscrimination between union and nonunion employees, union membership increased considerably.

In 1920 the railroads were returned to private hands. But the principle of nondiscrimination continued, and in 1926 it was made permanent by the passage of the Railway Labor Act. This was the first time that the government declared unqualifiedly the right of private employees to join (or not to join) unions without interference from their employers and also provided a mechanism for enforcing this right. It should be noted, however, that the railroad industry stood alone in its development of a means of dealing neutrally with the issues of unionization and collective bargaining. Throughout the 1920s, the remainder of private industry continued to use the courts as a primary vehicle in its drive against unionism.

Meanwhile, in response to a series of adverse court decisions, unions were pressing strongly for some restriction of injunctions. In 1928 both major political parties endorsed such a limitation, and in 1930 the Supreme Court upheld the pertinent sections of the Railway Labor Act by ordering the Texas and New Orleans Railroad to bargain with the Brotherhood of Railway Clerks instead of with a company-dominated union. The late 1920s clearly portended a reversal of the legal status of unions that had prevailed since the Cordwainers' case in 1806.

Although the period from roughly 1900 to 1932 was one of transition toward the acceptance of unions, actual restrictions on union activities were proceeding with mounting intensity. The tide of change visible by World War I did not actually arrive until 1932.

THE PERIOD OF SUPPORT

The Norris-LaGuardia Act

In 1932 Congress finally accomplished what it had apparently intended in 1914 in the Clayton Act. In nine carefully worded paragraphs, the Norris-LaGuardia Act denied to federal courts the right to forbid strikes, peaceful picketing, or other actions not illegal in themselves, such as publicizing a strike or raising and disbursing funds in its support. Labor injunctions were not entirely outlawed, but the conditions of their use were drastically limited. The yellow-dog contract was made unenforceable.

Although some lower courts continued to issue injunctions as before, the Supreme Court eventually sustained the Norris-LaGuardia Act.[18] Some 25 states, including most important industrial ones, had passed laws roughly similar to the Norris-LaGuardia Act restricting injunctions issued by state courts.[19]

On the other hand, many states passed no such laws, and state courts continued to issue injunctions on the old terms. The full potential of the Norris-LaGuardia Act was never to be felt, however, because of further legal developments that would continue the period of support for trade unionism.

The Wagner Act—High Point of Support

The Wagner Act, whose official title was the National Labor Relations Act (NLRA),[20] passed Congress in 1935 in a strong antibusiness atmosphere. Its central provisions are still part of our basic labor legislation and seem likely to remain so for many years. Hence the remainder of this chapter has contemporary, rather than merely historical, significance.

The Wagner Act was monolithic, in the sense that it contained only one central idea, with all other parts in direct support thereof. This central purpose was stated succinctly in Section 7:

> Employees shall have the right to self-organization, to form, join, or assist labor organizations, to bargain collectively through representatives of their own choosing, and to engage in concerted activities, for the purpose of collective bargaining or other mutual aid or protection.[21]

The "right to bargain collectively" is the core of the law. The phrase "through representatives of their own choosing" brought to labor the prerequisite of meaningful bargaining—that workers have complete, unilateral control over the selection of their own "attorneys" in a dispute, with no interference or control whatsoever by management. The law as passed did not make a parallel statement of management's right to select its own representatives because management's freedom on that score had not been seriously challenged by unions.

Experience had made it clear that a bare statement of workers' rights to organize would be meaningless because employers possessed effective devices for preventing organization. Therefore, the law in Section 8(a) listed five unfair labor practices in which employers were not allowed to engage. Prohibition of the first three prevented the employer from exercising influence on the employees' choice regarding unionization. The first denied the employer the freedom "to interfere with, restrain, or coerce employees in the exercise of the rights guaranteed in Section 7." The second made it unfair "to dominate or interfere with the formation or administration of any labor organization or contribute financial support to it,"[22] which is another way of saying that company unions are improper. The third prevented an employer from discriminating between union and nonunion employees in such a way as to encourage or discourage the joining of unions.

The listing of a fourth unfair labor practice was necessary if the first three prohibitions were to be enforced; employers were forbidden to discriminate against anyone who filed charges or gave testimony under the act. Regulation of a final unfair practice was necessary if the other four protections were to have any meaning. The fifth item prohibited an employer from refusing to recognize and bargain collectively with the representatives selected by his or her employees—the good-faith bargaining requirement.

Two additional things remained to be done. One was to furnish a mechanism for determining the employees' choice of bargaining representative. To this end, Section 9 of the law provided for a government-supervised secret-ballot election, in which the employees could choose between a union and no union or between two or more unions in the event of such a contest. Less formal methods, such as a count of the number of workers signing cards authorizing a union to represent them, could be used if both sides were satisfied as to their accuracy. The majority choice would prevail, and a union so selected would become the exclusive representative of all employees in the bargaining unit. Through this simple technique, the Wagner Act largely substitutes peaceful persuasion and the ballot box for the violence and bitterness of the typical organizing strike—a major contribution of the law.

Finally, a National Labor Relations Board (NLRB or Board) was established to enforce the law. Much of its work is delegated to regional offices, which conduct hearings and issue decisions on charges of unfair labor practices, subject to appeal to the national Board, and from there to the federal courts. The law is essentially remedial rather than punitive. A finding of guilt is handled by an order to cease and desist rather than by a penalty levied on the employer.

Needless to say, the Wagner Act was not viewed with joy by employers, particularly because the protections and guarantees accorded unions and employees were not accompanied by any restrictions on union activity or any protections for employers. The National Association of Manufacturers, in particular, conducted an intense campaign in which it alleged that the law was unconstitutional and advised its members to disregard it.

The psychological effect of the Wagner Act upon workers was apparent immediately, as union organizers tried to make them feel that the "government wants you to join." Real enforcement did not begin until the Supreme Court accepted the law as constitutional in 1937,[23] though its impact was widened by a number of states that passed "little Wagner Acts" to cover intrastate commerce. Employers immediately started a campaign to change the law, either by repealing it or by making it more balanced.

THE TRANSITION TO TAFT-HARTLEY

The Wagner Act was not destined to remain our basic labor legislation for long. Two broad causes led to its amendment by the Taft-Hartley Act in 1947.

First, at the tender age of 12, the Wagner Act was inherently not a whole labor policy. It was passed after a long period of intense anti-union activity by management, assisted by government. Unions were weak and much in need of protection from militant employers, who barred no holds in fighting them. The Wagner Act had a single purpose—to protect employees and unions from employers by identifying a series of "protected activities" and then preventing employers from interfering with those activities.

The Wagner Act was clearly a product of its time and reflected the negative image that then surrounded management. However, the law made no provision for the conditions it created. By restricting employer interference with the formation of unions, under an administration and before a public sympathetic to labor, the law enabled many unions to grow from fledgling bodies to large and powerful organizations. Some unions were now able not only to defend their own existence but also seriously to challenge and attack employers' authority. The labor movement as a whole grew from 4 million in 1935 to roughly 16 million in 1948, testifying to the impact of the Wagner Act. Some labor leaders developed more skill in acquiring power than in using it wisely, but the Wagner Act made no provision for controlling the results. For example, the law gave no protection to the employer, the public, or even the employees in a fight between two unions. The act had furthered the practice of collective bargaining by requiring an employer to bargain with a union of his or her employees, but it made no provision for a union's refusing to bargain and trying to force conditions unilaterally on an employer. Nor did the law provide for workers caught in a dictatorial union. These and other problems made it clear that the Wagner Act was not adequate as a complete, permanent labor policy.

A second major reason for revision was the vocal criticism of the law and of unions by business and the press. Employers had always objected loudly that the Wagner Act was one-sided. During World War II, despite a largely successful no-strike commitment on the part of organized labor, some strikes did occur. The vast majority were short, total time lost from strikes was low, and many were wildcats called in violation of union orders. Nevertheless, the press contrasted the safety and comfort of strikers with the conditions of soldiers in foxholes and exaggerated the injury caused by the strikes.

Given that some changes in the law were needed, labor leaders virtually guaranteed drastic modifications by adamantly rejecting minor adjustments while Congress was still sympathetic to labor. By the time the Republicans got control of both houses of the Congress in 1946, it was too late for minor concessions. As Representative Fred Hartley, sponsor of the new bill in the House of Representatives, made clear, it was the intent of its framers "to reverse the basic direction of our national labor policy," and the mood of the Congress was about as strongly anti-union as the Wagner Act Congress had been pro-union. The Taft-Hartley Act, officially the Labor-Management Relations Act of 1947, was passed over the veto of President Truman, who objected to the reversal of policy, though he had earlier approved strong legislation for curtailing national emergency strikes.

In contrast to the Wagner Act, the Taft-Hartley Act is complex. Its complexity resides largely in additions to the Wagner Act because much of the original Wagner Act still remains unchanged in Taft-Hartley. Whereas the Wagner Act protected employees and unions from employers, Taft-Hartley seeks to protect employees, unions, management, and the public from the acts of both unions and management. And, whereas the Wagner Act attempted to regulate only the relationship between unions and management, its successor also regulates some aspects of the labor contract, some internal affairs of unions, and other activities. In scope and framework, Taft-Hartley is capable of being a balanced labor policy. Whether or not it is so in fact, it unquestionably ushered in the era of control, as we shall see.

In 1959 Congress passed the Landrum-Griffin Act, which consisted of two major parts. One was the Labor-Management Reporting and Disclosure Act, which will be discussed separately later in this chapter. The other was a series of amendments to the Taft-Hartley Act, which will be incorporated into the discussion of that law in the following section.

THE PERIOD OF CONTROL: TAFT-HARTLEY AND MISCELLANEOUS LEGISLATION CURRENTLY IN FORCE

The Taft-Hartley Act launched the period of control, which seems a reasonably accurate name for the period since the act's passage in 1947. Other legislation discussed in the following pages also seems to fall properly under the heading of "control." In addition, we will look at decisions by the National Labor Relations Board and the courts because shifts in interpretation have often had consequences as important as if the statute had been changed. The discussion in this section represents the current state of the law.

The Taft-Hartley Act's Philosophy

In its preamble and statement of policy, Taft-Hartley retains the language of the Wagner Act in stating that it is the policy of the United States to encourage the practice and procedures of collective bargaining. The law accepts the major implication of this statement of policy by recognizing (1) that collective bargaining presumes the existence of unions and (2) that employers have considerable power and desire to prevent or destroy unions (and therefore collective bargaining), which power they will often exercise unless they are restrained.

The Taft-Hartley Act therefore retains the Wagner Act's Section 7 guarantee that employees "shall have the right to self-organization, to form, join, or assist labor organizations, to bargain collectively through representatives of their own choosing, and to engage in other concerted activities for the purpose of collective bargaining."[24] However, reflecting a perhaps contradictory philosophical underpinning of Taft-Hartley, the amended Section 7 also protects employees' right to refrain from engaging in collective activity.

Taft-Hartley is composed of parts of the distinctly pro–collective bargaining Wagner Act and newly drafted parts that reflect a philosophy emphasizing individual choice. One commentator has pointed to these conflicting statutory purposes to explain the wide range of possible interpretations of the law. This circumstance has enabled members of the National Labor Relations Board with differing political views to justify their decisions by referring to different parts of Taft-Hartley.[25]

Basic Content of the Taft-Hartley Act

Coverage

The Taft-Hartley Act's coverage is not universal in that it specifically excludes labor groups on the basis of the occupations or the industries in which they work. This exclusion from coverage of the act's protections therefore serves to discourage collective bargaining by these groups. The act explicitly excludes agricultural and domestic labor, supervisors in all industries, workers covered by the Railway Labor Act, individuals employed by spouses or parents, independent contractors, and government employees at all levels. The AFL-CIO has sought to extend the law to cover agricultural employees, whose employers in most states are free to use the wide range of "union-busting" devices of pre–Wagner Act days. An important exception is California, where in 1975 the California Agricultural Labor Relations Act established mechanisms for conducting representation elections for field workers. Relative peace has followed the new legislation after years of dispute among the United Farm Workers (UFW), the Teamsters, and the agricultural employers. Despite this success, it is unlikely that the Taft-Hartley Act will be expanded to cover agricultural labor in the near future.

Most government workers, as will be seen in Chapter 16, currently have collective bargaining rights, despite their absence from Taft-Hartley coverage. In the 1960s and 1970s, the federal government and most (though not all) states passed separate enabling legislation giving some version of collective bargaining rights to public employees.

As a federal law, in order to be constitutional, Taft-Hartley can apply only to employees of employers whose firms "affect interstate commerce." Because many states do not similarly protect the right to organize, such protection is largely nonexistent where not provided by federal law. The legislative jurisdiction of the NLRB was expanded in 1970 to labor relations in the U.S. Postal Service. In 1974 the NLRB was granted legislative authority over private hospitals and nursing homes. Over the years, the NLRB has expanded its jurisdiction to cover private colleges and universities, charitable institutions, day care centers, law firms, job corps centers, and hotels and motels.[26] The NLRB applies certain monetary norms that employers must satisfy before it will claim jurisdiction. In practice the Board confines its jurisdiction to firms that have annual outflow or inflow, direct or indirect, across state lines of at least $50,000. The Board has established, in general, a $500,000 annual gross revenue for retail enterprises. These norms vary among various categories of business, including hotels and taxicab companies. The following jurisdictional standards apply to other industries: public utilities and transportation companies, $250,000; newspapers, $200,000; communication companies, $100,000; nursing homes, $100,000; other health care facilities including hospitals, $250,000; and private colleges and symphony orchestras, $1,000,000.[27] In states without enabling legislation, employees in smaller firms not covered by Taft-Hartley in effect have no legal protection of the right to organize. Even in states that have their own legislation, the right may be tenuously held, as enforcement provisions and procedures are not well developed there.

Protection of the Right to Organize and Bargain

Except for one change affecting union security, prohibition of the closed shop, the Taft-Hartley Act restates the Wagner Act's five unfair labor practices that employers are prohibited from using to fight the existence of unions. To the extent that these five provisions (Section 8[a]) are enforced, they ensure that employees can have and be represented by unions if they so desire.

Taft-Hartley acknowledges that recognition of a union by an employer is a prerequisite of collective bargaining, and it requires employers to deal with unions that represent a majority of employees. In support of this requirement, each side must bargain with the other in good faith and must reduce the agreement to writing if the other side so desires. The law, of course, does not require either side to make concessions. But it does require that each give reasons for its position and make some counterproposals. In addition, an employer cannot discharge workers for making bargaining demands.

Protection of Mutual Independence in Bargaining

Meaningful collective bargaining requires that each side maintain complete independence in selecting and instructing its bargaining representatives. But a free-speech clause of the Taft-Hartley Act, as currently interpreted, may destroy some of this protection.

The full implication of this portion is often not recognized. Collective bargaining presupposes independent selection of bargaining representatives on both sides, and Section 7 of the law assures employees the right to representatives "of their own choosing." The law suggests that employers should not be able to interfere with their employees' right to unionize and, if they do, with their choice of union. This does not mean that employers have no interest in the matter. Given the chance, employers would presumably help employees opt for either no union or a weak one.

At the same time, information possessed by employers that would be useful to employees in deciding whether to unionize should not be withheld. The problem, then, is to prohibit employer statements that coerce but to allow those that inform or persuade, even if the latter are clearly anti-union. This is not an easy distinction to enforce. To be consistent, the law must, of course, also protect the employer's independence from the union in the opposite direction—a matter to be discussed later in this section.

Section 8(c) of the Taft-Hartley Act specifically provides employers full freedom of speech unless their expression "contains threat of reprisal or force or promise of benefit."[28] This provision deals mainly with words rather than their effects—with instruments rather than results. Prior to 1953, the NLRB gave much attention to the probably coercive effects of what an employer said. In 1953 the Board decided to protect employer speech and thus weaken a union organizing campaign. For example, it refused to set aside a representation election lost by the union, even though the employer had argued strongly against the union in a meeting held several days before the election, on company time and property (a so-called captive audience speech), with all workers requested to attend. Pro-union spokesmen were not allowed to reply.[29] The company also enforced a "no-solicitation" rule, which prevented employees or the union from seeking support or membership on company property. The Board considers it consistent with an atmosphere conducive to a free election for an employer to deliver a preelection speech on company time and property to massed assemblies of employees if the speech is given more than 24 hours before the election and if the employer has no rule prohibiting the union from soliciting off-duty workers on company premises. The NLRB held, in the Associated Milk Producers case,[30] that informal, anti-union remarks that a supervisor made to employees individually did not constitute a speech to a massed assembly merely because he made the remarks to every employee. The comments in question were made on the day of the election, yet they were not considered to violate the 24-hour rule, and the election results were sustained. According to the NLRB, an employer does not violate the law by talking to workers at voluntary meetings, in small groups, or individually, even 24 hours before an election.[31]

Over the years, the NLRB and the courts have rendered specific opinions on the limitations that an employer may lawfully impose on distribution of union literature and on union solicitations. These restrictions consider such factors as who does the solicitation and distribution—whether it is done by employees or by outside organizers. Other factors taken into account are whether the activity is conducted on or off the employer's premises and whether it takes place during or outside working hours.[32]

At one time, any interrogation of employees as to their union sympathies was considered by the Board as coercive and hence an unfair labor practice. Current law requires an inquiry into the circumstances surrounding the interrogation to determine if it is indeed coercive.[33] The U.S. Supreme Court, by establishing a standard for employer campaign communication, has attempted to harmonize the interest of employer and employees in free and full disclosure of information with the employee interest in an uncoerced decision on collective bargaining. Under the standard, an employer can state only what he or she reasonably believes will be the likely economic consequences of unionization that are out of the employer's control.[34]

The courts and the Board have not ignored the matter of a union's intrusive threats and promises during an election campaign; they are outlawed as much as are the employer's. Indeed, the Supreme Court set aside a union's narrow election victory because a waiver of union initiation fees was conditioned on joining immediately and not after the election. This waiver was analogized to the granting of gifts or benefits by a union or an employer while an election is pending.[35]

Section 8(b)(1) of Taft-Hartley makes it an unfair labor practice for a union to "restrain or coerce . . . an employer in the selection of his representatives for the purposes of collective bargaining or the adjustment of grievances."[36] It is also illegal for a union to engage in or encourage a strike or boycott to push an employer into an employer association, which presumably would then be his or her bargaining representative. Both of these provisions help preserve employers' independence in the selection of bargaining representatives.

It constitutes an unfair labor practice for a union to coerce employees in their selection of a bargaining representative or, except under a union security clause, to attempt to cause an employer to discriminate between union and nonunion workers. In addition, a union may not try to influence workers' freedom of choice by striking to force an employer to recognize one union when another is already duly certified. These are all reasonable rules for sound collective bargaining; they outlaw abuses that had been frequent under the Wagner Act.

It is extremely difficult to balance employer and union free-speech rights against the potentially coercive impact of some "free-speech" statements. Under current Board law, the parties themselves must counter the incorrect statements of their opponents. The Board apparently has faith that workers can recognize campaign propaganda for what it is. Each of these policy changes directly followed the appointment of a board member whose view differed with the existing precedent. One would have to view this issue as not permanently decided!

Representation rights under Taft-Hartley remain substantially unchanged from those under the Wagner Act, in that the bargaining agent designated by majority vote is the exclusive representative of the whole bargaining unit. That is, once the union has been certified as the representative for a particular bargaining unit, it has an obligation to represent fairly all workers in that unit whether or not they are union members.

Tension Between Collective and Individual Rights

Taft-Hartley emphasizes the rights of individual workers as against the organized group. In Section 9(a), which establishes the principle of exclusive representation, the law pauses to establish the right of any individual to present a grievance to the employer and have it settled without the intervention of the union, so long as the settlement does not violate the contract. And Section 7 guarantees the right of employees to refrain both from joining unions (except under a union shop) and from engaging in "other concerted activities."

It is also worth noting that Taft-Hartley guarantees workers' rights to engage in "protected, concerted" activity, not exclusively union activity. Thus there are two requirements for conduct to be encompassed by the act. First, the activity must be the kind of activity that was meant to be protected; that is, the issue of concern must be related to wages, hours, or other terms or conditions of employment. Second, the activity must be concerted; that is, it must generally be carried out by more than one employee. Thus, if three employees of a nonunion employer were discharged after jointly protesting the employer's pay policy, this would be considered a Taft-Hartley violation. This latter requirement has seemed to cause the most controversy over the years.

Jurisdictional Disputes

In the broadest sense, a jurisdictional dispute may take either of two forms. One is a contest between two unions as to which shall represent a group of workers, and the other is a contest over the assignment of particular work to one union or the other. A strike or boycott in either instance is an unfair labor practice. An employer is particularly helpless in the face of a jurisdictional strike because to satisfy one union automatically antagonizes the other. Jurisdictional fights involving work assignments are most common in craft unions, particularly in the building trades, where repeated changes in methods and materials make the boundary lines between crafts necessarily impermanent. To protect employers against union disputes related to job assignments, Section 8(6)(4)(D) of the Taft-Hartley Act considers it an unfair labor practice for a union to picket or strike an employer over work assignments to a particular group of employees. In addition, Section 10(k) of the act stipulates that, before the NLRB reviews the unfair labor practice charge of the dispute, the Board must first "determine the dispute." In arriving at that determination, the Board can make affirmative work jurisdiction awards regarding the disputed work. Furthermore, the act permits the parties to develop a method for voluntary adjustment of the dispute. The NLRB can, however, take over cases where the private adjustment mechanisms are not effective and have broken down.[37]

Legal restrictions on jurisdictional disputes certainly seem justified. Perhaps the law has indirectly encouraged a workable result, having led unions to develop techniques for settling such disputes within the labor movement by discussion, conference, and—if necessary—binding arbitration. Work assignment disputes among AFL-CIO unions are usually resolved by the AFL-CIO Impartial Jurisdictional Disputes Board. Although jurisdictional strikes have not been completely eliminated, they have declined to an insignificant fraction of their earlier level.

Supervisors

Under the Taft-Hartley Act, supervisors are permitted to join unions, but they are not protected in their right to do so. That is, their companies may legally discipline them if they join or engage in union activities.[38] The result has been the almost complete disappearance of supervisors' unions, which had become fairly numerous in the late 1930s and early 1940s. Although not explicitly mentioned in Taft-Hartley, managerial employees are also excluded from the protection of the act.[39]

THE LABOR-MANAGEMENT REPORTING AND DISCLOSURE ACT, 1959

On September 14, 1959, President Eisenhower signed the Landrum-Griffin Act into law. This statute consists of two major parts. One is a series of amendments to the Taft-Hartley Act, already discussed. The other is the Labor-Management Reporting and Disclosure Act (LMRDA), which we will now examine. Compared to the Kennedy-Ives, Kennedy-Ervin, Shelley, and Elliot bills, which had also been introduced to cover much the same ground, the Labor-Management Reporting and Disclosure Act was considered a relatively tough labor law.

The law grew out of the recommendations of the McClellan Committee for elimination of the corruption and racketeering found in certain unions. Through newspapers and television, employers waged an intense, dramatic, and highly coordinated campaign, which left the general impression that the sins of some parts of some five or six unions characterized all unions. By contrast, the union campaign was conflicting and disorganized. Some unions opposed any legislation and some wanted limited legislation, whereas the former CIO unions supported fairly strict legislation. There was also disagreement as to whether the law should cover the Railway Labor Act unions, which it does.

Provisions of LMRDA[40]

This section will describe first the law's provisions and then its rationale and effects. The law contains seven titles. Title I, called "Bill of Rights," asserts that "every member of a labor organization shall have equal rights and privileges within such organization" to nominate, vote, attend meetings, and participate. These equal rights are subject, however, to "reasonable rules," such as those denying apprentices or emeritus members full rights. Title I asserts freedom of speech and criticism about any candidate or policy, again subject to "reasonable rules" concerning responsibility to the organization and to its legal and contractual obligations. Dues, initiation fees, and assessments may not be raised except by secret ballot or other processes that ensure membership consent. No labor organization is to limit the right of any member to institute any action in a court or administrative agency, provided that the member may be required first to exhaust reasonable procedures (not to exceed four months) within the union before he or she may sue it, and provided that he or she does not accept employer help. Except for nonpayment of dues, a member may not be fined, suspended, expelled, or otherwise disciplined until after a full and fair hearing, preceded by written charges and time to prepare a defense. The union must also, on request, provide a copy of any union-management agreement to any member affected by the agreement. Any provisions of a union constitution or bylaws in conflict with Title I are void.

Title II requires each union to file a variety of reports with the Secretary of Labor. Each union must also make the same information available to any member who asks and must permit examination of union records for verification. Each officer is to report any investments or transactions that (briefly interpreted) involve a conflict of interest. Title II also requires employers to report (1) direct or indirect payments or loans to unions or to their officers or employees, (2) expenditures whose purpose is to interfere with or coerce employees in their rights to organize or bargain collectively or expenditures to spy on such activities, and (3) any payments made to either employees or outside entities (such as labor relations consultants) to get them to try to influence employees for or against unionization and collective bargaining. People who receive payments for such purpose must also report them.

Title III deals with trusteeships. Any trusteeship established by a union over any subordinate body, as by a national union over a local, must be reported within 30 days, and semiannually thereafter, with details and reasons. The purpose of the trusteeship must be legal, such as to remedy financial malpractice or undemocratic procedures, and it must be handled in accordance with the union's constitution and bylaws.

Title IV provides that elections in unions must be fair, open, honest, reasonably frequent, and secret. Complaints of improprieties may be filed with the Secretary of Labor if the plaintiff has unsuccessfully sought satisfaction within the union. The Secretary of Labor can take reasonable remedial action, including ordering a government-supervised reelection. Challenged elections are presumed valid pending final decision. Officers of local unions must stand for election not less frequently than every three years, those of intermediate bodies every four years, and those of national unions every five years.

Title V deals with two "Safeguards for Labor Organizations." The first affirmatively obligates people handling union funds to use them solely for the welfare of the members, subject to recovery suits by members and fine or imprisonment for improper conversion. The second prohibits any member of the Communist Party from being an officer or non-routine employee (such as an organizer) during or within five years after termination of party membership. This section was declared unconstitutional in 1964 as violating the First and Fifth Amendments.[41] For five years after conviction or end of imprisonment, it denies the same posts to persons convicted of most major felonies or "conspiracy to commit any such crimes."

Title VI covers miscellaneous provisions. Title VII consists of the Taft-Hartley amendments, which need not be elaborated here.

Some Broader Observations on LMRDA

Certainly, honest elections are desirable, and the law has almost unquestionably increased their number. However, before passage of LMRDA, there was not much evidence of election malfeasance occurring in more than a small number of cases. Aside from the matters of elections, trusteeships, and the disqualifications for office holding, the provisions of the law are predominantly procedural, not substantive. The election and trustee provisions have almost certainly had desirable results, of a sort that most leaders approve. The restrictions on office holding, although they have assisted in the removal of some undesirables, are of more doubtful value.

To pursue the question of procedure versus substance: The law, for example, does not require a strike vote; it merely requires that the union's rules concerning strike votes, if there are any, be properly implemented. The law does not prevent a union from disciplining a member for revealing union business if the rules stipulate that he or she may not reveal it; it merely says that the member may not be disciplined for such action without a fair hearing. In general, the Department of Labor and the courts have been reluctant to review the "reasonableness" of internal union rules. This arrangement reflects the basic philosophy of the LMRDA, which is to ensure union members certain democratic processes and to leave the rest to them.

Unions, however, do not have unlimited power to define internal policies and procedures. In 1991 the Seventh Circuit Court ruled that a union had breached the contract with its members when it modified the terms of the collective bargaining agreement. The union had conducted secret oral negotiations with the employer that had resulted in a modified agreement. The revised agreement was submitted without notice to the membership for ratification. The court decided that the union's conduct had violated the law.[42]

The law reflects a certain lack of realism in two respects. One is an exaggerated belief that most union members are held in the iron grip of union bosses. The other is that, if given the weapons of democracy, the union members would throw the rascals out and live happily ever after under grass-roots control. The overall view seems to be that the LMRDA has had conspicuous influence in a relatively small number of cases and moderate influence in a moderate number of cases but that its total impact has been relatively small. The student of organizations is apt to conclude that, no matter what the laws, unions are likely to remain essentially bureaucratic rather than either dictatorial or democratic—and not because they are unions but because they are large organizations. All this does not mean that wishes of members will be systematically ignored. It means that bureaucrats will implement members' wishes by keeping their ears to the ground, not by being voted out of office, although the latter also occurs from time to time. If a bureaucrat's ear is good, the process can be effective, presumably supplemented from time to time by the "engineering of consent."

THE 1974 HEALTH CARE AMENDMENTS

On August 25, 1974, the Taft-Hartley Act was amended to cover private nonprofit hospitals. Health care employees could now utilize all the representational and collective-bargaining mechanisms available since 1935 to other private-sector workers. Prior to 1974, employees in nonprofit hospitals had been denied the protection of the Taft-Hartley Act; consequently, most hospital administrations refused to recognize or negotiate with any unions. Because of the unique nature of the health care industry, Congress sought to balance the rights of employees to bargain against the right of the public to uninterrupted health care services. It did so by incorporating in the amendments special dispute settlement procedures. The enactment of the amendments to Taft-Hartley resulted in a significant amount of successful union organizing activity, which has continued ever since. The steady growth of the health care industry, together with the relative success of union organizational efforts in the past, should provide unions with a significant pool of potential members. In short, amendment of the Taft-Hartley Act has had and will continue to have significant effects on the extent of unionization of the health care industry.

CRITIQUE OF LABOR LAW AND ATTEMPTS AT REFORM

The current statutory framework has been subjected to severe criticism, especially from the labor movement. Lane Kirkland, the former president of the AFL-CIO, has said that it might be better to scrap the current labor laws completely and go back to "the law of the jungle" that existed prior to passage of the NLRA.[43] According to Thomas R. Donahue, the former secretary-treasurer and interim president of the AFL-CIO, current labor law encourages conflict, reduces cooperation between labor and management, and hampers collective bargaining. Donahue expressed the view that

> mere tinkering with the National Labor Relations Act's rules, procedures and remedies will not suffice. . . . Experience shows that these rules and remedies no longer encourage collective bargaining and no longer protect the exercise by workers of full freedom of association. . . . Nothing less than a fundamental reworking of the NLRA will make representation accessible to all workers and nothing less will enable employees to participate on an equal basis through collective bargaining in the decisions which critically affect their working lives.[44]

Donahue proposed the following changes to the current law: (1) legislating a card-check recognition system under which a union could be recognized as a bargaining agent on the basis of signed authorization cards (under the present law, such recognition is allowed, but the decisions belong to employees), (2) requiring arbitration as a last resort for subjects not agreed upon in negotiation of first contracts, (3) expanding coverage of the act to include new groups of workers, (4) eliminating delays and reducing costs in representation elections, (5) creating new mechanisms to redress the imbalance of power in negotiations, (6) ending double-breasting and enforcing pre-hire agreements, (7) providing protection for contingent workers, and (8) repealing laws that prevent union security agreements.[45] The labor movement is also very distressed over the absence of a federal statute that would make it illegal to hire strike replacements.

Delays in implementation of Board procedures and enforcement of Board orders are of immediate concern to unions. Management can exploit these delays and thus diminish workers' rights under Section 7. Certification delays provide employers inclined to such tactics with ample time to dissuade employees from exercising their right to representation.[46] Critics of the current labor law suggest that enlarging the Board could bring about speedier decisions.[47] More timely decisions from the Board could reduce uncertainty about the legality of a particular union or management action.[48]

In 1994 a new General Counsel (G.C.) was appointed to the NLRB. According to the new G.C., a major priority for the current Board is to reduce significantly the currently prevailing lengthy delays of some of the cases before it.[49]

Bills to amend the National Labor Relations Act and to alter the jurisdiction, procedures, or remedies of the NLRB have been considered at almost every session of Congress since 1935. Only a few have received serious attention, and even fewer have reached the floor. As a result, the NLRA has been amended only a few times since its passage.

In 1995 the Republican majority in Congress was giving serious consideration to the enactment of a new statute referred to as the TEAM Act. Although the sponsors of the bill claimed that the objective of this law was to encourage cooperative labor-management relations, many distinguished labor law scholars and researchers were opposed to this bill. The main reasons for the objections are very well summarized in the following excerpts from a letter to all members of Congress mailed out in 1995:[50]

> The stated purposes of this bill—promotion of legitimate employee involvement and genuine worker-management cooperation—are vital to the national interest. However, enactment of the TEAM Act would frustrate the realization of these goals by encouraging *illegitimate* forms of employee involvement and discouraging the legitimate expression of worker voice.
>
> For the past sixty years, it has been the policy of our labor law to encourage collective bargaining by protecting the right of workers to freely associate and select representatives of their own choosing. A cornerstone of that policy has been the prohibition, contained in Section 8(a)(2) of the National Labor Relations Act, on employer domination of employee organizations and employee representation plans. That section was central to the NLRA and was enacted because prior to the NLRA's enactment, employer control of employee organizations and representation plans had been used widely and effectively to impede workers from organizing independent labor unions.
>
> The proposed TEAM Act would negate the original purpose of Section 8(a)(2) by permitting without limitation a revival of the very practices against which Section 8(a)(2) was aimed. The legislation contains no safeguards to guarantee that employer-created representation plans function democratically and independently of the employer. Nor is there anything in the bill which would prevent employers from manipulating employer-controlled organizations in order to thwart genuine employee voice. As a result, we are persuaded that passage of the TEAM Act would quickly lead to the return of the kind of employer-dominated employee organizations and employee representation plans which existed in the 1920's and 1930's.
>
> Indeed, because the proposed legislation applies even to workplaces where the employees have selected a union as their exclusive representative, enactment of this bill would free unionized employers to destabilize bargaining relationships and undermine support for the elected representative.
>
> Employee involvement and worker-management cooperation can and should be fostered by means which do not further limit employees' freedom of association. The proposed TEAM Act represents a step backwards towards the discredited approaches of the 1920's and 1930's and away from true employee involvement and genuine worker-management co-operation. H.R. 473 and S.295 should not be enacted into law.[51]

On July 30, 1996, President Clinton successfully vetoed the TEAM Act. In his veto message, the president noted that the bill would have permitted "employers to establish company unions where no union currently exists and permitted company-dominated unions where employees are in the process of determining whether to be represented by a union."[52]

A SOURCE OF CONTROVERSY

Some large corporations have adapted comfortably, if reluctantly, to the institution of unionism, particularly some high-technology, capital-intensive corporations to which labor is a small fraction of cost. But many employers, particularly in the South and the Southwest, bitterly oppose unions and—in an atmosphere that supports right-to-work laws, which place limitations on union security clauses—have so far widely succeeded in avoiding unionization. Unions report feeling utterly frustrated by the many employers who allegedly violate the law so blatantly that their employees are afraid to assert their legal rights. Companies may engage in practices repeatedly reaffirmed by the Board and the courts to be gross and willful violations. Meanwhile, some of the same companies may continue to receive large government contracts, which unions construe as subsidies. These contracts are gained in part because the violations of the law enable these employers to underbid unionized competitors. In the end, unions claim that the costs of the remedial-only awards are so small that employers have in effect been rewarded by the government for violating the law. Only stiff punitive damages, claim the unions, can prevent such management behavior. On the general principle that "justice delayed is justice denied," the unions claim that unless the Board also speeds up its processing of cases, millions of workers will continue to receive no meaningful protection from the law.

The outside observer may see the Chamber of Commerce and the National Association of Manufacturers (NAM) as hewing closely to the line that the NAM first adopted around the turn of the century. For the most part, these organizations simply do not like unions and hold that, if the government sees fit to protect them, then the protection should at least be kept to a minimum. Increasingly candid reference to the goal of maintaining a "union-free environment" leaves the position of some firms unmistakably clear. This stance differs from that of some large corporations, which, seeing no likelihood of becoming nonunion again, presumably do not want to reenact the costly warfare of the 1930s and therefore "actively" stay out of the fight.

THE PERIOD OF TRANSFORMATION: THE 1990S

The labor relations system of the United States seems to be "in the throes of a profound transformation."[53] The Dunlop Commission,[54] in the first chapter of its report, discusses the changing environment of labor-management relations. Specifically, the commission addresses such issues as the changing economy, the changing work force, and the changing labor market outcomes. In the second chapter, the commission reviews employee participation and labor-management cooperation in American workplaces. The findings of the commission on these topics are presented in Chapter 17 of this text.

The changes currently taking place in the labor relations environment will undoubtedly affect the future status of labor policy and of labor legislation as well as its interpretation. Kaufman and Kleiner state that the transformation taking place is centered on "the role of employee representation in the workplace, and its appropriate institutional form."[55] They maintain that "academics, employers, unionists, and policy makers are confronted with some momentous issues,"[56] expressed as follows:

Does the United States currently have the optimal level of employee representation to promote maximum efficiency and equity? If not, what level and form of representation could better accomplish these goals?

Are trade unions and collective bargaining the most effective form of employee representation? What structural changes in the industrial relations system could improve the performance of collective bargaining?

Has union membership declined because workers no longer demand this type of representation, or is there still a large demand for union services but it is frustrated by employer resistance? What are the implications for labor law?

Is there a significant demand among American workers for some other type of employee representation? What form would this representation take? Would it be a substitute for, or complement to, trade unions?

Should the involvement of employees in the operation and governance of the firm be limited to plant-level human resource issues or should employees also have a voice in strategic business decisions?

Are European-style works councils an alternative system of employee representation that the United States should consider? What about enterprise-based unions? Codetermination?

Does the current corpus of American labor law promote the optimal level of labor-management cooperation? If not, how should the law be changed? Given the current legal system, what can firms and unions do to initiate and sustain cooperative efforts?

To what degree can employees achieve representation through the political process, rather than through a workplace-based institution? Can the political process effectively represent workers without a strong organized labor movement?[57]

According to Kaufman and Kleiner, the preceding issues "will be at the forefront of debate among policymakers and at the leading edge of research by industrial relations scholars in the 1990s."[58]

It is too early to tell what will be the legislative and public-policy outcomes of the transformation taking place in the American industrial relations system. We can only conclude that powerful forces are at work, forces that will disrupt the status quo of the current industrial relations system. In conclusion, a quote from Heraclitus may be appropriate: "Nothing endures but change."

SUMMARY

This chapter has surveyed the development of the law governing labor-management relations. We have examined the evolution of the legal framework across diverse eras: the period of opposition before World War I, the transition toward acceptance through the early 1930s, a brief period of support ending just after World War II, the era of control, and the period of transformation.

Labor law is dynamic. It changes not only with the enactment of new statutes but also with new decisions issued by the NLRB and by the courts. The composition of the courts and of the Board changes over time. Republican and Democratic presidents nominate to these bodies individuals whose ideologies are similar to their own. The views of these appointees obviously affect the decisions reached by the respective tribunals, decisions that can be of great significance to both unions and employers. These tribunals, through their decisions and precedents, introduce into the realm of labor-management relations new dimensions and new interpretations of the law.

The basic federal law governing current labor relations had its beginning with the passage of the Wagner Act of 1935, as amended by the Taft-Hartley Act in 1947 and the Landrum-Griffin Act in 1959. This body of law is interpreted by the National Labor Relations Board and by the courts. The legal labor relation system has strengths and weaknesses. Some scholars suggest that "because American society is litigious and dynamic, and because labor law will evolve and change in coming years, the deficiencies may receive greater attention"[59] in the future. Labor law never was nor will it ever be a static concept; it will always be in a state of change and evolution.

Notes

1. A substantial portion of English-American law consists of rulings made by judges in particular cases rather than laws passed by legislatures. Any judicial decision tends to establish a precedent and, in fact, normally constitutes the law with respect to the situation it covers until a contrary decision is rendered in a similar case or until legislation creates a new rule. The body of precedent thus established constitutes the common law, or judge-made law, and judges tend to follow these precedents until there arises some compelling reason to deviate. When a new kind of case arises, covered neither by legislation nor by closely related precedent, the judge will normally seek guidance either in a parallel relationship from a different field or in some general principle of law.

   The conspiracy doctrine, as applied to unions in the United States, was actually borrowed from prior English decisions of a similar nature. It reflected the economic belief that wages were set by the market and that a union could only destroy proper relationships. It also, of course, protected merchants and manufacturers, who were the dominant class of the time. Furthermore, American judges were aware that property owners could vote, while propertyless workers could not until between 1810 and 1843, depending on the state in which they resided.

2. *People v. Trequier et al., 1 Wheeler's Criminal Cases,* 1943 (1823).

3. "The Philadelphia Cordwainers, 1806," in *A Documentary History of American Industrial Society,* vol. 3, eds. John R. Commons et al. (Cleveland: Arthur H. Clark, 1910), p. 183.

4. Ibid.

5. Ibid., p. 233.

6. Edwin E. Witte, "Early American Labor Cases," *Yale Law Journal* 5 (1926), p. 827.

7. The terminology regarding these stages is not fully standardized. Hence, the reader may not find them called by the same names elsewhere.

8. 208 U.S. 274 (1908); 52 L.ed. 488.

9. Edward Berman, *Labor and the Sherman Act* (New York: Harper, 1930), p. 4.

10. In re Debs, 64 Fed. 724, 726 (1893). Emphasis added.

11. Clayton Act, Section 6, 1914; c. 323, 38 Stat. 730, as amended; 15 U.S.C.A. # 12.

12. Ibid., Section 20.

13. The intent of the Congress in passing Sections 6 and 20 of the Clayton Act may not have been as clear as the language of its paragraphs seems to indicate. In this connection, the reader should consult Charles O. Gregory, *Labor and the Law* (New York: Norton, 1946), pp. 158–174 and especially pp. 179 ff. It is difficult to believe, however, that the majority in Congress were aware of the subtleties that, Gregory reports, some crafty lawyers had used in wording the law. If they were not, the Congress as a whole must have intended the law to be taken at its face value. See also *Duplex v. Deering,* 254 U.S. 443 (1921), 65 L.ed. 349.

14. 245 U.S. 229 (1917).

15. The student will find a somewhat more extended though still brief description of the circumstances surrounding this decision in Fred Witney, *Government and Collective Bargaining* (Philadelphia: Lippincott, 1951), pp. 57–60.

16. *Adair v. United States,* 208 U.S. 161 (1908).

17. National War Labor Board, Bulletin 287 (Washington, DC: U.S. Department of Labor, Bureau of Labor Statistics), p. 32.

18. The basic validation of the law arose in the case of *Senn v. Tile Layers' Protective Union* under Wisconsin's "Little Norris-LaGuardia Act." See Gregory, op. cit., pp. 338 ff.

19. Benjamin J. Taylor and Fred Witney, *Labor Relations Law,* 5th ed. (Englewood Cliffs, NJ: Prentice Hall, 1987), p. 96.

20. 49 Stat. 449 (1935).

21. National Labor Relations Act. Also cited NLRA or the Act; 29 U.S.C., 151–169 [Title 29, Chapter 7, Subchapter II, *United States Code*].

22. National Labor Relations Act, Sections 7 and 8(a)(2).

23. In the case of *NLRB v. Jones & Laughlin Steel Corporation,* 301 U.S. 1 (1937), by a five-to-four decision.

24. Labor Management Relations Act. Also cited LMRA; 29 U.S.C. 141–197 [Title 29, Chapter 7, *United States Code*] cited as the Taft-Hartley Act.

25. James A. Gross, "Conflicting Statutory Purposes: Another Look at Fifty Years of NLRB Law Making," *Industrial and Labor Relations Review* 39 (October 1985), pp. 7–18.

26. Linda A. Kahn, *Primer of Labor Relations,* 25th ed. (Washington, DC: Bureau of National Affairs, 1994), p. 20.

27. *NLRB v. Fainlilart,* 306 US 60 (1935); *Siemons Mailing Service,* 122 NLRB 81, (1958). *Long-Stretch Youth Home, Inc. and Maryland State Employees Council 92,* 280 NLRB 678 (1986) and *Res-Care, Inc. and Indiana Joint Board, Retail, Wholesale and Department Store Union,* 280 NLRB 670 (1986). See also Bruce S. Feldacker, *Labor Guide to Labor Law,* 3rd ed. (Englewood Cliffs, NJ: Prentice Hall, 1990).

28. Taft-Hartley Act, or Labor Management Relations Act, Section 8(c).

29. *Livingston Shirt Corporation,* 107 NLRB 4001 (1953).

30. *Associated Milk Producers,* 237 NLRB (1978).

31. *Peerless Plywood Co.,* 107 NLRB, No. 106 (1953); *Land O' Frost,* 252 NLRB No. 1 (1980); and *Flex Products Inc.,* 280 NLRB, No. 61, (1986).

32. For a comprehensive list of cases covering solicitation and distribution rules, see Kahn, op. cit., pp. 26–28.

33. *Atlantic Forest Products, Inc.,* 282 NLRB (1987); *White Plains Lincoln Mercury, Inc.,* 288 NLRB 1133 (1988). *Rossmore House,* 269 NLRB 1176 (1989).

34. *TRW Electronic Component Division, TRW Inc.,* 169 NLRB 21 (1968). David P. Twomey, *Labor and Employment Law, Text & Cases,* 8th ed. (Cincinnati: South-Western Publishing Company, 1989), pp. 109–10.

35. *NLRB v. Savair Mfg. Co.,* 414 U.S. 270 (1973).

36. Taft-Hartley Act, Section 8(b)(1).

37. Kahn, op. cit., pp. 181–82.

38. *Parker and Robb Chevrolet, Inc.,* 262 NLRB 401 (1982).

39. Kahn, op. cit., p. 49.

40. Labor-Management Reporting and Disclosure Act, 1959, 73 Stat. 519.

41. *Brown v. U.S.,* CA9, June 19, 1964, 56 LRRM 2593.

42. William B. Gould IV, *A Primer on American Labor Law,* 3rd ed. (Cambridge, MA: MIT Press, 1993), pp. 165, 293. See also *Merk v. Jewel Food Stores,* 945 F.2d 889 (7th Cir. 1991). Cert. denied III S.CT. 1951, 1992.

43. Martin Tolchin, "AFL-CIO Chief Laments State of Labor Laws," *New York Times,* August 30, 1989, p. A20.

44. Testimony of AFL-CIO Secretary-Treasurer Thomas R. Donahue to the Dunlop Commission, *AFL-CIO News,* September 19, 1994, pp. 1–2.

45. Ibid.

46. Guillermo Grenier and Raymond L. Hogler, "Labor Law and Managerial Ideology: Employee Participation as a Social Control System," *Work and Occupations* 18, no. 3 (August 1991), pp. 313–42.

47. Sam F. Parig, Frank J. Cavaliere, and Joel L. Allen, "Labor Law and the Future of Organized Labor under the Clinton Administration," *Labor Law Journal* 44, no. 5 (May 1993), pp. 313–17.

48. Steve Gunderson, "Making a Case for a National Commission on American Labor Law and Competitiveness," *Labor Law Journal,* 41, no. 9 (September 1991), pp. 587–95.

49. Fred Feinstein, General Counsel for the NLRB, "Emerging Issues before the NLRB," presentation to the Greater Cincinnati Chapter of the Industrial Relations Research Association, September 19, 1994.

50. A 1995 letter sent to all members of Congress and signed by many scholars, researchers, and practitioners in the field of labor law who oppose the TEAM Act. Some of the signers were Professor Harry C. Katz, Cornell University; Professor Hoyt N. Wheeler, University of South Carolina; and Professor Clyde W. Summers, University of Pennsylvania.

51. Ibid.

52. *AFL-CIO News* 41, no. 14 (August 5, 1996).

53. Bruce E. Kaufman and Morris M. Kleiner, "Employee Representation: Alternatives and Future Direction" in *Employee Representation,* eds. Bruce E. Kaufman and Morris M. Kleiner (Madison, WI: Industrial Relations Research Association, 1993), p. 3.

54. The Dunlop Report, *Fact-Finding Report,* Commission on the Future of Worker-Management Relations (Washington, DC: U.S. Department of Labor and U.S. Department of Commerce, May 1994).

55. Kaufman and Kleiner, op. cit., p. 3.

56. Ibid.

57. Ibid., p. 394.

58. Ibid., p. 4.

59. Gould, op. cit., p. 213.

CHAPTER 4

Some Effects of the Law on Unions and Management

After reading this chapter, you should be able to

- ■ Describe the effects on bargaining power of a primary strike, a partial strike, and a slowdown.

- ■ Explain the use of lockouts and secondary boycotts and their current legal status.

- ■ Evaluate the current legal status of picketing.

- ■ Discuss the significance of Section 14(b) of the Taft-Hartley Act.

- ■ Review the measures unions can take to ensure internal discipline.

- ■ Explain and discuss the extent to which management security is affected by current law.

THE CONSEQUENCES OF THE LAW

For nearly 130 years, the government and the courts were strongly supportive of employers in their efforts to fight and prevent unions. However, despite anti-union activities of the courts and the government, strong unionization did develop and became accepted during that period in a number of industries. Under the 1935 Wagner Act, discussed in Chapter 3, the government became distinctly pro-union and strongly protective of workers' right to organize. In 1947 the Taft-Hartley act countered the Wagner Act's restrictions on employers with parallel restrictions on unions. In many respects, the interpretations and applications of the Wagner and the Taft-Hartley Acts by the National Labor Relations Board (NLRB) and the courts do much more to determine the actual impact of the law than does the wording of the legislation itself.

This chapter will first examine the impact of the law upon employees' right to organize. Do the law itself, the interpretations of the law by the NLRB, and the actions of the Board affect the outcomes of representation elections?

Next, the focus will shift to the question of bargaining power. The law makes no attempt to define *power* or *bargaining power* or to regulate it as such, although it does regulate many things that affect bargaining power. Assuming that collective bargaining has been established and continues under protection of the law, within that context does Taft-Hartley tend to skew bargaining power toward employers or toward unions?

The effect of the law on bargaining power will be discussed through an examination of union and management security, prevailing attitudes toward bargaining, and regulation of bargaining tactics and disputes. Finally, the role of the law in fostering "mature" bargaining relationships will be considered.

REGULATION OF CERTIFICATION CAMPAIGNS

One of the primary functions of the NLRB is to conduct representation elections, which give employees the option of being represented by unions for collective bargaining. NLRB policies can have an impact on election outcomes.

Before the NLRB will conduct an election, at least 30 percent of the employees in a unit appropriate for collective bargaining must show an interest in having such a vote. In determining which group or groups of employees should be eligible to vote, the NLRB can affect the level of union support. A consistent body of research confirms that a union is less likely to win an election when the population of voters is large.[1]

Another role of the NLRB in an election campaign is to provide an atmosphere in which the employees' right to organize is balanced against the employer's right of free speech. Through many case decisions, the Board has promulgated a set of rules that guide employer and union behavior during election campaigns.

The NLRB, as we stated in Chapter 3, has at times regulated the content of employer and union communications. It has done so to prevent deliberate lies and misstatements of fact from influencing employee choice regarding union representation. Although under current policy the board does not engage in such regulation, in the past it has set aside the results of elections on the basis of both employer and union lies.[2] The question currently at issue is whether the Board's present tilt toward free speech (implying even the freedom to lie) tends to favor employers or unions in their efforts to influence employee choice. The policy certainly could produce an undesirable outcome for one of the parties. A campaign in which distortions and outright lies are transmitted is probably less likely to focus on the issue of whether employees wish to participate in collective bargaining.

The Taft-Hartley Act permits dissemination of information during campaigns as long as no threat of reprisal or promise of benefit is made. Cases involving threats of reprisal have primarily rested upon issues of direct economic consequence to employees, such as a statement by an employer that the workplace would be closed in the event of a union victory in the election.[3] An employer's promise of benefits is distinguished from certain union promises because the employer, assuming a union loss, has the unilateral power to change conditions, whereas the union has the power only to negotiate changes.

The NLRB prescribes some restrictions on pre-election campaigns. "The Board repeatedly has said that it generally will not censor or police pre-election propaganda of the parties. But there are limitations: (1) reproduction of the official ballot, (2) forged documents, (3) speechmaking immediately before the election, and (4) racial, religious, or ethnic slurs."[4] The NLRB has also ruled on the issue of relative equality of access to employees for the purpose of campaigning. Captive-audience speeches, where employees are obligated to assemble on work time to hear employer speeches, are commonly held during certification campaigns. They are a protected form of employer free speech, provided that the speech is not made within the 24-hour period preceding the election[5] and the union has alternative means to communicate with employees.[6] These methods include visiting employees in their homes, soliciting employees during nonwork time, writing letters to employees, holding organizational meetings and inviting interested employees to attend, and advertising in newspapers and broadcast media.[7]

The NLRB has consistently refused to allow unions any sort of "equal time" to respond to employer captive-audience speeches.[8] It has, however, adopted rules to allow unions full opportunity to contact all eligible voters by means of a names-and-addresses policy.[9] Within seven days after the Board has scheduled a certification election, the employer must furnish to the Board the names and addresses of all employees eligible to vote in the election. This list is then turned over to the union leadership. The Board adopted this policy to counterbalance the captive-audience policies already in place, thus granting unions a potentially useful organizing tool. One can only speculate, however, about the relative effectiveness of captive-audience speeches compared to the methods available to unions.

The NLRB and the courts have established definite rules on union solicitation and distribution of literature during organizing drives. According to Linda S. Kahn, the key considerations in the Board and court decisions on those issues are "who is doing the soliciting or distribution, employees or outside organizers; where does it take place, on or off company property; and when does it take place, within or outside working time."[10]

A final area worth mentioning is the effect of the time involved in following NLRB procedures. A union organizing campaign is a fragile mixture of fact and emotion, and the timing of various events can affect the outcome of any campaign. Research by Roomkin and Block has shown that the longer the time between the petition for election and the actual election, the greater the likelihood that the union will lose.[11] Because challenges to proposed bargaining units and other legal matters often result in exactly the kind of delay that Roomkin and Block test, some have suggested that NLRB procedure itself may not be entirely neutral.

THE LAW AND BARGAINING POWER: REGULATION OF BARGAINING TACTICS

Legal Status of the Primary Strike and the Lockout

Section 7 of the National Labor Relations Act states, "Employees shall have the right to self-organization . . . to bargain collectively and . . . to engage in other concerted activities for the purpose of collective bargaining or other mutual aid or protection."[12] Section 13 adds, "Nothing in this Act, except as specifically provided herein, shall be construed so as either to interfere with or impede or diminish in any way the right to strike, or to affect the limitations or qualifications on that right."[13] Together these two sections provide the fundamental protection of the right to strike. In fact, despite the restrictions and injunctions of earlier years, the right to strike against one's own employer to extract concessions has generally been recognized ever since the demise of the conspiracy doctrine. The right of employers to operate during an economic strike, either with nonstriking regular employees or with newly hired replacements, has also been recognized.

To diagnose the law's effect on bargaining power, we must first establish some reference point from which deviations can be measured. Any such standard is necessarily subjective and arbitrary because bargaining power is a matter of degree and there is no such thing as a "correct" amount on either side. While remaining aware of the arbitrary judgment involved, for want of something better we will establish the *effective primary strike* as a "standard" power relationship in collective bargaining. An effective primary strike is one in which essentially all nonmanagerial productive activities in an organization cease because essentially all nonmanagerial employees stay away from work and are not replaced. The concept "essentially all" allows for certain emergency operations to continue. Such a strike reflects no inherent power bias toward either side and is accepted by the law. In an effective primary strike, both sides incur substantial costs. Workers receive no wages or benefits, and employers continue to incur significant costs while producing no goods or services to sell.

The situation with respect to the *partial strike* is more ambiguous. The Board and the courts have vacillated between giving the bargaining advantage to the employer and being neutral. Through a slowdown, the union can exert pressure on the employer at little or no cost to the employees. And by operating during a strike, the employer may bring costs to the strikers without incurring a commensurate loss of production. The freedom of the employer to turn a strike into a partial strike by recruiting strikebreakers has consistently been fully protected, though the action significantly reduces the bargaining power of the strikers. (Legal and societal protection should be differentiated here. The community's attitude toward a strike and the potential replacement of strikers do much to determine whether the employer's legal right can actually be exercised.) However, the freedom of employees to conduct a partial strike in the form of a slowdown was for some years ruled unlawful by both the courts and the Board.[14] The Board had also ruled as unlawful an off-again-on-again partial strike.

Slowdowns, extended rest periods, and "quickie" strikes have all been ruled to be forms of economic pressure that are not in themselves evidence of bad faith in bargaining.[15] The Supreme Court continues to counsel caution in condemning as unprotected by law stoppages that are part and parcel of proper collective bargaining. Yet even if "quickie" stoppages are treated as protected activity, the employer is not wholly deprived of recourse to self-help. In the *Polytech* case, the NLRB held that a single unannounced walkout would be presumed protected. However, the employees would be subject to discharge "when and only when the evidence demonstrates that the stoppage is part of a plan or pattern of intermittent action which is inconsistent with a genuine strike or genuine performance by employees of the work normally expected of them by the employer."[16] On this aspect of bargaining power, the law may now be regarded as formally neutral.

The Law and Lockouts

In a simple sense, the lockout is the management counterpart of the strike. However, its actual use is not simple. Generally speaking, a lockout with the purpose of undermining or breaking a union or preventing unionization is considered an unfair labor practice. On the other hand, equality of treatment would suggest that lockouts used solely for bargaining power be allowed under the same circumstances as are strikes.

Apparently, the NLRB now allows nonstruck firms in an employer association to lock out employees to avoid whipsawing by a union that strikes only one firm (or a few firms) in the association. An employer locking out may also attempt to operate with temporary replacements, just as in a strike. But for various reasons, the Board for years was inconsistent in its stance toward single employers who wanted to close down in a fashion tantamount to an employer-initiated strike. Whenever the employer is not allowed to lock out following a contract expiration, bargaining power is shifted to the union. Even though mutuality of pressure remains, as in a strike, such a rule permits the union to terminate the relationship at moments disadvantageous to the employer but prevents the employer from terminating at moments disadvantageous to the union. According to current Board policy, an employer is permitted to lock out employees in order to attain his or her objectives or in defense of a legitimate bargaining position.[17]

The Law and Secondary Boycotts

A boycott is a concerted withholding of some relationship with another party, typically a refusal to conduct certain kinds of business with an employer. It is primary if conducted directly against the party with whom one has a dispute. It is secondary if it is conducted indirectly against the primary party through action against some other "third" party. A boycott that withholds labor is usually called a strike. *Boycott* normally refers only to the withholding of purchases or sales of commodities. The Taft-Hartley Act places rather broad prohibitions on secondary boycotts by unions. Some loopholes in the prohibition were plugged in the 1959 revisions of the law.

A union does have the right to publicize its dispute with the primary employer at locations of neutral employers who sell the primary employer's product. Thus, a union of fruit and vegetable packers was permitted to picket a grocery store that sold the struck goods to the public. However, the picket signs had to state clearly that the dispute involved only the one product sold by the store and that customers were being asked to refrain from purchasing only that one product.[18] When a union seeks a boycott of one product of a multiproduct firm, the harm to the neutral employer is relatively small. However, when the struck product represents a major part of the neutral employer's business, the union's action would amount to an illegal secondary boycott.[19]

Several other aspects of the law seem to tilt bargaining power toward employers. Union unfair labor practices, like employer unfair labor practices, are subject to cease-and-desist orders. Secondary pressures by unions are also designated as unlawful acts, subject to suit in federal court. According to Section 303 of Taft-Hartley, whoever can prove loss "shall recover the damages by him sustained and the cost of the suit."[20] In addition, if an employer files a charge that a union is engaged in a secondary boycott or certain other unfair practices and if the NLRB "has reasonable cause to believe such charge is true," the Board must apply for a temporary restraining order pending resolution of the dispute before the Board. Further, according to Section 10(m), the preliminary investigation of such cases "shall be made forthwith and given priority over all other cases."[21] This means that if an office of the Board is processing unfair-labor-practice charges against an employer and the employer then files secondary boycott charges against the union, the office must give priority attention to the charges against the union.

Damage suits for unfair practices work in one direction only. The employer can legally recover any damage, however slight, caused by union unfair practices. However, except under unusual circumstances, if unfair practices of the employer destroy the union or deplete its treasury, the employer can be required only to cease and desist, without penalty. Employers are liable only for back wages to employees incurred through an unfair labor practice.

Picketing

Picketing is an adjunct to other organizational or bargaining tactics rather than a tactic in itself. This observation is not intended to suggest that picketing is unimportant. A picket line can use the persuasive method of making the "scab" feel like a peculiarly low creature or the coercive (and illegal) method of making that person fear for his or her safety or of physically preventing access to work. Seasoned unionists will stay off the job until ordered back by their leaders; for them a picket line is not essential. It is the weak union member and the nonmember who may be converted from strikebreakers to strikers by a healthy-looking picket line. Thus, the picket line becomes important—and so does the law concerning it—in a situation where (1) the employer tries to operate during the strike and (2) the union is weak and undisciplined.

Picketing thus resembles the secondary boycott in its relation to power. It is unimportant where the union is strong but may be crucial where the union is weak. Hence, restriction of picketing (other than to prevent acts illegal in themselves) probably pushes bargaining power away from the "standard" rather than toward it.

The Legality of Picketing

Under Norris-LaGuardia, picketing was clearly legalized unless violent. In the early 1930s, several states passed laws patterned on Norris-LaGuardia to provide the same protection in state courts. In 1940 the United States Supreme Court, in *Thornhill v. Alabama,*[22] virtually identified peaceful picketing with protected speech under the First Amendment. The state can regulate picketing, but a compelling state interest must be shown, and the legislation must be narrowly drawn to minimize restrictions on free speech. The state can regulate violence but has less latitude in preventing actions potentially leading to violence.[23]

Under Taft-Hartley and most state laws, peaceful picketing in support of a primary strike is legal. The Board does not permit "mass" picketing, even if it entails no violence, *mass* being interpreted to mean the blocking of passage. However, relying on the police powers of the state, the courts have often enjoined picketing involving more than just a few people even when it is not accompanied by violence, threats, or actual blockage. The reason given is that large numbers of pickets create a presumption of danger. The number of pickets that constitutes mass picketing has not been defined for this purpose and seems to depend on the judge in the individual case.

The Taft-Hartley Act gives strikebreakers and strikers equal protection through the combination of Sections 7 and 8(b)(1). The former guarantees not only the right to organize and strike but also "the right to refrain from any and all such activities";[24] the latter section makes it unfair for a union "to restrain or coerce employees in the exercise of the rights guaranteed in Section 7."[25] Unions that engage in illegal picketing may be enjoined, and individuals who participate may be fired without reinstatement rights. It constitutes no defense that the unlawful picketing is a self-defense against an employer's egregiously unfair practice. As a practical matter, however, it is often difficult for an employer to sustain a discharge based on improper conduct on a picket line, and it is even harder to hold a union responsible for such conduct as an entity. In consequence, employers may not actually receive the level of protection against improper picketing that the provisions of the law seem to call for.

Like other tactics, picketing can influence the existence or security of a union as well as its bargaining power. In the hotel, restaurant, and other industries composed of many small firms, it is common to find a nonunion establishment picketed by workers from other firms in an effort to unionize it. This practice is known as "stranger picketing." Certain courts have acknowledged that even unions that lack members among the employees of the picketed company are not necessarily "strangers" who have no economic interest in organization there.[26]

Unions sometimes try to elicit consumer boycotts, particularly against employers who refuse to recognize or bargain with the unions. Conspicuous examples have been the boycott campaigns against Farrah slacks, J. P. Stevens products, and grapes or lettuce from nonunion farms in California. It is essentially correct to say that any such boycott is legal so long as it does not involve picketing. To illustrate, a union may organize a newspaper campaign urging consumers to stop all purchases from a department store or chain in the hope of inducing it to stop handling one particular boycotted item. However, if pickets walk around the store, their signs may refer only to the single item being boycotted. In that case the boycott is technically primary—even though it is conducted on the premises of a merchandiser several steps removed from the source—because it is directed at the primary producer. If effective at that level, it has substantially the same result as would be achieved by an effective strike against the primary producer, in which case the store would have none of the struck merchandise to sell.

Picketing in Secondary Boycotts

Picketing in connection with secondary boycotts has almost always been illegal and enjoinable. The Taft-Hartley Act makes it an unfair labor practice for a union to engage in a secondary boycott or to "induce or encourage" one, and the general position of the law has been that if a secondary boycott is itself illegal, so is picketing in support of it.

The law and decisions about picketing are complex. One possible stance is that peaceful picketing is a form of communication, which should be scrupulously protected under the First Amendment. The other is that in a society conditioned not to cross picket lines, picketing is more than speech: It is a form of coercion, even if peaceful and non-threatening. Although the law has changed over the years, at present one must give great attention to intent, actual effects, and public policy toward the location being picketed. Interestingly, a secondary boycott carried out through activities other than picketing, such as handbilling or other forms of advertising, would be legal. However, employers can prohibit nonemployees from entering their property to engage in solicitation or handbilling.[27]

An interesting complication concerns common-situs picketing. To clarify by example, suppose that the primary employer is a supplier of ready-mixed concrete whose plant is struck and being picketed. The question then arises whether picket lines may also be placed at a distant construction site where the company's concrete is being poured, the construction site being the location of a secondary employer that has no dispute with its own employees. The standards have been established in the *Moore Dry Dock* case; we can summarize them by saying that such picketing is allowed if it is clearly confined to the times and locations of the primary employer's operations and is clearly identified as being directed against the primary, not the secondary, employer.[28]

EFFECTS OF THE LAW ON UNION AND MANAGEMENT SECURITY

Union and management security will be discussed in Chapter 6 in terms of each organization's ability to perform its institutional function without undue interference in that performance. Current legislation has certain effects on the security of unions and managements. The purpose of this section is to explore those effects briefly.

Assurance of Union Existence

The most fundamental conditions of union security are that the union exist and that it be accorded representation rights. By making raiding more difficult, the law makes a union's continued existence more secure; by requiring the employer to recognize and bargain in good faith with a certified union, the law establishes representation rights. Those two points were discussed earlier. Furthermore, short-term security of the union's representation status is assured in the provision that a new representation election may not be held sooner than one year after a valid election has been conducted. A union's status is also assured for the life of a current contract (to a maximum of three years). Regarding the more direct union security devices of compulsory membership or dues payment, current state legislation ranges from permissive to prohibitive. At no time in our history has membership or dues payment been required by law.

The union shop is the strongest legal form of union security permitted under Taft-Hartley. A new employee must be allowed 30 days after hiring, or after the effective date of the contract, to join the union, with a special provision of only 7 days in the construction industry. The closed shop, which requires union membership before hiring, is considered illegal under Taft-Hartley.

Because union security—or any collective bargaining at all—is difficult to achieve on any basis except a closed shop in such short-term employment as that of stevedores, construction workers, and some musicians (see Chapter 6 on union and management security), subterfuge forms of the closed shop have developed there with the knowledge and co-operation of employers. Some unions operate hiring halls, and although these are required by law to handle union and nonunion members alike, in actuality they do not. In practice, hiring halls usually apply seniority provisions that give preference to longer-term employees, who are nearly always union members. Thus, in reality, in some industries, the closed shop—now called the "hiring hall"—is still in existence today. "The use of Union hiring halls as employment agencies has been a common practice in industries where employment is casual or intermittent, such as the construction and longshoring industries."[29]

Under the original (1947) Taft-Hartley Act, a union shop could be negotiated with an employer only if approved by a majority of the bargaining unit members voting in an NLRB special union shop authorization election. Even an overwhelmingly affirmative vote did not automatically establish the union shop, however. It merely allowed the union to negotiate on the subject. Following a petition by 30 percent or more of the bargaining unit, a union shop deauthorization election could be held, and if a majority voted against the union shop, it was mandatorily eliminated. The 1951 amendments to Taft-Hartley eliminated the union shop authorization elections, thus giving the union the right to negotiate over the union shop unless the bargaining unit voted to remove that right.

The controversial Section 14(b) of Taft-Hartley permits individual states to outlaw all forms of compulsory union membership. Such state laws are called "right-to-work" laws (see Figure 4.1).

It is often felt that such laws restrict only unions. As we shall see in Chapter 6 in the discussion of management security, some managements feel that union security is of value to them as well. Hence, a prohibition of union security can constitute a restriction on management as well as on unions. The main drive for such restrictive legislation has traditionally come more from small- and medium-sized firms rather than from very large corporations.

Whatever the merits of the laws themselves, the "right-to-work" label misrepresents the issue. It is clear that a closed shop (or even a union shop), in conjunction with a closed union, interferes with the right to work and that the combination is presumably contrary to sound policy. The distortion arises when the right to work is presumed to be denied by a union shop when union membership is readily available and dues are reasonable. Then the employer is free to hire any worker, and any worker is free to hold any job. In such circumstances, the right that is primarily infringed on is the worker's "right not to pay dues"—a phrase that hardly has the appeal of the term "right to work." In all fairness, we should also point out that some workers may refuse to join unions on religious or ideological grounds.

Under right-to-work laws, it is easy for employees to reap the benefits of a union agreement without the need to pay union dues. This practice is referred to as "free riding." Some economists claim that right-to-work laws, by prohibiting union shops, foster free riding and therefore decrease union viability. Others allege that such laws are usually not implemented and "thereby represent local attitudes and employee characteristics which would encourage free riding in any case."[30] Davis and Huston argue that "when other factors which affect free riding are taken into account, the marginal impact of right-to-work laws remains significant."[31]

The obvious effect of right-to-work laws is to reduce or eliminate a union's formal assurance that its membership and dues income from its bargaining unit members will remain steady. The possible consequences of such financial insecurity will be discussed further in Chapter 6.

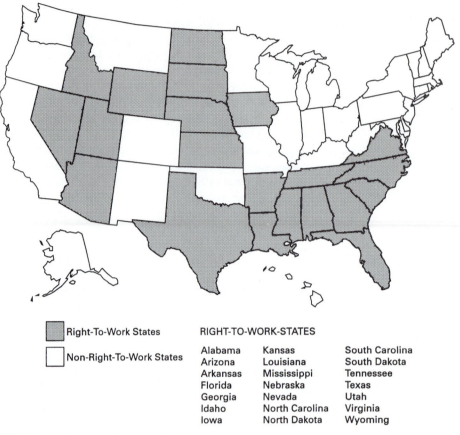

Right-To-Work States

Non-Right-To-Work States

RIGHT-TO-WORK-STATES

Alabama	Kansas	South Carolina
Arizona	Louisiana	South Dakota
Arkansas	Mississippi	Tennessee
Florida	Nebraska	Texas
Georgia	Nevada	Utah
Idaho	North Carolina	Virginia
Iowa	North Dakota	Wyoming

FIGURE 4.1 States with "Right-to-Work" Laws

Source: Reproduced with permission from *Human Resource Management,* published and copyrighted by Commerce Clearing House, Inc., 4025 W. Peterson Ave., Chicago, Illinois, 60646.

Statistical studies and the stated impressions of employers, employees, and unions indicate that right-to-work laws apparently have had little effect on unions.[32] In summary, although states that have adopted right-to-work laws hold significantly different attitudes regarding unionization than do the other states, there is no evidence of any significant impact on unionization of the right-to-work laws themselves.[33] Lumsden and Peterson,[34] in their study of the right-to-work laws, state, "We align ourselves with prevailing suspicions that the battle for right-to-work laws is one of symbol rather than substance." Because attitudes toward unionization do seem to have some effect, there is the chicken-egg question whether in certain states the attitudes produce the legislation or the legislation reinforces the attitudes. There is probably some of each.[35]

State versus Federal Laws on Union Security

Section 14(b) of Taft-Hartley establishes a relationship between state and federal law that weakens union security. Any type of union security that is permissible under federal law, such as union shop and maintenance of membership, is nevertheless illegal if prohibited by state law because the latter is then controlling. At the same time, any type of union security that is permissible under state law, as is the closed shop in some states, is nevertheless illegal if prohibited by federal law, which is then controlling. Although, in the mid-

1960s, Congresses were considered strongly sympathetic to organized labor, all attempts to repeal Section 14(b) failed, and none seems likely to succeed in the near future.

Dues checkoff is allowed by Taft-Hartley and by most states if individually authorized in writing by each employee. Because of a 1988 Supreme Court decision, however, some restrictions govern the collection by unions of dues and agency fees. This topic is elaborated on in Chapter 6, on management and union security.

The Taft-Hartley Act provides some union security in that a union's representation rights cannot be challenged for a year after it is certified. At the same time, the law weakens union security by providing for decertification elections on petition of 30 percent or more of employees or on petition of an employer faced with demands for recognition from two or more unions. Employers are prohibited from financing dissident employees' efforts to seek decertification elections or to sue the union, though the employer might do so indirectly through an outside organization, such as a right-to-work committee.

The Union's Ability to Function

In normal operation, the union has two major responsibilities: One is to formulate and implement bargaining strategy; the other is to uphold its side of the contract. Chapter 6 will describe how the discharge of both responsibilities requires internal discipline. Although a union can exert some discipline through social pressure, its most compelling formal disciplinary power would lie in making membership a condition for holding the job. In all states that prohibit union security, unions lack this type of formal disciplinary power. Even under a union shop, according to Section 8(a)(3) of Taft-Hartley, an employer may not discharge a worker for nonmembership except for failure "to tender the periodic dues and the initiation fees uniformly required as a condition of acquiring or retaining membership,"[36] nor may a union try to make an employer do so. Under current statutory provisions, union security relies primarily on income from dues. Over the years, union discipline was significantly weakened by NLRB rulings; according to some Board decisions, a union could not even enforce a fine for deliberate attempts to break the union, much less for nonattendance at union meetings.[37] In this respect, Taft-Hartley seemed to pursue two contradictory ends: to make unions more "responsible" by making them suable for unfair practices and breach of contract while simultaneously denying them the instruments through which responsibility is achieved and effectuated. However, in 1964 the Board held that no violation of the act occurs when a union fines members for crossing a picket line or for strikebreaking, and the courts could enforce payment of such fines.[38] A 1978 NLRB decision to fine constituents extended to supervisory members who crossed picket lines to do bargaining unit work.[39] The 1964 and 1978 decisions substantially enhanced the disciplinary powers of a union over its members.

In 1984 and 1985, the NLRB decided that union members could avoid imposition of any fines simply by resigning union membership before crossing the picket line. No notice period was required for such resignation.[40] These decisions clearly diminished the ability of unions to impose any form of internal discipline.[41]

Management Security

Neither state nor federal laws deal with management security as such, though some affect it indirectly. Management representatives have for years wanted the law to state which issues are bargainable and which are not. Such a law would greatly limit management security if its list of bargainable issues were very broad. Of course, managers who advocate such a list want it to be narrow, in which case management security would, in effect, be provided by law or at least be greatly enhanced. A "management rights clause" in a labor contract is neither required nor restricted by law, though it is assisted insofar as it has been ruled to be a mandatory issue about which a union may not refuse to bargain. Some state laws help in one way to enforce management rights clauses: They make unenforceable any arbitration decision that exceeds the arbitrator's authority and that thereby invades decision areas reserved to management.

According to most employers, the ultimate management security lies in preventing the formation of unions. By outlawing the major devices that management could employ to avoid unionization, the law in effect reduced employers' security. Although the law otherwise does not formally interfere with management security, the Board has steadily added to the list of issues over which management may not refuse to bargain. In consequence, many employers feel that their security has been substantially undermined by Board rulings.

In one sense, it is probably impossible to protect management security significantly by law—as by stating that some issues are nonbargainable. To make such a list would be naively to assume that bargainable issues are separable. In short, the law has very definite effects on the kinds of provisions that can be used to establish union security—but a rather uncertain effect on management security.

ATTITUDES TOWARD BARGAINING

In this section, we will categorize the attitudes of the parties toward bargaining. To determine how the law influences those attitudes, we will base our characterizations on a shortened and modified version of Selekman's description of the attitudes and of four types of relationships: conflict, power, accommodation, and cooperation.[42] The general tone of a relationship and the atmosphere in which it exists develop as a consequence of behaviors on both sides of the bargaining table. The four types sometimes represent four successive stages in the development of a given relationship. But a given relationship can start at any stage, shift in either direction, or stay in a particular pattern indefinitely.

Conflict

In the conflict relationship, management strongly opposes the union's very existence. It does everything it can to prevent unionization and does not always confine its opposition to legal means. The employer may subtly or blatantly blacklist or discriminate against union sympathizers, spurn union representatives, hire labor spies, engage professional strikebreakers, threaten to move the plant, utilize massive and sometimes scurrilous publicity against the union, seek the presence of hostile public and/or private police at union demonstrations, and organize "citizens' committees" of local residents and businesses to oppose unionism.

If a union manages to organize such an anti-union employer, management will negotiate with the union because legally it must; however, it will make no secret of its desire to eliminate the union. The employer will refuse any union security, try to discredit the union, and confine bargaining to the narrowest possible scope. If a strike occurs, management will try to break the union as well as the strike. Although the conflict attitude is usually more characteristic of small- and medium-sized firms, some large companies have evinced attitudes that can be described as hostile and conflictual toward unions.

Power Bargaining

The difference between conflict and power bargaining is roughly that between cold war and peaceful but competitive coexistence. In power bargaining as in conflict relations, management sees the union as an undesirable obstruction between itself and its employees. But it concludes that the union is there to stay and ceases open attempts to destroy it. Under pressure, management might even grant union security and possibly recognize that security for the union is not necessarily bad for management. It will nevertheless view union security as an unjustified boost to union power and an invasion of the individual's "right to work." Management will try to keep the union weak and defensive. Both sides will push their bargaining power to the limit, sometimes shortsightedly. Although the company would not hire professional strikebreakers, it will try to operate during a strike, possibly hire new employees to replace strikers, and appeal to union members over the heads of their leaders to return to work or accept a management-proposed contract.

The union may build large strike funds, engender antagonism toward the employer among members and the public, apply political pressures, or strike in disregard of the public interest. Typically, each side attempts to demonstrate that it cannot be pushed around. Personal relations are likely to be strident and caustic, and each side may impugn the motives or integrity of the opponent.

Accommodation Bargaining

In the accommodation approach, management does not necessarily like unions or assist in their expansion, but it accepts them as legitimate and seeks the best possible relationship with them. Perhaps most important, management views the union as a channel for dealing with employees rather than an obstacle to employee relations and tries to figure how best to use that channel. Management will not bypass the union leaders by going over their heads in appeals to the membership any more than management would expect the union to try to go over the heads of company executives to the stockholders. For example, job evaluation, merit rating, recreation plans, and other actions that directly affect employees are reviewed with the union.

In the accommodation spirit, management does not belittle the union and might even cite its cooperative attitude as a factor in the company's success, recognizing that high loyalty to the union often goes hand in hand with high loyalty to the company.[43] Both sides acknowledge that a tough relationship in which both throw their weight around benefits neither in the long run and can be psychologically and financially costly indeed.

Two points in the accommodation approach are notable. First, neither side challenges the essential security of the other. The second pertains to the conduct of a strike: Instead of viewing the strike as a rough struggle in which the union tries to keep bargaining-unit employees out of the plant while the company tries to get them in, management simply closes down production when a strike is called. Not only does this approach eliminate confrontations on the picket line, it in fact reduces the role of picketing to the transmittal of information only. It also tacitly acknowledges that the union is the source of authority from which employees receive their instructions about bargaining strategies, and it does not seek to abrogate any of that authority to management any more than it expects supervisors to take their instructions about the strike from the union. In similar spirit, the union will seek to prevent the strike from wreaking undue hardship, as when the Steelworkers bank and tend furnaces during a strike to keep their expensive linings from cracking or when transportation workers keep materials flowing to hospitals or other crucial locations. In accommodation, the parties do not eliminate warfare or particularly shift advantage within it, but they do limit its scope and reduce its casualties.

Cooperation

The cooperative approach brings the union and its members directly into the process of improving productivity and morale. It is more than a simple suggestion system. On the part of the union, it requires a recognition that union employees can benefit from cooperation and a willingness to encourage workers to help employers increase productivity and efficiency. On the part of management, it requires abandoning the attitude that workers "are not paid to think" and making an unqualified commitment that improvements initiated by workers will not lead to layoffs or pay cuts for anyone. In Chapter 9, we will refer to mutual gains or win-win bargaining. In addition, many unions and managements, under pressure of increased domestic and international competition, have begun to explore ways to save jobs through various forms of labor-management cooperation. Unions and managements do engage in many activities that are cooperative in the broad sense of the term. Joint efforts to improve the quality of working life, including job enrichment, may not only make life on the job more satisfying for employees; they may also improve productivity and morale in the long run. Joint safety efforts certainly can simultaneously protect workers and reduce costs to employers, and they are widespread. Some fringe benefits, like health and retirement benefits, are complex; these are often negotiated and worked out through a joint effort to find the best solution rather than through a contest of power. In due time, we might also see more joint efforts to study the environmental impact of certain production processes, though it would seem that the public might need representation as a third party in any such venture. Whether American unions and employers will ever move seriously toward codetermination, the European practice of having unions represented directly on corporate boards of directors, is yet to be seen; the question will be discussed in more detail in Chapter 6.

DOES THE LAW FOSTER "MATURE" BARGAINING?

As expressed in present legislation, what type of bargaining relationship does public policy tend to foster: conflict, power, accommodation, or cooperation? Although no consensus exists on this issue, unions and their supporters argue that there are a number of areas in which both federal and state laws advance conflict and power bargaining rather than promoting accommodation or cooperation. Such union advocates contend that the law furthers the conflict and power approaches by discouraging mutual acceptance of strike pressure. On the employer side, the law assists employers who seek to avoid the mutual pressure of the strike: It limits the number of peaceful pickets, gives as much protection to strikebreakers as to strikers, protects employers against secondary pressures if they attempt to break a strike, and permits the hiring of permanent strike replacements. On the union side, the law provides immunity for consumer boycotts against employers, no matter how remotely they may be connected to the dispute in question. On both sides, the law protects some kinds of partial strikes that seek to impose a cost on the opponent without having to endure some cost oneself. This is not to suggest that the law or the Board should rule differently in these situations but merely to identify the probable consequences of protecting certain kinds of activities.

The law also presents at least one potential impediment to labor-management cooperation. The Taft-Hartley Act makes employer domination of a labor organization an unfair labor practice. This provision was originally designed to prevent company unions, but in some instances it is also applied to other types of joint labor-management committees.[44]

In the 1980s, trends developed that are indicative of the state of great flux in the U.S. industrial relations system. On one hand, more and more employers chose to fight unions with every weapon available to them, even including the bankruptcy laws.[45] If we looked only at those situations, we might conclude that collective bargaining is becoming more conflict centered. On the other hand, a significant degree of union-employer cooperation began in some sectors of the economy. Likewise, if we looked only at those cases, we might conclude that there is a trend toward accommodation and cooperation. The fact that these two trends emerged at the same time only underscores the comments made at the beginning of this section that because of the complexity of the law, no simple answer describes the effect of our public policy on labor-management relations. Some observers have also pointed out that the same corporation may manifest differing attitudes toward unions at various corporate levels. For example, an employer may practice cooperation on the shop floor of its unionized operations while strategic-level decisions made by top management may reflect an attitude of hostility to unions.[46]

In recent years, U.S. companies have been initiating worker participation programs to increase employee involvement in workplace issues; to improve quality, efficiency, and productivity; and to advance worker commitment to company values and objectives. Worker participation groups function under a variety of names such as quality circles, total quality management programs, action committees, labor-management cooperation committees, work teams, and the like. But no matter what they are called, their goals remain very similar—to improve overall performance by increasing quality and productivity standards and to meet the needs of a highly competitive marketplace. Such groups often empower employees to make decisions once reserved exclusively for management. These decisions can cover such areas as ways in which work should be performed, working conditions, and rewards for high performance.[47]

Encouragement of such cooperation between management and labor has been supported by some labor unions, such as the United Auto Workers and the United Steel Workers.[48] In 1993 one president of an international union expressed the view that "employers must gather the courage to seek . . . changes, in order to foster the labor-management cooperation necessary to compete in the global economy."[49]

Former U.S. Secretary of Labor Robert Reich expressed similar sentiments when he recognized the significant contributions of employees to the effectiveness of organizations by stating, "The most successful businesses in the country today are the ones that give their employees more responsibility and more voice in the product."[50]

Although the benefits of increased worker participation appear to have been embraced by many companies and labor leaders, there are still problems associated with the formation of worker participation groups. For instance, increased employee participation in traditionally management-driven areas is a source of conflict among labor unions. Some labor organizations maintain that worker participation groups act only to undermine the efforts of unions themselves while increasing management's control over workplace issues. Thus they resist the establishment of such groups.[51]

Present labor law may deter the formation of worker participation groups. According to some experts, current interpretation of the law may contribute to an adversarial relationship between unions and management because it discourages worker participation.[52] Section 8(a)(2) of the National Labor Relations Act prohibits employers from dominating, interfering with, or contributing financially or otherwise to the support of a labor organization. When 8(a)(2) was enacted, it was intended to prevent employers from forming employer-dominated labor organizations that would successfully keep legitimate unions from organizing workers.[53] Now the same legislation may actually inhibit the formation of employee participation programs (EPP) and thus may impede labor-management cooperation.

In attempts to become more efficient and competitive, some U.S. employers have tried to establish EPPs. Ironically, however, some NLRB decisions may discourage the formation of such programs. In a 1992 decision, the Board found in the case of Electromation, a nonunion company, that the employer violated the act through the formation and support of five in-house employee action committees.[54] Also in 1993, the NRLB determined that E. I. DuPont de Nemours and Company had violated the act when it established six safety committees. The DuPont company was unionized, and its employees were represented by the Chemical Workers Association, Inc., International Brotherhood of DuPont Workers. The central issues in this case were whether the committees were employer-dominated labor organizations within the meaning of Section 2(5) and Section 8(a)(2) of the National Labor Relations Act and whether the respondent had bypassed the union in dealing with the committees. In May 1993, the NLRB ruled that the company had violated Section 8(a)(2) of the act.[55]

According to Thomas Kochan, member of the Commission on the Future of Worker-Management Relations, "The role of government may need to be reinvented to support changes in labor-management cooperation and employee participation in the workplace."[56]

Proponents of worker participation believe that both management and workers can benefit from the process. Yet the Electromation and DuPont decisions make it apparent that when employers establish worker participation groups, they must be careful not to violate the current law. Such groups cannot address any issues related to hours, wages, or terms and conditions of employment.[57] However, in spite of some legal obstacles, it appears that increased employee participation will continue to be an important element in the future success of U.S. companies. The topic of labor-management cooperation will be discussed at greater length in Chapter 17, covering the findings of the Commission on the Future of Worker-Management Relations, known as the Dunlop Report.

SUMMARY

The overall effect of law on the bargaining relationship is somewhat ambiguous. The law has made it possible for employers to weaken or avoid unions in the private sector where unions are comparatively small, weak, or absent to begin with. This effect can be attributed to difficulties of enforcement and to weak remedies rather than to specific provisions of the law, and the ability of unions to gain recognition is probably affected far more than is their bargaining power when they do exist. Meanwhile, unions have been very successful in the public sector at both state and local levels, even in states that prohibit strikes and provide no legal protection for the right to organize. The laws governing unionization in the public sector will be covered in Chapter 16 of this text.

Viewed overall, one of the most appealing aspects of the law is its provision that questions of representation are to be settled by secret ballot of the affected employees, not by no-holds-barred confrontation between workers and employers. By making any union thus selected the exclusive representative of the employees in the bargaining unit, the law has removed an important source of friction among unions within a potential bargaining unit. Finally, the requirement of good-faith bargaining is another stabilizing aspect of the law, particularly as the requirement has been broadened over the years. All of these provisions help foster relationships of accommodation rather than of power or conflict.

Notes

1. Herbert G. Heneman and Marcus H. Sandver, "Predicting the Outcomes of Union Certification Elections: A Review of the Literature," *Industrial and Labor Relations Review* 36 (July 1983), pp. 537–59.

2. *Midland National Life Insurance Co.,* 263 NLRB 24 (1982); *General Knit of California,* 239 NLRB 101 (1978).

3. *Atlantic Forest Products, Inc.,* 282 NLRB 855 (1987); *White Plains Lincoln Mercury, Inc.,* 288 NLRB 1133 (1988) and *Rossmore House,* 169 NLRB 1166 (1989).

4. Linda G. Kahn, *Primer of Labor Relations,* 25th ed. (Washington, DC: Bureau of National Affairs, 1994), pp. 57–58.

5. *Peerless Plywood Co.,* 107 NLRB 428 (1953).

6. *Livingston Shirt,* 107 NLRB 400 (1953).

7. Benjamin J. Taylor and Fred Witney, *Labor Relations Law,* 5th ed. (Englewood Cliffs, NJ: Prentice Hall, 1987), pp. 301–2.

8. Except in some cases when the employer has committed unfair practices or where employees are legitimately restricted from solicitation during nonwork time. See *Montgomery Ward & Co., Inc.,* 145 NLRB 846 (1964) and *Livingston Shirt,* op. cit.

9. *Excelsior Underwear, Inc.,* 156 NLRB 1236 (1966).

10. For a good summary of solicitation and distribution rules and a listing of the most recent NLRB and court cases on these topics, see Kahn, op. cit., pp. 26–28.

11. Myron Roomkin and Richard Block, "Case Processing Time and Outcome of Elections: Some Empirical Evidence," *University of Illinois Law Review* 1, no. 1 (1981), pp. 75–97.

12. National Labor Relations Act, Section 7.

13. Ibid., Section 13.

14. 25 LRRM 806 and 26 LRRM 1493.

15. *NLRB v. Insurance Agents' International Union,* 361 U.S. 477.

16. *Polytech, Inc.,* 195 NLRB 695 (1972), 321.

17. For a good summary of the most recent NLRB and court cases governing lockouts, see Kahn, op. cit., pp. 124–26.

18. *NLRB v. Fruit and Vegetable Packers and Warehousemen, Local 760,* 377 U.S. 58 (1964).

19. *NLRB v. Retail Clerks, Local 1001,* 447 U.S. 607 (1980).

20. Labor Management Relations Act or Taft-Hartley, Section 303.

21. Ibid., Section 10(m).

22. 310 U.S. 88 (1940).

23. *Nash et al. v. The State of Texas,* 632 T. Supp. 951 (1986).

24. Taft-Hartley Act, Section 7.

25. Ibid., Section 8(b)(1).

26. Robert A. Gorman, *Basic Text on Labor Law: Unionization and Collective Bargaining* (St. Paul, MN: West, 1976), p. 220.

27. *DeBartolo Corp. (DeBartolo II) v. Florida Gulf Coast Building and Construction Trades Council,* 108 S.Ct. 1392 (1988). *Lechmere, Inc. v. NLRB* (12 S. Ct. 841, 1992).

28. For a good summary of the most recent NLRB and court opinions governing picketing, see Kahn, op. cit., pp. 108–14. The legal statuses of strikes, picketing, and lockouts are covered by Louis B. Livingston, "Strikes, Picketing and Lockouts" in *Labor and Employment Law: Resource Materials,* 6th ed., ed. Peter M. Panken (Philadelphia: American Law Institute–American Bar Association Committee on Continuing Professional Education, 1992), pp. 1482–97.

29. Kahn, op. cit., p. 95.

30. Joe C. Davis and John H. Huston, "Right-to-Work Laws and Free Riding," *Economic Inquiry* 31 (January 1993), p. 52.

31. Ibid.

32. Keith Lumsden and Craig Peterson, "The Effect of Right-to-Work Laws on Unionization in the United States," *Journal of Political Economy* (October 1975), pp. 1237–48.

33. Ibid., p. 1247.

34. Ibid., p. 1248.

35. William J. Moore and Robert J. Newman, "The Effects of Right-to-Work Laws: A Review of the Literature," *Industrial and Labor Relations Review* 38 (July 1985), pp. 571–87.

36. National Labor Relations Act, Section 8(a)(3).

37. *Bloomingdale's and William P. Ward v. Distributive, Processing, and Office Workers of America (Independent),* 33 LRRM 1093.

38. *Local 833, UAW (Allis-Chalmers Manufacturing Company),* 149 NLRB 67 (1964).

39. *American Broadcasting Companies v. Writers Guild of America,* 437 U.S. 411 (1978).

40. *Machinists' Local 1414 v. Neufeld Porsche-Audi, Inc.,* 270 NLRB 1330 (1984) and *Pattern Markers' League v. NLRB,* 105 Sup. Ct. 3064 (1985).

41. For a good discussion of union discipline, see William B. Gould IV, *A Primer on American Labor Law,* 3rd ed. (Cambridge, MA: MIT Press, 1993), pp. 160–62.

42. Benjamin H. Selekman, "Varieties of Labor Relations," *Harvard Business Review* (March 1949), pp. 175–99. Descriptions of these attitudes also appear in the introduction to Benjamin Selekman, Sylvia K. Selekman, and Stephen H. Fuller, *Problems in Labor Relations* (New York: McGraw Hill, 1950) and subsequent editions.

43. For studies indicating that loyalties to company and union tend to go up and down together, see Ross Stagner, W. E. Chalmers, and Milton Derber, "Guttman-Type Scales for Union and Management Attitudes Toward Each Other," *Journal of Applied Psychology* (October 1958), p. 299.

44. Donna Sockell, "The Legality of Employee-Participation Programs in Unionized Firms," *Industrial and Labor Relations Review* 37 (July 1984), pp. 541–56.

45. Many firms, including Continental Airlines and Wilson Foods, in the early 1980s used the bankruptcy provision fundamentally to alter their relationships with their unions.

46. Thomas A. Kochan, Harry Katz, and Robert McKersie, *The Transformation of American Industrial Relations* (New York: Basic Books, 1986).

47. Arthur F. Silbergeld and Thomas T. Liu, "Employee Participation Programs under the National Labor Relations Act," *Employment Relations Today* 18, no. 4 (winter 1991/92), pp. 505–14.

48. Ibid., pp. 505–6.

49. "Reich Commission Attacked as Pro-Labor," *Labor Relations Reporter, The Bureau of National Affairs,* May 5, 1993: 143 LRR 48–53 (51).

50. "Workplace Commission Seeks Win-Win Solutions," *Labor Relations Reporter, The Bureau of National Affairs,* May 31, 1993: 143 LRR 153–154 (153).

51. Silbergeld, op. cit., 505, 506.

52. "Recent NLRB Findings May Have Chilling Effect," *Labor Relations Reporter, The Bureau of National Affairs,* July 12, 1993: 143 LRR 346–347 (346).

53. Kenneth A. Jenero and Christopher P. Lyons, "Employee Participation Programs: Prudent or Prohibited," *Employee Relations Law Journal* 17, no. 4 (spring 1992), pp. 535–66 (536).

54. For a more comprehensive discussion of this topic, see "NLRB General Counsel's Memorandum on Employee Participation," *Labor Relations Reporter, The Bureau of National Affairs,* May 13, 1993: 14:201–11; Harold J. Datz, "Employee Participation Programs," *Labor Relations Reporter, The Bureau of National Affairs,* May 13, 1993: 14:221–25; Raymond L. Hogler, "Employee Involvement and Electromation, Inc: An Analysis and a Proposal for Statutory Change," *Labor Law Journal* 44, no. 5 (May 1993), pp. 261–75. 309 NLRB No. 163, 1992–93 CCH NLRB 17, 609, 142 LRRM 1001 (1992).

55. *E. I. DuPont de Nemours and Company and Chemical Workers Association, Inc. International Brotherhood of DuPont Workers and National Labor Relations Board.* 4-CA-18737-1,-2,-3, -5,-6,-7. 4-CA-18792, 4-CA-18835, 4-CA-18840-2, 4-CA-19078. 1993 NLRB Lexis 637; 311 NLRB No. 88 May 23, 1993.

56. "Reich Commission Attacked as Pro-Labor," op. cit., p. 51.

57. "News and Background: Electromation Creates Risks for Employers," *Labor Relations Reporter, The Bureau of National Affairs,* May 31, 1993: 143 LRR 141–142 (142).

CHAPTER 5

Union and Employer Organizational Structure in the Private Sector

After reading this chapter, you should be able to

■ Identify the differences between craft and industrial unions.

■ Explain the functions of local unions, internationals, and the AFL-CIO.

■ Discuss the effects of a democratic workplace on union democracy.

■ Explain how individuals become union leaders and what they must do to stay in office.

■ Explain how competitive pressures affect the attitudes of business toward unions.

■ Explain how the size of a firm affects its attitude toward unions.

■ Review the effects on collective bargaining of corporate mergers and the growth of conglomerates.

■ Explain how multinational corporations have affected bargaining structures.

ORGANIZATIONAL STRUCTURE

The way an organization is structured tends to reflect its values and goals as well as how likely it is to accomplish those goals. Although there is significant variation in the ways unions and business firms organize themselves for purposes of collective bargaining, some patterns do emerge.

Organizational structure also reflects past experience: It tends to incorporate what seemed to work and abandons what did not. Given the changing environment of labor-management relations, it is likely that the structure of the labor movement will continue to evolve. If, for example, some employers continue to pursue a policy of cooperation with their unions and seek to focus on work rules and other plant-specific issues, authority in those unions might become more decentralized.

The last 15 years have witnessed numerous trends (mergers, acquisitions, joint ventures, internationalization) that have made corporate structure far more complex. We might expect to see this trend continue if it proves to be successful. On the other hand, the debt burden and complexity of these operations may lead to major sale of subsidiaries and decentralization of decision making.

The primary purpose of unions is to represent workers in collective bargaining with their employers. For this reason, the employers' organizational structures influence the ways unions choose to organize themselves. As employer structures change, unions, to sustain their viability, must anticipate those changes and adapt accordingly.

PART I: UNION STRUCTURE

THE MEMBERSHIP BASE: CRAFT, INDUSTRIAL, AND RELATED TYPES OF UNIONS

A *craft union* represents a group of workers who have as a common bond the same set of skills, the same occupation. An *industrial union* represents workers with a variety of different skills, provided that they are all in the same industry. Pure craft and pure industrial unions are rare in the United States; almost every union represents a compromise.

Some organizations that are called unions are in reality hybrid organizations—at times representing workers as employees, and at times representing the interest of these workers as self-employed individuals. Craft organizations such as those of plumbers and barbers, for example, simultaneously negotiate the wages and benefits they receive when they work as "employees" for others, and also establish the prices they charge customers for their labor when they are self-employed. A plumbers' union acts more like a traditional union when it negotiates the wages and benefits of plumbers employed by contractors working on large commercial projects. However, this same plumbers' organization acts more like a medieval guild when it establishes the price of labor that a self-employed plumber will charge his or her own customers. The rationale for the hybrid approach is quite pragmatic: Workers such as bricklayers, carpenters, electricians, paperhangers, and other building craftspeople often move readily between being employees and being self-employed.

More common are unions combining several related crafts, generally known as *amalgamated craft unions.* An example is the International Brotherhood of Boilermakers, Iron Ship Builders, Blacksmiths, Forgers, and Helpers, a union whose membership has declined significantly over the years. Such unions retain the essential orientation of craft unionism. However, if a particular industry employs workers with only a limited number of different skills, an amalgamation of the unions covering those skills may result in an industrial union or a close approximation thereof. For example, much of the men's clothing industry originally was organized into separate craft unions of stitchers, pressers, cutters, trimmers, and so on. When these groups were combined into the Amalgamated Clothing and Textile Workers Union (ACTWU), they became a true industrial union. The ACTWU and the International Ladies' Garment Workers' Union (ILGWU) typically bargain as a complete industrial union for all organized employees in a given company. The United Steelworkers of America followed the same pattern in many of their plants.

In the last ten years, structural and financial challenges in the clothing, steel, and rubber industries have brought additional adaptations. In 1995 the two New York–based clothing unions, the International Ladies Garment Workers and the Amalgamated Clothing and Textile Workers, merged to become UNITE—Union of Needletrades Industrial and Textile Employees. The United Steelworkers took over the financially troubled rubber workers.

If industrial unions extend their coverage, they become multi-industrial. Such extension is illustrated by the names of several unions: the Gas, Coke, and Chemical Workers (subsequently merged into the International Union of Oil, Chemical, and Atomic Workers); the United International Union of Automobile, Aerospace, and Agricultural Implement Workers of America (generally known as the UAW); and the United Rubber, Cork, Linoleum, and Plastic Workers of America (URW). Unions often extend their jurisdictions without changing their names to match. For example, the Teamsters (International Brotherhood of Teamsters, Chauffeurs, Warehousemen, and Helpers of America) includes many brewery workers and retail clerks, among others. The International Brotherhood of Electrical Workers is a hybrid; it is definitely a craft union in the building trades and an industrial union in electrical manufacturing.

Amalgamations often reflect obvious relations, as between plumbers and steamfitters or gas and coke workers. The relationships on which other amalgamations are based are less obvious. Machinists in a factory presumably have a choice between a craft union of machinists and an industrial union of factory workers. They may have no practical choice, however, if an industrial union organizes the rest of the plant but the Machinists have no locals in the area. And choice may be eliminated if the National Labor Relations Board (NLRB), on the basis of a hearing, decides that all shop workers in the plant constitute an appropriate bargaining unit and, after an election, certifies the industrial union as the exclusive bargaining representative. If workers have a free choice, they may choose the union with the most vigorous leaders rather than the one that seems abstractly more logical. In many cases, the union selected is simply the one that got there first or conducted the most effective campaign. Many brewery workers, dairy workers, and retail clerks belong to the Teamsters because the Teamsters had already organized the drivers in their firms and were ready, willing, and able to organize the workers inside the plant. Small clothing firms in coal-mining towns have sometimes been represented by the United Mine Workers "because the union was there." Viewed broadly rather than within rigid formal patterns, unions in many respects organize in the directions and areas that seem most likely to bring them members.

A difficult jurisdictional problem may arise during the transition from a craft operation to an industrial one. Under older construction techniques, carpenters were carpenters and plasterers were plasterers. But in many contemporary buildings, the walls consist of machine-made panels. In the installation of such a wall, the distinction between a "carpenter" and a "plasterer" may have to be made on some niggling basis—such as whether the panel is nailed or cemented into place. In many respects, building construction has ceased to be group of crafts and has become an industry, and many of its difficult problems of technology and of industrial relations may never be adequately solved unless industrial unions supplant the craft unions currently in place. In the last 20 years, unions in the building trades have tried to achieve more concerted action in dealing with large construction firms. This coordination approaches industrial unionization in fact if not in form. Meanwhile, such jobs as steamfitter, stone mason, and electrician retain much of their original skill requirements in all kinds of construction, and nearly all building crafts retain their identities in small construction and in repair and maintenance.

Historically, the issue of organizing on a craft versus an industrial basis was very important. Most of the early unions in the United States were craft based, and their concerns and interests were recognized and taken into account in the establishment in 1886 of the AFL. When the CIO came into existence during the 1930s, it was composed almost exclusively of industrial unions. As a consequence, one of the most difficult issues the AFL and the CIO faced before they could merge in 1956 was the need to resolve the conflicts that arose over their differing views and approaches to unionism.

ORGANIZATION AND GOVERNANCE

The Local Union

Nearly all union structure in the United States is built on the basic local unit. The local is normally confined to a geographical area small enough for all members to attend a single meeting. This criterion may mean ten locals of a given union in a large city or only one local for the whole of a sparsely populated county. In industrial unions, a local usually covers a single plant or a number of small plants. It may carry the employer's name. Years ago, ethnic groups formed separate locals, as in the case of Italian and Jewish locals of clothing workers in New York City. In the South, in the past, locals of some unions were based on race.

Unlike management, a union is structured as a formally constituted, democratic organization, with ultimate power vested in its members. The bylaws of each local define the number, terms, duties, election, and salaries (if any) of local officers. They also cover procedural matters, such as calling and termination of strikes, ratification of contracts, selection of convention delegates, frequency of meetings, auditing, dues, fees, and other details. Many locals elect or appoint business agents to do the detailed work. In larger locals, the president and/or the secretary-treasurer may be full-time officers, with salaries, offices, and staffs. Salaries of local officers vary considerably from union to union, but they tend to run about even with the top rates earned on the job by union members. Membership meetings, plus referendums, constitute the legislative branch; the officers constitute the executive branch. Some locals have executive boards to make certain interim decisions between meetings.

The president, vice-president, and secretary-treasurer perform the duties typical of those offices and are elected by members of the local. In a small local, the officers may serve as contract negotiators, though a staff representative from the national union or its appropriate district is the usual principal negotiator. In the latter case, it is typically the function of the officers to inform the district representative of the special problems and desires of the local membership. It is often their additional function to "sell" the membership on the nature of the possible contract gains, as contrasted with what the members would like or think they ought to have. The president normally participates in a final effort to settle grievances before they go to arbitration.

Shop stewards are normally elected, ideally in sufficient numbers that they can consult with employees who have or think they have grievances; a shop steward usually accompanies an aggrieved employee in presenting the grievance to the supervisor in the initial step of the grievance procedure. Because the steward presumably is familiar with any grievance from its inception, he or she usually follows the grievance through all of its steps, including being present and probably testifying at an arbitration of the grievance. There is also a grievance committee, usually elected, that sits with management representatives in an effort to resolve grievances. In a union that operates a hiring hall, as is often the case with the longshoremen, people in building trades, and musicians, some person(s) must also be in charge of keeping records of members and of referring them to jobs when requests are received.

In unions of nonfactory workers, including construction workers, hotel and restaurant workers, barbers and beauticians, and others who function in scattered small groups, the primary work of the local is done by a business agent, who may be elected or appointed and is nearly always paid. The business agent may negotiate contracts, settle grievances, preserve jurisdictions, recruit new members, and handle correspondence and accounting. Among longshoremen on the dock, the walking delegate performs these functions.

Initiation fees, which represent a union member's initial financial obligation, are required by most unions and may be set either by the national organization or by an individual local subject to limits in the national constitution. Monthly dues are required by all labor organizations; some apply a single rate, whereas others utilize a varying rate structure, often a percentage of earnings. The maximum dues payment among unions is usually determined by local units. Most unions exempt unemployed members from paying dues; a smaller percentage exempt retirees, workers temporarily laid off, and apprentices. Per capita taxes, which are contributions by local affiliates of national unions to the parent organizations, are required almost uniformly.

The International Union

Because the primary role of labor unions is collective bargaining, the national or the international (if the union has locals in Canada) union is the locus of power in the labor movement. Locals are bound to the national and operate under its constitution. They also pay dues to the national for each local member. National unions may be affiliated with the AFL-CIO. The AFL-CIO, however, has little authority over most of the activities of its affiliated nationals.

The legislative power of national unions is vested in the convention. The Landrum-Griffin Act requires that conventions be held at least every five years, but most unions hold them more often. Local unions send representatives called delegates to the national convention. Delegates also come from city, state, and district bodies, which will be described shortly. Between conventions, the international's affairs are run by an executive board. National officers are usually elected either by the convention or by referendum; they normally include a president, a vice-president, and a secretary-treasurer, all working on a full-time basis.

A national union may hire a staff of as many as several hundred. Members of the executive board usually have specific areas of personal assignment, such as organization and membership, contacts with locals, economic policy, political action, negotiations, and public relations.

There may also be district, state, county, or city divisions of an international union, known as joint boards, county councils, state councils, and the like. They coordinate the work of locals within their areas. They also link the international and the local, breaking down the administrative task of the international into more convenient units. In some unions, each member of the executive board is responsible for a certain geographical area. The organizational levels between the local and the international are normally secondary in importance, although (especially in industries comprising numerous small firms, such as clothing or building construction) the joint board or local trades council sometimes does the real collective bargaining.

Election of Union Officers

Under the Labor-Management Reporting and Disclosure Act (LMRDA),

> Every national or international labor organization . . . shall elect its officers not less often than once every five years. . . . Every local labor organization shall elect its officers not less often than once every three years. Officers of intermediate bodies, such as general committees, system boards, joint boards, or joint councils, shall be elected not less often than once every four years.[1]

The statute also outlines the procedures that must be followed during such elections.

The Whole Union

The entity referred to as "a union" is normally the totality of the national or international office; the state or regional offices, if any; and all the locals. It is difficult to generalize about behavior or structure because of the many differences among unions. In industries or companies operating on a national scale, the national officers of the union do most of the important negotiating with employers, as has traditionally been the case with the United Automobile Workers, the United Steelworkers of America, and the United Mine Workers. By contrast, where there is little or no competition among geographically separated firms, negotiations with employers are usually carried on by the officers of the local unions. If a regional or national representative participates in negotiations, his or her function may be more to provide experience and negotiating skill than to influence the outcome toward any national pattern. Negotiations in building trades, transit companies, bakeries, and laundries are normally conducted at the local level by the local union.

Creation of new local unions is the principal purpose of organizing activities, which are relatively expensive. It is customary for organizers' salaries and expenses to be paid by the regional or national union. Whereas workers in some other industrialized nations take unionization for granted and do not wait to be recruited, American workers usually do not form a union until they feel an explicit need for one. An organizer's typical initial move is therefore to uncover and publicize grievances and dissatisfactions in order to build up potential support for the union. If and when the plant is organized, the actual process of negotiating contracts and of processing grievances may be left to the local union.

THE AFL-CIO—FORMAL STRUCTURE

The history and background of the American Federation of Labor (AFL) and the Congress of Industrial Organizations (CIO) were discussed in Chapter 2. As stated previously, the AFL-CIO merged into one federation in 1955. The federation is guided by its constitution, which was adopted at its founding convention in 1958. The AFL-CIO network consists of its national headquarters, eight regional divisions, and 50 state federations.[2] Any national union accepting the principles and objectives of the AFL-CIO can apply for and obtain membership in the federation. A local union may affiliate directly with the federation if there is no national union in its field; it is then known as a federal union.

It should be clearly understood that the AFL-CIO is not a union, nor were the separate federations preceding it. It does not engage in collective bargaining, nor can an individual join it except indirectly as a member of an affiliated union. The function of the AFL-CIO is to bring about organized cooperation of the constituent unions on behalf of labor as a whole. It has been found advantageous, for example, to pool forces for lobbying and electioneering. The central body is highly useful for settling jurisdictional disputes between national unions and has worked out a set of procedures for this purpose.

When the government seeks a representative from organized labor to serve on some board or commission, it is usually the federation that selects that person in the name of all labor. Policies regarding emergency wage controls, minimum wage legislation, social security, immigration, or tariffs can be executed better by a central organization. The federation publishes a newspaper and a variety of periodicals and pamphlets covering news of interest to labor as a whole. In brief, the federation carries on the class-wide functions of the labor movement. Some money and effort for organizing drives also come from the federation. The AFL-CIO receives its income from a per capita tax on the affiliated unions.

The top governing body of the federation is the biennial convention, which technically has final authority in virtually all matters, including establishment of broad policy, acceptance or expulsion of affiliated unions, and selection of federation officers. Historically, the top officers of the federation made decisions on most matters, and any internal disagreements were resolved in private. This situation changed dramatically in 1995, when a group of Executive Council members publicly criticized the leadership of the AFL-CIO and, as was stated in Chapter 2, forced the resignation of the federation president and his executive officers, including the secretary-treasurer and the executive vice-president. Fifty-one vice-presidents jointly constitute the Executive Council. The Executive Council acts as the governing, policy-making body of the federation between conventions. The Council must meet a minimum of three times a year. It proposes and reviews legislation and also formulates positions on national and international subjects.

Another AFL-CIO policy-making entity is the General Board, which includes the Executive Council plus principal officers of each affiliated national and international union and department. The Board makes decisions on matters of policy referred to it by the Executive Council or by the executive officers. The members of the General Board vote as representatives of their unions; in this respect they differ from members of the Executive Council, who vote as representatives of the AFL-CIO.[3] Figure 5.1 shows the structure of the AFL-CIO and its affiliate unions.

Subject to some qualification, the federation is loose; any member union can withdraw if it feels that the advantages of freedom outweigh those of affiliation. The UAW, for example, disaffiliated from the AFL-CIO in 1968 and rejoined in 1981. The federation has little power over its constituent unions.

The major functions of the federation are reflected in its list of standing committees: legislation, civil rights, political education, international affairs, education (within the unions as well as in the nation in general), social security, economic policy, community services, housing, research, public relations, safety and occupational health, and organization and field services. Provisions are also in place for discouraging the raiding of one union by another and for settling jurisdictional disputes.

The AFL-CIO also has subdivisions called departments, which coordinate groups of unions that face related problems. There is one department each for building trades, food trades, industrial unions, maritime trades, metal trades, transportation trades, professional employees, public employees, and union label. These departments are, in effect, subfederations. Each has its constitution and officers, accepts or rejects unions for membership, and collects its own per capita tax. A national union may belong to more than one department but need not join any. If only a portion of the union's membership is qualified for affiliation, the union may affiliate with respect to that fraction. Table 5.1 provides statistical data on AFL-CIO membership.

Among the AFL-CIO departments, the Industrial Union Department (IUD) has special significance. In 1955 the former CIO entered the merged federation almost intact as the IUD. It brought along its president and secretary-treasurer (Walter Reuther and James B. Carey, respectively) and its $1.25 million treasury. Some 35 former AFL unions joined the IUD with all or part of their memberships. The IUD carries considerable weight in the AFL-CIO but by no means dominates it. An important function of the IUD is to coordinate bargaining strategies of two or more unions dealing with the same employer.

The AFL-CIO and Member Unions

The AFL-CIO constitution gives the organization more formal control over its member unions than did the constitution of the AFL, and in this respect the present federation more nearly resembles the old CIO. The original federations reflected their respective histories: The AFL grew from a group of existing unions, whereas the large unions—steel, autos, and rubber—were themselves created by the CIO. Four areas in which the AFL-

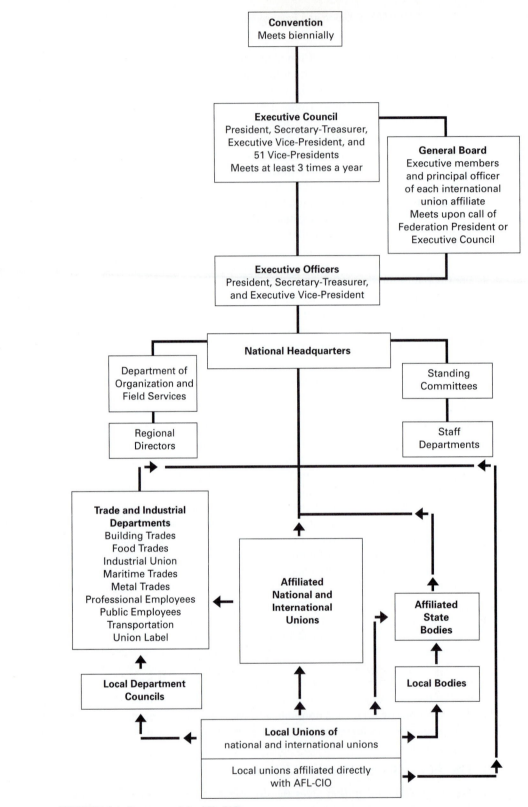

FIGURE 5.1 Structure of the AFL-CIO

Source: C. D. Gifford, ed., *Directory of U.S. Labor Organizations, 1996 Edition,* Bureau of National Affairs (Washington, DC: 1996), p. 2.

TABLE 5.1 AFL-CIO Membership Data
American Federation of Labor and Congress of Industrial Organizations Paid Membership

The following table shows the average per capita membership of current affiliates paid to the AFL-CIO for the year 1955, two-year periods ending in 1965, 1975, 1985, and subsequent conventions. The 1995 figures are based on the two-year period ending June 30, 1995.

Organizations	Thousands of Members								
	1955	1965	1975	1985	1987	1989	1991	1993	1995
Actors and Artistes of America, Associated	34	61	76	100	95	97	99	93	80
Air Line Pilots Association	9	18	47	33	31	31	35	31	35
Aluminum, Brick and Glass Workers, International Union				49	45	44	42	38	37
Asbestos Workers, International Association of Heat and Frost Insulators and	9	12	13	12	12	12	12	12	12
Automobile, Aerospace and Agricultural Implement Workers of America, International Union	1,260	1,150	a.	974	998	917	840	771	751
Bakery, Confectionery and Tobacco Workers International Union				115	109	103	101	99	96
Boilermakers, Iron Ship Builders, Blacksmiths, Forgers and Helpers, International Brotherhood of	151	108	123	110	90	75	66	58	42
Bricklayers and Allied Craftsmen, International Union of	120	120	143	95	84	84	84	84	84
Broadcast Employees and Technicians, National Association of	4	4	5	5	5	5	5	5	s.
Carpenters and Joiners of America, United Brotherhood of	750	700	700	609	609	613	494	408	378
Chemical Workers Union, International	79	70	b.58	40	35	34	40	38	34
Clothing and Textile Workers Union, Amalgamated				228	195	180	154	143	129
Communications Workers of America	249	288	476	524	515	492	492	472	478
Coopers International Union of North America	3	2	2	1	1	1	1	p.	
Distillery, Wine and Allied Workers International Union, AFL-CIO/CLC				14	13	11	10	8	8
Electronic, Electrical, Salaried, Machine and Furniture Workers, AFL-CIO, International Union of					185	171	160	143	135
Electrical Workers, International Brotherhood of	460	616	856	791	765	744	730	710	679
Elevator Constructors, International Union of	10	12	13	20	21	22	22	22	20
Engineers, International Union of Operating	200	270	300	330	330	330	330	305	298
Farm Workers of America, AFL-CIO, United			14	12	9	11	15	16	16
Fire Fighters, International Association of	72	87	123	142	142	142	151	151	151
Firemen and Oilers, International Brotherhood of	57	44	40	25	25	25	25	25	t.
Flight Attendants, Association of				c.17	20	21	24	28	31
Flight Engineers' International Association	1	1	2	1	1	1	1	1	1
Food and Commercial Workers International Union, United				989	1,000	999	997	997	983

TABLE 5.1 (cont.)

| | Thousands of Members | | | | | | | | |
Organizations	1955	1965	1975	1985	1987	1989	1991	1993	1995
Garment Workers of America, United	40	35	32	28	26	24	21	20	u.
Garment Workers Union, International Ladies'	383	363	363	210	173	153	143	133	123
Glass, Molders, Pottery, Plastics and Allied Workers International Union			35	72	65	86	80	73	69
Glass Workers Union, American Flint	28	31	35	24	22	20	22	20	20
Government Employees, American Federation of	47	132	255	199	157	156	151	149	153
Grain Millers, American Federation of	33	25	29	30	28	28	27	26	20
Graphic Communications International Union				141	136	124	113	95	94
Horseshoers of United States and Canada, International Union of Journeymen	1	1	1	1	1	1	1	1	1
Hospital and Health Care Employees, National Union of				d.23	60	d.58			
Hotel Employees and Restaurant Employees International Union	300	300	421	327	293	278	269	258	241
Industrial Workers of America, International Union, Allied		71	93	63	61	60	53	48	v.
Iron Workers, International Association of Bridge, Structural and Ornamental	133	132	160	140	122	111	101	91	82
Laborers' International Union of North America		403	475	383	371	406	406	408	352
Laundry and Dry Cleaning International Union, AFL–CIO		22	20	15	14	14	14	12	11
Leather Goods, Plastics and Novelty Workers Union, International	30	34	39	21	19	15	12	6	5
Leather Workers International Union of America	2	5	2	1	e.1				
Letter Carriers, National Association of	100	130	151	186	200	201	210	210	210
Locomotive Engineers, Brotherhood of						f.3	20	20	19
Longshoremen's Association, AFL–CIO, International		50	60	65	64	62	60	58	61
Longshoremen's and Warehousemen's Union, International						g.16	45	40	36
Machinists and Aerospace Workers, International Association of	627	663	780	520	509	517	534	474	448
Maintenance of Way Employees, Brotherhood of	159	77	71	61	58	48	42	33	31
Marine and Shipbuilding Workers of America, Industrial Union of	27	22	22	17	12	h.			
Marine Engineers' Beneficial Association, National	9	9	20	22	22	48	53	52	w.
Marine Engineers' Beneficial Association									27
Maritime Union of America, National	37	45	35	17	18	i.			
Maritime Union, National							3	3	21
Mechanics Educational Society of America	49	37	23	5	4	4	3	3	3

TABLE 5.1 (cont.)

	Thousands of Members								
Organizations	1955	1965	1975	1985	1987	1989	1991	1993	1995
Metal Polishers, Buffers, Platers and Allied Workers International Union	15	11	9	5	5	5	4	4	3
Mine Workers of America, United						j.	0.82	75	75
Molders and Allied Workers Union, AFL-CIO, International	67	50	50	32	32				
Musicians of the United States and Canada, American Federation of	250	225	215	671	601	54	51	47	35
Newspaper Guild, The	21	23	26	24	25	25	25	21	20
Novelty and Production Workers, International Union of Allied				23	23	23	23	23	20
Office and Professional Employees International Union	44	52	74	90	86	84	89	89	86
Oil, Chemical and Atomic Workers International Union	160	140	145	108	96	71	90	86	83
Painters and Allied Trades of the United States and Canada, International Brotherhood of	182	160	160	133	128	128	124	106	95
Paperworkers International Union, United			275	232	221	210	202	188	233
Pattern Makers League of North America	11	10	10	8	8	7	7	q.	
Plasterers' and Cement Masons' International Association of the United States and Canada, Operative	60	68	55	46	43	39	39	35	29
Plate Printers, Die Stampers & Engravers Union of North America, International	1	1	1	1	1	1	1	1	1
Plumbing and Pipe Fitting Industry of the United States and Canada, United Association of Journeymen and Apprentices of the	200	217	228	226	220	220	220	220	220
Police Associations, International Union				14	13	15	18	22	26
Postal Workers Union, AFL-CIO, American			249	232	230	213	228	249	261
Professional Athletes, Federation of				2	1	1	1	1	2
Professional and Technical Engineers, International Federation of			14	19	20	21	21	23	22
Radio Association, American	2	2	1	1	1	1	1	1	1
Retail, Wholesale and Department Store Union	97	114	118	106	140	137	128	80	76
Roofers, Waterproofers and Allied Workers, United Union of				26	25	23	21	20	21
Rubber, Cork, Linoleum and Plastic Workers of America, United	163	153	173	106	97	92	89	81	79
School Administrators, American Federation of			7	9	9	9	9	11	11
Seafarers International Union of North America	42	80	80	80	80	80	80	80	80
Service Employees International Union, AFL-CIO			480	688	762	762	881	919	1,027

TABLE 5.1 (cont.)

Organizations	Thousands of Members								
	1955	1965	1975	1985	1987	1989	1991	1993	1995
Sheet Metal Workers International Association	50	100	120	108	108	108	108	108	106
Siderographers, International Association of	1	1	1	1	1	1	1	r.	
Signalmen, Brotherhood of Railroad	15	11	10	11	11	10	10	10	10
Stage Employees and Moving Picture Machine Operators of the United States and Canada, International Alliance of Theatrical	46	50	50	50	50	50	50	51	51
State, County and Municipal Employees, American Federation of	99	237	647	997	1,032	1,090	1,191	1,167	1,183
Steelworkers of America, United	980	876	1,062	572	494	481	459	421	403
Stove, Furnace and Allied Appliance Workers International Union of North America	10	9	3	3	3	4	5	4	x.
Teachers, American Federation of	40	97	396	470	499	544	573	574	613
Teamsters, Chauffeurs, Warehousemen and Helpers of America, International Brotherhood of						k.l.161	1,379	1,316	1,285
Textile Workers of America, United	49	36	36	23	20	20	18	17	15
Tile, Marble, Terrazzo, Finishers, Shopworkers and Granite Cutters International Union, AFL-CIO				7	8	l.	2	2	2
Train Dispatchers Association, America		3	3	3	3	2	2	2	2
Transit Union, Amalgamated		98	90	94	94	96	98	94	95
Transport Workers Union of America	80	80	95	85	85	85	85	78	75
Transportation-Communications International Union					113	86	73	49	58
Transportation Union, United			134	88	m.	m.	64	60	58
Utility Workers Union of America	53	50	52	52	54	51	55	47	46
Woodworkers of America, International	91	49	52	34	26	23	21	19	y.
Writers Guild of America, East. Inc.						n.	3	3	3

a. Disaffiliated 7/1/68. Reaffiliated 7/1/81.

b. Chemical Workers charter revoked by convention, 10/3/69, and reinstated by Executive Council 5/12/71.

c. Flight Attendants charter granted 2/23/84.

d. Hospital and Health Care Employees charter granted 10/1/84. Merged into Service Employees International Union and American Federation of State, County and Municipal Employees on 6/1/89.

e. The membership figure shown is based on one month's per capita tax and this union was suspended in accordance with Article XV, Section 5, of the AFL-CIO Constitution.

f. Locomotive Engineers charter granted 4/1/89.

g. Longshoremen's and Warehousemen's Union charter granted 8/22/88.

h. Marine and Shipbuilding Workers of America merged with International Association of Machinists and Aerospace Workers on 10/17/88.

i. Maritime Union of America, National, merged with National Marine Engineers' Beneficial Association on 3/29/88.

j. Molders and Allied Workers Union merged with Glass, Molders, Pottery, Plastics and Allied Workers International Union on 5/1/88.

TABLE 5.1 (cont.)

k. Teamsters, Chauffeurs, Warehousemen and Helpers of America affiliated 11/1/87.

l. Tile, Marble, Terrazzo, Finishers, Shopworkers and Granite Cutters International Union merged with United Brotherhood of Carpenters and Joiners of America on 11/10/88.

m. Transportation Union reaffiliated 8/1/89. Date of disaffiliation was 4/1 86.

n. Writers Guild of America, East, Inc. affiliated 8/19/89.

o. Mine Workers of America, United affiliated 10/1/89.

p. Coopers International Union of North America merged with Glass, Molders, Pottery, Plastics and Allied Workers International Union on 9/1/92.

q. Pattern Makers League of North America merged with International Association of Machinists and Aerospace Workers on 10/1/91.

r. Siderographers, International Association of merged with International Association of Machinists and Aerospace Workers on 9/15/92.

s. Broadcast Employees and Technicians, National Association of merged with Communication Workers of America on 1/1/94.

t. Firemen and Oilers, International Brotherhood of merged with Service Employees International Union, AFL-CIO on 2/1/95.

u. Garment Workers of America, United merged with Food and Commercial Workers International Union, United on 12/1/94.

v. Industrial Workers of America, International Union, Allied merged with Paperworkers International Union, United on 1/1/94.

w. The AFL-CIO Executive Council at the February 1995 meeting agreed that henceforth the National Marine Engineers' Beneficial Association would become two separate entities: the Marine Engineers' Beneficial Association and the National Maritime Union.

x. Stove, Furnace and Allied Appliance Workers International Union of North America merged with Boilermakers, Ironship Builders, Blacksmiths, Forgers and Helpers International Brotherhood of on 10/1/94.

y. Woodworkers of America, International merged with Machinists and Aerospace Workers, International Association of on 5/1/94.

Source: Report of the Executive Council of the AFL-CIO to the Constitutional Convention (New York: October 1995) in *Directory of U.S. Labor Organizations, 1996 Edition,* C.D. Gifford, ed., (Washington, DC: Bureau of National Affairs, 1996), pp. 83–85. Reprinted with permission.

CIO has sought influence have been solution of jurisdictional disputes, elimination of corruption, opposition to communism (an issue of historical interest), and protection of civil rights.

Although the federation can set standards of behavior for member unions, it cannot replace their officers, change their rules, discipline their members, or curtail their incomes. Its ultimate disciplinary power lies solely in suspension or expulsion. Though the AFL-CIO is important to the labor movement as a whole, in the short run an individual union is not significantly affected by nonaffiliation. For example, if the federation successfully lobbies for an increased minimum wage, an expelled union benefits as much as a member union. A nonaffiliated union may lose some prestige, but this may not be overly important to a strong, functioning union. The United Mine Workers, in fact, may for a time have benefited from its voluntary independent status. In 1989 the "house of labor" became significantly more unified with the affiliation of the United Mine Workers and the Teamsters, two of the most important previously unaffiliated unions. Both of these unions sought the advantages of labor unity in times of need. The Mine Workers were locked in a bitter struggle with the Pittston Coal Company; the Teamsters at that time faced a federal government suit aimed at removing their leadership.

However, when the federation charters a new union that is in a position successfully to raid the expelled one, it wields significant power. For example, in 1949 the CIO expelled the United Electrical Workers (UE) for alleged communist domination. It then chartered a new union, the International Union of Electrical, Radio, and Machine Workers (IUE), which eventually captured much of the UE's original membership. By contrast, after expelling the International Longshoremen's Association (ILA) for corruption, the AFL was almost totally unsuccessful in recruiting its members into the replacement union. Eventually, however, the combined efforts of the AFL-CIO, the federal government, the state of New York, the city of New York, the Waterfront Commission, and assorted other agencies cleaned up the union enough that it could qualify for reentry into the federation.

The AFL-CIO was able to eliminate corruption in several smaller unions following actual or threatened expulsion. Probably the main effect of the federation's action in these cases was to strengthen the position of reform groups within the affected unions. On the whole, as a result of the combined effects of the federation's disciplinary actions, the Ethical Practices Code of the federation, and the law, corruption seems to have dropped to an insignificant level within AFL-CIO unions.

In the case of the Teamsters, the federation felt that it was hopeless even to try to establish a rival union. And by expelling the Teamsters in 1957 for corruption, the AFL-CIO gave up all formal authority over them. The 1987 reaffiliation of the Teamsters with the AFL-CIO provided the federation with an opportunity successfully to influence that union in a positive direction.

Race, Communism, and Jurisdiction

No union may be a member of the AFL-CIO if its constitution or bylaws contain racially discriminatory provisions. The federation also attempts to exert influence over its affiliated unions in several other areas. The separate actions of the AFL and CIO in removing communist elements were successful enough that, in the Communist Control Act of 1954, Congress declared affiliation with either federation (and by implication with the AFL-CIO) to be prima facie evidence of noncommunist control.

Jurisdictional problems take two forms. The first is work assignment: Should the metal molding on a wooden cabinet be installed by the metalworkers (because it is metal) or by the carpenters (because it is on a wooden object)? The second issue concerns representation rights. Here the question is which union is appropriate to organize a particular group of employees.

The AFL-CIO constitution (Article XX) requires its members to accept established bargaining units and respect the collective bargaining and work relationships of every one of its affiliates. In the event of a dispute, the case goes to a mediator selected from a panel of mediators knowledgeable about the labor movement. If he or she cannot settle the dispute within 14 days, it is referred to an impartial umpire selected from a panel of "prominent and respected persons," whose decisions can be appealed to the Executive Council for a final ruling. Penalties levied on a union that does not comply with the final decision include loss of the right to use the appeals machinery, possible suspension, and provision of assistance by the federation to the plaintiff union.

Miscellaneous Union Organizations

Not all labor organizations are affiliated with the AFL-CIO. A number of national or international unions do not come under the AFL-CIO umbrella and are referred to as independent. For a period of time, two of the largest unions, the Teamsters and the United Auto Workers, were independent of the federation. A number of local unions have never affiliated with either a national or international union or a federation. Usually such unions are confined to a single establishment, employer, or locality. The AFL-CIO is considered the official voice of the labor movement.

DEMOCRACY IN UNIONS

Some Problems of Democracy in General

Democracy in its ideal state requires many things: informed citizens, intelligent awareness of one's own self-interest, awareness of the rights of others, willingness to accept wise leadership, and a mechanism that informs leaders of the wishes of the electorate and replaces those leaders if they do not respond. The technical apparatus of democracy includes secret ballots, freedom to oppose, and a judicial system that protects individuals and restrains officials.

Anyone who has observed democratic organizations at close range, particularly private ones, knows that a vast gulf often exists between the ideal and the actual. Reluctance to attend meetings, impatience with the business part of the meeting, unwillingness to serve on committees, and greater readiness to criticize leaders than to help them—these phenomena are observed almost anywhere that democratic organizations operate. Often they reflect a feeling that the "business" is unimportant or that the member does not understand it well enough to cast an intelligent vote. When important discussions do reach the floor, many members hesitate to speak, some get off the subject, and others cannot be heard. Officers get reelected because no one wants to hurt their feelings, or because they pull the strings and decisions gravitate to those who will make them. In organizations other than governments, the unopposed slate, elected by acclamation, is common.

In government, voters often know little about the candidates. Some citizens shrink from politics as from a loathsome disease, and others are indifferent. Though the issues may seem important, they also often seem unfamiliar and hopelessly complex. Many people never bother to vote. The nonparticipation of most corporate stockholders is too well known to deserve comment. Much the same may be observed for professional, charitable, fraternal, and civic organizations.

These inadequacies appear even where people are honest and sincere, and they are greatly aggravated if leaders or voters are self-seeking or dishonest. Unions are spared none of these difficulties and add a few of their own. In the following pages we will raise the questions: How much democracy is there in unions? How much ought there to be? What can be done to eliminate the discrepancies? Incidentally, except at the stockholder level, these questions do not arise on the management side; the basic structure of management is authoritarian, with power flowing down from the top.

The legal response to concerns about union democracy was the enactment of the Labor-Management Reporting and Disclosure Act of 1959, discussed in Chapter 3.

Special Problems of Democracy in Unions

Plant Government versus Union Government

Democracy is concerned with making government responsive to those governed. In unions a complication arises at the outset. What the employee is really concerned about is his or her plant government—the rules and regulations, wages, and conditions surrounding the job. If the union, in conjunction with management, creates a good plant government, the member may care little about how the union itself is run. That is, the member may see him- or herself less as a participant in the union than as a customer buying a service from it, and if the service is good, he or she may not care whether the "supplier" is honest or democratic.

Solidarity and the External Nature of the Union's Problems

The union itself does not provide for the member's wants but merely bargains for him or her with a third party, the employer. In many organizations, disagreement and criticism about internal matters are allowed, even encouraged. But in conflicts with outsiders, the factions are expected to close into a solid front. This expectation is heightened during negotiations and is greatest during a strike. At a strike rally, the union leader is both chair of a discussion group and captain of an army. Experience shows that he or she is more vulnerable if lack of toughness loses a strike than if victory comes from suppression of dissent. For the union's most important business, the ground rules are those not of domestic policy but of foreign policy during war, when dissent is made to seem treasonous.

All this means not that democratic practices are absent but merely that they face special obstacles. Many union contracts run for two or three years and greatly extend the noncrisis periods between negotiations. Furthermore, union security provisions place the existence of labor unions out of immediate jeopardy and improve the conditions for toleration of dissent.

The Absence of Conflict over Policy

The major business of democratic government is to accommodate disagreements over policy, whereas questions of means tend to be left to elected leaders and their appointees. In reality, contests over candidates are often policy contests in disguise.

In the past, the union's main policy was traditionally simple and uncontested—to obtain more from employers. The remaining concerns were mainly technical—how much to ask, when and whether to strike, whether to act tough or reasonable. But these were really matters of tactical significance, not policy, and we normally do not select tactics by elections. It should be pointed out, however, that a large union with a diverse membership may have many policy conflicts over bargaining goals. The traditional, relatively simple union policy of asking for more has undergone major changes, and become more complex, during the last 10 years. Declining membership, downsizing, competitive pressures, employee participation in the workplace, changes in the environment of worker-management relations, and emergence of a new model of work organization[4] have forced unions to reevaluate their past policies toward employers. This topic is discussed at greater length in Chapter 17, which contains the major findings of the Dunlop Commission.

Management Reactions and Democracy

Management's preference is a factor that militates against rank-and-file democracy and control over union decisions. Although employers often accuse unions of being undemocratic, much of this criticism arises from a simple desire to find fault with unionism. When employers negotiate with unions, generally they prefer ones with strong leadership. They want to deal with representatives on a "businesslike basis" and are annoyed when unions must repeatedly go back to their members for approval. On details an employer may prefer to talk matters over with the business agent, reach a conclusion, and know that things are settled. By contrast, democratic processes "rock the boat."

The Psychology and Politics of Leadership

Union members usually distrust leaders who have not come up through the ranks. Election to a salaried union post brings a sharp change in the quality of life of a labor leader. He or she now spends time in offices, conference rooms, planes, and hotels, and not in the work environment of the union members. The leader's income is probably larger and more regular than theirs, with an expense account added. Many of the leader's contacts are now with people of higher status—the officers of the company, the higher officials of the union, the school board, the United Way, and the city council. Though leaders may tell the members how much simpler life was at regular work, most resist returning to their previous occupations.

Meanwhile, the leader acquires experience at a difficult and demanding job. The cost of on-the-job training for union leaders is probably as high as for corporate executives, particularly when the issues in bargaining are as complex as pensions, job evaluations, health plans, automation, and bankruptcies. Union members see no more logic in discarding experienced executives every few years than does a corporate board of directors. Besides, the corporation probably has a larger pool to draw from. "Effective union leaders are relatively scarce; and experienced, proven union leaders not in office are even scarcer."[5] This is one reason leaders are returned election after election, sometimes without opposition, at least at the national level. Turnover of local officers by contrast, is often quite high.

At the national-union level, the union president traditionally is very powerful and usually unchallenged. The techniques union presidents utilize to hold power are standard and well known—patronage, prestige, constitutional authority, publicity, and the seduction of potential rivals into attractive invisible posts. A competent president of an international union can often keep his or her position until death or retirement.

Democracy cannot be measured quantitatively, and it is difficult to say how large a proportion of the labor movement actually represents it, as contrasted to the fractions in which democracy merely meets with obstacles or functions reasonably well. Some past abuses have been flagrant.[6] William Hutcheson was elected president of the Carpenters for life and appointed his son Maurice to replace him when he retired. At one point, James Caesar Petrillo not only was elected the Musicians' president for life but was granted authority to change the union constitution at will. However, when opposition later became strong, he was replaced and the constitution was normalized. While president of the United Mine Workers, John L. Lewis held dissident locals in line by ousting their elected presidents and replacing them with his trustees. Well-grounded fears for physical safety have quieted occasional rivals in the Teamsters, Mine Workers, International Longshoremen, and scattered other unions.

Petty tyrants crop up in union offices (just as they have among supervisors, office managers, and corporate executives), and some have fined, expelled, or denied jobs to members who criticized them. Historically, the task of protecting workers from management so greatly overshadowed that of protecting them from the union that little thought was given to the latter—although many leaders have worked hard to protect members' rights. Managements may criticize dictatorial leadership. But the kind of labor leader most in need of the criticism could fend it off with "Whatever management criticizes must be good for the workers." Historically, at least in some unions, the internal procedures for protecting members against improper discipline from the union itself have been woefully inadequate. For example, under a local union's bylaws, a member who appealed his discipline for criticizing the president of the local might find the president sitting as judge. Other appeals procedures, though not essentially unfair, were often so cumbersome that only a masochist would use them. The international convention is the court of final appeal in most unions. But this body may meet only every two or three years, and it is too large and unwieldy to handle essentially judicial matters.

PUBLIC REVIEW BOARDS

Some unions have established public review boards, their founding motivated in part as a move to erase the smear that corrupt unions have left on the whole American labor movement. They are also in part a frank recognition that the protection of members' rights is not all it could be, even in unions with long-standing reputations for honesty and strong membership participation. In 1957 the UAW created a Public Review Board (PRB)

> for the purpose of insuring a continuation of high moral and ethical standards in the administrative and operative practices of the International Union and its subordinate bodies, and to further strengthen the democratic processes and appeal procedures within the Union as they affect the rights and privileges of individual members of subordinate bodies.[7]

The PRB consists of seven distinguished citizens not connected with the union. The board members are proposed by the international president, with the approval of the International Executive Board, to the delegates of each constitutional convention of the union. The PRB, together with the Convention Appeals Committee, acts as the final appellate authority under the internal remedial procedures provided by the union constitution. In addition, it is the exclusive appellate authority for claims of violation of the Ethical Practices Codes. The PRB has the authority to make final and binding decisions on cases from aggrieved members of subordinate bodies of the union.

Unions in general are apprehensive over the creation of such tribunals because of their reluctance to give to outsiders final and binding authority over internal matters. The courts are traditionally also disinclined to address internal matters of private organizations. At present, it seems unlikely that other unions will follow the UAW in establishing public review boards.

PART II: THE EMPLOYER ORGANIZATIONAL STRUCTURE

AN OVERVIEW OF THE ISSUES

In this section we will examine management as an organization. In the preceding section we did the same for union organization, but we may immediately note an important difference. Although there is wide disagreement as to whether any particular employer needs such a thing as a union organization, no one—not even the union—seriously questions the need for management. Many forces, both inside and outside the organization, determine how its management will treat its employees—how the management will accept the prospect of having its employees organize into a union and how the management will behave toward a union if and when one is organized. In some organizations, employers use sophisticated methods to avoid unionization. The discussion of this subject is postponed to Chapter 6, on union and management security.

We will look first at some of the relations of the firm with its environment. On one side are the input relations, in which the firm takes in such things as labor, materials, and capital from its environment. On the other side are the output relations, in which the firm releases such things as manufactured products, services, advertising, wages, and other payments to its environment. Speaking broadly, the study of these input and output relations falls mainly within the subject matter of economics.

Second, and by contrast, we will look at relationships inside the firm. These involve strategies, aspirations, likes and dislikes, and flows of information within the company. The internal politics and organizational structure of the firm are also relevant. This second group of forces would be thought of as behavioral rather than economic. Though many of these relations, both economic and behavioral, are universal, our analysis will be confined to the United States.

To understand the intraorganizational and interorganizational aspects of a business firm, as well as its labor relations, we must utilize an interdisciplinary approach. The subject of labor relations stands, so to speak, with one foot in market analysis and the other in the behavioral sciences and related disciplines.

THE ENVIRONMENT AND CONSTRAINTS ON THE FIRM

The Private Profit Economy

There has been increasing dispute in the last three decades whether firms seek to maximize profits, as economists generally have argued (or at least find useful for their models), or whether they "satisfice" profits, as argued by Herbert Simon and others who view firms through the eyes of organization theory. We need not settle this point to be reasonably confident that over any extended period, the management of a firm must ensure that its income equals or exceeds its expenditures. Although the relation may not be quite as widely recognized there, the same is true for most government agencies, nonprofit service organizations, and labor unions viewed as employers, not to mention individual colleges or departments within a university. True, these entities may derive their income from taxation or contributions rather than from sale of products. And the "revenue" may take the form of a budget allocation rather than a return on sales, the budget allocation being secured through persuasion of higher levels of administration rather than persuasion of customers. Yet the imperative of keeping expenditures within budget constraints may be no less binding. In fact, in this respect the whole of a nonprofit organization may operate under much the same logic as does a subdivision within a profit-seeking firm.

In the United States, both sides in collective bargaining operate under a limited contractual relationship. In contrast to some relations in Japan and Latin America, the employer usually does not assume responsibility for the economic welfare of the employee or the employee's family beyond payment of the contracted wage and related fringe benefits for as long as the employee continues to perform satisfactorily and is needed by the employer. Some employers have contractual pension and health benefit obligations toward some of their retirees. The employee also has no responsibility for the economic welfare of the employer beyond the satisfactory performance of specified tasks. The employer usually has no obligation to keep an employee on the payroll unless it is considered in the economic interests of the firm to do so. The situation is softened somewhat by various court decisions and employee security provisions under union contracts. Overall, however, neither the laws nor the customs of our country obligate an employer to retain unneeded employees. A major exception to this is the 1988 plant closing law, which requires large employers (defined as having 100 or more full-time employees) to provide 60 days' notice to employees of foreseeable mass layoffs.[8]

Numerous kinds of regulations may affect employers in their relations with employees. For example, public utilities may need utility commission permission before passing increased wage costs on to consumers in the form of increased utility bills. Safety regulations may require larger crews of employees than the employer may think are necessary. These regulations may affect the level at which the employer will be seeking to balance costs and incomes. But they do not remove the imperative of keeping them balanced.

The Input Side

Cost structure refers to the percentage of total costs occasioned by particular inputs, such as wages, materials, power, advertising, and the like. In some industries, labor constitutes a high percentage of total cost. The labor percentage has been high in such industries as construction, transit, handmade pottery, education, and service. On the other hand, in some highly automated, capital-intensive industries like petroleum refining, labor costs may represent a very small proportion of total costs. Needless to say, managements are under greater pressure to avoid large wage increases in labor-intensive than in capital-intensive industries.

An employer also has a particular labor structure, which means the numbers and ratios of different types of employees. Some industries employ only one or a few dominant types. The trucking industry employs mainly drivers, and an industry as complex as building construction is dominated by representatives of fewer than a dozen specific crafts. By contrast, a large manufacturing plant making complex items engages many unskilled and semiskilled workers whose abilities can be used just as easily to put together ships as automobiles, radios as pumps. In addition, manufacturing relies on a variety of skilled jobs, with a sprinkling from nearly every occupation. For example, firms in steel, automobiles, chemicals, textiles, and paper all include their quotas of computer technicians, electricians, carpenters, machinists, crane operators, truck drivers, plumbers, and many others—if not for production, then at least for maintenance work. Illustrative of the scope of skills exercised in large modern industry is a steel plant's having several agricultural economists on its staff because some of its waste products contain ingredients for fertilizers.

The homogeneous group of employees poses to management a different set of problems from that posed by the occupationally cosmopolitan group. The employer with only a few types of labor has a simple wage structure. It is easy to make comparisons with the wages competing employers are paying for the same kinds of labor, and for competitive reasons it is important that they pay about the same.

The large firm with a variety of workers may find it more important to maintain proper differentials among the jobs within its own organization than to pay the same as other employers. These internal differences are important for keeping status structures and lines of promotion clear and for motivating employees to prepare themselves for higher positions. Furthermore, it is difficult to compare general wage levels of two firms that include many kinds of employees in widely differing proportions. The total (or the average) wage measures the employer's labor cost. Employers can bargain effectively over the total (or average) wage bill only if they bargain simultaneously with all employees. If employers were to deal with different groups separately, they might deal most generously with those who hold "bottleneck" jobs and whose actions could seriously curtail the output of the whole organization. Or they might treat best those who negotiate first and put the real "squeeze" on the later groups in order to keep the total wage bill within a given amount. In either event, severe discontent of some groups will almost certainly follow. Both strategically and practically, employers in mass production industries generally find it preferable to deal with a single union for all employees rather than with a separate union for each group. Therefore, in most instances, they tend to prefer a single union of the industrial type. At the same time, there seems to be a tendency, both in the United States and globally, to restructure single-employer-single-union bargaining, often to the level of the business division. The decentralization due to the evolution in corporate business strategy toward local profit centers, budget compliance, and greater autonomy for business unit managers has led to changes in the scope and structure of bargaining.[9]

Unions have been successful in organizing workers in factories, offices, retail stores, and schools and at all levels of government. In most of these sectors, people work in essentially unchanging workplaces for a regular work week. There are many workplaces, however, which other circumstances prevail. Dunlop covered this topic extensively in his classic book *Industrial Relations Systems.*[10] In the airlines, the railroads, and over-the-road bus and truck transportation, employees eat and sleep away from home much of the time, and their associated costs must be absorbed or paid for by the employers. These industries also face scheduling problems in getting employees to their homes from time to time, either in the course of their work runs or with "deadhead" transportation provided. The work of local bus drivers is concentrated in the first part of the morning and the last part of the afternoon; this scheduling raises questions as to whether they should be paid for the largely unusable time in between. Construction workers are often employed a month here, two days there, and a week somewhere else, sometimes by the same construction firm and sometimes by different firms. Hence, union-management contracts are nearly useless unless they encompass essentially all employers with whom a given individual is likely to work. In addition, contracts must include provisions for days when employees report to work and then are sent home because of bad weather. And to be feasible, such fringe benefits as vacations and pensions must be negotiated on a multiemployer basis.

Lumberjacks in logging camps typically live for extended periods in facilities provided by their employers, and their contracts may need to deal with quality of food and beds, sanitation, transportation out of camp, medical care, or even the number of movies per week. Migrant farm workers have much the same problem but in more severe form because they change employers much more often. Construction engineers may be moved by their employers from coast to coast or to foreign nations at perhaps two- to five-year intervals. Aprons, outer clothing, safety goggles, hard hats, and tools are required in many jobs, and decisions must be negotiated about who is to pay for them and how often they are to be cleaned or replaced. The role of tips as part of pay must be determined for many service workers, as must be the role of royalties for those whose recorded commercials or artistic performances are replayed many times. Garment workers are subject to seasonal employment, and movie actors and technicians face some very special problems when working on location. College professors may need to negotiate about academic freedom, class size, teaching loads, or free tuition for their families. In the last 15 years, the issue of workplace privacy has been gaining increased attention. Surreptitious monitoring on occasions beyond the ordinary course of business is of concern to unions as well as to employees. The issue is being brought more and more often before the courts.[11] Finally, entirely new issues are raised by the new technologies many workers utilize. Examples include extended exposure to video display terminals, use of electronic monitoring of productivity, and the details of telecommuting (working from home or remote locations through use of modems and facsimile machines). In 1991 about 20 million U.S. workers performed portions of their primary jobs at home. A large proportion of these at-home workers were self-employed (28 percent), but even more (61 percent) were simply "taking work home from the office" without being compensated for their work at home.[12]

Although this book deals mostly with the more obvious types of relationships, readers should keep in mind that the subject matter of collective bargaining contracts is complex and varied.

The Output Side

The output of a firm is its product and/or service. The main problem on the output side is the state of competition. Many small-to-medium-sized firms are in such industries as clothing, construction, trucking, and retailing. Competition is vigorous and often breaks out in price cutting. Prices tend to run close to costs, leaving little margin for profit. Each firm is extremely reluctant to agree to anything that might raise its costs above its competitors', and the pressure to get costs below that level is strong. Because many of these industries tend to have fairly high labor costs, wage cutting is an obvious way to reduce costs. In addition, it is easy for new firms to enter the industry and for old ones to move to low-wage areas. Under these circumstances, employers may desire some stabilizing force to keep competitors from obtaining a cost advantage based solely on wage cutting. The labor union is one device for attaining wage stability. Despite objections to some specific union actions, an employer in such an industry will often recognize that a strong union covering all competitors may benefit the individual employer as well as his or her employees. The union, if it is to stabilize wage rates in such an industry, must be large. In fact, it will almost necessarily be more powerful than any single employer. It may be able to win from employers virtually anything the industry is able to give, in which case the only way the union can get "more" is to make the industry more prosperous. Union leaders may therefore become interested in reducing costs, increasing sales, and generally improving the welfare of employers. Employer willingness to accept the union's stabilizing effects on costs is thus augmented by the fact that union leaders may view the problems of the industry in much the same light as does management. Where industries consist of many comparatively small employers, they may form an employer association and engage in multiemployer bargaining, which we will examine in more detail in Chapter 7, on bargaining structure.

In short, when management sells its output in an environment of vigorous competition among many small firms, it tends to resist unionization less if the union is strong, if the union covers all important competitors, and if all competing firms can bargain simultaneously through a single employer association. Although the union tends to dominate this relationship, it also tends to show restraint, which grows out of its understanding of the economic limitations of the industry.

At the opposite end of the spectrum are the industrial giants, whose profits sometimes run into billions. Though some exceptions exist, uniformity of wage rates among competing firms of this sort is less pressing than in the price-competitive industries. This does not mean, however, that large companies in the same industry sign widely different labor contracts. Because differences among large employers are sometimes more important than their similarities, the industrial giants usually bargain singly, sometimes negotiating separately with a variety of different unions. These firms are large enough that bargaining between any one of them and even a large and strong union is by no means one-sided.

The foregoing discussion of management's relation to its environment on the input and output sides is by no means comprehensive. Obviously, such additional factors as rate of growth, rate of technological change, seasonal and cyclical regularity or irregularity, economic conditions, antitrust policy, foreign competition, and government policy—to mention only a few—will have consequences for a firm or industry. These need not be detailed. However, one consequence is that, more than almost anything else, management wants flexibility and freedom of action to adapt to the vicissitudes of organizational life.

SOME INTERNAL ASPECTS OF THE FIRM

There are many ways a firm must adjust to the input and output sides of its environment. A significant amount of management's work is concerned with people. They must be located, selected, recruited, trained, placed, and evaluated. They must also be motivated and induced to work on their tasks and with one another. As products and processes change, the methods and content of jobs must be modified and redescribed, and their relative rates of pay must be reevaluated. Any change in product or process may also change the relative numbers of different skills that the firm employs. A major change in job mix may require lengthy advance planning so that new employees can be recruited or existing ones retrained. An orderly reduction in force must also be planned long in advance to minimize hardship to employees, comply with plant-closing legislation, avoid penalty rates for unemployment compensation, hold down severance costs, and stay within the constraints of the seniority rules and affirmative action guidelines—to mention only the more conspicuous considerations. Many of these adjustments can be facilitated by specialists, who may be either hired or engaged as consultants. For example, industrial engineers specialize in arranging physical layouts and muscular motions for optimum efficiency. Other specialists deal in such areas as job evaluation, merit rating, recruitment, employee testing, interviewing, and employee record keeping. To say that there are specialists in these areas does not assume merely the availability of experienced people. It also presupposes large bodies of knowledge stored in libraries and computer memories, taught in university courses, and acquired through numerous experiments designed to evaluate different methods of doing things.

As a consequence, managements, at least in large firms, have access to a large body of expertise about the effective utilization of human resources. Among many other things, this expertise addresses such issues as authoritarian versus participatory supervision, effective use of grievance procedures, strengths and weaknesses of participative decision making, job simplification, and job enrichment, and potential ways to reduce turnover rates. Listing these issues does not imply that we know precisely how to utilize the available knowledge. It does mean, however, that management has access to information and tools for addressing a variety of human resource management problems and issues.

While recognizing the importance of individual differences, management at times assumes that there are known or knowable ways of making the most effective use of human beings as factors in production. Unions seem to thwart the related moves that management may consider sensible in dealing with employees. First, the general union objective, insofar as it has one in this area, is to make work life more satisfactory for employees. This aim may or may not coincide with that of the employer as to the most effective use of employees as factors of production. Second, union officers or negotiators usually do not have the human resource expertise available to management. This fact may leave the union representatives feeling defensive when negotiating over human resource management issues, and the consequence may be the kind of aggressive response that sometimes arises from insecurity. Third, union leaders and members observe the way firms use applied psychology in their advertising to mold consumer perceptions into seeing the advantages but not the disadvantages of the products they are marketing. Unions are concerned that management's professional use of applied psychology in the workplace may also have a "brainwashing" purpose in attempts to shift workers' loyalties from the union to management. Management's assurance that the various experts are objective and impartial in dealing with employees is apt to be met with the stereotypical "The company's paying them, aren't they?"

This aspect of the relationship sometimes goes a step further. Not only can management acquire expert help in dealing with employees, it may now seem worthwhile to enlist ultrasophisticated advice for handling the union itself. This expertise may cover evasions of the law through minute knowledge of its loopholes and technicalities. For example, management might "accidentally" delay delivery of certain information in ways that will hamstring the union's preparation for negotiations and then be "understandingly patient" while union attorneys frustratedly try to ascertain whether they can compel the employer to provide the necessary information. The employer's sophistication may lie in making such moves seem utterly natural and legal, certainly not subject to prosecution, and then generously offering the requested materials at an inconveniently late date as a gesture of goodwill. The union representatives may thus be frustrated and left "off base" because they cannot be sure whether management's behavior involved an honest mistake or a very clever bargaining ploy. The subject of employers' anti-union activities is discussed further in Chapter 6, on management and union security.

Many employers believe that their human resource management (HRM) departments can protect the welfare and interests of their employees better than unions can, primarily because those departments employ professionals and have resources usually not available to unions. A management with this perspective will tend to see unionization as the effort of an outside group to challenge and frustrate its HRM activities. Other employers may view things differently. They may conclude that the employee can never fully trust the HRM department because it is controlled by management. Such employers recognize the inherent limits of their ability to deal with all their employees' needs and accept the necessity for employees to have a union as an advocate for their interests.

In short, some employers may see the union as a frustrating barrier to the relationship between management and its employees. Others may see it as the appropriate channel for that relationship and may even consider the union as a legitimate performer of some of the functions normally reserved for HRM departments.

Some researchers view managerial structure with respect to industrial relations as having three tiers. The highest tier, called the *strategic level,* is where the most fundamental business decisions are made, such as what business the firm should be in, where organizational expansion and contraction should take place, and what corporate values are. The middle tier, called the *functional level,* is the organizational level where collective bargaining may actually take place. The third tier is the *workplace* or *shop floor level.* This is the the scene of actual day-to-day interaction between workers and their supervisors. The implementation of most agreements takes place at this level.[13] The attitudes toward unions of management representatives at these three levels need not be, and indeed frequently are not, the same.

ATTITUDES TOWARD UNIONS: SMALL AND LARGE EMPLOYERS

The Small Individual Enterprise

To understand the negative attitudes of some small employers toward unions, it is necessary to review some elements in the background of the small firm. To illustrate, we may imagine a well-established, successful small enterprise such as might be found in retailing, wholesaling, small manufacturing, trucking, real estate, or a wide variety of other industries. The entrepreneur's success is probably the product of a lifetime of worries, sacrifices, near bankruptcies, baffling decisions involving both money and ethics, grueling work, and heart attacks and ulcers. It may be the fruit of the owner's being caught up in some "crazy" idea in which he or she alone had faith—plus the persistence to make it work. For many years this person may have been founder, investor, president, foreman, laborer, advertising manager, and office helper, doubling as maintenance person on weekends. Before starting a business, he or she may have worked for someone else, receiving wages, salary, or commission. This person may have disliked having to take orders based on decisions he or she had not helped to make and probably winced to think of someone else's hand on the valve that controlled the income flow. At great personal sacrifice and with a risk only vaguely guessed at, he or she started a business.

The company may be more familiar to this person than home and more important in his or her thinking. The employees may be better known than his or her family, and their welfare may be more important. The employer may always have treated them as well as the condition of the business permitted—often better. As the number of employees grew to 10, 20, 50, and 100, the employer continued to have as much interest in and affection for them as his or her spreading attention permitted.

To such an employer, the idea that employees should form a union to bargain (or even strike) and ask to participate in the making of decisions about which he or she knows so much more than they can ever know is utterly shattering. "It is my company" (and "my" may be spoken with pleading rather than arrogance), in a sense and to a degree that no one else can ever appreciate. The employer sees unionization as the utter antithesis of everything he or she has built and stood for. It introduces outsiders between employer and employees and threatens to embitter a relationship that has always seemed good. The owner is dismayed that the employees feel they have not been treated as well as possible.

Business dealings have shown the owner that many people are shrewd in their selfishness, ready to take advantage of a technicality. He or she may have disagreed with their ethics but understood their motives. Unions, on the other hand, have often seemed to pursue tactics that not only are costly to employers but may not always make economic sense to the union or its members. The employer knows how to protect against the shrewd operator but is baffled and frightened by the prospect of dealing with the unpredictable actions of a union that does not even seem always to pursue economic self-interest. In addition, the union seems to threaten the employer's freedom to manage his or her own firm according to a personal concept of what is right and wise—a freedom that may be the most cherished thing in the employer's life.

If the company is forced to deal with a union, the entrepreneur will probably feel bitter about it for many years—perhaps until his or her death. The employer will be angry at the union and will also direct that anger inward, feeling that the failure was somehow his or her own. He or she will be slow to adjust to the new method of operation. It will be long before it is accepted as an accomplished fact, and it will probably never really be understood. The entrepreneur may strike out blindly at the union or may even liquidate the business rather than deal with it. With the arrogance that sometimes marks the self-made entrepreneur, the employer's anger and retaliatory actions against the union may know no bounds. Such a successful, small individual enterprise represents one extreme situation into which a union may be introduced.

The Large Corporation

Despite the obvious contrast in size between the small individual enterprise and the large corporation, size is probably one of the less important differences. The ownership and structure of the large corporation tend to give it a different outlook and philosophy in its relation to unions.

Pride of ownership is likely to be minimal or nonexistent. The enterprise may be owned collectively by hundreds of thousands of stockholders. It may be almost completely "inside" controlled, in which case hired management has superseded ownership as the controlling force. Unlike the income of the proprietor-owner of the small enterprise, the salaries of the corporation officers are charged to the company as expenses, not paid out of profits—although profit-sharing plans often tie some considerable part of the officials' incomes to profits. Because the officers are themselves employees, they have an important psychological bond with the rank and file.

Officers of a corporation have normally been promoted from within. They have learned to take orders as well as give them and have often had to accept and implement policies of which they themselves disapproved. They have observed that neither the world nor their firm fell to ashes when their judgment was overruled. To people trained in this school, the union is merely one more pressure among the dozens to which they have already adapted. Although any new pressure may mean another headache or ulcer, they assume that they can learn to live with it.

The division of labor within the large corporation simplifies the problem. The obvious way to deal with the union is to create a new vice-presidency, complete with staff and office, to handle labor relations. Although this statement oversimplifies, something rather similar has happened in many large American corporations. A budget appropriation is made for the department, some dividends are withheld for the contingency of a strike, and the enterprise goes on.

When the problem of labor relations is assignable to a special department as a staff function, it takes on a psychological quality quite different from that in the individual enterprise. It becomes a technical problem to be investigated, pondered, and—if possible—solved. It is usually interesting, often frustrating, certainly challenging. In brief, the task of dealing with the union becomes professionalized. The union creates a job to be done, not an insult to be vindicated.

This professionalization underlies an additional psychological reaction. In the absence of unions, departments of labor or human relations would have been long in arriving and might still be nonexistent in many firms. In a very real sense, the employees of such departments owe their jobs to unions and must recognize, at least subconsciously, that the disappearance of unions would threaten their personal security. Perhaps one of the miscellaneous forces tending to perpetuate unions is that a professional arm of management has a vested interest in their continuance.

Intermediate Types

The two pictures just drawn of the small and the large firm represent extremes. Actual cases demonstrate a voluminous variety of reactions. Some individual proprietors accept unions without too many reservations, whereas some corporate officers display fierce proprietary interest and take personal offense at unionization. Emotional biases picked up from parents, friends, or other sources often add complications, as do the convictions of some that unions will destroy their organizations and the economy. The important point to remember is this: Many employers view unionization as a challenge and an interference. Others see it as a reasonable expression of workers' desire for representation and take the union in stride. Still others show mixed and intermediate reactions. In general, however, the large corporation is probably better equipped psychologically and organizationally to make this adjustment than is the small individual enterprise or the closely held corporation.

Every management, however, knows the need for discipline, and it is a rare employer who does not see in unionization at least a potential, and at worst an impossible, obstacle to prompt and effective disciplinary action. But, as we shall see later, management may also find through the union a better grievance procedure than management alone can provide.

COMPLEX ORGANIZATIONAL STRUCTURES

One generally may think of an employer as being in some particular industry and as being an independently acting unit. Actually, the real world includes many variations on organizational structure. Among the various possibilities, we will consider joint bargaining by a number of employers (multiple-employer bargaining), firms that cross industries (conglomerates), and firms that cross national boundaries (multinationals). The first of these will be discussed in Chapter 7, on bargaining structure. Conglomerates and multinationals are discussed next.

Conglomerates, Mergers, and Collective Bargaining

Although the literature in both economics and law contains conflicting reports on the overall desirability of formation of conglomerates through mergers, many labor relations experts and union officials think that conglomerates have shifted bargaining power to management. The anticonglomerate arguments advanced by unions are as follows: (1) The conglomerate can "whipsaw" unions because it can shift production to other plants when one is struck, and (2) the conglomerate usually has greater capital reserves ("deep pockets") and therefore can more easily absorb the costs of a strike.[14] On the other hand, corporate acquisitions financed by leveraged buyouts through the sale of high-interest junk bonds may render some conglomerates quite weak indeed.

Recognizing the possible deleterious effects of sustained conglomerate growth in the absence of countervailing union tactics, the AFL-CIO formed a special committee of the Industrial Union Department charged with the development of coalition bargaining between a single firm and a combination of several different international unions representing its employees. Coalition bargaining will be discussed in more detail in Chapter 7.

One study indicates that the rationale behind coalition bargaining may be based on faulty assumptions about conglomerate bargaining leverage. Hendricks states that the impact of conglomerates on union power, if measured by wage level, appears to have been neutral.[15] Moreover, according to Hendricks, the union coalition response to conglomerate mergers has been motivated by various factors other than power shifts. Hendricks believes that scale economies in the provision of fringe benefits and workers' concern over wage variation among member firms of a conglomerate can explain the real impetus behind coalition bargaining. For example, following a conglomerate merger, workers may initiate among themselves wage comparisons that were never contemplated in the past. Equity theory holds that employees are concerned with the perceived fairness of pay, based on an individual's comparisons between (1) his or her own input into the job and pay and (2) the inputs and pay of others doing comparable work. Consequently, dissatisfaction arising from a perception of pay inequity might partially explain the push behind coalition bargaining.

Multinationals and Industrial Relations

The multinational corporation (MNC) represents a major challenge and a distinct threat to unions and their members. MNCs can frustrate unions through their ability to (1) deplete union membership in one country by transferring job opportunities to foreign operations, (2) ship production from nonstriking countries to customers in a striking country, (3) threaten to move production or to reduce domestic production and to expand foreign

operations, (4) cover losses from domestic strikes through profits from foreign operations, and (5) weaken bargaining authority of domestic managers because of complex
decision-making structures. Bargaining with MNCs is made more complicated because
of the difficulties in obtaining financial data, the differences in labor law among countries, and the distinct labor relations practices corporations use in various countries. All of
these factors weaken the bargaining power of labor unions.[16]

As noted in Chapter 1, improvements in transportation and communication resulted
during the 1800s in a widening of product markets, which necessitated the formation of
national unions from the existing locals. Changes in production processes in the early
1900s required the labor movement to organize on an industrial basis rather than along the
traditional craft lines. Perhaps the growth of MNCs represents another development to
which labor must respond to remain viable. Barriers of language, culture, law, custom,
and ideology will make any transformation to truly international unions more difficult
than the two earlier transitions.

Labor's response to the continuing growth of MNCs has been varied. It has included
support for international labor standards, restrictions on trade, sharing of information on
corporate strategy, and innovative collective bargaining. The problems that MNCs pose
for U.S. workers go beyond the impact of finished goods from abroad, which have historically been the target of trade barriers. Domestic firms export capital and subsequently
import foreign components for final assembly in the United States. In many industries
this foreign outsourcing is a much greater cause of job loss than imports of final products.[17] Whereas restrictions on trade pit one country's workers against those of another,
MNCs integrate workers in different countries into one production process.[18] This practice provides the opportunity and indeed perhaps the necessity for workers to establish
unified strategies when dealing with multinational employers. This issue will become
more significant in the future because of the 1994 NAFTA trade treaty with Canada and
Mexico and the reduction of tariffs under the recent GATT treaty.

Contacts have been established across national borders between unions in the same
industry or dealing with the same employer. Examples of such contacts resulting in cooperative efforts include the International Union of Food and Allied Workers Association's
support for Guatemalan employees of Coca-Cola; the International Commission for Coordination of Solidarity among Sugar Workers, with representatives from 30 sugar-
producing countries; an organization called Transnational Information Exchange, which
is a network of research and labor groups interested in autos, information technology, and
agribusiness; and separate international networks of labor organizations representing
workers employed by General Motors, Ford, and IBM.[19]

One example of the use of the autoworkers' information network occurred when
GM locked out workers in Ireland and tried to shift its Irish production to its Bedford,
England, facility. Upon learning how they had come to get the work, the Bedford workers
refused to do it. General Motors then shifted the work to an outside contractor in West
Germany. West German GM workers were able to convince the outside contractor's em-
ployees not to perform that work.[20]

Transnational bargaining is another potential response of unions to the multinational
corporation. Available evidence indicates, however, that this response has had very limited
success. Except for Canadian and multinational union agreements with the Belgian
Glaverbel Glass Company and BSN–Gervais Danone in France, transnational bargaining
is hampered by conflicting approaches to collective bargaining among trade unions. Direct
negotiation with multinational corporations in host countries, along with innovative techniques like European codetermination between management and workers, appears to offer
trade unions some opportunity to countervail the power of multinationals.[21]

Unless international labor reaches some consensus about optimal strategy, and unless innovative techniques produce significant results, trade unions will presumably rely on conventional weapons. These include union organizing attempts in countries that have rudimentary industrial relations policies, pressure on multinational corporate headquarters to bargain with "source unions," limitations on overtime to prevent crossnational shifts in production during a strike, and consumer boycotts.

To put it mildly, the task of unions in dealing successfully with truly multinational corporations is several orders of magnitude more difficult than dealing with managements in conventional intranational relations. For example, even some powerful and well-established American unions have faced almost insurmountable difficulties in extending union conditions from the Snowbelt to the Sunbelt within the United States. When we add differences among cultures, laws, currencies, taxes, languages, ideologies, and other conditions, taken in conjunction with the fact that the international trade union structure has nowhere near the cohesion possessed by a multinational corporation, it is not surprising that unions feel rather discouraged at their prospects of successful negotiation with multinational corporations.

SUMMARY

The purpose of this chapter has been to review the major components of the private-sector organizational structure of unions and employers. The first part of the chapter discussed union structure. Subjects considered included the membership base of unions, with particular attention to craft and industrial unions; the functions and operations of local and international unions; the structure of the AFL-CIO; and the special problems of democracy in unions. The second part of the chapter covered the organizational structures of private employers. The environment and the constraints to which an employer may be exposed were analyzed. The input and output sides of an employer's enterprise and their impact on labor relations were evaluated. This part also treated labor-intensive versus capital-intensive industries, the labor structure and the numbers of different occupational groups employed by firms, the size and location of employment, the outputs of companies and the state of competition in their product markets, and the ways in which employers can respond and adjust to the input and output sides of their environments.

The chapter also surveyed different types of management and their attitudes towards unions. It looked at the small individual enterprise as well as the large corporation. The philosophies and reactions toward unions of different types of firms were reviewed and interpreted. The final part of the chapter concerned unionization activities in conglomerates and in multinational corporations.

Notes

1. Labor-Management Reporting and Disclosure Act of 1959, Title IV, Section 401.
2. C. D. Gifford, ed., *Directory of U.S. Labor Organizations, 1996 Edition* (Washington, DC: Bureau of National Affairs, 1996), p. 1.
3. Ibid., p. 4.
4. *The New American Work Place: A Labor Perspective,* a report by the AFL-CIO Committee on the Evolution of Work, Washington, DC, February 1994.
5. Benson Soffer, "Collective Bargaining and Federal Regulation of Union Government" in *Regulating Union Government,* Martin S. Estey, Philip Taft, and Martin Wagners, eds. (New York: Harper & Row, for Industrial Relations Research Association, 1964), p. 103.
6. For a symposium on corruption and organized labor, see "Attacking Corruption in Union-Management Relations," *Industrial and Labor Relations Review* 42 (July 1989), pp. 501–65.

7. For more detailed information on the UAW's public review board, see *Public Review Board, Annual Report* (Detroit: UAW, published annually).

8. Worker Adjustment and Retraining Notification Act, 102 STAT. 890.

9. John Purcell, "How to Manage Decentralized Bargaining," *Personnel Management* 21, no. 5 (May 1989), pp. 53–55.

10. John T. Dunlop, *Industrial Relations Systems* (New York: Holt, 1958).

11. *Workplace Privacy Gains Attention, Bulletin to Management,* BNA Policy and Practice Series, vol. 44, no. 1, Jan. 7, 1993.

12. *Many Employees Perform Work at Home, Bulletin to Management,* BNA Policy and Practice Series, vol. 44, no. 2, Jan. 28, 1993, p. 28.

13. Thomas A. Kochan, Harry C. Katz, and Robert B. McKersie, *The Transformation of American Industrial Relations* (New York: Basic Books, 1986).

14. Wallace Hendricks, "Conglomerate Mergers and Collective Bargaining," *Industrial Relations* 15 (February 1976), p. 77.

15. Ibid., pp. 75–88.

16. Donald L. Levison Jr. and Robert C. Maddox, "Multinational Corporations and Labor Relations: Changes in the Wind?" *Personnel* (May–June 1982), pp. 70–77.

17. Kim Moody, *An Injury to All: The Decline of American Unionism* (London: Verso, 1988), p. 296.

18. Ibid.

19. Ibid., pp. 297–302.

20. Ibid., p. 300.

21. Robert F. Banks and Jack Stieber, *Multinationals, Unions, and Labor Relations in Industrialized Countries* (New York: Cornell University, New York State School of Industrial and Labor Relations, 1977), p. 11; "Easier Said Than Done," *The Economist* (October 15, 1977), p. 90.

CHAPTER 6

Management and Union Security

After reading this chapter, you should be able to

- Identify the issues that employees tend to consider as management prerogatives.

- Review some arguments regarding the issue of management prerogatives.

- Explain how interest in the outcome of a decision and the party's ability to make that decision affect participation in decision making.

- Discuss decision-making issues in worker-owned firms and discuss the protest function.

- Evaluate the impact on management of having union representatives on corporate boards.

- Explain and evaluate the significance of union security and its effects on union leaders and on their bargaining demands.

- Explain why some employers support strong union security provisions, whereas others object to such provisions.

SURVIVAL

The focus in this chapter is on the fact that when management and unions bargain, they must also consider survival. A union cannot achieve concessions and advantages for its members unless it continues to exist, and in a conflict between the two it will almost necessarily choose survival over advantage. Management's survival in collective bargaining refers to its ability to remain master in its own house and to retain managerial authority, without which it ceases to be management. In the event of conflict, management too will choose survival. Because the mere continuance of an organization's existence is of little consequence if it cannot perform its basic functions, the security of union or management means the condition in which survival of its ability to function is assured.

For this analysis, it is assumed that survival and advantage can be separated into relatively "pure" specimens. This does not mean that they are separable in fact or that unions and managements isolate them in their own minds. However, there is a distinct difference in logic between the two subjects, and they can be better understood when they are separated for purposes of discussion.

PART I: MANAGEMENT SECURITY

THE NATURE AND STATUS OF THE PROBLEM

When a firm buys typewriters or electricity, the sellers (if paid) do not care if the electricity is wasted or the typewriters are abused. Nor do the typewriters and electricity complain. But when an employee sells his or her time, ability, and effort, he or she goes with them. The employee cares how they are used, and part of a union's job is to see that the conditions of use are satisfactory to the employee. The employee's continued presence gives almost any management action potential influence on the employee and leads in turn to the employee's potential desire to influence almost any management action. This interconnection is an important element in the management security problem.

Management security refers to the freedom of management to make managerial decisions—that is, to perform the function of management—without interference from the union. Management's freedom to make decisions about employees is expressed in the following hypothetical management security clause (similar text appears in many contracts): "The right to hire, lay off, discharge for cause, promote, or transfer employees is the exclusive prerogative of management, except as otherwise provided in this contract." But the very purpose of a union is to "interfere" with management's decisions and to bring them more into accord with the desires of the employees. Hence, if unions are to function at all, they necessarily interfere to some degree with management's freedom by introducing the exceptions referred to in the preceding clause. The real problem is to find out what constitutes "managerial" decisions, why and whether management should make them, and how much freedom management should have in doing so. The problem is crucial: On its outcome depend much of the nature of the union-management relationship and some important characteristics of the private enterprise system.

In hiring a housekeeper, for example, the employer discusses with the applicant such matters as wages, duties, and days off. If the discussion is satisfactory, the two will reach an agreement specifying conditions that are mutually acceptable and that may not be changed except by mutual consent. The wages, hours, duties, and conditions of work are said to be bargainable issues. They fall within the scope of bargaining and are subject to joint determination.

But if the housekeeper were to suggest that the employer discuss the color of the living room walls and that the two reach an agreement about color as they did about wages, the housekeeper might be informed that this was none of his or her business. The employer need not necessarily disapprove of the housekeeper's choice of color or the housekeeper's objection to magenta walls, but the employer may deny the housekeeper's right to be consulted. The employer asserts that the room color falls outside the scope of bargaining. The employer considers it his or her exclusive prerogative to determine the color by unilateral decision. The housekeeper, in turn, would normally assert that it was his or her exclusive prerogative to decide unilaterally how to spend leisure time or income.

The housekeeper scenario illustrates three kinds of decisions found in employer-employee relationships. Some seem to belong exclusively to the employer, some belong exclusively to the employee (or the union), and some involve joint determination. Over time, unions have steadily increased the number of questions subject to joint determination, narrowing the areas of unilateral management decision. Hence, the problem is also said to involve the scope of collective bargaining. Management often asserts that many decisions are prerogatives of management by the inherent right of owners to manage their property as they see fit. For this reason, the problem is also known as the management prerogative issue; it is illustrated graphically in Figure 6.1.

The traditional division of decision-making authority in the United States was codified in the Wagner Act. Management was required to bargain with unions over wages, hours, and other terms and conditions of employment. This legal requirement formalized the American tradition of business unionism. Labor sought to improve the material conditions of workers by increasing compensation, improving working conditions, and protecting employees from arbitrary managerial decision making. All other decisions, such as level of employment, production methods, product design, plant location, pricing, and advertising, were traditionally considered strictly management prerogatives.

As stated at several points in this book, various pressures on organized labor and management are leading some to explore the path of greater cooperation. If this new relationship is to work, and if workers are to participate more fully in the operation of their companies, the traditional scope of bargaining must necessarily expand. In exchange for work rule concessions and greater loyalty and effort on workers' part, they must be given the opportunity to participate in decisions taken by employers. Among companies and unions engaged in a high level of cooperation, the issues of scope of bargaining and management prerogative may be less significant than for the vast majority of unions and employers, for whom these subjects are very important.

The approach of some employers to their security has changed significantly in the last 10 years. This change is "driven in part by international and domestic competition, technology and workforce developments."[1] According to the *Fact-Finding Report* of the Dunlop Commission,

> External forces are interacting with a growing recognition that achieving a high productivity/high wage economy requires changing traditional methods of labor management relations and the organization of work in ways that more fully develop the skills, knowledge and motivation of the workforce and that share the gains produced. . . .
>
> Since the 1980s, there has been a substantial expansion in the number and variety of employee participation efforts and workplace committees in both establishments governed by collective bargaining agreements and those without union representation. These arrangements take a wide variety of forms such as: quality circles, employee participation teams, total quality management teams, team-based work structures with a variety of responsibilities, safety and health committees, gain sharing plans, joint labor management training programs, information sharing forums, joint task forces for a variety of problems, employee ownership programs, and worker representation on corporate boards of directors. . . . Surveys in 1987 and 1990 of the Fortune 1000 firms . . . report that 86 percent of these large firms . . . report some experience with employee involvement. . . .

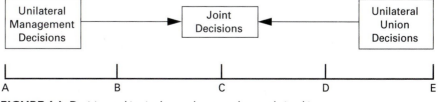

FIGURE 6.1 Decision making in the employer-employee relationship

Employee participation, in a wide variety of forms, is growing and is partially diffused across the economy and the workforce, extending to upwards of one-fifth to one-third of the workforce. Adding the more informal styles of communication and involvement found in many small establishments would likely increase the number covered.[2]

Employee participation, labor-management cooperation, and empowerment of employees affect the traditional view of management security. Many employers have decided, in response to economic pressures, to involve their employees in numerous decision processes traditionally reserved for management. In essence, in many instances, management was willing to trade off some of its managerial prerogatives and its management security in exchange for employee involvement and participation. The objective of this approach is to strengthen the economic security of the enterprise. According to the Dunlop Commission, "Employee participation will have to expand to more workplaces if the American economy is to be more competitive at high standards of living in the 21st century."[3] For further discussion of the subject of employee participation, see Chapter 17, which presents the findings of the Dunlop Commission.

Employee participation poses legal issues for both unions and employees. Some of these issues were addressed in the *Electromation* case[4] and in the *DuPont* case. The Electromation case is discussed in some detail in the Dunlop fact-finding report and recommendations, to be covered in Chapter 17 of this text. In the *DuPont* case,[5] the employer was charged with an unfair labor practice for establishing six safety committees and one fitness committee. The employer was accused of violating the National Labor Relations Act and with bypassing the union in dealing directly with employees on mandatory bargaining subjects. After reviewing the case, the National Labor Relations Board (NLRB) held that the company had unlawfully dealt with the seven committees and ordered that the committees be dissolved. The NLRB determined that the committees had been designed to circumvent the Chemical Workers Association Union.

In labor-management relations, there are three kinds of decisions: those made unilaterally by management, joint decisions, and those made unilaterally by unions. The law divides some of these decisions into mandatory and voluntary subjects of bargaining.[6] The only topics over which bargaining is legally required are included under the heading "wages, hours, and other terms and conditions of employment." All other legal subjects of bargaining are referred to as voluntary because bargaining over them is not mandated by law. Mandatory and voluntary subjects of bargaining will be discussed in Chapter 9.

RATIONALES FOR MANAGEMENT PREROGATIVES

Economic Efficiency

One argument for giving management unconstrained decision-making authority over most issues was economic efficiency. This argument seems to assume that bargaining slows down the allocation of resources to their most productive uses and that labor can generate no information or ideas for alternatives that might contribute to efficiency.[7]

During the last few years, the efficiency argument has lost its potency. Many firms have recognized the value of labor-management cooperation. Employers have realized that labor can make significant contributions to efficiency when it participates in the decision-making process. A major example of such an approach is the Saturn Corporation Project, referred to briefly later in this chapter as well as in appendix B to Chapter 9.

Private Property

Private property is the second argument in defense of managerial prerogatives. According to this argument, owners (or managers) should have unrestricted authority over their own property and therefore should not have to bargain over business decisions. Under the free enterprise system, the entrepreneur should be in total control of his or her firm's resources. The acceptance of this rationale would make all subjects of bargaining permissive. This argument seems to conflict directly with existing labor law, which in effect precludes unilateral entrepreneurial control over wages, hours, and working conditions. This argument also raises the question of where to draw the line between mandatory and permissive subjects.[8]

Presumed Futility of Collective Bargaining

A third argument for limiting the scope of bargaining is based on the assumption that negotiations would serve no useful purpose. Sound business decisions based on conditions faced by the firm should not be reversed as a result of labor negotiations. Accompanying this notion is the idea that labor lacks the expertise to participate fully in today's complex business environment. Moreover, many business decisions have only tangential or uncertain implications for labor.[9] If it were true, however, that many business decisions are necessary and not amenable to change through negotiation, what harm would be done if these decisions were made mandatory subjects of bargaining? After negotiating over them to the point of impasse, management would simply implement the decision it had originally made. The idea that labor is unqualified to contribute to decision making because of a lack of business acumen seems paternalistic and contradicts the often-heard claim, "People are a firm's greatest resource."

Despite the persuasiveness of some of the philosophical arguments, organizations are becoming increasingly receptive to employee involvement on a larger scale because it is effective. In unionized plants, the impetus for employee participation on a wide range of issues frequently comes from management rather than from unions.

Unilateral Control of Strategy

If bargaining is to have any meaning, each party must control its own strategy and leadership in dealing with the other. Entirely on its own, the union must formulate its demands, decide when or whether to strike, select its bargaining representatives, accept or reject the company's offer, and so on. Similarly, management cannot share with the union decisions about how much it will offer, who is to sit on its negotiating committee, whether it will force a strike rather than concede, and the like.

Interest and Decision Making

The Nature and Types of Interest

Beyond the necessity that each party control its own bargaining strategy, it is difficult to find any kind of decision that falls neatly into the realm of either joint or unilateral determination. One can, however, discern some factors that would seem to determine how hard a party will fight either to secure participation in a decision or to keep the other party from participating. The two most conspicuous criteria for allocating decision-making powers seem to be interest and ability.

The *interest criterion* concerns the degree to which a party is affected by a decision. The concept of the interest criterion is explored indirectly in the discussion of mutual gains bargaining, covered in Chapter 9, on the negotiation process. A party strongly affected by a given decision will have a strong interest and presumably be willing to fight hard to influence it.

To illustrate, management normally has a high interest in having its machines properly cared for, whereas most employees may not care whether the machines last 1 year or 20. Normally, it seems reasonable for management to decide unilaterally whether to maintain the machines in good shape or instead to spend the money on replacing them more frequently. But if the machine happens to be a large, unsafe, high-speed grinding wheel that may fly apart and kill the operator, the employee has a more intense interest in its condition than does management. It might then be reasonable, not only for union and management to determine maintenance policy jointly, but even to allow the employee to refuse to operate the machine unless it is properly maintained.

The same principle operates in other areas. Management normally determines which machines will be used in processing, say, a diesel crankshaft through a machine shop. If a batch of crankshafts is followed by a batch of compressor pistons, the employees may have to be reassigned to different machines. Management has a high interest in the efficient use of the workers and the equipment. If each person in the shop is an all-round machinist and if the pay is the same on all machines, the employees have only a slight interest in who is assigned to which job. Under these circumstances, the job assignments could logically be decided unilaterally by management. But if the rates of pay are different on different machines, or if transfer may involve loss of seniority, the employees have a definite interest in the assignments. The effect of job transfers on wage rates and seniority may then logically become a matter for joint determination.

The attempt to settle work assignment problems on the basis of "prerogatives" or "inherent rights" holds the prospect of extended futile disagreement. An approach based on interests can bring a settlement that is both logical and realistic.

Ability and Decision Making

The Nature of the Ability Criterion

The *ability criterion* means that either party will tend to insist on participating in a decision in proportion to its ability in the subject matter involved—assuming that it also has an interest. We need not raise the question of whether representatives of union or management are better or wiser people; we need simply note that we live in a world of specialization. One's interest in one's own health is presumably greater than a doctor's interest in it. But in decision making, the patient's stronger interest will give way to the physician's superior ability. The same kind of reasoning applies to some management decisions. Policies regarding prices, advertising, methods of production, financing, sources of materials, internal organization, and so forth can be made and coordinated only by those familiar with all aspects of the firm's operations. Usually, only management officials possess this kind of knowledge and information. This situation is changing: In some firms, employees get involved and do participate in the decision-making processes. For further discussion of this subject, consult the Dunlop Report, covered in Chapter 17.

Modifications of the Ability Criterion

Many employers presume that employees or unions should not participate in management decisions because they do not have the background and expertise to make such decisions wisely. This generalization is observed rather strictly in many union-management relationships, but it is subject to two reservations. First, the engineer's ideal plan is often modified by nonengineers because the ideal method is too costly, is unattractive, or impinges seriously on the environment. Patients often deviate from their doctors' advice because of costs, whims, or convenience. In short, even if the manager definitely has superior knowledge in management matters, it does not follow that his or her judgment should not be modified for nonmanagerial reasons.

Second, in some industries, union leaders have had considerable competence in dealing with management problems. For example, in the clothing industry, some union leaders have owned and operated their own firms, and some union officers probably have as much know-how as many clothing executives. In fact, the unions in both men's and women's clothing maintained their own management engineering departments to give technical advice and assistance to managements, and both have made loans to employers. In brief, ability does not always necessarily lie entirely with management.

Analysis versus Practice

The reader should be aware that the interest and ability criteria represent the outside analyst's view, not the views of the parties. Their approach is apt to be catch-as-catch-can, with full exploitation of bargaining power. It seems that unions sometimes fight to participate in decisions that affect them little or regarding which they have little competence. And managements sometimes seem to defend to the last ditch their "right" to make undiluted decisions in areas where bargaining would not hurt them. A management's attitude toward decision making will depend much on its general attitudes toward unions, toward some broader ideological problems, and toward "principle for principle's sake" as contrasted to "realistic adaptation to reality."

INHERENT DIVERGENCE OF INTERESTS

Decision Making in a Worker-Owned Plant

The Development of a Management

A simple way to discover that the need for strong management security is based on something more than abstract "rights of ownership" is to assume that the employees purchase a controlling share of stock of the corporation they work for. The board of directors will then be selected by the employees, and if there are such things as inherent rights, the employees will possess all of them. This new board of directors will shortly discover that, as top management, it desires certain conditions that conflict directly with the immediate wishes of the employees who elected them. For example, the manager's desire to keep prices low enough to meet competition and sell the firm's product may run directly counter to the employees' desire to raise wages. The new managers might study the market conditions and report them to the workers, who could then balance their desire for higher wages against their desire to stay in business and set the price accordingly.

Sound price policies, however, depend not only on wages and market conditions but on costs of materials, locations of customers, rates of depreciation, and many other factors, including some highly discretionary aspects of cost accounting. Workers might eventually recognize their inability to vote intelligently on such complex decisions and then logically give the board unilateral control over prices, subject only to the ultimate threat of loss of office. In due time, similar arrangements would be made for decisions about maintenance policy, the borrowing of money, and the negotiation of leases; eventually, the board might be assigned simply the broad responsibility of keeping the firm in sound condition.

The board would have to insist, in turn, that if given responsibility for keeping the firm solvent, it must also have the authority to make the decisions affecting solvency. In brief, officers elected by the employees would shortly be found behaving like management for the simple reason that they are management. Their desire for freedom to make certain decisions grows from their interest in the job they do, not from the nature of the group they represent. Soon their experience will also give them superior ability compared to the rank and file.[10]

The Development of a Protest Function

At the same time, the rank-and-file workers would make some interesting discoveries. They too could find their interest as owners conflicting with their interest as workers. For example, a worker's health may fail, producing a marked decline in productivity. As an owner, he or she would want inefficient producers weeded out. But as a worker, he or she wants desperately to keep the job and, if possible, the previous rate of pay. Because wage income is probably many times dividend income, the worker's interest greatly outweighs the owner's interest. In this and many other situations, the employer takes a worker's point of view and in due time may try to get the managers to give overriding consideration to employee welfare. But the managers cannot do this without abdicating their responsibility for all the other factors that affect solvency.

The workers would also discover—as all democracies do—that to elect leaders does not guarantee that they will not be arbitrary, careless, or inclined to play favorites. A government, therefore, establishes a judicial system through which citizens may redress unfair or discriminatory acts by their elected officials. So too in the worker-owned plant, in the promotion, transfer, discipline, and replacement of individuals, there would almost certainly arise charges of favoritism and stupidity against the supervisors. For this eventuality, some channel could be established through which to handle the function of protest against management without having to throw out the managers. This organized method of protest might not take the form of a union, but it could easily do so.

It seems significant that ordinary citizens get redress against their government through the judicial branch of the government. But those who are also employees of government have joined unions in fairly large numbers to protect their employee interests against the employers they helped elect. Similarly, many employees of unions are also organized and bargain collectively with the unions that employ them. The officers of unions at first showed no greater enthusiasm for this development than did "capitalist" managements, but under pressure they have now accepted it.

The essential point is that, in this respect, there are two functions within the organization. One is that of managing; the other is that of protesting against the management in the name of those managed. The need for management arises out of the nature of the organization and the need for someone to assume the responsibility for keeping income equal to or greater than expenses. The need for the protest function arises because managers, being human, are less than perfect in dealing with their subordinates and because the welfare of the employees is not and cannot be the sole, or even the primary, concern of the managers.

In short, management must necessarily think of labor as a factor of production and therefore as a cost. The job of the union is to think of labor as a collection of human beings and to insist that they be treated as such. To some extent the two views coincide because persons who are treated well also produce better. But there are many ways in which human beings desire good treatment above and beyond those that bring a return to management. Even the most enlightened management will presumably not venture into these areas on its own initiative. This distinction exists equally, whether the managers are appointed by private capitalists, by the workers, or by a socialist state.

THE CORE OF MANAGEMENT SECURITY

Despite the apparent impossibility of drawing a sharp line to delineate the scope of bargaining in general terms, there is a line in each operation at any given moment, and there is considerable uniformity as to its location throughout American industry, particularly among large firms. The following is an example of a management clause:

ARTICLE 2 RIGHTS OF MANAGEMENT
Section 2.1 Management of Company. The management of the Company and the direction of the work force is vested exclusively in the company subject to the terms of this Agreement. All matters specifically and expressly covered or treated by the language of this Agreement may be administered for its duration by the Company in accordance with such policy or procedure as the Company from time to time may determine.[11]

If management achieves, regularly reviews, and vigorously enforces a strong management clause, the executives will know that if the enterprise goes bankrupt it was their fault, not the union's. Elsewhere in the contract are clauses covering wages, hours, pensions, seniority, holidays, and other items of interest to the employees. Many of these cost the company money and can therefore have an adverse effect on its balance sheet. But the same thing can be said of raw materials, energy, and rent, for which the firm may also pay high prices despite strenuous bargaining. The price it pays for labor (including benefits) is merely one of many items in the firm's economic environment. The important fact is that under a strong management clause, rigorously guarded and enforced, the executives are free to study that environment and decide how best to live with it and then to carry out those decisions without interference from the union. That is the core of management security.

PATTERNS AND TRENDS IN MANAGEMENT SECURITY

A "basic patterns" study of 400 contracts by the Bureau of National Affairs indicates the frequency with which various management prerogative subjects are covered in contracts containing such provisions (see Table 6.1). It is interesting to note the significant differences in

TABLE 6.1 Management Rights Provisions (frequency expressed as percentage of 320* management rights statements)			
	All Industries	*Manufacturing*	*Nonmanufacturing*
Direct Work Force	76	77	73
Manage Business	74	77	69
Frame Company Rules	43	43	43
Control Production	39	50	18
Determine Employees' Duties	28	24	33
Close or Relocate Plant	17	19	14
Change Technology	16	19	12

*Includes 209 manufacturing and 111 non-manufacturing provisions.

Source: Basic Patterns in Union Contracts, Fourteenth Edition (Washington, DC: Bureau of National Affairs, 1995), p. 79.

TABLE 6.2	Restrictions on Management Rights (frequency expressed as percentage of contracts)		
	All Industries	*Manufacturing*	*Nonmanufacturing*
General Statement	57	60	52
Subcontracting	55	54	58
Supervisory Performance of Work	58	75	32
Technological Changes	26	27	24
Plant Shutdown or Relocation	23	29	13

Source: Basic Patterns in Union Contracts, Fourteenth Edition (Washington, DC: Bureau of National Affairs, 1995), p. 81.

managerial prerogative in various areas. Whereas in 76 percent of the contracts with management-rights clauses, the direction of the work was a managerial prerogative, instituting technological change was allowed a managerial prerogative in only 16 percent of the clauses, and plant closing or relocation was allowed in 17 percent of such provisions.[12]

Some contracts place definite restrictions on managerial prerogatives. As shown in Table 6.2, some contracts contain general statements limiting managerial rights; others set restrictions in such areas as subcontracting, performance of work by supervisors, technological changes, and plant shutdown or relocation.

UNION REPRESENTATION ON CORPORATE BOARDS

Traditionally, labor unions and employers in the United States have objected to union presence on corporate boards of directors. Both sides have preferred instead to utilize the adversarial negotiation process. Some authors suggest that the reason for unions' objections to board representation stems from their apprehension that such participation may decrease the importance of collective bargaining and reduce their independence.[13] Despite these concerns, in 1973 the first union gained representation on the board of directors of the Providence and Worcester Railroad. Only 20 workers were affected by this pioneering official union entry into the corporate boardroom.[14] In 1980, in a precedent-setting side agreement with the UAW, Chrysler Corporation appointed UAW president D. A. Fraser to the board of directors of the corporation. This was a unique nomination for a major U.S. union leader. Boards have very broad powers in establishing corporate policies in all areas of activity, including labor relations. Being on the board may present a union leader with a conflict of interest between his or her responsibilities to the corporation and to the union. The Fraser appointment was not well received by other firms in the auto industry. Mr. Fraser's staff associates at UAW's Solidarity House also questioned his new role. Other union leaders resisted or at best were neutral to the Fraser appointment.

A recent settlement gave the Steelworkers Union a seat on the board of directors of LTV Steel. Similar agreements were reached with four other major steel makers.[15]

Other industries in which unions have gained board representation include several airlines, some trucking firms, and various manufacturing establishments.[16] Of course, greater employee stock ownership also affords labor a greater voice in board composition. In the last 10 years, some union leaders have become more receptive to the concept of boardroom representation. The change in attitudes is traceable to various developments: large permanent layoffs of union members in a number of industries, decreasing union membership as a percentage of the work force, automation, increased anti-union activities by management coupled with more sophisticated anti-union personnel policies, increasing management resistance to union demands, and growth of management bargaining power relative to union power. The growth of European-owned industry in the United States could also encourage the importation of codetermination, or representation by workers on boards of directors, into this country. Union members on the boards of directors of European companies may favor codetermination for the U.S. subsidiaries. Also, many U.S. firms have European branches that operate under codetermination.

Although initially some union leaders objected to union representation in boardrooms, others currently see a possible benefit to such appointments. Lynn Williams, former president of the United Steelworkers of America (USWA), advocated union membership on corporate boards. According to Williams, corporations in the United States tend to be overly concerned about short-term profitability as opposed to the long-term effects of their decisions on employees. However, it is the long-term effects of corporate decisions that have the greatest potential for negative impact on the work force. Employees are more interested in maintaining long-term job stability, even in the face of a loss in short-term income. This interest explains why employees through their representation bring a long-term perspective to the table.[17]

Douglas Fraser, former UAW president and corporate board member for the Chrysler Corporation, believed that union representation on corporate boards would grow in the future. "In contrast to the old approach, unions and workers alike now realize they have to work together—the consequences of not working together are far too serious."[18]

Does union representation on corporate boards actually benefit workers—or, for that matter, management? One study suggests that union representatives on corporate boards face different role expectations from their CEOs and their union constituents: CEOs believed that worker representatives serve merely to communicate board decisions to workers; union constituents viewed the task of protecting worker interests as being paramount. These differing role expectations may prevent the worker board member from being effective. However, other authors suggest that union board members can increase their effectiveness by adopting persuasive bargaining techniques and building power bases among board and union members rather than relying on the traditional distributive bargaining approach common to union negotiations.[19]

According to some experts, union representatives on corporate boards actually play an informational role, providing a voice for worker concerns.[20] However, if the union board representative's *only* role is to serve as an employee voice, other problems can develop. Some suggest that the union board member's lack of real decision-making influence often leads to a sense of disillusionment and the conclusion that codetermination is a "hopeless game in which labor is a minor partner."[21] Some authors suggest that union participation on boards of directors may adversely affect company management by curtailing employers' opportunistic tendencies toward meeting their own needs.[22]

Including union representatives on a corporate board opens a two-way channel of communication. Information can be transmitted to and from both labor and management. Representation of both union and management on corporate boards offers new opportunities for each side to gain from the experience of the other.[23] It should be noted that current labor and antitrust law does not encourage the full participation of union representatives on corporate boards.[24]

Overview of Some Legal and Practical Aspects

As noted earlier, where employees are represented by a union, the Taft-Hartley Act requires the employer to bargain with respect to "wages, hours, and other terms and conditions of employment." Because the highest possible degree of management security is to bargain about nothing, to the degree that the law requires management to bargain at all, it reduces management security. The precise boundary line defining what management will and will not be required to bargain about is determined by the National Labor Relations Board and the courts. Many managements feel, however, that the interpretations of mandatory subjects of bargaining have been much too broad.

Those managements would like to have the law define the bargainable area specifically, prescribing either a short list of bargainable issues or a long list of nonbargainable ones. How much good this would do for management is problematic. First, a legal obligation to bargain is explicitly not an obligation to concede. Its presence may simply change the wording from "I refuse to discuss a pension" to "I refuse (after due bargaining) to grant a pension." It is easy enough to pass a law stating, for example, that wages are bargainable and methods of production are not. But what happens to the nonbargainability of production methods if the union proposes to substitute a change in methods for a wage increase—a not unknown situation? Despite the existence of some marginal cases, if it is in the employer's interest to bargain about methods, he or she will probably do so, whether the law requires it or not. And if it is sufficiently in the employer's interest to reject the union proposals about methods, he or she will probably do so, even if the law requires bargaining about them. (If the employer really needs the housekeeper and the housekeeper is nauseated by magenta walls, the employer may have to bargain over the wall color.)

Indications are that the future will bring considerable diversity in approaches to management security. Some managements will refuse to discuss certain issues "on principle." Others will experiment with joint approaches to a wide variety of problems. After World War II, Walter Reuther, then president of the United Automobile Workers, sought to break with tradition and demanded that General Motors apply union wage concessions made at the bargaining table toward a lowering of car prices. That proposal, viewed as radical and setting a dangerous precedent for involving unions in topics that were strictly managerial prerogatives, caused a long strike ultimately won by the company. As a sign of a change in the thinking of at least some employers, in 1981 General Motors agreed in principle to just such an arrangement.[25] Among the most celebrated departures from the traditional division of managerial decision making occurred in the Saturn Corporation, a subsidiary of General Motors. Here, union representatives are actively involved at all levels of management including strategic planning, manufacturing, marketing, and hiring of employees.[26] It remains to be seen whether the Saturn experience becomes a model for the future or simply ends up as a one-time experiment.

PART II: UNION SECURITY

THE MEANING OF UNION SECURITY

Union security has a number of meanings. It refers to the continued existence of the union as an organization. It means the continued existence of the union as a bargaining agent for each bargaining unit it represents. Union security can also be defined as the union's freedom to perform the function of collectively representing employees without interference from management or other sources. The last definition parallels that of management security in that both are based on freedom to function. One difference should be noted. Dealing with the union is merely one of management's many functions, and for all practical purposes only those interferences with management function that come from the union are significant to the union-management relation. By contrast, the function of collectively representing employees is so overwhelmingly important in the union's life that, normally, the union goes promptly out of existence if this function ceases. Hence, any clear threat to the union's continued status as bargaining agent, whether from management or from other sources, is directly relevant to the union-management relation. Thus, the phrase "or from other sources" appears in the definition of union—but not management—security.

Whether a protest function is necessary or desirable in the enterprise and whether the union is its appropriate instrument will not be debated here. Freeman and Rogers to some extent address this issue in their article on employee representation in a nonunion market.[27] Within the organized sector, the union is still the established agent of bargaining unit members in performing the protest function. The major questions that arise are these: How much and what kind of security is necessary for the union to function properly? How is it achieved? Does it interfere with management security? Does it interfere with the workers' interest, public interest, or bargaining power? What standards, if any, should a union be required to meet before being accorded a secure position?

SOME THREATS TO UNION SECURITY

Before discussing whether a union should be made secure and by what methods, it is necessary to note what forces threaten its security and how serious they are.

The Nonessentiality of Unions and the Likelihood of Management Opposition

One basic threat to the security of a union is so obvious that it is sometimes overlooked. Although an enterprise cannot operate without a management, it can operate without a union. The steel industry without a union is a tenable concept, and in fact that situation prevailed for some 50 years. But the United Steelworkers without the steel industry would be senseless. However logical and desirable the protest function and the union may be, they are dispensable. The members may from time to time question whether they really need a union. And many employers feel that they can perform the function of looking after the needs of their employees better than the union. This subordinate position is the starting point of the problem of union security and partially explains many characteristics of union behavior.

In many places, management dislike of unions takes active forms and keeps the union's existence in perpetual jeopardy. Although the law prohibits the practice, numerous employers nevertheless succeed in systematically weeding union members or leaders out of their organizations.

Anti-union labor attorneys help employers operate within the law while at the same time making it very difficult for unions to gain recognition. Some anti-union employers engage the services of industrial psychologists and other social scientists who, in the anti-union activities, apply such concepts as "positive reinforcement, organizational and individual effectiveness, employee value systems, negative feedback, problem-solving orientations, and performance through motivation."[28] Other consultants advise management on hiring procedures that can help filter out potential union sympathizers and activists. As a result, in many firms it is difficult for employees to join unions. This lack of freedom, too, is a threat to the union's security. Employers' anti-union attitude was illustrated in a survey showing that 45 percent of responding firms admitted that being nonunion was their major labor relations objective.

Anti-Union Activities

Many in the labor movement hold that unions are the target of a large-scale propaganda offensive conducted by management, whose familiar refrain is that "labor is a narrow special interest group; that union bosses are dictators; that union members are their tools; that American workers are overpaid; that American unions have priced themselves out of the market."[29]

The use of so-called union-busting consultants in organizing drives is quite widespread. A survey of employers shows that 41 percent of firms use such consultants, whereas union organizers situate that figure at closer to 70 percent of campaigns. Management consultants who specialize in defeating unions include lawyers, representatives of employer and trade associations, psychologists, detectives, and nonprofit anti-union organizations. Some of these experts have degrees in labor relations, psychology, and other social sciences.

There are a number of reasons for the increase in anti-union activities by employers and for the recent popularity of anti-union experts. First, a significant proportion of union organizing activity has been taking place in the anti-union South. Thus, the increase in anti-union drives is a direct response to an increase in organizational campaigns by unions in that part of the country. Second, organizational activity is usually conducted by large and strong unions; employers, fearing that such unions may force them to provide large wage concessions, try therefore to prevent unionization. Third, the anti-union methods applied by contemporary anti-union specialists are considerably more sophisticated and legal, and thus more attractive to employers, than the lockouts and the violence of the 1930s. One way employers motivate managers to resist unionization vigorously is by making future career opportunities contingent on success in the campaign and subsequent negotiations. In some cases, for managers of plants where organizing drives occur, the likelihood of being fired increases and of being promoted decreases, especially if the union wins.[30]

Decertification Elections

Another anti-union weapon is the decertification election. The Taft-Hartley Act specifies a procedure for decertifying a labor union. A labor organization's NLRB certification to represent all employees in a bargaining unit for collective bargaining purposes can be challenged only after one year. After the year has elapsed, employees within the unit can request a decertification election, provided a contract is not in force. A labor agreement acts as a bar to a representation election for up to three years. A decertification election must be requested during the 30-day period from 90 to 60 days before the contract expiration date.

Generally, only employees can petition the NLRB for a decertification election, and they must do so without the assistance or encouragement of the employer. However, when an employer has an objective reason to doubt the continued majority status of an incumbent union, he or she may also petition the NLRB.[31]

Researchers have conducted studies of union decertification elections,[32] which represent a relatively small proportion of total elections. Unions win only about a quarter of decertification elections.[33] According to a 1995 paper by Borgers, unions lose the majority of decertification elections because of "employee dissatisfaction with, and rejection of unions that are perceived as not providing effective servicing for employees in smaller union units."[34]

Loss of Membership and Income: The Basic Problem

The outsider may wonder why a problem of membership exists. If employees want union representation, they will join the union and get it. If not, they will stay out and do without representation. And if only a minority wants a union, it should certainly not be able to force unionization on the majority. Unfortunately, the problem is not so simple, and unions face a fundamental difficulty. According to law, a contract between union and employer must apply equally to all persons in the area covered by the contract (the bargaining unit), whether they belong to the union or not. Therefore, when a union bargains with management, it is negotiating just as much for the nonunion employees as for the union members. It is illegal to do otherwise because the employer is prohibited by law from discriminating between union and nonunion employees. Even if the law were silent on the matter, one can imagine the problems that would arise if an employer tried to favor either group. Furthermore, such differentials are also outlawed by the legal definition of a majority union as the "exclusive representative" of all employees within the bargaining unit. A union's ability to organize workers and collect dues is complicated further by right-to-work laws, which prohibit compulsory union membership in many states. By a ruling of the NLRB, the union, as exclusive bargaining agent, must process the grievance of any individual employee against the employer, including arbitration if necessary, even if the employee is not a union member and pays no dues.[35]

Thus the union faces a difficult problem. Employees get the same representation, at least the same contract terms, whether they belong to the union or not. If a person desires the benefits a union can secure, it is attractive from a purely economic point of view to work in a unionized plant without joining the union or paying any union dues. Although nonmembers cannot vote in elections of union officers or on contract ratifications, the number of employees placing a high value on that privilege is not large enough to alter this situation very much. Theoretically, a group of employees could vote unanimously to be represented by a union without any of them joining or paying dues.

This problem is reflected clearly in the typical union appeals that membership be maintained and dues paid. Appeals for "solidarity," "participation," and "being a good union member," as well as the virulent denunciation of the "free rider," all parallel the means a tax collector would have to use if payment of tax bills could not be enforced. When the nonessentiality of membership for any one individual is added to the nonessentiality of the union itself, it is little wonder that heads of unions tend to be "jumpy" about threats to the security of the union and its income.

Loss of Membership: Additional Factors

Employees may avoid the union for reasons other than a desire to "ride free." Some object to unions in principle. Others think the dues are too high or are misused, and some feel the pinch of even reasonable dues. Inertia counts others out. Some see no positive value in unions or think them mainly negative and objectionable. Others fear that joining may displease the boss. In addition, factional differences may bring membership below the majority point and put the union out of existence.

Anything less than full membership means a proportionate loss of dues. Studies suggest that between 6 and 15 percent of the employees will stay out, if they can, in companies where the union is well established and the work force is stable. The percentage may be much higher where there is a high labor turnover and a less clearly established union. To a large national union, the difference between the voluntary level of membership and full membership may be significant.[36]

Because a continuous membership is necessary for the union's security and because there are so many reasons why membership may be avoided, unions have come to view compulsory membership as the chief device for achieving security. In fact, it is not uncommon to find the terms *union security* and *compulsory membership* used interchangeably.

UNION SECURITY AND SOUND LABOR RELATIONS

The meaning of *sound labor relations* is vague and need not be detailed here. In general, however, the term implies that in protecting the interests of their constituents, both union and management behave with restraint and intelligence, recognize the rights of others, and realize that what is good for the opponent is not necessarily bad for oneself.

To state the conclusion before the evidence is presented, it seems safe to say that sound relations between union and management are impossible unless both management and union possess a rather high degree of security.

It has already been observed that survival must take priority over interests. Threats to survival often arouse intense emotions and push logic into the background. People who are drowning may grab their rescuers around the neck, though in calmer circumstances they would know better. Thus management, if it feels that its freedom to manage will thereby be constrained, may resist a simple proposal that greatly benefits the employees and costs management little. Likewise, a union may reject the most sensible proposal from management if it feels that the change will reduce membership loyalty or solidarity. Wisdom and moderation are not characteristic of people or organizations whose lives are in jeopardy.

Insecurity puts union leaders under constant pressure to "sell" the union. Now, while selling oneself or one's product is normally considered commendable in a market economy, a notable difference between the union (as an agent of protest) and the company (as an agent of production) may be overlooked. One marvels at the masochism of the employer who objects to union security and proclaims, "Let the union sell itself." The employer is implicitly recommending that the union improve its product. Now, the product that the union sells is concessions from the employer, and a better product is bigger concessions. Freely translated, "Let the union sell itself" means "Come on. Beat me till I give you bigger concessions."

The employer will have to pay for the union's advertising in the form of a frequently renewed display of shiny, big concessions. Selling also involves making the prospective customer dissatisfied with what he or she has, which for the insecure union means perpetual criticism of management. The insecure union, like the insecure individual, often tends to be permanently aggressive and belligerent. This tendency involves seeking unreasonable concessions as well as reasonable ones. It means inventing grievances and pressing every grievance, whether real or imagined. It means calling management nasty names and imputing improper motives to it. Whatever else such activities may do, they do not make for pleasant or sound relations between a company and its union.

MANAGEMENT AND UNION SECURITY

It is often assumed that employers universally and automatically oppose union security. Actually, the employer may see distinct advantages in a secure union—assuming there already is a union. This attitude is more marked in large firms and among those who have dealt longest with unions.

First, if all employees belong to the union, disciplinary action can be viewed on its merits, not as possible anti-union discrimination. We noted earlier that management security is closely linked to the ability to maintain discipline; in this respect, union security may make it easier for management to defend its security. Second, it is destructive to morale to have resentment, distrust, and argumentation between union members and non-members; mandatory membership removes this friction. Third, if membership actually drops below a majority, the union may disappear, only to wage a new organizing campaign to get back in. Such on-again, off-again relations can be extremely disruptive. Fourth, a union leader free from the worry of holding members has more time to work with management on difficult problems. The leader is also freer to consider solutions on their merits, not on their effects on membership. Fifth, union security removes any suspicion that management will look with disfavor on employees who join the union. In the absence of union security, the more responsible employees may stay out and leave the union to the "hotheads."

An important reservation expressed by managements is that compulsory membership makes the union too strong. This reaction is most evident among employers who have some hope of preventing or eliminating unions. To such employers, the signing of a union security clause means that the union is there to stay and its position is obviously much "stronger." But if by strength we mean bargaining power, then it is not at all clear that a secure union is able to win larger concessions than an insecure one.

Once management accepts that the union will be with it indefinitely, the alternatives change. It is then no longer a question of secure union versus no union but of secure union versus insecure union, both equally real and permanent. At this point, there is no apparent reason why formal union security will necessarily reduce management security. In fact, the secure union may be more willing to sign a strong management security clause than will an insecure one. If the union is under less pressure to sell itself, it can more safely relax and let management be management.

THE FORMS AND EXTENT OF UNION SECURITY

Of the many ways to establish union security, most involve some form of compulsory membership. This section discusses the most prominent forms.

The Closed Shop

A closed shop, which is prohibited by law but tolerated in certain situations, is one in which each employee must be a union member before being hired. Often the union functions as the employment office through a hiring hall; this practice is legal. In clothing, printing, construction, and longshoring occupations, for example, an employer who wants employees may simply call the union, which sends him or her the number requested from a rotating list at the hiring hall. If preferred, the union will send extras so that the employer has a choice.

A closed shop is workable only where one or a limited number of clearly defined skills are involved and where preselection, such as apprenticeship or experience, assures that everyone on the list is qualified. Strictly speaking, a closed shop limits employers' discretion because they cannot hire anyone who is not already a member of the union. Whether or not employers suffer thereby depends on whether the union can provide an adequate supply of competent workers. If all competent crafts workers are already union members (as was the case with the building trades in some cities), a formal closed shop adds no restriction not already created by comprehensive unionization.

In occupations where people typically work only for short periods for different employers in succession, there could be no union security—indeed, perhaps no collective bargaining—except under the closed shop or the hiring hall arrangement. As was widely predicted, the closed shop has continued virtually intact among longshoremen, building crafts workers, and one-night-stand musicians, despite the prohibitions in the Taft-Hartley Act and the laws of many states. The prohibition is probably unenforceable in such jobs short of elimination of collective bargaining itself.

The Union Shop, the Agency Shop, and Maintenance of Membership

The Labor Management Relations Act of 1947 (LMRA) allows the following types of union security provisions, some of which, however, may be disallowed by state law under Section 14(b) of the LMRA: union shop, modified union shop, maintenance of membership, and agency shop.

The **union shop** requires membership in the union after hiring but not before. It places no restriction on the employer's freedom to hire. The restriction is instead on the employee, who must usually join the union within 30 days, the minimum period allowed by the Taft-Hartley Act, except for the 7-day provision in the construction industry.

Union shop is the strictest type of compulsory membership feasible in a mass production industry. The employer in such an industry would hardly tolerate the hiring restrictions of a closed shop. Furthermore, the closed shop could damage the union if it had to decide which of its members to send out for each of dozens of different kinds of jobs. The closed shop is no more applicable to mass production industry than the union shop with a 30-day waiting period is to longshoring.

Several varieties of **modified union shop** have also appeared. The most common provision requires union membership of all workers except those who were not union members before the effective date of the agreement. The provision requires new employees to join and members to maintain their membership.

An **agency shop** requires all employees in the bargaining unit to pay dues to the union but not to become members. Its practical effect is nearly identical to that of a union shop because most people who pay the dues feel that they may as well get voting rights as well. Nevertheless, it preserves an option for those who for some reason are distressed by membership as such. Moreover, the courts define union membership under a union shop clause as the paying of dues. Thus, under either a union or an agency shop, the only obligation for employees is payment of dues or of an equivalent fee.

Maintenance of membership provides a lesser degree of union security than does the union shop. It does not require anyone to join the union unwillingly. But it does require anyone who is a member, as of some specified date, to remain a member and pay dues for some specified period, usually the duration of the contract. At the end of each contract period, there is usually a 15- to 30-day escape period during which any member may resign and thereafter stay out of the union.

The checkoff of union dues from a worker's paycheck is partly a security and partly a bookkeeping device. It protects the union against loss of dues and possible loss of members through inadvertence or recalcitrance.

Several other terms describe the absence of security rather than its presence. The open shop, strictly defined, is open on equal terms to union members and nonmembers. If members constitute less than a majority, no collective bargaining occurs and no contract is signed; the shop remains nonunion. If a majority want the union, it becomes a unionized shop, with the union as bargaining agent. As Table 6.3 shows, 64 percent of contracts sampled by the Bureau of National Affairs in a survey of all industries contained union shop clauses. The next most common form of union security clause in private-sector labor contracts is the modified union shop, which is present in 10 percent of contracts. Over time, as existing employees are replaced by newly hired workers, the modified union shop becomes a union shop. This brings the total to about three-fourths of all contracts requiring union membership as a condition of employment. Agency shop and maintenance of membership provisions are much less common. Provisions for checkoff are contained in 95 percent of contracts.[37]

There is significant regional variation in the distribution of union shop clauses. Only about 15 percent of sampled contracts in the Southeast and Southwest provide for

TABLE 6.3 Union Security Provisions (frequency expressed as percentage of contracts)

	Union Shop	Modified Union Shop	Agency Shop Only	Maintenance of Membership	Hiring	Checkoff
All Industries	64	10	4	4	23	95
Manufacturing	61	13	2	5	10	98
Apparel	89	—	—	—	44	100
Chemicals	56	6	—	13	6	100
Electrical machinery	70	25	—	—	5	100
Fabricated metals	47	16	15	16	5	95
Foods	71	10	—	5	24	100
Furniture	50	—	17	—	—	100
Leather	50	—	—	—	25	100
Lumber	43	—	—	—	—	100
Machinery	65	23	4	—	—	100
Paper	57	14	—	7	—	100
Petroleum	—	—	—	29	29	100
Primary metals	44	32	—	4	—	100
Printing	100	—	—	—	63	50
Rubber	83	—	—	—	—	100
Stone, clay, & glass	69	23	—	—	8	100
Textiles	30	—	—	20	—	100
Transportation equipment	76	3	3	—	9	100
Nonmanufacturing	67	7	7	3	43	90
Communications	40	—	40	—	10	100
Construction	83	7	—	—	90	76
Insurance & finance	57	14	—	14	—	100
Maritime	50	—	13	13	100	38
Mining	33	8	—	—	—	100
Retail	85	11	—	—	44	89
Services	78	4	7	4	56	96
Transportation	64	—	12	4	8	100
Utilities	40	20	10	10	20	100

Source: Basic Patterns in Union Contracts, Fourteenth Edition (Washington, DC: Bureau of National Affairs, 1995), p. 98.

this form of union security.[38] The reason for this is the concentration of so-called "right-to-work" states in these regions. In 21 states, most of which are in these regions, compulsory union membership is illegal. Figure 4.1 in Chapter 4 shows the regional pattern of right-to-work states.

A 1988 Supreme Court decision in the *Beck* case has important implications with regard to the use of dues and agency fees collected from those required to pay them under union and agency shop provisions. The Court decided that those who object to such payments can be forced to pay only that proportion of dues or agency fees that goes toward "collective bargaining, contract administration or grievance adjustment."[39] The NLRB General Counsel has issued some implementation guidelines based on the *Beck* decision. Each union having a contract with a union security clause must provide an annual accounting of the percentage of its funds spent on representational and nonrepresentational

TABLE 6.4 Representational and Nonrepresentational Expenses

Representational Expenses

1. Collective bargaining, contract administration, and grievance arbitration.
2. Litigation expenses incident to items in number 1, fulfilling the duty of fair representation, handling jurisdictional disputes, and conducting litigation concerning bargaining unit employees.
3. National conventions.
4. Union business meetings and social activities open to member and nonmember employees.
5. Cost of union benefits available to members and nonmembers alike.

Nonrepresentational Expenses

1. Union organizing activities, either in the represented unit or outside of it.
2. Litigation expenses not directly concerning the bargaining unit.
3. Union publications to the extent that they report nonrepresentational activities.
4. Costs of union benefits not available to nonmembers.
5. Costs of a union building fund.
6. Lobbying.
7. Promotion or defeat of legislation.
8. Political campaigns.
9. Advertising relating to nonchargeable matters.

Source: Rosemary M. Collyer, General Counsel of the National Labor Relations Board. "Memorandum to all Regional Directors, Officers-in-Charge, and Resident Officers, on Guidelines Concerning *CWA v Beck,*" Memorandum GC 88–14. November 15, 1988, pp. 6–7.

activities. Employees who object to paying the nonrepresentational proportion of the dues are entitled to have those charges waived. For example, suppose that only 80 percent of a union's funds are spent on representational activities; if monthly dues are $10, those who object can meet their obligation to the union by paying only $8 per month. Employees who disagree with the accounting for representational and nonrepresentational activities are entitled to challenge that determination.[40] Table 6.4 lists the general types of activities believed to be chargeable to those who object (representational expenses) and those that cannot be imposed on objectors (nonrepresentational expenses). Again, these are just administrative agency guidelines; there may be much litigation in this area before final rules are devised to distinguish representational from nonrepresentational expenses.

THE BASIC CONTROVERSY SURROUNDING UNION SECURITY

The basic conflict over union security is now clear. On the one hand, union security seems to be a requisite condition for sound industrial relations. On the other, compulsory membership curtails the individual's freedom of choice. The choice between a particular type of freedom and a workable system of industrial relations is a value judgment and hence cannot be decided by rational analysis alone. As is often argued, the choice seems to be between two incompatible principles: (1) that no person should be required to join or pay dues to any private organization as a condition of holding his or her job and (2) that any person who is in fact represented by a union and who lives under the contract it negotiates should contribute to its support. Disconcertingly, it is logically possible to believe in both principles, taken separately. There would be no problem, of course, if everyone—or nearly everyone—joined voluntarily. This has long been the situation through much of British industry, where in the past compulsory membership was neither prohibited nor needed. In many crafts and industries, workers simply took for granted that they would join, and the nonunion worker was so offensive that no one would work next to him or her.

Compulsory Membership, Union Democracy, and Individual Rights

Labor contract articles on union security usually stipulate that an employee who fails or refuses to join a union or maintain union membership is subject to discharge.[41] The following contract provisions illustrate this point:

> **CAUSE FOR DISCHARGE**
> - Failure to tender dues and initiation fee
>
>> (c) The Union will accept into membership each employee, covered by this Agreement, who tenders to the Union the periodic dues and initiation fee uniformly required as a condition of acquiring or retaining membership in the Union.
>> (6) Upon receipt of notice, from the Local Union having jurisdiction of the employee, that an employee has failed to comply with the above provisions, the employee shall be dismissed. (Iowa Industries Inc. and Auto Workers; exp. 2/92)
>
> - Failure to maintain membership
>
>> Should an employee fail or refuse to join the Union or maintain membership therein as hereinbefore provided, the Union may request the Company to discharge such employee. . . . (The Connecticut Light and Power Co. and Electrical Workers [IBEW]; exp. 6/92)
>
> - Loss of good standing membership in union
>
>> Employees losing their good standing membership in the union, who may for such loss of good standing membership in the union be legally discharged, will not be retained in the employ of the Company. . . . (Muskegon Piston Ring Co. and Auto Workers; exp. 8/92)[42]

If union membership is compulsory, a serious problem can arise. In unions not characterized by high-level democracy, individual rights may be infringed on in two ways. First, in the past, some unions restricted their membership by admitting only friends or relatives of present members, and others placed numerical restrictions on membership. If membership is both required and unavailable, the applicant is denied the right to work in the job being sought. Because of legal developments during the last few decades, this is no longer a problem in unionized organizations. Whatever other controversy exists about compulsory membership, there is broad agreement that if membership is required, it must also be available to any qualified applicant. That is, whatever one might think about either a closed shop (which is illegal) or a closed union taken separately, a combination of the two would be unacceptable to most Americans.

As to the second possible infringement of individual rights, if a union is operated undemocratically, the closed or union shop might free workers from the arbitrary control of the employer only to bring them under the arbitrary control of the union. If unions are allowed to require membership, it would seem reasonable to require them in turn to guarantee members' rights and freedom from arbitrary discipline within the union. These rights are, to some extent, protected under the Labor Management Reporting and Disclosure Act, discussed in Chapter 3.

Most legislation concerning union security since World War II has moved in the direction of prohibiting compulsory membership. This, of course, prevents the abuse of the union's disciplinary power by abolishing it. For example, the Taft-Hartley Act is written so that a union shop contract cannot, in fact, compel membership; it can merely require the payment of dues. We should note in this connection that there is no necessary conflict between democracy and disciplinary power. For although democracy implies the right to participate in the formulating of rules, it does not include the right to violate them. Absence of discipline is anarchy, not democracy. The way our legislation has handled this thorny problem of the relationship among compulsory membership, union democracy, and union responsibility shows more evidence of political jockeying than of rationality.

SUMMARY

Union and management security share an important trait. If either is approached as a question of principle or inherent right, debate on it can be endless. But if either is approached as a technique for achieving satisfactory performance of an organizational function, rational criteria can be applied and mutually acceptable conclusions reached. Which approach is "proper" is, of course, a value judgment. The actual developments are nevertheless clear: Both management security and union security have in fact been established in the majority of areas now subject to collective bargaining. This situation could have resulted from mutual acceptance of mutual security on a problem-solving basis. It could also have resulted from each side's victory for its own version of the principle of its own security. Although the espousers of principle are more visible to the public, they have probably not had the most actual influence. Though in the minority, the number of areas in which insecurity still prevails on both sides remains significantly large.

Notes

1. The Dunlop Report, *Fact-Finding Report,* Commission on the Future of Worker-Management Relations (Washington, DC: U.S. Department of Labor and U.S. Department of Commerce, May 1994), p. 29.

2. Ibid., pp. 29–30, 34, 55.

3. The Dunlop Report, *Report and Recommendations,* Commission on the Future of Worker-Management Relations (Washington, DC: U.S. Department of Labor and U.S. Department of Commerce, December 1994), p. 12.

4. *Electromation Inc. and Teamsters, Local 1049,* AFL-CIO, 142 LRRM 1001–1024.

5. Betty Southard Murphy, Wayne E. Barlow, and D. Diane Hatch, "Manager's Newsfront," *Personnel Journal* 72, no. 8 (August 1993), p. 24. *E.I. du Pont de Nemours Co. v Chemical Workers Assoc., Inc.* 311 NLRB No. 88 (1993), 143 LRRM 1121 (1993), 143 LRRM 1268 (1993).

6. *NLRB v. Wooster, Division of Borg Warner Corporation,* 356 vs. 341 (1958).

7. Donna Sockell, "The Scope of Mandatory Bargaining: A Critique and a Proposal," *Industrial and Labor Relations Review* 40 (October 1986), p. 24.

8. Ibid., p. 26.

9. Ibid., p. 26.

10. This conclusion may need to be softened somewhat if the entire work force is well educated. See, for example, the discussion of the kibbutz in Arnold S. Tannenbaum et al., *Hierarchy in Organizations* (San Francisco: Jossey-Bass, 1974).

11. Boeing Co. and Machinists Union, contract expires October 3, 1995 (Washington, DC: Bureau of National Affairs), no. 1244, 20:5–20:6, 2-4-93, pp. 49–50.

12. *Basic Patterns in Union Contracts,* 14th ed. (Washington, DC: Bureau of National Affairs, 1995), pp. 79–81.

13. Brian Hamer, "Serving Two Masters: Union Representation on Corporate Boards of Directors," *Columbia Law Review* 81 (April 1981), p. 639.

14. *Wall Street Journal,* February 16, 1973, p. 5. Sources: *Columbia Law Review,* op. cit., p. 640; D. M. Douglas, "Labor Unions in the Boardroom: An Antitrust Dilemma," *The Yale Law Journal* 92, no. 106 (November 1982), p. 106.

15. *Monthly Labor Review,* October 1994, p. 61. See also *Monthly Labor Review,* January 1994, pp. 21–23.

16. Thomas A. Kochan and Harry C. Katz, *Collective Bargaining and Industrial Relations,* 2nd ed. (Homewood, IL: Irwin, 1988), p. 410.

17. Barbara Presley Noble, "Reinventing Labor: An Interview with Union President Lynn Williams," *Harvard Business Review* 71, no. 4 (July/August 1993), pp. 114–23.

18. Douglas Fraser, speaking at a meeting of the Industrial Relations Research Association, Cincinnati, November 15, 1993.

19. Tove H. Hammer, Steven C. Currall, and Robert N. Stern, "Worker Representation on Boards of Directors: A Study of Competing Roles," *Industrial and Labor Relations Review* 44, no. 4 (July 1991), pp. 661–80.

20. Everett M. Kassalow, "Foreign Labor Developments, Employee Representation on Corporate Boards," *Monthly Labor Review,* September 1989, pp. 39–42.

21. David A. Dilts and Robert J. Paul, "Employee Ownership of Unionized Firms: Collective Bargaining or Codetermination?" *Business and Society* 29, no. 1 (Spring 1990), pp. 19–27.

22. Stephen C. Smith, "On the Economic Rationale for Codetermination Law," *Journal of Economic Behavior and Organization* 16, no. 3 (1992), pp. 261–81.

23. Ibid.

24. Robert N. Stern, "Participation by Representation," *Work and Occupations* 14, no. 4 (November 1988), pp. 396–422.

25. Charles C. Heckscher, *The New Unionism* (New York: Basic Books, 1988), p. 119.

26. Kochan and Katz, op. cit., pp. 408–9.

27. Richard B. Freeman and Joel Rogers, "Who Speaks for Us?" in *Employee Representation,* Bruce E. Kaufman and Morris M. Kleiner, eds. (Madison, WI: Industrial Relations Research Association, 1993), pp. 13–79.

28. Richard B. Freeman and Morris M. Kleiner, "Employer Behavior in the Face of Union Organizing Drives," *Industrial and Labor Relations Review* 43 (April 1990), p. 351.

29. Ibid., p. 355.

30. Ibid., p. 363.

31. Lisa M. Lynch and Marcus H. Sandver, "Determinants of the Decertification Process: Evidence from Employer-Initiated Elections," *Journal of Labor Research* 8 (Winter 1987), pp. 86–87.

32. Thomas G. Pearce and Richard B. Peterson, "Regionality in NLRB Decertification Cases," *Journal of Labor Research* 8 (Summer 1987), pp. 253–69. John G. Kilgour, "Decertifying a Union: A Matter of Choice," *Personnel Administrator* 32 (July 1987), p. 45. Lynch and Sandver, op. cit. For a comprehensive list of older research in this area, see E. Edward Herman, Alfred Kuhn, and Ronald L. Seeber, *Collective Bargaining and Labor Relations,* 2nd ed. (Englewood Cliffs, NJ: Prentice Hall, 1987), pp. 387–88.

33. National Labor Relations Board, *Fifty-Fourth Annual Report of the National Labor Relations Board* for fiscal year 1990 (Washington, DC: U.S. Government Printing Office, 1992), p. 12. Kilgour, op. cit., p. 45.

34. Frank Borgers, "Union Decertification: Process and Outcome," *Proceedings of the Forty-Sixth Annual Meeting,* Industrial Relations Research Association, Boston, January 6–8, 1995, p. 7.

35. *Hughes Tool Company,* 147 NLRB 166.

36. William J. Moore and Robert J. Newman, "The Effects of Right-to-Work Laws: A Review of the Literature," *Industrial and Labor Relations Review* 38 (July 1986), pp. 571–85. Daniel

Quinn Mills, *Labor-Management Relations,* 4th ed. (New York: McGraw-Hill, 1989), pp. 443–46.

37. *Basic Patterns in Union Contracts,* op. cit., p. 102.

38. *Basic Patterns in Union Contracts,* 13th ed. (Washington, DC: Bureau of National Affairs, 1991), p. 101.

39. *Communication Workers of America* v. *Beck,* 128 LRRM 2729 (1988); *Communication Workers of America* v. *Beck,* 4870S 7356 (1993). See also David A. Lebowitz, "Limits on the Use of Agency Fees: The Revival of Communication Workers of America v Beck," *Employee Relations Law Journal* 18, no. 3 (Winter 1992–1993), pp. 437–60. Kenneth A. Kovach, "The Use of Union Dues for Political Purposes," *Labor Law Journal* (October 1993), pp. 607–14.

40. Rosemary M. Collyer, General Counsel of the National Labor Relations Board, "Memorandum to all Regional Directors, Officers-in-Charge, and Resident Officers, on Guidelines Concerning CWA v Beck," Memorandum GC 88-14 (issued November 15, 1988), pp. 3–4.

41. *Collective Bargaining Negotiations and Contracts* (Washington, DC: Bureau of National Affairs), 11.1.90, no. 1185, 87:321, p. 29.

42. Ibid.

CHAPTER 7

Bargaining Structure

After reading this chapter, you should be able to

- Comprehend the criteria applied by the NLRB in defining appropriateness of bargaining units.

- Understand the advantages and disadvantages to employers and unions of both craft and industrial bargaining units.

- Explain the multiemployer bargaining unit: its effects on employers, unions, and the public's interest.

- Explain coordinated bargaining: its impact on employers and its significance for unions.

- Understand how new forms of business structure affect the collective bargaining process.

COMPONENTS OF BARGAINING STRUCTURE

According to Weber, bargaining structure can be seen as consisting of four not necessarily distinct components: (1) the informal work group, (2) the election district, (3) the negotiation unit, and (4) the unit of direct impact.[1] We will discuss these components in order, from the smallest to the largest.

The Informal Work Group

The smallest grouping of workers has been referred to as the informal work group, whose members would tend to have a common view of the work environment. This informal group may consist of workers in one or more occupations who come into frequent contact with one another.

The Election District or Election Unit

The election district or election unit is the group or groups of workers that the National Labor Relations Board (NLRB) considers appropriate for the purpose of collective bargaining. The election unit may consist of one or more informal work groups. In a certification election, only those employees who are in the election unit are eligible to vote. If a union is successful in a certification election, the election unit becomes the certified bargaining unit.

Election units differ in scope of coverage. Three main categories are the single-employer, single-location unit; the single-employer, multilocation unit; and the multiemployer unit. Each of these units in turn may include different clusters of jobs or job classifications.

The single-employer, single-location unit can cover all workers eligible for certification in a single establishment[2] or any particular category of employees such as craft, clerical, professional, production and maintenance, or any other specific employee classification that the NLRB finds eligible for separate certification.

A multilocation unit encompasses employees who work in a number of locations, such as plants, stores, warehouses, or offices of a single employer, either in a single geographical area or in scattered areas. A multiemployer unit embraces the employees of a number of employers and is rarely considered appropriate for certification by the NLRB.[3]

The Negotiation Unit

Although the negotiation unit can be the same as the election unit, the negotiation unit can include more than one election unit if both parties agree to a broader unit. A negotiation unit may encompass multiple election units in a single location, several locations of the same employer, or employees of more than one employer. Such units have typically involved only workers organized by the same union. Coalition bargaining, where multiple unions negotiate together, is discussed later in this chapter.

A great deal of confusion surrounds bargaining structure because the Wagner Act refers to the election unit as the appropriate bargaining unit. As we just discussed, the actual group of people involved in direct negotiations may or may not be the same group as those who voted in an election to have union representation. It is unfortunate that the term *bargaining unit* was used in this way.

The Unit of Direct Impact

The unit of direct impact extends beyond the boundaries of the negotiation unit. It may cover more than one industry, as when a settlement by an auto company has direct impact on auto parts companies. Such pattern relationships also exist in the rubber industry, in steel fabrication, and in a variety of other industries. The concept of a unit of direct impact is not limited to the private sector. In the case of municipal bargaining, terms agreed upon by a large municipality may have a direct effect on neighboring communities. Furthermore, a negotiating unit in the public sector may be directly affected by negotiations in the private sector, and possibly the reverse may occur. Industrial relations systems are highly interdependent, and every agreement may eventually have some impact on every other negotiating unit.

THE NLRB AND THE APPROPRIATE ELECTION BARGAINING UNIT

Before passage of the Wagner Act of 1935, many labor disputes arose over refusal of employers to recognize labor unions. The process of certification through secret-ballot elections largely eliminated this source of conflict. Unless an employer voluntarily agrees to recognize a union, before a union can be elected and certified as the representative of a group of employees, the NLRB must determine the appropriate bargaining unit that the union is to represent. Dunlop notes that "determination of the bargaining unit is the most significant responsibility exercised by the National Labor Relations Board for the future of collective bargaining."[4] Gorman likewise states that "unit determination is at the heart of our system of collective bargaining."[5]

In general, except for the statutory limitations to be discussed shortly, if the union and the employer can agree on which employees should be in the election unit, the Board will run the election in that unit. This reflects the value placed by the NLRB on voluntary settlement of disputes by the concerned parties. It is only in situations where the union proposes one election unit and the employer insists on a different one that the Board is forced to make an independent determination.

Because the Taft-Hartley Act provides few guidelines for unit determination, over time the Board has developed its own standards. These are mutuality or community of interest, geography or physical proximity, employer organizational structure[6] and administrative or territorial divisions, functional integration, interchange of employees, bargaining history, employee desires, and extent of organization.[7] Other criteria that the Board sometimes applies are "organization and representation of employees";[8] "similarity of duties, skills, interests and working conditions of the employees";[9] similarity in the scale and manner of determining earnings "common supervision and determination of labor relations policy."[10]

In a study of the NLRB and the appropriate bargaining unit, Abodeely et al. state that

> the NLRB has properly identified a number of factors germane to determining an appropriate bargaining unit. The problem lies with the Board's application of these factors. The inconsistent case-to-case manner in which the Board uses the individual factors invites speculation that the Board is using the factors to support rather than to reach its determinations.[11]

Thus, in the final analysis, value judgments of Board members may be the most important criterion that determines appropriateness of bargaining units.

Section 9(b) of the National Labor Relations Act (NLRA) gives the NLRB broad discretionary authority in determining the appropriateness of bargaining units. The only limitation on the Board's authority relates to professional, craft, and guard employees. Specifically, in a case affecting professional employees, the Board is not allowed to include both professional and nonprofessional employees in the same bargaining unit "unless a majority of such professional employees vote for inclusion in such unit" (Section 9[b][1], NLRA). In craft certification cases, the Board is prohibited from deciding "that any craft unit is inappropriate for such purposes on the ground that a different unit has been established by a prior Board determination" (Section 9[b][2], NLRA). And in guard certification cases, the Board is not permitted to certify guards in the same units as nonguards. In addition, no labor organization can be certified as a representative of guards if it is affiliated or "admits to membership employees other than guards" (Section 9[b][3], NLRA).

The role of the NLRB in determining bargaining units needs clarification in several respects. First, although charged with determining appropriateness of bargaining units, the Board is not required to seek and certify the "most appropriate or optimal unit." Thus, the Board theoretically has broad discretion. Second, the unit is based on "jobs or job classifications"[12] and not on specific individuals employed in these classifications. Thus, turnover of employees does not change the legal status of a unit. Third, membership in the unit and in the union are not necessarily the same. Employees in the bargaining unit need not be members of the union, except under a union shop or related union security provision. Under Section 9(a) of the NLRA, labor organizations "selected for the purpose of collective bargaining by the majority of the employees in a unit . . . shall be the exclusive representatives of all the employees in such unit." Thus, it is possible for a union to be elected as the representative of a group of employees, the majority of whom may not belong to it (and conceivably none might belong). The union would still have the legal obligation to bargain for and fairly represent all employees in the unit regardless of their union affiliation.

THE CRAFT BARGAINING UNIT

The purpose of this section is to examine the status of craft employees within the context of the collective bargaining structure. In the *American Potash and Chemical Corporation* case, the NLRB in 1954 defined a true craft unit as

> a distinct and homogeneous group of skilled journeymen, craftsmen, working as such, together with their apprentices and/or helpers. To be a journeyman craftsman an individual must have . . . a substantial period of apprenticeship or comparable training. . . . Furthermore such craftsmen must be primarily engaged in the performance of tasks requiring the exercise of their craft skills.[13]

Craft employees can be found in all sectors of the economy. They are employed as electricians, plumbers, tool makers, and stationary engineers and in a variety of other trades. In some firms, they form their own units and bargain separately from the other employees. In other firms, they are included in large, comprehensive units together with unskilled and semiskilled workers. The bargaining status of craft employees within a firm depends on the nature of the craft, the type of industry, the collective bargaining history in the industry, and, most important, the policies and practices of the NLRB.

If given the choice, most craft workers would probably opt for separate craft units, because such units would give them more bargaining power and status than they could obtain within a comprehensive industrial unit. A union representing a small unit of electricians can normally obtain better contract terms than an industrial union representing many different categories of employees. However, from the point of view of industrial unions, it is not desirable to permit craft workers separate representation. The bargaining power of an industrial union could erode significantly if it allowed some of the critical crafts to depart from the unit. In case of a strike, it is much easier to replace semiskilled than skilled workers. A strike by a small, strategic craft union could easily close down a large operation and thus deprive the great majority of industrial workers of work. Thus, the right of self-determination for craft workers may in effect reduce some of the rights of the majority. The bargaining power of an industrial union tends to vary directly with the size of its constituency. It is therefore in the interest of the industrial union to represent as large a constituency as possible, in terms of both absolute size and skills.

The industrial union is a political entity, and its elected officials must be responsive to the demands of the majority of its members. This majority usually consists of unskilled and semiskilled people. The industrial union, however, cannot entirely ignore the interests of the craft minority because to do so could lead to wildcat strikes, petition to the NLRB for severance, and a general level of internal turmoil and dissatisfaction. Such developments would be detrimental to the industrial union and to all members of the bargaining unit.

Some industrial unions, to protect the rights of craft workers within the industrial unit, grant them a limited right to vote separately on labor contract ratification, particularly on issues directly affecting them.[14]

Employers and the Appropriate Unit for Craft Employees

Employers do not hold a unified position concerning the most appropriate bargaining unit for craft employees. Although some employers prefer to bargain separately with their craft workers, the majority probably prefer to bargain with as few unions as possible.

There are a number of reasons why some firms may favor separate bargaining with their crafts. In some cases, having a craft submerged in a comprehensive unit could create industrial relations and personnel problems for the employer. Also, the separate approach may appeal to employers who subscribe to the divide-and-conquer strategy, who think that by depriving the industrial union of strategic crafts they can gain financially at the bargaining table. Management may be willing to pay craft employees more than they would earn if they belonged to an industrial union, but the extra cost may be more than offset by the employer's lower total wage costs for the majority of employees, the semiskilled and unskilled workers.

Separate bargaining units for craft employees may, nevertheless, have drawbacks for the employer. A firm negotiating with a number of different unions becomes vulnerable to "whipsawing."[15] Bargaining with many unions increases administrative costs and makes it more difficult to plan reliable production and marketing schedules. Usually, continuity of production is more secure with fewer unions.

The NLRB and the Craft Bargaining Unit

Under the Wagner Act of 1935, the NLRB has been vested with the authority to certify craft bargaining units. The craft bargaining unit cases facing the NLRB can be divided into two broad categories: (1) initial certification cases involving craft employees who were never represented in a collective bargaining relationship with a particular firm and (2) severance cases involving craft employees who request the Board to separate them from existing industrial units. In both instances, the NLRB must decide whether the craft satisfies the NLRB criteria for certification. It is easier for a craft to gain separate certification rights when there is no history of successful collective bargaining within the context of a larger unit.

The NLRB is willing to certify craft employees in separate bargaining units when some of the following conditions are met: The craft employees are unrepresented, they are engaged in traditional craft work that they perform in a separate and distinct location apart from other employees, they have a separate community of interest and do not "interchange with other employees,"[16] and the union seeking recognition is a craft union traditionally representing the craft in question.

Craft certifications are governed by criteria laid down in the *Mallinckrodt Chemical Works* case. Under the policy proclaimed in the *Mallinckrodt* case, all petitions for craft severance were to be decided on a case-by-case basis, regardless of the industry in which they occurred. In such cases, the NLRB applies the following criteria:

1. Whether or not the proposed unit consists of a distinct and homogeneous group of skilled journeymen craftsmen
2. The history of collective bargaining of the employees sought
3. The extent to which the employees in the proposed unit have established and maintained their separate identity during the period of inclusion in a broader unit
4. The history and pattern of collective bargaining in the industry involved
5. The degree of integration of the employer's production processes
6. The qualifications of the union seeking to "carve out" a separate unit[17]

The craft certification criteria that emerged in the *Mallinckrodt* case and their application did not improve the position or the future outlook of craft unions. Laurence J. Cohen, who reviewed the Board's decision under the Mallinckrodt doctrine, states that

> the future for separate craft of departmental units seems dim in general and positively bleak where severance is attempted. For one thing, the very application of the doctrine to

date will tend to inhibit the filing of new petitions for severance. And, when such petitions are filed, the history of the Mallinckrodt doctrine to date affords little hope that those petitions will be granted.[18]

The NLRB, confronted with the dilemma between the right of self-determination of craft employees and a potential threat to stability in industrial relations, is willing to trade off self-determination for industrial peace. The Board's position on this issue is very well summarized in the *Mallinckrodt* case. The Board states that, in the making of unit determination in severance cases, the nature of the issue underlying such determination

> is the need to balance the interest of the employer and the total employee complement in maintaining the industrial stability and resulting benefits of a historical plant-wide bargaining unit as against the interest of a portion of such complement in having an opportunity to break away from the historical unit by a vote for separate representation.[19]

A discussion of craft bargaining units would be incomplete without a consideration of the impact of technological change.[20] New technology has simplified some production techniques, thus opening work previously performed by craft workers to semiskilled people. In some instances, sophisticated machinery has supplanted certain craft categories, as in the printing industry. In still other situations, new technology has put new demands on craft employees, forcing them to upgrade their technical competence and training. The industrial electrician who services automated and computerized equipment must be much better trained now than in the past. Some unions have responded to the technological challenge by merging with related craft unions. Others have begun organizing semiskilled workers, thus increasing their bargaining and organizational strength.

Technology is not standing still, and craft workers everywhere will experience new pressures for change in their traditional bargaining structures. The construction industry has been one of the major targets of change. Currently, the industry is organized and bargains on a craft, or multicraft, basis. The development of factory, prefabricated, and modular housing that can be built by semiskilled people may force construction crafts to adjust to the new conditions and form different structures for bargaining purposes.

Technological change may confront the NLRB with new challenges in the form of more applications for separate units from new crafts and groups of technical workers. As Chamberlain and Kuhn observe, "We may well see in the coming years more skilled and technical employees seeking narrow bargaining units and excluding other types of workers."[21] If the past is a guide to the future, the NLRB will probably be very reluctant to sanction these new skilled workers as separate entities for collective bargaining—especially if some of them have been members of comprehensive bargaining units with relatively stable histories of collective bargaining.

THE SIGNIFICANCE OF NLRB ELECTION UNIT DECISIONS FOR UNIONS AND MANAGEMENT

The importance of NLRB authority to determine the appropriateness of bargaining units is apparent from the following statement by Barbash: "The NLRB's early support of more inclusive units accelerated the ascendancy of industrial unionism, exemplified . . . in steel, coal and electrical products."[22] The certification process not only acts as a catalyst to collective bargaining, but it also influences collective bargaining outcomes. The existence of certification machinery eliminates the recognition dispute and transfers the determination of the initial bargaining unit from the bargaining parties to the NLRB. Although the parties have the freedom to expand units established by the Board, these initial NLRB units are the basic building blocks upon which the parties, through bargaining, can build more inclusive structures for actual negotiations. However, the bargaining units that the NLRB determines as appropriate are not necessarily the same as those the parties would have established, sometimes through power confrontations, had there been no certification machinery. Bargaining outcomes are affected by the bargaining power held by each party; this power in turn is influenced by the dimensions of the bargaining units. Because the NLRB is the major force in determining the dimensions of initial units, it follows that NLRB decisions would have an impact on bargaining outcomes.

From the union's point of view, Board decisions are often crucial. Whether the Board establishes a single- or a multilocation election unit can make the difference between winning and losing a certification election and bargaining rights. For example, for many years unions encountered difficulties in winning certification elections among units of multiple retail stores. Things changed dramatically in favor of unions with the *Save-On Drugs, Inc.* case,[23] in which the NLRB recognized the easier-to-organize single store as an appropriate unit for certification.

As stated previously, the initiative in forming a bargaining unit is usually taken by a labor organization; it presents to management or to the NLRB its version of an appropriate unit. The unit favored by a labor organization may be confined to a single occupation, a single department, several occupations or departments in a single location, multiple locations of a single employer, or, under rare circumstances, the same type of employees of multiple employers. A union considers several factors when deciding on its desired unit. Traditionally, the most important factor has probably been the union's self-proclaimed jurisdictional mandate in its charter. This statement would set out which type or types of employees and in which industries the union would seek to organize. The predominant factor determining a union's desired unit seems to be its ability to win an election. This may involve representing workers in small units, which are easier to win but more expensive to represent. It sometimes requires agreeing to an employer's desired unit to get a prompt election, which also increases the chances of a union victory. A third set of factors involves attempts to maximize the unit's potential bargaining power. These factors comprise the administrative, competitive, and operational structures of the firm, including the degree of centralization of its industrial relations activities. Here, the union may try to mirror its structure to that of the corporation. Because unions try to "take wages out of competition," the ideal bargaining unit from the union's perspective might be coextensive with the firm's labor or product market.

NLRB policies are significant for management. Employers favor election units in which it would be difficult for a union to organize and obtain a majority. In proposing the boundaries of bargaining units, the parties obviously take opposing positions. In responding to union initiatives, employers take into account the same factors influencing union policies, but typically with opposite preferences. For, whereas unions measure success by the frequency of their recognition as bargaining agents, employers measure success by their ability to keep unions out, and either party's potential for victory often hinges on the dimension of the election bargaining unit.

Under the NLRA, an employer is free to recognize and bargain with a labor organization without its being certified as a representative of some group of employees. Under such voluntary recognition, the unit that emerges is essentially determined through bargaining. Because of NLRB policies and court decisions, as well as employers' desires to remain nonunion or at least delay unionization as long as possible, employers have selected formal election and certification over voluntary methods in determining representation rights.

The certification machinery gives employers an opportunity to counter the union initiative in proposing bargaining units. When a union petitions for certification, employers are notified and allowed to respond. The response may be acceptance, rejection, or proposed modification. Although the NLRB is not legally obliged to receive management proposals, employer arguments are thoroughly reviewed, the weight given to them depending on the circumstances of each case.

Employers usually favor large election units primarily because it is more difficult for unions to win elections in such units. In addition, employers like larger units, rather than numerous small units, because of the decreased administrative costs resulting from larger units. Also, the interests of large, heterogeneous groups are likely to be more diverse than those of small, homogeneous ones. The consequence is a reduction of solidarity within larger units, a development welcomed by employers. Finally, management has more staffing flexibility when all of its employees are in one large unit.

The importance attached by the NLRB to management views regarding size of bargaining units may be influenced by the composition of the board. NLRB members are presidential appointees, and those appointed by Republican presidents may be more pro-management than those appointed by Democrats. Thus, which side has the upper hand in determining size of bargaining units may depend on the Board's political coloration at the moment.

THE STRUCTURE OF COLLECTIVE BARGAINING IN THE UNITED STATES

In the previous section, we chiefly discussed the appropriate election unit. As stated earlier, the union and management can, if both agree, decide to negotiate contracts in a unit covering more than one election district. In an early estimate, Dunlop noted that two-thirds of "employees covered by collective bargaining agreements are in situations where the actual negotiation area, represented by the people sitting at the bargaining table, is different from the area covered by the NLRB certifications."[24]

Kochan and Katz have developed a matrix to characterize bargaining structure on the basis of union and management interests. The union interest is described as being either narrow, as in a craft union representing workers with a narrow group of skills, or broad, as in an industrial union representing all employees in an industry. Management interests are either centralized, as in multiemployer or single-employer multiplant negotiations, or decentralized, as in single-employer, single-plant bargaining.[25] Most industries and occupations can be characterized as falling into one of the four categories: narrow, centralized; narrow, decentralized; broad, centralized; and broad, decentralized (see Table 7.1).

Bargaining in the airline industry offers an example of a narrow, centralized unit. Unions organize workers on a craft or occupational basis, with separate organizations representing pilots, flight attendants, and mechanics. For the employers' part, negotiations are carried out separately for each airline company at the corporate level.

An example of broad, centralized bargaining is that in the underground coal mining industry. The United Mine Workers is an industrial union representing all types of mine employees. The employers have formed a multiemployer bargaining association to negotiate contracts with the union covering their unionized employees.

In printing and publishing, unions are organized on a narrow, decentralized basis. Employees are represented by various craft unions; as a result, some employers must negotiate with a few different unions. Newspaper publishers, even though some own papers throughout the country, negotiate on a decentralized basis, with separate negotiations taking place at each paper.

TABLE 7.1   The Four Main Types of Bargaining Units, with Industrial and Occupational Examples

Employee Interests Covered	Employer Interests Covered	
	Centralized	*Decentralized*
Narrow	Airlines	Federal employees
	Construction trades	Firefighters
	Hotel associations	Police officers
	Interstate trucking	Printing and publishing
	Longshoring	Teachers
	Railroad crafts	
Broad	Automobiles	Chemicals
	Coal mining (underground)	Oil refineries
	Electrical machinery	Public utilities
	Farm equipment	Many small manufacturing plants
	Paper	and industrial unions
	Retail food	
	State government	
	Steel	

Source: Thomas A. Kochan and Harry C. Katz, *Collective Bargaining and Industrial Relations,* 2nd ed. (Homewood. IL: Irwin, 1988), p. 120, figure 4–1.

In oil refineries and in the chemical industry, negotiations are conducted on a broad and decentralized level. Employees in both industries are represented by industrial unions, which negotiate separate contracts for each location.

Determinants of Bargaining Structure

Arnold R. Weber states that the term *bargaining structure* denotes "a multiplicity of units tied together in a complicated network of relationships by social, legal, administrative and economic factors." In his view, the structure "may be described by the scope of the units of which it is comprised and the system of decision making adopted by the parties on both sides of the bargaining table." Many factors determine the bargaining structure. According to Weber, these can be classified as "market factors, the nature of bargaining issues, representational factors, governmental policies and power tactics in the bargaining process."[26]

Market Factors

Both employers and unions take into account the market context when devising the dimensions of bargaining structures. Employers are sensitive to competitive pressures when developing appropriate boundaries for bargaining structures. Under conditions of severe product market competition, some employers have opted for multiemployer bargaining to reduce at least one aspect of competitive pressure. Weber states that unions have tried to shape "bargaining structures that are co-extensive with the specific market(s) encompassed by their jurisdiction." A distinction can be drawn between the approaches of industrial and craft unions in determining appropriate bargaining structures. For industrial unions, usually, output or "the scope of the product market" is important. For craft unions, inputs or "labor market considerations" are of greater significance.[27]

Bargaining Issues and Structure

Bargaining issues can be classified as market-wide, company-wide, or local. Weber points out that wages have "market-wide implications," and fringe benefits like pensions and insurance plans usually have "company-wide" implications.[28] Issues such as safety, work rules, and wash-up times are related to local working conditions and are usually treated at the local level. The collective bargaining structures emerging in various industries reflect the nature and significance of the issues to be negotiated. Thus, in some industries, issues such as wages and major fringe benefits are negotiated at the national level and local issues are left to local bargaining. The bargaining structure in the automobile industry is an example of such a dual approach. Weber states that when

> the important issues are market wide in nature, such as wages, there will be strong pressures for expanding the scope of the negotiating unit and centralizing decision-making power within the unit to avoid variations among plants or firms. Conversely, demand for decentralized or even fractionalized bargaining are likely to develop when local problems are paramount.[29]

According to Walton et al., in recent years negotiations "have been characterized by a . . . devolution from industry to company level and from company to plant level."[30] Way states that "over the past fifteen years collective bargaining has become . . . more decentralized."[31]

Representational Factors

Individual firms or unions are sometimes willing to enter into comprehensive alliances in order to increase their bargaining power. Weber points out that "the formation of the common front inevitably involves a partial relinquishing of individual group goals."[32] The cost of a "common front" normally is a reduction of local autonomy. A smaller employer in a multiemployer unit composed of small and large firms may decide that the cost of being a small fish in a big pond is too high and that he or she would rather protect his or her autonomy and remain independent. When a union bargaining structure embraces too many heterogeneous groups and it becomes unworkable, the union may attempt either to restructure the existing framework or to develop new decision-making procedures to accommodate the conflicting pressures.

The Impact of Government

Bargaining structures do not operate in a vacuum; legislation, the courts, and government administrative agencies all influence the dimensions of bargaining structures. The bargaining unit decisions of the NLRB undoubtedly shape and influence the nature and characteristics of the present bargaining structures.

Power Tactics

Weber states that "each party will seek to devise a structure that will maximize its capacity for inflicting real or expected costs on the other party in the course of the bargaining process."[33] Both unions and employers attempt to develop bargaining structures that would maximize their bargaining power. Sometimes lengthy strikes result from labor-management confrontations over dimensions of bargaining structures.

For a multiplant employer engaged in the production of the same product in a number of plants, the optimal structure may consist of individual single-plant bargaining units. Such units may optimize the employer's bargaining power in negotiations. Thus, if a strike develops in any one plant, the other plants can continue production. Furthermore, some production can be transferred from striking to nonstriking facilities. Obviously, in such a firm, a union would tactically desire multiplant bargaining for the same reason that the employer would strongly oppose such a structure. In such situations, according to Weber, "The union inevitably will seek to broaden the negotiating unit to encompass all the production facilities."[34]

In the case of multiplant vertically integrated production, where each plant is engaged in a different phase of the total production process, the employer may be inclined to centralize bargaining, whereas the union may object to that arrangement. In such an operation, a strike in one plant could bring all the plants to a standstill; thus, the union would not need a multiplant bargaining unit in order to achieve its bargaining objectives.

Weber claims that tactical bargaining structure considerations "are not determinate in the evolution of bargaining but they may exercise an important influence in individual cases, especially in the early stages of the bargaining relationship."[35]

Perry and Angle have expressed the view that bargaining unit structure can have organizational outcomes. They evaluated the effects of different unit structures on "union affairs, labor-management relations, organizational performance, and employee attitudes." Their study was based on a sample of public mass transit organizations. The authors concluded that although structure of units "may have temporary or passing dysfunctional effects on organizational and individual outcomes," over time the parties adjust to structural limitations. Other authors have also recognized that bargaining structure may affect bargaining outcomes. According to Mills, decentralized structures can increase strike activity. Weber states that bargaining structure has an impact on economic leverage, on bargaining power, and on worker satisfaction. Hendricks and Kahn suggest that "some portion of the relationship often found between structural variables (such as firm size, concentration, labor intensity, and union rivalry) and bargaining outcomes (such as relative wage levels) may occur indirectly through the formation of different bargaining units." According to Weber, the structure of collective bargaining can be viewed as the "vital element in a chain of interdependence linking together the aspirations and demands of the parties, the bargaining process and the external environment.[36]

Individual Employee Influence

Another determinant and consequence of bargaining structure is the amount of influence individuals wish to have over decisions affecting them. It is a simple principle of mathematics that the smaller the bargaining unit, the greater the influence one vote will have on a democratically made decision. Beyond that, small groups of people doing the same kinds of work or working under the same conditions for the same employer are likely to have similar interests compared to workers with different skills, working conditions, and employers. As a result, individual influence is perhaps greatest in narrow, decentralized bargaining units where the union represents only one occupation and negotiations are with a single employer, perhaps at the plant level.

A drawback of narrow units might be the difficulty the parties experience in responding to technological change. For example, a union consisting only of railroad firemen would be more threatened by the introduction of diesel locomotives than would a broad unit comprising all railroad employees.

From a societal viewpoint, another disadvantage of narrow, decentralized units is the strike potential. The larger the number of units, the greater the potential for strikes. These strikes would, however, tend to involve fewer employees.

Although workers are likely to have more voice in narrow, decentralized units, their unions may lack the bargaining power to achieve their members' objectives effectively. Thus, there may be a trade-off involving the ability of individual union members to influence union bargaining goals and the union's bargaining power, a trade-off that may be necessary to achieve members' objectives at the bargaining table.

THE MULTIEMPLOYER BARGAINING UNIT

When a number of employers join forces for purposes of collective bargaining, the unit structure is described as a multiemployer bargaining unit. Sometimes agreements negotiated by a few large employers are also signed by smaller employers, who may agree to essentially the same terms as those approved by the large employers. Multiemployer bargaining may take place within many different geographical subdivisions: a metropolitan area, a region, or the whole country. Some of these arrangements embrace the whole industry within a particular geographical area; others cover only a portion of such an industry.

Effects of Multiemployer Units on Employers and Unions

The advantages and disadvantages of multiemployer bargaining units have been covered in great detail in many publications.[37] The purpose of this section is to review briefly some of the effects of multiemployer bargaining on unions and management. Competitive pressures are the dominant force encouraging both unions and employers to enter into multiemployer or industry-wide bargaining relationships. In some industries, such as apparel, both unions and employers may want to see uniformity of wages. Multiemployer bargaining could help the parties reach this objective.

Small employers in highly competitive and labor-intensive fields may find it easier to operate with uniformity of labor cost. The unionized employer subjected to intensive competition from the nonunionized sector may be highly supportive of multiemployer bargaining units, particularly if such units could affect the nonunionized employers who use substandard wages to undercut prices in the product market. Employers of such broader units would not have to be too concerned about some employers within the unit paying their workers less than the agreed-upon scale. Union supervision would ensure compliance with contract terms.

The multiemployer unit is particularly advantageous to both sides in industries composed of many small, financially weak employers. In such industries, there are bargainable issues, such as health and pension plans, that may be difficult to negotiate and implement through single-employer bargaining. Small employers, apart from the fact that they may lack the professional personnel necessary for negotiation of complex fringe-benefit programs, may also be concerned with the cost and competitive implications of introducing such programs. The fear of increased costs, to which their firms' competitors would not be subjected, would be a strong deterrent against the introduction of major benefit programs. Thus, in some industries, multiemployer bargaining undoubtedly overcomes a major stumbling block in negotiation of fringe-benefit programs.

Multiemployer bargaining provides both management and unions with significant cost savings in negotiation of labor agreements. It is cheaper to negotiate one master multiemployer agreement than a number of single-employer agreements. There are, however, considerations other than costs, such as intraorganizational issues, that the parties take into account before opting for multiemployer units. Multiemployer bargaining may not only overlook the needs of various employee groups but also ignore particular requirements of individual employers. In some cases, bargaining may become more intensive among the various employers within the extended group than between the employers' group and the union. This certainly appears to be the case in major-league baseball, where great differences exist between large-market teams with cable television deals, such as the New York Yankees and the Atlanta Braves, and small-market teams like the Pittsburgh Pirates. Production costs and organizational structures are not uniform among firms. Thus, what may be readily acceptable to one employer may be considered financially disastrous by another. The marginal firm in the multiemployer unit is more vulnerable under that arrangement than it would have been had it bargained on its own.

Arriving at multiemployer agreements is much more difficult than arriving at single-employer contracts. The expanded size of the unit comprising many heterogeneous groups leads to intensive intraorganizational bargaining both on the union's and on the employer's side. At times, these intraorganizational pressures may lead to lengthy delays in negotiation and even to a breakdown of bargaining. A uniform master contract covering the employees of a number of firms may overlook the requirements of the component units. The desires and needs of employees within a bargaining unit are not homogeneous. As in other organizations, the larger the unit, the greater the diversity that must be suppressed for the sake of uniformity. In some multiemployer units, to protect the aspirations of different groups of employees, master contracts cover only items such as wages and major fringe benefits, with other issues being negotiated on a local level.

Bargaining Power in the Multiemployer Bargaining Unit

Emergence of multiemployer bargaining units has a direct implication for the levels of bargaining power retained by the parties. The possibility that one side may be able to strengthen or equalize its bargaining power through the formation of multiemployer units may set in motion the forces necessary for the creation of such bargaining frameworks. This process is not always peaceful; sometimes it is accompanied by confrontation, friction, and work stoppage.

There are a number of reasons for employers' forming multiemployer units: In some instances, employers are willing to give up bargaining power in order to lessen competition in the product market or to achieve industrial peace and greater stability in labor relations. Employers' need for a countervailing power in the face of strong unions may also be a catalyst for the formation of industry-wide multiemployer bargaining units. In highly competitive labor-intensive industries composed of many small employers with a high degree of unionization concentrated in a few unions, the only way for employers to have significant bargaining power is to form industry-wide bargaining units. In such industries, an individual employer who bargains independently may be at a disadvantage. Strong unions may concentrate their initial bargaining against firms that are likely to be the most generous. The contracts thus concluded can then be used as a basis for pattern following by the rest of the industry. Such conditions provide a strong impetus for employers to try to improve their bargaining strength by creating multiemployer frameworks.

Some unions may favor multiemployer bargaining as a means of increasing their bargaining power. A union's ability to strike all employers within an industry would give it a significant amount of power at the bargaining table; the union would not have to concern itself with the possibility of a struck employer's being assisted by nonstriking firms. Additionally, the union could devote its limited resources to one large negotiation rather than to many small ones. Multiemployer bargaining, especially if market-wide, also eliminates one employer rationale for refusing union demands: that such concessions will make the firm uncompetitive.

In some instances, the bargaining power of a union may decline under industry-wide bargaining. Supplying strike benefits to employees of a whole industry may strain significantly the financial resources of a union and thus lessen its bargaining power. Also, if all employers are targeted in a strike, individual employers need not concern themselves with the danger of losing market share to their nonstriking competitors. Cox et al. conclude that industry-wide bargaining may strengthen employers because "the industry as a whole can face strike threats which might be disastrous to a single employer through the loss of his market."[38] Union bargaining power under industry-wide bargaining may also be reduced by pressure of public opinion and threat of government interference. In some industries, however, if bargaining were conducted on a single-employer basis, the union would be the weaker partner. The waterfront and the Longshoremen's Union represent a case in point. The union's bargaining position improved significantly when collective bargaining moved from a single- to a multiemployer level. The broader structure improved coordination among the longshoremen; it became impossible for the employers "to play one port against the other."[39]

In some instances, it may be in the union's interest to give up some of its power as a means of satisfying its other objectives. Improving the survival rate of firms in the industry, thus maintaining employment opportunities for union members, is a union goal for which it may be worth sacrificing some bargaining power in the short run. In the past, in New York's cutthroat, bankruptcy-ridden garment industry, the union welcomed multiemployer bargaining as a means of improving the financial health and lifespans of firms in the industry. The union was willing to sacrifice some of its short-run power for other considerations that could benefit the union and its members over the long haul.

The Pros and Cons of Multiemployer Bargaining from the Public's Point of View

One consequence of multiemployer bargaining is uniformity of contract terms. There is opposition to such standardization on the grounds that it may be detrimental to the public interest. Some scholars claim that multiemployer bargaining could strengthen monopolistic forces in the economy and lessen competition. Reduced competition in turn could lead to lower levels of output and higher prices, easier to pass on to the consumer. Uniform contract terms in such units "squeeze out marginal firms, discourage the entry of new small firms, and allow, if not encourage, collusion between union and management leaders at the expense of the public."[40]

Scholars are not unanimous in their opinions on the effects of multiemployer bargaining on industry competitiveness. Although industry-wide bargaining sets wage scales for the whole industry, this circumstance does not stop competition. The competition, rather than being based on the lowering of wages, would be based on "developing increased productivity . . . more effective use of . . . modern machinery . . . better distribution and . . . better reaching of markets."[41]

Another major criticism of multiemployer bargaining is that it broadens the extent of labor conflict. A strike in a multiemployer bargaining unit, whether the unit is national or local in scale, can have serious implications for affected consumers if the unit is the primary supplier of a particular service or product.

One major argument directed against critics of multiemployer bargaining rests on the proposition that, under expanded bargaining frameworks, the frequency of strikes diminishes and that labor relations in such units are more stable and mature. The participants are more sensitive and responsive to public opinion and government pressures. The expertise and sophistication of negotiators on both sides are considerably greater than in an industry consisting of many small firms bargaining individually.

Labor Law and the Multiemployer Unit

Although multiemployer units are established on a consensual basis, the NLRB does impose some constraints on union and management behavior. At one time, employers or unions could withdraw from multiemployer bargaining at any point they wished, even during negotiations. Under current Supreme Court law, either party may withdraw at any time before negotiations actually begin as long as that party gives notice to the other side. After negotiations begin, however, withdrawal is permitted only by "mutual consent" of the parties or under "unusual circumstances."[42] The Court has determined that a negotiating impasse is not considered an unusual circumstance.

The Decentralization of the Bargaining Structure

The current trend seems to be away from multiemployer bargaining, at least on the basis of experience in several major industries. When a firm's principal competitive threat comes from domestic unionized firms, multiemployer bargaining offers a way to ensure mutual survival. When, on the other hand, the threat comes mainly from nonunion companies and foreign competition, the advantages of multiemployer bargaining may be outweighed by its costs. If the key issues continue to be those best addressed at the firm or plant level, such as productivity, job classifications, work rules, performance-based pay, and job security, the trend toward decentralization of bargaining may be expected to continue.

In the last 15 years, there has been a strong movement away from multiemployer toward single-employer bargaining. According to Way, "Multiemployer bargaining in nonmanufacturing determined employment conditions in just over one-third of units in 1988, as compared to approximately two-thirds of units in 1980, while multiemployer bargaining in manufacturing had all but disappeared."[43]

The numbers of employers and workers covered by multiemployer labor contracts have declined significantly in the last 15 years. Katz[44] provides two examples of such developments, the trucking industry and the underground coal mining industry. In trucking, there was a master freight agreement between the Teamsters' Union and the Employers' Association. The agreement covered intercity truck drivers. During the last 10 years, some trucking firms decided to withdraw from the master agreement. In the mining industry, the United Mine Workers had a master agreement with the Bituminous Coal Operators Association. Here also some firms decided to pull out from the master agreement and negotiate their own contracts.

Katz[45] reports a large-scale shift of negotiations away from company-wide to plant-level bargaining. This phenomenon, observed in the auto, tire, and airline industries, had an impact on local pay and also resulted in some work rule concessions. A number of hypotheses have been advanced to explain why the structure of collective bargaining has been decentralizing in recent years. According to Katz, the three leading hypotheses are "the shift in bargaining power, . . . the spread of new work organization that puts a premium on flexibility and employee participation, and . . . a decentralization of corporate structure and diversification of worker preferences."[46] For a comprehensive discussion of these three hypotheses, see Katz's article as well as the extensive references it includes.

Changes in multiemployer and association bargaining are not confined to the United States. In 1993, in British Columbia, Canada, the pulp and paper companies that had been negotiating industry-wide agreements for about 50 years decided to terminate the system-wide approach to bargaining. These negotiations, on behalf of 14 firms, had been conducted through the Pulp and Paper Industrial Relations Bureau (PPIRB). According to the president of PPIRB, Mr. Mitterndorfer, the diverse economics of pulp and paper mills in the group made such industry-wide negotiations "out of date." Mr. Mitterndorfer stated that "today, British Columbia pulp operations are competing individually against producers all over the world in contrast to past days when the competitors sat at the same bargaining table and everyone was bound by the same rules."[47]

The pressures of global markets are experienced by Canadian as well as by U.S. employers in most sectors of the economy. These global developments will probably contribute to further decentralization of the collective bargaining structure in the United States.

COORDINATION OR COALITION BARGAINING

In this section, the terms *coalition* and *coordination* will be considered interchangeable. For purposes of consistency, and when there is no conflict with direct quotations, we will primarily use the term *coordination*. This term refers to two or more unions seeking to negotiate similar terms with an employer. The strongest form of coordination would be the signing of one master agreement covering all employees of all unions. A weaker form might just involve a set of common goals to be pursued in separate negotiations by all unions within the coalition.

Coordination was first practiced by craft unions as early as the 1880s,[48] and it still continues in some situations. However, not all joint bargaining is coordinated bargaining. Chernish[49] states that coalition bargaining "is a new industrial relations development" that is to be distinguished from other forms of joint bargaining:

> The most important differentiating feature of coalition bargaining as contrasted to other forms of joint bargaining is that the other efforts have come about as a result of voluntary agreement between the employer and the union. Coalition bargaining programs are designed to force an employer to bargain with a representative of the various participating locals on a joint basis.[50]

Why Do Unions Want Coordinated Bargaining?

The union target of coordinated bargaining is the large multiplant corporation; the process is an attempt by unions to increase their bargaining power with large employers. In the last 30 years, coordinated bargaining has been utilized by unions "as a weapon in bargaining with Union Carbide, Campbell Soup, the major companies in the copper industry, American Home Products, Olin, and General Telephone, among others."[51] The coordinated bargaining approach was first applied formally "in the 1966 General Electric and Westinghouse negotiations, and has been reapplied there in each triennial negotiation ever since."[52] Hildebrand states that "the coalition movement has come from a combination of union weakness in bargaining in some situations and a thrust for more power from some large aggressive labor organizations."[53]

Large-scale union efforts toward coordinated bargaining began in the mid-1960s, when conditions seemed ripe. There was little unemployment and little excess capacity. When confronted with uniform demands from coalition groups, employers were at a disadvantage because they could not readily shift production from the affected plants to other plants within their companies. Furthermore, the union movement had dynamic leaders like the late Walter Reuther, who was willing to fight for coalition bargaining and was referred to as the "intellectual father of coalition bargaining." The 1960s were also a period of major corporate changes that potentially strengthened managements relative to unions and that unions wanted to counter. Many mergers occurred; it was the era of conglomerates and multinationals. Many large corporations also experienced rapid growth. In response to these developments, the Industrial Union Department (IUD) of the AFL-CIO established a coordinated bargaining program. Its purpose has been to provide coordination in negotiations for different unions that have collective bargaining relationships with the same employer. The IUD establishes committees of representatives of unions that are interested in working together. The committees are responsible for development of "a program for cooperative and coordinated bargaining."[54] According to Howard D. Samuel, IUD president, the growth of conglomerates contributed to the development of coordinated bargaining. As Bok and Dunlop state,

> In an era of rapidly growing conglomerates it is understandable that the unions should be seriously concerned over the ability of companies to sustain a strike by continuing pro-

duction in other plants not involved in the dispute and by maintaining profits through diversified operations in other divisions of the enterprise.[55]

Along with local labor relations offices, the large multiplant corporations have corporate headquarters labor relations departments that coordinate and centralize labor relations for the whole corporation. Coordinated bargaining is the unions' response to employer orchestration of labor relations throughout a corporation or even an industry.

When the potential for coordinated bargaining is discerned in a particular situation, the IUD develops a detailed plan of action for the interested unions. An IUD pamphlet on coordination states that the IUD "at the request of the involved unions . . . helps organize and implement joint negotiations for any company or industry." Under such a program, all the involved unions get together, establish a procedure, compare notes, agree on common objectives, and plan bargaining strategy. When they cannot negotiate jointly, they exchange information, either by having representatives of other unions sit on their bargaining teams as observers, or through frequent coordinating committee meetings, or both.[56]

The current and future challenge to the labor movement is to increase coordination among unions in different countries that bargain with the same multinational corporations. Given the ease with which technology is transferred and production shifted from one country to another, unions need to think and operate globally as corporations already do.[57]

Employer Opposition to Coordinated Bargaining

The main reason for employers' opposition to coordinated bargaining is the potential loss of bargaining power[58]—the same reason that makes coordination attractive to unions. Why, asks Northrup, "should a company whose employees have chosen different unions to represent them open up the company to more encompassing strikes by agreeing to widen the bargaining basis?"[59]

The objective of unions is to negotiate, through coordination, master agreements or local agreements with identical termination dates. Such agreements would give unions the ability to strike simultaneously a multiplant company or even an entire industry. Such strikes would be more costly to the employer and thus could strengthen union bargaining power. Some employers think that the ultimate goal of coordination is centralization. This is a one-way street because it may be difficult for employers to move back to smaller bargaining structures from company-wide or industry-wide units.[60]

Multiplant companies that bargain locally sometimes benefit from interplant wage differentials that reflect differences in local labor markets. Coordination that aims at uniformity would make it more difficult to sustain such plant differentials.

Not all employers oppose coordinated bargaining. Some multiemployer bargaining frameworks include coordination among unions in an arrangement that both unions and employers approve as mutually beneficial. The multiemployer, multiunion bargaining framework may be seen in industries composed of many small employers who find it easier to negotiate with a number of unions. However, employer consent to coordinated bargaining does not extend to most large multiplant employers, who "want no part of coalition bargaining, and will continue to fight it."[61]

PATTERN BARGAINING

Another aspect of bargaining structure of concern in this chapter is the influence of settlements in one set of negotiations on bargaining outcomes regarding other employers. Pattern bargaining can be defined as "an informal means for spreading the terms and conditions of employment negotiated in one formal bargaining structure to another. It is an informal substitute for centralized bargaining."[62] Pattern bargaining is exemplified when a settlement in the auto industry influences subsequent settlements in the steel, auto parts, and rubber industries.

Throughout the 1980s, it was widely reported that the extent of pattern bargaining had diminished greatly.[63] This conclusion was largely based on surveys of managers who were asked what factors influenced their company wage and benefit objectives during negotiations. A large number of respondents claimed that they were not influenced by factors external to the firm itself.

In a 1994 book, *Contemporary Collective Bargaining in the Private Sector,* Paula B. Voos observes that many

> authors note a decreased use of multi-employer bargaining in recent years, a loosening of bargaining patterns, an increased tendency of collective agreements to be "tailored" to a particular company or particular operation's economic situation and a greater importance of locally bargained work rules in situations where companies are pursuing shopfloor participation or team production strategies. Bargaining has become more decentralized and patterns have loosened in aerospace, meatpacking, automobiles, and other sectors.

According to Voos, the "shifts demonstrate the adaptability and resiliency of collective bargaining in the face of changed conditions."[64]

THE COLLECTIVE BARGAINING STRUCTURE AND NEW FORMS OF BUSINESS ORGANIZATIONS

In a 1994 book, Howard Wial discusses the relationship between the structure of collective bargaining and the major structural transformation of American business organizations. He contends that the changes taking place in business organizations affect "the viability of existing collective bargaining relationships."[65]

Wial describes the new emerging business structures "as a locus of business decision-making networks of loosely linked business units."[66] These units may be simultaneously competing with one another in the marketplace and sharing new technology or even interchanging workers.[67] Business decisions made within such networks can have impact on employees who are scattered over the firms within the network. Wial suggests that the emerging network form of business organization may require the formation of new network-based bargaining structures.

In the traditional model of business organizations, most firms were considered as vertically integrated, hierarchical entities whose interactions with other companies were conducted as "arm's length market transactions."[68] In the last 10 years, the vertical integration model has been undergoing important changes. Many functions that in the past were carried out within the vertically integrated firm are now delivered by "specialized subcontractors."[69] Furthermore, organizations that historically operated at arm's length from each other have now "formed cooperative relationships, such as joint ventures, consortia, and long-term alliances, with suppliers, customers, or distributors."[70] As a result of these developments, the demarcation line between "the people and activities that are inside the firm and those that are outside"[71] is now blurred.

The vertical model has been modified by the trend toward more subcontracting as well as by increased cooperation in business relationships among firms. These developments raise important questions regarding collective bargaining and the appropriateness of existing bargaining structures for coping and functioning effectively within the context of the new forms of business organizations. Wial[72] suggests that such bargaining issues as allocation of work, wage inequality, and wage competition cannot be solved by single-employer units and should be negotiated in multiemployer units. He recognizes, however, that the trend in the United States, as discussed earlier, is away from centralized and multiemployer bargaining units.[73]

Wial claims that current labor law "inhibits the expansion of the scope of the bargaining unit beyond the certified unit, . . . where the certified unit is restricted to a single employer."[74] As a result, most bargaining takes place at the level of the single firm.

Because network structures of business organizations, discussed earlier, are a relatively recent phenomenon in most sectors of the economy, multiemployer bargaining paralleling network boundaries is not present. According to Wial,[75] it is unlikely under the current law governing unit determination that multiemployer bargaining structured along network boundaries will develop. To encourage network-based bargaining, the law would have to be amended, and NLRB policies regarding bargaining structures would have to be revised—an unlikely development in the near future.

SUMMARY

This chapter has introduced the concept of bargaining structure as consisting of the informal work group, the election district or election unit, the negotiation unit, and the unit of direct impact. The first and last of these are informal in nature. The reader should understand how the election district and negotiation unit are established; what factors influence the desirability of the various structures; and the consequences of these structures for employees, unions, employers, and the general public. After reading this chapter, one should also be able to discuss the bargaining structures in several major industries or occupations.

The chapter reviewed in some depth the election and negotiation unit configurations. Craft units merit special mention because of their importance in labor union history. The issue of craft units also illustrates the potential problems of merging small groups of employees into larger ones. Finally, the evaluation of multiemployer bargaining units is important because such units have the potential to affect significantly the extent of industrial conflict.

Notes

1. Arnold Weber, "Stability and Change in the Structure of Collective Bargaining," in *Challenges to Collective Bargaining,* Lloyd Ulman, ed. (Englewood Cliffs, NJ: Prentice Hall, 1967), pp. 13–36.
2. Subject to legislative restrictions under Section 9(b)(2) of the National Labor Relations Act regarding crafts, guards, and professional employees.
3. Such an election unit would usually only be found appropriate on the basis of a history of bargaining prior to a certification election.
4. John T. Dunlop, *Collective Bargaining* (Chicago: Irwin, 1949), p. 27.
5. Robert A. Gorman, *Basic Text on Labor Law, Unionization and Collective Bargaining* (St. Paul, MN: West, 1976), p. 67.
6. Bruce S. Feldacker, *Labor Guide to Labor Law,* 3rd ed. (Englewood Cliffs, NJ: Prentice Hall, 1990), p. 40.
7. John E. Abodeely, Randi C. Hammer, and Andrew L. Sandler, *The NLRB and the Appropriate Bargaining Unit,* rev. ed. (Philadelphia: Industrial Research Unit, The Wharton School, University of Pennsylvania, 1981), pp. 11–83.
8. *Labor Law Course,* 23rd ed. (Chicago: Commerce Clearing House, 1976), p. 1825.

9. *Fifteenth Annual Report of the NLRB,* 1950 (Washington, DC: U.S. Government Printing Office, 1951), p. 39.

10. Gorman, op. cit., p. 69.

11. Abodeely et al., op. cit., p. 14.

12. Archibald Cox, Derek Curtis Bok, and Robert A. Gorman, *Cases and Materials on Labor Law* (Mineola, NY: Foundation Press, 1977), p. 295.

13. 107 NLRB 1418 (1954).

14. Interview with Nathan Headd, UAW Research Department, Detroit, Michigan.

15. "Whipsawing—union stratagem seeking to obtain benefits from a number or group of employers by applying pressure to one, the objective being to win favorable terms from the one employer and then use this as a pattern or perhaps a base to obtain the same or greater benefits from the other employers, under the same threat of pressure (including a strike) used against the first one." *Source:* Harold S. Roberts, *Roberts' Dictionary of Industrial Relations,* rev. ed. (Washington, DC: BNA, 1971), p. 581. The same strategy can be applied by an employer against unions or by several unions against an employer.

16. *St. Vincent's Hospital,* 223 NLRB 98. Source: *Forty-First Annual Report of the NLRB,* 1976, pp. 56–57.

17. 162 NLRB 387 (1966).

18. Laurence J. Cohen, "Two Years under Mallinckrodt: A Review of the Board's Latest Craft Unit Policy," *Labor Law Journal* 20, no. 4 (April 1969), pp. 195–215.

19. 162 NLRB 387 (1966).

20. Abodeely, et al., op. cit., p. 111.

21. Neil W. Chamberlain and James W. Kuhn, *Collective Bargaining,* 2nd ed. (New York: McGraw-Hill, 1965), p. 250.

22. Jack Barbash, "Collective Bargaining: Contemporary American Experience—A Commentary" in *Collective Bargaining: Contemporary American Experience,* Gerald G. Somers, ed. (Madison, WI: Industrial Relations Research Association, 1980), p. 579. Douglas V. Brown and George P. Schultz, "Public Policy and the Structure of Collective Bargaining" in *The Structure of Collective Bargaining,* Arnold R. Weber, ed. (New York: Free Press of Glencoe, 1961), p. 314.

23. *Save-On Drugs, Inc.,* 138 NLRB 1032 (1962). Source: E. Edward Herman and Gordon S. Skinner, *Labor Law* (New York: Random House, 1972), pp. 156–60.

24. John T. Dunlop in Arnold R. Weber, ed., *The Structure of Collective Bargaining* (New York: Free Press of Glencoe, 1961), p. 28.

25. Thomas A. Kochan and Harry C. Katz, *Collective Bargaining and Industrial Relations,* 2nd ed. (Homewood, IL: Irwin, 1988), p. 120.

26. Weber, "Stability and Change in the Structure of Collective Bargaining," op. cit.

27. Ibid., p. 15.

28. Ibid., p. 17.

29. Ibid.

30. Richard E. Walton, Joel E. Cuther-Gershenfeld, and Robert B. McKersie, *Strategic Negotiations* (Boston: Harvard Business School Press, 1994), pp. 52, 65.

31. Philip K. Way, "The International Decentralization of Collective Bargaining: Convergence or Divergence?" paper presented at the annual meeting of the Industrial Relations Research Association, Washington, DC, 1995.

32. Weber, op. cit., p. 18.

33. Ibid., p. 20.

34. Ibid., p. 21.

35. Ibid.

36. James L. Perry and Harold L. Angle, "Bargaining Unit Structure and Organizational Outcomes," *Industrial Relations* 20 (Winter 1981), pp. 47–59. Weber, *The Structure of Collective*

Bargaining, op. cit., pp. 3–18. Daniel Quinn Mills, *Labor-Management Relations* (New York: McGraw-Hill, 1978), p. 404. Wallace E. Hendricks and Lawrence M. Kahn, "The Determinants of Bargaining Structure in U.S. Manufacturing Industries," *Industrial and Labor Relations Review* 35, no. 2 (January 1982), pp. 181–95. Arnold Weber, "Stability and Change in the Structure of Collective Bargaining," op. cit., pp. 15–32.

37. Neil W. Chamberlain, *Collective Bargaining* (New York: McGraw-Hill, 1951), Chapters 8 and 9. Chamberlain and Kuhn, op. cit., Chapter 10. See also Jesse Freidin, *The Taft-Hartley Act and Multi-Employer Bargaining,* Industry-Wide Collective Bargaining Series (Philadelphia: University of Pennsylvania Press, 1948). Clark Kerr and Lloyd H. Fisher, "Multiple Employer Bargaining: The San Francisco Experience," in *Insights into Labor Issues,* R. A. Lester and J. Shister, eds. (New York: Macmillan, 1948).

38. Cox et al., op. cit., p. 329.

39. *Pacific Longshore Case,* 7 NLRB 1008 (1938). Source: Chamberlain, op. cit., p. 180.

40. Chamberlain and Kuhn, op. cit., p. 245. See also David A. McCabe, "Problems of Industry-Wide or Regional Trade Agreements," *American Economic Review* 33, supplement (1943), pp. 163–73; and John Van Sickle, "Industry-Wide Collective Bargaining and the Public Interest" in *Unions, Management, and the Public,* E. Wight Bakke and Clark Kerr, eds. (New York: Harcourt, Brace World, 1948), pp. 521–25.

41. Labor Relations Programs, Hearings on S. 55 and S. J. Res 22, 80th Cong., 1st sess., Part 1, p. 577. Source: Chamberlain, op. cit., p. 207.

42. *Bonanno Linen Service v. NLRB,* 454 U.S. 404 (1982).

43. Way, op. cit.

44. Harry C. Katz, "The Decentralization of Collective Bargaining: A Literature Review and Comparative Analysis," *Industrial and Labor Relations Review,* October 1993, p. 11. Harry C. Katz and Thomas A. Kochan, *An Introduction to Collective Bargaining and Industrial Relations* (New York, McGraw Hill, 1992), pp. 195–97. Harry C. Katz, Thomas A. Kochan, and Robert B. McKersie, *The Transformation of American Industrial Relations* (New York: Basic Books, 1986), pp. 128–30.

45. Katz, op. cit., p. 11.

46. Ibid., p. 13.

47. *Pulp and Paper,* March 1993, p. 29.

48. Phillip J. Schwarz, *Coalition Bargaining* (Ithaca, NY: Cornell University Press, 1970), p. 2.

49. William N. Chernish, *Coalition Bargaining* (Philadelphia: University of Pennsylvania Press, 1969), p. 7.

50. Ibid., p. 271.

51. Arthur A. Sloane and Fred Witney, *Labor Relations,* 8th ed. (Englewood Cliffs, NJ: Prentice Hall, 1994), p. 244.

52. Ibid.

53. George H. Hildebrand, "Cloudy Future for Coalition Bargaining" in *Readings in Labor Economics and Labor Relations,* rev. ed., Richard L. Rowan, ed. (New York: Irwin-Dorsey, 1972), pp. 301, 304–5.

54. *Coordinated Bargaining,* pamphlet issued by the IUD Department, AFL-CIO, Washington, DC, p. 1.

55. Derek C. Bok and John T. Dunlop, *Labor and the American Community* (New York: Simon & Schuster, 1970), p. 258.

56. *Coordinated Bargaining,* op. cit., p. 14.

57. Robert B. Wood, *The Mobility of Work among Multinational Corporations,* paper presented at the AFL-CIO/Cornell University Conference on Changing Challenges for Unions, October 1989.

58. Hildebrand, op. cit., p. 311.

59. Herbert R. Northrup, "Boulwarism v. Coalitionism—The 1966 G.E. Negotiation," *Management of Personnel Quarterly* 5, no. 2 (summer 1966), p. 8.

60. Hildebrand, op. cit., pp. 311–12.

61. Schwarz, op. cit., p. 23.

62. Kochan and Katz, op. cit., pp. 136–37.

63. See, for example, Audrey Freedman and William E. Fulmer, "Last Rites of Pattern Bargaining," *Harvard Business Review* (March–April 1982), pp. 30 ff. Audrey Freedman, *The New Look in Wage Policy and Employee Relations* (New York: The Conference Board, 1985). Thomas A. Kochan, Harry C. Katz, and Robert B. McKersie, *The Transformation of American Industrial Relations* (New York: Basic Books, 1986), p. 134.

64. Paula B. Voos, ed., *Contemporary Collective Bargaining in the Private Sector* (Madison, WI: Industrial Relations Research Association, 1994), pp. 6, 7.

65. Howard Wial, "New Bargaining Structures for New Forms of Business Organization" in *Restoring the Promise of American Labor Law,* Sheldon Friedman, Richard W. Hurd, Rudolph A. Oswald, and Ronald L. Seeber, eds. (Ithaca, NY: ILR Press, 1994), p. 303. See also Howard Wial, *Rethinking the Microeconomic Foundations of Worker Representation and Its Legal Regulation: From Asset-Specificity to Collective Goods,* paper presented at the annual meeting of the Industrial Relations Research Association, Washington, DC, January 1995.

66. Ibid., pp. 305–6.

67. Ibid.

68. Ibid.

69. Ibid.

70. Ibid.

71. Ibid.

72. Ibid.

73. Ibid.

74. Ibid., p. 310.

75. Ibid.

CHAPTER 8

Preparation for Bargaining

After reading this chapter, you should be able to

■ Identify the factors that management and unions consider in selecting their bargaining teams.

■ Explain and evaluate the advantages and drawbacks of bargaining books.

■ Discuss the methodology for collecting bargaining information from supervisors and stewards.

■ Identify major sources of bargaining data used in preparation for negotiations.

■ Understand diverse interests within unions and management and their effects on bargaining demands.

THE COLLECTIVE BARGAINING PROCESS

This chapter will examine the collective bargaining process, focusing on the practical steps the parties take prior to negotiations. The process is influenced by factors such as the characteristics of the bargaining unit, the organizational structures of the union and of the employer, and the nature of the labor-management relationship. The membership composition of a bargaining unit affects the size and constitution of bargaining teams, the methods used in formulating bargaining demands, and the content of those demands. The degree of sophistication of bargaining preparations varies significantly with the available resources and the size of the union and the employer. A large union or a large employer with a sizable staff and a centralized approach to negotiation can spend considerably more time and effort on preparation than can a union or an employer lacking adequate resources. Another factor influencing preparation for bargaining is the prevailing labor-management relationship. In a cooperative relationship, preparations may be characterized by a joint search for objective information sources. In contrast, when conflict is intense, each side may seek to use information as a weapon to bolster partisan arguments and coerce concessions.

The character of the bargaining process, its outcomes, and its failures or successes can all be influenced by the quality of the preparation procedures. The purpose of this chapter is to review in some detail the steps that the parties can take in preparing for bargaining. It should be recognized, however, that the full range of preparations outlined are typical of only the most sophisticated negotiators—usually large employers and large unions negotiating contracts covering substantial numbers of employees. It would be less common for negotiators to engage in elaborate preparations, particularly when smaller units are involved.

BARGAINING TEAMS

Management

The bargaining structure directly affects the composition of the bargaining team. In the case of multiemployer bargaining, the team may include representatives appointed by the various employers within the bargaining unit. In some cases, bargaining in such a unit is delegated to an association that appoints its own team. In the case of single-employer, multilocation bargaining, the team may be composed of only head office staff, or it may include some local representation. In the case of a multilocation employer bargaining separately for each location, the team may be confined to local management, or it may include a representative from the firm's head office. In single-employer, single-location bargaining, the team may consist of the top management of the company.

In selecting a team, management must decide whether to appoint an insider or an outsider, and a lawyer or a nonlawyer. Management must also choose other members of the negotiating committee. The committee must include a note taker, a language draftperson, and people with operating and costing expertise, as well as representatives of various constituencies that would be affected by the negotiation outcome. Management must also determine how much authority to delegate to negotiators.[1]

Some firms engage in dual bargaining, in which a master contract and a local contract are negotiated separately. Major issues such as wages and fringe benefits are negotiated at the corporate level by head office staff, and issues of local interest are resolved by local officials with assistance from the head office.

The composition, size, and selection of the management team in terms of expertise, personality, and level of militancy is influenced by the complexity of the contract being negotiated and the nature of the opposition. In union-management relations, the history of the relationship plays a major role, and each party reacts to that history and the behavior of its opposition. Unfriendly or militant behavior on the part of union or management may create a desire in the other party to choose team members who can respond in kind. Cooperative behavior such as mutual gains or win-win bargaining can cause both teams to take the more abrasive personalities away from the bargaining table.

The effectiveness of a bargaining team is determined not by its size but by its ability, knowledge, and experience. A team well versed in tactics, strategy, and timing would be in a better position to avoid impasses and strikes and would end up with a better agreement than a team composed of inexperienced people.

The bargaining process, the behavior and conduct of negotiators at the bargaining table, and the teams agreed upon all have impact on the structure of the institutional relationship that evolves between the parties. Experienced negotiators will attempt to use the bargaining process as a means of building the type of relationship structure desired by the principals in their organizations.

The most important member of the bargaining team is usually its spokesperson. That individual is responsible for representing major positions, communicating priorities, timing concessions, making threats and commitments, and determining the responsibilities of each team member. The spokesperson is like an orchestra conductor, coordinating and timing the activities of the various individuals toward the achievement of a common objective.

Union

Union bargaining teams, like management teams, come in various sizes. There are cases where a business agent alone represents membership in bargaining, and there are cases where the full bargaining team or committee may include up to a hundred people. When a committee is that large, negotiations are usually delegated to a much smaller subcommittee. The larger group maintains contact with the subcommittee and provides assistance, but it does not participate directly in negotiations. Approval of the larger group becomes necessary, however, before the contract can be finalized.

Union teams, like management teams, also require assistance from experts in various fields. Economists, benefits specialists, actuaries, and attorneys are all background participants in the bargaining process.

The bargaining structure and the size and dimensions of the bargaining unit have direct impact on the size and composition of the union bargaining team. In national negotiations, the union team is usually large and is composed of officers of the national union, staff experts from the national, and some representatives from local unions. In local bargaining, the negotiating committee is relatively small. If the bargaining committee is elected by the local, it typically includes union officers, a business agent, and some shop stewards. In some instances, a representative of a national union may assist a local union either as an advisor or as a full-time member of the bargaining team. The representative of the national union helps locals formulate demands and assists them in the negotiation process. National unions are concerned with maintaining some uniformity of contract terms within the industries that they represent. It is usually the responsibility of the national representative to maintain such uniformity and prevent local concessions from falling below the minimum industry norm established by the national union. With the increased complexity of contract terms, the trend has been for national unions to assume a larger role in local negotiations.

The issue of bargaining team size is more significant for unions than for management. In appointing a bargaining team, management is primarily interested in having an effective negotiating group. A union, however, also must consider the political implications of size and composition. As a democratic organization, the union must have enough people on the team to accommodate the various views and agendas of its members. Bargaining units are composed of heterogeneous groups of employees. If the contract is to be ratified, it is important that these divergent interests be represented at the bargaining table.

PREPARATION OF BARGAINING DATA

In this section, we will outline some of the data that can be helpful to both sides at the bargaining table. Careful preparation of proposals can reduce uncertainty and improve communication, thus contributing to effective bargaining. Better preparation provides the parties with broader perspectives, which, in turn, increase flexibility and can accelerate the negotiation process.

Understanding the opposition is an important ingredient in bargaining. Before bargaining starts, management may attempt to find out everything it can about the union: its financial strength, its organizational structure, any internal problems, its formal and informal power structures, bargaining experience of other employers with the union, and the types of settlements arrived at elsewhere. Information on some of these subjects can be obtained informally through conversations with union leaders, discussions with labor relations officers of other firms who have dealt with a particular union, published Bureau of Labor Statistics (BLS) survey data, union publications or newspapers, union contracts, and published reports from the Bureau of National Affairs. Under the Reporting and Disclosure Act of 1959 (Landrum-Griffin Act), every labor organization must file a financial report annually with the Secretary of Labor. These reports are in the public domain and are a good source of financial information about unions.

Unions, like management, try to find out as much as possible about the weaknesses and strengths of employers. The following management data can be helpful to union negotiators: financial information on the company and the industry, annual reports, financial reports to stockholders, Dun and Bradstreet credit reports, and reports filed with the Securities and Exchange Commission. Other useful sources are U.S. Department of Commerce reports, trade journals, and industry association reports. An AFL-CIO publication suggests that union negotiators should not only examine company profits but also obtain information on sales, production, pricing policies, new technology, new products, investment plans, and trends in new orders.[2] If a company is publicly owned and traded on one of the exchanges, information can also be obtained from such stock market services and publications as Moody's, Standard and Poor's, Value Line, *Commercial and Financial Chronicle, Wall Street Journal, Barron's, Forbes, Business Week,* and *Fortune.* Individual firms are also reviewed by some of the large brokerage houses such as Merrill Lynch, Dean Witter Reynolds, and PaineWebber.

Knowledge of the opposition is not confined solely to an understanding of that organization's economic strengths and weaknesses. Part of the preparation can be an investigation of the personalities involved and the pressures to which the other side is subject. A thorough preparation for bargaining "may not point to specific answers in the bargaining. [It] can, however, help narrow the difference, reduce the area of controversy, and indicate the general range of a reasonable settlement."[3]

Sources of Data

Both sides usually compile economic data for bargaining purposes. Although the nature of the data varies, there is a basic statistical package that most negotiators find helpful. They try to assemble data on business conditions, the state of the economy, and terms of settlement in the region and the industry in question. They also gather statistics on wages, benefits, profitability, productivity, family budgets, and the Consumer Price Index. Data internal and external to the firm are also important to the bargaining process, both for the purpose of effective negotiations and for accurate costing of the agreement (see Table 8.1).

Before sitting down across the table, both sides have a fairly accurate picture of the cost of the existing bargaining package. In the case of a first contract, a breakdown of all existing labor costs is prepared. It is much easier for an employer than for a union to gather such data. In some instances, however, employers may be willing or compelled by the NLRB to share such information with their unions.[4] In preparing for bargaining, both parties attach importance to prevailing wage rates and benefits outside the bargaining unit. They try to gather such data from recent labor contracts negotiated within their labor market, their industry, and the economy at large. Sometimes employers compile such information from wage and benefit surveys. Under NLRB rulings, management may be compelled to share the results of such surveys with their unions. In a General Electric case, the company was directed to "furnish to the union correlated information concerning the respondent's area wage surveys and other information necessary to enable the union to bargain intelligently on rates of pay."[5]

Wage and benefit surveys can be useful tools for formulating wage proposals and anticipating the opposition's moves. Many employers conduct wage and benefit surveys by telephone or by mail. They usually seek information on base pay rates of various job classifications and on benefits. These surveys are commonly confined to the local area of the employer.

There are many additional sources for data that can be helpful to parties preparing for negotiations. According to Henderson, "Thousands of organizations annually collect data on jobs in various industries, on kinds of work performed and on specific occupations".[6] The U.S. Department of Labor, Bureau of Labor Statistics (BLS) is the cheapest

TABLE 8.1 Useful Bargaining Data

Internal to the Firm	*External to the Firm*
(1) Number of workers in each job classification	(1) Comparative industry wage rates
(2) Compensation per worker	(2) Comparative occupational wage rates
(3) Minimum and maximum pay in each job classification	(3) Comparative fringe benefits
(4) Overtime pay per hour and number of annual overtime hours worked by job classification	(4) Consumer price index
(5) Number of employees, by categories, who work on each shift[1]	(5) Patterns of relevant bargaining settlements
(6) Cost of shift differential premiums[1]	
(7) History of recent negotiations	
(8) Cost of fringe benefits	
(9) Cost-of-living increases	
(10) Vacation costs by years of service of employees	
(11) Demographic data on the bargaining unit members by sex, age, and seniority	
(12) Cost and duration of lunch breaks and rest periods	
(13) An outline of incentive, progression, evaluation, training, safety, and promotion plans[1]	
(14) Grievance and arbitration awards	

[1]If applicable.

and most acceptable source of survey results, wage and benefit data, and other pertinent information for collective bargaining purposes. The following BLS resources can be helpful to negotiators: *Compensation and Working Conditions, Industry Wage Surveys, Area Wage Surveys, Employment and Earnings,* and *News Releases on the Consumer Price Index* (CPI), a monthly report on consumer price movements.

A large number of organizations are engaged in wage survey activities. These include individual firms, employer and trade associations, Chambers of Commerce, the American Management Association, the Conference Board, private national and metropolitan consulting firms, unions, and the AFL-CIO, which enters the information collected in its computer bank. Other data sources are national publishers such as the Bureau of National Affairs (BNA) and Prentice Hall, which publish survey results concerning compensation practices. Henderson[7] provides an extensive list of business and professional journals, magazines, and organizations that conduct various types of compensation surveys.

Perhaps the most comprehensive source of comparative wage data is the federal government.

Industry Wage Surveys are a continuing series of reports based on BLS surveys of employment, occupational earnings, established practices, and supplementary benefits of nonsupervisory workers in selected large manufacturing and nonmanufacturing industries.[8]

Occupational Compensation Surveys are a series of BLS reports covering earnings and supplementary benefits for selected occupations. A major objective of the surveys is to describe the levels and distributions of occupational pay in a variety of the nation's local labor markets. Another goal of these surveys is to publish information on the incidence of employee benefits among and within local labor markets.[9]

Employment and Earnings (E.E.) is a monthly publication containing information on developments in employment and unemployment. The E.E. includes some of the following statistical tables: household data on employment status, characteristics of the employed and the unemployed and establishment data on national and state employment and on national hours and earnings by major industry and manufacturing group.[10]

The *Consumer Price Index (CPI) Detailed Report* is a monthly publication providing information on consumer price movements. The report covers two indexes: the CPI for all urban consumers (CPI-U) and the CPI for wage earners and clerical workers (CPI-W). The indexes reflect data for the U.S. city average and selected areas.[11]

THE VALUE OF ECONOMIC DATA

A word of caution is appropriate regarding the use of economic data: Too much stress on such data may involve the parties in long academic debates regarding value and applicability of data and methodology rather than in negotiations over the terms of the contract. Economic data, even if elaborately compiled and impressively presented, are not necessarily applicable or pertinent to every argument at the bargaining table. Some of the available government statistics are outdated, and presentation based on such data may be irrelevant. Probably the most important function of data collection lies in enabling the parties to place the economic terms of the contract in a comparative framework. Relevant data allow them to compare the wages and benefits of the bargaining unit members to others in similar occupations, industries, and areas of the country.

Negotiators tend to present biased statistical data and to leave out material that could provide a balanced picture. A deterrent to that approach would be an agreement between the parties, at the beginning of negotiations, on sources of economic data to be utilized. Such an agreement could provide an incentive for negotiators to use data selectively to support specific arguments rather than applying it in a shotgun manner.

It is advisable for negotiators not to rely on one-sided data or on weak and questionable statistics. To do so can be counterproductive and lead to a loss of credibility, an important ingredient at the bargaining table. One author states that "being caught in an error means losing the initiative."[12] Apart from presenting arguments based on their own data, negotiators should also be prepared to respond to unfavorable material presented by the opposition.

Preparation of economic data for bargaining purposes is a major task for both union and management. Negotiators differ on the importance of such material in negotiations. Some union and employer representatives claim that economic data are useless at the bargaining table, that the only thing that counts is bargaining power. This view is not shared by the majority of negotiators. Some management negotiators consider economic data a means of keeping union demands "within competitive limits." Some feel that "without factual information, the results may easily be less satisfactory to all."[13]

According to most negotiators, the bargaining status of economic data is not as prominent as it should be. This situation, however, is changing. In the last 10 years, negotiators have begun referring to economic data with much greater frequency, and this trend is most likely to continue. Escalating health care costs, cost-of-living provisions, supplementary unemployment benefits, guaranteed annual income programs, pensions, and other benefit plans all contribute to the significance of economic data in bargaining. Such data provide important constraints within which the parties must operate.

Although today's negotiators are armed with considerably more economic data and statistics than were their counterparts 20 or 30 years ago, the data, still used in a partisan manner, are seldom utilized by both sides "as the basis for arriving at agreement."[14] The parties spend an inordinate amount of time arguing over relevancy, validity, assumptions, and interpretation of statistics. This preoccupation with data can slow down the bargaining process and at times can impose unnecessary obstacles to potential settlements.

Chamberlain and Kuhn suggest that the bargaining process is adversely affected if economic data are used primarily as ammunition for debate. That approach leads to reliance on one-sided material, which may be valuable for scoring debating points, but its usefulness in obtaining bargaining concessions is highly questionable. As a result, credibility of all material can become suspect even if it is obtained from independent research sources.

Some negotiators claim that economic data can be beneficial to both sides and can help build a better relationship between unions and management. A first step in this direction could be the involvement of the parties in joint research activities. Together they could develop a data bank of economic information that both sides could use. Chamberlain and Kuhn suggest that parties establish "joint fact-finding commissions, either permanent or ad hoc in nature; or joint employment of impartial third-party investigators."[15] The availability of data acceptable to both sides would help reduce conflict over data, but without eliminating it completely. Even the most legitimate data are subject to different interpretations and value judgments, each side trying to interpret the data on terms that will be most advantageous to its bargaining position. Even where a firm is willing to open its financial records to the union in order to prove its weak financial condition, there is still disagreement over the interpretation of such records, and the assistance of outside parties might prove very useful in the context of preparation for bargaining.

BARGAINING BOOKS

Over the years, labor agreements have grown in complexity, size, and number of clauses. To cope with the vast quantity of data, many negotiators keep records or journals of all relevant information regarding each clause or section of a contract. The content of such journals is sometimes compiled into a comprehensive set of materials referred to as the *bargaining book* ("B book").[16]

The B book can be organized into binders or into separate files on a personal computer disk. The information can be separated by subject matter or by contract article. With proper indexing, the data required can be quickly retrieved, updated, replaced, or deleted. The personal computer has helped many negotiators not only in organizing information but also in preparing and modifying bargaining proposals. The computer disk can also be used for storage of negotiating documents, rough notes, minutes of negotiation sessions, and information on costs of various proposals. Although the balance of this section refers to bargaining books, many negotiators now use personal computers rather than paper binders for maintaining bargaining records.

Some B books include detailed instructions and outlines for negotiators; however, few organizations preprogram their negotiators with detailed scripts. As a guideline for negotiators, some B books contain a priority designation code for each clause of the contract.

B books can be structured in a number of different ways. The National Industrial Conference Board[17] illustrates several ways for negotiators to organize them. A bargaining book may contain only existing contract clauses and proposed changes (with reasons for the changes) but exclude any known or anticipated demands from the other side. Sometimes negotiators will retain the existing wording of a particular clause while changing its interpretation. The new interpretation would be included in the book and could be a subject of discussion at the bargaining table. Some books are structured according to anticipated or known demands from the other side together with the party's intended responses and reasons. In some books, evaluation of contract clauses extends to comparisons with contract terms in other bargaining units. Some B books contain internal payroll data, demographic factors, and other relevant statistics generated within the organization. Such books may also encompass economic and statistical data, evaluations of earnings, cost of living information, wage trends, and benefits developments within the industry and the overall economy.

A study of management preparation for collective bargaining by Ryder et al.[18] states that B books of some large corporations may include the following material for each contract clause: (1) the wording and history of each clause as it has appeared in successive contracts; (2) evaluation of similarities and differences between the clause and its counterparts in other contracts in the industry; (3) internal inputs regarding the clause such as special problems, interpretations, correspondence, grievances, and their disposition; (4) legal status of the clause in terms of NLRB and court decisions; (5) suggested changes in determination of maximum and minimum positions; (6) outline of past union demands and arguments relevant to the clause, as well as management's response, with reasons; (7) statistical evidence and cost estimates, where applicable, and any other material upholding a particular bargaining position; and (8) status of negotiations regarding each clause and copies of any drafts and arguments presented at the table.

B books are advantageous to negotiators before, during, at the conclusion of, and after negotiations.[19] Before the start of negotiations, the book helps negotiators focus on problem areas that may arise in negotiations. It also helps them anticipate and respond to the moves of the opposition. The book can facilitate the conduct of negotiations in a more organized and orderly manner. Through its cross-reference system, it can help negotiators obtain pertinent information quickly.

According to a study by the Conference Board,[20] B books encourage concentration on one item at a time. Negotiators can avoid bringing up too many items simultaneously for fear of forgetting them. A well-organized book protects negotiators and gives them a certain sense of security. They know that nothing will be overlooked, that each item will be discussed at the proper time if they follow the B book outline.

In some negotiations, significant time is devoted to arguments about the date when a particular clause was amended or adopted, and a B book containing background on each clause can reduce debates over issues that are readily verifiable. The book can also help avert impasses over troublesome or emotional issues. Problems can be put aside and resurrected when the chances for an agreement are improved. The B book can help speed the bargaining process. Issues can be resolved faster if research has been completed in advance and if there is no need for long postponements to gather data. Also, the presence of a data file on each clause brings the parties down from generalities to specifics.

The B book permits negotiators to review at any time the overall status of negotiations and the progress made toward an agreement. This review is facilitated by blank spaces in the book in which negotiators can make notes on clauses on which agreement has been reached.

Poorly prepared negotiators tend to be defensive. This attitude in turn can lead to stalemates, accusations, confrontations, and emotionalism, all of which impede bargaining. The B book can be a confidence builder for negotiators. By providing them with information and arguments for answering the opposition, it bolsters their sense of security and self-assurance, a valuable asset at the bargaining table.

The book can reduce the workload of the chief negotiator by making it possible to divide responsibility for different parts of the contract among members of the bargaining team. Also, in case someone departs from the team, it facilitates the task of familiarizing the successor with the responsibilities of the position.

The B book can also be of value at the end of negotiations and during the life of the contract. It is much easier and faster to draft the final version of the contract if all changes and agreed-upon clauses can be abstracted from one central source. Also, many questions and problems relating to the interpretation and administration of the contract are raised during its life. The B book, if it includes summaries of intent and arguments, can provide valuable guidance and assistance in contract administration.

Although both sides may have at their disposal comprehensive B books (or computer disks), those resources are not necessarily brought to the bargaining table. Negotiators usually like to approach the table with as little material as possible. They may simply bring along folders covering clauses on the day's bargaining agenda, or they may have laptop computers. Comprehensive B books, when available, are usually kept out of sight. Many negotiators feel that their counterparts would view such material as a crutch, and this in turn could reduce their effectiveness at the table. When neutral territory like a hotel is chosen as the negotiation site, both parties may house their research and advisory staffs and keep their B books and/or computer disks in adjoining rooms. In case a team needs to consult those sources, it can call a recess and adjourn to the next room.

Not everyone is convinced of the value of B books. Some negotiators and their principals claim to be familiar enough with the contract that they do not need B books. Some negotiators and their superiors feel that the cost of preparation of B books is higher than the benefits obtained. When such material is brought to negotiations, it creates a formal atmosphere, which may have an adverse effect on spontaneity and creativity, restricting the parties in their search for new solutions to existing problems. Because it is more common for management to come equipped with bargaining books, the union team may feel threatened by a too-well-prepared opposition. Its insecurity may express itself in aggressive behavior that could lead to a breakdown of negotiations. One employer representative who was critical of B books stated that such a book gives the union team "the impression that all the company arguments are manufactured and are ersatz, and makes the presentation too formal when it should be casual."[21]

To conclude, a B book or a computer disk is a useful source of information; one should probably be prepared by each side and be updated continuously. It should be kept away from the bargaining table and out of sight of the opposition. The negotiators should bring to the bargaining table only data necessary for the day's discussion. Recently, in many organizations, the B book has been superseded by the personal computer and the B disk.

OTHER DATA USED IN PREPARATION FOR BARGAINING

In preparation for bargaining and as a guideline for formulation of bargaining proposals, unions and managements collect and review information on labor relations and wages as well as financial, statistical, and economic data. In addition, one of the best guides for preparation of bargaining proposals is the study of existing contracts. Useful sources of information about the strength and weakness of an existing agreement include (1) analysis of grievances and arbitration awards, (2) review of the content of other agreements and exchange of information with other firms and unions, and (3) input from supervisors, employees, and stewards. In the following sections, these three sources are examined.

Grievances and Arbitration Awards

An examination of grievances and inside arbitration awards is an important phase of bargaining preparations. Grievances can be analyzed for problem areas related to text or ambiguity of contract language; specifically, they can be examined as to content and causes.

Grievances can reflect difficulties in contract administration and interpretation. A study of grievances enables management and unions to develop contract modification proposals.

Grievances can be classified according to the contract clauses under which they are filed. If a particular clause is responsible for too many grievances, either side may try to have it modified. To obtain a quick reference to troublesome areas, management sometimes prepares a frequency distribution of grievances by the contract provisions under which they occur. An evaluation of this subject need not be confined to contract provisions that contribute to the filing of grievances. Such review can also extend to clauses that have the potential to generate grievances but have not yet done so. Moreover, trouble-free provisions may provide valuable lessons for the drafting of future contract language.

A study of in-house arbitration awards can provide useful guidelines for revision of existing agreements. Unfavorable awards provide clues as to weaknesses and needs for modification of contract language. Furthermore, some understandings reached during arbitration proceedings can be incorporated into new contracts.

The analysis of grievances and arbitration awards can be supplemented by an examination of contract violations, such as work stoppages, slowdowns, and activities leading to disciplinary sanctions. Contract violations may be symptomatic of employee discontent with the contract.

Content of Other Contracts and Exchange of Information with Other Organizations

In preparing for negotiations, both sides pay considerable attention to wages and benefits specified in other contracts. Management monitors labor relations developments in other organizations by reviewing labor contracts as well as by interacting and exchanging information with officials of other firms. Labor relations executives communicate by telephone, at meetings, and through surveys of employers in a particular region or industry. In some industries, the trade or industry association can act as a clearinghouse for labor relations data. Conventions and periodic meetings of labor relations professionals provide further opportunities for exchange of information. Correspondingly, unions also share data and intelligence with other unions and among their own locals. Pattern developments within industries or new approaches to difficult topics of bargaining are communicated during union conventions and through the offices of the AFL-CIO.

Input from Supervisors and Stewards

No labor agreement is perfect, and none can incorporate answers to all possible problems that may arise during contract administration. However, as Santayana once said, those who do not learn from history are condemned to repeat it. If an existing contract has generated too many operating problems, one way of reducing them is to find out which contract clauses are responsible and try to modify them in future agreements.

Because first-line supervisors and stewards most frequently encounter and respond to potential problems related to a collective agreement, they can be an invaluable source of information regarding contract weaknesses and strengths. Their reactions and views can be helpful in the formulation of bargaining proposals. The National Industrial Conference Board cites four methods for soliciting input from supervisors: the meeting, the questionnaire, the interview, and the contract booklet.[22] Although unions tend to be much less formal in their approach to information gathering of this type, the regular stewards' meeting can serve the same function and can provide important information on the existing labor agreement. The stewards' knowledge of the viability of the contract tends to parallel that of first-line supervisors.

One approach for gathering contract information from supervisors is a small-group meeting with a discussion leader who facilitates a critical examination of each provision of the agreement. In a variation on this approach, a number of small committees meet to evaluate the content of the contract, then report to a general meeting of all supervisors. The recommendations of all the committees are discussed, evaluated, modified, ignored, supplemented with additional suggestions, and possibly adopted. The resulting recommendations for action are forwarded to the appropriate officials. Still another way to gather input from supervisors is continuously to monitor their reactions to and views on the current contract. This is a preferable avenue of action because it minimizes the possibility of arriving at recommendations in an atmosphere charged with emotion, such as frequently prevails before negotiations.

Some employers, instead of conducting meetings or as a supplement to meetings, use questionnaires to elicit supervisors' reactions to various parts of the contract. Such a questionnaire would list certain contract provisions and ask supervisors to approve, disapprove, or suggest modification of the clauses in question.[23] A variation on the questionnaire is the use of professional interviewers. The advantage of this approach is that skilled professionals meeting with supervisors can obtain information that is potentially more valuable than data acquired through questionnaires. The main disadvantage is cost.

The self-esteem of lower-level supervisors improves when they are asked to participate; they feel part of management. Some employers also report that suggestions from supervisors are helpful in the areas of discipline, seniority, and wage payment as well as in the clarification and interpretation of contract language. Not every employer considers the input from supervisors to be useful for purposes of proposal formulation. Some managers feel that lower-level supervisors are concerned primarily with the impact of the contract on their own operations and tend to ignore cost implications. Some employers also see supervisors as too emotional to be helpful. Despite these criticisms, supervisors can make valuable contributions in the formulation of bargaining proposals.

FORMULATION OF PROPOSALS

Unions and management exhibit similarities and differences in proposal preparation. Both sides carefully review the current contract, searching for weaknesses, strengths, and potential modifications. Changes in legislation may also necessitate amendment of existing contract terms.

In the past, unions were on the offensive, with management attempting to maintain the status quo. In the last 15 years, management has become more aggressive, demanding contract revisions not only as a negotiation tactic and as a trading currency but in a real and, at times, successful effort to change existing contract terms.

One similarity between union and management in contract preparation involves sources of information. Management seeks information from the foreman and the first-line supervisors; the union is briefed by shop stewards and business agents. Here, however, the parallelism ends. A union, as a democratic organization with elected officers, devotes more attention to internal responses than does management. The employer is essentially authoritarian, with the highest levels of management ultimately deciding on the offer to be made to the union. This does not mean, however, that the upper echelons of a large organization can ignore internal reactions to a potential contract. Although upper management possesses a high degree of authority, as a matter of good governance it tries not to be too arbitrary or dictatorial. To manage effectively, top executives must consider the interests of the various pressure groups that exist within every organization. Interests and personalities differ considerably among divisions and departments; interests may need to be reconciled and personalities addressed for purposes of contract negotiation.

Failure to take account of these needs could lead to internal conflict and adverse consequences. This matter is particularly important in view of the recent trend towards empowerment and implementation of workplace participation processes.

Formulation of Management Proposals

A firm is a dynamic entity, and its production methods, equipment, technology, labor-to-capital ratio, product mix, and organizational structure are subject to change. These changes must be taken into account when proposals are prepared.

When asked how far in advance they start preparing for a forthcoming negotiation, labor relations officers usually state, "The day after the current agreement is signed."[24] Although this may be the case in some companies, in most firms preparations begin three to nine months before the start of negotiations. The average preparation period for large multiplant companies is nine months.[25] Smaller firms employing professional negotiators spend three to four months in preparation for bargaining.

In a 1993 article, Thomas and Wisdom[26] propose a number of steps for management to take in preparation for negotiation in the nineties. The authors consider preparation an investment and not just a cost.[27] Preparation is not only a process of collecting data on legal developments, economic trends, grievance activity, and the like; it also provides a means of obtaining a better view of any organizational problems that may require some remedial action. The authors suggest that the organizational mission be identified. The offers made by management should be governed by "organizational goals and objectives."[28] The bargaining book, or a "clause book,"[29] which contains a chronology of revisions of contract language, can help negotiators clarify organizational aspirations. The article suggests that preparation for labor negotiations should not only be the responsibility of labor relations staff, corporate attorneys, and labor consultants but should involve the whole management team in deciding on bargaining goals.

Management's preparation of proposals is a two-stage process. In the first stage, data are collected and analyzed. In the second stage, decisions are made as to the types of proposals to be presented at the bargaining table. Responsibility for the first stage of preparation usually rests with the labor relations department, which is charged with the drafting of contract proposals. The text may be sent for review and comments to various levels of management. Furthermore, the text is reviewed and, if necessary, modified by in-house or outside lawyers. Negotiators do not always appreciate the legal contribution because lawyers tend to introduce too much technical jargon and legalism into bargaining. In some negotiations, opposing lawyers battle over language and technicalities rather than over substance. Extensive participation of lawyers in bargaining not only is costly but may also be detrimental to the negotiating process.

Large multiplant corporations have labor relations departments at the corporate, division, and local plant levels; the distribution of responsibility among these departments depends on the organizational and bargaining structure of the corporation. In some firms, the major responsibility for bargaining preparation is vested with the corporate-level department; in others, the focus of activity may be at the divisional or plant level. Local autonomy would be more common in firms that negotiate separate agreements for each division or plant rather than having master contracts.

Management's decision-making mechanisms vary considerably among firms. Ryder et al.[30] state that in firms where one international union represents a large proportion of the company's blue-collar work force, corporate executives participate fully in the decision-making process. In firms organized on a divisional basis, where each division serves a different product market and union strength is confined to individual divisions, the decision-making authority is vested at the local level. In the latter situation, corporate officers and labor relations experts provide guidelines and act as consultants to local management. In some firms, labor relations departments are responsible for formulating proposals subject to approval from above. In other firms, various aspects of the contract are reviewed by different groups, which collect and analyze data and prepare recommendations on contract proposals. Such groups may be composed of representatives from labor relations, production, finance, and marketing.[31]

According to Ryder et al.,[32] labor relations managers exert a major influence on "management's pre-bargaining decisions," particularly in the area of noneconomic aspects of the contract, but their influence also extends to economic issues.

Within the corporate structure, authority for the final decision usually rests with corporate officers, particularly the president. Although the president usually has the final say, in some large firms many contract decisions are made by various executives. Boards of directors commonly stay out of labor relations, particularly in the prebargaining stage. In many firms, decisions regarding bargaining proposals are made by labor relations officers or executive committees trusted by top management.[33]

Some contracts are negotiated by employer associations. The association negotiators frequently possess broad discretion in the noneconomic area. They are also influential in decisions regarding economic issues, but the final word rests with their clients.

Opinions differ among labor relations managers as to whether it is productive to formulate specific contract language ahead of negotiations. An objection is that doing so hardens the positions of negotiators before issues are properly reviewed. Contract provisions prepared in advance can be counterproductive when creative solutions are needed. In situations where management negotiators do prepare written contract articles preceding negotiations, they first explore the subject matter before presenting their written terms to the other side. Some management negotiators offer written proposals only in response to union demands. Another argument against advance preparation of written articles is the potential for leaks, which can produce unnecessary accusations before the start of bargaining. There is also the fear that written proposals may generate a strong union counterattack.[34] Although there are lengthy discussions among labor relations experts regarding the value of written proposals, many employers nevertheless prepare written contract language in advance, as well as fallback positions in case their first choices are rejected.

Employers preparing written contract language find the process useful for purposes of critical evaluation of any potential agreement. Some employers submit their version of the contract to the union in the early stages of bargaining, claiming that it provides a better focus for negotiations. Some negotiators favor an exchange of written proposals, which makes it easier to detect and concentrate on problem areas. Some employers also think that unions with a tendency to distort employers' positions publicly have more difficulty doing so when proposals are in written form.

Formulation of Union Proposals

Unions require data from a variety of sources in formulating bargaining demands. For example, in formulating its demands, the UAW considers the following factors: level of economic activity, stage of the business cycle, economic forecasts, relationship between prices and wages, real earnings of workers, and unemployment levels within specific groups and in the overall economy. Although "the data are not the primary determinant of the demands" that a union makes, they do help the union to "find solutions to problems that arise in shaping demands at the bargaining table."[35]

The UAW wants its negotiators to have all the financial and economic data that will be significant for negotiations. The necessary data are gathered from such sources as company reports to stockholders and to the Securities and Exchange Commission; registration statements; prospectuses; industry statistics; and any materials providing information on sales, profits, financial resources, employment prospects, and industry trends.

One problem confronted by all users of data is that of availability and reliability. It is probably more of a problem for unions than for employers because of the confidential nature of employer materials. Unions have difficulty obtaining from employers productivity figures as well as other information that would be relevant for bargaining. The problem of availability is particularly acute when it comes to negotiation of new programs or modifications of old ones: In some cases, the necessary data have never been compiled.

Corporate publications could be more helpful to unions in negotiations if they contained the following: information on profitability, labor costs, and plant and corporate productivity; separate data for wages, salaries, and fringes; breakdowns between direct and indirect labor costs; figures on hours worked and hours compensated; statistics on prices, sales, and distribution expenses; data on advertising costs and on research and development expenses; information on management compensation packages; clear separations between operating and nonoperating revenues and expenses; and more detail on specific product line and geographic breakdowns.[36]

Another problem facing unions concerns the reliability and consistency of accounting reports. Accounting procedures are not standardized among firms, and the lack of uniformity makes intercompany comparisons difficult. Firms do not use identical inventory valuation procedures or depreciation methods. Differences in accounting methodology can account for differences in reported profits rather than in "underlying profitability."

The reliability of employment and unemployment statistics published by the U.S. Department of Labor can also be questioned. There is a discrepancy between the two employment series, one based on household interviews, the other on a survey of establishment payrolls. Unions would like to see these two series more compatible. Another problem for unions is the availability of current government data; most of the data are out of date at release time.

Unions turn to many sources in formulating their demands. They consider economic conditions; their own accomplishments with other employers; and contracts negotiated by other unions within the region, the industry, and the economy. They study grievances, complaints, and arbitration awards for clues to problem areas under existing contracts. To determine rank-and-file priorities and expectations, they hold membership meetings; conduct employee surveys; and interview shop stewards, business agents, and active union members.

The process of formulating demands differs among single- and multilocation and multiemployer bargaining units.[37] Some single-location units appoint committees charged with proposal formulation. If the unit is affiliated with a national union, a representative of the national will usually be a committee member. Such a committee, after arriving at a set of proposals, presents them at a regular or special general membership meeting for discussion, amendment, rejection, or adoption. Proposals approved by the membership are presented as demands to the employer. Rank and file do not necessarily participate directly in the formulation of demands in every union local. In some instances, membership meetings are just formalities, and membership input is obtained informally and selectively. In such a bargaining unit, the demand formulation committee plays a crucial role in deciding on the types of demands to be presented to the employer.[38] In some local unions, formulation of demands is left to business agents, who consult one another as well as union officers and rank-and-file members. This approach is utilized in the construction industry,[39] whose nature in terms of seasonality, major fluctuations in labor force, and mobility of workers among job sites and employers makes the business agent a stable force in a mobile environment.

Formulation of demands is more complex in multilocation units. In those units, the town meeting approach, which may be appropriate in a single unit, has been modified in favor of a representative government model. Under that model, the bargaining proposal committee is composed of elected representatives of all the locals within the multilocation unit. The larger the multilocation unit, the more complex the process of delegating authority. In some instances, locals elect representatives to regional committees, which in turn make recommendations to a national committee that is responsible for formulating final proposals for submission to management.

Although the rank and file in multilocation units do not participate directly in the approval of final bargaining demands, the membership provides input in the initial stages. Usually, local committees formulate proposals subject to membership approval. The local demands are communicated upward to local delegates appointed to regional or national committees. These delegates are expected to defend and represent local interests.

The national union, even when negotiations are conducted locally, exerts significant influence on local demand formulation, particularly on complex issues. The national can also provide representation at the bargaining table, offer research and computer facilities, supply advice, set minimum standards on specific issues, and extend negotiation help. In general, the national may exercise its authority on the nature and content of major demands.

Two types of union demands appear at the bargaining table. First are the traditional demands for improvement in existing wages and benefits and requests for concession on noneconomic issues. Such demands include a union attempt to keep up with the achievements of other bargaining units. Second are the pioneering demands that a union may present. These are proposals for concessions never before granted to the union or to any other union. Although bargaining may be intense on the first type of demands, the hardest task confronting negotiators is achieving a breakthrough on pioneering demands. It is much harder to convince management to grant concessions on provisions that do not appear in other contracts. No firm wants to be the first to give in on a new issue. In some instances, the foundation for a new demand is built over a number of years, and the theme is repeated in successive negotiations. When a new demand is introduced for the first time, both sides usually recognize that no agreement will be reached. However, a gradual approach helps lower management's resistance and eventually may culminate in union success. Hence, the more sophisticated unions engage in long-term planning in formulating and presenting innovative demands. They usually avoid building up high membership expectations and keep a low profile on such issues. This approach averts face-saving problems on proposals that may be difficult to deliver on the first round.

STRATEGIC PREPARATIONS FOR BARGAINING

Unions' and employers' preparations for bargaining are not confined to data collection and proposal formulation. They also extend to strategic moves by both parties. According to Walton and McKersie,[40] the purpose of these strategies is to manipulate the "strike cost of party and opponent."

Thomas and Wisdom[41] recommend that management be prepared for a potential strike. To reduce the possibility of a strike and be ready for it if it materializes, management can take a number of precautionary measures: (1) It can build up inventories; (2) it can train managers and nonunion employees to substitute for striking employees; (3) it can locate subcontractors who could do some of the work of the striking employees; (4) it can make plans for hiring replacements for the striking employees (a very sensitive issue for union-management relations); and (5) in negotiating a contract, it can try to time the contract expiration date to fall in a relatively slow season and thus increase its bargaining power. Other prenegotiation tactics that employers can use are transfer of production to plants not affected by negotiations, mutual assistance agreements with other firms in the industry, and buildup of financial resources.

Inventory stockpiling cannot be employed in every industry, and not every firm that might benefit from it has the necessary financial resources to use it. It has been applied in steel and coal but would be futile in the fashion or perishable goods industry. The size of the inventory buildup can communicate to the union the duration of a potential strike that an employer could tolerate. Modern production and just-in-time inventory control methods will likely make stockpiling a more problematic bargaining tactic.

The effectiveness of the threat of transfer of production to other facilities depends on the likelihood of its being carried out. A threat of a transfer of cement production from Maine to Oregon would obviously lack credibility because cement, because of high transportation cost, is usually produced relatively close to its markets. However, the presence of a geographically close cement plant with excess capacity would make such a threat plausible and effective. Thus, the potency of this strategy depends on the capacity and location of alternative production sites that would not be directly affected by the outcome of negotiations. As a prenegotiation strategy, it is not necessary actually to transfer any production; it is usually sufficient for an employer to make the appropriate transfer arrangements and communicate them to the union.

An assistance pact with other firms in the same industry is still another strategy available to employers. The assistance can take the form of financial or production aid. In the airline industry, prior to 1979, struck firms were eligible for financial help from other companies in the industry. In 1979 Congress, in enacting the Air Deregulation Act, outlawed the mutual aid pact in this industry.

A further strategy utilized by employers is building up financial resources before the start of negotiations. This can be accomplished in a number of ways. The firm may issue new stock or bonds, or it may announce an increased line of bank credit. The intent of such a move is to communicate to the opposition the ability to tolerate a strike. The company, in effect, tells the union, "If you push us too far, we have the financial stamina to absorb the work stoppage."

The union, for its part, has an arsenal of strategies to weaken employer resistance. Accumulating a large strike fund, entering into mutual assistance pacts, increasing workers' solidarity, conducting strike votes, encouraging savings, securing other sources of income,[42] and accumulating grievances are examples of union bargaining strategies.

A usual first step for unions is the buildup of large strike funds. Special membership assessments or mutual assistance pacts with other unions can help out the union treasury. Although the strike fund may seem large in absolute dollars, in many instances such a fund contains only enough money to cover a few weeks' wages. Another approach to the building up of union financial resources is the Dubinsky approach, from the garment industry:

> Tradition has it that David Dubinsky sometimes opened a campaign to organize garment workers in a new area by depositing a substantial sum to the account of the union in a leading local bank. His well-founded assumption was that word of the deposit would reach the ears of the local garment manufacturer who would assume that the union was able to finance a long strike and [the manufacturer] would capitulate. Too late did they learn that the entire sum was borrowed on the express condition that it be returned intact after serving its psychological purpose.[43]

Before negotiations, the union builds up rank-and-file support and worker solidarity. Membership meetings, letters to members, articles in the union press, and informal discussions all emphasize the significance of solidarity and warn of the danger of divisiveness and factionalism. Usually, the most impressive statement of union cohesiveness is the strike vote, which a union may seek before the start of negotiations. A vote in which a high percentage of voters authorize strike action is interpreted as an expression of solidarity and confidence in the union. The outcome of such a vote is quickly communicated to management. In most such votes, the majority of union members provide the union with the necessary strike authorization not because they are willing to strike but in order to strengthen the union's hand in bargaining.

To strengthen workers' ability to survive financially during a strike, unions urge workers to build up their savings accounts. Union newspapers and union officers plead with members to step up their rate of saving. Members receive guidelines on amounts to put aside. In smaller communities, word of the success of such campaigns and of any increases in employee savings is quickly passed on by the local bankers to the affected employers.

In some communities, advance arrangements are made with local merchants, landlords, and financial institutions so they will assist the workers financially in case of a strike. This approach strengthens the union's bargaining position and communicates to the opposition its willingness to strike if a satisfactory settlement cannot be secured.

In some small communities with strong local and family ties, union officers try to find private sponsors who, in case of a strike, would provide support to striking employees. Under such sponsorship arrangements, families whose members work for nonstriking firms accept responsibility for helping out striking workers.

As additional insurance against hardships during strikes and as a strategic measure, unions try to develop other sources of income for their members. They can accomplish this by finding alternative employment opportunities or persuading legislators to provide strikers with better unemployment benefits. Still another prenegotiation strategy that is popular with some unions is the accumulation of grievances just before negotiations, to be used as a trading currency in bargaining.

SUMMARY

This chapter detailed the procedures that unions and managements can follow in preparation for collective bargaining. The parties have many important decisions to make before negotiations begin; those decisions can profoundly affect the success of bargaining.

Each side must decide who will sit on the negotiating committee and what each person's role should be. Bargaining proposals must be carefully formulated and thoroughly researched to be effective. An example of what can happen if proposals are not worded carefully occurred in the 1987 negotiations between the United Auto Workers and General Motors. That contract guaranteed that no plants would be closed during the life of the agreement. The UAW was quite upset when four plants were permanently idled "but not closed."[44]

The chapter examined the value of economic data in bargaining, reviewed the application of bargaining books and computers to negotiations, and evaluated strategic preparations. A more extensive discussion of bargaining strategy and tactics will be presented in Chapter 9.

Notes

1. Charles S. Loughran, *Negotiating a Labor Contract: A Management Handbook,* 2nd ed. (Washington, DC: Bureau of National Affairs, 1992), pp. 50–61.

2. *Collective Bargaining: Lining Up the Facts,* pamphlet reprinted from AFL-CIO *American Federationist,* March 1972.

3. Ibid.

4. John Gaal, "The Disclosure of Financial Information: Competitiveness and the Current Requirements of the Duty to Bargain in Good Faith," *Labor Law Journal* 10 (September 1987), pp. 562–73.

5. *General Electric Co. & International Union of Electrical, Radio and Machine Workers, AFL-CIO,* 192 NLRB 68 (July 14, 1971).

6. Richard I. Henderson, *Compensation Management,* 6th ed. (Englewood Cliffs, NJ: Prentice Hall, 1994), p. 343.

7. Ibid., pp. 348–52.

8. *Industry Wage Surveys,* published by the U.S. Department of Labor, Bureau of Labor Statistics: a series of bulletins covering various industries, e.g., department stores, petroleum refining, hospitals, and many others. See also *BLS Publication Index* and *American Statistics Index,* Congressional Information Service Inc. (CIS), a comprehensive guide to the statistical publications of the U.S. Government.

9. *Occupational Compensation Surveys on Local Labor Markets;* a series of separate bulletins published by the U.S. Department of Labor, Bureau of Labor Statistics. See also the CIS guide described in note 8.

10. *Employment and Earnings* (Washington DC: U.S. Department of Labor, Bureau of Labor Statistics), monthly.

11. *CPI Detailed Report* (Washington, DC: U.S. Department of Labor, Bureau of Labor Statistics), monthly.

12. James F. Honzik, "Assembling the Facts" in *Dealing with a Union,* LeRoy Marceau, ed. (New York: American Management Association, 1969), p. 65.

13. Neil W. Chamberlain and James W. Kuhn, *Collective Bargaining,* 2nd ed. (New York: McGraw-Hill, 1965), p. 75.

14. Ibid.

15. Ibid., p. 78.

16. Meyer S. Ryder, Charles M. Rhemus, and Sanford Cohen, *Management Preparation for Collective Bargaining* (Homewood, IL: Dow Jones–Irwin, 1966), p. 62. See also Maurice B. Better, *Contract Bargaining Handbook for Local Union Leaders* (Washington, DC:) Bureau of National Affairs, 1993), p. 54. See also Loughran, op. cit.

17. *Preparing for Collective Bargaining,* Studies in Personnel Policy No. 172 (New York: National Industrial Conference Board, 1959), pp. 35–39.

18. Ryder et al., op. cit., pp. 64, 65.

19. James J. Bambrick Jr. and Marie P. Dorbandt, "The Use of Bargaining Books in Negotiations," *Management Record* 19, no. 4 (April 1957), pp. 118–45.

20. *Preparing for Collective Bargaining,* op. cit., p. 36.

21. Ibid., p. 37.

22. Ibid., pp. 46–48.

23. Ibid.

24. Ryder et al., op. cit., p. 45.

25. Ibid., p. 48.

26. Steven L. Thomas and Barry L. Wisdom, "Labor Negotiations in the Nineties: Five Steps toward Total Preparation," *SAM Advanced Management Journal* 58, no. 4 (Autumn 1993), pp. 32–47.

27. Ibid., p. 33.

28. Ibid.

29. Ibid.

30. Ryder et al., op. cit., p. 27.

31. Ibid., p. 25.

32. Ibid., p. 43.

33. Ibid., p. 44.

34. Ibid., p. 55.

35. Odessa Komer, International Vice-President, United Auto Workers, "The Role of Data in Collective Bargaining," *1978 Proceedings, Sixth Annual Meeting, Society of Professionals in Dispute Resolution,* October 29–November 1, 1978, pp. 118–24.

36. Ibid.

37. Robert R. France, *Union Decisions in Collective Bargaining* (Princeton, NJ: Princeton University, Industrial Relations Section, 1955), pp. 18–20.

38. Ibid., pp. 19–20.

39. Bevars D. Mabry, *Labor Relations and Collective Bargaining* (New York: Ronald Press, 1966), p. 300.

40. Richard E. Walton and Robert B. McKersie, *Behavioral Theory of Labor Negotiations,* 2nd ed. (Ithaca, NY: ILR Press, 1991), pp. 75–82.

41. Thomas and Wisdom, op. cit.

42. Walton and McKersie, op. cit., pp. 79–81.

43. Alfred Kuhn, *Labor Institutions and Economics,* rev. ed. (New York: Harcourt, Brace & World, 1967), p. 171.

44. Gregory A. Patterson and Joseph B. White, "GM-UAW Pact Allows Company to Cut Payroll in Return for Worker Buy-Outs," *Wall Street Journal,* September 19, 1990, p. 3; Doron P. Levin, "Contract Enhancing Job Security Is Agreed On by Union and G.M.," *New York Times,* September 18, 1990, p. A20.

CHAPTER 9

The Negotiation Process

After reading this chapter, you should be able to

- Explain why the location of negotiations has tactical implications.

- Identify the important factors relevant to the bargaining procedure and their effects on bargaining.

- Distinguish among illegal, voluntary, and mandatory subjects of bargaining and give examples of each.

- Discuss and describe the four stages of the negotiation process.

- Explain and review the integrative aspects of bargaining, referring to Follett and to Walton and McKersie.

- Discuss and evaluate the criticisms of mutual gains bargaining.

BARGAINING PROCEDURE

This section reviews procedural issues that negotiations must address before bargaining over substance can begin. The parties must agree on a mutually acceptable bargaining procedure. The following can be classified as procedural issues: (1) bargaining location; (2) agenda sequence; (3) authority to make firm commitments; (4) working draft to be used; and (5) procedure during negotiations—schedule, caucuses, record keeping, confidentiality, and status of articles settled.

Bargaining Location

One of the first issues to be resolved in any negotiations is where the talks will occur. The three obvious possibilities are on the territory of one side or the other or on a neutral site. The neutral site could be a hotel or any other public or private facility. The location depends to some extent on the level of negotiations. In multiplant or multiemployer bargaining, the parties usually select a neutral site. On the other hand, small single-plant employers usually negotiate on their own premises.

There are a number of advantages and disadvantages to holding negotiations in the workplace. First, using an "inside" location can reduce the cost of bargaining: There are no rental costs for hotel rooms and no need to compensate people for travel expenses. Second, union democracy is fostered because union negotiators tend to be more sensitive to the needs of their constituents if they are in close geographical proximity to them. Third, the location is more convenient for management because materials and personnel are readily available.

There are, however, a number of drawbacks to on-site bargaining. First, if negotiators interact with the rank and file, there is a greater possibility of gossip and rumor, which can distort information and exert unnecessary pressure on negotiators. Second, the union team may feel patronized and resentful if bargaining takes place on employer premises. Whether this feeling is founded on fact or on imagination is immaterial if it is detrimental to the bargaining process.[1] Furthermore, employer and union negotiators alike may be unwilling to meet in the other side's facility, perceiving a "psychological disadvantage in doing so."[2] Also, union representatives may refuse to meet on the employer's premises because in case of a strike they would not be able to continue meeting there as doing so would involve crossing picket lines.[3]

Bargaining away from employer premises also has drawbacks. First, issues tend to be magnified. Negotiators may feel that being away on an expense account requires extracting larger concessions from the opposition. This attitude at times increases the significance of minor issues and results in extensive discussion over topics that should have been settled in a relatively short time. Second, being away from the workplace can lead to "less sober bargaining,"[4] being conducive to evening drinking and subsequent hangovers. Third, neutral-site negotiations frequently feature marathon sessions conducted to the point of exhaustion and provide a bargaining advantage to the side with the greater physical stamina. In such an atmosphere, the goal of reaching an agreement dominates behavior and becomes an end unto itself. As a result, the final product may be less than adequate from the point of view of both sides. Fourth, because the parties are removed from the daily problems that exist under the current contract, they may push aside and ignore some of those problems. They would find it more difficult to do so if negotiations took place in closer proximity to their constituents. Finally, it is much harder to avoid the press on a neutral site. The negotiators face a dilemma: If they refuse comments to the media, they end up with bad press coverage. If they make comments to the media, they may still end up with bad coverage. If they make a statement, it may be blown out of proportion or taken out of context and thus may be detrimental. A comment to a reporter by one side forces a response from the opposition. This fact at times leads to collective bargaining in the news media rather than at the bargaining table.

Research on the effects of negotiation site on process and outcomes has not been extensive or conclusive. Some have argued that those hosting negotiations gain a perceived status advantage.[5] In a laboratory experiment using college students, negotiators got a "better deal" when negotiating on their own territory.[6] In a more recent field study of union and management negotiators, however, those bargaining in the other party's offices reported being more competitive then when they bargained on neutral ground or in their own offices. Those playing host to negotiations also reported being more accommodating.[7] Consistent with these findings, Fisher and Ury suggest accepting an invitation to meet on the opponents' territory, particularly if the other side "tends to feel insecure"[8]; this may put them at ease and possibly make them more open to the other side's position.

Bargaining on one's own territory provides the benefit of designing the physical environment to one's advantage. In addition, one can more easily manipulate the timing of interruptions—from phone calls for example—when negotiating in one's own office.[9] On the other hand, an advantage of being a visitor is the ease with which one could walk out—a circumstance that can be used as a bargaining tactic.[10]

Whatever the site, any facility must meet a number of requirements. It must be free from disruption. The room must have chairs, tables, chalkboard and chalk, paper, pencils, water, plenty of coffee, and sufficient illumination. It must be accessible at all hours and should be near eating and refreshment facilities. It should also have adjoining caucus rooms that can be made available to both sides.

Agenda Sequence

Another procedural issue to be resolved at the beginning of negotiations is the sequence of the bargaining agenda. The typical approach is for the parties to negotiate over minor issues first, the rationale being that it is difficult to resolve minor issues if they are left for later stages of negotiation. If major issues are agreed upon first, there is less incentive for the parties to settle anything else because each side usually assumes that the other would not risk a strike over minor issues. The strike threat is not always necessary for the resolution of minor problems. In some instances, the parties may be willing to accommodate each other not because of threats but because they may want a better relationship. Typically, however, neither side is willing to rely on the goodwill of the opposition and therefore prefers to resolve minor issues early.

Authority to Make Firm Commitments

Under the law, the parties are under obligation to bargain in good faith; according to National Labor Relations Board (NLRB) rulings, this means that negotiators must have the authority to make firm commitments on behalf of their principals. In spite of these legal requirements, the power of negotiators varies considerably. Therefore, it is advisable to clarify the authority of both sides at the outset, thus reducing potential misinterpretations later.

Some union negotiators have full authority to conclude a final agreement, subject to membership ratification. Others require the approval of an executive committee before they can sign.

Some management negotiators are fully empowered to reach agreement, subject to almost automatic approval from top management. By contrast, in some firms negotiators must clear each concession with their superiors.[11] The negotiators who must check each move with their principals have the perfect "out" when cornered. However, such lack of authority, apart from its questionable legality, makes it more difficult to extract concessions from the opposition and weakens bargaining effectiveness.

Working Draft to Be Used

In some bargaining situations, the parties exchange draft agreements. This raises a procedural question as to whether to negotiate from the union draft, the employer draft, or the existing agreement. Because negotiators prefer working from their own drafts in the belief that it gives them a bargaining advantage, a procedural argument could develop over this issue.

Procedures During Negotiations

Certain procedural rules should be established during the first bargaining session. The parties should establish a schedule and determine the duration of negotiation sessions. Time of day or day of the week can have an impact on negotiations: Sessions that start in the afternoon are preferable to negotiations confined to evening hours, as negotiators may be tired and irritable during the evening. At times, weekend negotiations may be most effective.

In the early stages of bargaining, it is advisable to limit sessions to a few hours per day. When sessions go on too long, tempers grow short, fatigue sets in, the law of diminishing returns starts operating, and the extra hours of negotiation can prove counterproductive. This does not suggest that long sessions are always detrimental. In the last stages of bargaining, marathon sessions may be necessary for concluding an agreement, particularly if both sides desire to reach a settlement by a certain deadline.

There can be conflict of interest between the two sides over frequency of bargaining sessions. Management negotiators sometimes find it advantageous to schedule a reduced number of meetings. Their purpose would be to provide the union less negotiation time before contract expiration. As the contract deadline approaches, the rank and file and union negotiators may become impatient. Such a development could strengthen management's bargaining position.

Another scheduling issue involves timeouts for caucuses. Typically, the parties agree to call caucuses as often as necessary.

A procedural point usually resolved during the first session concerns the taking of minutes or record-keeping arrangements. A number of options are open to the parties. They may decide that each side will keep its own records, they may employ a stenographer, they may install a recording machine, or they may dispense with record keeping altogether. Because formality in record keeping can be detrimental to the bargaining process, the parties are probably better off without any stenographic assistance.

Another issue closely related to record keeping is the matter of confidentiality. In some cases, the parties agree to keep all proceedings confidential until an agreement is reached, thus reducing the outside pressures on negotiators during bargaining. In other situations, there is a constant flow of news releases. This type of news media bargaining could have an adverse effect on the bargaining process.

A variety of views exist on the issue of confidentiality. Some suggest that the rank and file should be informed of developments at the bargaining table. The logic of this position is that the bargaining team enjoys more trust from its constituency if communications are always open. The other side of the coin is that too much openness is counterproductive for the bargaining process. When proceedings are out in the open, the parties are afraid to explore new ideas, and flexibility suffers. Negotiations become an exercise in public relations and are directed to the audience rather than to the issues. Parties then tend to become more formal and commit themselves to specific positions. This development can lead to impasses and to breakdowns of bargaining. Successful bargaining requires some confidentiality; if it is absent in formal sessions, it is sometimes replaced by off-the-record meetings between the representatives of unions and management. The final agreement, rather than being arrived at by the bargaining teams, may be hammered out in confidential meetings between the representatives of the two sides. Some state jurisdictions governing public employees have "sunshine laws" requiring that all formal collective bargaining sessions between the government and its unions be held in public. In these states much of the actual bargaining is thought to occur in confidential, informal meetings.

Another procedural point that the parties must resolve concerns the status of articles on which agreement has been reached. Typically, the parties come to an understanding that each issue agreed upon is tentative and nonbinding until a complete agreement on all issues has been reached.

LEGAL BARGAINING GUIDELINES

Section 8(d) of the National Labor Relations Act states that the employer and the representative of the employees have an obligation to "confer in good faith with respect to wages, hours, and other terms and conditions of employment or the negotiation of an agreement or any question arising thereunder . . . but such obligation does not compel either party to agree to a proposal or require the making of a concession."[12] The National Labor Relations Board (NLRB)[13] and the courts, including the U.S. Supreme Court in the *Borg Warner* decision, have recognized three classes of bargaining proposals: mandatory, voluntary, and illegal subjects of bargaining.[14]

> *Illegal Subjects.* These are the demands that would be illegal and forbidden under the Act, such as a proposal for a closed shop. Bargaining on these subjects may not be required, and they may not be included in the contract even if the other party agrees.

Voluntary Subjects. These are the topics that fall outside the mandatory category of "wages, hours, and other terms and conditions of employment." They may be placed on the bargaining table for voluntary bargaining and agreement. The other party, however, may not be required to bargain on them or agree to their inclusion in a contract. Insistence on them as a condition to the execution of a contract will be a violation of the bargaining duty.

Mandatory Subjects. These are the subjects that fall within the category of "wages, hours, and other terms and conditions of employment." Both the employer and the union are required to bargain in good faith with respect to them.[15]

Mandatory Bargaining Subjects

The category of mandatory subjects of bargaining has been given specific meaning in many NLRB and court decisions. Included in the category are the following topics:

- Discharge of employees . . .
- Seniority, grievances, and working schedules . . .
- Union security and checkoff . . .
- Vacations and individual merit raises . . .
- Retirement and pension and group insurance plans . . .
- Christmas bonuses and profit-sharing retirement plan . . .
- Employee stock purchase plan providing for employer contributions and making benefits partly dependent on length of service . . .
- A nondiscriminatory union hiring hall . . .
- Plant rules on rest or lunch periods . . .
- Safety rules, even though the employer may be under legal obligation to provide safe and healthful conditions of employment . . .
- Company-owned houses occupied by the employees, as well as the rent paid for the houses . . .
- No-strike clauses binding on all employees in the bargaining unit . . .
- Physical examinations employees are required to take . . .
- Insurance plans, even though the employer proposed to improve the insurance programs and the expiring agreement contained no provisions concerning the plans . . .
- The privilege of exclusive hunting on a reserved portion of the company's forest preserve, a privilege that had existed for 20 years before the company proposed to discontinue it . . .
- A "bar list" maintained by an oil company of former employees and others who were barred from entering the company's refineries . . .
- "Most favored nation" clauses . . .
- Polygraph (lie detector) tests for employees . . .
- A "zipper clause" closing out bargaining during the term of the contract and making the contract the exclusive statement of the parties' rights and obligations . . .
- Jury-duty rights . . .
- The preparation, use, and sharing of costs of official transcripts of arbitration hearings . . .
- A plan under which employees could purchase the employer's products at a discount . . .
- A recreation fund that subsidized activities suggested by employees, even though the fund was established unilaterally by the employer that had sole discretion over disbursements . . .
- Whether a security guard is to carry a weapon . . .
- The prohibition of smoking on company premises during working hours regardless of whether the incumbent union seeks to obtain such a ban or to limit or eliminate it . . .
- An employer whose in-plant food services are managed by an independent caterer must bargain over in-plant food services and prices. . . .
- Alcohol and drug testing of current employees who suffer work-related injuries that require medical treatment is a mandatory subject of bargaining.[16]

Voluntary Bargaining Subjects

There has been less delineation of voluntary subjects of bargaining—those that may be advanced but not insisted upon as a condition of an agreement. The following items, however, have been placed in this category:

- A clause making the local union the exclusive bargaining agent, even though the international union was the certified agent . . .
- A clause requiring a secret ballot vote among the employees on the employer's last offer before a strike could be called . . .
- A clause fixing the size and membership of the union grievance committee . . .
- A requirement that a contract must be ratified by a secret employee ballot . . .
- A clause providing that a contract will become void whenever more than 50 percent of the employees fail to authorize dues checkoff . . .
- A requirement that the union post a performance bond or an indemnity bond to compensate the employer for losses caused by picketing by other unions . . .
- A requirement that employers post a cash bond to cover any assessment for wages or fringe payments due under the contract, or guarantee to pay to the union a sum equivalent to the initiation fees the union would have received for each employee not included in the bargaining unit if the employer violated a clause barring subcontracting to employers not parties to the master contract . . .
- A clause fixing terms and conditions of employment for workers hired to replace strikers . . .
- Strike insurance obtained by employers to guard against the financial risks involved in a strike . . .
- Benefits for retirees . . .
- Interest-arbitration clauses calling for arbitration of disputes over terms of a new contract . . .
- Use of a court reporter to transcribe negotiating sessions . . .
- Inclusion in a collective bargaining contract of a union "bug" indicating that the contract was printed by union-represented employees . . .
- Promotion of employees to supervisory positions . . .
- A no-strike clause under which employees would waive their right to seek redress from the NLRB for discipline imposed on strikers who are replaced . . .
- An employer's proposal concerning a buyout of lifetime job guarantees employees had received earlier . . .
- Information relevant to the amount of the agency fee to be charged nonmembers . . .
- Taping employees giving their opinions on an employer's newly formulated management principles.[17]

In determining whether the parties are bargaining in good faith, the NLRB relies on its totality-of-conduct concept rather than looking at individual actions. Among the factors the Board examines as part of this totality of conduct are willingness of the parties to meet at reasonable times and places, rejection of the other side's proposals without extension of a counterproposals, refusal to discuss mandatory bargaining issues, and failure to provide the other side with information that is relevant to bargaining. After examining these and all other actions that constitute a party's totality of conduct regarding negotiations, the Board determines whether the party is bargaining in good faith.

Labor contracts contain clauses regulating such subjects as grounds for discipline and discharge; grievance and arbitration procedures; restrictions on hours of work and overtime; rules governing layoffs, recalls, and bumping rights; leaves of absence; management and union rights; subcontracting; seniority; strikes and lockouts; union security; and working conditions and safety. Table 9.1 shows the frequency of these and other clauses in major union contracts in 1995. (The table covers only noncompensation contract clauses.)

TABLE 9.1. Survey of Contract Provisions and Their Frequency in Collective Bargaining Agreements

Contract Clause	Percent Containing Contract Clause
CONTRACT TERM	
1 year	1
2 years	5
3 years	64
4 or more years	30
Contract reopeners	9
Automatic renewal	90
DISCIPLINE AND DISCHARGE	
General grounds for discharge	97
Specific grounds for discharge	82
GRIEVANCE AND ARBITRATION	
Steps specified	99
Arbitration as final step	99
HOURS AND OVERTIME	
Daily work schedules	87
Weekly work schedules	71
Overtime premiums	98
LAYOFF, REHIRING, AND WORK SHARING	
Seniority as criterion	88
Seniority as sole factor	43
Notice to employees required	49
Bumping permitted	63
Recall rights	85
Work sharing	17
LEAVE OF ABSENCE	
Personal	76
Union	78
Family	36
Funeral	86
Paid sick	31
Unpaid sick	50
Military	75
MANAGEMENT AND UNION RIGHTS	
Management rights statement	80
Subcontracting	55
Supervisory work	58
Technological change	26
Plant shutdown or relocation	23
Union access to plant	54
Union bulletin boards	71
Union right to information	56

TABLE 9.1. (cont.)	
Contract Clause	*Percent Containing Contract Clause*
SENIORITY	
Probationary periods at hire	83
Loss of seniority	80
Seniority lists	65
As factor in promotion	67
As factor in transfer	57
STRIKES AND LOCKOUTS	
Unconditional no-strike pledges	63
Unconditional no-lockout pledges	70
UNION SECURITY	
Union shop	64
Modified union shop	10
Agency shop	10
Maintenance of membership	4
Hiring provisions	23
Checkoff	95
WORKING CONDITIONS AND SAFETY	
Occupational safety and health	89
Hazardous work acceptance	27
Safety and health committees	53
Safety equipment provided	43

Source: Basic Patterns in Union Contracts, Fourteenth Edition. (Washington, DC: Bureau of National Affairs, 1995).

CONTRACT DRAFTING

Thorough preparations for bargaining, along with careful contract costing and the most effective negotiating techniques, tactics, and strategies, will not prevail over a sloppy and poorly drafted contract. Unless the contract language is clear and unambiguous, what either side thought it won at the bargaining table may be lost during contract administration or in subsequent arbitration decisions. To avoid future disputes, it is important during negotiations to take the necessary time to prepare a well-drafted agreement.[18]

The person or persons who will draft the contract should be at the bargaining table. Their presence can help capture the letter and spirit of the settlement. Drafting during or toward the end of negotiations can prevent or reduce future friction. Most parties draft the language as they agree to each clause; some may decide to negotiate from sets of alternative clauses.

To avoid future problems, particularly those that might arise during arbitration, both sides need to define terms identically and clearly. This task can be quite tedious and difficult in the face of the excitement and fatigue that accompany an approaching contract expiration deadline. There are times, however, when the parties intentionally leave language ambiguous because doing so may be the only way to avoid an unwanted impasse or strike. In contract interpretation cases, arbitrators face difficult decisions when language is vague and there has been an incomplete meeting of the minds during negotiations.

Once bargaining has commenced, the ongoing negotiations often tend to fall into patterns that are similar. For the purposes of analysis, we shall refer to these patterns as stages.

STAGES OF THE NEGOTIATION PROCESS

Many negotiation processes, with some overlap, can be broadly divided into four stages: the opening stage, the settling-in stage, the consolidation stage, and the finalization stage.[19] These stages are characterized by variations in the behaviors of the negotiating parties, in the level and intensity of the discussions, and in the extent of actual bargaining (or trading) that occurs.

Opening

The opening stage includes the first meeting or set of meetings between union and management. Typically, the union first presents all its demands. Frequently, in important negotiations, press conferences are convened for the opening of contract talks. Following the presentation of union demands, a recess commonly is called for, often for days or even weeks. The recess gives management the necessary time to formulate its initial proposals as well as to prepare its responses to the union demands. At the next meeting, management customarily comes back with its response to the union proposals; it may also present its own set of demands.

The union may not always be the first to introduce its proposals. Generally, the objective of the union is to improve the status quo; this compels management to play a defensive role. There have been changes in this approach in the last 15 years, with management being the party on the offensive, requesting revisions in the terms of the collective agreement.

In the early stage of the negotiation process, the agenda of issues to be negotiated has usually been determined by the parties. Each side has probably decided, internally, what would be the best outcome on each issue presented at the bargaining table. It is considered a faux pas to bring up any completely new issue after the opening stage of negotiation.

The number of proposals that the union presents at the bargaining table can vary from a few to a few hundred. Frequently, the list of demands grows with the size and heterogeneity of the bargaining unit. This does not mean, however, that small, homogeneous units always confine themselves to a small number of demands.

A common feature of many types of negotiations, including those between labor and management, is that in the early stages each side takes positions more extreme than it knows it will ultimately accept. This feature applies to both the number and the magnitude of demands. Because both sides are aware of this pattern, one might well ask why it is so commonly followed.

One answer is that because it is expected, if either party changed its past behavior pattern and decided not to exaggerate its demands, it would still have difficulty overcoming the skepticism and distrust of the other side. One way out of this traditional approach is to utilize win-win negotiations, a technique explained in a later section.

Another reason, particularly for unions, that so many demands are presented at the bargaining table is the democratic nature of the union. Presenting all rank-and-file demands provides maximum membership input, making the approach politically attractive to union leaders. If, for example, a member suggests a proposal that is very unlikely to be acceptable to management, it may still be advisable for the union leader to let management deny the demand.

Introduction of novel bargaining demands, even if they are rejected during contract negotiations, may still be advantageous to the introducer. The idea of a new demand planted with the opposition may bear fruit over time: The other side is forced to start thinking seriously about the demand. At times, it may take a few contract negotiations before a new demand is accepted and becomes part of a labor agreement.

Proposals more extreme than what one expects to settle upon are attractive for a number of reasons. First, because each party is uncertain what the other side will agree to, it seems easiest to test the opponent's resistance points through this approach. Each side wants to extract the maximum concession; if management would be willing to grant a five-percent wage increase but the union only demands four percent, one percent of a potential gain is lost to the bargaining unit members. Also, extracting concessions from the other side justifies negotiators' jobs to their constituents and may also make them feel good. Imagine, for example, that you offer a used car dealer $5,000 for a car and he or she accepts immediately; you may drive away feeling that you paid too much—that you were taken advantage of. The same car priced at $6,000 and purchased at $5,000 would let you drive away with the satisfied feeling that you did not overpay and indeed got a good buy.

The tradition of presenting an extensive list of demands is not without its problems. Bargaining can be adversely affected by union officers' abdicating their leadership responsibilities in favor of rank-and-file wishes. Too many demands can lead to confusion and may generate erroneous signals to the other side. Unnecessary impasses can result when the opposition attaches mistaken values to particular demands.

Not all negotiators follow the excessive, many-issues approach. Some are reluctant to submit too many proposals to the opposition, particularly if certain proposals are to be used for trading purposes. They feel that such action can lead to misinterpretation of signals. The other party could underestimate the importance of some proposals and perhaps infer that all issues are tradeable. Including additional proposals just for use as bargaining chips may not work if they are perceived as such. Making a concession sometimes induces the other side to respond in kind. However, when a concession does not involve giving up on an important issue, the other side may not feel compelled to reciprocate.

Settling In

The second stage of negotiations is the settling-in stage. Whereas during the opening stage, the parties have defined the limits of what will be negotiated, during the settling-in stage they have the opportunity to discuss each issue in some depth. Each party presents data to the opposition in support of its position. Each side makes a significant effort to identify what the other side really wants. This attempt to discover the other party's priorities often involves comprehensive discussion of the issues and presentation of supporting materials related to those issues. Preparation of bargaining data was discussed in some detail in Chapter 8, on preparation for bargaining. To justify wage increases, unions present detailed analyses of industry and local wage trends and national price trends as well as other relevant background material. In response, management may make a presentation delimiting the cost increases that the firm is willing to absorb over the life of the proposed contract. The employer may present detailed data on labor cost structures, pricing structures, and competition within the industry, along with other supporting data. During discussion of some of the issues, experts may be invited to present data in support of certain arguments or to educate both sides at the table. For example, in the area of pensions and health or life insurance, there usually are third-party carriers who provide coverage for the members of the bargaining unit. Representatives from HMOs and health and life insurance companies may be asked to provide detailed cost figures for the various proposals under consideration.

During the settling-in stage of negotiations, the parties try to resolve issues on which agreement can be reached easily. Some subjects merely require a full discussion of the concerns surrounding a particular proposal, after which both sides may discover mutual interests. This knowledge in turn may help them find quick solutions to specific problems. Usually both sides attempt first to resolve the easy issues as well as to dispose of some of the "blue-sky" issues that are presented only for trade-off purposes. Thus, by the end of the settling-in stage, only real issues are left on the bargaining table—issues that may be difficult to resolve.

Consolidation

The third stage of negotiations is the consolidation stage. Although most of the basic arguments and supportive information have been presented at the preceding stage, certain issues may require further elaboration or reiteration of positions. Some progress may be occurring at this time as each side begins to offer concessions to the other. Some trade-offs of smaller items from each side's priority list may be taking place. A discussion of the economic package usually begins in the consolidation stage.

In most negotiations, wages and benefits are combined and referred to as the economic package. Management may at times not care whether there is a pension improvement or an equivalent wage increase. Because employers are more concerned with total labor cost than with its allocation, they prefer to discuss all wage and benefit changes as a whole package. In some instances, this allocation question is extremely important, particularly when the employer negotiates with a number of different unions. A relatively inexpensive pension concession, for example, might become prohibitively expensive for the employer if other unions with which it negotiates received the same benefit. Some authors suggest that managerial indifference to the structure and various components of a benefits package (aside from its cost) is ill-advised; some research results indicate that benefits such as pensions can constitute incentives that may positively affect employee behavior.[20]

By the end of the consolidation stage, most of the less important items or the more easily settled issues have been taken off the bargaining table either through agreement or by intentional omission. Thus, at the end of this stage, each side has a fairly good understanding of the opposition's true priorities.

Finalization

Finalization is the last stage of the collective bargaining process. At this stage, only a few items may be left on the bargaining table. These items are usually very significant to both sides and difficult to resolve; otherwise they would have been settled or disposed of earlier. Generally, at this stage, the parties have a good idea as to whether an impasse or a strike is likely. If a strike is imminent, both sides begin serious strike preparations. During the finalization stage, a mediator may be called in to assist the parties in resolving an impasse and reaching an agreement without a work stoppage. The finalization stage is accompanied by a change from routine bargaining sessions to what may be called crisis negotiations. Crisis bargaining affects the behavior of the parties. Both sides are aware of the rapidly approaching deadline. In response, the pace of bargaining accelerates and the negotiators bargain much more intensely, meeting daily and for much longer periods.

PLAN OF ACTION

Every negotiating team, to be successful, must develop a comprehensive plan of action. Each party must have some idea, prior to negotiations, where it is going, where it would like to be, and how it intends to get there. Without a plan and an overview, a team may be successful in settling individual issues but at the end of negotiations may find itself dissatisfied with the final settlement. A plan is like a road map: It provides the team with guidelines and clear mileposts toward the achievement of its overall goals.

During negotiations each side attempts to satisfy the interests of its various constituents. On the union side, there are a number of distinct groups that are interested in and follow closely the negotiation outcomes. One is the union leadership, which, though not always present at the bargaining table, is responsible for bargaining settlements. Another is the negotiating committee itself; for its members, failure can mean loss of position, prestige, and the next election. Individual political needs play an important role at the bargaining table, with respect both to the types of issues introduced and to the conduct of negotiations over these issues. An important group to which the union must pay close attention during negotiations is its membership. Almost all collective bargaining agreements require rank-and-file ratification. Union members must be satisfied with the negotiated contract terms because they are the final decision makers as to the acceptability of the negotiated contract.

The negotiating team on the management side must likewise attend to the interests of various groups and principals who are not present at the bargaining table. The team leader has to know if "there is someone in management outside the negotiating committee who needs to review or approve proposals, contract language, or offers."[21] In many negotiations, the leader "does not have full and unencumbered authority to make any and all agreements he or she wishes. The principal normally retains the right to make final decisions on key issues. . . . The negotiation between the management spokesperson and his or her principal(s) is frequently as difficult as that with the union."[22] When the parties finally have arrived at a contract, it is important that managers and supervisors who were not participants in the negotiations be briefed on all the terms of the contract being negotiated. Because they must administer the agreement, "It is vital that they understand . . . changes in the contract . . . the intent of the parties . . . and how the new contract provisions are to be administered."[23]

A very comprehensive discussion of the dynamics of the actual negotiation process is reviewed in the Colosi model in Appendix A. The model examines bilateral and multilateral negotiations, it evaluates interaction at the bargaining table, and it discusses the structure of union and management bargaining teams.

NEGOTIATION TACTICS AND TECHNIQUES

Because of the complexity of the bargaining process, a number of organizations have written guides to help their negotiators identify appropriate tactics and techniques to use during negotiations. A particularly instructive guide developed by the American Federation of State, County and Municipal Employees (AFSCME) offers the following advice to its negotiators:[24] Discussions should begin with areas where agreement is most likely rather than more controversial matters. Such an approach, it is suggested, will lead to initial success on which the parties can "build and will find that subsequent accommodations are more easily reached on disputed issues."[25] Negotiators are urged to be gracious and to allow for face saving. "To gloat and chortle over minor victories . . . may make it impossible for the other side to offer reasonable compromises without resentment and embarrassment."[26]

The AFSCME guide offers advice based on mutual gains bargaining (MGB) guidelines. MGB is discussed in more detail in the next section. In this approach, negotiators are urged to explain the advantages of their proposals to the other side. At times, for example, union demands may contain proposals that can also be advantageous to the employer. Also, negotiators are advised to focus their presentations on the problems at hand rather than on personalities. The AFSCME guide states that "by far the most fruitful atmosphere for reaching sound agreements is the recognition by the parties of mutual interest in solving problems of common concern."[27]

Although these guides offer general frameworks for behavior rather than step-by-step instructions, they can assist the parties in reaching a settlement.

MUTUAL GAINS BARGAINING

A discussion of the negotiation process would be incomplete without a more comprehensive examination of recent experimentations with win-win or mutual gains bargaining (MGB). These approaches are also referred to as principled negotiations, collective gaining, unconditionally constructive relationships, integrative bargaining, target-specific bargaining, and interest-based bargaining. All these styles of bargaining have a common core that contains the following components: "sharing information fully; focusing on underlying interests, not stated positions; and creating options that would result in mutual gains."[28] For purposes of this section, the term *MGB* will be considered interchangeable with and a proxy for all the other terms commonly used to describe the process.

Integrative Bargaining

MGB is not a new concept. As early as the 1900s, Mary Parker Follett discussed the idea of integrative bargaining, or MGB;[29] her work is considered the genesis of MGB literature. In reviewing integration, Follett distinguished it from the notion of a compromise. She wrote,

> There is a way beginning now to be recognized at last, and even occasionally followed: When the desires are integrated, that means that a solution has been found in which both desires have found a place, that neither side has had to sacrifice anything. Let us take a very simple illustration. In the Harvard Library one day, in one of the smaller rooms, someone wanted the window open, I wanted it shut. We opened the window in the next room, where no one was sitting. This was not a compromise, because there was no curtailing of desire; we both got what we really wanted. For I did not want a closed room, I simply did not want the north wind to blow directly on me; likewise the other occupant did not want that particular window open, he merely wanted more air in the room.[30]

Follett, writing about negotiations between unions and employers, points out that collective bargaining settlements usually are the results of compromise. Follett makes a distinction between compromise and integration. She suggests that *compromise* means a giving up of something, whereas *integration* implies an attempt to satisfy the needs of both sides. "Compromise does not create, it deals with what already exists; integration creates something new."[31]

In 1965 Walton and McKersie, in their classic work *A Behavioral Theory of Labor Negotiations,*[32] presented a comprehensive model of integrative bargaining. Their model will be discussed in more detail in Chapter 10, on bargaining theory and bargaining power. During the 1980s, the concept of integrative bargaining was popularized, particularly by publication of Fisher and Ury's *Getting to Yes.*[33] The philosophy of integrative bargaining stresses a participative working relationship between labor and management and a joint problem-solving approach to collective bargaining.

Principled and Traditional Negotiations

Fisher and Ury developed an alternative approach to the traditional bargaining model, which is often referred to as distributive positional or zero-sum-game negotiations. They named their method *principled negotiation.* Their methodology stresses four basic points:

people, interests, options, and criteria.[34] *People* means focusing on problems and separating the individuals from the issues. *Interests* implies concentrating on interests rather than on positions. *Options* suggests that participants should invent jointly options that can meet their mutual as well as their separate interests. Finally, negotiators are to "frame each issue as a joint search for objective criteria."[35] Figure 9.1 shows how Fisher and Ury compare traditional positional bargaining, which can be either soft or hard, with their model of principled negotiation.

Win-Win Bargaining

According to Fisher and Ury,

> The soft negotiator wants to avoid personal conflict and so makes concessions readily in order to reach agreement. He wants an amicable resolution; yet he often ends up exploited and feeling bitter. The hard negotiator sees any situation as a contest of wills in which the side that takes the more extreme position and holds out longer fares better. He wants to win; yet he often ends up producing an equally hard response which exhausts him and his resources and harms his relationship with the other side. Other standard negotiating strategies fall between hard and soft, but each involves an attempted trade-off between getting what you want and getting along with people.[36]

FIGURE 9.1 The Game of Negotiation

PROBLEM		SOLUTION
Positional Bargaining: *Which Game Should you Play?*		*Change the Game—* *Negotiate on the Merits*
Soft	*Hard*	*Principled*
Participants are friends.	Participants are adversaries.	Participants are problem solvers.
The goal is agreement.	The goal is victory.	The goal is a wise outcome reached efficiently and amicably.
Make concessions to cultivate the relationship.	Demand concessions as a condition of the relationship.	Separate the people from the problem.
Be soft on the people and the problem.	Be hard on the problem and the people.	Be soft on the people, hard on the problem.
Trust others.	Distrust others.	Proceed independent of trust.
Change your position easily.	Dig in your position.	Focus on interests, not positions.
Make offers.	Make threats.	Explore interests.
Disclose your bottom line.	Mislead as to your bottom line.	Avoid having a bottom line.
Accept one-sided losses to reach agreement.	Demand one-sided gains as the price of agreement.	Invent options for mutual gain.
Search for the single answer; the one they will accept.	Search for the single answer; the one you will accept.	Develop multiple options to choose from; decide later.
Insist on agreement.	Insist on your position.	Insist on using objective criteria.
Try to avoid a contest of will.	Try to win a contest of will.	Try to reach a result based on standards independent of will.
Yield to pressure.	Apply pressure.	Reason and be open to reason; yield to principle, not pressure.

Source: Roger Fisher and William Ury, *Getting to Yes* (New York: Houghton Mifflin, 1981), p. 13.

Fisher and Ury claim that traditional, distributive bargaining "produces unwise agreements";[37] it is inefficient and jeopardizes existing relationships.

Traditional or distributive bargaining "refers to the activity of dividing limited resources. It occurs in situations in which one party wins what the other party loses."[38] In traditional bargaining, negotiators typically conceal their true positions. The other side usually has a good idea what it would take to reach settlement, but they can never be certain. There is always the possibility of misreading the other party's potential bottom line.

In collective bargaining, negotiators routinely participate in positional or distributive bargaining. Each party assumes a position and argues for it, and after making some concessions, the parties reach a settlement by compromise.

In traditional confrontational bargaining, the parties believe that they face a fixed pie or a zero-sum game—"Your gain is my loss." In integrative bargaining, the objectives of the negotiators are not considered "mutually exclusive."[39] One team's achievement does not necessarily dismantle the other team's share.

Integrative bargaining offers an alternative bargaining method. It is based "on the distinction between interests and positions."[40] According to Fisher and Ury, "Interests define the problems. The basic problem in a negotiation lies . . . in the conflict between each side's needs, desires, concerns and fears. . . . [I]nterests motivate people . . . the most powerful interests are basic human needs."[41] Integrative bargaining is a process that attempts "to build into the model of negotiations a safe way of sharing more ideas and information than is typical of negotiations."[42]

Fisher et al. challenge the notion that the only two options open to negotiators are soft and hard styles of positional bargaining. They suggest that their "principled negotiation" model is superior to the positional model. In principled negotiations, both sides are trying to find ways to realize mutual gains. They seek objective data sources to settle disagreements on mutually agreeable terms without the necessity for one side to lose face. Negotiations are viewed as problem-solving challenges. Both parties are expected to face their problems together as a team. The emphasis is on each party's interests rather than on their positions.

Parties are urged to come to the table with open minds rather than committing to specific positions early in negotiations. Although negotiations should, to the extent possible, be kept on a rational basis, the emotional aspects of the process must be acknowledged. Each party is encouraged to step into the other's shoes and try to understand the other party's interests. The emphasis in principled negotiations is on persuasion rather than on coercion. Also, each side is expected to act in a reliable, predictable, and trustworthy manner while maintaining a healthy skepticism of the other.

The principled negotiations model and win-win techniques stress the significance of the quality of the relationship among the parties. The model separates relationship issues from substantive interests. When the parties are engaged in win-win negotiations, their relationship is expected to be nurtured on a continual basis, not just during bargaining. Information is to be shared, ideas are to be sought and objectively evaluated, and communication is to be frequent and frank.

Joint Gains and Win-Win Agreements

According to Fisher and Ury, principled negotiations can produce joint gains and create value. They believe that joint gains are possible because of different degrees of significance placed by the parties on time and because of differences in beliefs, forecasts, and aversion to risk.[43] The subject of joint gains or creation of value is also addressed by Lax and Sebenius. They suggest that creating or discovering value, or arriving at win-win agreements, can be traced to the following factors: First, achieving any settlement that is better than the no-settlement option "creates value relative to the alternatives. Second, negotiators create potential value with respect to one negotiated outcome by finding another that all prefer."[44] And, finally, the parties may come upon an alternative that may create more potential value than previously anticipated.

Pruitt and Carnevale suggest that "there are three general ways to construct win-win agreements: expanding the pie, exchanging concessions, and solving underlying concerns. Each leads to a different kind of agreement and requires a different set of problem solving tactics."[45] First, the expanding-the-pie approach is self-explanatory: If available resources can be expanded, both sides may be able to satisfy their needs. Second, an exchange of concessions or trade-offs is based on the assumption that parties assign different values or priorities to the same issues. Third, solving underlying concerns means discovering and understanding the interests and concerns of the other party. In searching for solutions, the parties must first surmount some of their apprehensions about each other. At times, asking the right questions may overcome the parties' unease. The frequently quoted example of two children fighting over the same orange illustrates this point: The conflict is resolved when one child states that the orange is wanted for eating; the other child wants the orange to use the peel in baking a cake.[46]

Criticisms of Mutual Gains Bargaining

Mutual gains bargaining has its share of both supporters and critics. So far, the emphasis of this section has been on the positive dimension of MGB; we will now review some criticisms of this approach.

In a 1994 article, Lobel,[47] a federal mediator, expressed some serious reservations about MGB, or interest-based (win-win) bargaining. In Lobel's view, advocates of MGB make the following dangerous implicit assumptions: (1) In traditional, positional bargaining, negotiators are oblivious to the interests of their counterparts; (2) in traditional bargaining, participants do not search for imaginative solutions to joint problems; (3) power should not be applied in negotiation; (4) there are satisfactory solutions to most problems as long as negotiators devote enough time to discussing and seeking them; (5) the amount of available funds over which the parties negotiate will expand as a result of creative problem-solving activities; and, finally, (6) relationships are adversely affected by dissent. In accepting these assumptions, negotiators may be entering into MGB with false expectations that the process may not be able to satisfy. The result may be frustration, the long-term relationship may be jeopardized. "If the negotiation does not result in a mutually satisfactory solution, one side will feel abused or taken advantage of."[48]

According to Lobel, MGB problem-solving activities do not necessarily result in a bigger pie. The parties do not operate in a vacuum; in some sectors of the economy, external forces may prevent the parties, regardless of their good intentions and creativity, from expanding the pie. "With good problem solving . . . the decline may be slowed. When interest-based negotiators claim that the pie may increase, they are establishing an expectation that negotiation can eliminate outside variables."[49] The MGB approach as presented in Fisher and Ury's *Getting to Yes* stresses objective standards or criteria;[50] it does not address directly the issue of power. According to Lobel, in bargaining "power plays an important and indispensable role. To suggest otherwise is to ignore reality."[51]

Proponents of MGB assume that when all alternatives are reviewed and discussed long enough, a mutually satisfactory solution can be achieved. "What is not mentioned is that the solution can be mutually unsatisfactory or unsatisfactory to only one side."[52] According to supporters of MGB or interest-based bargaining, creativity is repressed when parties engage in positional bargaining. Lobel states that creativity is restrained only "by negotiators who hold inflexible positions. Good negotiators do not blindly hold to positions, but continually explore various alternatives."[53] Although Lobel is critical of MGB, he recognizes some of its advantages, such as (1) warning negotiators not to apply power irresponsibly, (2) addressing the need for civility to be observed at the bargaining table, (3) taking into account the interests of both parties, and (4) creating an environment that is conducive to creativity and to the joint search for solutions to common problems.

Advocates of MGB or interest-based bargaining recommend that the parties refrain from expressing positions and instead concentrate on interests. Lobel argues that "traditional negotiators" utilize positions as a means of bargaining over interests. "These positions can be used to help both sides to understand, clarify and develop their respective interests."[54]

Negotiation of a labor contract

> is only one part of the interaction between a union and an employer. The relationship between the parties during the life of a contract is probably as significant if not more so than the relationship between the two sides during collective bargaining. The process is not a panacea. . . . Attaching words to the negotiation process will not change the basic nature of bargaining. Power will still be a factor; solutions may be unsatisfactory and the pie may get smaller. In today's economy, a new style of bargaining or new words will not change these realities . . . saying that changing the form of the negotiations will help make the problem go away may be developing an expectation that no system of bargaining can achieve.[55]

Is Bargaining Integrative or Distributive?

In the last 10 years, the discussion of mutual gains bargaining in its various manifestations has served to focus attention on areas of potential harmony between unions and employers. Similarly, most observers on both sides of the bargaining table would likely agree that in our increasingly competitive and international market system, the attempt to work together on many issues of mutual concern is absolutely essential. It would be naive, however, to assume that parties can discover or achieve mutually beneficial solutions on all subjects under negotiation simply by implementing the proper bargaining techniques, which are part of the MGB approach. Despite the increased focus on and attention paid to MGB and to integrative bargaining, many issues do not lend themselves completely to MGB solutions.

A review of the last 10 years of negotiations over health insurance terms reveals that very significant distributive bargaining issues still prevail in this area. Unions and employers have jointly identified a variety of methods for reducing health insurance costs to their mutual benefit. Initiatives undertaken by the parties such as self-insurance, wellness programs, employee assistance plans, and early detection of health problems have often provided improved coverage to employees at lower cost to their employers. However, many other health insurance issues clearly continue to be distributive; a gain for one side can be achieved only if the other side incurs a loss. Management proposals to decrease the employer's contribution to health care from 90 to 75 percent; to discontinue paying premiums for retirees; to remove coverage for allergy treatments, dental care, or prescriptions—all are examples of bargaining topics that continue to be distributive rather than integrative.

THE TRANSFORMATION OF THE TRADITIONAL LABOR-MANAGEMENT SYSTEM AND ITS IMPACT ON MGB

Under the traditional labor-management system, at the strategic level, the employer managed and the union abstained from participating in business decisions. Under this workplace model, the leitmotif "has been job control with grievance systems culminating in arbitration."[56] As a consequence of this system, labor unions are now faced with the responsibility of administering complex contracts.

In the last 10 years, a transformation has been taking place in the traditional system. This transformation has contributed to a number of major changes in the system: The parties have started developing new forms of governance; in some companies, union representatives have been appointed to boards of directors; unions have become more involved and have begun to participate "in major business decisions."[57] In negotiating labor contracts, unions have started placing more emphasis on employment security, with gain sharing also becoming a more frequent topic of bargaining. Furthermore, because of pressures from the nonunionized sector, labor unions are willing to negotiate more flexibility at the workplace level. The transformation of the traditional labor-management system has a number of causes: foreign and domestic competition, deregulation, changing labor market conditions, decline of unions, and pressure from nonunionized employers.

All these factors contributed to the need for unions and employers to find a more effective bargaining model. The result has been the emergence of mutual gains bargaining (MGB), discussed in the previous section. As Heckscher states, "The economic developments of the past decade have produced some important value shifts."[58] Many more employees than in the past accept the proposition that their interests are linked to the prosperity of their employers. Furthermore, workers are more aware of the impact of market competition on their employers and therefore on their employment security. During the last 10 years, a growing number of employers have started empowering workers to make shop floor decisions and to participate in the operation and, to some extent, in the management of the enterprise. These developments and value shifts have influenced the attitudes of labor unions toward MGB. "The labor movement, which is closely bound to its constituencies, is beginning to reflect these shifts, and as it does, it has started to develop more frequently the mechanisms of decentralized discussion and planning that . . . are crucial to the success of mutual gains bargaining."[59] These contextual changes may have a major impact "on the dynamics of adversarial collective bargaining."[60] The transformation that is taking place may provide the foundation for more labor-management cooperation in the future. According to Heckscher, "There is more desire for cooperation than ability to create it; mutual gains techniques have been effective in closing the gap."[61]

In a new book titled *The Mutual Gains Enterprise,* Kochan and Osterman write "that the majority of American workplaces have experimented with some form of workplace innovations."[62] They deduce "that innovations have spread to at least one-third of American workplaces."[63] But they also point out that not all employers who embrace innovations will preserve them over time. Furthermore, Kochan and Osterman state that "human resource innovations do not stand alone but are most effective and most often a part of a larger transformation of production and service delivery strategies that emphasize production quality and innovations."[64] They do not assume that "all jobs, firms or professions must adhere to . . . mutual gains principles or be doomed to be inefficient."[65] In their view, mutual gains principles are not "the silver bullet or simple solution"[66] to all the problems facing the American economy and the individual enterprise. They do not view mutual gains principles "as necessarily fitting all employment settings. They are not a universalistic 'one best way' to structure employment relationships."[67]

Despite the ever-expanding research and literature advocating the application of collaborative negotiation techniques, this approach is still viewed with suspicion by many unions and employers. Appendix B to this chapter presents innovative collective bargaining provisions that were achieved because of a spirit of partnership. These contract articles were arrived at because labor and management concentrated on "common goals and joint strategies necessary for enterprise survival and prosperity."[68] It is interesting to note that one of the labor agreements quoted in Appendix B addresses the issue of reduction in force by utilizing interest-based bargaining procedures.[69]

Over the years, there have been many efforts to reform labor negotiations. The objective of these efforts was to move away from positional bargaining and confrontation and to adopt "problem solving negotiation. . . . Yet in the end, these innovations have never made significant inroads. . . . This is a sobering note in the current symphony of enthusiasm for mutual gains bargaining."[70]

To conclude, there are no ideal bargaining models or processes that would be appropriate for all bargaining parties. There are no paradigms that would work well in all organizations. In the final analysis, the parties must be eclectic in deciding which bargaining approach would work best in their particular circumstances.

SUMMARY

This chapter has reviewed the negotiation process. It began with a discussion of the typical procedural aspects of bargaining, from evaluation of the appropriate bargaining location and determination of the bargaining agenda to record keeping. This discussion was followed by an examination of legal bargaining guidelines, mandatory and voluntary bargaining subjects, and the concept of good-faith bargaining. We looked at noncompensation contract clauses and contract drafting, then surveyed the four stages of the negotiation process, particularly the change in the content and intensity of negotiations with the approach of the contract expiration deadline. Finally, mutual gains, integrative, or win-win bargaining—as an alternative to the traditional, distributive, adversarial method of negotiations—was examined.

Appendix A to this chapter presents the Colosi Bargaining Model, which reviews the composition of bargaining teams; examines horizontal, vertical shadow, and sunshine bargaining; and evaluates the dynamics of the bargaining process. Appendix B includes a number of innovative provisions from collective agreements as well as a statement issued by the AFL-CIO on the new American workplace.

Notes

1. *Preparing for Collective Bargaining, Studies in Personnel Policy,* no. 172 (New York: National Industrial Conference Board, 1959), p. 20.
2. Maurice B. Better, *Contract Bargaining Handbook for Local Union Leaders* (Washington, DC: Bureau of National Affairs, 1993), pp. 17–18.
3. Charles S. Loughran, *Negotiating a Labor Contract. A Management Handbook,* 2nd ed. (Washington, DC: Bureau of National Affairs, 1992), pp. 87–88.
4. Ibid., p. 21.
5. J. Z. Rubin and B. R. Brown, *The Social Psychology of Bargaining and Negotiations* (New York: Academic Press, 1975) and R. J. Lewicki and J. A. Litterer, *Negotiation* (Homewood, IL: Richard D. Irwin, 1985).
6. D. A. Martindale, "Territorial Dominance Behavior in Dyadic Verbal Interactions," *Proceedings of the 79th Annual Convention of the American Psychological Association,* 1971.

7. Michael J. Duane, Ross E. Azevedo, and Yin Sog Rhee, "Location of Negotiations and Bargaining Behavior: My Place or Yours," *Journal of Collective Negotiations* 16 (1987), pp. 377–83.

8. Roger Fisher and William Ury, *Getting to Yes* (New York: Penguin Books, 1983), p. 140.

9. Duane et al., op. cit., pp. 377–78.

10. Fisher and Ury, op. cit., p. 140.

11. Thomas A. Kochan and Harry C. Katz, *Collective Bargaining and Industrial Relations,* 2nd ed. (Homewood, IL: Richard D. Irwin, 1988), pp. 201–5.

12. National Labor Relations Act, Section 8(d).

13. *NLRB v. Wooster Division of Borg-Warner Corporation,* 356 US 342 (1958).

14. Linda G. Kahn, *Primer of Labor Relations,* 25th ed. (Washington, DC: Bureau of National Affairs, 1994), pp. 67–75.

15. Ibid.

16. Ibid.

17. Ibid.

18. The suggestions on contract drafting come from James R. Redeker, "Contract Drafting to Avoid Disputes" in *Collective Bargaining Negotiations and Contracts* (Washington, DC: Bureau of National Affairs, 1992), no. 1234, 14:51–14:54, pp. 61–64.

19. Reed C. Richardson, *Collective Bargaining by Objectives,* 2nd ed. (Englewood Cliffs, NJ: Prentice Hall, 1985), pp. 166–67.

20. Alan L. Gustman and Olivia S. Mitchell, "Pensions and Labor Force Activity" in *Pensions and the U.S. Economy: The Need for Good Data* (Philadelphia: Irwin, 1990).

21. Loughran, op. cit., p. 61.

22. Ibid., p. 201.

23. Ibid., p. 453.

24. *Bargaining Guide for Negotiators,* prepared by the Education Department of the American Federation of State, County and Municipal Employees (Washington, DC: Bureau of National Affairs, 1987), Collective Bargaining Negotiation and Contracts, nos. 1099, 1100, 14:31–14:39, pp. 54–57.

25. Ibid.

26. Ibid.

27. Ibid.

28. Richard E. Walton, Joel E. Cutcher-Gershenfeld, and Robert B. McKersie, *Strategic Negotiations* (Boston: Harvard Business School Press, 1994), p. 308.

29. M. P. Follett, "Constructive Conflict" in *Dynamic Administrator: The Collected Papers of Mary Parker Follett,* H. C. Metcalf and L. Urwick, eds. (New York: Harper, 1940). *Source:* Interview with Mary Parker Follett by Albie M. Davis in *Negotiation Theory and Practice,* J. William Breslin and Jeffrey Z. Rubin, eds. (Cambridge, MA: The Program on Negotiation, Harvard Law School, 1991), pp. 13–24. See also Richard E. Walton and Robert B. McKersie, *A Behavioral Theory of Labor Negotiations,* 2nd ed. (Ithaca, NY: SLR Press, 1991), p. 7.

30. Albie M. Davis, op. cit., pp. 14–15.

31. Mary Parker Follett, *Dynamic Administration: The Collected Papers of Mary Parker Follett,* H. C. Metcalf and L. Urwick, eds. (New York: Harper & Row, 1942), pp. 34–35, cited in Walton and McKersie, op. cit., p. 128.

32. Walton and McKersie, 1991, op. cit., pp. 126–83.

33. Fisher and Ury, op. cit. See also Fisher and Ury with Bruce Patton, *Getting to Yes,* 2nd ed. (New York: Penguin Books, 1991).

34. Fisher et al., 1991, op. cit., pp. 10–11. See also Jerome Barrett, "A Briefing Paper on the Past Version of Win-Win Bargaining" in *Collective Bargaining Negotiations and Contracts* (Washington, DC: Bureau of National Affairs, 1992), no. 1212, pp. 14:71–14:74.

35. Fisher et al., 1991, op. cit., p. 193.

36. Ibid., pp. xviii, 13.

37. Ibid., p. 4.

38. Walton and McKersie, 1991, op cit., p. 11.

39. Roy J. Lewicki, Joseph A. Litterer, John W. Minton, and David M. Saunders, *Negotiation* (Burr Ridge, IL: Irwin, 1994), p. 80.

40. Raymond A Friedman, "Bringing Mutual Gains Bargaining to Labor Negotiations: The Role of Trust, Understanding and Control," *Human Resource Management* 32 (winter 1993), p. 436.

41. Fisher et al., 1991, op. cit. pp. 40–41, 48.

42. Friedman, op. cit., p. 455.

43. Fisher et al., 1991, op. cit., pp. 74–75.

44. David A. Lax and James K. Sebenius, *The Manager as Negotiator* (New York: Free Press, 1986), p. 89.

45. Dean G. Pruitt and Peter J. Carnevale, *Negotiation in Social Conflict* (Pacific Grove, CA: Brooks/Cole, 1993), pp. 36–38.

46. Fisher et al., 1991, op. cit., p. 57.

47. Ira B. Lobel, "Realities of Interest Based (Win-Win) Bargaining," *Labor Law Journal,* December 1994, pp. 771–78.

48. Ibid., p. 772.

49. Ibid., p. 775.

50. Fisher et al., 1991, op. cit., pp. 81–94.

51. Lobel, op. cit., p. 774.

52. Ibid., p. 775.

53. Ibid., p. 773.

54. Ibid., p. 772.

55. Ibid., p. 778.

56. Robert B. McKersie, "Why the Labor Management Scene is Contentious" in *Negotiation. Strategies for Mutual Gain,* Lavinia Hall, ed. (Newbury Park, London: Sage, 1993), p. 78.

57. Ibid., p. 79.

58. Charles C. Heckscher, "Searching for Mutual Gains in Labor Relations" in Hall, *Strategies for Mutual Gain,* op. cit., p. 103.

59. Ibid.

60. Ibid.

61. Ibid.

62. Thomas A. Kochan and Paul Osterman, *The Mutual Gains Enterprise* (Boston: Harvard Business School Press, 1994), p. 107.

63. Ibid.

64. Ibid., p. 76.

65. Ibid.

66. Ibid., p. 45.

67. Ibid., p. 76.

68. *Guidelines: Innovative Collective Bargaining Contract Provisions,* (Federal Mediation and Conciliation Service, U.S. Department of Labor) issue no. 1 (January 1995), p. 1.

69. Ibid., pp. 31–32.

70. Heckscher op. cit., p. 86.

APPENDIX A

The Colosi Bargaining Model

Most discussions of collective bargaining focus on the skills, techniques, and knowledge necessary to prevail in labor negotiations. The Colosi Model examines the actual negotiating process and reviews the interactions that take place across and around the bargaining table. This model examines the structure of bilateral and multilateral negotiations, explores the structure of the bargaining team, identifies bargaining configurations, and analyzes the dynamics of the bargaining process.

BARGAINING STRUCTURE

When a negotiation such as arms control talks or collective bargaining is reported in the media, the press usually depicts the negotiation as a meeting of two basically undifferentiated sides sitting across a table from each other. A reporter might describe the situation by commenting, "The United Auto Workers and Chrysler have suspended their contract talks for an indefinite period" or "The baseball owners and players convened again today in New York."

This description oversimplifies the negotiation process and portrays its structure as a one-dimensional, two-party process that occurs only in the media spotlight; the process is more complex than that. Collective bargaining is an intricate ritual with many players and various configurations. In order to understand the complexities of the bilateral collective bargaining process, one needs to examine not only the various bargaining configurations but the structure of the bargaining team itself.

BARGAINING TEAM

Members of each bargaining team can be divided into four classifications: stabilizers, destabilizers, quasi mediators, and ratifiers. Each category has its own role and function in the bargaining process.

Stabilizers

Stabilizers are those team members committed to the table process and oriented toward reaching agreement, sometimes at any cost. They see negotiation as a way to avoid a war, a court battle, or a strike; they tend to be averse to conflict. Roger Fisher and William Ury, in their book *Getting to Yes,* identify stabilizers as "soft" negotiators, referring to the fact that they are soft on the people and soft on the issues.

Stabilizers tend to trust others, even when the trust isn't warranted. Stabilizers demonstrate their agreeability with their words and with their deeds. They also demon-

---

The model was written by Thomas R. Colosi, Vice President for National Affairs, The American Arbitration Association. Assistance was provided by Lois Gant.

strate their assent with their body language by frequently nodding their heads. They usually fall into line when authority is applied, regardless of which side applies it. They are easy to work with, and they are easy for the other side to work with. That is not necessarily an advantage for either side unless the stabilizers on a team can be managed.

Destabilizers

Destabilizers, on the other hand, are generally not averse to conflict. They don't like the negotiation process. They don't trust the other team. They are more verbal. Destabilizers tend to drive hard bargains. They tend to be what Fisher and Ury call "hard" negotiators—hard on the people and hard on the issues.

Destabilizers tend to mistrust the other side and those on their own team who want to negotiate a deal. Destabilizers frequently resist authority, and they don't listen very well to anyone else's point of view. If left unchecked, destabilizers can overpower, intimidate, create mistrust, and ultimately sabotage the internal working relationship of a bargaining team or the entire negotiation process.

Quasi Mediators

The quasi mediators on the bargaining team have several roles. Usually, they are the team leaders, the chief negotiators. As advocates for the interests of their side, they must harmonize not only the interests across the table but the interests of the stabilizers and destabilizers within their own team. Although clearly an advocate, the quasi mediator is interested in achieving a settlement that is not only workable, but one that both sides can live with.

Fisher and Ury refer to quasi mediators as "principled negotiators," soft on the people yet hard on the issues. The quasi mediators orchestrate the negotiation process and usually fully understand the process.

Although all three classifications of bargaining team members act in specific roles—as stabilizers, destabilizers, and quasi mediators—their roles can and often do change during the negotiating process. On certain issues, all three categories of members may be transformed into destabilizers. An example might be the union team's response to a management proposal to have employees contribute to a previously noncontributory health insurance plan. This proposal may strike the union as a backward, negative move to the extent that all negotiating team members may agree that a strike, if necessary to defeat the proposal, would be totally justified.

Similarly, as a result of a lengthy strike that completely closes company operations, management negotiating team members may revise their positions. Ardent foes of the proposed agreement (the destabilizers) may, after several months of a strike, become more settlement oriented, if only out of desperation, and a previously unacceptable position may now be acceptable. For example, the company's proposal that employees contribute to their health insurance plan may simply not seem worth many months of lost production and sales, even to those who proposed it initially. Indeed, after a lengthy strike, everyone, on both sides, may well be classified as a stabilizer, in that everyone wishes as rapid a settlement as possible. The price of continued strife may be seen as too high, whatever the settlement costs.

Ratifiers

Ratifiers, although not official members of the bargaining team, play a very important role in internal team negotiations. Often, the negotiations between the ratifiers and the negotiators may be very contentious. No matter how well managed the bargaining team, the relationship with those who have ratification authority must also be effectively managed.

The "bottom line" of any negotiation is a line that is more than theoretically drawn by the people with the power and authority to approve a settlement.

Unlike other members of the bargaining team, ratifiers are very rarely present at the bargaining table. Leverage in the negotiation process rests with the negotiators rather than the ratifiers. Having the ratifiers present at the table puts the team at a great disadvantage: Emotional detachment between the negotiators and the ratifiers is critical because emotional involvement can cloud thinking and decision making.

The process of buying a car provides a practical illustration of the way having the negotiator and ratifier present constitutes a disadvantage for the team. Typically, when a couple decides to buy a car, one partner cannot finalize a deal until the decision is ratified by the other partner, who may be distant from the negotiations. When both partners are present, the team has lost the leverage advantage of having the ultimate decision rest with someone who is away from the negotiation.

BARGAINING CONFIGURATIONS

Horizontal Bargaining

Horizontal bargaining, negotiations that occur across the table, is often highly structured and formalized. It may appear that a great deal of bargaining takes place across the table. This is not necessarily so. In fact, in difficult negotiations, very little actual bargaining occurs in this horizontal configuration. What does occur across the table is by no means unimportant. Whereas often the activity itself is not negotiation, it may set the tone for future negotiation. The activity across the table may include information sharing (discovery and evaluation), posturing, education, oration, yelling, cursing, threats, crying (demonstrating intensity), and the like. Most of the real bargaining occurs mainly within the bargaining teams themselves, away from the table, in caucus, where the decisions are made about what to promise, when to promise, and who shall promise.

Within each team, active intraorganizational negotiations are constantly being conducted. As previously noted, different members may be very adamant about their respective roles and positions. In addition, it must be recognized that team members' positions may vary from issue to issue.

Thus, away from the bargaining table, in caucus, each team must deal with the questions of what movement, if any, to make; how much of a movement to make; when to make it; and how to make it. Predictably, the destabilizers resist movement; the stabilizers encourage movement; and the quasi mediators facilitate (and negotiate) the making of the decision, implement it, and seek to keep the team unified.

Vertical Bargaining

Each team must not only bargain internally; it must also bargain with its own hierarchy, its constituencies and those whose interest they represent. This bargaining configuration is also called *constituencies bargaining*. The plural is used intentionally; each party is composed of numerous subgroups of constituencies with unique interests that must be satisfied. For example, in the 1980s when the United Auto Workers negotiated a new master contract with General Motors, the union had to pay attention to skilled and unskilled workers, males and females, younger and older workers, and Americans and Canadians. Furthermore, within each group, multiple constituencies are present.

Vertical, or constituencies, bargaining can be of great significance, especially when the proposed agreement has to be ratified by the membership. At times, a proposed agreement reached and recommended by the union negotiating team is voted down by the membership, sometimes overwhelmingly. The ratification vote may be negative because the negotiating team failed to convey the reality of the bargaining situation to the membership—and most especially to the opinion leaders, such as shop stewards and other union activists—or perhaps because the union negotiating team simply misread its constituencies or overlooked the needs of a key subgroup.

Shadow Bargaining

The term *shadow bargaining* describes the informal negotiating process that occurs away from the bargaining table, formal caucuses, or official constituent meetings. The negotiating may not necessarily occur in the "shadows," but it often does. The principals of each side may meet privately to see if a deal can be reached, and frequently they are successful because, with no observers, neither person has to engage in rhetoric or expound publicly on the virtues of his or her proposals.

Sometimes, but not always, the shadow meetings are fully authorized by team members or key hierarchy members. There are dangers when meetings are not authorized. Any deal reached during shadow negotiation may be rejected by the constituents, who may suspect a "sellout." This in turn could create a barrier to reaching an agreement in the future. Unauthorized and secret shadow bargaining presents risks and therefore is not too often utilized by negotiators.

Nonetheless, well-intentioned individuals may take it upon themselves to meet with similarly inclined individuals from the other side in an effort to facilitate agreement. Unless each side's mandate is clear and its authority agreed upon in advance, such meetings are likely to result in misunderstandings and frustrations.

"Sunshine" Bargaining

In the aftermath of the secrecy and closed atmosphere of the Watergate era, and as a reaction against the negative feelings it engendered, legislators began to enact open-meeting "sunshine" laws providing that all public sector deliberations must be conducted within public view. Although these laws originally applied only to meetings of governmental boards and regulatory bodies, the state of Florida applied the sunshine law to all meetings, including collective negotiations for public employees.

The idea underlying these laws is that the government, which belongs to all the people, should make its important decisions in the open, where taxpayers and voters can observe that process and the dynamics behind it. Decisions must not be presented as *faits accomplis.*

Many jurisdictions have enacted sunshine laws for governmental meetings, and a few have adopted sunshine bargaining laws. The rationale for these laws is that the use of public monies to pay public employees gives the public the right to observe the process by which labor-management contracts are reached. It is claimed that if people are free to observe the negotiations, they will more likely support these contracts, as opposed to agreements produced in closed or secret negotiations. Public officials who negotiate agreements can have their performance more easily evaluated; thus, a better assessment of their conduct can be made by the electorate, their "employers."

Criticism of Sunshine Laws

Opponents of sunshine bargaining argue that it creates more problems than it solves. The physical presence of the public affects adversely the atmosphere of negotiations and makes real bargaining more difficult. Very often, parties in the public spotlight make speeches rather than resolve issues and reach agreements. Further, a public presence results in often uninformed value judgments. The following factors need to be considered when one evaluates sunshine laws.

First, sunshine bargaining incorrectly assumes that horizontal (across-the-table) negotiations are the key to reaching an agreement. Internal and vertical bargaining are not specifically covered by these sunshine laws, and, as mentioned previously, they are vital parts of the negotiation process. Shadow bargaining is presumably barred by sunshine laws. It is important to note that the open-meeting laws do not eliminate shadow bargaining in the private sector; the laws cover only the public sector.

Second, the cathartic release of the horizontal negotiation process is hampered by the public's presence. The normal give and take, the floating of possible settlements, is hindered by the presence of a large, and possibly boisterous, audience or by the presence of the media. Candor is inhibited and posturing encouraged.

Third, critics point out that the very legislators who enact sunshine bargaining laws do not themselves "deliberate" over such laws "in the sunshine." Indeed, most sunshine bargaining laws are crafted, "deliberated," and enacted behind the closed doors of a legislative caucus session.

Veteran negotiators prefer that agreements be made public and subject to public scrutiny only after they are reached. Closed negotiations are not necessarily sinister or even contrary to the public interest. To some extent, they are often more effective, efficient, and equitable than open negotiations.

THE DYNAMICS OF THE TABLE

Collective Bargaining as a Ceremony

Collective bargaining is simultaneously a ritual, a game, a catharsis, and a problem-solving process. Just as ritual is an integral part of religion, it is an integral part of the collective bargaining process. We all take some comfort in the familiarity of ritual, and this is especially true in tense negotiation sessions. The union may begin by announcing its initial demands, which may be unrealistically high. No one on the union team seriously expects to receive so high a settlement. We can then anticipate management to react negatively and make disparaging remarks about the probable outcome of negotiations, given the unreasonable posture of the union. Management will usually point out the severe economic consequences of such a proposed settlement. It is a ritual, one with which most participants are quite familiar.

Collective Bargaining Rules

Collective bargaining is an activity pursued according to certain rules. The rules are both of the written statutory variety and the unwritten behavioral variety. For example, we expect the parties, upon reaching agreement, to execute a written agreement. Indeed, the refusal to commit the agreement to writing is considered an unfair labor practice by the National Labor Relations Board. An unwritten rule is the practice of the union's presenting its demands first.

In conflict situations, the presence of rules of the process directs the parties' behavior into predictable and safer channels. It should also be noted that many veterans of negotiation recall past situations with humor and fondness. For example, negotiating committee members may remember how seven years ago they bargained for 37 hours straight until they reached agreement. Although at the time they were probably frustrated and fatigued, now they remember the experience fondly, the way one recalls a championship football game. It is not coincidental that the word *team* is used to describe each side. This "win-lose" mind-set is alive and well, as demonstrated in the 1994–95 baseball strike. However, more enlightened parties are moving to an "I can live with it–I can live without it" mind-set.

Collective Bargaining as an Emotional Release

A catharsis is an emotional release, and clearly the negotiating table provides an opportunity for this. Psychologists report that bottling up one's emotions is unhealthy. The bargaining table provides a reasonably safe outlet for strong feelings. Often, the outsider—the company attorney or the union representative—may be the most vocal and outspoken participant.

If negative feelings are to be expressed, it is less destructive to have outsiders—those who do not have to live with one another—express these sentiments. They can provide "vicarious catharsis." Long after the contract is reached and the problems solved, the harsh words between two adversaries may be remembered and may be a potential source of friction.

The Role of Hostile Behavior in Collective Bargaining

Hostile behaviors, unless one can predict their results, are usually not productive. Very few professional negotiators are at all affected by such actions, and most generally attempt not to behave that way themselves at the table. They usually dismiss negative phrases as meaningless. Although some authors urge readers to Win by Intimidation, such behavior may be at cross-purposes with a negotiator's real goals: reaching agreement and having those on the other side eventually advocate to their ratifiers the approval of the settlement.

The following two factors contextualize the function of hostility in bargaining. First, hostility is frequently expected and accepted as part of the negotiating process between the parties. If so, it can be viewed as an appropriate channel for release of tension and catharsis. It is also a predictable form of behavior that is anticipated by the other side. Second, even though hostility clearly has its negative consequences, it can have positive aspects as well. As previously stated, each bargaining team is composed of individuals who have emotional commitments to their side. These strong emotions need to be dealt with if the negotiations are to move toward an agreement, and verbalizing antagonism may be a way of accomplishing that objective.

Like any other aspect of the collective bargaining process, whatever is said or done must be placed in the overall context of the desired goals. Expressing hostility, therefore, can be, in the final analysis, either constructive or destructive, depending on how and why it is used.

Exchange of Information

Amidst the often emotionally charged atmosphere present in negotiations, it is easy to underestimate the role of information exchange between the parties. The negotiating table presents the parties with a unique opportunity for face-to-face communication and for clarification of positions, policies, and proposals for change.

For union negotiators, especially rank-and-file employees who are members of the bargaining team, this may be a rare opportunity to communicate with management officials, many of whom they would never have met but for their participation in negotiations. In some instances, when union negotiators are presented with a clear rationale for management proposals, they may be more willing to accept them. For example, when the vice-president of finance explains that the company must now bid on contracts for work that will not commence until three years hence, perhaps the union team may be more favorably disposed toward the company's proposal for a three-year agreement that would allow more accurate forecasting of labor costs for that period. At the very least, such an instructional opportunity serves to personalize that vague, amorphous entity called management and provides a different view of negotiable issues.

Similarly, management negotiators, some of whom may be removed from the day-to-day workplace, are given an opportunity to learn what employee concerns are and how their policies are viewed by those on the receiving end of memos and procedural bulletins.

The Role of Trust and Integrity

It is important to note the vital role of trust and integrity in labor relations. It is the ongoing, close daily relationship of the parties that distinguishes collective bargaining from many other negotiating relationships. It not only means that the parties must reach agreement; they must live up to their agreements—both those reduced to writing and, more important, those expressed verbally.

No agreement, no matter how extensive, can possibly cover all potential situations. Ultimately, certain matters must be left to the parties' trust and integrity. If a contested matter should end up in arbitration, the handwritten notes from negotiations, as well as the parties' oral testimony about their recollections, may be very pertinent. In fact, most grievance matters never reach the arbitration stage because the parties usually honor their oral agreements. The negotiator who lies or bends the truth and cites the absence of a written agreement may well emerge victorious—once. Because labor relations is an ongoing process, he or she wins the battle but loses the war. Henceforth, his or her word is valueless, and his or her reputation may be damaged beyond repair.

People in the labor relations field are not necessarily any more virtuous than people in other fields. However, ethically, the system is based upon integrity, predictability, and trust. To lose one's integrity and the trust of others is as shortsighted as it is impractical if one intends to remain in the labor relations profession.

APPENDIX B

Innovative Collective Bargaining Contract Provisions and the New American Workplace

The *Report and Recommendations* of the Commission on the Future of Worker-Management Relations,[1] known as the Dunlop Commission, states that one of the goals for the twenty-first-century workplace should be to "expand coverage of employee participation and labor-management partnerships to more workers and more workplaces and to a broader array of decisions."[2] The following innovative provisions from current labor contracts suggest that some employers have already started implementing employee participation programs and labor-management partnerships in their organizations. The source of these contract provisions is a new publication of the Federal Mediation and Conciliation Service (FMCS), U.S. Department of Labor, entitled *Guidelines: Innovative Collective Bargaining Contract Provisions*.[3] The FMCS guidelines also include a statement from the AFL-CIO on the new American workplace; that statement is included in this appendix.

The next few sections include innovative articles from current labor agreements as well as a labor perspective on "the new American workplace."

UNITED MINE WORKERS OF AMERICA AND THE BITUMINOUS COAL OPERATORS ASSOCIATION

[Exp. August 1, 1998]

G. UMWA-BCOA Labor-Management Positive Change Process ("LMPCP")

Section 1. Establishment of Purpose

The parties recognize that, just as the coal industry has changed, and continues to change, so too must a new and different relationship be fostered between labor and management. The parties recognize that the Union's goals of increased job and employment opportunity and security for its members goes hand-in-hand with, and indeed depends upon, the increased and continuous competitiveness and financial stability of the Employers. It is further recognized that the mutual objectives of the parties can best be attained by a joint commitment to continuous improvement of working relationships, productivity, health, safety, training, education, and investment in technology and, most importantly, human resources. In this light, the parties must discard old ways of dealing with each other in an atmosphere of mistrust, and foster a new environment of mutual trust and a good-faith acceptance of their respective institutions. For, in truth, the parties have a major responsibility to the same resource: the Union, to its members, and the Employers, to their employees. In order to achieve these objectives, the parties recognize the need for new and creative approaches to labor-management relations, to the increasing involvement of Employees in the success of mining operations, and for changes to be made at the mine sites to allow the Employers to better compete in today's global marketplace.

Accordingly, to promote joint efforts addressing those needs, and to enhance existing efforts to improve labor-management cooperation, the parties here establish the UMWA-BCOA Labor-Management Positive Change Process (LMPCP). . . .

H. UMWA-BCOA Labor-Management Policy Committee

The parties recognize that the coal industry is at a critical juncture. It operates in a global economy and faces the challenges of environmental legislation as well as fierce domestic and foreign competition. These challenges are likely to increase rather than subside during the next several years. Mutual cooperation at the highest levels and a sincere commitment to communication and problem solving are therefore critical for the industry to maintain and enhance its competitive position.

To address these concerns, the parties hereby establish a "UMWA-BCOA Labor-Management Policy Committee." This Committee shall operate as a labor-management committee within the meaning of Section 302(c)(9) of the LMRA, as amended, established and functioning so as to fulfill one or more of the purposes set forth in Section 6 of the Labor Management Cooperation Act of 1978. The Committee shall have the full support and commitment of both the UMWA and the BCOA in the Committee's efforts to identify problems, formulate plans to solve these problems and, where appropriate, conduct joint activities designed to implement the plans.

The Committee shall be comprised of four high-level representatives of the UMWA; four high-level representatives designated by the BCOA; and one neutral Chairman who shall be selected by the other members of the Committee. The Chairman will have authority to assist the Committee in carrying out its purposes, which shall include: (a) opening lines of communication that will serve to promote the objectives outlined in this Agreement, and (b) addressing the major issues facing the industry, such as legislation, the environment, technological changes, and similar issues.

SATURN CORPORATION AND THE UNITED AUTO WORKERS

[No expiration—living document]

Saturn Philosophy

We believe that all people want to be involved in decisions that affect them, care about their jobs and each other, take pride in themselves and in their contributions, and want to share in the success of their efforts.

By creating an atmosphere of mutual trust and respect, recognizing and utilizing individual expertise and knowledge in innovative ways, and providing the technologies and education for each individual, we will enjoy a successful relationship and sense of belonging to an integrated business system capable of achieving our common goals, which insures security for our people and success for our business communities. . . .

Consensus Guidelines

The structure described in [the section on Saturn Philosophy] is intended to make the Union a full partner in Saturn.

The consensus technique is the basic support methodology for Saturn decision-making and conflict resolution processes.

The parties agree that the consensus process, as outlined below, is the primary method for making decisions and resolving disagreements.

In the context of Saturn's philosophy and mission, decisions and disagreements will be resolved within the following guidelines:

- Resolution is achieved through the joint efforts of the parties in discovering the "best" solution.
- The solution must provide a high level of acceptance for all parties.
- Once agreement is reached, the parties must be totally committed to the solution.
- Any of the parties may block a potential decision. However, the party blocking the decision must search for alternatives.
- In the event an alternative solution is not forthcoming, the blocking party must reevaluate the position in the context of the philosophy and mission.
- Voting, "trading" and compromise are not part of this process.
- The joint effort is aimed at discovering the best decision/resolution within the context of Saturn's philosophy and mission while, at the same time, satisfying the stakes and equities of all major shareholders.

Saturn Conflict Resolution Procedure

There is a four-step problem-solving procedure, the last step of which involves final and binding arbitration. Conflicts may be reinstated in those instances where the International Union, UAW, by its Executive Board, Public Review Board, or Constitutional Convention Appeals Committee finds the conflict was improperly resolved by the Union or the Union representative.

INTERNATIONAL BROTHERHOOD OF TEAMSTERS NATIONAL MASTER FREIGHT AGREEMENT COVERING OVER-THE-ROAD AND LOCAL CARTAGE EMPLOYEES OF PRIVATE COMMON, CONTRACT AND LOCAL CARTAGE CARRIERS

[Exp. March 31, 1998]

Article 20 Section 2. Joint Industry Development Committee

The Parties recognize that the unionized LTL industry is losing market share and jobs to competitors. The parties recognize that it is in the interest of the Union and the Employers to return the LTL industry to health and to foster its growth. Only if the industry prospers and grows will the industry's employees, whom the Union represents, achieve true job and economic security. Only if the industry prospers and grows will the industry have access to the resources it needs to capitalize and be competitive.

Recognizing that returning the industry to health should be a cooperative, long-term effort, the Teamsters National Freight Industry Negotiating Committee ("TNFINC") and the Employer Association agree to establish a Joint Industry Development Committee to serve as a vehicle for this effort. The purpose of the Committee will be to perform the following tasks: address the principles of an intermodal truck load agreement as a means of capturing new market and creating additional city/P&D jobs; develop data to evaluate and monitor industry and competitor productivity, costs and operations; catalogue, compare and evaluate workrules, practices and procedures among the various NMFA supplements and the Employer Association's companies; make joint recommendations to the parties about any changes in the NMFA and its supplements that the Committee believes should be considered in the next round of negotiations for the new NMFA; solicit grants for joint activities that benefit the industry and its bargaining unit employees, such as driver training schools; and monitor pending legislation and executive action on the national, state and local level that may affect the welfare of the industry and, where appropriate, jointly recommend actions that further the interests of the industry and its bargaining unit employees and jointly present the views of the Joint Committee to legislative and executive bodies.

The Committee shall operate as a labor-management committee within the meaning of Section 302(c)(9) of the LMRA, as amended . . . so as to fulfill one or more of the purposes set forth in Section 6 of the Labor Management Cooperation Act of 1978. The Committee shall have the full support of both the International Brotherhood of Teamsters and the Employer Association in the Committee's efforts to identify problems, formulate plans to solve those problems and, where appropriate, conduct joint activities designed to implement the plans. The Chairman of TNFINC will appoint [5] Union representatives to the Joint Committee. The Employer Association will appoint [5] Employer representatives to the Joint Committee. Appointments to the Joint Committee will be made in a manner to assure that there are persons serving who are familiar with the full range of operations undertaken by the Employer Association's carriers under all supplemental agreements. The Joint Committee shall meet at least quarterly and may appoint continuing subcommittees to carry out specific tasks. The Union and Employer representatives to the Joint Committee will establish procedures for the operation of this Committee.

THE NEW AMERICAN WORKPLACE: A LABOR PERSPECTIVE

[Adopted by the AFL-CIO Committee on the Evolution of Work, February 22, 1994]

The time has come for labor and management to surmount past enmities and forge the kind of partnerships which can generate more productive, democratic and humane systems of work. . . .

[I]t is possible to discern five principles which together define a model for a new system of work organization. . . .

First, the model begins by rejecting the traditional dichotomy between thinking and doing, conception and execution. . . . This . . . requires a fundamental redistribution of decision-making authority from management to teams of workers. . . .

Second, in the new model, jobs are redesigned to include a greater variety of skills and tasks and, more importantly, greater responsibility for the ultimate output of the organization. . . . Moreover, workers are given the authority, and the training, to exercise discretion, judgment and creativity on the job. . . .

Third, this new model of work organization substitutes for the traditional, multi-layered, hierarchy a flatter management structure. . . . The aim is to enable workers to be self-managers who are responsible for their own performance, and the work teams are often self-managed with responsibility for scheduling work, ordering materials, hiring workers and the like. . . .

Fourth, the new model goes beyond the workplace level to insist that workers, through their unions, are entitled to a decision-making role at all levels of the enterprise. . . . Moreover, as stakeholders in the enterprise, workers have a vital interest in the strategic decisions which ultimately determine how much work will be done, where and by whom. Because workers have long-term ties to their jobs, they bring a long-term perspective and can be counted on to promote policies designed to insure that businesses have long-term futures and can provide long-term employment at decent wages. Thus, in this new model such strategic decisions are to be jointly made by workers—acting through their unions—and the other stakeholders.

Fifth, . . . the new model of work organization calls for the rewards realized from transforming the work organization to be distributed on equitable terms agreed upon through negotiations between labor and management. This means in the first instance, a negotiated agreement to protect income and employment security to the maximum extent possible.

These five principles form an integrated whole—a vision of a new system of work organization. They combine individual participation through restructured work processes and redesigned jobs, with collective representation, through restructured decision-making processes from the shop floor to corporate headquarters. The aim of this approach is to achieve work organizations which at one and the same time are more productive and more democratic. Therein lies the source of its legitimacy and its power.

Notes

1. Commission on the Future of Worker-Management Relations, *Fact-Finding Report* issued May 1994; *Final Report and Recommendations* issued December 1994.
2. Commission on the Future of Worker-Management Relations, *Final Report and Recommendations* (Washington, DC: U.S. Department of Labor and U.S. Department of Commerce, December 1994), p. xxii.
3. Issue no. 1, January 1995, pp. 3–13.

CHAPTER 10

Bargaining Theory and Bargaining Power

After reading this chapter, you should be able to

■ Explain what is meant in the Walton and McKersie Model by the following terms: *distributive bargaining, integrative bargaining, attitudinal structuring,* and *intraorganizational bargaining.*

■ Comprehend the roles of power and transactions in the Kuhn model of bargaining.

■ Review the roles of tactics, strategies, and strikes in the Kuhn model.

■ Evaluate the significance of *goods* and *bads* in the bargaining process.

■ Explain why arbitration is not a viable alternative to a strike

This chapter is about the theory of collective bargaining. The literature describes numerous theories of bargaining; we will focus our attention on only two. The first is the behavioral theory of Walton and McKersie; the second is the exchange theory of Alfred Kuhn. Walton and McKersie divide bargaining into four subprocesses and examine the interrelationships among these four sets of activities. Kuhn elucidates the concepts of power and bargaining power and evaluates the various strategies and tactics available to negotiating parties.

BARGAINING THEORY

Bargaining theorists try to understand the process and predict the outcomes of negotiations between parties. For example, when a consumer sets out to purchase an automobile, it is theoretically possible for any of a fairly wide range of prices to be the end point at which the seller and the buyer finally agree. After watching a number of consumers purchase autos, however, we may observe that the actual range of prices paid for the automobiles is fairly narrow. Nonetheless, differences do exist. Why is it that different consumers end up paying different prices? In our day-to-day lives, we encounter bargaining transactions like the automobile purchase situation discussed later. In addition, each of us makes intuitive observations and has an understanding of the nature of the bargaining problem, at least as conceptualized in the purchase of an automobile. We know that some consumers and some automobile dealers are better bargainers than others. Some automobiles are in shorter supply than are others. Some consumers live in cities that offer a wide choice of dealers for the same automobile. At a particular time, some consumers have greater need for automobiles, just as at some times, some dealers have greater need to sell them. All these factors play roles in the predicted final price to be settled upon by the buyer and the seller.

It is clear from this simple example that a predictive model or theory of bargaining outcomes incorporating all potential influences would be impossibly complex. Bargaining theorists make simplifying assumptions that make their task manageable. Although some of these assumptions are unrealistic, the true test of any theory is how well it predicts reality.[1]

A BEHAVIORAL THEORY OF LABOR NEGOTIATIONS: THE WALTON AND MCKERSIE MODEL

In their classic work, *A Behavioral Theory of Labor Negotiations,* Walton and McKersie advanced the proposition that the process of labor-management negotiation comprises four different subprocesses: distributive bargaining, integrative bargaining, attitudinal structuring, and intraorganizational bargaining.[2]

In the first subprocess, the parties bargain over division of a particular pie, and one party's gain is a direct loss for the opponent. In theoretical terms, this approach can be described as a fixed-sum game, or as distributive bargaining.

As contrasted with distributive bargaining, in the integrative bargaining subprocess, both sides search for solutions that would increase the size of the pie. In game theory models, this approach is referred to as a variable-sum game. In this subprocess, the objectives of both parties need not necessarily be in conflict, as they are in distributive bargaining. An example of a problem that might be solved through integrative bargaining is the development of an employee assistance program, which would serve bargaining unit members with substance abuse or other personal problems. Such a program could help management improve productivity while providing help for union members.

The third subprocess in the Walton and McKersie model is attitudinal structuring. Unlike distributive and integrative bargaining, which refer to negotiations between unions and management, attitudinal structuring represents a major departure from components represented in other bargaining theories. This negotiation subprocess defines the quality and type of relationship between labor and management. Attitudinal structuring encompasses the parties' efforts, intended and unintended, to shape their opponents' behaviors. Although Walton and McKersie acknowledge that attitudinal structuring can be influenced by such factors as the technical and economic context of the workplace, the social value system, and the personalities of negotiators, they hypothesize that the negotiators' own behaviors can influence the attitudes and behaviors of their opponents.[3] An understanding of this subprocess is important because the history and past behavior of negotiators can influence the success of current bargaining: A conflict-prone relationship may embody a set of attitudes that will make it difficult for the parties to move to a more cooperative relationship. In contrast to tactics used in distributive or integrative bargaining, in which the objective of a tactical move is to change the other party's position on a particular issue, attitudinal structuring may entail activities unrelated to specific bargaining issues. An example is the granting of a concession as a means of gaining the other party's trust. The first two bargaining subprocesses can be thought of as issue-oriented decision-making processes, whereas attitudinal structuring concerns the mood and atmosphere prevailing at the bargaining table and the tactics the parties can use to change the atmosphere.

The fourth subprocess, intraorganizational bargaining, is the only one of the four bargaining subprocesses that takes place largely away from the bargaining table. Intraorganizational bargaining refers to the internal negotiations that occur within the respective organizations. Walton and McKersie recognize that neither the union nor management represents a homogeneous constituency. On each side are individuals with conflicting views and interests. Each side must resolve some of these internal conflicts before it can reach a settlement with its bargaining opponent. On the management side, intraorganizational bargaining takes place among various staff and departmental interests. On the union side, industrial units representing different occupations, skills, age groups, and minorities provide union negotiators with ample opportunities for intraorganizational bargaining. Of course, the larger the bargaining unit, the greater the potential for internal conflict.

Walton and McKersie, in their theoretical and tactical framework for the four subprocesses of labor-management negotiation, make an important contribution to the literature of bargaining theory. First, they allow us to view collective negotiations not as a unidimensional contest of labor versus management but rather as a complex, interrelated process of distributive, integrative, and intraorganizational bargaining—as well as attitudinal structuring. Second, they suggest the existence of strong links among bargaining behaviors, tactical decisions, and the goals of the negotiating parties. In their view, by observing behaviors we can infer much about the agendas and objectives of the parties. Walton and McKersie claim that "the behaviors which we call distributive bargaining are indices for inferring goal conflict or perceived goal conflict."[4] Third, their framework suggests that any single action by a union or a management negotiator can evoke a multiplicity of responses within the four subprocesses. For example, a threat made by a negotiator may further that negotiator's goal on a single issue in the distributive bargaining subprocess. At the same time, the threat may diminish the potential for future discussion of a problem within the integrative bargaining subprocess, making it difficult or even impossible to engage in integrative bargaining. Further, that same threat may have an adverse effect on the attitudinal structuring subprocess; thus it may have negative repercussions for current and, perhaps, even future negotiations. Finally, that same threat may either satisfy or dissatisfy the constituency of the party making the threat, thus influencing the content of intraorganizational bargaining. Therefore, Walton and McKersie suggest that if union or management negotiators focus solely on a particular tactic within one subprocess, ignoring the linkages among the subprocesses, they may set off an unintended chain reaction with unwanted adverse effects.

Another important and useful concept discussed by Walton and McKersie is the notion of a contract zone. The zone can have a positive or a negative range. Its outer limits are determined by the bargaining parties. For example, in the case of a potential automobile transaction, there is a price at which the buyer would rather walk than drive. Correspondingly, there is a price at which the seller would rather keep than sell the automobile. The range of potential outcomes in this example may be limited by the dealer's choices and costs and the buyer's perception of the costs of alternative forms of transportation. A hypothetical automobile transaction is examined in some detail in the next section. In general, the outer limits of the contract zone are defined by the points outside which the parties would prefer not to settle. Consider the issue of wages in labor-management negotiations: There is a wage at which management would be losing money and therefore might have no incentive to remain in business and employ workers. On the other end of the scale, there is a level of compensation at which workers would decide to look for alternative employment rather than work at that wage. Within each contract zone, the par-

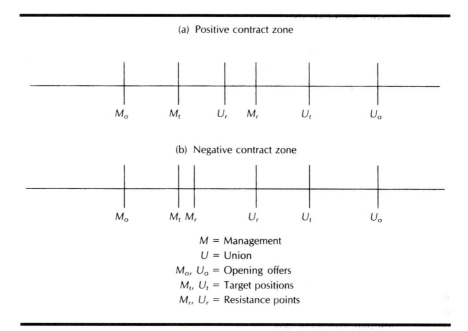

FIGURE 10.1 Contract Zones for Wages

Source: Richard E. Walton and Robert B. McKersie. *A Behavioral Theory of Labor Negotiations* (New York: McGraw-Hill, 1965), pp. 42–45.

ties have opening offers, target positions, and resistance points. A resistance point within the range of potential solutions indicates the minimum settlement level that the party would be willing to accept. Beyond that point, the party would refuse to settle and thus would be willing to recognize and respond to the economic consequences of an impasse. Figure 10.1 details the two possible positions of resistance points in labor-management negotiations. In the case of a positive contract zone, Figure 10.1(a), the union and management resistance points overlap; there is a range of possible settlements that the parties would prefer to a strike. A negative contract zone, Figure 10.1(b), is said to exist whenever the resistance points do not overlap.

To conclude, Walton and McKersie provide us with "a conceptual framework for organizing thinking about the dynamics of negotiations."[5] Their four subprocesses "account for almost all the behavior in negotiations."[6]

THE BASICS OF TRANSACTIONS AND OF POWER: THE KUHN MODEL

Workers' loss of power during the industrial revolution sparked the formation of unions, and the relative power of employers and unionized workers has been a central concern in their relationship ever since. The basic nature of power is much the same across many areas. Hence, in studying power in connection with union-management relations, we will also be acquiring some understanding about important aspects of relations in general— between nations, firms, husband and wife, or the president and the Congress.

In the model developed by Alfred Kuhn,[7] several terms are pertinent to the analysis of power. Things people want affirmatively are *goods*. Goods can also be seen as things of value, the ones to get and the ones to give up. By contrast, things people want to avoid or get rid of are *bads*. These are things one may give something of value to prevent or to have removed. As we shall see, power is concerned with the kinds and quantities of goods and bads involved in interactions between parties.

Goods and bads have very broad meanings here. Goods include not only such marketable items as bread, automobiles, or haircuts, but also such relatively personal and nonmarketable things as praise, affection, self-esteem, or friendship. Bads are not marketable in the same sense as goods because people will not give anything of value in exchange for them. The varieties of bads will be detailed later in connection with a discussion of their uses.

Transactions

A transaction is any interaction between parties in which goods or bads are exchanged. Any set of negotiations in which a union and management establish the terms on which labor will be sold is a transaction. Power and bargaining power are aspects of the analysis of transactions. *Power* is the ability to get wanted goods from another party, and *bargaining power* is the ability to get them on good terms—that is, by giving relatively little in return. The meanings of these terms will be amplified in the following discussion.

In making a decision, one weighs costs and benefits. If the benefits of a transaction outweigh its costs, one can rationally accept it. If costs exceed benefits, the transaction would be rejected on rational grounds. For a transaction to occur, each of two parties must make a decision; the transaction will not be concluded unless the benefits equal or exceed the costs simultaneously for both parties. A transaction is thus seen to involve two mutually contingent decisions. Note, however, that two mutually contingent decisions are not the same decision. In fact, the two decisions must be different, or there can be no transaction. For example, in an exchange of my boa constrictor for your trailer hitch, I must decide whether to give up the boa and receive the hitch, and you must decide whether to give up the hitch and receive the boa. One might say loosely that we both agree to the same thing, the exchange. But, more strictly, we can jointly agree on the exchange only if we separately decide that to me the hitch is worth more than the boa and to you the boa is worth more than the hitch. Only if the benefits equal or exceed the costs to each of us separately will the transaction be concluded. Hence, our analysis will focus on two separate but mutually contingent decisions.

Let us confine attention for the moment to transactions in goods, calling the two parties A and B and the two goods X and Y. Party A already possesses X, and B already possesses Y. To A the benefit of the exchange is that A acquires Y. The cost is that A must give up X. Thus, A will decide to make the exchange if to him or her the value of Y (the benefit of the exchange) exceeds the value of X (the cost of the exchange). For the moment, we will ignore possible costs or benefits of the exchange process itself, as well as some other items that we will return to later. A transaction cannot take place on the basis of A's decision alone; B must also agree. This B will do if to him or her the value of X (the benefit of the exchange) exceeds the value of Y (the cost of the exchange). If to either party the cost and benefit are exactly equal, that party is indifferent as to completing or not completing the transaction. For simplicity, we will assume arbitrarily that all cases of indifference are resolved in favor of completing the exchange.

In short, if the benefits exceed (or equal) the costs for A and if the benefits exceed (or equal) the costs for B, then and only then will the exchange of X for Y take place. Thus, the exchange depends on four values: the value of X to A, the value of Y to A, the value of X to B, and the value of Y to B. We will call these four values, respectively, AX, AY, BX, and BY, and identify each more explicitly. For those who prefer it, utility may be substituted for value in any of these usages. Even more specifically, we may think of subjective expected utility if we wish to remind ourselves that all costs and benefits are ultimately subjective and that actions are based on images and expectations rather than on reality as such. The following list describes the companions and the dynamics of transactions:

AX: The value of X to A. If X is a commodity, AX can also be described as A's desire to keep X or as his or her reluctance to give it up. If X is a service, AX is A's desire not to perform it or his or her reluctance to do so. "Desire not to perform" means such costs to A as the time, effort, risk, frustration, money, materials, or adverse side effects of performing the service. AX is the cost to A of going through with the transaction.

AY: The value of Y to A. If Y is a commodity, AY is A's desire to have it. If Y is a service, AY is A's desire that B perform it. In either case, AY is the benefit to A of going through with the transaction.

BX: The value of X to B. With appropriate substitution of terms, this is the parallel of AY.

BY: The value of Y to B. With appropriate substitution of terms, this is the parallel of AX.

We can now express the relation more simply:

$$\text{If } AY \geq AX,$$

$$\text{and if } BX \geq BY,$$

then the exchange of X for Y will take place. If those conditions prevail, we can thus say that A has the power to get Y while B also has the power to get X. In this approach, power is never a trait or characteristic of one party taken alone but is always the position of one party in a particular relation with some other party. Furthermore, the greater the amount by which AY exceeds AX and/or the greater the amount by which BX exceeds BY, (1) the greater is the likelihood that the transaction will actually go through and (2) the greater is the potential gain in utility to one or both parties. We can also say that the greater the likelihood that the transaction will take place, the greater is the power of A to get Y and the greater is the power of B to get X.

Thus, we see the core of power—that one party holds something valued by another party, which he or she can give or do if the other in return will give or do something wanted by the first party. More briefly, power resides in the ability to grant or withhold things wanted by others. We will see later why this statement also holds for power based on bads, like strikes, threats, or violence.

We said earlier that the greater the amount by which AY exceeds AX, the greater is the likelihood that the transaction will take place, and hence the greater is A's power to get Y.[8] This means that A's power to get Y increases as AY increases. A's power to get Y also increases as AX decreases because the less reluctant A is to give up X, the more likely A is to do so and thus to get Y. On B's side, we can make parallel statements about the way his or her power increases in proportion to the amount by which BX exceeds BY.

Another conclusion follows. If A's power to get Y rises, and if A gets Y by giving X to B, then B's power to get X also rises along with A's power to get Y. That is, in an exchange of goods, A's power and B's power rise and fall together; one does not rise at the expense of the other. In this respect, the dynamic differs sharply from bargaining power, to which we now turn.

Bargaining Power

So far we have dealt with transactions as if the goods involved were indivisible—a boa constrictor for a trailer hitch, a bowie knife for a hunting bow, a naval base for a treaty of friendship. We next discuss the terms of the exchange—the question of how much X will be given in return for how much Y. That is the question of bargaining power, which is the ability to get relatively much in return for relatively little—to get favorable terms in a transaction. We will illustrate with a transaction in which X is a divisible good, money; Y is an indivisible good, an automobile; A is a potential buyer; and B is the seller.

Each party must choose between two goods, the one to get and the one to give up. For convenience, we can join these two items for each party and say that one party's effective preference is his or her net desire for the good held by the other. For A, this means A's desire for Y, or AY, minus A's desire to keep X, or AX. If effective preference is shortened hereinafter to EP, A's desire for Y can be referred to as A's EP for Y, or simply as A's EP. This is desire backed by purchasing power, in which A's desire for Y is the demand, or preference aspect, and the X offered in return is the purchasing power, or effective aspect. The explanation of B's EP parallels that of A. We will illustrate bargaining power with the purchase of a used car because the price of a car is typically both negotiable and worth bargaining about.

You, A, are looking at a used car. You have examined its condition, and your desire for the car (AY) and your desire not to part with your money (AX) are such that you would be willing to give as much as $2,600. As shown in Figure 10.2, this means that your EP

FIGURE 10.2 Potential EPs for Buyers and Sellers of a Used Car

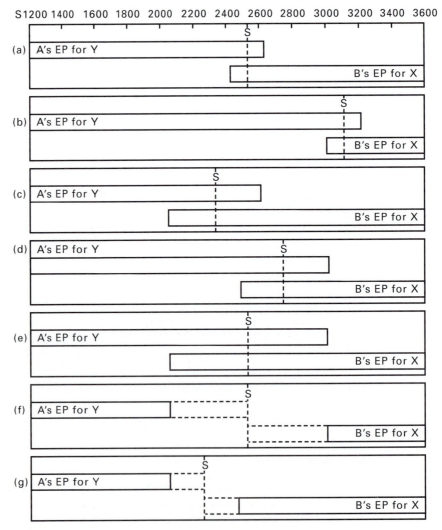

for the car extends to $2,600, which may also be thought of as your reservation price, or the price above which you would rather keep your money than acquire the automobile. A reservation price is the most a buyer will give for an item or the least a seller will accept. Given the dealer's desire for money (BX) and his or her desire not to give up the car (BY), he or she would be willing to sell for as little as $2,400. That is the reservation price, presumably reflecting the dealer's best assessment of what he or she thinks can be gotten from someone else. We will assume for the moment that you and the dealer are equally good negotiators. You eventually split the difference and settle for $2,500, at S, as in Figure 10.2(a).

Suppose that your EP extends instead to $3,200 and the dealer's extends to $3,000. After negotiations you settle for $3,100, as in Figure 10.2(b). The terms are better for you in 10.2(a) ($2,500) than in 10.2(b) ($3,100). That is, you get a lower price in the first case than in the second; your bargaining power is better (greater). By contrast, the dealer would get better terms in the second case, which means that his or her bargaining power is greater in Figure 10.2(b) than in 10.2(a). Thus, unlike "plain" power, the bargaining powers of the two parties move in opposite directions. The dealer's goes up as yours goes down, and vice versa.

Let us examine some other situations. In Figure 10.2(c) we show your EP back in its original position at $2,600. But the dealer's EP is now longer than in 10.2(a), extending to $2,000 instead of to $2,400. Still assuming that you are equally good negotiators and split the difference, what are the consequences? The settlement S now occurs at $2,300, compared to $2,500 in Figure 10.2(a). By contrast, 10.2(d) shows the dealer's EP back to its original position of $2,400 but shows your EP extended to $3,000. Now the midpoint settlement has risen to $2,700.

The main principles about bargaining power are now clear. Starting from any given position and with relative bargaining skills unchanged, either party's bargaining power rises with an increase in the other party's EP and decreases with an increase in his or her own EP. That is, the more intensely the other party wants what you have, the greater is your bargaining power, and the more intensely you want what the other has, the less is your bargaining power. More formally, each party's bargaining power varies directly with the other party's EP and inversely with his or her own. These generalizations are equally true if one party is consistently more skilled at negotiation. The settlement terms S in Figure 10.2 then fall consistently toward one end of the overlap rather than at the midpoint. But S moves with changing EPs in the same way as previously stated, as you can readily test for yourself.

What happens if both EPs increase? If they increase by the same amount, no change in bargaining power results, as we can see by comparing Figure 10.2(a) with 10.2(e). Both EPs have increased by $400, but the midpoint has remained unchanged at $2,500. If the EPs change by different amounts, bargaining power shifts in favor of the party whose EP increases less, as you can readily confirm. Incidentally, one cannot relate power or bargaining power to the lengths of EPs because the length of the EP depends on the wholly arbitrary point of origin in the diagram. It is relevant, of course, to note which EP changes most during negotiations and whether either EP extends to some particular point, such as a set of terms proposed by a mediator.

We now shift to a transaction that will not necessarily go through. In Figure 10.2(f), your EP extends to $2,000 while the dealer's extends to $3,000. There is no overlap, and if the EPs stay where they are, no transaction is possible. We can call this gap between EPs a negative overlap of $1,000.

In one sense, it seems pointless to talk of bargaining power when there are no terms on which you can get the car or the dealer can get your money. But let us compare Figure 10.2(f) with 10.2(g). In 10.2(g), your EP remains at $2,000 while the dealer's increases to

$2,400. And, whereas the midpoint terms in 10.2(f) are $2,500, in 10.2(g) they have dropped to $2,200. Though this is of no use to either party if matters stop there, certainly A's prospects look better in 10.2(g) than in 10.2(f). Thus, the previous generalization still holds: that A's bargaining power is improved by an increase in B's EP.

The same reasoning can be applied to "plain" power. For any given EP of B that does not overlap A's, the longer A's EP, the closer A will be to overlapping B's and getting the car. The longer A's EP, the less distance A must yet move to get the car, or the lower the hurdle that will remain to be overcome. If the EPs do overlap, then the greater A's EP, the greater is A's assurance that he or she will get the car, even if at a higher price. With this background, we can now state the relationship between power and bargaining power more simply. In transactions where terms are not already given (are negotiable), then, other things being equal, the more you want something from someone else, the more likely you are to get it, but the more you will probably give for it. The more the other party wants what you have, the more likely you are to get what he has, and the less you will probably have to give for it. In short, with respect to a given transaction, an increase in the other party's EP is all in your favor; an increase in your own EP is a mixed blessing. Parallel statements apply to B.

TACTICS AND STRATEGY

We have examined the effects of EPs and of changes in EPs on power and bargaining power. We now shift from that general analysis to the question of how a party to a particular transaction can improve its position relative to that of the other party. Within the framework established previously, two questions arise that are logically distinct, even if the means of answering them are often not clearly distinguished. Expressed from A's point of view, the first question is this: Assuming that the EPs of both A and B are given and are unlikely to change during negotiations, what can A do to achieve a settlement as near as possible to his or her own end of the existing overlap of EPs? We will use the term *tactics* to refer to such attempts to achieve the best possible settlement for oneself within a given set of EPs. We next remove the assumption about EPs being given, to arrive at the second question: How can A seek to change one or both EPs to gain an advantage? We will use the term *strategy* for any attempt by a party to alter the EPs themselves as a means of achieving a more satisfactory outcome. Although these definitions are somewhat more specific, they parallel the general usage in which *strategy* refers to a relatively long-range or wide-scope action, whereas *tactics* typically accept the "strategic" situation as given and operate more narrowly within its limitations. We can summarize the difference between tactics and strategies by saying that the purpose of strategies is to influence the position of the overlap of EPs, whereas the purpose of tactics is to influence the location of the settlement within a given overlap. Given these clarifications, we can now define *negotiation* more precisely as the use of tactics and strategies to improve one's power or bargaining power in a transaction.

Let us note first some situations in which the EPs may be essentially immovable and tactics alone could be brought to bear. One example would be negotiations over the price of a car, in which the buyer's upper limit is firm because he or she can acquire an identical automobile for that amount just down the street. The dealer's EP is also firm at a price that has already been offered by another customer, who is still eager to buy. Another example might occur if the negotiators were agents whose principals had set firm limits on the terms that they could accept.

Strictly speaking, tactics deal with perceptions about the magnitudes of EPs, not with their actual magnitudes, and with attempts to manipulate those perceptions. The normal use of tactics is to try to learn the true length of the opponent's EP and then either to conceal one's own EP or to understate it as just meeting or barely overlapping the opponent's. The party who can successfully effectuate that tactic will achieve a settlement near its own end of the overlap and channel to itself nearly all of the jointly available gain of utility from the transaction. The most obvious use of strategy is to try to lengthen the opponent's EP while resisting any increase in one's own, or possibly shortening it. Given the complexities of human relationships, there is no limit to the ways in which tactics and strategies can be used. It is also possible that a move designed to have one effect might also produce the other instead or in addition. For example, a union leader might say, "You know, the strike isn't really hurting our members very much!" intending the remark as a tactic to impress management that the union's EP for an early settlement is quite short. But the remark might cause management to think more carefully than it had before about the real consequences of a long strike. Here we see a strategic effect of a move intended as a tactic. It is probable that the parties often take certain actions with only an intuitive feel for their effects on the other party. And it is highly improbable that the parties think consciously of their actions as tactical or strategic. That is the language of the textbook, not of the parties. Nevertheless, it is good for the reader to know that there is a definite logical difference in nature and effect between tactics and strategy.

Hostility, Generosity, and Assorted Other Motives

Bargainers sometimes are out to get what they can and do not care whether the other party is pleased or displeased. The desire to get as much and give as little as possible is a self-centered stance. Not caring whether the other party is pleased or displeased, helped or hurt, is an indifferent state. Much union-management bargaining is self-centered. But bargainers are not always indifferent. Because of liking or sympathy, they may want to help the other party, or they may want to hurt him or her out of anger or frustration. We will call the first attitude generous and the second hostile. Both can easily be accommodated in the Kuhn model. One's desire to help the other is represented by a generous extension of one's own EP, long if the generosity is large and short if it is small. Conversely, a desire to hurt the opponent contracts one's EP. This variation is similar to the attitudinal structuring of the Walton and McKersie model, discussed earlier.

Other motives can similarly be accommodated; just one is cited. If A wants to create the impression of being a tough bargainer, A will seek better terms than his or her EP for Y alone might call for. This is logically the same as a greater reluctance to give up what A has. It shortens A's EP and thereby raises A's bargaining power but decreases his or her power to get Y. A desire to appear "reasonable" would have the opposite effect. Other motives, like impatience to finish the negotiations, can similarly be traced.

Bads as Strategies

We have defined *strategy* as the attempt to change EPs, usually by increasing the other party's desire for the good one has to offer. Sometimes, however, a party can alter an EP by imposing bads on the other party. Bads include criticism or insult, fear, pain, destruction, frustration, insecurity, disease, noise, distraction, ugliness, and invasion of privacy. A bad can also lie in withdrawing or reducing the rate at which a good is provided, as in reducing a worker's pay, turning off a tenant's utilities, or calling a strike. Although pain and destruction are bads for almost everyone, what constitutes goods or bads often depends on the people and the situation.

A bad is almost necessarily a "service" rather than a commodity, as with inflicting pain, blowing up a truck, or calling a strike. Bads are not so much things as circumstances—the fact, say, that garbage has been dumped on your lawn, your tires have been slashed, or your income has been cut off. Bads can play a large role in union-management relations.

A Unique Property of Union-Management Relations

To have power or bargaining power, a party must be able to withhold something wanted by the other. When a union bargains with a management over, for example, a wage increase, the thing wanted by the union is the increase, which management can withhold until the union can provide a sufficient inducement. The other half of the relationship, however, is unusual. The thing wanted by management is labor. But whereas the union bargains on behalf of workers, it does not own labor in the same sense that management owns money or the factory.

The union cannot get what it wants, such as a wage increase, without first winning the agreement of the employer. But by the acts of hiring and operating from day to day, management can obtain the thing it wants, labor, without even consulting the union, much less winning its agreement. Because the employer can withhold what the union wants but the union cannot withhold what the employer wants, the goods-based bargaining power in this basic relation usually rests with the employer.

There are, of course, exceptions, as when employees must be recruited through a union hiring hall or the union effectively restricts the supply of workers. In any case, these exceptions do not undercut the statement that an employer generally can increase or decrease his or her work force without winning agreement from the union. A union cannot withhold labor in the same simple way that a car dealer withholds the car if you do not pay an acceptable price. The employer already "has" the labor. The only way the union can exert power, as contrasted to simple persuasion, is to be conspicuously unpleasant—to impose a bad on the employer in the form of a strike. As with any other bad, its purpose is to lengthen the employer's EP; hence, it constitutes a strategy.

Strategic bads involve two stages, imposition and relief. Whether one party imposes a bad on the other or both parties impose bads reciprocally, they do not negotiate about imposing the bads; rather, they negotiate about relieving them. The bargaining about relief can come either before or after the bad is imposed. In a stress transaction, the bad is imposed first, and the parties negotiate about relieving it. In a threat transaction, the parties negotiate first, and the relief consists of not imposing the bad later if satisfactory terms are negotiated.

To provide power or bargaining power, a bad must be relievable, the relief being the good, relatively speaking, that is bargained for. Kidnappers or hijackers, for example, destroy their power if they kill their hostages, as they then lose the ability to undo or relieve the bad. The bad of a threat to burn a house actually lies in the promised good of not burning it if the threatener's terms are met. One must, of course, have the capacity to provide (produce) the bad, even as one can acquire power through goods only if one can produce the goods. To return to the main point, it is not unionization, as such, that provides bargaining power to workers; it is the ability through collective action to cut off the flow of labor to the employer—the ability to withhold—that provides the power.

Union-management relations typically involve both threat and stress. The threat comes first—"Agree to this or there will be a strike." As we shall see, the threat is nearly always present implicitly, even if no one ever mentions it. If the threat does not produce agreement, it is eventually converted into the stress of an actual strike. The threat stage involves the implied promise not to apply the bad if agreement is forthcoming. The stress stage involves the promise to relieve the bad if agreement is reached. The typical union-management relation is that of a threat that can later be converted into a stress. A strike can do this because it is relievable. By contrast, a threat to burn your house cannot be converted to stress because it is not relievable. Whereas a struck employer can be changed back to an unstruck employer, a burned house cannot be similarly changed back to an unburned one.

APPLICATION OF KUHN'S MODEL TO COLLECTIVE BARGAINING

In this section we take Kuhn's general model[9] and see how it can be applied to the negotiation of a new collective bargaining agreement. We discuss some of the complexities of actual negotiations to illustrate how they can be accommodated in the model; we consider the question of wages. Management thinks that a 5 percent raise would be about appropriate in light of labor and product market conditions and the recent rate of inflation, but it would be willing to go to 7 percent as a gesture of goodwill. The union thinks that company productivity has risen much faster than the national average and that workers should enjoy some increase in real earnings over and above an adjustment for inflation. The union is initially unwilling to settle for less than 15 percent. As shown in Figure 10.3(A), the initial actual EPs of management and union extend to 7 and 15 percent, respectively. The parties are bargaining on wages alone for the moment.

Each party's own EP is the same as what Walton and McKersie call its resistance point.[10] It represents that party's minimum acceptable terms. Walton and McKersie also use the concept of target, or the amount each side will aim for. "The target of one is usually selected in a way that represents the best estimate about the other's resistance point"[11]—that is, one party's best estimate of the other's EP.

APPLYING TACTICS AND STRATEGIES

The negotiating parties obviously do not open by stating their true EPs. Management opens with an offer of 4 percent and the union demands 20, as shown in Figure 10.3(A). Each side knows that its opening proposal understates its own EP and confidently assumes that the same is true of the opponent. Hence, the opening proposals are not really credible. Each side is untruthful when it states that its opening proposal is the "most it will give." Whether at this or some subsequent point, the core problem of tactics is to be able to retreat from a given position (i.e., acknowledge that you were misrepresenting the true position of your EP) but nevertheless to remain maximally credible the next time you state a position. If by retreating you have revealed that you were distorting the truth the first time, why should the opponent not assume that you are equivocating this time, too?

Because tactics interweave with strategy, let us shift for the moment to strategy, which usually is the attempt by one party to lengthen the EP of the other. The union may assemble data to show that the present wage not only has failed to keep pace with the cost of living but also has fallen behind both other employers and the labor market. If the data are convincing, the employer may come to realize that it will take a larger wage than anticipated to meet his or her own objectives. Quite regardless of what the employer considers a good tactical move at the moment, the consequence may be an increase of his or her actual EP, say to 8 percent. On the other hand, the employer might be able to gather data to show that it is already above other employers and that unless it slows down in the rate of wage increases, local union members may lose jobs. If the employer's data are convincing, the union's EP may grow longer—that is, the union may be willing to accept a lower wage than before.

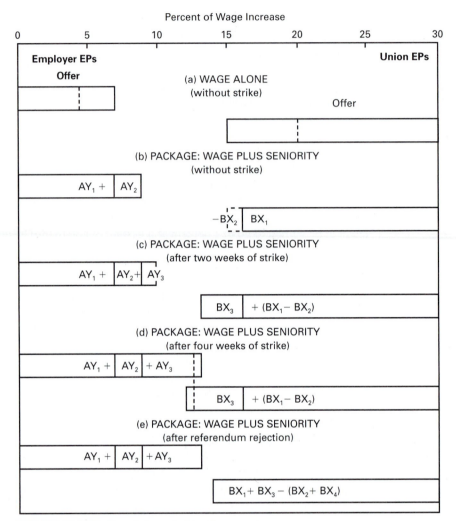

FIGURE 10.3(A) Negotiations of a New Agreement

Now let us look at some possible interplay of tactics and strategy. Whether or not they convincingly support strategies, the data may play a tactical role. Management representatives could pretend to look thoughtfully at the union's data and then caucus. On returning they could say, "We were not really aware of how we stood relative to others. On the basis of this new information, we are willing to offer you 6 percent." By pretending to learn something new, management could thus retreat without losing face—that is, without implicitly admitting that its prior statement of its position was false. The union might similarly use management's data to rationalize a graceful retreat.

But still further subtleties can surround the use of data. Suppose one side submits certain statistics in the belief, possibly correct, that the other party is not fully aware of particular relevant facts. If the statistics are to have their strategic effect of actually lengthening the other party's EP, they must be "good." That is, under critical examination they must demonstrate what the party submitting them says they demonstrate. Therein, however, lies a risk. You cannot expect your opponent to be influenced by the logic of data without implying that you yourself would be convinced by them. But suppose that after you have submitted data, the opponent can demonstrate that they are wrong or that they mean something different from what you said. Your position may then be weaker than if you had not submitted the data at all. In short, do not press arguments based on statistics too hard unless you are sure they are solid, or you may get caught in their backlash.

Let us trace just one more stage of subtleties. To fulfill a bona fide strategic purpose, data must be "good," as stated. If the purpose is to cover a tactical retreat under the face-saving guise of "new information," it does not matter directly whether the data are good or weak. However, if the union's figures are so obviously flawed that management could not reasonably have been convinced by them, it is then clear that for management to attribute a retreat to "new information" found in the union data is pure face saving. And that conclusion leads to the next step—that if some move is very obviously a face-saving device, it will not save much face. But even that is not the end of the line. If the union negotiator sees through the face-saving device, should the negotiator nevertheless pretend that he or she did not and accept management's new position as a sincere change of heart? Although there may be exceptions, the general answer would be yes. The reason is that although you strengthen your own position by making it difficult for yourself to concede, you also strengthen it by making it easy for the opponent to concede. In simple behaviorist's terms, reward the kinds of concessions you want to encourage; don't punish them. These observations, of course, are all reciprocal.

What one communicates is crucial. In this respect, the stances one takes and the concessions one makes or does not make may communicate far more than one's arguments. For example, once a party has stated a position, there is a double edge to concession.[12] The first edge is the "appeasement" effect. The concession may be taken as evidence of weakness, suggesting that the conceding party's EP is much longer than claimed. And it may give the opponent a scent of victory and bring a shortening of his or her EP. Either effect will tend to produce a hardening of the opponent's position and reduce the likelihood of counterconcessions. The opposite edge tends to soften the opponent. It may suggest that the conceding party is strong and confident enough to be reasonable but will make no further concessions unless there first are some counterconcessions from the opponent. Any concession by one party comes closer to being acceptable to the other and may raise the latter's hope of an early settlement. Nothing in Kuhn's theory gives any clue as to which edge of concession will cut. Intimate knowledge of the personalities and the situation can be helpful, but even that is not infallible.

Commitment—As Tactic and Strategy

Suppose you say during negotiations, "This much will I concede, but no more." If your opponent feels absolutely sure that you will not concede any more, that is a fact of life that must be accommodated. By contrast, if your opponent believes that your brave words are pure tactical bluff, he or she will not make further concessions, at least not until some additional ones have been extracted from you. Thus, there is great value in being credible when you take a firm stand. The question then is this: How can you make your position credible when there are such obvious reasons for you to bluff? The answer is to demonstrate that you cannot afford to go back on your word. The way to do so is to make clear that there is some stake you will lose if you do not keep your word and that you would lose more from forfeiting the stake than you would gain by breaking your word.[13] The act of putting yourself in a position to lose a stake is called commitment, and it is a crucial factor in many negotiations. Because a stake is a thing of value, its introduction into the bargaining relation affects the length of at least one EP and hence is a strategic ingredient.

The negotiator's own position could be at stake. "The union members (or top management) would throw me out on my ear if I give another inch," if credible, is one way to show that a negotiator cannot afford to make another concession. "I have gone on record that I will resign if I concede any more than this offer" may lend credibility to a stance, especially if accompanied by a confirming headline in the local paper. "The union members simply won't work for less than 15 percent" is no less credible, just because both sides know that the union negotiators have deliberately worked them into believing they deserve that much and can surely get it if they are tough enough. Commitment by the company could take the form of a well-publicized announcement that it will close the plant and move elsewhere rather than pay more than it has already offered.

In an ongoing successful relationship, the presence of credibility is a crucial factor. Once having made a commitment, a negotiator will lose trustworthiness if he or she backs down. Hence, a commitment may carry weight for no reason except that the opponent recognizes that the first party's reliability is at risk. The tactics utilized around commitment are mainly the following. The first is to avoid making a commitment until you are sure you are prepared to adhere to it. A second and related tactic is to have planned a way to back out of the commitment—a way known to yourself but not to the opponent. The third is to prevent the opponent from making a commitment, and the fourth is to find a way for the other side to get out of the commitment gracefully if one is made.

Not making a commitment hardly needs illustration, though the temptation to "get tough" is not always easy to resist. One way to back down from a commitment is to have couched it in words that sounded firm but were actually flexible. "I will not budge till hell freezes over" could be followed eventually with "I hear the fuel shortage has even reached down there!" Another way is to invoke some previously unsuspected third party: "My doctor just told me my blood pressure will not allow stringing these negotiations out any longer"; "I heard the president's speech last night about inflation, and I guess we all have to sacrifice a little"; or "We just got a new report from accounting that shows things are a bit better than we thought." (These third-party retreats are also variations of the "new information" tactic.) One way to stall off the opponent's commitment is to appear to stay flexible enough that the opponent does not seem to need a commitment. Another way to avoid the opponent's commitment, which is also a way to make it seem reversible, is to ignore or downplay it, perhaps by rewording it. For example, if the opponent says, "I absolutely will not budge one more step!" one can reduce the seeming firmness of this commitment by responding, "I fully understand why you said you would not want to go beyond your present offer." One might also subtly refer to some third party whom the opponent could use as a scapegoat to cover a retreat. We will shortly observe other devices in the relationships between the negotiators and their principals.

Once one party has made an irrevocable commitment, the other party can hurt only itself if it makes a parallel but nonoverlapping countercommitment. The unique feature of a union-management negotiation is that usually the parties try to reach a settlement. The consequence is that, even if one party seizes the initiative by making an irrevocable commitment, the other may be just cantankerous enough to respond with its own commitment. If this happens, one or both may eventually have to back down. The dilemma of commitment is that it is most effective if there is no way out—but it is risky indeed to leave no way out.

More than One Issue

Another complexity of labor-management negotiations lies in multiple bargaining issues. We will first assume that there are only two issues: The union wants a wage increase, and management wants a relaxation of seniority rules. On a cost basis, employers would prefer no wage increases. But management knows that it must be able to hold and recruit employees, and it also wants to avoid the withholding of effort that may follow if employees feel they are not receiving a reasonable wage. The union may attempt to obtain as high a wage as possible, but it also must take into account that the company, to remain competitive, might have to demand a great deal of workers if wages are too high. As to seniority, the union would prefer to keep the present clauses, but the issue may not be overly significant for its members. Management concludes that more flexible seniority rules could reduce the wage bill by about 2 percent.

Although any translation of a nonmonetary provision into money value is conjectural, let us assume that the union would grant a loosening of rules in return for an additional 1 percent in wages. Regarding the package of "wage plus loosened seniority," in Figure 10.3(B) AY_2 represents the additional amount the company would give for the loosened seniority. The EP is extended because the package is worth more to management than is the wage settlement alone. By contrast, the union's EP is shortened by 1 percent (marked $-BX_2$) to 16 because the package is worth less to the union than was the wage alone. The gap between the EPs has narrowed by one point because the management's EP has grown by two and the union's has shrunk by only one. But they still do not touch.

We can similarly include any number of additional issues in this system by simply extending or shortening each EP, depending on whether the item has positive or negative value to the party. The difficulties of actually keeping track of all the issues and their interrelations will probably rise much faster than the number of issues. But no new principles are needed to understand the logic of more complex sets of issues.

Strike as Strategy

It is obviously possible that the EPs of the parties could have been different from those shown in the preceding section, that they could have overlapped, and a settlement could have been reached. But we left the parties with a gap between their EPs. Let us assume that they have continued to negotiate for a long time and that it is clear they will not agree. What next?

We now come to the crucial difference between the union-management relationship and most other purchase and sale relationships. If you go to an automobile dealer and fail to reach an agreement on price and trade-in, after a reasonable amount of discussion you leave. You do not make the purchase. The dealer does not make the sale. You part company, perhaps permanently.

The unique feature of the union-management contract is that in most instances the parties must agree—even if they do not agree—primarily because the alternative, a divorce, is too costly. In some cases, however, the parties have no choice but to terminate the relationship. In view of this fact, we might pose the following question: How, in a free society, can we encourage and assist the disagreeing parties to agree and to continue their association? In terms of the present model, what can be done to extend one or both EPs until they overlap?

Changing the EPs is a question in strategy, so the question is thus one of finding an effective strategy. This will be the strike or the perceived possibility of a strike. After failing to agree, the union and management part company. And, as in most other relation-

FIGURE 10.3(B) Negotiations of a New Agreement

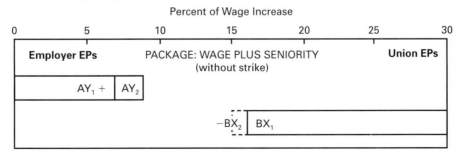

ships, it is the seller's stopping delivery, rather than the buyer's refusing it, that constitutes the overt act of breaking the relation. The seller stops because he or she has not been promised an acceptable price.

But there the similarity ends. Whereas the break in an ordinary commercial relationship may be permanent, this one is viewed from the outset as temporary—not a termination of the relation but a pause that will strategically push EPs until agreement is reached. The EPs grow because the strike has costs. These costs lengthen the EPs in the same way that the employer's desire to remove the costs of a tight seniority clause lengthened his or her EP.

The strike was traditionally thought of as a union weapon. In a disagreement over contract renewal in an established relationship, it is at least a mutual weapon. The costs it imposes on both parties are the inescapable consequence of a failure to agree. There is no a priori reason to assume that the strike is the fault of one party or the other because either side could have avoided it by asking less or conceding more. The employer could, of course, initiate a lockout. But we have seen that it is normally the seller (the union) who stops delivery.

Costs as a Strike Continues

Any attempt to recalibrate the cost of a continuing strike with a given amount of wage change is likely to be oversimplified and conjectural. But, however inaccurately, people do—in fact, must—make such conversions. For the ensuing discussion, we assume not that these estimates are necessarily accurate but that they are the best the parties can do and that they do serve as a basis for their behavior. We need not detail here whether the costs to management are those of lost sales, lost production, customer ill will, deterioration of raw materials or equipment, continuing fixed expenses, or permanent loss of some customers. We also need not detail whether the costs to the union are those of lost income to employees, depleted union treasury, political battles within the union, loss of public sympathy, or something else. Again, we will simply assume that the decision makers for both sides can compare the costs of continuing the strike with the benefits of settling it and can translate those costs and benefits into some equivalence with contract terms.

Let us now assume that a strike has been in effect for two weeks. The company has been able to make deliveries to its customers out of inventory, and it expects to be able to continue to do so for another two weeks. The main anticipated financial burden of a strike lasting that long will be some overtime costs to rebuild inventory after the strike ends. These costs are calculated at about 1 percent of the annual wage bill. As shown in Figure 10.3(C), that amount is represented by AY_3, which, when added to the company's EP, extends it to 10 percent.

The union members get no strike benefits from the national for the first several weeks of the strike. Hence, the strike is shown as imposing a significant financial burden

FIGURE 10.3(C) Negotiations of a New Agreement

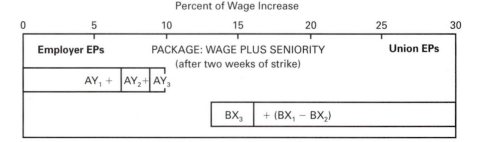

Percent of Wage Increase

0	5	10	15	20	25	30

Employer EPs	PACKAGE: WAGE PLUS SENIORITY (after two weeks of strike)	Union EPs

$AY_1 +$ | $AY_2 +$ | AY_3

BX_3 | $+ (BX_1 - BX_2)$

on them. The amount of that burden, represented as BX_3, in Figure 10.3(C), extends the union EP to 13 percent. The gap between the union and management EPs is still 3 percent, so no settlement occurs.

Two weeks later, the company EP has grown considerably because inventories are used up and customers are starting to shift to other suppliers. AY_3 is therefore enlarged, so that the entire company EP now extends to 13 percent, as shown in Figure 10.3(D). On the union side, BX_3 has grown by only one point, mainly because the national union has started paying strike benefits. However, the EPs now overlap, and after some rounds of tactical maneuvering, the parties agree on 12.5 percent.

Before going into a further complication, let us restate a central aspect of the preceding. The purpose of strategic moves is to lengthen the opponent's EP and possibly to shorten one's own. The portion of each party's EP that is directly related to the strike is a direct function of its own cost of continuing the strike. Hence, the frequent statement that the greater the cost one can impose on the opponent (lengthening EP) and the less the cost to oneself of imposing it (limiting one's own EP), the greater is one's bargaining power. The related tactic is to pretend that one's EP is shorter than it actually is, which means giving the impression that one is not really hurting very much from the strike. If credible, this tactic increases the opponent's estimate of how long he or she must endure and, with it, his or her willingness to settle.

Some Added Complications

Earlier we stated the relationship between power and bargaining power in negotiable transactions as "The more you want something from someone else, the more likely you are to get it, but the more you will probably pay for it." Where there is no strike, the union's intense desire (large BX) for an item (X) to be received from management lengthens the union's EP and makes it willing to give more of other items (Ys) as concessions to management. The larger the BX, the more the union is willing to give up to obtain it. Management is in a position to gain something of value in exchange for X. When a strategic threat has been imposed in the form of a strike, however, the cost the union takes on to obtain its goal is the willingness to endure a long strike. Thus an intense desire on the part of the union can cut either way. It improves management's position in seeking a settlement without a strike, but it can worsen management's position once a strike begins.

We have now demonstrated the significant role of the strike in union-management relations. It is the crucial strategic ingredient that lengthens one or both EPs far enough that the parties who must agree eventually will do so, with rare exceptions. Those who contemplate outlawing strikes had better think carefully about what they would substitute for this force in a free society. The alternatives are not as easy to identify as they might seem, as we will see in Chapter 14, on dispute resolution and regulation.

FIGURE 10.3(D). Negotiations of a New Agreement

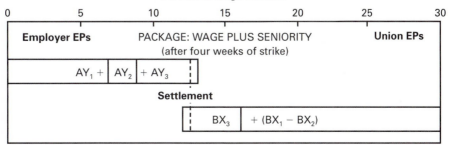

FURTHER EXTENSIONS OF THE MODEL

Principal and Agent Relations

Let us assume that the terms agreed upon by the negotiators must be submitted to the union membership for ratification. The rank and file turn down the 12.5 percent, but the vote does not specify what they would accept. After some inquiry, the union negotiators conclude that the members would probably accept 14 percent. Therefore, they return to postreferendum negotiations with an EP extending to that amount, as shown in Figure 10.3(E). The members' reluctance, designated BX_4, is introduced as a negative quantity, shortening the union's EP. Management's remains at 13. There is the additional possibility that a settlement agreed to by the management negotiator will be turned down at the top level, but this is far less common because it is easier for negotiators to keep in touch with the small number of top decision makers on the employer side than with the large number of members on the union side. Hence, management negotiators can more easily avoid agreeing to a settlement without advance assurance that it will be accepted.

There is no need to pursue the details thereafter. Management's EP may extend further as the costs of the strike continue to rise. Meanwhile, the union EP might start to grow again as the strike grinds on and members begin facing foreclosed mortgages and repossessed cars. Conversely, the workers may grow highly hostile toward the employer, swallow their losses, and shrink their collective EP. In any event, at some point a settlement ensues.

In addition to ratifications, another tactic negotiators can use is the relation between agents and principals. One form of this tactic is a relatively weak commitment, as in "I can't accept your proposal because I am positive my constituents would not accept it." The reverse is to use the relation as a means of backing out of a commitment, as in "I personally can't accept your proposal, and I feel sure my constituents won't either. But for whatever it may be worth, I'll take it back and ask them." The negotiator could then return to the constituents with any of three main approaches. One is a simple question: "Are you willing to accept this?" The second is a sub rosa recommendation that the constituents reject the proposal if the negotiator feels that a tough refusal will bring greater concessions from the opponent. The third is a recommendation to accept if the negotiator is convinced there will be no further concessions by the other side. When the negotiator returns from the constituents to deal again with the opponent, the face-saving description could be "They sure surprised me. They accepted (rejected) even though I felt sure they would reject (accept)." This face-saving tactic can be used even if the constituents did exactly what the negotiator expected them to do—in fact, even if they precisely followed the negotiator's advice.

Suppose the union is insecure and faces a decertification election in the near future. This condition will almost certainly affect the union's EP, though in which direction will depend on the circumstances. If the members have been thinking of the union as ineffec-

FIGURE 10.3(E) Negotiations of a New Agreement

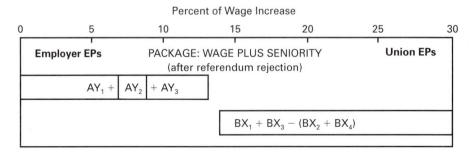

tive and weak in dealing with management, the effect may be to shorten the union EP. If management wants the union to be voted out, its EP will shorten or lengthen, depending on which move seems most likely to turn the members against the union. On the other hand, if the company wants to build a secure and peaceable relation with the union, its EP will move in the direction that would solidify support for the union. These dynamics, incidentally, illustrate why it is not possible to enforce literally the idea in the law that the employer should exert no power at all, as contrasted to persuasion, on the workers' choice of bargaining agent. If, instead, the company faces imminent closing unless it can save money and become more competitive, and if the employees need their jobs as much as many employees do, the union's EP will lengthen considerably.

Negotiators' Security

Suppose that a union election is coming up in several weeks. In this election, the union president must run against an insurgent who has raised considerable support for his assertion that the incumbent is soft on management and generally not aggressive and militant enough. The incumbent, a principal negotiator, is now under pressure to "really do something" for the members. The result will be a shortening of the union's EP. If management likes the present union president and dislikes the challenger, its EP will lengthen by the amount of that preference. If management likes the challenger but not the incumbent, its EP may shorten. The consequences of any of these changes for the relative bargaining powers of the parties can readily be traced.

Interrelated Negotiations: Effects over Time and Space

A complication in bargaining is that the parties pay attention to the possible tactical or strategic effects of their present negotiations on any other negotiations, whether involving parties other than themselves or themselves at some future time.

With regard to tactics, their core is credibility. At least for the kinds of negotiations we are considering here, credibility is apt to be associated more closely with a person than with an organization. To illustrate with an obvious behavior, if a negotiator opens with grandiose demands and then later retreats great distances without even arguing very much, at the next contract expiration the other party will not take the opening demands seriously. Hence, a negotiator must examine tactics, not only for their present effects but in light of their probable consequences over the years ahead. In fact, even one single outstandingly brilliant, senseless, considerate, or insensitive behavior may affect the responses of others for decades.

Negotiators who develop high-level trust and understanding can cut through, perhaps avoid entirely, vast displays of window dressing and quickly get to the real core of the issues. Often, they can thereby speed agreement. Even if not, it can be immensely helpful to have early identification of the exact points of agreement and disagreement. Some negotiators who have repeatedly worked opposite each other report that they achieve subtle but reliable means of communicating with each other, of which even they may not be consciously aware. Of crucial importance are signals that say, "Ignore this, it's just for effect" as contrasted to "I'm serious about this one, so pay close attention."

There are strategic as well as tactical relationships among successive bargains. If one side has won a very advantageous settlement in a given year, it may relax and feel a duty to go a bit easy (display a longer EP) the next time. If the union accepted a substandard settlement one year because the employer was in economic difficulty, it may expect reciprocal generosity in the future when management is in a better financial position; in many cases the employer may feel obliged to respond. By the same token, if the union is confident that the employer will be generous later when it has more money, the union will be more willing to accept a low settlement now. In short, not only do present behaviors affect expectations about the future, but expectations affect present behaviors.

There are also interrelations among different negotiations going on more or less simultaneously but with different employers, whether those employers deal with the same or a different union. Pattern setting is one such relation. Typically, the EPs of both parties are shorter if they are aware that they are pattern setters than if they are bargaining solely on their own behalf. For in the former case, any concession made by either union or management means a potential loss, not merely to the principals immediately involved but to all other unions or managements, respectively, that follow the pattern. Knowledge that one will be a hero with unions or managements elsewhere for putting up a successful fight may further shorten a negotiator's EP.

Pattern followers tend to have their EPs move at the outset of bargaining to roughly the positions already set elsewhere. Because each party then knows at the outset approximately where the opponent's EP is, pattern-following bargaining is typically easier and quicker. Even a pattern follower, however, can have unique problems that drag out the negotiations. And some supposed pattern followers may hold out for something better (for the union or the management) than appears in the pattern. But the opponent's argument, "Others did it. Why can't you?" may be hard to answer convincingly.

Backing Away from the Strike

One might infer from the preceding discussion that most contract settlements come only as the result of a strike. The contrary is the case: Most contracts are renegotiated without a strike. Why?

The first reason is that, in some cases, the EPs of the parties overlap without a strike or a strike threat. The second reason is more compelling. It is the mutual knowledge that if a settlement is not reached, a strike will occur. Instead of waiting to feel the actual lengthening of EP that comes with a strike, the parties can imagine or compute its approximate magnitude, and then negotiate as if the EPs already were of that magnitude. All this is simple and effective in principle, and it works much of the time. But why does it sometimes fail? Again, the answers are those of tactics or strategies.

As to tactics, either party may underestimate its own EP and/or overestimate the opponent's as those EPs would be during a strike. Hence, that party may reject the last offer that would avert the strike. Either side may also make a tactical error in thinking that its own adamant stance will bring a last-minute capitulation by the other party and then fear excessive loss of face from its own last-moment concession.

In addition to misjudgment and miscalculation, there may be various other reasons for a strike. An employer may accept a strike as a way of liquidating an excessive inventory or as a means of weakening or even destroying the union. The union may decide that it has no alternative to a strike, particularly if the employer's offer is unacceptable to the union leadership, to the membership, or to both.

The real pressure of a potential strike often is not felt very strongly until the strike deadline gets close. During the last hours, the relation is much like a game of chicken. Each side may fervently hope that a strike will not ensue and may actually be willing to concede enough to prevent it. But each hopes that if it sits tight, the other will lose nerve first and concede. So both sides sometimes watch sadly as the pickets start to march, each wondering if it acted recklessly in holding out too long. Sometimes the parties stop the clock just before midnight and furiously work toward a settlement that they may achieve within the next few hours—but "before midnight."

As the strike deadline approaches, another complication arises. Unless it seems clear that the parties will succeed in reaching agreement before the deadline, each must start making overt preparations for the strike. These preparations have both tactical and strategic effects. One such preparation is for the company to start building its inventory of finished goods, possibly by operating overtime. The tactical effect is to make credible the company's statements that it will take a strike rather than increase its offer. Its credibility is further enhanced if the required overtime involves higher unit costs. The strategic effect is to shorten management's EP once a strike starts because its ability to sell out of inventory will decrease its costs from the strike. The union's building of a large strike fund has parallel tactical and strategic effects.

Strike preparations also have a two-edged psychological strategic effect. One edge is to sharpen awareness of the seriousness of the situation, lengthen EPs, and make the parties work harder for a settlement. The opposite edge arises from the fact that the precise purpose of a strike (including management's "taking" of a strike) is to make life unpleasant for the other party—to impose costs. As each party watches the other preparing to harm it, tempers are apt to flare up. The direct effect is to shorten EPs and reduce the likelihood of a settlement.

What about Arbitration?

The potential strike costs can allow the parties to reach agreement without a strike for what they think they would have settled for if a strike had occurred. This relation leaves the intriguing question, Why not have the parties agree in advance to binding arbitration if they fail to settle? If, as it sometimes does, the strike threat should fail, then the dispute would get settled peaceably by arbitration, without the losses of a strike. Several factors preclude this option. The first relates to the content of the agreement. With or without a strike, a settlement reached by the parties is a mutually accepted accommodation. Even if one or both were reluctant to sign it, each separately preferred the benefit of the accord to the cost of a strike. By contrast, an arbitrator may hand down a decision that may be unacceptable to one of the parties, possibly to both. Although arbitrators may be expected to be sensible, it is nevertheless possible that in an extreme case, an arbitrator's award could bankrupt the company or destroy the union. And once the parties have agreed to arbitrate, they lose control over the terms of the settlement. Few in the private sector are willing to risk it.

Second, whereas it is usually possible to estimate the approximate cost of a strike, and thus the value of a settlement necessary to prevent it, the terms of an arbitrator's award are much more difficult to predict. Hence, the strike's logic of "Settle for this now, since that's about what you're going to settle for eventually anyway" is much harder to apply to a prospective arbitration.

Finally, the parties know that without arbitration they will eventually have to reach some agreement, even if doing so will necessitate reducing or abandoning some of their demands. Hence, they tend to agree, at least tentatively, on various issues just to get a settlement. With arbitration as an alternative, they do not have to agree on anything. These observations underscore even more strongly the role of the strike, or the prospective strike, as the pressure that produces an agreement between parties without the need for arbitration.

IMPLEMENTS OF BARGAINING POWER IN COLLECTIVE BARGAINING

Violence as a Union Weapon

The history of violence is long and checkered. Violence by employees against company property, customers' plants, or even company officials has occurred from time to time through the history of the labor movement. As used against employers, violence tends to be counterproductive. Violence already executed holds no power or bargaining power. It can, of course, fulfill the tactical function of making the threat of subsequent violence more credible, but it is perhaps more likely to bring a hostile contraction of the employer's EP. If used by strikers against employees who continue to work, it may intimidate them into staying home and thereby increase the pressure on the employer. Through most of our history before the 1930s, local police, private detectives, company guards, the army, or the National Guard typically supported management and often used coercive methods to break strikes and intimidate strikers. Harlan County, Kentucky, was by no means the only place where a union organizer stood a large chance of being shot or beaten. Historically, in many places, attempts to unionize were viewed as criminal activity and were treated by the authorities accordingly. Prior to the protections introduced by the Wagner Act, violence against union members or organizers was often effective. Violence by labor is typically sporadic and usually done without union approval, its usual effect being to turn the public and the police against the employees. There is evidence that, particularly during the 1930s, employers sometimes secretly arranged to have their own properties damaged (slightly!) because of the adverse publicity the union would receive in consequence.

Employer Weapons

Employer "weapons" fall into two distinct categories. The first is the prevention or elimination of the union's very existence. The second category of management weapons comprises those aimed at increasing the employer's bargaining power in labor negotiations without seeking to undermine or eliminate the union. Some companies have apparently automated further than production costs alone would justify, to make themselves almost strike-proof. Some petroleum refineries and telephone exchanges, for example, can operate almost indefinitely without their unionized work forces, even if certain repair, maintenance, and installation services must be postponed. Multiple plants performing the same function (horizontal integration) make a company less vulnerable, as it can produce and ship goods from nonstruck plants if others are struck. Large textile companies have been the most conspicuous examples, though some food processing, auto parts, and retailing are also involved. Diversification, or conglomerate structure, is a variation on the same theme. Even though the whole of a conglomerate's production of one product may be shut down, profits overall may be little affected because other subdivisions may be operating. Multinational operation is a still more extended version of the same concept. Employers sometimes threaten to close plants and move their operations elsewhere, to the South or the Southwest or to other countries. Actual movements take place often enough to lend those threats credibility. Occasionally, a plant is sold to a larger and stronger employer. Anticipatory inventory accumulation can help minimize a firm's costs during a strike.

A final question about weapons involves management's response to a strike. Some employers fully accept the mutual nature of the strike pressure. When a strike is called, the company simply stops production until agreement is reached, in a behavior that is the core of the "accommodation" approach. Others attempt to operate despite the strike, perhaps using broad publicity to urge strikers to return to work before a settlement has been reached with the union, or even hiring new employees. When pursuing this course of action, employers typically appeal to employees over the heads of their leaders, seeking to drive a wedge between the employees and their union. This approach is really an effort to get rid of the union, rather than an attempt merely to increase the company's bargaining power.

Union Weapons

Union weapons also fall into two categories. The first is the effective primary strike, with all other weapons falling into the second category. In essence, the union weapon is shutting down the employer's operations—stopping production. This is the union's means of using power to win bargaining gains from the employer. Except for what is already "in the pipelines," an effective strike stops the flow of income to the employer. However, if the employer continues to operate during the strike, using either regular employees or striker replacements, this primary strike is not fully effective. (*Primary* here means that the employees who have a complaint act directly upon the employer from whom they want concessions.) When the primary pressure is not effective, secondary pressures may be attempted. On the input side, such pressures seek to enlist the cooperation of employers or unions who produce or deliver materials to the primary employer: They are asked to stop doing so. For example, if the primary employer is a clothing manufacturer, a textile mill supplier might stop weaving or shipping cloth, or truckers might refuse to deliver it. On the output side, consumers might be asked to stop buying the struck clothing, retail stores might be asked to stop handling it, or (again) truckers might be asked to stop delivering it. These indirect actions are known as secondary boycotts, though some more strictly resemble strikes. As stated in Chapter 4, most of these devices are illegal. It is important to note that secondary pressures only seek to do what the primary strike has failed to do—stop the primary employer's operations. If the primary strike is fully effective, secondary pressures are largely irrelevant.

Picketing is purely symbolic, or informational, if the employer shuts down when struck. No one is trying to enter the plant to work, so pickets are not needed to persuade them to stay out. On the other hand, if the employer seeks to operate during the strike, the presence or absence of a convincing-looking picket line may determine whether workers stay out or go in.

Several variations on strikes are used at times. In a slowdown, employees stay on their jobs but work at a much-reduced pace, sometimes by the simple stratagem of meticulously following every detail of the employer's rules and regulations. Because the employees come to work and get paid, this strategy is effective if they can get away with it, as it can hurt the employer considerably while costing the employees nothing. A "sick-in" is often used by professional or public employees, particularly if they are legally forbidden to strike. Here, many employees call in sick instead of coming to work. These and other strike substitutes are essentially partial work stoppages.

SUMMARY

Negotiations are the process of carrying through transactions under conditions of uncertainty. The chapter first reviewed the four subprocesses of Walton and McKersie's behavioral theory of labor negotiations. These subprocesses are distributive bargaining, integrative bargaining, attitudinal structuring, and intraorganizational bargaining. Different strategies and tactics are appropriate for goal accomplishment in each of these four subprocesses.

The next part of the chapter reviewed in some detail Kuhn's general theory of transactions. The theory was applied to labor-management negotiations. The roles of strategy and tactics and their effects on each side's bargaining power and the position of its effective preferences (EPs) were discussed at some length.

The purpose of presenting the theories in this chapter is to give the reader a better comprehension of the negotiation process. The chapter assumes that improving understanding can improve performance.

Notes

1. Milton Friedman, *Essays on Positive Economics* (Chicago: University of Chicago Press, 1953).
2. Richard E. Walton and Robert B. McKersie, *A Behavioral Theory of Labor Negotiations,* 2nd ed. (Ithaca, NY: ILR Press, 1991), pp. 4–6.
3. Ibid., p. 5.
4. Ibid., p. 9.
5. Ibid., p. xii.
6. Ibid., p. xv.
7. Alfred Kuhn, *The Logic of Social Systems. A Unified, Deductive System-Based Approach to Social Science* (San Francisco: Jossey-Bass, 1974).
8. All statements of relationships presented in this section are to be construed as assuming that other relevant factors remain unchanged—the traditional "ceteris paribus" assumption applied in economics.
9. Alfred Kuhn, *The Study of Society. A Unified Approach* (Homewood, IL: Irwin, and Dorsey Press, 1963), Chapter 17.
10. Walton and McKersie, op. cit., p. 43.
11. Ibid.
12. Allan M. Carter, *Theory of Wages and Employment* (Homewood, IL: Irwin, 1959), p. 122.
13. Kuhn, op. cit., p. 193.

CHAPTER 11

Costing of Labor Contracts

After reading this chapter, you should be able to

■ Explain why many articles in a labor agreement, regardless of whether they cover economic or noneconomic issues, can have cost implications.

■ Comprehend the different financial components that constitute the total compensation package.

■ Explain the concepts and the significance of demographic, accounting, and financial data for costing of contracts.

■ Discuss information sharing and collective bargaining.

■ Review the most common methods for computing the costs of union wage demands.

■ Explain procedures for costing employee benefits.

■ Explain the concept of new money and its value in costing of contracts.

■ Critically evaluate existing methods for costing of labor contracts.

■ Discuss and explain some of the factors that employers consider in formulating their financial proposals.

■ Explain and define *elasticity of demand.*

■ Explain and evaluate the relationships among the following components: increased contracts costs, elasticity of demand, and prices to consumers.

■ Explain the concept of present value.

■ Explain the implications of present value for costing of labor contracts and for facilitation of settlements.

■ Explain the discounted cash flow model and evaluate its potential strengths and weaknesses for costing of labor contracts.

CONTRACT COSTING

Many articles in a labor agreement, regardless of whether they apply to economic or noneconomic issues, can have cost implications. Some direct costs such as wages and benefits are relatively easy to measure. Some indirect costs resulting from contract provisions governing such topics as seniority, layoffs, and grievance and arbitration procedures are more difficult to estimate. Even more complex to measure are the interrelationships among changes in labor costs and such fields of corporate activity as capacity utilization, costing and pricing of output, labor productivity, product mix, capital-to-labor ratio, and profitability. Because changes in compensation affect worker behavior, other cost considerations include the motivational level of employees, absenteeism, turnover, need for close supervision, ease of recruitment, and quality of applicants.

Clearly, no single chapter can provide a formula for accurately accounting for all these costs. Our goal in this chapter is twofold. First, we will illustrate the computations that unions and management make in estimating the financial consequences of various bargaining proposals. Second, we will discuss the indirect consequences of changes in contract terms to help illustrate the difficulty of fully assessing the cost implications of most proposals. Although it may not be possible to determine exact dollar costs for the indirect effects, an estimate of the magnitude of such effects provides useful information for the structuring of proposals to accomplish organizational goals.

Estimates of potential costs can help both parties evaluate the impact of a settlement on employment, output, pricing, sales, product mix, and substitution of capital for labor. Consideration of these factors can benefit unions, management, and the bargaining process itself. The union, by increasing its level of sophistication in the application of costing procedures, can formulate better contract demands as well as improve its ability to refute management's arguments. Better understanding of labor costs can help management defend its positions in bargaining and assist it in arriving at more advantageous contract offers. Good costing procedures can give both sides a better understanding of financial costs and can also help them compare the levels of satisfaction or utility that different sets of proposals contain. Better understanding of these factors can facilitate negotiations and lead to more judicious use of power at the bargaining table.

A conversation that the author of this book had with a contract costing manager for a very large corporation revealed that this particular firm has utilized a complex model for the costing of its contracts. The model had taken many years to develop. Although its detailed components are confidential, it was suggested to the author that the model was based partly on art and partly on science. The costing personnel undergo a lengthy apprenticeship period during which they are taught to develop a feel for the indirect implications of contract costs.

LABOR COSTS AND THEIR COMPONENTS

The importance of contract costing depends on the share of a company's total costs expended on labor costs. Industries vary greatly in degree of labor intensity. Consider a simple example of two firms, each having total costs of $100 million per year. Assume that in the more labor-intensive firm, 70 percent of total costs consist of labor costs. A 10-percent miscalculation in labor costs could amount to a $7 million–dollar mistake. The same 10-percent miscalculation in a capital-intensive firm, where labor costs are only 10 percent of total costs, would amount to only $1 million. Obviously, the computation of total cost and labor cost is considerably more complex in the real world than in our illustration.

To arrive at the total cost of an agreement, it is necessary to calculate the many different financial components that constitute labor costs. The total compensation package consists of direct pay and employee benefits. The major part of the package is the direct paycheck disbursed to each employee. Direct pay may consist of hourly, daily, weekly, or monthly pay. It may also include incentive payments; commissions; mileage payments; automatic and merit increases stipulated in progression plans; travel allowances; clothing, tool, and safety equipment allowances; various nonproduction bonuses; profit sharing; differentials for shift work, hazardous work, and abnormal conditions; cost-of-living allowances; deferred wage increases; and overtime and premium pay.

Benefits

The 1996 edition of *Employee Benefits,* a survey published by the U.S. Chamber of Commerce, reports that the average payment for benefits (including retirees and former workers) was 42.0 percent as a percent of payroll in 1995. Figure 11.1 shows how the benefit dollars were spent in 1995, Figure 11.2 presents employee benefits as percent of payroll by industry groups, and Figure 11.3 provides data on average annual employee benefits and earnings in 1995.[1]

There is no universal definition of employee benefits. Generally, employee benefits can be categorized into two broad groups: time-not-worked benefits and security and health benefits. The first category consists of compensation for time not worked during regular employment periods. Items under this heading can include: vacation; holidays; sick and funeral leaves; time for jury duty and court witness appearances; military service; reporting pay; call-in and call-back pay; paid meal periods; rest periods; washup, cleanup, and clothes-changing time; and time spent on union business. The second category of benefits may include life, medical, and accident insurance; workers' compensation insurance; sick leave pay; pensions; social security; unemployment insurance; guaranteed annual income; supplemental unemployment benefits; and severance pay allowances.

As Table 11.1 shows, the U.S. Chamber of Commerce annual benefit survey divides benefits into the following seven categories: (1) legally required benefits such as social security, unemployment insurance, and workers' compensation; (2) retirement and savings, where employers' shares of pensions and profit sharing are counted; (3) life insurance and death benefit payments; (4) medical benefits, which include hospital and short- and long-term disability insurance; (5) paid rest periods like coffee breaks, lunches, and washup time; (6) payments for time not worked, consisting of vacations, holidays, and sick pay; and (7) miscellaneous other benefit payments such as employee meals, education expenses, and child care.[2]

In the last 10 years, both employers and unions have invested great attention and effort in attempting to reduce the escalating cost of health care benefits. Henderson writes that "possibly no compensation topic created more interest among both human resources specialists and top levels of management than the continued increase in health care costs."[3] In 1970 such costs represented 6.4 percent of the gross national product (GNP); by 1990 this percentage had gone up to 10.7 percent of GNP.

Although health care costs have been "increasing at the slowest rate in several years,"[4] they still exceed the inflation rate. During the last 10 years, health care costs have become a major negotiation issue that has generated a great amount of friction at the bargaining table. One study reports that in 1986, 30 percent of strikes were health benefit related; this total increased to 60 percent in 1989.[5] Employees and unions try to curb health care cost increases by concentrating on three areas: "funding of benefits, delivery of benefits and emphasis on preventive care or wellness."[6]

The first approach to be discussed is funding. Funding of benefits has been changing in the last 10 years, with many more employees paying portions of their health benefits premiums for the first time. In addition to augmenting or increasing contributions, many benefit plans require employees to pay higher deductibles. Although the "AFL-CIO advises local unions to resist accepting or increasing deductibles and co-payment of insurance premiums . . . a number of employers and unions have negotiated changes in contributions."[7]

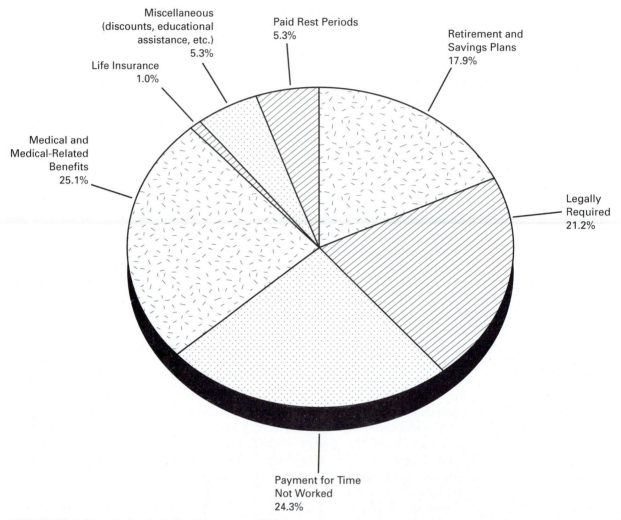

FIGURE 11.1 How the Benefit Dollars Were Spent—1995

Source: Employee Benefits, 1996 Edition, U.S. Chamber of Commerce, Research Center, Washington, DC (December 1996), p. 2. Reprinted with permission from the U.S. Chamber of Commerce from the 1996 Edition of *Employee Benefits. Employee Benefits* may be ordered by calling 1-800-638-6582.

The second cost containment measure to be reviewed is delivery of benefits. This area also has seen many changes in the last 10 years. Both parties are trying to reduce costs by changing the system for delivery of health benefits. "Growing in popularity are managed care programs, flexible benefit plans, on site medical facilities, and carve outs."[8] A carve out is a stand-alone plan that attempts to identify a major segment of health care costs and encompass that component under a separate plan or policy. Typically, carve outs cover such areas as mental health and substance abuse programs.

The third area of health care cost containment relates to prevention and wellness. Although programs in that area are more common in nonunion settings, a 1992 survey of employer bargaining objectives found that 28 percent of the contracts of the survey participants contained wellness provisions. Furthermore, 12 percent of participants stated that they would try to negotiate wellness programs.[9]

There are differences between the percentages of union and nonunion employees

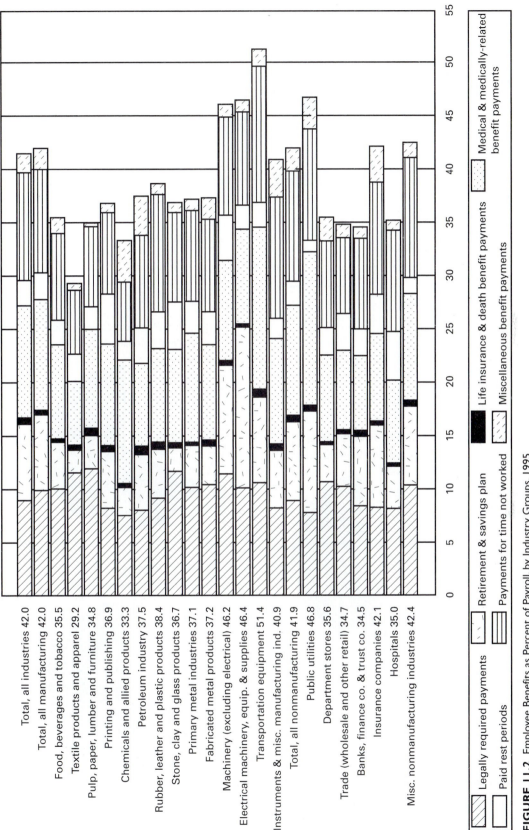

FIGURE 11.2 Employee Benefits as Percent of Payroll, by Industry Groups, 1995

Source: Employee Benefits, 1996 Edition, U.S. Chamber of Commerce, Research Center, Washington, DC (December 1996), p. 21. Reprinted with permission from the U.S. Chamber of Commerce from the 1996 Edition of *Employee Benefits*. *Employee Benefits* may be ordered by calling 1-800-638-6582.

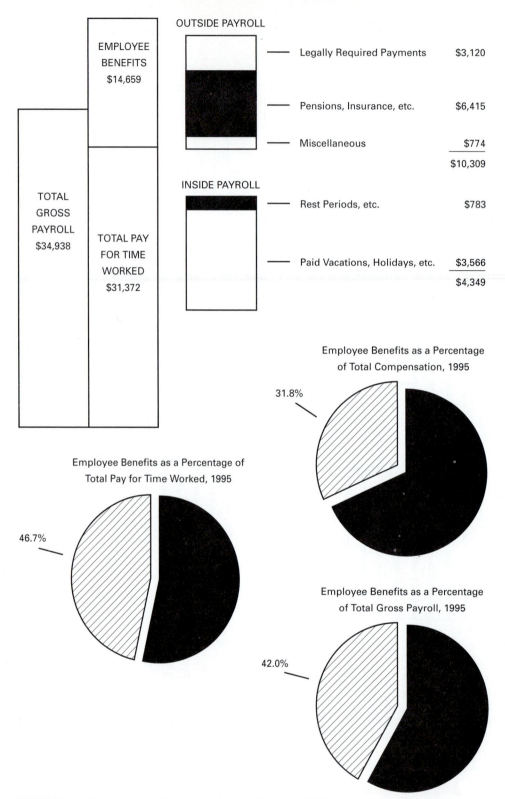

FIGURE 11.3 Average Annual Employee Benefits and Earnings, 1995

Source: Employee Benefits, 1996 Edition, U.S. Chamber of Commerce, Research Center, Washington, DC (December 1996), p. 38. Reprinted with permission from the U.S. Chamber of Commerce from the 1996 Edition of *Employee Benefits. Employee Benefits* may be ordered by calling 1-800-638-6582.

TABLE 11.1 Employee Benefits, by Type of Benefit: All Employees, 1995

Type of Benefit	Total, All Companies	Total, All Manufacturing	Total, All Nonmanufacturing
Total employee benefits as percent of payroll	42.0	42.0	41.9
1. Legally required payments (employers' share only)	8.9	9.6	8.8
a. Old-age, survivors, disability, and health insurance (employer FICA taxes) and railroad retirement tax	7.3	7.3	7.4
b. Unemployment compensation	0.6	0.9	0.5
c. Workers' compensation (including estimated cost of self-insured)	0.9	1.3	0.9
d. State sickness benefit insurance and other	0.0	0.0	0.1
2. Retirement and savings plan payments (employers' share only)	7.5	7.3	7.5
a. Defined benefit pension plan contributions	4.1	2.5	4.4
b. Defined contribution plan payments (401(k) type)	1.7	1.7	1.7
c. Profit sharing	0.6	1.8	0.3
d. Stock bonus and employee stock ownership plans (ESOP)	0.2	0.9	0.1
e. Pension plan premiums (net) under insurance and annuity contracts (insured and trusted)	0.6	0.0	0.7
f. Administrative and other costs	0.4	0.4	0.3
3. Life insurance and death benefit payments (employers' share only)	0.4	0.4	0.4
4. Medical and medically-related benefit payments (employers' share only)	10.5	10.5	10.5
a. Hospital, surgical, medical, and major medical insurance premiums (net)	7.1	6.9	7.2
b. Retiree (payments for retired employees) hospital, surgical, medical, and major medical insurance premiums (net)	1.7	1.8	1.7
c. Short-term disability, sickness or accident insurance (company plan or insured plan)	0.5	0.3	0.5
d. Long-term disability or wage continuation (insured, self-administered, or trusts)	0.2	0.3	0.2
e. Dental insurance premiums	0.5	0.6	0.5
f. Other (vision care, physical and mental fitness benefits for former employees)	0.5	0.7	0.4
5. Paid rest periods, coffee breaks, lunch periods, wash-up time, travel time, clothes-change time, get ready time, etc.	2.2	2.5	2.2
6. Payments for time not worked	10.2	9.8	10.3
a. Payment for or in lieu of vacations	5.4	5.4	5.4
b. Payment for or in lieu of holidays	3.3	3.1	3.3
c. Sick leave pay	1.2	0.7	1.3
d. Parental leave (maternity and paternity leave payments)	0.0	0.0	0.0
e. Other	0.4	0.5	0.3
7. Miscellaneous benefit payments	2.2	2.0	2.3
a. Discounts on goods and services purchased from company by employees	0.2	0.0	0.3
b. Employee meals furnished by company	0.2	0.0	0.2
c. Employee education expenditures	0.3	0.2	0.3
d. Child care	0.0	0.0	0.0
e. Other	1.6	1.7	1.5
Total employee benefits as cents per hour	708.9¢	821.4¢	690.1¢
Total employee benefits as dollars per year per employee	$14,659	$17,313	$14,227

Source: Employee Benefits, 1996 Edition, U.S. Chamber of Commerce, Research Center, Washington, DC (December 1996), p. 12. Reprinted with permission from the U.S. Chamber of Commerce from the 1996 Edition of *Employee Benefits. Employee Benefits* may be ordered by calling 1-800-638-6582.

who receive medical and dental care benefits. Among full-time unionized workers, 9 out of 10 were provided with medical care plans, compared with 8 of 10 full-time nonunionized employees. In the dental care area, 7 of 10 unionized employees had access to plans, whereas only 6 out of 10 nonunionized employees participated in such plans. One proposed explanation for the higher rates of participation of union employees is the difference in compulsory contribution toward plan premiums. Whereas only 3 out of 10 union employees had to contribute for individual coverage, 6 out of 10 nonunion employees were required to make contributions toward plan premiums.[10]

The methodology for costing health care benefits is beyond the scope of this book. Health plan costing is complex because of the many surrounding assumptions and uncertainties. At the bargaining table, the parties are faced with a variety of options for health care plans, each with different cost components. These choices generate confrontations and contribute to tension and to impasses in the negotiation process. To conclude, "Most experts believe that health cost will remain a major bargaining issue into the 21st century"[11] as the parties seek new methods for restraining rising costs.

DATA UTILIZED IN CONTRACT COSTING

The data used in the costing of labor agreements can be classified into three major categories: demographic, accounting, and financial. Demographic data supply a breakdown and a statistical profile of the labor force in terms of such criteria as age, sex, seniority, and marital status. Accounting data provide payroll information on the work force regarding such specifics as direct pay, overtime, vacation, and holiday pay. Financial data furnish figures on projected revenues, output, product mix, and nonlabor costs.[12]

Some firms focus primarily on demographic data in costing contracts and do not consider financial and accounting information. Such firms try to negotiate the lowest "direct dollars-and-cents-per-hour cost" and disregard the impact of union demands on future profitability, which can be calculated from accounting and financial material. In such firms, general economic data and settlements by other companies, rather than financial and accounting inputs, are the important factors in contract costing.[13]

Some firms utilize both demographic and accounting data in estimating contract costs but disregard financial data. Such companies not only are concerned with total labor costs based on demographic factors but also consider the proportions of total cost disbursed for direct labor, for time-not-worked benefits, and for security and health benefits, including workers' compensation and Social Security taxes. Costs are also allocated to product lines, departments, and divisions. Such tabulations are based on historical accounting data. These calculations ignore financial inputs and thus by implication assume that product mix, level of output, relationship between overtime and straight time, and many other variables are not affected by the contract.

Some firms utilize all three sets of data: demographic, accounting, and financial. However, the financial data are used more as a broad guideline concerning potential costs than as a detailed printout for a course of action. Company negotiators who rely on "financial data" are more sensitive to the effects of contracts on profitability and on their employers' strategic objectives. They are more likely to structure bargaining terms to minimize the financial effects of settlements. For example, if a firm's profit projections are more optimistic for the second than for the first year of a contract, they may try to delay the major portion of an increase to the second year. Availability of financial data may make it easier for a negotiator to sell a particular package not only to opponents, but also to principals.[14]

INFORMATION SHARING AND COLLECTIVE BARGAINING

The costing of labor contracts and the process of negotiation can be facilitated by a sharing of financial information between labor and management and by joint fact-finding activities. Some negotiators claim that such an approach can benefit both sides and can help build a better relationship between union and management. A first step in this direction could be the involvement of the parties in a joint search for data. The parties could develop a data bank of financial information accessible to be both sides. In 1965, Chamberlain and Kuhn suggested that the parties gather information by establishing "joint fact finding commissions, either permanent or ad hoc in nature; or joint employment of impartial third party investigators."[15]

Although access to data that could be provided through sharing and joint activities could reduce friction at the bargaining table, it could not eliminate it completely. Even the most legitimate and objective data would still be subject to different interpretations and value judgements; each side would still attempt to interpret the data on terms that would be most advantageous to its bargaining position. Even where a firm would be willing to open its financial records to the union in order to prove weak financial status, there still could arise serious disagreements over the interpretation of those records.

Kochan and Katz[16] have incorporated in their model of industrial relations the strategic sharing of information between management and labor, suggesting "a broader role for information sharing between management and worker representatives." They point out that at some General Motors plants, workers and union leaders have participated "in solving production and quality problems as they arise." Information sharing is not a new phenomenon; it has been utilized indirectly in many situations, particularly where the parties required the assistance of mediation to reach a settlement. According to Kochan and Katz, "One major function of mediation is to allow . . . information sharing to take place, either directly between the parties or indirectly by both parties' sharing confidential information . . . with the mediator."[17]

In general, apart from mediation and the legal disclosure requirements of the Wagner and Taft-Hartley Acts, "few accepted mechanisms exist for firm-level labor-management information sharing."[18] One reasons that information sharing has not become more popular may be its perceived effect on bargaining power. A study by Kleiner and Bouillon[19] concluded that information sharing can increase union bargaining power. Obviously, employers who feel that they will diminish their power at the bargaining table by providing financial data to unions will not be willing to share such information. Some employers, particularly those in financial difficulty, may want to share the bad news with their unions in order to obtain some concessions. But even in such situations, there may be a strong resistance to sharing. Management may be reluctant to establish precedents for future bargaining.

Not all employers object to the sharing of information. One settlement negotiated in 1994 by the Kroger Company, one of the largest grocery chains in the United States, was greatly facilitated by information sharing. In this instance, the company and the union established joint teams of labor and management representatives who were responsible for gathering information to be shared. This procedure was followed at all the company stores in Nashville, Tennessee. In this particular bargaining unit, the company and the union, Local 1557 of the United Food and Commercial Workers International Union (UFCW), agreed to bargain by using a method called target-specific bargaining (TSB). One of the major components of TSB is joint fact finding and "mutual disclosure of bottom line for core issues"[20] as well as an exploration of the reasoning underlying the parties' positions. So far the parties have been pleased with the operation of TSB, which contributed to their 1994 settlement.

The concept of information sharing in collective bargaining has been put into practice in other countries as well. In Canada, in the federal public sector, the government established the Canadian Pay Research Bureau (CPRB). The CPRB was created after Canadian federal employees were granted full collective bargaining rights in 1966; most of them were also given the right to strike. The role of the CPRB was to provide the bargaining parties with research findings on rates of pay, employee earnings, conditions of employment, and related practices prevailing both within and outside the public sector. The director of the bureau was expected to consult regularly with representatives of both sides and to make certain that, as far as possible, their needs would be considered in CPRB research activities. According to recent inquiries with various offices of the Canadian government, the CPRB is no longer in existence.

In Japan "information sharing is a much more pervasive practice . . . than in the United States."[21] Morishima, in a study of information sharing in Japan, found that "the Japanese industrial relations system has developed and widely institutionalized labor management information sharing through a mechanism called the joint consultation system." Morishima[22] concludes that the Japanese approach benefits both union and management by reducing difficulties over wage negotiations and shortening the time necessary for reaching a wage settlement. There is, however, a cost to union members when information is shared. Morishima states that "negotiation outcomes show that a shorter and easier negotiation process seems to come about at the expense of the union's ability to deliver a high wage settlement for its membership."[23]

As a trade-off for smaller wage increases, the Japanese unions may be obtaining "long term employment security."[24] Management, in exchange for strategic information sharing, apart from securing moderate wage increases may also be lessening "union militancy."[25] There are some lessons in the Morishima study for both unions and management in the United States. By sharing information, Morishima management may actually attain more cooperation and less militancy from its unions. This result in turn could contribute to higher productivity. Unions may also benefit from information sharing by reducing the number and severity of confrontations, bargaining impasses, and strikes. This approach could also empower union members and give them a stronger voice in the operation of the enterprise, a development that many employees may welcome.

METHODS FOR COSTING CONTRACTS

The four common methods for calculating the costs of union wage demands are based on (1) total annual cost of demands, (2) annual cost of demands per employee, (3) cost of total demands as a percentage of payroll, and (4) cost of demands in cents per hour. The major advantages of these methods are simplicity, ease of computation, and ability to communicate bargaining results clearly to bargaining unit members.[26]

One estimates the annual cost of demands by totaling on an annualized basis all the union demands, in terms of wages as well as benefits.

To determine the annual cost increase of union demands per employee, one divides the total annual cost by the size of the labor force. This total can be computed in two ways: It may be based on the actual number of employees in the bargaining unit at the time the contract is negotiated, or it may be based on the average of the labor force for the year. The following illustration is a simplified calculation of annual increased labor costs per employee. Assuming a labor force of 100 workers and a cost of demands of $150,000, the average increased annual labor cost per employee would be $1,500.

One calculates the cost of total annual demands as a percentage of payroll by dividing the total cost of demands by the total payroll. Thus, if the total payroll is $1.5 million and the demands amount to $150,000, then the result is 10 percent.

To arrive at the cost of demands in cents per hour, one divides the total demands by the total hours worked. Thus, if there are 100 employees working on average 40 hours per week, 52 weeks per year—or 2,080 hours per employee—total hours worked are 208,000. If total demands are $150,000, then the cost of the demands in cents per hour would be

$$\frac{150,000}{208,000} = 0.72, \text{ or } 72 \text{ cents}$$

In his study of contract costing, Granof found that all company negotiators interviewed reported their primary objective was "to minimize the cents-per-hour direct wage increase." Also of reported concern was the actual cost of increases per productive hour. To calculate these costs, the company negotiators multiplied agreed-upon cents-per-hour increases by an average number of hours for which each person had been paid in the previous year. The sum of this calculation was then divided by an average number of productive hours, "or an arbitrary number of annual hours such as 1,900 or 2,000" per person. Calculations of productive hours exclude from total hours periods during which no work is accomplished, such as holidays, sick leave, and so on.[27]

The following illustration converts the cost of cents-per-hour increases into the cost of these increases per productive hour. If the negotiated direct wage increase is 50 cents per hour and in the previous year the company paid its workers for 240,000 hours, out of which only 200,000 were productive, then the actual increase per productive hour is 60 cents.

$$240,000 \times 0.50 = \$120,000$$

$$\frac{\$120,000}{200,000} = 0.60, \text{ or } 60 \text{ cents per productive hour}$$

Provisions for overtime premiums and shift differentials can be found in many contracts. Cost-of-living allowances are included in some. Methods for calculating the costs of these wage-related provisions vary among firms. In the case of cost of living, some firms negotiate provisions imposing a ceiling on increases within the contract term. In estimating the future costs of such provisions, some firms assume that the ceiling will be reached. Others try to project the level of the cost-of-living index and estimate cost as being either the index or the ceiling, whichever is lower.[28] Some employers' estimates of overtime premiums and shift differentials are based on historical data rather than on future projections. Many firms assume that the same number of premium hours that prevailed in the past will continue into the future.[29]

Procedures for Costing Employee Benefits

Methodology similar to that for calculating wage costs also applies to benefit costing. It can be based on (1) annual cost of each benefit and service for all employees, (2) annual cost per employee, (3) benefit costs as a percentage of payroll, or (4) per-employee cost in dollars and cents per hour.[30] The first two methods are fairly straightforward. The third approach, which computes benefit costs as a percentage of payroll, divides the total annual cost of benefits by the annual payroll. Thus, if the total payroll is $1.5 million and the total benefits are $450,000, then benefits represent 30 percent of payroll:

$$\frac{450,000}{1,500,000} = 0.30, \text{ or } 30\%$$

A company employing this approach faces the problem of deciding what to include in the payroll total. Certain items such as premium pay or bonuses are considered payroll by some employers, whereas others classify these as benefits. The percentage figure obtained would obviously vary depending on the definition of *payroll* applied. According to Henderson, "This problem emphasizes the importance of identifying and defining benefits and services and often requires major policy decisions by senior management."[31] The percentage approach is helpful for comparing benefit costs with those of other firms.

The fourth approach is based on the hourly cost of benefits per worker. This is the computation most frequently applied "in expressing the cost of benefits."[32] One reason for its popularity is ease of calculation. Another reason is its public relations value. It is relatively simple and meaningful to communicate value of benefits in cents per hour to bargaining unit members. The cents-per-hour approach is also useful in informing employees of the cost of benefits; it enables workers to assess the value of benefits in relation to their hourly pay. Henderson points out, however, that this amount may not always have much meaning for the employee whose hourly pay is very low. "A service worker being paid $5 an hour may not attach much significance to the fact that the company paid $2 in benefit costs for each hour worked. On the other hand, the significance of the benefit may seem greater if the figure is given as $4,160 a year ($2 × 2,080 hours/year)."[33] One calculates the per-hour cost of benefits by dividing the total cost of benefits by the number of hours. Thus, if the total annual cost of benefits is $450,000 and the total number of hours worked is 200,000, the cost of benefits is $2.25 per hour:

$$\frac{\$450,000}{200,000} = \$2.25$$

One difficulty with this approach is arriving at an appropriate number of hours worked. Some firms use the actual hours worked by the labor force; others use only productive hours.

> The cents-per-hour figure varies among organizations because of the different ways to identify and define the term hour. To one organization, hours may mean an arbitrary figure calculated by multiplying the days that the organization operated during the year by 8 hours (260 × 8 hours = 2,080 hours); to another company, it may mean the actual hours worked by the employee. In the latter case, it is possible to calculate cents per hour by dividing the total benefit costs by the total number of hours worked during the year.[34]

Companies employ a number of methods for calculating additional vacation hours, resulting from negotiated settlements. Some firms arrive at extra vacation costs by multiplying the increase in vacation hours by base wage rates. Thus, if additional vacation time amounts to 4,000 hours and the base rate is $8 per hour, then the extra cost is $32,000. Some companies base their calculations on the cost of making up time lost through extra vacation hours. Thus, if 4,000 extra hours are allocated to vacations and the cost of making up the vacation time through holiday and overtime pay would average $12 per hour, then the cost is not $32,000, as in the previous example, but $48,000. Increased vacation may have additional costs that are more difficult to measure, such as the cost of recruiting new employees to offset the additional vacation time. Also, new employees may initially be less efficient than the existing work force.

Firms utilize a variety of procedures for calculating the costs of extra holidays.[35] The simplest approach is to multiply additional holiday hours by a base wage rate; thus, if additional holidays amount to 800 hours and the base wage is $8 per hour, then the cost of holidays is $6,400. Another consideration applied to costing of holidays, the sum in addition to the cost of extra holidays at regular rates, is the sum of premiums that may have to be paid to those employees who will be required to work during the holidays at premium rates, as in firms with continuous operations. Thus, if there are 800 hours of additional holidays with the base rate of $8 per hour, and we assume that 400 of these hours must be made up at overtime rates of $12 per hour, then the cost of the additional holidays is $8,000 rather than $6,400, as in the previous illustration. Increasing the number of holidays does not always result in the hiring of extra workers. In some firms, the additional holidays are offset by a loss of production, which may have an adverse effect on cost and profitability. Costs of additional holidays are also influenced by the numbers of employees who exercise the option to work during holidays at premium pay, assuming that a contract contains such an option.

Costing of benefits such as pensions, life insurance, and various health plans is sometimes so complex that companies engage outside experts to help them estimate the costs.

Another approach to contract costing is the total-cost concept suggested by Walter A. Hazelton.[36] According to Hazelton, in the negotiation of most labor agreements, there is a strong dependence "on comparison of average labor rates . . . to norms." These norms are based on local, industry, or national averages. As contrasted with wage comparisons, benefit comparisons are frequently "handled subjectively." Hazelton holds that benefits, like wages, "should also be compared to norms" or be calculated as benefit costs per hour, to be added to hourly labor rates; such total hourly costs could then be compared to industry norms.

NEW MONEY

Some negotiators use the expression "new money" to denote

> a newly negotiated wage or benefit improvement that has a cost impact. It is distinguished from previously negotiated wage or benefit provisions that continue to have a cost impact. For example, if management agrees to pay its employees 5 percent more than wages in effect under the previous contract, the 5 percent represents "new money." The wages paid under the previous contract are considered "old money." Also, the concept of new money means that an employer will only "take credit" for the additional wage or fringe benefit *for the first year* the new wage or benefit is in effect. Although the 5 percent wage increase in the first year of a three-year contract is paid each year, it is normally only counted for labor negotiations purposes in the first year of the contract.[37]

The term *new money* is not used only with respect to wages; it is also applied to benefits.

In applying the concept of new money, the parties cannot ignore the impact of both old and new money on the total cost of the settlement. According to Loughran,

> The general costing rule is that if management negotiates any improvement in wages or benefits which has a cost impact during the term of the contract being negotiated, or agrees to continue a wage or benefit provision which will have a higher cost under the new contract than under the prior contract, that impact should be estimated and included as part of management's settlement package cost estimate.[38]

For an excellent discussion of the concept of new money, the reader is referred to Loughran's book, *Negotiating a Labor Contract*.[39]

Criticisms of Existing Methods for Costing Contracts

The existing contract costing methods are inadequate. Current approaches do not take into account the impact of increased contract costs on the firm as a total entity. The costing analysis employed is usually static rather than dynamic; it assumes that when labor costs go up, ceteris paribus (other things being equal) conditions prevail. Existing procedures are based on the assumption that the past will be repeated in the future. Also, current methods usually do not take into account the value of money over time, a concept that will be discussed in some detail later in this chapter.[40]

The total costs of settlements are not always reflected in labor costs paid out to bargaining unit members. A frequently overlooked cost implication of new contract terms is the ripple effect it may have on compensation for the company's nonunion employees.[41] Increased contract costs may contribute to a reduction in profits due to a decline in output and sales. Granof illustrates this point with a hypothetical company operating at capacity and agreeing to provide its employees with two 15-minute rest periods per day. Typically, one computes the cost of the rest period by multiplying the number of workers by days worked by rest period by hourly wage. In reality, the cost to the firm could be higher. If our hypothetical firm, operating at capacity, is not in a position to increase its labor force without additional investment and cannot offset the rest period through higher productivity, then the extra rest period will be detrimental to the firm's output, sales, and profitability.

In multiproduct firms, the percentages of labor cost may vary among products. Some products require high labor and low capital input, whereas for others the opposite is the case. Although, for bargaining purposes, it is important for a firm to arrive at a detailed breakdown of cost on an individual product basis, not many firms do so. An employer who can determine the cost impact of a labor contract for each item of the product line is in a better position to improve performance in such decision areas as pricing, substitution of labor by capital, changes in product mix, discontinuation of unprofitable products, and introduction of new technology.

Threats to some companies' survival arise "not because of union pressure or strikes, but because they negotiated without an understanding of the probable results of offers made across the table." Management's emphasis should be not on "What is necessary to avoid a strike?" but rather on "What is necessary for the company to survive either a settlement or strike, and prosper?"[42]

FINANCIAL DIMENSIONS OF MANAGEMENT PROPOSALS

The financial dimensions of management bargaining offers are influenced by a variety of factors: labor contract terms prevailing in the industry, competitive conditions in other input and output markets, technical possibilities in the production of different outputs, and demand for the output of the industry and of the firm. In markets where the firm has some control over output price, the firm's ability to pass on higher costs to consumers in the form of higher prices can influence significantly the size of management's offer. In the past, potential consumer responses to price changes were usually not a significant topic of negotiation. In today's highly competitive environment, where unions have concerns over employment security, discussions about product pricing and market share are no longer uncommon during negotiations.

The impact of the decision-making mechanism on sizes of bargaining offers, pricing policies, plant capacity, and levels of output varies significantly among firms. In smaller companies, managers or manager-owners may be wearing many different hats, assuming responsibility for bargaining, costing of the contract, and costing and pricing of output. In large corporations, these functions are scattered among different departments. Production and finance departments are responsible for computing the impact of various cost increases on cost of output; they also compute cost per unit of output at different hypothetical levels of output. On the product pricing side, marketing managers and economists try to answer the question of how consumers will respond to price increases. On the basis of data received from an army of experts, top managers make final decisions regarding optimum levels of output and pricing and on the appropriate size of the bargaining offer to be made to the union.

According to economic theory, the objective of the firm is to maximize equity return to stockholders; this can be conceptualized as long-run profit maximization. Expected profits are maximized in the short run when the revenues expected from output and pricing decisions under existing markets are largest relative to the expected costs of producing that output with existing plants and factor markets. This relationship is often expressed in terms of marginal (incremental) revenue and costs. Under existing conditions of industry structure and plant capacity, firms will continue to expand output until the expected extra revenue is equal to the expected increase in costs, and no longer. Firms maximizing profits successfully will behave as if they were equating marginal revenue and marginal cost,[43] even if they do not or cannot determine these magnitudes precisely.

Equity (long-run profits) maximization recognizes the price, output, and investment decisions that will generate expected revenue and cost streams in both the short and the long run. Maximization of the difference between the present values of these expected streams of revenue and cost is equity or long-run profit maximization. Such maximization involves decisions about plant capacity, plant location, technologies utilized, capital structure, product mix, and research and development expenditures on new processes and products, as well as short-run pricing and output decisions.

The collective bargaining process is part of this short-run and long-run decision process. The size of management's offer will reflect the assessments of the impact of that offer on short-run profitability and the long-run equity position of the firm. The correct costing of contracts should reflect all these factors. Relatively few labor relations experts have the perspective, information, or skills to make such determinations. Proper contract costing requires a combined knowledge of accounting, finance, marketing, economics, and production. The better the labor relations specialist can communicate and interact with the specialists in these areas, the more involved they will be in the process of determining the management offer to produce a "costing" with credibility throughout the firm.

ELASTICITY OF DEMAND

Firms often try to pass increased contract costs on to consumers as higher prices. The extent to which an individual firm can do this depends on the elasticity of demand for its product or service. The elasticity of demand is a measure of the sensitivity or responsiveness of quantity demanded to changes in price.

Both products in Figure 11.4 experience a 25-percent rise in price, from $4 to $5 per unit. The quantity sold of the elastic product represented in panel A decreases from four to two units, a decline of 50 percent. The sales decline for the inelastic product, panel B, is only about 17 percent, from six to five units.

In individual bargaining situations, a firm's ability to transfer increased costs to consumers would depend upon the elasticity of its demand curve. The firm's demand curve depends on the competitive relationship among firms in the industry, reflecting the degree of competition in the firm's product market. The demand curve faced by individual firms is usually thought to be more elastic than the demand curve of the entire industry. The reason for this is that more substitutes are available for one firm's products than for those of the industry as a whole. This is one reason why unions and even some firms prefer to negotiate on an industry-wide basis.

We can illustrate the importance of the concept of elasticity by relating it to total revenue. Total revenue is price times quantity (TR = P × Q). If 100,000 widgets are sold

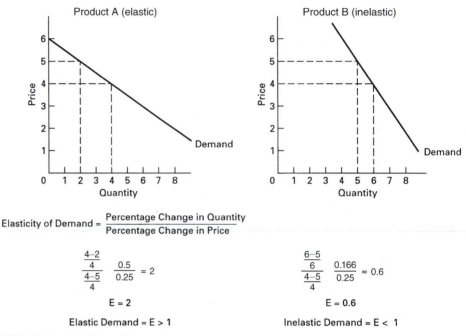

Elasticity of Demand = $\dfrac{\text{Percentage Change in Quantity}}{\text{Percentage Change in Price}}$

$$\dfrac{\dfrac{4-2}{4}}{\dfrac{4-5}{4}} \quad \dfrac{0.5}{0.25} = 2$$

$$E = 2$$

Elastic Demand = E > 1

$$\dfrac{\dfrac{6-5}{6}}{\dfrac{4-5}{4}} \quad \dfrac{0.166}{0.25} = 0.6$$

$$E = 0.6$$

Inelastic Demand = E < 1

FIGURE 11.4 Elasticity of Demand

at $2.00 each, total revenue will be $200,000. If firms in the widget industry attempt to transfer the costs of a labor settlement of 10 percent of total costs by increasing prices 10 percent (to $2.20), what will happen to total revenues? (1) If the demand for widgets is elastic, the percentage decrease in quantity will be greater than the percentage increase in price; therefore, total revenue will fall. Not only will the firms fail to recover their increased costs, their revenue will be less; for example, if we assume that at $2.20 only 80,000 widgets will be sold, total revenue will be $176,000. (2) If the demand is inelastic, the percentage decrease in quantity will be less than the percentage increase in price. Whether the increased revenue will equal the settlement depends on how inelastic the demand is; for example, if we assume that at $2.20, 98,000 widgets will be sold, total revenue will be $215,600, or $15,600 higher than before the price increase. We should point out that the increased costs of a labor settlement would be affected by demand for widgets. A decline in demand may decrease the number of employees required; thus, the final cost effect of a labor settlement may be different from the 10-percent increase assumed earlier. The preceding conclusions may also be modified by dynamic factors in the economy such as productivity gains and coincidental increases in the prices of substitute and complementary products. A discussion of these factors is beyond the scope of this book.

As just shown, some understanding of the concept of elasticity of demand is important at the bargaining table. A firm that plans to pass increased contract costs on to its customers but finds itself confronted with an elastic market demand could experience a decrease not only in revenues and profits but also in employment. It is important, therefore, for both management and unions to be aware of elasticity of demand in developing strategies and tactics at the bargaining table. In some major corporations, economists with expertise in calculation of elasticity prepare estimates of the potential impact of higher prices on sales. Such professional help is often not available to the smaller company, which must then rely on the judgment of its marketing managers.

Although the concept of elasticity is unfamiliar to many labor relations practitioners, its impact on the results of the bargaining process is real. As illustrated earlier, the more elastic the firm's or the industry's demand, the more difficult it will be to pass increased costs on to consumers without adverse effects on profits and employment. This relationship should be a factor for all parties to consider in bargaining.

THE PRESENT VALUE CONCEPT

An important tool in the field of finance and economics is the concept of present value.

Economists discuss marginal efficiency of capital as an investment determinant. Financial analysts have a variety of present worth valuation theories, and corporate financial officers utilize present value formulas in their investment decisions. All these approaches have a common denominator, which is the concept of the time value of money. The present value of $100 to be received one year from now is worth less than $100 to be received immediately. In other words, $100 is worth more today than the present value of $100 one year from now because a return can be earned on it during the year. According to Loughran, present value analysis can "be a valuable tool for labor contract costing."[44] The present value methodology is extensively covered by Granof.[45] The concept is a useful method for telling the parties the present value of future obligations assumed under an agreement. Its formula is as follows:

$$PV = \frac{S}{(1 + i)^n} = S(1 + i)^{-n}$$

PV = present value of a given obligation
S = future value of the same obligation
i = discount rate
n = number of periods

Assume that a hypothetical company considers giving its employees a one-time raise of $1 million, to take effect at the beginning of the third year of the contract. The present value of that raise, based on present value tables[46] and a 10-percent discount rate,[47] would be $826,000, rather than the $1 million it would be worth if received now:

$$\$826,000 = \frac{1,000,000}{(1 + 0.10)^2} = 1,000,000 (1 + 0.10)^{-2}$$

The basic formula can be modified to take into account a variety of contract terms. If a union demanded for its members a lump-sum contract-signing bonus that amounted to $1 million, the employer could save $174,000 ($1,000,000 − $826,000) by getting the union to accept payment at the end of the two-year contract instead of at the beginning.

THE DISCOUNTED CASH FLOW MODEL

Labor contract costs have many implications for employers. As stated earlier, they may have an impact on prices charged, on volume produced and sold, on product mix, and on capital-to-labor ratio. Current contract costing procedures have been called inadequate because many firms still "base computations on historical, as opposed to projected, levels of operations."[48] This situation is changing, however, as more firms stress strategic planning and as some unions participate in strategic business decisions.[49] The past is relevant as an information base but not as a decision base.

Granof suggests that firms cost contracts by utilizing the discounted cash flow (DCF) model.[50] The model is based on the time value of money, which is measured by present value formulas. The DCF model is currently used by employers making investment decisions. In arriving at these decisions, management considers all future cash inflows and outflows that accompany investment expenditures and discounts these cash flows to their present value. The formula is as follows:

$$DCF = \sum_{n=0}^{N} \frac{(\text{cash inflow}_n)}{(1 + i)^n} - \sum_{n=0}^{N} \frac{(\text{cash outflow}_n)}{(1 + i)^n}$$

The DCF model utilizes investment evaluation techniques in costing of labor contracts. The model utilizes present value formulas for the costing of settlements, but, rather than just applying these formulas to projected costs, it also applies them to projected receipts. In bargaining, the parties consider settlement packages of various compositions. In some instances, a union may feel indifferent about two management proposals and view both as equally acceptable. An application of the DCF model could reveal that one proposal is less expensive than the other. The model also looks beyond the direct cost of a labor contract to examine the overall impact of a settlement on a firm. Under the model, all projected receipts and expenditures are discounted to their present value, and on this basis the most attractive bargaining package can be selected. Cash flows may differ among bargaining proposals; the model, through its present value approach, provides a common denominator enabling the parties to compare the costs of different options.

The model not only is important for management, it could also be useful to unions. It could highlight the employment implications of various union proposals. One difficulty that unions would have in utilizing the model would be a lack of necessary financial data. Union contract analysts would have to engage in intelligent guesswork to come up with the financial ingredients necessary for the structuring of a DCF model. The model could help unions anticipate management's reactions to their demands; it could also help them formulate better proposals. In a labor-management relationship based on cooperation and trust, confidential information necessary to implementation of the DCF model could be shared.

So far, the DCF model has not been very popular in the collective bargaining domain. According to Granof, the following reasons are responsible for its absence from the bargaining scene. First, the model stresses a single objective, the maximization of net present value of projected cash flow. In reality, a company may have numerous objectives, some of which may differ from those implied by Granof, the model. For a particular firm, it may be important to achieve a given annual earning per share, and this aim could be incompatible with results obtained under a DCF model. Second, the present value formula utilized in the model contains a discount rate that must be determined arbitrarily. The most commonly used rate is the cost of capital. However, that rate is difficult to define. Third, the DCF model is based on projections of future cash flows; firms find it difficult to arrive at accurate long-term cash flow forecasts.[51] Furthermore, we should point out that economic concessions in collective bargaining affect people and therefore cannot always be viewed as if they were simply competing alternative investment decisions. Despite the foregoing limitations, the model has some potential for collective bargaining.

Contemporary college graduates entering the world of work are equipped with quantitative and computer skills that their predecessors, even 10 years ago, did not possess. This development and major breakthroughs in computer technology have increased the application of sophisticated costing technique to collective bargaining.

COSTING A COLLECTIVE BARGAINING AGREEMENT BY AN EMPLOYER[52]

In the old days of collective bargaining, a company negotiator had a pad of paper, the current labor contract, a calculator, and a deck of cards in his or her briefcase. The cards were used to pass the time during the long union and company caucuses.

In today's collective bargaining world, it is not uncommon for the company's negotiator to come with a laptop computer. The computer is loaded with employment, wage, hour, and benefit data from the company's human resources information system (HRIS) and various spreadsheet formulas that enable the negotiator to cost any union proposal immediately. The negotiator can assess how much a proposed wage increase will cost, what financial impact a benefit change will have, and what the company will have to pay for a possible change in certain working conditions. For example, in a labor-intensive workplace, such as a unionized retail chain with many different classifications, wage progressions, part-time and full-time workers, and a variety of benefit plans and working conditions, the computer can be an invaluable tool in negotiations.

In most cases, the negotiator, working with the company team, establishes a costing goal or limit for the new contract. This may be represented by a simple incremental cost amount that the company believes it can afford over the term of the contract. In some cases, the goal is expressed as a percentage of sales target, such as "Total wage costs should be no more than 10 percent of total sales at the end of the contract." In other cases, the goal can be a targeted average hourly base compensation rate, which includes all wage and benefit costs divided by the number of hours worked; the rate is then projected through the end of the contract term.

The establishment of goals and a costing methodology require a sophisticated human resources information system that shows the negotiator how many hours are worked by each person in each classification. It also shows wage rates and progressions for all hours worked; pay for hours not worked, such as vacation and sick pay; and incidents of premium pay, such as overtime. Additionally, it reveals taxes such as FICA and Medicare, benefit costs per hour, and other relevant data.

The negotiator then applies a spreadsheet software program to integrate the wage data with HRIS, which calculates the "flow-through" effects of any change in hours, pay, working conditions, or benefits. "Flow-through" or "roll-up" is simply a method that takes into account the full impact of a wage increase. For example, let's say a classification of workers receives a 50-cents-per-hour increase each year for the three-year term of the contract. Each 50 cents affects the wage rate, which is multiplied by the hours worked by each person. It also affects the company's obligation to pay additional FICA and Medicare contributions and a higher rate for the employees' vacations, sick pay, and overtime or premium pay. Depending on the design of the plans, it could also affect the cost of pension or other retirement and benefit plans. The software includes these additional factors in the costing.

Furthermore, assumptions must be inserted into the software to estimate gains or changes in productivity, the rate of turnover, the hours projected to be worked over the future years of the contract, and the impact of work restrictions that the union is proposing. With respect to restrictions, the company must have some estimate of their cost on a per-hour basis and then project them for all hours worked. For example, if a union representing employees of a retail food store wants a clause limiting the use of outside vendors to set up or stock shelves, the cost of this proposal will be added to the total calculation and will be expressed as cents per hour for all hours worked. Also, if lump sum versus rate increases are to be used, or if some type of incentive pay is being considered, the software will have formulas to estimate the cost impact of these pay changes.

If the negotiator has a target that involves compensation costs as a percent of sales, estimates must be made of real versus inflationary sales gains over the term of the contract, the impact of additional stores, and the change in the mix of employees who will work in the new stores. Presumably, newer employees with less seniority and lower pay will work many of the hours in the newer facilities; thus, the total compensation costs for these facilities and "new sales" will have a different base compensation rate.

In some cases where the bargaining relationship is mature and cooperative, both sides can agree on a total compensation cost target for the full term of the contract. Then they work with a variety of contract proposals, or scenarios, to determine the cost impact of each. When they reach the total costing goal by combining a variety of proposals and counterproposals, a memorandum of agreement is signed and presented to the membership for ratification. This represents the ultimate utility and value of "knowing the numbers" in collective bargaining. Once the parties agree on a total cost goal, or "what the company can afford," the rest of the bargaining is fairly simple.

While the traditions and traits of collective bargaining—and the rituals attendant thereto—continue in most settings, if trust becomes the controlling factor in a relationship between the company and the union, the laptop computer becomes the instrument of compromise and agreement.

THE COMPUTER AND CONTRACT COSTING

The computer is an important tool for the costing of labor contracts. Chapter 12 of this book will provide a comprehensive review of the role of computers in collective bargaining. That chapter will also review various software programs that are currently available for facilitating the collective bargaining process.

SUMMARY

Both labor and management could benefit from more open discussion of methods and assumptions applied in the costing of new proposals. Unions, by applying different assumptions, may find out that the actual costs of some of their demands are much higher than they anticipated, and this information may induce them to revise demands or shift to less expensive options. Managements, by subjecting their cost methodologies to review and criticism from unions, may find out that their approaches and assumptions are flawed, and this information may persuade them to revise their offers or counteroffers. Such revisions, at times, could make the difference between a strike and a settlement.

Contract-costing procedures could be upgraded through more extensive reliance on financial and economic concepts. Existing procedures use accounting methodology and are based primarily on the assumption that the future is a repetition of the past. Management sometimes ignores such important ideas as the time value of money, considering as outlays only labor costs directly attributed to its employees. A firm however, is a total entity; whatever happens in any subsystem can affect the total system. In reality, costs resulting from new settlements may be considerably higher than the actual totals paid out to labor in the form of higher wages and fringe benefits.

The costing of contracts poses major challenges to negotiators, who are not always familiar with finance, production, and pricing of output, all of which influence management's offer. In many firms, these decisions are heavily influenced by finance people who have no background in labor relations. Greater familiarity with these areas could give negotiators more influence over the composition and magnitude of the bargaining package.

For this possibility to be realized, however, labor relations experts would require better training in finance, accounting, and economics. As management negotiators gain further expertise in costing, unions will have to respond in kind. Union negotiators will also have to become better trained in quantitative skills. Union and management negotiators will need to acquire sophistication and understanding of the quantitative tools currently applied by actuaries, accountants, economists, and financial experts. This is necessary to prevent these quantitatively, but usually not labor-relations-oriented, professionals from assuming greater influence over labor relations in the future.

For additional information on costing, review Appendix A to this chapter, "Elementary Steps in Costing a Contract." The appendix provides examples of the actual mechanics of contract-costing provisions. It advances the discussion from the conceptual approach taken within the chapter to the practical level required for direct application of costing methods.

Notes

1. *Employee Benefits, 1996 Edition* (Washington, DC: U.S. Chamber of Commerce Research Center, 1996), pp. 2, 12, 21, 38.

2. Ibid., p. 10.

3. Richard I. Henderson, *Compensation Management,* 6th ed. (Englewood Cliffs, NJ: Prentice Hall, 1994), p. 550.

4. William E. Lissy, "Currents in Compensation and Benefits," *Compensation & Benefits Review,* 26, no. 5 (September 1994), p. 15.

5. *Employee Benefit Plan Review,* May 1990, p. 64.

6. "Current Bargaining Issues," *Health Care Cost Containment Measures,* Bureau of National Affairs, 1992, no. 1227, 16:381.

7. Ibid.

8. Ibid., 16:386

9. Ibid., 16:393.

10. William J. Wiatrowski, "Employee Benefits for Union and Non-Union Workers," *Monthly Labor Review* 117, no. 2 (February 1994), pp. 35–36.

11. "Current Bargaining Issues," op. cit., 16:381.

12. Michael H. Granof, *How to Cost Your Labor Contract* (Washington, DC: Bureau of National Affairs, 1973), pp. 20–21.

13. Ibid.

14. Ibid.

15. Neil W. Chamberlain and James W. Kuhn, *Collective Bargaining,* 2nd ed. (New York: McGraw Hill, 1965), p. 75.

16. Thomas A. Kochan and Harry C. Katz, *Collective Bargaining and Industrial Relations,* 2nd ed. (Homewood, IL: Richard D. Irwin, 1988), pp. 267, 408, 465–66.

17. Ibid.; see also Carl M. Stevens, *Strategy and Collective Bargaining Negotiation* (New York: McGraw Hill, 1963), pp. 142–46.

18. Motohiro Morishima, "Information Sharing and Collective Bargaining in Japan: Effects on Wage Negotiation," *Industrial and Labor Relations Review* 44, no. 3 (April 1991), p. 469.

19. Morris M. Kleiner and Marvin L. Bouillon, "Providing Business Information to Production Workers: Correlates of Compensation and Profitability," *Industrial and Labor Relations Review* 41, no. 4 (July 1988), pp. 605–17. See also Morishima, op. cit., pp. 469, 480.

20. Mimeographed notes, Human Resource and Labor Relations Conference, Peachtree Executive Conference Center, Peachtree City, Georgia, September 26–29, 1994.

21. Morishima, op. cit., p. 480.

22. Ibid., p. 469.

23. Ibid., p. 481.

24. Ibid., p. 481.

25. Ibid.

26. Granof, op. cit., pp. 5–6.

27. Ibid., p. 34.

28. Ibid., p. 40.

29. Ibid., p. 42.

30. Harold Stieglitz, *Computing the Cost of Fringe Benefits,* Studies in Personnel Policy, no. 128 (New York: National Industrial Conference Board, 1952), pp. 7, 10. See also Henderson, op. cit., pp. 566–68.

31. Henderson, op. cit., p. 567.

32. Ibid., pp. 566–68.

33. Ibid., p. 567.

34. Ibid.

35. Granof, op. cit., p. 50.

36. Walter A. Hazelton, "How to Cost Labor Settlements," *Management Accounting* (May 1979), pp. 19–23.

37. Charles S. Loughran, *Negotiating a Labor Contract. A Management Handbook,* 2nd ed. (Washington, DC: Bureau of National Affairs, 1992), pp. 294–96.

38. Ibid.

39. Ibid.

40. Granof, op. cit., pp. 4, 7.

41. Neil M. Frank and Akshay K. Talwar, "The Accountant's Role in Labor Negotiations," *The CPA Journal* (December 1988), p. 60.

42. Ibid., pp. 56, 59.

43. For further discussion of this topic, see any introductory text in economics.

44. Loughran, op. cit., pp. 318–20.

45. Granof, op. cit., pp. 80–128.

46. Financial tables are included in most mathematics of finance texts.

47. *Discount rate* refers to the rate applied to calculation from future to present. The term *interest rate* is utilized for calculations from the present to the future. The discount rate used depends on prevailing money market conditions and interest rates. Granof, op. cit., suggests that the discount rate used be the cost of capital rate (p. 110).

48. Granof, op. cit., p. 127.

49. Thomas A. Kochan, Harry C. Katz, and Robert B. McKersie, *The Transformation of American Industrial Relations* (Ithaca, NY: ILR Press, 1994), pp. 178–205.

50. Granof, op. cit., p. 90.

51. Alexander A. Robichek, Donald G. Ogilvie, and John D. C. Roach, "Capital Budgeting: A Pragmatic Approach," *Financial Executive* 37 (April 1969), pp. 26–39. Eugene M. Lerner and Alfred Rappaport, "Limit DCF in Capital Budgeting," *Harvard Business Review* 46 (September–October 1968), pp. 133–39. *Source:* Granof, op. cit., p. 90.

52. *Source:* Thomas E. Murphy, Group Vice President, and Brad Tomich, Manager of Labor Relations, the Kroger Co., Cincinnati, Ohio.

APPENDIX A*

Elementary Steps in Contract Costing

Perhaps no other issue in collective bargaining more easily defies precision and yet looms larger in the minds of negotiators than cost of the economic package. A review of the literature on the subject leads quickly to the conclusion that there are many approaches to costing the package. Yet the need for both labor and management to determine, with considerable accuracy, the financial consequences of labor contract proposals is of critical importance to the success of the collective bargaining process. Labor costs are among the largest costs incurred by most corporations, and the cost of labor depends not only on the overall size of the compensation package but on its component parts as well. For a labor union, negotiating benefits for its members represents one of its major functions. Unions are, therefore, keenly interested in obtaining the best settlements possible.

The job of evaluating the cost of contract proposals is no easy one. Every item in the agreement—the benefit package, changes in work schedules and job classifications, seniority rules, and other contract changes—must be examined to determine the actual cost to the company and the benefit to the union membership. An understanding of these factors is essential to negotiators to enable them to trade one item of a proposal or counterproposal for another.

This understanding is as crucial to the effective mediator as it is to the negotiators. The mediator who understands the importance of being able to cost out a proposal accurately and who can aid the parties in developing the figures enhances his or her ability to develop alternatives that can mean the difference between a settlement and a strike.

The material for this collection of examples was originally gathered by Edward F. O'Brien, Regional Director, Region 4, of the Federal Mediation and Conciliation Service. The purpose of these data is to aid members of the Service in better understanding the methods by which the parties may compute costs. It is also intended to be a guide for the career development of new mediators and to provide resource material for those who are familiar with costing practices.

Although the Office of Technical Services would encourage mediators to utilize this costing information, at the outset it should be emphasized that the material is only a guide and that it in no way purports to be the best approach or an approach advocated by the Service.

The methods of costing presented in this Appendix are intended to indicate how the cost of one aspect of the total package may influence other aspects of the contract and how such costing can be accomplished. In the final analysis, however, the mediator must use his or her professional judgment as to the appropriate application of this information in contract negotiations.

Wages

Wage rates and wage increases vary greatly by industry, occupation, and union status. Wage rates and wage rate changes are published monthly by the Bureau of Labor Statistics.[†] Shown here are a few simple methods for calculating wage increases.

---

*The material for this appendix was prepared by Edward F. O'Brien, Regional Director, Region 4, and by the Division of Research, Planning and Development, Office of Technical Services, Federal Mediation and Conciliation Service.

†Two Bureau of Labor Statistics publications that contain such information are *Monthly Labor Review* and *Employment and Earnings.*

There are at least two basic methods by which to calculate the direct cents-per-hour cost of a wage increase.

Method 1. If a wage increase of $0.45 per hour is granted, the cost is then $0.45. If the increase is not a flat across-the-board increase but rather an average increase of $0.45, then the increases are weighted.

100 workers with increases of $0.40
80 workers with increases of $0.45
50 workers with increases of $0.50

$$
\begin{array}{rl}
100 \times \$0.40 = & \$\ 40 \\
80 \times\ \ \ 0.45 = & \ \ \ 36 \\
\underline{\ 50} \times\ \ \ 0.50 = & \ \ \underline{\ \ 25} \\
230 & \$101
\end{array}
\qquad \frac{101}{230} = \$0.44
$$

1. Hourly cost per employee = $0.44

2. Total annual cost = $210,496

Average hourly increase × number of hours paid × number of employees
$$0.44 \times 2{,}080 \times 230 = \$210{,}496$$

3. Annual cost per employee = $915.20

$$\frac{\text{Annual total cost}}{\text{Number of employees}} \quad \frac{\$210{,}496}{230} = \$915.20$$

Method 2. This method takes into account hours paid for but not worked. The total increase in wages is divided by either the total projected or total estimated number of productive hours to be worked. Assume a standard number of paid hours, 2,080, for the workers in this above example:

$$
\begin{array}{rl}
100 \times 2080 \times \$0.40 = & \$83{,}200 \\
80 \times 2080 \times\ \ \ 0.45 = & 74{,}880 \\
50 \times 2080 \times\ \ \ 0.50 = & 52{,}000 \\
\text{Total increase in wages} = & \$210{,}080
\end{array}
$$

This is then divided by the total numbers of projected productive hours. (Assume each employee works 2,000 hours per year.)

Total number of productive hours = number of employees × number of productive hours for each worker.

$$230 \times 2000 = 460{,}000$$

$$\frac{\text{Average cost}}{\text{Productive hours}} \quad \frac{\$210{,}080}{460{,}000} = \$0.46 \text{ per hour}$$

Note: If productive hours had been determined to be 1,900, the increase would have been $0.48. Generally, the previous year's average number of productive hours per employee is used.

Method 3. In order to determine the average hourly cost of a wage increase of a multiyear contract, calculate the increase by the number of years or months each increase will be in effect and divide by the total number of years or months of the contract.

A three-year contract provides for the following increases. (This calculation utilizes 2,080 hours per year, as does Method 1.)

December 1, [1995] = $0.50 per hour
December 1, [1996] = 0.45 per hour
December 1, [1997] = 0.40 per hour
$1.35

TABLE A.1

	In Years			In Months	
$ Per Hour		Years in Effect	$ Per Hour		Months in Effect
0.50	×	3 = $1.50	0.50	×	36 = $18.00
0.45	×	2 = .90	0.45	×	24 = 10.80
0.40	×	1 = .40	0.40	×	12 = 4.80
		$2.80			$33.60

$\dfrac{\$2.80 \text{ years}}{3} = \$0.93 \text{ per hour}$ $\dfrac{\$33.60 \text{ months}}{36} = \$0.93 \text{ per hour}$

Method 4. An alternative method for calculating the average hourly cost of the wage increase over the life of the contract is to sum the total wage increase over the period in which it is in effect and then divide this sum by the total time period of the contract.

For example:

TABLE A.2

	$ Per Hour		Months in Effect
First 12 months	$0.50	×	12 = $ 6.00
Second 12 months			
$0.50 + $0.45	0.95	×	12 = 11.40
Third 12 months			
$0.50 + $0.45 + $0.40	1.35	×	12 = 16.20
			$33.60

$\dfrac{\$33.60}{36 \text{ months}} = \$0.93 \text{ per hour}$

(*Note:* This method assumes 2,080 hours per year, as does Method 1.)

The technique of computing increases by the number of months for which an increase is to remain in effect is particularly useful when the company is attempting to stay within certain cost limitations and the union is influenced by the total package increase as opposed to the actual money in hand. For example, a $1.50 total wage increase over three years of $0.25 at six-month intervals may be more acceptable than one that is front loaded but does not yield as high a wage increase over the same period as a $0.50–$0.50–$0.20 package. In fact, the first package may even become an acceptable compromise if the company is willing to increase the wage rate over the period by the $1.50 amount but is unable or unwilling to front load the package.

This approach has often been used in instances where the parties desire to create or expand a differential between different bargaining units. The parties can stay within the same average cost for all bargaining units and end up with varying wage rates. By applying this method in certain situations, such as delaying a second- or third-year increase for a month or two, it is often possible to persuade the parties to apply the savings to a fringe demand costing one or two cents per hour.

Method 5. This method determines the average yearly wage increase over the term of the contract and is frequently used by the parties to describe a wage settlement. The same three-year contract and increases given in Method 3 apply to this example.

TABLE A.3

In Years			In Months		
$ Per Hour		Years in Effect	$ Per Hour		Months in Effect
0.50	×	3 = $1.50	0.50	×	36 = $18.00
0.45	×	2 = 0.90	0.45	×	24 = 10.80
0.40	×	1 = 0.40	0.40	×	12 = 4.80
		$2.80			$33.60

$$\frac{\$2.80}{6 \text{ years}} = \$0.47 \text{ per hour} \qquad \frac{\$33.60}{72 \text{ months}} = \$0.47 \text{ per hour}$$

Reduction in Hours

About 70 percent of all major collective bargaining agreements provide for a 40-hour scheduled work week. Another 8 percent of such agreements specifically schedule work weeks of less than 40 hours. Over the years, the work week has declined, and a demand for a reduction in the work week is not uncommon.

A reduction in the work week with no loss in weekly pay represents an increased hourly pay. If the work week were to be cut from 40 hours to 35 hours, the increase in hourly wages needed to provide the same pay received for 40 would be approximately 14 percent.

For a specific example in dollar-and-cents terms: If hourly wages average $5.00, weekly pay for 40 hours is $200; then a reduction in hours to 35 would require an hourly increase of 71¢ to maintain the weekly wage of $200, a 14.2-percent hourly wage increase. If the hours reduction in this example were only to $37\frac{1}{2}$ hours, the hourly increase needed to maintain the weekly wage of $200 would be 33¢, a 6.6-percent hourly wage increase.

Cost-of-Living Clauses

Basically, the COLA is a means of maintaining the existing ratio between the Consumer Price Index (CPI) and average hourly earnings. Such agreements have traditionally been popular during periods of rapid inflation. Regardless of the basic differences in COLA language found in collective bargaining contracts, each COLA provision contains the same basic elements. These elements are (1) selection of the actual index to be used (most agreements use the Consumer Price Index published by the Bureau of Labor Statistics or some variation of it), (2) selection of the base year upon which changes in the COLA are to be measured, (3) agreement on the length of time that shall elapse between wage-adjustment periods, (4) agreement on whether the adjustment shall be incorporated into the actual wage rate or shall be paid apart from basic wages, (5) agreement as to whether upward wage adjustments will be unlimited or capped during the duration of the agreement, and (6) adoption of a formula to determine the amount of the wage adjustment to be made.

In estimating the total cost of an escalator clause, the anticipated rise in inflation or the CPI for the contract duration must also be projected. (*Note:* Most experts have repeatedly failed accurately to predict yearly inflationary rates, so the costing of a COLA clause is at best a rough approximation.)

In the following costing example, the length of time between COLA adjustments is quarterly; the adjustments are unlimited or uncapped; the wage adjustments formula is a $0.01 hourly wage increase for each 0.3-point quarterly rise in the CPI; the length of the agreement is 15 months; and the CPI is expected to increase by 10 points yearly with quarterly increases as listed below. The estimated cost to the employer of such a COLA agreement would be calculated as shown in Table A.4.

TABLE A.4

	CPI Level	Point Change	Quarterly Cents per Hour Increase
Base period	155.4	—	—
End of 1st quarter	157.8	2.4	$0.08
End of 2nd quarter	160.6	2.8	0.093
End of 3rd quarter	163.1	2.5	0.083
End of 4th quarter	165.5	2.4	0.08
Total		10.1	0.336

The first quarterly COLA adjustment would take place three months after the effective contract date and would be in effect for 12 months because the example uses an agreement of 15 months' duration. The second increase would be six months after the start of the contract and would be in effect for nine months, or three-fourths of a year. The third increase would be in effect for six months, or one-half year, and the fourth would be in effect for three months or one-fourth of a year.

The estimated cost of each of the four quarterly increases is equal to

Hourly increase × number of hours paid × number of employees.

TABLE A.5

Cost of Each Quarterly Adjustment			
First quarterly adjustment	$0.08 × (2080) × 230	=	$ 38,272
Second quarterly adjustment	0.093 × $3/4$(2080) × 230	=	33,368
Third quarterly adjustment	0.083 × $1/2$(2080) × 230	=	19,854
Fourth quarterly adjustment	0.08 × $1/4$(2080) × 230	=	9,568
Estimated total cost of COLA adjustments		=	$101,062

If the contract were for 12 months and the CPI were assumed to rise in the same manner as the above example, the quarterly adjustments over this contract period would be calculated as shown in Table A.6.

TABLE A.6

	Cost of Each Quarterly Adjustment		
First quarterly adjustment	$0.08 × ¼(2080) × 230	=	$28,704
Second quarterly adjustment	0.093 × ½(2080) × 230	=	22,246
Third quarterly adjustment	0.083 × ¼(2080) × 230	=	9,927
Estimated total cost of COLA adjustments		=	$60,877

(*Note:* The first quarterly increase would be in effect for nine months, or three-fourths of a year, the second for six months, and the third for three months. The fourth quarterly increase would not go into effect until the end of the year and does not appear as a cost in these calculations.)

Some contracts provide for a limit or cap on the amount to be paid under COLA. Such a cap may be $0.10 or $0.20 during a year or over the life of a contract. Other contracts state that the cost of living would have to exceed a certain predetermined percentage before any adjustment would be made.

Fringe Benefits

According to a study by the Conference Board, a private research firm, a large number of U.S. companies have liberalized their employee benefits, which now account for $0.327 of every payroll dollar. The study reported two major trends: (1) companies increasingly are paying the full cost of employee benefits, and (2) more and more firms are providing the same benefits to all employees, rather than differentiating between blue- and white-collar workers. Because fringes are becoming more important to the bargaining process, a few examples on costing of such benefit increases may be helpful.

Holidays

According to the Bureau of National Affairs (BNA), in union contracts covering 5,000 or more workers, paid holidays were provided in 99 percent of the agreements. The median number of paid holidays was 10 in manufacturing contracts and 8 in nonmanufacturing contracts.

The determinants in costing an additional holiday are the number of workers affected, the average rate, and the number of hours of holiday pay, which is usually eight. Examples are shown next.

1. Total annual cost

   Number of workers (230) × average hourly rate, assume ($5.00) × number of paid holiday hours, assume (8).

$$230 × \$5.00 × 8 = \$9200$$
Total annual cost is $9200

2. Hourly cost per employee per year

$$\frac{(\text{Annual cost} = \$9200)}{\text{Average hours paid per year (2080)} × \text{number of workers (230)}}$$

$$\frac{\$9200}{478,400} = \$0.019 \text{ per hour cost}$$

3. Annual cost per employee

$$\frac{\text{Annual cost (\$9200)}}{\text{Number of workers (230)}} = \$40$$

Overtime Premiums

Ninety percent of all major contracts provide for daily overtime rates, and 65 percent provide for weekly overtime rates. Generally, in manufacturing contracts, time and one-half is specified for work after the normal day and/or work week. Double or triple time is generally paid for work during normal leisure periods, such as Saturdays, Sundays, and holidays. In costing any increase in overtime, Saturday, Sunday, or holiday work, it is standard to assume that the number of hours paid at premium rates will be the same as in prior years. Once the number of hours paid at premium rate is determined, the cost is calculated by multiplying the change in rates by the number of hours.

If, for example, the company paid time and one-half for all work on Saturday and this was increased to double time for Saturday work and the number of Saturday hours worked the previous year was 38,800, the increase would be calculated as follows. Also, assume a wage rate of $5.00 per hour and a work force of 230 employees.

Current Cost of Overtime Payments

1. Total annual cost

$$\text{Wage rate} \times 1\tfrac{1}{2} \times \left(\begin{array}{c} \text{number of hours worked on} \\ \text{Saturday in the previous year} \end{array} \right) =$$

$$\$5.00 \times 1\tfrac{1}{2} \times 38{,}800 = \$291{,}000$$

2. Hourly cost per employee per year

$$\frac{\text{Total cost}}{\text{Total number of hours paid} \times \text{number of employees}} =$$

$$\frac{\$291{,}000}{2080 \times 230} = \$0.61$$

3. Annual cost per employee

$$\frac{\text{Total cost}}{\text{Number of employees}} = \frac{\$291{,}000}{230} = \$1265$$

Anticipated Cost of Overtime Payments

1. Total annual cost

$$\text{Wage rate} \times 2 \times \text{number of Saturday hours worked}$$
$$= \$5.00 \times 2 \times 38{,}800 = \$388{,}000$$

2. Hourly cost per employee per year

$$\frac{\text{Total cost}}{\text{Total number of hours paid} \times \text{number of employees}} =$$

$$\frac{\$388{,}000}{2080 \times 230} = \$0.81$$

3. Annual cost per employee

$$\frac{\text{Total cost}}{\text{Number of employees}} = \frac{\$388,000}{230} = \$1687$$

Increased Cost of Anticipated Overtime Payments

1. Increased total costs

$$\$388,000 - 291,000 = \$97,000$$

2. Increased hourly cost

$$\$0.81 - 0.61 = \$0.20$$

3. Increased annual cost per employee

$$\$1687 - 1265 = \$422$$

Shift Differentials

Premiums are frequently paid for shifts, either as flat cents per hour or on a percent calculation of the average straight-time hourly rate. Work performed in the third shift is generally paid at a higher rate.

Calculation of Shift Differentials

Shift 1—no premiums for 100 workers
Shift 2—$0.20 per hour for 65 workers
Shift 3—$0.40 per hour for 65 workers

1. Total annual cost

$$65 \text{ workers} \times 2080 \text{ hours} \times \$0.20 = \$27,040$$
$$65 \text{ workers} \times 2080 \text{ hours} \times \$0.40 = \underline{\$54,080}$$
$$\text{Total annual cost is } \$81,120$$

2. Hourly cost per employee per year

$$\frac{\$81,120}{230 \times 2080} = \$0.17$$

3. Annual cost per employee

$$\frac{\$81,120}{230} = \$352.70$$

Vacation Pay

Vacation policy varies by industry and company. More leisure time is frequently a demand, and in order to calculate an additional week of paid vacation, it is helpful to know the present vacation eligibility, the average hourly rate of each group of workers in each eligibility classification, and the hours of vacation.

Present Vacation Eligibility

15 workers—less than 1 year—no vacation
50 workers—   1 year—40 hours
100 workers—   1–2 years—80 hours
65 workers—   3–10 years—120 hours

TABLE A.7

1. *Total Annual Cost*

Workers		Average Hourly Rate		Vacation Hours		Current Annual Cost
50	×	$4.50	×	40	=	$ 9,000
100	×	5.00	×	80	=	40,000
65	×	5.50	×	120	=	42,900
				Total annual cost		$91,900

2. Average hourly cost per employee per year

$$\frac{\text{Annual cost (\$91,900)}}{\text{Hours paid per year (2080)} \times \text{number of workers (230)}} = \$0.193$$

3. Annual cost per employee

$$\frac{\$91,900}{230} = \$399.57$$

Example 1. Additional cost of providing additional week or 40 hours after 15 years.

$$
\begin{array}{l}
15 \times \$4.00 \times \text{no vacation eligibility} \\
\;50 \times \;\;4.50 \times \;\;40 = \$ \;\;9,000 \\
100 \times \;\;5.00 \times \;\;80 = \;\;40,000 \\
\;40 \times \;\;5.50 \times 120 = \;\;26,400 \\
\;25 \times \;\;5.50 \times 160 = \;\;\underline{22,000} \\
\hphantom{25 \times \;\;5.50 \times 160 = \;\;}\$97,400
\end{array}
$$

1. *New* total annual cost $97,400
    Old total annual cost   −91,900
    Additional annual cost $5,500

2. Additional hourly cost $\dfrac{\$5,500}{478,400} = \$0.012$
    (2080 hours × 230 employees)

3. Annual cost per employee

$$\frac{\$5,500}{230} = \$23.91$$

Example 2. Providing 1 week after 6 months.

$$
\begin{array}{l}
\;\;5 \times \$4.00 \times \text{no vacation eligibility} \\
\;10 \times \;\;4.375 \times \;\;40 = \$ \;\;1,750 \\
\;50 \times \;\;4.50 \;\;\times \;\;40 = \;\;\;\;9,000 \\
100 \times \;\;5.00 \;\;\times \;\;80 = \;\;40,000 \\
\;65 \times \;\;5.50 \;\;\times 120 = \;\;\underline{42,900} \\
\hphantom{65 \times \;\;5.50 \;\;\times 120 = \;\;}\$93,650
\end{array}
$$

1. *New* total annual cost $93,650
    Old total annual cost   −91,900
    Additional annual cost $ 1,750

2. Additional hourly cost

$$\frac{\$1,750}{478,400} = \$0.0037$$

Supplemental Unemployment Benefits and Severance Pay

Unlike most other benefits, supplemental unemployment benefits (SUB), or some form of unemployment pay, have not been widely negotiated. About 30 percent of all workers covered by major collective bargaining agreements are covered by a SUB provision or wage protection plan. About the same number are covered by severance pay plans. Generally, SUB funding is based on a specified time for which benefits will be paid and at a certain percentage of current pay. Length of service benefit variations and dependent allowances are also built into the costing. Severance plans, on the other hand, generally provide a flat week's pay for service benefit, which may vary by length of service, such as ten weeks' pay for five years' service.

Rest Periods

In order to calculate the cost of including two 10-minute rest periods, which may or may not be written into a contract, the basic formula includes the number of workers $\times$ average hourly rate $\times$ annual number of rest hours.

1. Total annual cost $99,670.50

$$230 \times \$5.00 \times 86.67^* = \$99,670.50$$

2. Cost in cents per hour

$$\frac{\$99,670.50}{2080 \times 230} = \$0.21$$

3. Per year cost per employee

$$\frac{\$99,670.50}{230} = \$433.35$$

Other Pay-for-Time-Not-Worked Benefits

A number of fringe benefits fall into this pay-for-time-not worked category, in addition to holidays, vacations, and rest periods: paid sick leave (aside from sickness and accident benefits provided under health insurance coverage); funeral leave; jury duty; military duty leave; paid meal periods; and wash-up, clean-up time. Sick leave benefits, for example, are provided by about one-third of all major contracts and cover the same percentage of workers.

Sick leave benefits and provisions vary greatly and may be based on length of service—for example, 1 day after 1 year, 2 days after 2 years, and so forth, to a maximum of 12 days. Other contracts might provide a flat number of days for all employees after a certain period of service. Benefits not used during the year may be either lost, accumulated,

---

*The two rest periods a day represent 100 minutes a week and 5,200 minutes per year, or 86.67 hours per year.

$$(20 \text{ minutes} \times 5 \text{ work days} \times 52 \text{ weeks}) = \frac{5,200}{60} \text{ minutes} = 86.67$$

or paid for. If, for example, the parties agree to give all employees 3 days of sick leave per year, the total annual cost would be

1. Total annual cost

$$230 \times (\$5.00 \text{ per hour} \times 24 \text{ hours}) = \$27,600$$

2. Hourly cost per employee per year

$$\frac{\$27,600}{478,400} = \$0.06 \text{ per-hour cost}$$

3. Annual cost per employee

$$\frac{\$27,600}{230} = \$120 \text{ per employee}$$

Pension

Increased benefits and improvements in pension plans are generally costed by actuarial firms. It should be noted, however, that protections and guarantees for workers covered under private pension plans are provided in the Employee Retirement Income Security Act of 1974.

Insurance

Sickness and accident, hospitalization, and life insurance plans, whether a firm is establishing new plans or improving benefits, are best left to the actuarial experts.

Spillover

One element in contract costing that may be discussed is the effect that wage and benefit changes have on nonbargaining-unit employees or other represented workers. For example, pension and/or health and welfare increases or improvements may have to be extended to other employees in separate units or not represented if the company has only one plan. Similarly, an additional holiday closing would affect the entire work force.

If historical wage differentials exist between bargaining-unit and nonbargaining-unit employees, a wage increase in one may affect the other's rates.

Roll-Up

The terms *roll-up, impact, creep,* and *add-on* are commonly used to describe the costs that must be added to the wage-and-benefit package in order to reflect accurately the ultimate labor cost for a given contract term.

Some parties talk about a 10-cent-per-hour wage increase, plus an additional holiday at 1 cent, as an 11-cent package. However, at some point in negotiations or afterward, the total cost of that change in wages and benefits must be calculated. The following are typical factors that may automatically increase when the hourly wage rate is increased:

Overtime

Weekend and holiday premium pay

Vacations

Holidays

Sick leave

Life insurance

Sickness and accident benefits (in some cases)

Pensions (in some cases)

Simply stated, roll-up is a factor (total cost of old wages divided by total cost of old fringes) used to calculate the new fringe benefits based on the new contract. A simple example is provided for illustration. In this example, the company employs 230 people who receive an average wage rate of $5.00 per hour and fringe benefits of $1.50 per hour. The total worker-hours paid to the 230 was 478,400 (230 × 2080). The wage increase to be granted is 44 cents per hour, and new fringes will equal 67 cents.

Shown below are two measurements of roll-up. Wage roll-up computes the increased costs of current benefits as a result of the wage increase. Package roll-up is a further refinement and costs out the newly negotiated fringes at the higher wage rate. Because the proposed new fringes were costed at the old rate, it is appropriate to calculate the new cost.

1. Wage-increase-only roll-up:
   (a) Determine for the prior year the total cost of fringes that vary with changes in the wage rate. For example, $1.50 multiplied by hours paid, 478,400, equals $717,600.
   (b) Determine the prior year's total direct wages. Average hourly earnings multiplied by hours paid, $5.00 × 478,400, equals $2,392,000.
   (c) Divide total fringe costs by wages to get the roll-up percentage.

$$\frac{\$717,600}{2,392,000} = 30\%$$

   (d) Multiply the proposed direct hourly wage increase by this percentage roll-up figure to get indirect labor costs increase.

$$\$210,496 \times 0.30 = \$63,149$$

This represents the increase in the cost of fringe benefits attributable to the increase in the wage rate or the wage roll-up.

2. Package roll-up: Steps **(a)(b)(c)**
   (d) Divide the total cost of proposed fringe improvements* by the total direct wages for the prior year to determine the percent fringe roll-up.

$$\$0.67 \times 478,400 = \$320,528$$

$$\frac{\$320,528}{2,392,000} = 13.4\%$$

   (e) Multiply the cost of the wage increase, $210,496, by 13.4% = $28,206. This represents the increase in cost of proposed benefits attributable to the increase in the base wage rate or the package roll-up.
   Note: In making quick comparisons, the roll-up percentages may be applied to the cents-per-hour wage or fringe costs, as contrasted with the calculations in dollar costs.

First-Year Cost of Package

A number of hypothetical benefit changes have been presented, and—in order to determine the package costs—all negotiated items should be listed. The costs shown represent only one year of increased costs, and if the contract is for a two- or three-year duration,

---

*Since COLA is a flat cents-per-hour amount, it does not vary with fluctuations in wages. It is not subject to roll-up.

TABLE A.8

Benefits Negotiated	Total Annual Cost Increase	Hourly per Employee Cost Increase	Annual Cost Increase per Employee
1. One additional holiday	9,200	0.02	40
2. Double pay for Saturday or sixth day of week	97,000	0.20	422
3. Shift differential	81,120	0.17	353
4. Inclusion of two 10-minute rest periods	99,670	0.21	433
5. Three days of sick leave per worker	27,600	0.06	120
6. Additional vacation week after 15 years	5,500	0.01	24
Subtotal of proposed fringe improvements	$320,090	$0.67	$1392
7. Wage increase (taken from method 1)	$210,496	$0.44	$ 915
8. Roll-up	$ 63,149	$0.13	$ 275
(a) Cost of existing benefits as a result of wage gain			
(b) Increase in proposed benefits as a result of new wage rate	28,206	0.06	130
9. Cost of living estimates	60,877	0.13	265
10. Pension and insurance cost charges		unknown	
11. **Grand Total**	$682,818	$1.43	$2977

this should be calculated. Similarly, not all benefits may become effective the same year, and this would be taken into consideration in costing the package.

Table A.9 gives the cost of 0.005¢ to 50¢ hourly increases over periods ranging from one day to three years and is particularly useful in demonstrating long-term costs of hourly increases to the parties.

TABLE A.9   Cost Chart in Dollars

Lump Sum Amounts for Periods Indicated

Cents Per Hour	3 Years 6240 Hours	2½ Years 5200 Hours	2 Years 4160 Hours	1½ Years 3120 Hours	1 Year 2080 Hours	½ Year 1040 Hours	1 Month 173.33 Hours	1 Week 40 Hours	1 Day 8 Hours
0.005	$ 31.20	$ 26.00	$ 20.80	$ 15.60	$ 10.40	$ 5.20	$ 0.87	$ 0.20	$0.04
0.01	62.40	52.00	41.60	31.20	20.80	10.40	1.73	0.40	0.08
0.02	124.80	104.00	83.20	62.40	41.60	20.80	3.47	0.80	0.16
0.03	187.20	156.00	124.80	93.60	62.40	31.20	5.20	1.20	0.24
0.04	249.60	203.00	166.30	124.80	83.20	41.60	6.93	1.60	0.32
0.05	312.00	260.00	208.00	156.00	104.00	52.00	8.67	2.00	0.40
0.06	374.40	312.00	249.60	187.20	124.80	62.40	10.40	2.40	0.48
0.07	436.80	364.00	291.20	218.40	145.60	72.80	12.13	2.80	0.56
0.08	499.20	416.00	332.80	249.60	166.40	83.20	13.87	3.20	0.64
0.09	561.60	468.00	374.40	280.80	187.20	93.60	15.60	3.60	0.72
0.10	624.00	520.00	416.00	312.00	208.80	104.00	17.33	4.00	0.80
0.11	685.40	572.00	457.60	343.20	228.80	114.40	19.07	4.40	0.88
0.12	748.80	624.00	499.20	374.40	249.60	124.80	20.80	4.80	0.96

TABLE A.9 *(cont.)*

Lump Sum Amounts for Periods Indicated

Cents Per Hour	3 Years 6240 Hours	2½ Years 5200 Hours	2 Years 4160 Hours	1½ Years 3120 Hours	1 Year 2080 Hours	½ Year 1040 Hours	1 Month 173.33 Hours	1 Week 40 Hours	1 Day 8 Hours
0.13	811.20	676.00	540.80	405.60	270.40	135.20	22.53	5.20	1.04
0.14	873.60	728.00	582.40	436.80	291.20	145.60	24.27	5.60	1.12
0.15	936.00	780.00	624.00	468.00	312.00	156.00	26.00	6.00	1.20
0.16	998.40	832.00	665.60	499.20	332.80	166.40	27.73	6.40	1.28
0.17	1060.80	834.00	707.20	530.40	353.60	176.80	29.47	6.80	1.36
0.18	1123.20	936.00	748.80	561.60	374.40	187.20	31.20	7.20	1.44
0.19	1185.60	988.00	790.40	592.80	395.20	197.60	32.93	7.60	1.52
0.20	1248.00	1040.00	832.00	624.00	416.00	208.00	34.67	8.00	1.60
0.21	1310.40	1092.00	873.60	655.20	436.80	218.40	36.40	8.40	1.68
0.22	1372.80	1144.00	915.20	686.40	457.60	228.80	38.13	8.80	1.76
0.23	1435.20	1196.00	956.80	717.60	478.40	239.20	39.87	9.20	1.84
0.24	1497.60	1248.00	998.40	748.80	499.20	249.60	41.60	9.60	1.92
0.25	1560.00	1300.00	1040.00	780.00	520.00	260.00	43.33	10.00	2.00
0.26	1622.40	1352.00	1061.60	811.20	540.80	270.40	45.07	10.40	2.08
0.27	1684.80	1404.00	1123.20	842.40	561.60	280.80	46.80	10.80	2.16
0.28	1747.20	1456.00	1164.80	873.60	582.40	291.20	48.53	11.20	2.24
0.29	1809.60	1508.00	1206.40	904.80	603.20	301.60	50.27	11.60	2.32
0.30	1872.00	1560.00	1248.00	936.00	624.00	312.00	52.00	12.00	2.40
0.31	1934.40	1612.00	1289.60	967.20	644.80	322.40	53.73	12.40	2.48
0.32	1996.80	1664.00	1331.20	988.40	665.60	332.80	55.47	12.80	2.56
0.33	2059.20	1716.00	1372.80	1029.60	686.40	343.20	57.20	13.20	2.64
0.34	2121.60	1768.00	1414.40	1060.80	707.20	353.60	58.93	13.60	2.72
0.35	2184.00	1820.00	1456.00	1092.00	728.00	364.00	60.67	14.00	2.80
0.36	2246.40	1872.00	1497.60	1123.20	748.80	374.40	62.40	14.40	2.88
0.37	2308.80	1924.00	1539.20	1154.40	769.60	384.80	64.13	14.80	2.96
0.38	2371.20	1976.00	1580.80	1185.60	790.40	395.20	65.87	15.20	3.04
0.39	2433.60	2028.00	1622.40	1216.80	811.20	405.60	67.60	15.60	3.12
0.40	2496.00	2080.00	1664.00	1248.00	832.00	416.00	69.33	16.00	3.20
0.41	2558.40	2132.00	1705.60	1279.20	852.80	426.40	71.07	16.40	3.28
0.42	2620.80	2184.00	1747.20	1310.40	873.60	436.80	72.80	16.80	3.36
0.43	2683.20	2236.00	1788.80	1341.60	894.40	447.20	74.53	17.20	3.44
0.44	2745.60	2288.00	1830.40	1372.80	915.20	457.60	76.27	17.60	3.52
0.45	2808.00	2340.00	1872.00	1404.00	936.00	468.00	78.00	18.00	3.60
0.46	2870.00	2392.00	1913.60	1435.20	956.80	478.40	79.73	18.40	3.68
0.47	2932.80	2444.00	1955.20	1466.40	977.60	488.80	81.47	18.80	3.76
0.48	2995.20	2496.00	1996.80	1497.60	998.40	499.20	83.20	19.20	3.84
0.49	3057.60	2548.00	2038.40	1528.80	1019.20	509.60	84.93	19.60	3.92
0.50	3120.00	2600.00	2080.00	1560.00	1040.00	520.00	86.67	20.00	4.00

CHAPTER 12

The Computer and the Collective Bargaining Process

After reading this chapter, you should be able to

■ Describe the advantages a computer may bring to the bargaining process.

■ Comprehend some of the drawbacks of using computers.

■ Explain the use of the Electronic Meeting System.

■ Describe, on the basis of the research of Broderick and Boudreau, the three types of computer applications that can be of assistance in bargaining.

■ Evaluate the benefits of using a computer to draft the agreement.

THE IMPACT OF COMPUTERS ON COLLECTIVE BARGAINING

In one of the early works on the impact of computers on collective bargaining, published in 1969, Dunlop expressed the view that "the computer has a comparative advantage and its advantages are greatest when you can get joint agreement in its use.... It is most likely to be useful in questions where large masses of data are relevant."[1] These observations are as applicable today as they were well before computer technology reached anything approaching its current level of sophistication.

The author's recent discussions with labor relations practitioners indicate that both union and management negotiators have recognized the value and significance of computer technology. They are relying on it with increasing frequency when negotiating and costing labor agreements.

In the course of bargaining, the parties to negotiation often revise their wage and benefit offers. Negotiators require estimates of the cost of each new proposal and its potential effect on the total cost of an agreement. The computer can be very helpful in supplying expeditious computations of each new financial package. This resource in turn accelerates negotiation and provides an opportunity for the parties to be more creative in discovering mutually acceptable contract terms.

A good software program can help negotiators evaluate different combinations of wage and benefit proposals. The availability of such information may be particularly significant in the last stages of bargaining, when the parties—in order to reach a settlement—engage in intense trading of different items of the package. At these times, instantaneous access to cost estimates for alternatives can make the difference between an agreement and a strike. Some employers and unions have developed software programs tailored to their own needs.

Computers enable the parties to follow trends within their industry and among industries. Some unions, like the United Food and Commercial Workers Union and the Service Employees International Union, have been storing all of their local contracts on computer. This type of storage gives them access to the necessary data to follow settlement trends in the industries with which they negotiate.[2]

Merlin P. Breaux of the Gulf Oil Corporation in Houston summarized the importance of computers to negotiation:

> Access to computer data banks has significantly shortened our research time prior to negotiations. And the application of software spread sheets has made contract cost analysis a much easier and more accurate process. In the future of collective bargaining, more development of computer skills is a necessity.[3]

During the last 10 years, many employers have developed or purchased software to implement a computerized human resource information system (HRIS). Such a system usually can "acquire, store, manipulate, analyze, retrieve, and distribute pertinent information regarding human resources."[4] An HRIS system includes the following elements: "A computerized data-based management system. Screens for inputting data. Programs for cross-checking data and transaction accuracy. Modules for performing specific functions . . . such as . . . compensation costs. Query programs for requesting special information combinations or what if analyses."[5] Although HRIS is a management system, some employers are willing to share selective information with their unions. In response to the emergence of HRIS, some unions have developed their own computerized programs to assist them in the negotiation process. Undoubtedly, a well-structured HRIS model can provide both sides with a significant amount of information for costing and analysis of various proposals at the bargaining table.

Computers offer the parties the necessary technology for preparing a complete and accurate database containing information from both internal and external sources. Such a database is significant for two reasons: "First, it is needed to accurately cost proposals and counterproposals. Second . . . a data base provides the raw material for developing arguments for one's own bargaining position and discounting 'facts' presented by others."[6]

Negotiators require demographic, accounting, and financial data; these three categories of internal data were reviewed in Chapter 11, on contract costing. A good source for such data is the Human Resource Information System, just described. Although the types of information needed by individual employers may vary, all employers and unions require certain statistics: industry and area wage data, cost-of-living statistics, and comparative information on industry contract terms. The various sources for such information were noted in Chapter 8, on preparation for bargaining. A well-prepared database helps the parties anticipate each other's proposals, speeds up the costing process, and in general improves the climate and efficiency of the negotiations.

The ubiquity of computers and the constantly expanding universe of software programs have led to increased utilization and acceptance of computer technology in labor-management negotiations. With the ever-increasing complexity of costing—particularly of some parts of the labor contract, such as health care coverage—and the need for more hard data for decision making, the computer has become an indispensable tool at the bargaining table.

Computer technology and a variety of on-line computer services have improved significantly the quality of information available to both unions and employers. A convenient avenue of access to large amounts of relevant information is LEXIS/NEXIS, an on-line database that contains the full texts of hundreds of specialized business periodicals, business-related wire service stories, specialized newsletters, current legislative initiatives, brokerage house reports on firms, and much more.

CAVEATS FOR COMPUTER USERS

Goldman discusses some of the following "Computer Traps for the Unwary":[7] The first one is GIGO—garbage in, garbage out. The relevance and significance of the output depend on the quality of the input from the user. Second, there are some tasks that can be performed better and faster manually than through a computer. Third, mistakes in calculation, in assumptions, and in data entry may be magnified and at times more difficult to detect when computers are used. Fourth, the software or the hardware may have some internal design problems that may generate wrong results. Fifth, there is always the risk that stored data will be lost, destroyed, or infected by a virus. Finally, the probability that information may end up with the opposition or the press is greater when computers are used.[8] Some computer users tend to produce too many copies of confidential printouts, creating opportunities for sensitive information to fall into the wrong hands.[9] Furthermore, at times, unauthorized users gain access to confidential computer files. In response, the parties can and do employ a variety of safeguards to maintain security and to prevent the other side from accessing restricted data.

Computers have some other disadvantages as well. They may reduce the necessity of "mental gymnastics which can often help the negotiator to see a solution or tradeoff that might not occur to him or her if the calculations are done by computer."[10] Although computers provide the perfect technology for costing and for obtaining information quickly, Nyerges finds that they have two major drawbacks: "Unlike people, computers do not have fears, nor do they entertain hopes. Computers merely reflect experience gained from situations and judgements. . . . One word of warning: Quick assessment does not always mean a quick answer. . . . [A]ssessment . . . must be subordinated to tactical considerations."[11]

THE ELECTRONIC MEETING SYSTEM

Computers not only can be effective in the costing of labor contracts, as we indicated in the first section, but they can also enhance the efficiency of the negotiation process if installed in the area where negotiations are to be conducted. Herniter et al. refer to such an arrangement as an "electronic meeting room" (EMR);[12] others call it an electronic meeting system (EMS). The EMS is "a computer supported group work environment that provides computer hardware and software, audio and video technology, and a host of new group work methods and procedures. . . . EMS are now being augmented with negotiation-specific modules to provide Negotiation Support Systems."[13] The EMR offers the parties a number of advantages, such as

> reducing language ambiguities, reducing misunderstanding and mistrust, reducing note-taking and typing chores, providing convenience, introducing one central point of reference

for all participants, tracking progress and status, increasing accuracy, enforcing momentum, saving time between sessions, and saving time after the conclusion of contract talks.[14]

The Department of Management Information at the University of Arizona reviewed the significance of the EMS for purposes of labor negotiations. They tested the value of an electronic meeting room in negotiations between two employers and two locals of two large national labor unions. The first negotiation was conducted between Sun Trans, a Tucson bus company, and the Teamsters union; the second negotiation involved El Rio, a nonprofit health facility in Tucson, and the American Federation of State, County and Municipal Employees. Both contracts were concluded without work stoppage; the agreements were ratified by union membership. In their negotiations, the parties utilized a Group Systems (GS) software that concentrated "on text and agenda to rationalize and structure the interaction of meeting participants through various group-dynamics techniques." Through the GS software, the parties developed the following bargaining tools: "A contract log, an electronic bargaining book (EBB), an article checklist, and a proposal editor."[15]

"A contract log is a computerized audit trail . . . an accounting term."[16] The log encompasses all sections and articles of a labor agreement. All new proposals are entered into the system by a facilitator and classified according to the applicable articles and sections. The date and time of each entry is recorded. The electronic bargaining book (EBB) is similar to the bargaining book discussed in Chapter 8, except that the information is entered into the computer. The source for the EBB entries is the contract log. The article checklist maintains a record of articles by categories, providing the parties with a continuous status report on each article.

The fourth device for electronic bargaining is the "proposal editor," a word processing system. Each team has access to a computer containing such an editor. These computers are installed in the caucus rooms of the respective teams. All the proposals developed by the teams are shown on a public screen accessible to both sides. In the Sun Trans case, the article checklist and the EBB were helpful to negotiators; the parties used both tools extensively. Negotiators were able to follow the progress of negotiations on a publicly accessible screen.[17]

The electronic meeting room saved time not only between bargaining sessions, but also after the contract was agreed upon. In many negotiations, even after an agreement is attained, the parties may differ on the language describing the contract terms. In the Sun Trans case, there were just two minor disagreements over language at the conclusion of negotiations. The parties were able to send the contract to the printers within a few weeks after arriving at the agreement. Frequently, the process of clarifying language may take months. The electronic meeting room permits the parties to resolve most language issues during negotiations.

Initially, the union representatives who participated in the University of Arizona negotiation project were apprehensive about using the EMS approach. Their concerns were primarily due to their relative inexperience with computers, as compared with management negotiators. They were fearful that they might be taken advantage of because of their weak computer backgrounds. The union team was also worried that confidentiality might be breached and text altered when information was entered into the computer. The facilitators who participated in the process were able to allay the union negotiators' fears by providing them with a brief computer tutorial. According to information obtained in a postnegotiation debriefing and analysis session, "Union members' computer anxiety does not affect the outcome of electronic bargaining."[18]

In both the Sun Trans case and the El Rio case, the researchers attempted to obtain answers to a number of significant questions: (1) Does the computer technology have a positive effect on the outcome? (2) Can it contribute to a better long-term contract?

(3) Can the technology decrease costs and the effort and time required for negotiations? and (4) Can this approach increase satisfaction?

In the Sun Trans case, the electronic dimension did not contribute to a qualitative difference in the outcome. The participants noted, however, that they saved time. They also expressed the view that the setting had a positive effect on the tone of the negotiations.

In the El Rio case, "the computer and the setting,"[19] as well as the assistance of the facilitators and the application of integrative bargaining, "all helped change the outcome of the agreement."[20] The facilitators had a very important function in both sets of negotiations. Without their expertise and assistance, the outcomes would most likely have been different.

Using Computer Technology for Brainstorming or for Generating Options During Negotiation

According to various researchers, the efficiency of the negotiation process can be improved when the following principles are applied to bargaining: "(1) Improve communication among participants; (2) generate many alternatives before judging; (3) separate the personalities from the problem; and (4) use objective data and criteria."[21] Nunamaker et al. suggest that EMS, together "with negotiation specific models to provide Negotiation Support Systems (NSS),"[22] can help the parties apply these four principles to negotiation. Together, EMS and NSS can assist negotiators in generating options.

Application of the four principles was tested in a study conducted at the University of Arizona. The researchers provided each participant with a networked microcomputer workstation. In the initial stages of the study, all communication for generating options was conducted electronically; computer workstations alone were utilized, and no verbal communication occurred. In later stages of the process, the parties used both verbal and electronic communication. When the negotiating parties began generating options, the EMS provided support in at least four areas: "(1) parallel communication; (2) group memory; (3) anonymity; and (4) a structured pattern of discussion."[23]

Parallel communication can assist the parties in easing "production blocking,"[24] one of the most significant constraints on the development of options in the traditional approach, where individuals take turns expressing their views. This approach can restrain creativity in three ways: (1) Negotiators may either forget or suppress ideas if they cannot express them immediately; (2) when negotiators delay expressing their suggestions, they concentrate on remembering the ideas not expressed rather than developing new ones; and (3) when negotiators focus on listening to others, they are diverted from proposing their own opinions. These drawbacks can be diminished through parallel communication.[25]

EMS offers a group memory that makes it possible to record all electronic comments. This gives negotiators the opportunity to stop, reflect, and comment electronically on other people's ideas. Furthermore, this approach is conducive to gains from "synergy"[26] or from the combined effort of negotiators working together.

The anonymity that EMS provides helps separate the people from the problems, thus stimulating the presentation of new ideas. The potential for critical evaluation by others and pressure to conform are removed. Also, face saving is not an issue when ideas are presented through EMS.

EMS can provide a structured pattern for discussion. In the Arizona EMS study, each negotiator was able to take part in a number of parallel but distinct conversations. The negotiators were "randomly switched between separate conversations. This reduces cognitive inertia (the tendency . . . to focus on one option)."[27]

Although EMS has many advantages, it also has some drawbacks: Speaking is usually faster than electronic typing, although listening is slower than reading.[28] One area in which EMS is not helpful is in resolving conflicting points of view; for this process, the computer is a poor substitute for people. Furthermore, some negotiators are very uncomfortable around computers; some do not even type. For such individuals, computer technology is more a liability than an asset.

The impact of EMS was evaluated in a number of field studies concerning effectiveness, efficiency, and user satisfaction. These evaluations were conducted at a few IBM locations as well as at the University of Arizona.[29] The participants in the field studies were "practicing managers and professionals from both large and small public and private sector organizations."[30] According to the research findings, the experience of the participants was very positive. It suggested that Electronic Brainstorming Software (EBS)[31] was more productive and "more satisfying than other option generation approaches used by these groups."[32] The most frequently cited advantages of EBS were its anonymity and the freedom of expression that it offered to participants.[33]

Another important conclusion from these studies relates to the impact of group size on effectiveness. Non-EMS studies of group option generation indicate that the larger the group, the lower are "effectiveness, efficiency and satisfaction."[34] In contrast to these findings, with EMS "larger groups outperformed the small groups."[35] Synergy is one reason given for these results. "Larger groups are more likely to experience synergy, as they have more members with more options"[36] (see Figure 12.1). "Although . . . much more research remains to be done . . . EMS technology can enhance the initial phase of negotiation to improve the generation of options for mutual gains."[37]

The Electronic Brainstorming Software developed by Nunamaker et al. was also tested at Queen's University in Canada. One of the major findings was that "using computers increased the production of ideas."[38] The researchers concluded, however, that individuals who generated ideas electronically on their own, and then combined their ideas with those of others who were also working on their own, were not less productive than the people who utilized the electronic interactive technique.[39]

In the final analysis, "the human component of the electronic meeting room pack-

FIGURE 12.1 Group Size and Group Performance

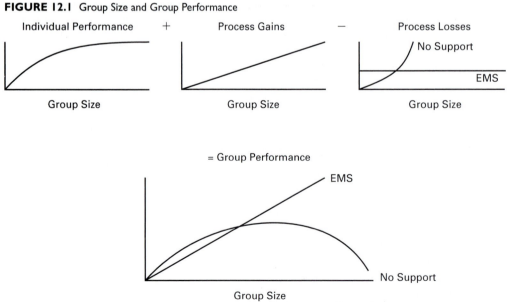

Source: J. F. Nunamaker Jr., Alan R. Dennis, Joseph S. Valacich, and Douglas R. Vogel, "Information Technology for Negotiating Groups: Generating Options for Mutual Gains," *Management Science* 37, no. 10 (October 1991), p. 1340.

age plays a critical role. The computer can't produce a significant change in meeting dynamics by itself. It isn't a panacea—it must be used as part of a package that includes people and their negotiating methods."[40]

COMPUTERS FOR TRANSACTION PROCESSING, EXPERT SYSTEMS, AND DECISION SUPPORT SYSTEMS

Another way to look at the potential value of computers in negotiations is to utilize the model proposed by Broderick and Boudreau in their article, "Human Resource Management, Information Technology, and the Competitive Edge."[41] These authors propose three types of computer applications: "Transaction Processing/Reporting/Tracking Systems . . . Expert Systems and Decision Support Systems"[42] (see Figure 12.2). Each of these three types of applications is further subdivided, as shown in Figure 12.2. Each of the three broad categories is associated with different demands on the user's analytic and computer expertise. The highest level of sophistication is expected of those who would use computer assistance for decision making. Figure 12.2 illustrates a model that offers a number of guidelines for ways negotiators could match computer applications with their needs and objectives.

The first category, transaction processing, reporting, and tracking, could be applied for routine, high-volume information needs such as computation of overtime pay, pension benefits, payroll levels, and the like.[43] The second category, expert systems, can "improve decisions for which the 'right' outcomes are determined through expert knowledge and experience. . . . Expert system applications are based on rules, but the rules are complex, derived from careful analysis of expert decisions."[44] For example, do labor market factors justify a particular wage scale? All negotiators, and new ones in particular, could benefit from utilizing expert systems. There are a number of expert system applications of which the

FIGURE 12.2 Types of Computer Applications

Transaction Processing/Reporting/Tracking Systems

BEST AT:	High Volume Sorts, Lists, Merges
	Editing
	Simple Calculations
	Displaying Information
	Auditing & Spotting Discrepancies

Expert Systems

BEST AT:	Codifying Knowledge & Experience
	Distributing Expertise
	Recommending Action
	Education

Decision Support Systems

BEST AT:	Supporting Research
	Optimizing Decision Alternatives
	Speeding Up Discovery

Source: Renae Broderick and John W. Boudreau, "Human Resource Management, Information Technology, and the Competitive Edge," *Academy of Management Executive* 6, no. 2 (May 1992), pp. 7–17.

most common are "black box" and training. In the black-box approach, a recommended decision on a particular issue is provided, but participants are not informed as to how the "experts" arrived at the decision. As an illustration, the negotiator might input two different vacation plans to the computer and be told that plan A is better than plan B but receive no explanation as to how that decision was made. In the training application approach to expert systems, users are guided "through a series of questions and information displays designed to educate them on the reasoning experts use in reaching a decision."[45]

The third category in Figure 12.2 is the decision support system (DSS), whose purpose is to "improve decisions for which the rules are changing or are not well defined, and the 'right' outcomes are unknown." Decision support systems "package computer tools that allow a user to pull together information, analyze it, and represent it in many forms (graphs, reports, etc.), and also assist the user with electronic memory aids and references."[46] Decision support systems could be of great assistance to negotiators, but they are expensive to develop. It may take some time before the DSS becomes part of the labor negotiator's toolbox. One example of the application of the computerized DSS is group brainstorming, discussed earlier. Such a system allows individuals at different locations to be connected by computer with one another. Brainstorming software enables people to share, exchange, and evaluate ideas of all the members of a particular group.[47]

COMPUTER SOFTWARE FOR DRAFTING AGREEMENTS

Electronic tools can also help negotiating parties expedite the drafting of contracts. This facility in turn can give them more time to focus on other aspects of the negotiation process.

Although the computer is useful for typing documents, because of its word processing capacity its real untapped potential is the application of expert systems to the drafting of labor contracts. Contract drafting systems are available for various commercial transactions. One such system is used at Nynex[48] for drafting of custom purchase agreements. Nynex is saving time and legal costs by creating is own customized contracts. "The preprogrammed 'expertise' of these systems"[49] permits the user to connect to "a highly developed decision tree that can include hundreds of variations on the document being created."[50]

A number of companies have developed software authoring tools to automate the drafting of various forms, legal documents, and contracts. Such software can assist users in drafting employment and termination agreements.[51]

Currently, many labor contracts are "ill drafted."[52] The expert system and the computer could help negotiating parties write contracts that are clear, precise, direct, and simple. Such contracts could reduce the number of grievances and arbitration cases and thus minimize future disputes over contract meaning and interpretation.

Labor contracts in the public and private sectors and in various firms and industries contain standard clauses as well as some unique contract terms. Most likely, in the near future the marketplace will provide employers and unions with more software and expert systems that will help them refine the contract-drafting process.

RESTRUCTURING OF PROBLEMS DURING NEGOTIATIONS

To reach agreement during the negotiation process, negotiators must be willing to be flexible and to make concessions. According to Sycara, concession making is "a sequential decision process where the next decision of a party depends on the current state, the magnitude of concessions already made, and anticipated responses of the other party(ies)."[53]

Impasses are reached in negotiations. One approach for resolving stalemates is problem restructuring. Sycara suggests a computer program named Persuader, which can assist in problem restructuring. "The Persuader simulates hypothetical labor-management negotiations."[54] The program utilizes the concepts and techniques of artificial intelligence. "The Persuader engages in the following type of problem restructuring: (1) introduction of new goals, (2) goal substitution, (3) goal abandonment, and (4) changing the reservation prices of the negotiating parties."[55] Sycara claims that a major problem during bargaining, particularly distributive bargaining, is problem restructuring. In her view, the restructuring process can be automated through artificial intelligence technology. Sycara recognizes the creative dimension of restructuring, which relies on the "experience and insights of the negotiators."[56] The Persuader takes all this into account and "acts as an automated labor mediator in hypothetical negotiations."[57]

SOFTWARE PROGRAMS FOR COLLECTIVE BARGAINING

Software programs can provide support to negotiators in a variety of areas, including preparation for negotiation, development of an action plan, record keeping associated with grievances and arbitration, costing, administrative chores, and information retrieval. These "so-called expert-in-a-box . . . software programs . . . tap the unique expertise of the individual or group"[58] and synthesize it into hundreds of rules that can be accessed from the computer.

The computer software currently available could be of assistance to parties in negotiation.[59] Although most of the programs were developed for employers, with relatively minor modifications some of this software could also be useful for labor unions. A number of software programs are described briefly in Appendix A to this chapter.

SUMMARY

Computers will most likely assume a much larger role in collective bargaining and will be utilized by more employers and unions in the future. Computers offer negotiating parties many advantages: word processing, costing through spreadsheets, option-generation capacity through the electronic meeting room, quick access to information for decision making, and expert systems. Computers save time and are very fast. However, with all its advantages, the computer does have limitations. Determination of the actual content of contract terms and interpersonal dynamics cannot be taken over by computers.

The following statement by Cascio summarizes well the future collective bargaining role of computers:

> To the extent that computer models could track accurately union and management preference curves for particular settlements, then ultimately collective bargaining would cease to exist as we know it. The issues would become mere pawns in a computerized chess game, and the political aspects of the process would be scuttled. Since that prospect seems rather remote at this time, the most likely role of computers in collective bargaining for the foreseeable future will probably be to help the parties make decisions regarding content issues.[60]

To conclude, no expert system or any other software program can substitute for the experience, decision-making abilities, and people skills of individual labor-management negotiators. "No computer can codify human behavior,"[61] which is "an art, not the sum of the analytical we have learned to embed in software."[62]

According to D. O. Cantrell of Gulf Oil Corp.,

> Technology may enhance the collective bargaining process, but a computer will never replace the cigar-chewing, table-thumping, red-eyed, human being–type negotiator. Why? Collective bargaining is a dynamic process, subject to the strong influence of personalities and politics. It is not a science; it is an art—specifically, the art of persuasion, practiced with high stakes—the lives and well-being of fellow employees. Collective bargaining is entered into to solve human problems. Its dimension can never be fully contained and analyzed in a computer. A computer can never make the judgment call at 3:30 a.m. that is the difference between a strike and a settlement. Only a seasoned negotiator has that sixth sense, gut-feel for the timing to make the final offer that both sides can live with. . . . A computer may help us negotiate smarter and even faster, but it is only a small part of the synergy of the collective bargaining process. We will always need the expertise of the human negotiators to make it happen.[63]

For information on electronic resources such as Web sites, listservers, and CD/ROMs, consult the bibliography at the end of this book.

Notes

1. "The Computer in Dispute Settlement: A Panel and General Discussion." Panel members: George W. Taylor, David L. Cole, and John T. Dunlop. *Source: The Impact of Computers on Collective Bargaining,* A. J. Siegel, ed. (Cambridge, MA: MIT Press, 1969).

2. Wayne F. Cascio, *Costing Human Resources: The Financial Impact of Behavior in Organizations* (Boston: PWS-Kent, 1991), p. 167. Also *"Labor Letter,"* Wall Street Journal, November 20, 1984, p. 1.

3. Michael R. Carrell and Christina Heavrin, *Labor Relations and Collective Bargaining,* 4th ed. (Englewood Cliffs, NJ: Prentice Hall, 1995), p. 340.

4. Michael J. Kavanagh, Hal G. Gueutal, and Scott I. Tannenbaum, *Human Resource Information Systems: Development and Application* (Boston: PWS-Kent, 1990), p. 29.

5. Cynthia D. Fisher, Lyle F. Schoenfeldt, and James B. Shaw, *Human Resource Management,* 2nd ed. (Boston: Houghton Mifflin, 1993), p. 350.

6. Steven L. Thomas and Barry L. Wisdom, "Labor Negotiations in the Nineties: Five Steps toward Total Preparation," *SAM Advanced Management Journal* 58, no. 4 (Autumn 1993), pp. 4, 32–37.

7. Alvin L. Goldman, *Settling for More* (Washington, DC: Bureau of National Affairs, 1991), pp. 215–17. All rights reserved.

8. Ibid.

9. Charles S. Loughran, *Negotiating a Labor Contract,* 2nd ed. (Washington, DC: Bureau of National Affairs, 1992), p. 293.

10. Ibid.

11. Janus Nyerges, "Ten Commandments for a Negotiator" in *Negotiation Theory and Practice,* J. William Breslin and Jeffrey Z. Rubin, eds. (Cambridge, MA: Program on Negotiation, Harvard Law School, 1991), p. 189.

12. Bruce C. Herniter, Erran Carmel, and Jay F. Nunamaker Jr., "Computers Improve Efficiency of the Negotiation Process," *Personnel Journal* 72, no. 4 (April 1993), p. 93.

13. J. F. Nunamaker Jr., Alan R. Dennis, Joseph S. Valacich, and Douglas R. Vogel, "Information Technology for Negotiating Groups: Generating Options for Mutual Gains," *Management Science* 37, no. 10 (October 1991), pp. 1325–26.

14. Herniter et al., op. cit., p. 93.

15. Ibid., p. 93.

16. Ibid.

17. Ibid., p. 97.

18. Ibid., p. 98.

19. Ibid.

20. Ibid.

21. Ibid. See also R. Anson and M. T. Jelassi, "A Development Framework for Computer-Supported Conflict Resolution," *European Journal of Operational Research* 46, no. 2 (May 25, 1990), pp. 181–99. R. Fisher and W. Ury, *Getting to Yes: Negotiating Agreement without Giving In* (Boston: Houghton Mifflin, 1981). A. Foroughi and M. T. Jelassi, "NSS Solutions to Major Negotiation Stumbling Blocks," *Proceedings of the 23rd Annual Hawaii International Conference on System Sciences,* vol. 4, 1990, pp. 2–11. M. Jarke, M. T. Jelassi, and M. F. Shakun, "MEDIATOR: Towards a Negotiation Support System," *European Journal of Operational Research* 31, no. 3 (September 1987), pp. 314–34. M. T. Jelassi and A. Foroughi, "Negotiation Support Systems: An Overview of Design Issues and Existing Software," *Decision Support Systems* 5.2 (1989), pp. 167–81. R. J. Lewicki and J. A. Litterer, *Negotiations* (Homewood, IL: R. D. Irwin, 1985). R. J. Lewicki, J. W. Minton, and D. M. Saunders, *Negotiation,* 2nd ed. (Burr Ridge, IL: Irwin, 1994). M. F. Shakun, *Evolutionary Systems Design: Policy Making under Complexity and Group Decision Support Systems* (San Francisco: Holden Day, 1988).

22. Nunamaker et al., op. cit., p. 1326.

23. Ibid.

24. Ibid.

25. Ibid.

26. Ibid.

27. Ibid.

28. Ibid.

29. Ibid., p. 1334.

30. Ibid., p. 1329.

31. Ibid.

32. Ibid., p. 1334.

33. Ibid., p. 1338.

34. Ibid., p. 1340.

35. Ibid.

36. Ibid.

37. Ibid., p. 1344.

38. R. Brent Gallupe, Lana M. Bastianutti, and William H. Cooper, "Unblocking Brainstorms," *Journal of Applied Psychology* 76, no. 1 (February 1991), p. 140.

39. Ibid.

40. Herniter et al., op. cit., p. 99.

41. Renae Broderick and John W. Boudreau, "Human Resource Management, Information Technology, and the Competitive Edge," *Academy of Management Executive* 6, no. 2 (May 1992), pp. 7–17.

42. Ibid.

43. Ibid.

44. Ibid.

45. Ibid.

46. Ibid.

47. Ibid. See also Gallupe et al., op. cit., pp. 137–42.

48. Mike France, "Smart Contracts," *Forbes,* August, 19, 1994, pp. 117–18.

49. Ibid.

50. Ibid.

51. Ibid.

52. James R. Redeker, "Contract Drafting to Avoid Disputes" in *Collective Bargaining Negotiations and Contracts* (Washington, DC: Bureau of National Affairs, 1992), no. 1234, 14:51–1454, pp. 61–64.

53. Katia P. Sycara, "Problem Restructuring in Negotiation," *Management Science* 37, no. 10 (October 1991), p. 1248.

54. Ibid., pp. 1248–49.

55. Ibid., p. 1249.

56. Ibid., p. 1267.

57. Ibid.

58. Nancy K. Austin, "MBA-in-a-Box," *Working Woman* 18, no. 11 (November 1993), p. 30.

59. See the 1994 *Personnel Software Census,* a directory of software for human resource management. Advanced Personnel Systems, P.O. Box 1438, Roseville, CA 95678, 916-781-2900.

60. Cascio, op. cit., p. 118.

61. Austin, op. cit., p. 30.

62. Ibid.

63. Deborah O. Cantrell, "Computers Come to the Bargaining Table," *Personnel Journal* (September 1984), pp. 27–30.

APPENDIX A

Software Programs for Negotiations and Labor Relations

The Labor Relations System Program[1]

The Labor Relations System Program (LRSP) was developed to provide the labor relations professional with a comprehensive software tool to track, review, and analyze data on grievances, arbitrations, and disciplinary cases.

In preparation for and during collective bargaining, labor relations professionals require data on grievance histories and patterns, arbitration, and disciplinary cases. Without automation, the compiling of this data would be both time-consuming and tedious. The LRSP instantaneously provides users with data for formulation of strategy during the collective bargaining process.

The LRSP opens to a main menu containing three options that each take the user to submenus for the Grievances, Arbitration, and Disciplinary modules. Each of these submenus allows the negotiator to enter and edit the pertinent data, run various comprehensive reports, and back each database up onto a floppy disk. The program is designed for ease in moving from one module to another. The LRSP is a DOS-based product that requires an IBM-compatible computer and at least 640K of RAM.

The Negotiator[2]

The Negotiator provides one-time input of employee profile information and company data and unlimited analysis of alternatives (each available within seconds). This program operates on MS-DOS and is user-friendly, menu driven, self-contained on a single diskette, and supplied with an extensive user's manual and tutorial.

In addition to providing instant analyses of labor costs on a cost-per-productive-hour basis for labor negotiation, the software can also be used to forecast salary and benefit costs on the basis of varying assumptions, identify approaches for improving productivity, model different skill mixes to optimize labor costs, and conduct competitive analyses of labor costs and productivity. The software incorporates all standard variables with the ability to add more. It is available in both U.S. and Canadian editions to allow for differences in pensions, workers' compensation, and the like.

Three Negotiation Spreadsheets: ContractCoster, TotalComp Offer Analyzer, and UnitCost[3]

The ContractCoster spreadsheet template allows users to arrive at different combinations of percentage increases and compares these with the negotiators' parameters or authority. The negotiators can front load, back load, try to split increases, offer no increases, or propose any combination toward reaching an agreement. Within split seconds of entering their proposals, negotiators know if their potential offers exceed their authority! ContractCoster can help negotiators develop a series of multiyear proposals that are in line with their negotiating authority.

TotalComp OfferAnalyzer, another spreadsheet template, permits users to develop annual total compensation costs and to monitor any cost increases resulting from concessions during negotiations. The program, which provides a structured, simple-to-follow format for gathering the costs of salaries as well as salary-related and non-salary-related benefits, covers up to five bargaining units. The program also helps track all salary and benefit cost increases. TotalComp permits quick comparisons among proposals made in different bargaining units. Users can also monitor offers made during negotiations.

A third spreadsheet template, UnitCost, captures data negotiators require to cost out proposals efficiently and to arrive at the amounts of current costs. UnitCost lists all of the common benefits (both fixed and variable within the bargaining unit). It allows the inclusion of benefits that may be unique to a particular employer. The program's special feature is its breakdown of total costs for the average employee and the amount of money paid for time not worked (e.g., vacation, holiday, sick leave, etc.).

The Art of Negotiating[4]

The Art of Negotiating is an interactive software program that can help users prepare for negotiation. The program, developed by Gerald I. Nierenberg, guides negotiators through major areas of preparation for bargaining. In each section, the program asks an integrated series of questions and thus stimulates the negotiators' thinking about the situation and about people at the bargaining table. The program also records important data for use in negotiations.

In its treatment of *subject matter,* the program helps users establish who the other negotiators are and what the issues are. It supports negotiators by focusing on the following six topics:

1. *Objectives:* Determine what each side wants from the negotiation.
2. *Issues:* Understand the issues that normally divide the parties. Identify emotional issues and reword them in neutral ways. Plan questions to guide the negotiation.
3. *Needs:* Develop new negotiating alternatives based on the needs of each side. Evaluate the strengths, weaknesses, and risks of options before offering them at the table.
4. *Climates:* Monitor and control the emotional environment of the negotiation. Transform a negative situation into a positive one.
5. *Strategies:* Consider how, where, and when to approach the opponent and the opponent's potential countering moves, to prepare in advance counterstrategies.

6. *Agenda:* Prepare an agenda.

7. *Reports:* Print out customized reports about the negotiation. Share them with teammates and other authorized parties.

This program runs on IBM PC, XT, AT PS/2, or compatible computers. It requires DOS 2.0 or higher and 256K of RAM. Diskette Format is $5^1/_4$ inches or $3^1/_2$ inches.

The Art of Negotiating is not an expert system; it does not provide answers. The user supplies answers to questions, and the program stimulates thought processes and acts as a catalyst for new ideas. The software helps negotiators develop a plan of action.

The Idea Generator Plus[5]

The Idea Generator Plus is one of the expert-in-a-box software programs based on the unique knowledge of experts and synthesized into hundreds of rules that can be retrieved from a computer. The program relies on an interactive format; it offers a structured approach to creativity. The program assists users in developing creative options for problem solving. The software helps users evaluate the concepts generated and determine which ideas to consider.[6]

Preparing for Key Negotiations[7]

Preparing for Key Negotiations focuses on results based on the users' personal resources and experiences. This program can help negotiators to solve problems, to think, and to make decisions on critical issues. It treats the computer as a communication medium for guiding users in their tasks by utilizing their own knowledge and experience.

Negotiators' most valuable asset consists of the information and experience stored in their memories. The software enables users to access and apply their knowledge to negotiations. It prompts users to define their objectives and to consider all factors, including people and personalities, that might help or hinder them in the achievement of their goals. Users are instructed to consult their own judgment and imaginations in responding to a variety of issues.

In addition to enhancing users' understanding of specific problems on which they are working, the program also clarifies the implications of potential courses of action. The software can help users improve their performance in four areas:

1. Reorganizing facts and ideas under consideration

2. Reviving forgotten experiences, impressions, and other relevant information

3. Developing and creating new concepts and insights by linking knowledge stored in their memory banks; this in turn can assist them in generating new inferences, deductions, and associations

4. Applying their judgment in selecting the best approaches for implementable actions or conclusions

PC novices can use this software: Users do not need any previous experience with computers or operating systems. They need not spend time learning a new technology by immersing themselves in manuals and instructions. The program guides users through the entire session with prompts and questions, rather as an actual consultant would. All users need do is enter the answers in response to prompts.

The software makes it possible to develop custom programs quickly and economically and to disseminate the organization's most effective expertise among all users.

Negotiator Pro for Labor-Management Negotiations[8]

Negotiator Pro (N.P.) is a negotiation support software system that can be used with DOS and Windows as well as with Mac computers. The software can assist negotiators by offering them a checklist of key questions and issues that arise in negotiations. The more complex the negotiation, the easier it is to overlook important matters, but N.P. keeps issues from getting lost. The software covers both minor and major negotiation topics. It is a database of significant negotiation subjects as well as a mentoring tool that prompts the user to be more creative.

The software adopts the interest-based bargaining approach, which has been used by a wide range of organizations. N.P. instructs negotiators to define the interests of all the parties and assists them in identifying interests that are overlapping or conflicting. N.P. has been used by labor and management negotiators. It contains questions and minitutorials based on publications and on research carried out by many negotiation experts. The program refers to an extensive negotiation bibliography from various fields including psychology and game theory.

N.P. incorporates an expert system that considers the personality as well as the negotiation style of the user. The program classifies personality types into four categories: (1) pragmatic, (2) analytic, (3) extroverted, and (4) amiable. In addition to providing users feedback on their personality types, the program can help them determine whether they are effective or ineffective, competitive or cooperative negotiators (nomenclature based on research by Williams).[9] The objective of this expert system is to give the user some perspective on interpersonal issues and problems that inevitably emerge in negotiation. N.P. offers suggestions for overcoming some of these problems.

Notes

1. Human Resource Solutions, Inc., P.O. Box 4254, Cherry Hill, NJ 08034. Tel.: 609-751-4651. Contact: Mike Sweeney.

2. A demonstration disk and information package are available from Industrial Relations Products Ltd., The Clifford Group, Suite 1810 Oceanic Plaza, 1066 W. Hastings St., Vancouver, BC, Canada V6E 3X1. Tel.: 604-687-6211, 604-688-6468. Fax: 604-687-0023. Contact: R. N. Crooks.

3. Becker & Bell Inc., 2149-C Portola Rd., Ventura, CA 93003. Tel.: 916-626-6010, 916-626-8201. Contact: Gene Bell.

4. Experience in Software Inc., 2000 Hearst Ave., Suite 202, Berkeley, CA, 94709-2176. Tel.: 800-678-7008 or 510-644-0694. Fax: 510-644-3823. Contact: Carolyn Burd.

5. Ibid.

6. Nancy K. Austin, "MBA-in-a-Box," *Working Woman* 18, no. 11 (November 1993), p. 30.

7. Winsight Inc., 72 Dempsey Avenue, Princeton, NJ 08540. Voice: 609-921-6486. Fax: 609-921-6579.

8. *Source:* Daniel Burnstein, Beacon Expert Systems, Inc., 35 Gardner Road Brookline, MA 02146. Tel.: 800-448-3308 or 617-738-9300. Fax: 617-734-3308. The designer of the software, Daniel Burnstein, worked for the United Electrical Workers. He also designed multimedia lessons as director of the Harvard Law School interactive video project. He has written frequently on negotiation topics, coauthored a curriculum on negotiation for the American Management Association, and taught negotiation skills in a wide variety of settings. He also is chair of the Negotiation Skills Interest Group of the American Bar Association.

9. Gerald R. Williams, *Legal Negotiation and Settlement* (St. Paul, MN: West, 1983).

CHAPTER 13

Ethical and Unethical Conduct and the Collective Bargaining Process

To everyone who proposes to have a good career, moral philosophy is indispensable.

—Cicero, *De Officiis,* 44 B.C.

After reading this chapter, you should be able to

■ Identify ethically questionable behavior in distributive bargaining.

■ Comprehend ethically questionable behavior in integrative bargaining.

■ Understand whether trusting the other party in negotiations may adversely affect your bargaining position.

■ Evaluate the advantages of a Pre-Negotiation Ethics Workshop.

■ Describe what it means to be an ethically responsible negotiator.

■ Explain bargaining behavior and procedures that are unethical and should be regarded as unfair.

ETHICAL BEHAVIOR AND A NUMBER OF BARGAINING BEHAVIOR MODELS

This chapter will attempt to highlight the connections between ethics and ethical behavior and distributive, integrative, and mixed-motive bargaining (for definitions of terms, see Walton and McKersie).[1]

Its objectives are as follows: to explore tactics and strategies of distributive, integrative, and mixed-motive bargaining that present opportunities for unethical conduct; to

This chapter was coauthored by E. Edward Herman and Robert Faaborg. Parts of the chapter were published in the *Proceedings of the Forty-fifth Annual IRRA Meetings,* Anaheim, CA, January 1993, pp. 207–14. This material was also published in a working paper series by the Harvard Law School, Program on Negotiation, July 1993.

evaluate the relations between ethics and trust and the dilemmas of distributive and integrative bargaining; to discuss the significance of trust and ethical behavior as catalysts for integrative and mixed-motive bargaining; to review the potential positive effects of such bargaining on joint gains and on the efficiency of bargaining outcomes; and to propose a methodology for and the formation of a Pre-Negotiation Ethics Workshop (PNEW) that could help the parties develop their own ground rules and a code of ethical behavior before the start of bargaining.

The chapter is based on the following assumptions and arguments:

1. The collective bargaining process includes some aspects of both distributive bargaining (where the parties are in conflict) and integrative bargaining (where they have common interests).

2. Integrative bargaining can lead to more efficient settlements because it allows for larger joint gains.

3. Understanding and applying ethical concepts can improve the payoff for the bargaining parties.

4. Trust plays a very important role in integrative, problem-solving bargaining. Higher levels of trust can increase the integrative component of the distributive-integrative continuum.

5. In general, the more that negotiations are conducted according to explicit rules of ethical behavior, the more likely is the development of a trusting relationship between the principals.

6. A joint Pre-Negotiation Ethics Workshop devoted to the discussion of a mutually acceptable code of ethical conduct will tend to increase trust between the parties.

7. Finally, providing training for organizations and for negotiators in ethical concepts and behavior, establishing acceptable norms and ground rules of ethical conduct, and developing an organizational code of ethics could increase the integrative—and thus reduce the distributive—component of collective bargaining.

ETHICAL BEHAVIOR IN NEGOTIATIONS: A BRIEF REVIEW OF THE LITERATURE

In Dante's *Divine Comedy,* the eighth circle of hell is reserved for "falsifiers of all sorts" and for those "false in words."[2] Under Dante's criterion, some negotiators could qualify for admission to hell.

Some scholars state that "various forms of lying and deceit are an integral part of negotiation"[3] and that although negotiations are not always unethical, "the opportunity to engage in unethical behavior is almost always present in bargaining."[4] One author lists five forms of deception and disguise that appear in negotiations. These are misrepresentation, bluffing, falsification, deception, and selective disclosure.[5] As paradoxical as it may sound, whereas misrepresentation is seemingly regarded as part of the negotiation process, it is important to stress that negotiators value highly their integrity and reputations. This finding is based on conversations with federal mediators and arbitrators, as well as with many negotiators. A number of opinion polls conducted among professionals also support this conclusion.[6] Poker bluffing is acceptable; cheating by marking cards or through other means is not. The same is true of negotiations; puffing is generally regarded as acceptable, but outright falsification of records or threatening bodily harm is clearly not.

Kelley and Lewicki state that honesty and integrity are necessary parts of "a successful negotiations relationship."[7] But they also suggest that "deception and disguise of one's true position are essential to maximizing objectives."[8] The second statement would probably be challenged by proponents of mutual gains bargaining, who would claim that deception, disguise, and dissimulation of one's true interests are detrimental to the process of principled negotiation.

Misrepresentation strategies and tactics are often followed by both sides at the bargaining table. Negotiators typically distort their initial proposals. They do not tell each other at the outset what they would really be willing to settle for. They may threaten strike action over an issue that they are actually willing to concede. All this behavior seems to be part of the ritual or dance of the negotiation process.

Henry Taylor, the British statesman, expressed the view that "falsehood ceases to be falsehood when it is understood on all sides that the truth is not expected to be spoken."[9] In many negotiations, misrepresentation is expected by both sides. This fact brings up an important question: Are there any limits or boundaries to misrepresentation? Are some actions ethically acceptable whereas others are not?

Some authors express the view that ethical appropriateness does not mandate telling the truth. What it requires is for the parties to understand and acknowledge the boundaries within which misrepresenting, puffing, bluffing, or lying is acceptable. Some scholars address the question thus: What is meant by telling the truth?[10] They suggest that telling the truth is not just an issue of moral character but is related to the situation in which one finds oneself.

Fisher et al.,[11] proponents of principled negotiation, suggest that "less than full disclosure is not the same as deception. . . . Good faith negotiation does not require full disclosure."[12] This statement is criticized by White, who suggests that Fisher et al. do not acknowledge "that between 'full disclosure' and 'deliberate deception' was a continuum, not a yawning chasm." White claims that negotiators "at least passively" mislead their opponents about their "settling points" even when their behavior is ethical.[13] A cursory review of the literature indicates that there is little agreement as to what does and does not constitute unethical behavior in the course of negotiations. Next we turn to the negotiation process itself.

THE NEGOTIATION PROCESS

Over the years, the negotiation process has been studied and researched by economists, psychologists, sociologists, political scientists, anthropologists, game theorists, philosophers, and practitioners, and by scholars from various disciplines, including law, industrial relations, management, and communications. Of all the books, monographs, and articles published on this subject during the last few decades, one of the most significant contributions was made by Walton and McKersie in *A Behavioral Theory of Labor Negotiations*.[14] The book presents a conceptual framework of labor-management negotiations. It is an abstraction and analysis of "four sets of activities or subprocesses, which together account for almost all the behavior in negotiations."[15] These four subprocesses are distributive bargaining, integrative bargaining, attitudinal structuring, and intraorganizational bargaining (discussed in Chapter 10). This chapter addresses only the first two of these subprocesses. Within the context of both integrative and distributive bargaining, there is also a subprocess referred to as mixed-motive bargaining.

Before examining, the ethical dimensions of these two subprocesses, let us define the following terms or agenda items, which we will refer to in our discussion of distributive and integrative bargaining: *issues, problems,* and *mixed items.* In distributive bargaining, the parties negotiate over issues. A pure issue is defined as a fixed-sum payoff; a gain by one side corresponds to a loss by the other side. The parties negotiate over a fixed pie; if one side gets a larger slice, it is always at the expense of the other side. In integrative bargaining, the parties negotiate over problems. In this subprocess, the objective of the parties is to increase joint gain or the size of the pie. In collective bargaining, very few agenda items can be categorized as pure issues or pure problems. Not too many issues can be settled by "pure" conflict, and very few "pure" problems can provide the parties with direct mutual gain. Most agendas contain mixed items that represent both issues and problems.[16] We refer to negotiations over these items as mixed-motive bargaining. The coexistence of these two elements in integrative bargaining was first recognized by Walton and McKersie, who refer to those common situations as mixed-motive situations.[17]

Scholars and practitioners of the negotiation process adopt three different approaches to negotiations. Some advocate a distributive approach to bargaining. They are referred to as value claimers; they consider those who participate in integrative problem-solving approaches as "naive and weak minded."[18] Others favor an integrative, problem-solving, win-win, mutual gains approach to negotiation. They are referred to as value creators and principled negotiators.[19] Still others,[20] including the authors of this chapter, assume that negotiations encompass both collaboration and competition, that some aspects can be common whereas others represent conflicting issues. Integrative and distributive bargaining are both intertwined parts of the labor negotiation process.

THE DISTRIBUTIVE BARGAINING MODEL:
TACTICS AND STRATEGIES

Under the distributive model, negotiating parties behave in a competitive manner. Their objective is to resolve conflicts of interest and to influence, to their own advantage, the distribution of fixed resources.

The distributive approach[21] recognizes some of the following strategies and tactics that can be utilized in bargaining: assessing the opponent's utilities of outcomes and strike costs, modifying the opponent's perceptions of the party's utilities, manipulating strike costs, communicating the party's commitment and making it credible, preventing the opponent from becoming committed, enabling the other side to revise its commitments, and abandoning commitments made.[22] Each of these tactics and strategies presents opportunities for unethical behavior.

In assessing their opponents' utilities for outcomes and strike costs, parties may apply a variety of tactics, some of which "flow along ethically questionable channels and may involve cloak-and-dagger operations."[23] In attempting to modify an opponent's perception of the party's utilities, negotiators try to minimize clues, sometimes by "appearing uninformed" or by appointing to negotiating committees people who do not know their party's resistance points. Other tactics for modifying perceptions may involve the submission of a large number of proposals in order not to reveal too early the relative significance of various issues. Sometimes, in trying to convey "deliberate impressions," negotiators overstate or even grossly exaggerate the significance of a particular demand. There are ethical problems "as well as . . . risks in communicating misinformation . . . spiraling of misinformation can lead to greater uncertainty and miscalculation."[24] The boundary between misrepresentation and lies is very vague; the former may be acceptable as "natural"; the latter may provoke hostility. According to Walton and McKersie, "collective bargaining is a continuing relationship[;] abuses . . . will eventually receive their due."[25]

Manipulating strike costs of the party and the opponent presents various opportunities for misleading the other side, some of which could be considered ethically problematic. One example of such manipulation was the deposit by an international union of a significant amount of money in a local bank in a small community.[26] The objective of the deposit was to create the impression that the union had the monetary resources to finance a lengthy strike. In reality, the money could not be used by the local union; its primary objective was to create the impression of strength.

Commitment tactics, particularly when a party is communicating firmness or flexibility, present many opportunities for misleading the other side. Walton and McKersie[27] break down commitment declarations into three elements: (1) degree of finality, (2) specificity, and (3) consequence or threat accompanying each commitment. Each element of the commitment statement offers opportunities for unethical conduct.

Some of the tactics discussed so far are regarded as ethically questionable. Goldman[28] argues that others are unacceptable. These include "false statement of law or fact" and distortion of truth, which violate the criminal code.

INTEGRATIVE BARGAINING

Integrative bargaining is characterized by a process in which both parties stress common interests, joint gains, and problem-solving activities, but the opportunity for unethical tactics is nonetheless still present.

Raiffa, who supports use of the problem-solving model, states that most negotiations are conducted in a distributive rather than in an integrative mode and that therefore the resulting agreements are inefficient. Raiffa also emphasizes the significance of the ethical component in negotiations. He states that "ethical reflections should be a continuing imperative" of negotiations. Although Raiffa offers some observations on how to think about "ethically laden choices," he does not provide specific procedures or details for incorporating ethics into the negotiation process.[29]

Scholars in this field point out that when parties engage in integrative bargaining, they cannot totally distance themselves from the distributive dimension, primarily because some items are both collaborative and conflictual. This fact presents negotiators with a variety of dilemmas, some of which have ethical implications. One point of this chapter is to suggest that the understanding and mutual acceptance of ethical norms and ethical behavior can help the parties increase the integrative and reduce the distributive components of collective bargaining. Ethics could be the catalyst or one of the spans of the bridge connecting and moving the parties from distributive toward integrative bargaining. It is interesting to note that whereas literature on integrative bargaining acknowledges the joint gain potential of this model, it does not cover in sufficient depth the significance and effects of ethical behavior on this process.

The success of problem-solving outcomes in the context of collective bargaining is affected by resolution of dilemmas produced by the simultaneous, and to some extent conflicting, needs of integrative and distributive bargaining. In many instances, tactics effective in pure distributive bargaining conflict with pure integrative bargaining. In pure distributive bargaining, the parties try to minimize openness and disclosure of information. The opposite conduct is desirable for success of pure integrative negotiations. Walton and McKersie[30] discuss a number of these dilemmas, but we will explore only some of these. One dilemma of integrative bargaining is problem identification. That process necessitates communication and exchange of data. Release of information may offer the recipients useful clues for distributive bargaining and provide them with indirect assessments of the other side's weaknesses and strengths. Thus, it may assist them in assessing the sender's utility curve.[31] Identifying a problem may expose a weakness that the other side may exploit in other areas of bargaining. It may also offer the other side an opportunity to concentrate on solving its own problems while pretending to work on joint problems. Integrative bargaining, through its open communication channels, can also provide senders with opportunities to release misleading information in order to enhance their position in distributive bargaining. Obviously, such behavior is ethically problematic.

Another dilemma facing negotiators is the content of the agenda for integrative bargaining. In distributive bargaining, the parties frequently include in their agenda additional issues. They do this for two reasons: to hide true utilities and to produce "trading horses."[32] The temptation to misrepresent by introducing such "trading horses" into the integrative process is always present. Some negotiators hope to achieve greater payoffs for themselves from such behavior. In most instances, that approach is detrimental to the relationship and may have negative effects on the bargaining process.

Still another dilemma of integrative bargaining is "preference ordering." An integrative approach requires the ranking of alternatives from most to least attractive. It also necessitates an honest comparison of the utilities of the two sides. Walton and McKersie suggest that "there is often an incentive for a party to misrepresent his own utilities so as to make one favored 'integrative solution' appear to better balance the party's interest than the other solutions."[33] In proposing the negotiation agenda and in stating utility functions, negotiators can distort the utility of various items and represent items of low utility to themselves as major sacrifices, thus extracting large concessions at low cost. Integrative bargaining, unless it addresses purely integrative problems like any other negotiation process, entails the issues of "interinstitutional and interpersonal utility comparisons."[34] This in turn brings up the difficult issue of comparison of the costs and benefits of each solution. For integrative bargaining to be successful, it is important that both sides honestly state their preferred solutions or utility functions.[35] Unfortunately, at this stage, there is a temptation to misrepresent one's interests. This in turn can undermine trust, an important element of integrative negotiations.

Another dilemma of integrative bargaining involves determining how to negotiate mixed-agenda items. One possible approach is the employment of a two-level mixed bargaining strategy. At one level, the parties could address problems and attempt to increase joint gains. At another level, they could negotiate distributively over the allocation of potential gains. One approach for resolving potential conflict over distribution of gains is for the parties to agree on allocation standards, some of which could be based on the following criteria: equal distribution, division proportionate to each party's contribution or to each side's status, and allocation according to each party's needs or according to each side's bargaining power.[36]

In negotiating over mixed items, the parties can employ a number of different strategies. Two of these are (1) an integrative approach combined with a soft strategy in allocating shares and (2) an integrative strategy aimed at enlarging joint gains, followed by hard bargaining over share allocation. The first strategy presents risks because the soft negotiator may be taken advantage of by the other side when the parties must decide on the distribution of gains. The second strategy presents difficulty because the "party can never be sure that behind the guise of searching for larger sums opponent is not merely introducing the subjects which have 'solutions' that give opponent disproportionate share."[37] Thus, negotiations over mixed items create opportunities for unethical behavior.

TRUST

An ingredient important for the success of problem solving within the context of integrative bargaining is mutual trust.[38] The four subprocesses—distributive bargaining, integrative bargaining, attitudinal structuring, and intraorganizational bargaining—interact with one another, and the level of trust within the integrative subprocess is affected by the degree of trust present in the other subprocesses.

Negotiators are reluctant to be open, to disclose data, and to participate in problem-solving activities if they are concerned that some of their information may be applied against them. A relationship based on trust can help negotiators resolve dilemmas that develop in mixed-motive bargaining. It is easier to be cooperative during the problem-solving phase if there is trust.

To protect themselves against trust violations, negotiators can utilize a number of safeguards. They can agree to ground rules on confidentiality, news blackout, and privacy. They can conduct their sessions on an off-the-record basis. They can agree to "separate inventing from deciding."[39] Other possible safeguards include establishing small subcommittees addressing separate topics, appointing different negotiators who would utilize different bargaining processes regarding the same items assigning integrative problem-solving agenda items to committees at the lower level of the organization and distributive bargaining items to upper-level personnel, and seeking assistance from mediators or facilitators.[40]

Trust, however, cannot be separated from ethical conduct; the two are closely intertwined. The level of trust is affected by the behavior and interactions of the negotiators in the four negotiation subprocesses. It is moved by the behavior of labor and management in the course of negotiations as well as by developments occurring during the life of an agreement. It is also influenced by the history of the relationship, by personality characteristics and backgrounds of the major participants, and by the organizational culture and climate.

It is beyond the scope of this chapter to deal fully with the dynamics of trust building, which must address the function of language, potential penalties for violation, and means for assisting the other side to overcome past transgressions.

Peterson and Tracy[41] developed a conceptual model in order to identify factors that promote problem solving in labor negotiations. They tested the model empirically through a survey and discovered that one of the five significant relationships between perceived success in problem solving and a cooperative working relationship between parties was trust. According to the survey respondents, trust was "knowing that the other side is telling the truth, is playing the game fairly, and can and will deliver." We should note that all of these elements of trust—truthfulness, fairness, and following up on commitments—are essentially ethical notions; this demonstrates the intrinsic relationship between trust and morality. The Peterson and Tracy study confirms Walton and McKersie's conclusions that trust is one of the factors that facilitate joint problem-solving activities.[42]

A minimum level of trust is necessary for problem solving to be successful.[43] The importance of trust in enlarging the "mythical fixed pie" is also recognized by Bazerman and Neale,[44] who stress its importance for creating integrative agreements. Kimmel et al.[45] conducted an empirical study on the effects of trust on cooperative behavior and on outcomes that benefit both sides. According to their findings, a high level of trust is a necessary ingredient for cooperative problem-solving behavior in negotiations. Success depends on the parties' willingness to be open with one another and to exchange information about their needs and priorities. Without trust, some negotiators develop low-risk approaches to integrative bargaining. Others give up the problem-solving process in favor of distributive bargaining.

TRUST AND ETHICS

Unethical behavior undermines trust. Negotiators who are not open with each other during the integrative phase of bargaining will not benefit from the process.[46] As Walton and McKersie state, "Integrative solutions cannot emerge if both sides are not candid with each other."[47] According to Raiffa, "Disputants often fare poorly when they each act greedily and deceptively. . . . [T]hey can all jointly gain if they would be less greedy and more open and honest with one another."[48] The process of problem solving in negotiations is very fragile and can easily be derailed by misunderstandings and differences in perception. It mandates openness and exchange of information. In our view, trust cannot be developed and maintained in a bargaining relationship without adherence to some implicit or explicit ethical norms within an organization as well as among negotiators. Without ethics trust will remain an elusive commodity.

It is our hope that a Pre-Negotiation Ethics Workshop (PNEW), which we will propose in the next section, may help increase the likelihood that individuals involved in negotiations will develop the degree of trust necessary for satisfactory resolution of those negotiations. Familiarity with some of the literature on the psychological and sociological dynamics of trust might also be helpful. It is essential for all of us to understand the peculiar logic of trust and distrust and especially the extent to which both are social constructs that are in large part socially created facts.

It is by now well established that for most people, the *belief* in or *perception* of ethical behavior and intentions on the part of others strongly influences the likelihood of ethical behavior in oneself.[49] The more we believe that others with whom we interact are acting ethically, the more we are inclined to act ethically. Conversely, if we believe that others are trying to take advantage of us and frequently act unfairly toward us, we are likely to respond in kind. In general, each of us would prefer to act honestly; this preference is reinforced by a perception that others around us are also not trying to cheat us in our transactions.[50] Thus, to a large degree, the belief that others will behave ethically is self-reinforcing. To this extent, ethical behavior is a social construct.

What is true of ethics in general applies even more to trust. Trust exhibits what has been called the *intentional paradox*. If we mutually intend to trust, that intention by itself increases trusting behavior and our perception of trusting behavior, which lead to even more trust and confirm our original intention. And, of course, distrust has the opposite effect. If we both initially distrust each other, this leads us to look for negative behavior, which, once again, is self-reinforcing. Dasgupta argues that the mere fact that someone has placed his or her trust in us makes us feel obligated, and this makes it harder to betray that trust.[51] One feels a sense of obligation not to betray someone who has placed trust in us.

On the other hand, Jones points out that "expectations of hostility or competitiveness tend to breed hostility or competitiveness in response."[52] He calls this *correspondence bias*—the tendency for people who initially expect X to be untrustworthy to treat X as untrustworthy; if X shows some sign of untrustworthiness, I attribute this to a latent character flaw in X rather than a setup by me. This correspondence bias is further evidence of the extent to which trust and distrust are social constructs. We in part *create* the conditions required for trust and successful negotiations. "Social beliefs can and do create their own social reality."[53] Dasgupta concludes, "If people are somewhat cynical about one another, everyone will emerge worse off than if people trust one another."[54]

Unfortunately, this initial trust must confront such psychological phenomena as that which Messick and Sentis call the *egocentric fairness bias*,[55] the tendency for people to see arrangements that favor themselves over others as fairer than arrangements that favor others. Rempel et al. reported that even among trusting relationships, "there was a tendency for people to view their own motives as less self-centered."[56] If people could be made more aware of their own egocentric biases and everyone's tendency to engage in the correspondence bias, perhaps they would be a bit more likely to begin negotiations with at least a presumption *not* to distrust the motives and intentions of the other party.

It might also be helpful for negotiators to be made aware of the literature showing the existence of what is called *false consensus bias*. This is the common tendency for people to believe that whereas they themselves or people from their group generally act morally, others are not nearly as ethical. Of course, if one just *thinks* about this general belief, it immediately becomes obvious that it *cannot* be true. Yet it has been well documented in studies by Michalos,[57] Goethals,[58] Ferrel and Weaver,[59] and others. Beltramini reports that in a study using questions "concerning relatively unethical competitive information acquisition strategies . . . [i]n every case, more respondents thought other companies were less scrupulous than their own company and themselves."[60] These results were replicated by Cohen and Czepier,[61] Vitell and Festervand,[62] and Finn et al.[63]

Thus, all of these studies, representing such diverse populations as undergraduate students, business managers, and CPAs, are consistent. Every single one makes the same point: Most people think most people are not as nice as they are themselves and, therefore, cannot be trusted to behave as well. Taking respondents at their word, the same studies provided clear evidence that most people were wrong about most people.[64]

We believe that if one becomes aware of the existence of the correspondence bias, the egocentric fairness bias, and the false consensus bias, it is only reasonable to apply these biases to oneself. Thus, for each of us, the chances are that others' demands upon us are fairer than we initially perceive them to be. More important, it is likely for each of us that others, including the individuals making up the other negotiating party, are more moral than we are initially inclined to believe they are. A rational response to the facts of these commonplace biases should result in an increase in trust between the parties to negotiation.

We believe that an even stronger result follows from an understanding of the intentional paradox and the fact that trust is a social construct. Qualities like moral virtue, generosity, and trustfulness are social goods. The more people display their trustfulness, the more others are inclined to be trustworthy. Moral virtues in general, and trust in particular, feed on themselves.[65] Because trust is a necessary condition for people's being in fact trustworthy, it follows that we should try to be trustful. We have argued earlier that it is prudent for negotiating parties, as for all of us, to engage in trusting and trustworthy behavior. We now claim that it is equally *morally correct* to adopt a strategy of trust. Just as the general perception of ethical behavior in others increases the likelihood of our own ethical behavior and reinforces ethics in general, so, in negotiations, the belief that others will behave so as to deserve our trust is a necessary condition for such trustworthy behavior and is self-reinforcing. In our view, a Pre-Negotiation Ethics Workshop may be a good way to encourage trust, understanding, success, and mutual fulfillment of expectations during subsequent negotiations.

THE PRE-NEGOTIATION ETHICS WORKSHOP (PNEW)

Given our assumptions (1) that increasing the level of trust in negotiations tends to influence bargaining toward the integrative end of the distributive-integrative continuum and (2) that increasing the level of perceived and actual ethical behavior tends to increase the level of trust, we propose as part of the bargaining process that the parties participate in a Pre-Negotiation Ethics Workshop (PNEW) to address ethical issues, problems, and dilemmas that arise during negotiation. The objectives and benefits of the PNEW would be as follows: (1) provide an introductory understanding of the traditional ethical theories and basic ethical concepts relevant to negotiations, such as impartiality or fairness, respect for rights, issues surrounding deception and misrepresentation, and professional rights and responsibilities; (2) help the parties reach consensus on a general "code of ethics" to be followed during the subsequent negotiations; (3) help acclimate individuals who will be involved in negotiations to each other, their communication styles, their personalities, and so on; and, especially, (4) raise group awareness of individual differences in ethical standards, perspectives, cultural assumptions, and backgrounds. This last process may become extremely valuable in avoiding potential misunderstandings that might decrease the level of trust between the parties. Our belief is that a general shared discussion of the meaning and importance of specific professional ethical standards will enable participants to become aware of what matters to each of them personally. This awareness in turn should help to increase trust and understanding among negotiators.

The details of such an ethics prenegotiation workshop must, of necessity, be determined by those involved in the negotiations and may be subject to considerable time and cost constraints; however, we believe that even an afternoon devoted to ethics and the development of a consensus about ethical procedures to be followed in negotiations will prove valuable to the parties. In our view, the specific topics and procedures are not nearly as important as the fact that the participants devote attention to ethics and to their beliefs and expectations about what is unethical behavior and what is ethically desirable in negotiations.

Nearly everyone in our society agrees on the crucial importance of ethics and moral behavior, but almost no one agrees on anything else. It is essential that any discussion of ethics avoid the pitfalls of ending in unresolvable arguments. Consequently, we urge that prenegotiation discussion center on two questions: (1) What does it mean to be an ethically responsible negotiator? and (2) What behavior and procedures during the course of negotiations should be ethically prohibited or regarded as unfair? Of course, there is much more involved in the ethics of negotiations (e.g., "externalities"—issues concerning effects of the conduct and outcome of negotiations on parties not represented at the table); furthermore, negotiators may wish to consider issues in the PNEW not stipulated in this chapter.

To address the first question, concerning what it means to be an ethically responsible negotiator, we suggest that workshop planners might choose topics from among the following: Integrity, Confidentiality, Avoiding Conflict of Interest, Justice, Fairness, Loyalty, Respectfulness, Candidness, Responsibility to Clients' Welfare, Empathy (understanding others' needs), Listening Skills, Flexibility, Competency/Hard Work, Fiduciary Responsibility, Keeping Commitments/Promises, and Balancing Demands of Conflicting Personal and Professional Obligations. The second and principal question that we suggest be discussed centers on what behavior and procedures should be prohibited during the course of negotiations. This topic is explored further in the following sections. However, what follows should be regarded only as tentative suggestions for the theme of the PNEW and for guidelines in developing a prenegotiation code of ethics.

ROLE RESPONSIBILITY/PROFESSIONAL ETHICS

We believe that the ethics of negotiations can benefit from the model of ethical obligation advanced by some contemporary theorists of business ethics.[66] Specifically, this model abstracts from the ethical and legal fact that in most advanced societies, contractual rights and duties provide a foundation for the special duties a person assumes in voluntarily accepting a position or role within a legitimate social organization such as a business or a profession. Business and professional ethics center around such duties or responsibilities, which one takes on when one contracts for a job.[67] Crucially, role responsibility or professional ethics points us toward our prima facie duties as professionals or in our career roles. Sadly, few professional and still fewer nonprofessional career roles have well-developed and detailed codes of ethics. And, of course, notoriously, our prima facie professional or job duties may clash at times with our prima facie general ethical duties.

Moreover, we all occupy several roles, which may involve potentially conflicting duties. Thus, one's role as a parent may directly clash with one's professional obligations.

Professional rights and responsibilities arise out of the specific nature of a given profession. Professions exist to solve certain problems, serve certain interests, or fill certain needs. These moral purposes of a profession have resulting ethical consequences involving both positive and negative obligations as well as making it permissible in specific contexts to ignore or even violate general prima facie obligations. A professional may sometimes do to a client what even a spouse or parent may not do. For example, surgeons may be obligated to perform actions that risk the death of their patients and that would be tantamount to murder if attempted by the rest of us.

Thus, special roles create special moral rights and duties. Becoming sensitive to these responsibilities, increasing one's awareness of the possibility of ethical conflicts, and attempting to analyze and resolve such clashes are the essence of applied ethics. The professional model helps us see what is *not* our responsibility. Thus, it is *not* the duty of the negotiator to "do good," to maximize everyone's utility. In fact, the negotiator's role entails a primary responsibility to the client's interests; it would be highly immoral, not to mention illegal, for a negotiator to act as Mother Teresa.

Of course, it is crucial that the professional or business role one chooses to undertake be itself morally legitimate. But the professional model avoids the supererogatory requirements of traditional ethical theory and concentrates professional and career ethics on the explicit and implicit contractual duties associated with one's profession or career and on the general duties not to harm others, to prevent avoidable harm, and to compensate for harm caused. Of course, these are themselves abstract and minimal responsibilities, but at least this role responsibility/professional model allows us to concentrate on the genuine and pragmatic ethical dilemmas specific to our professions that arise out of the agreements we have with our employers, co-workers, clients, and customers.

Consequently, we suggest that the PNEW not try to tackle the morass of traditional ethical theory, ignore utilitarian ethics altogether, and instead concentrate on two questions: (1) What does it mean to be an ethically responsible professional negotiator? and, especially, (2) What behavior and procedures during the course of negotiations should be ethically prohibited or regarded as unfair?

TWO REQUIREMENTS OF ETHICS: IMPARTIALITY (UNIVERSALITY) AND RESPECT FOR RIGHTS

Impartiality

Ethics is *not* a matter of an individual's taste, judgment, or choice, nor is it a matter of what is prudent for an individual to do or what maximizes his or her self-interest. In fact, one essential requirement of any genuine ethical theory is that it distinguish between actions that are egoistically prudential and ethical obligations. Ethics is intrinsically universal in application. One logical feature of ethical principles is their objectivity, impartiality, fairness, or universality. This feature is associated with the ethics of the philosopher Immanuel Kant.[68] According to Kant, a person performs every rational, voluntary action according to some reason, to achieve some purpose. Kant argued that an action is moral only when this reason can be made universal—that is, when this reason is one on which we would be willing to have *everyone* act in relevantly similar circumstance. This condition is sometimes referred to as reversibility because people's reasons for action must be "reversible"; people must be willing to have others use the same reasons, even against themselves. Thus, immoral people violate the principle of impartiality or universality;

they wrongly want to make special exceptions of themselves. For example, they wish to break contracts when it suits their own interest, but they would not allow others to do the same to them. Their stance violates the essential conceptual point: Obligation is universal. If someone has a duty or obligation to act a certain way in a given circumstance, then *everyone* similarly suited who finds him- or herself in the same circumstance has the same obligation or duty.

Consider the following example, which might prove useful in understanding this requirement of impartiality or universality. Suppose Smith decides to enter into a contract, knowing he cannot possibly meet the deadline required by its terms. Smith's rationale might be this: "My firm badly needs this contract to pay its debts, and, anyway, the other party won't know I'm lying about meeting the deadline until it's too late." Could Smith universalize his rationale? Could he consistently be willing to have *everyone* break contracts whenever it suited their purposes? The answer is clearly negative because the very practice of contracting requires for its existence that people trust one another to adhere to contract terms. If *everyone* acted according to Smith's rationale and broke contracts on a whim whenever it suited them, no one would ever enter into the contractual relationship. The very practice of contracting would collapse. Thus, Smith's action cannot be universalized; it is seen to be immoral once one applies the test of universality.

It might prove helpful, when applying this principle of impartiality or universality to a specific negotiating tactic or rule of procedure, to conduct the following mental exercise: Place yourself in the position of all potentially affected individuals, especially that of those who are likely to be harmed the most or who benefit the least or whose legal or moral rights may be violated or encroached upon. If you were in their position, would you choose to proceed in this way? What alternatives, if any, might be preferable to those people?

Rawls's[69] "veil of ignorance" procedure is helpful here: Imagine that you do not know beforehand which group of affected individuals you belong to. For example, suppose you were the opponent party subject to a given procedure or action in negotiations. Would that alter your choice of tactics? In other words, in considering all of these issues, ask yourself whether you are trying to make an exception of yourself, your client, or a certain subclass of preferred individuals. Is the decision fair to all those affected? Is it just? Would they perceive it as just?

Ask yourself further: To help determine the answers to these questions, should these potentially harmed individuals be consulted? If not, why not? What consequences might result from their learning of the decision before it has been made? What are the probable *perceived* results of each alternative?

Some correctly see a similarity in all of this to the common-sense moral principle known as the golden rule: "Do unto others as you would be done unto yourself." However, especially in a field as competitive as negotiations, it is important to realize the limitations of the golden rule. For example, if you are a negotiator who is young, callous, high-risk-taking, reckless, and even uncaring toward yourself, applying the golden rule may lead to approving of aggressive, even manipulative and deceptive behavior. The principle of impartiality or universality and Rawls's procedural "veil of ignorance" are designed to avoid such results. In formulating ethical principles and procedures, one is not permitted to adopt rules designed only to give advantage to oneself or individuals like oneself.

Respect for Individual Rights

In addition to impartiality or universality, respect for humanity—for the individual's rights, dignity, and autonomy—is central to ethics. In fact, Kant believed that such respect follows from considerations of universality because he thought that everyone would choose to be treated with such respect. Again, we will avoid advancing specific ethical principles or rights; however, we emphasize that respect for individuals' rights does *not* mean merely respect for their *legal* rights. This principle is not limited, as some may think, to a call for nondiscrimination. Rather, it requires respect for the value of each individual as a free, rational, autonomous agent who should be free to choose actions consistent with respect for others' freedom. In Kant's words, we should treat humanity as an end in itself and never merely as a means to our own ends.

Thus, respect for persons would prohibit ad hominem abusive attacks on or threats against individuals. Instead, negotiations should be conducted so as to emphasize the use of reasons and justifications, what some call "legitimacy."[70] Notice that if someone alters another's choice set by deceptive or manipulative statements or behavior, then he or she has violated that person's freedom to choose, whether the motives for such violation were paternalistic or governed purely by self-interest. Again, we hope that the specifics of such behavior will be discussed in the PNEW and agreement reached concerning just what sorts of behavior will be regarded as permissible.

Of course, impartiality and generalized respect for individuals and individual rights do not exhaust ethical considerations. As we have suggested, following Bowie's[71] model of professional ethics, we all have the general duties to (1) do no harm, (2) attempt to prevent harm, and (3) compensate for unavoidable or unintended harm that we may cause in the performance of our professional responsibilities. However, it is beyond the scope of this chapter to try to apply these admittedly general and vague principles to negotiation ethics; most important, these are just the kinds of decisions we would prefer to leave to the PNEW. And, again, it is important to keep in mind that the goal of a PNEW is not to arrive at specific conclusions or agreements about ethical principles but to build and encourage the kind of mutual respect, trust, and understanding that, we have argued, is most likely to produce successful negotiations. What is ethically most important is not the substance or specific content of PNEW decisions but that they (1) be made openly and made known to all involved and (2) be agreed to by all parties to the negotiations and their second tables. (These second tables are the hierarchy and constituency that each team represents and to which it is answerable.)

The importance in negotiations of the existence of "known and accepted" rules has been stressed by Lax and Sebenius[72] in their discussion of the ethical dimension of negotiations. Some of the literature on ethics and negotiations makes vague reference to the "rules of the game," often citing Carr's[73] ill-founded analogy to bluffing and poker. Such an analogy fails because the rules of poker are generally well known, detailed, and agreed upon in advance. The alleged "rules" of negotiation are vague and context dependent. Their interpretation and detail—and even acknowledgment of their existence—vary from individual to individual. Much of the misunderstanding, mistrust, and conflict involved in negotiations arises because of these conflicting beliefs about its so-called unwritten "rules." We believe one of the principal benefits of the PNEW should be its contribution toward making some of these rules explicit and understood by all sides. This should help increase the trust and mutual understanding between the parties during the negotiation process.

Lax and Sebenius[74] also offer some principles that might prove helpful in the PNEW discussion. In the determination of tactics to be regarded as ethically permissible, they propose the criterion of "self-image." Citing Peter Drucker,[75] they suggest that one ask oneself the following question: When you look at yourself in the mirror the morning following the use of such tactics, will you like the person you see? Lax and Sebenius[76] also cite the ethical guideline often called the Publicity Test: Would you be comfortable if your use of such tactics were publicized? To the press? To your clients? To your religious leader? Your parents? They also suggest the Advising Test: Would you be comfortable advising another to use this tactic? A junior colleague? Your potential opponents in future negotiations?

SUMMARY

In this chapter we reviewed some of the tactics, strategies, and dilemmas of distributive, integrative, and mixed-motive bargaining that offer opportunities for unethical behavior. We also discussed reasons for the parties to behave ethically. Some proposed tactics may seem ethically suspect because they appear to fail the test of impartiality, universality, or respect for individuals' rights. Alternatively, some individuals may just feel uneasy about a tactic that appears to them to be in the gray area of ethical permissibility. When these problems arise, the negotiating parties should try to find creative alternative rules of procedure that are less objectionable.

The actual content and substance of the ethical rules of procedure agreed upon by the parties are not what is crucial. What is significant, as we stated in the introduction, is our belief that awareness and application of ethical rules and procedures will tend to increase the trust and understanding between the parties involved in negotiation. We have argued that increased trust and understanding should in turn increase the integrative component of the distributive-integrative continuum, resulting in larger joint gains and more efficient settlements.

Of course, our proposed Pre-Negotiation Ethics Workshop is only one possible means toward the end of increasing ethical conduct during negotiations. But, in our view, whatever means are adopted, both negotiators and their clients will benefit from increased attention to ethics.

Notes

1. Richard E. Walton and Robert B. McKersie, *A Behavioral Theory of Labor Negotiations,* 2nd ed. (Ithaca, NY: ILR Press, 1991).

2. Charles Eliot Norton, trans., *The Divine Comedy of Dante Alighieri* (Boston: Houghton Mifflin, 1920), pp. 194–207.

3. Roy J. Lewicki and Joseph A. Litterer, *Negotiation* (Burr Rose, IL: Irwin, 1985), p. 324.

4. J. Keith Murnighan, *The Dynamics of Bargaining Games* (Englewood Cliffs, NJ: Prentice Hall, 1991), p. 187.

5. Roy J. Lewicki, "Lying and Deception" in *Negotiating in Organizations,* Max H. Bazerman and Roy J. Lewicki, eds. (Beverly Hills, CA: Sage, 1983), pp. 68–90.

6. Chester L. Karrass, *The Negotiating Game* (New York: Thomas Y. Crowell, 1970), p. 36.

7. Harold H. Kelley, "A Classroom Study of the Dilemmas in Interpersonal Negotiations" in K. Archibald, ed., *Strategic Interaction and Conflict* (Berkeley: University of California Press, 1966), pp. 49–73.

8. Lewicki, 1983, op. cit., pp. 69–70.

9. Albert Z. Carr, "Is Business Bluffing Ethical?" *Harvard Business Review* 46, no. 9 (1968), p. 143; David A. Lax and James K. Sebenius, *The Manager as Negotiator* (New York: Free Press, 1986), p. 148.

10. Dietrich Bonhoeffer, "What Is Meant by 'Telling the Truth'?" in *Ethics,* Eberhard Bethge, ed. (New York: Macmillan, 1965), pp. 363–72; Sissela Bok, *Lying* (New York: Pantheon Books, 1978), p. 282.

11. Roger Fisher and William Ury with Bruce Patton, ed., *Getting to Yes,* 2nd ed. (New York: Penguin Books, 1991), p. 135.

12. Ibid.

13. James J. White, "The Pros and Cons of 'Getting to YES'," *Journal of Legal Education* 120 (1984), p. 118.

14. Walton and McKersie, op. cit.

15. Ibid., p. xv.

16. Ibid., pp. 13, 127–28, 161–62.

17. Ibid., pp. xi–xii.

18. Lax and Sebenius, op. cit., p. 32.

19. Ibid., and Fisher et al., 1991, op. cit.

20. Ibid., and Walton and McKersie, op. cit.

21. Walton and McKersie, op. cit.

22. Ibid., pp. 58–125.

23. Ibid., pp. 61–63.

24. Ibid., pp. 71–72.

25. Ibid., p. 72.

26. Alfred Kuhn, *Labor Institutions and Economics* (New York: Holt, Rinehart & Winston, 1958), p. 171.

27. Walton and McKersie, op. cit., p. 93.

28. Alvin L. Goldman, *Settling for More* (Washington, DC: Bureau of National Affairs, 1991).

29. Howard Raiffa, *The Art and Science of Negotiation* (Cambridge, MA: Belknap Press, Harvard University Press, 1982), pp. 344–55, 358–59.

30. Walton and McKersie, op. cit., p. 161.

31. Ibid., p. 154.

32. Ibid., p. 170.

33. Ibid., p. 175.

34. Ibid., p. 154.

35. Ibid., p. 153.

36. Richard E. Walton and Robert M. McKersie, "Behavioral Dilemmas in Mixed-Motive Decision Making," *Behavioral Sciences* 11 (1966), pp. 382–83.

37. Walton and McKersie, 1991, op. cit., p. 166.

38. Ibid., pp. 141, 143. K. Gergen, *The Psychology of Behavior Exchange* (Reading, PA: Addison-Wesley, 1969). R. B. Peterson and L. N. Tracy, "A Behavioural Model of Problem-Solving in Labour Negotiations," *British Journal of Industrial Relations* 24, no. 2 (July 1976), pp. 159–73.

39. Fisher and Ury, op. cit., p. 60.

40. Walton and McKersie, 1966, op. cit., pp. 381–82; 1991, op. cit., p. 159.

41. Peterson and Tracy, op. cit., pp. 165–66.

42. Walton and McKersie, 1991, op. cit., pp. 141, 159, 181–82.

43. Ibid., p. 143.

44. Max H. Bazerman and Margaret A. Neale, *Negotiating Rationally* (New York: Free Press, 1992), pp. 89–101.

45. Melvin J. Kimmel, Dean G. Pruitt, John M. Magenau, Ellen Konar-Goldband, and Peter J. D. Carnevale, "Effects of Trust, Aspiration, and Gender on Negotiation Tactics," *Journal of Personality and Social Psychology* 38, no. 1 (1980), pp. 9–22.

46. Mary Parker Follett, *Dynamic Administration: The Collected Papers of Mary Parker Follett*, Y. C. Metcalf and L. Urwick, eds. (New York: Harper & Row, 1942).

47. Walton and McKersie, 1991, op. cit., p. 148.

48. Raiffa, op. cit., p. 345.

49. Alex Michalos, "The Impact of Trust on Business, International Security and the Quality of Life," *Journal of Business Ethics* 9 (1990), pp. 619–38.

50. Partha Dasgupta, "Trust as a Commodity" in *Trust: Making and Breaking Cooperative Relations,* Diego Gambetta, ed. (Padstow, England, and New York: Basil Blackwell, 1988), p. 56.

51. Ibid.

52. E. E. Jones, "Interpreting Interpersonal Behavior: The Effects of Expectancies," *Science* 234 (1986), pp. 41–46.

53. M. Snyder, "When Belief Creates Reality," *Advances in Experimental Social Psychology* 18 (1984), pp. 247–305.

54. Dasgupta, op. cit., p. 56.

55. D. M. Messick and K. P. Sentis, "Fairness, Preference and Fairness Biases" in *Equity Theory: Psychological and Sociological Perspectives,* D. M. Messick and K. S. Cook, eds. (New York: Praeger, 1983), pp. 61–94.

56. J. K. Rempel, J. G. Holmes, and M. P. Zanna, "Trust in Close Relationships," *Journal of Personality and Social Psychology* 49 (1985), pp. 95–112.

57. Michalos, op. cit.

58. G. R. Goethals, "Fabricating and Ignoring Social Reality: Self-Serving Estimates of Consensus," *Relative Deprivation and Social Comparison,* J. M. Olson, C. P. Herman, and M. P. Zanna, eds. (Hillsdale, NJ: Earlbaum, 1986), pp. 139–59.

59. O. C. Ferrel and K. M. Weaver, "Ethical Beliefs of Marketing Managers," *Journal of Marketing* 41 (1978), pp. 69–73.

60. R. F. Beltramini, "Ethics and the Use of Competitive Information Acquisition Strategies," *Journal of Business Ethics* 5 (1986), pp. 307–12.

61. W. Cohen and H. Czepier, "The Role of Ethics in Gathering Corporate Intelligence," *Journal of Business Ethics* 7 (1988), pp. 199–204.

62. S. J. Vitell and T. A. Festervand, "Business Ethics: Conflicts, Practices and Beliefs of Industrial Executives," *Journal of Business Ethics* 6 (1987), pp. 111–22.

63. D. W. Finn, L. B. Chonko, and S. D. Hunt, "Ethical Problems in Public Accounting: The View from the Top," *Journal of Business Ethics* 7 (1988), pp. 605–15.

64. Michalos, op. cit.

65. Jones, op. cit.

66. Norman Bowie, *Business Ethics,* 2nd ed. (Englewood Cliffs, NJ: Prentice Hall, 1982).

67. Ibid.

68. Those with training in ethical theory will recognize the following as a common sense version of Kant's categorical imperative and the concept of universalizability. See also Tom L. Beauchamp, *Philosophical Ethics: An Introduction to Moral Philosophy,* 2nd ed. (New York: McGraw Hill, 1991).

69. John Rawls, *The Theory of Justice* (Cambridge, MA: Belknap Press, Harvard University Press, 1971).

70. Fisher and Ury, op. cit.

71. Bowie, op. cit.

72. Lax and Sebenius, op. cit.

73. Carr, op. cit.

74. Lax and Sebenius, op. cit.

75. Peter F. Drucker, "What Is Business Ethics?" *The Public Interest* 63 (1981), pp. 18–36.

76. Lax and Sebenius, op. cit.

CHAPTER 14

Dispute Resolution and Regulation

After reading this chapter, you should be able to

■ Understand the difference between interest disputes and rights disputes.

■ Identify trends of strike activity in the United States and understand the reasons for these trends.

■ Explain corporate campaigns and review factors that determine the effectiveness of such campaigns.

■ Review the role of mediators in resolving disputes.

■ Comprehend and discuss the emergency dispute procedures contained in the Taft-Hartley Act.

AN OVERVIEW OF TECHNIQUES APPLIED TO RIGHTS AND INTEREST DISPUTES

Interest disputes arise during contract negotiations when the parties cannot agree on the terms of a new contract. Rights disputes, on the other hand, occur during the term of an existing contract. Disputes over rights involve disagreements over interpretation of the contract. One can think of interest disputes as bargaining over the contract and rights disputes as bargaining under the contract. Using a governmental analogy, we can say that interest disputes involve the legislative aspects of labor-management relations, and rights disputes more closely resemble the activities of the judicial branches of government.

In this chapter we will review various techniques for resolving disputes and impasses. Some of these techniques prohibit strikes or at least delay them; others utilize third parties as mediators, fact finders, and arbitrators of interest disputes.

Historically, the strike has been the primary manifestation of the labor dispute. The historical pattern of strikes and their causes are discussed in some detail in the next few sections. Ultimately, in determining what public policy should be toward strikes, one must assess the cost of strikes to society, along with the alternatives and their implications for a free-market economy.

	Private Sector	*Public Sector*
Interest		
	Mediation	Mediation
	Strikes	Fact finding
		Arbitration
		Strikes (in some states for nonessential employees only)
Rights		
	Grievance procedure	Grievance procedure
	Arbitration as a final step	Arbitration as a final step

FIGURE 14.1 Interest and Rights Dispute Resolution Techniques for Impasses in the Public and Private Sectors

DIVERSITY IN IMPASSE RESOLUTION

The type of dispute resolution procedure used by parties in conflict depends on two factors: whether the dispute is an interest or a rights dispute and whether the employer is in the public or the private sector. Figure 14.1 presents the framework of a typical dispute resolution procedure for interest and rights disputes.

Grievance procedures are widely used to resolve most rights disputes. Disputes not resolved in the prearbitration stage of the grievance procedure are submitted to a third party for final and binding resolution. In the United States, a strike during the term of a contract is relatively uncommon. This fact is due primarily to the existence of grievance procedures and arbitration provisions in most U.S. labor agreements. Private-sector rights disputes will be more fully discussed in Chapter 15, on contract administration. Public-sector rights disputes, as well as other public-sector topics, will be treated separately in Chapter 16.

In the private sector, the strike is the last recourse for the resolution of interest disputes that the parties cannot settle either through direct negotiation or through mediation. (Although strikes are not always thought of as a dispute resolution technique, they do serve that particular purpose.)

In the public sector, there have emerged a wide array of interest dispute resolution techniques; these differ among states, and within states by jurisdictions and by occupational categories. Some of these techniques are reviewed in a later section. The primary focus of this chapter, however, is on interest disputes in the private sector, or on the northwest quadrant of Figure 14.1.

STRIKE ACTIVITY IN THE UNITED STATES

Strike activity can be measured on the following dimensions: the number of stoppages during a calendar year, the total number of workers involved, and the total number of idle days during the year. Table 14.1 presents historical data on strike activity in the United States from 1947 to 1996. The number of stoppages originating each year is reported in the first double column of the table. The second double column contains data on the numbers

TABLE 14.1 Work Stoppages Involving 1,000 Workers or More, 1947–96[1]

Period	Number of Stoppages		Workers Involved		Days Idle	
	Beginning in Period	In Effect During Period	Beginning in Period (thousands)	In Effect during Period (thousands)	Number (thousands)	Percent of Estimated Working Time[2]
1947	270	—	1,629	—	25,720	([3])
1948	245	—	1,435	—	26,127	0.22
1949	262	—	2,537	—	43,420	.38
1950	424	—	1,698	—	30,390	.26
1951	415	—	1,462	—	15,070	.12
1952	470	—	2,746	—	48,820	.38
1953	437	—	1,623	—	18,130	.14
1954	265	—	1,075	—	16,630	.13
1955	363	—	2,055	—	21,180	.16
1956	287	—	1,370	—	26,840	.20
1957	279	—	887	—	10,340	.07
1958	332	—	1,587	—	17,900	.13
1959	245	—	1,381	—	60,850	.43
1960	222	—	896	—	13,260	.09
1961	195	—	1,031	—	10,140	.07
1962	211	—	793	—	11,760	.08
1963	181	—	512	—	10,020	.07
1964	246	—	1,183	—	16,220	.11
1965	268	—	999	—	15,140	.10
1966	321	—	1,300	—	16,000	.10
1967	381	—	2,192	—	31,320	.18
1968	392	—	1,855	—	35,367	.20
1969	412	—	1,576	—	29,397	.16
1970	381	—	2,468	—	52,761	.29
1971	298	—	2,516	—	35,538	.19
1972	250	—	975	—	16,764	.09
1973	317	—	1,400	—	16,260	.08
1974	424	—	1,796	—	31,809	.16
1975	235	—	965	—	17,563	.09
1976	231	—	1,519	—	23,962	.12
1977	298	—	1,212	—	21,258	.10
1978	219	—	1,006	—	23,774	.11
1979	235	—	1,021	—	20,409	.09
1980	187	—	795	—	20,844	.09
1981	145	—	729	—	16,908	.07
1982	96	—	656	—	9,061	.04
1983	81	—	909	—	17,461	.08
1984	62	—	376	—	8,499	.04
1985	54	—	324	—	7,079	.03

TABLE 14.1 *(cont.)*

Period	Number of Stoppages		Workers Involved		Days Idle	
	Beginning in Period	*In Effect During Period*	*Beginning in Period (thousands)*	*In Effect during Period (thousands)*	*Number (thousands)*	*Percent of Estimated Working Time[2]*
1986	69	—	533	—	11,861	.05
1987	46	—	174	—	4,481	.02
1988	40	—	118	—	4,381	.02
1989	51	—	452	—	16,996	.07
1990	44	—	185	—	5,926	.02
1991	40	—	392	—	4,584	.02
1992	35	—	364	—	3,989	.01
1993	35	—	182	—	3,981	.01
1994	45	—	322	—	5,021	.02
1995	35	—	192	—	5,771	.02
1996[p] Through February	6	7	43.4	45.9	839.6	.01

[1]The numbers of stoppages and workers related to stoppages that began in the year. Days of idleness include all stoppages in effect. Workers are counted more than once if they are involved in more than one stoppage during the year.

[2]Agricultural government employees are included in the total employed and total working time; private households, forestry, and fishery employees are excluded.

[3]Data not available.

p = preliminary.

Source: Compensation and Working Conditions (CWC), U.S. Department of Labor, Bureau of Labor Statistics, Washington, DC (February-March 1996), p. 151.

of workers involved in stoppages and gives a better perspective on year-to-year variation in stoppage activity. We must use caution in interpreting statistical stoppage data. For example, column 1 of Table 14.1 indicates that there were more strikes in 1990 than in 1992, but the impact of the stoppage activity may have been greater in 1992 because more workers were on strike in 1992 than in 1990.

Another measure of strike activity is the propensity to strike and its relationship to the number of negotiations taking place during any particular period. Such totals can be derived from statistics contained in Table 14.1 and from contract expiration notices received by the Federal Mediation and Conciliation Service (FMCS). The National Labor Relations Act requires that parties to a contract notify the FMCS 30 days prior to the contract's expiration. Unions have authorized strikes in about two to three percent of the cases for which notice was submitted to the FMCS.[1]

Major Work Stoppages in 1995

All measures of work stoppage activity were down in 1995, according to the U.S. Department of Labor's Bureau of Labor Statistics.[2] Most of these measures had been at record lows in 1995. Thirty-one major stoppages began during 1995, idling 192,000 workers and resulting in about 5.8 million days of idleness (about 2 out of every 10,000 available work days). Comparable figures for 1994 were 45 stoppages, 322,000 workers, and 5.0 million days of idleness (see Table 14.1 and Figures 14.2–4). The series of reports yielding these figures, which dates back to 1947, covers strikes and lockouts involving 1,000 workers or more and lasting at least one shift. The term *major work stoppage* includes worker-initiated strikes, as well as lockouts of workers by their employers, involving 1,000 workers or more. The bureau does not attempt to distinguish between strikes and lockouts in its statistics.

FIGURE 14.2 Work Stoppages Involving 1,000 Workers or More, 1947–95

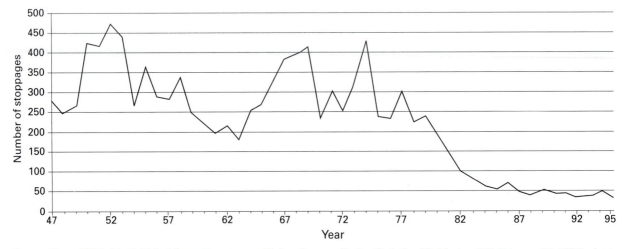

Source: News, USDL 96–59, United States Department of Labor, Bureau of Labor Statistics, Washington, DC (February 21, 1996); chart created from information in data tables.

FIGURE 14.3 Workers Involved in Major Work Stoppages, 1947–95

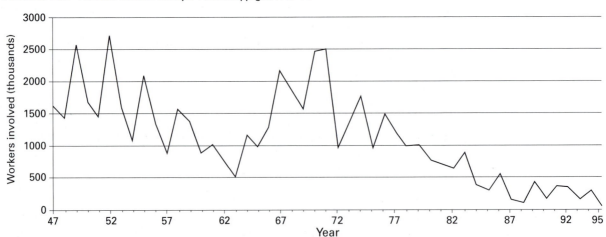

Source: News, USDL 96–59, United States Department of Labor, Bureau of Labor Statistics, Washington, DC (February 21, 1996); chart created from information in data tables.

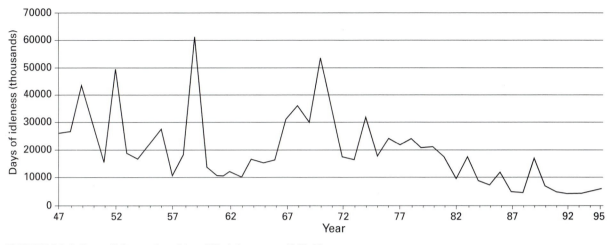

FIGURE 14.4 Days of Idleness from Major Work Stoppages, 1947–95

Source: News, USDL 96–59, United States Department of Labor, Bureau of Labor Statistics, Washington, DC (February 21, 1996); chart created from information in data tables.

EXPLANATORY MODELS OF STRIKE ACTIVITY

Industrial relations scholars have expended significant research effort toward understanding why and when strikes occur. Strike trends within the United States have been related primarily to fluctuations in the business cycle as represented by unemployment and inflation rates. Studies of strike activity at the aggregate level indicate that strike activity increases during periods of low unemployment and high inflation.[3] At such times, it is harder for employers to find replacement workers and easier for strikers to find temporary employment during a work stoppage. When strikes occur during high unemployment, they are likely to last longer.[4] During such periods, employers tend to ask for union concessions (give-backs from unions of previously granted wage increases, benefits, work rules, or other contract terms). Unmet demands for concessions can contribute to strike actions.[5]

Wage and price increases in the economy build up pressures for higher wages in each bargaining unit. An inflationary environment is usually accompanied by unanswered wage expectations, which can be conducive to strike activity. The size of the labor movement and the prevailing political attitudes toward unionism can also affect the level of aggregate strike activity in the economy.[6]

Studies of strikes reveal certain causal factors. Strikes take place in highly unionized regions of the country. Strikes are more likely in large bargaining units including high proportions of males. Strikes are less likely where bargaining unit wages have kept up with inflation. Additionally, strike activity correlates positively with more labor-intensive industries and with declines in product market demand.[7] Research also seems to indicate that strikes in previous contract rounds decrease the probability of strikes in subsequent negotiations.[8] Individual willingness to strike for higher pay has been found to correlate positively with youth, minority status, and the absence of expected financial hardship incurred by striking.[9] Another interesting relationship is between strikes over contract rights and productivity. The frequency of strikes during the terms of contracts is positively related to periods of rapid increase in productivity. On the other hand, such strikes cause reduced rates of productivity growth.[10]

The foregoing relationships suggest the need for development of a conceptual framework that would provide us with selective conflict resolution procedures and remedies, one that could target specific situations where the propensity to strike is higher.

We must conclude that more research is required to give us a better understanding of the reasons for strikes. It is possible that strikes are idiosyncratic—that is, that they occur where negotiations are beset by structural difficulties or by antagonistic negotiators. Current industrial relations theory does not provide us with the necessary tools for predicting accurately whether a strike would ensue in any given set of negotiations.

Work stoppages are undoubtedly also influenced by employers' ability to hire temporary or permanent strike replacements.

CORPORATE CAMPAIGNS: STRIKE SUBSTITUTES AND SUPPLEMENTS

There has been a significant decrease in strike activity during the last 15 years. One reason for the decline seems to be the growing ineffectiveness of strikes. In the 1980s, more firms continued to operate during strikes; they recruited workers who were willing to cross picket lines, and they were able to sell their products to customers who did not object to anti-union activities by employers.

Because the strike as a source of union power had lost its potency, the labor movement began searching for new methods for regaining power. One such method has been the union corporate campaign. Although it is subject to varying definitions, the corporate campaign generally consists of the use of nontraditional tactics to pressure management. Examples of such tactics include appealing for help from outside parties having interests in the employer's organization, such as creditors, stockholders, interlocking directors, and the public; running sophisticated public relations campaigns; building coalitions with other unions and nonlabor groups; conducting boycotts; lobbying legislative and regulatory bodies; employing nonstrike in-plant actions, such as lunch-hour picketing; and doing anything else that will put pressure on corporate management.[11]

One of the most notorious labor disputes in modern labor history was between the Amalgamated Clothing and Textile Workers Union (ACTWU) and the J. P. Stevens Company. The ultimate successful resolution, from the union's point of view, of this long-standing dispute was achieved through a corporate campaign.

A study of 28 corporate campaigns examined their use in three types of situations: as a complement to an organizing drive, as a supplement to the traditional strike, and as a strike substitute in a bargaining dispute. The authors of the study concluded that corporate campaigns are most successful from the union's perspective when they are used to complement organizing drives. Unions had limited success in strike substitute situations, and failures occurred when corporate campaigns were used to supplement strikes.[12]

IMPASSE RESOLUTION

In addressing the issue of impasse resolution, it is necessary to consider the causes of the impasse. A particularly difficult problem occurs when one of the parties does not want a settlement: A management, for example, might want to break the union. Such a management might conclude that even a settlement quite favorable to the employer could nevertheless add credibility to the union presence. In that case, no concession from the union would be accepted by management. A management might also hope that protracted tension would split the union membership, undermine its leaders, or empty its treasury. There is also the possibility, particularly in a family-owned company, that the owners would rather go out of business than grant some demand that the union considers basic. On the other side, the union might want to avoid settlement until a favorable pattern is set elsewhere, or it might use a strike to publicize its position on a particular issue.

Either side might use toughness to "punish" the opponent for some past negotiating behavior or to demonstrate for the next negotiations or to its own constituents that it is not a "pushover." Impasse resolution techniques are not too effective when a settlement is not desired by both parties.

The term *impasse* suggests that the parties have not been able to reach an agreement. In some situations, negotiators may conclude that an impasse has been reached when, in reality, there is still room for further negotiation. In such cases, additional exploration of options may prove productive. In particular, a candid disclosure by the parties of their real goals and interests may reveal alternatives that were not considered previously.

To start with the improbable, if a party's real objective is to display its toughness, it can hardly open an exploratory discussion with "Our real goal is to impress you with how tough we are. Can you suggest any better ways to do this?" By contrast, if a union openly admits in a post-impasse discussion that its real objective is to break some government policy, it is possible that management also has gripes about "government interference" and that together they could have greater impact by joining forces. Or perhaps joint discussion might reveal that severance pay could better achieve a kind of worker security that the union has sought to implement through stricter seniority.

The Nonparticipative Observer

Sometimes it helps a discussion merely to have an outside observer present. Much as when husband and wife or parent and child discuss a disagreement, expressions of anger and departures from logic are tempered because their unproductiveness would be obvious to a disinterested observer.

A third party can sometimes be tactically useful merely by encouraging both sides' negotiators to talk. For example, suppose negotiations have broken off with each saying, "We have nothing further to offer. If and when you are ready to make concessions, let us know." Following such a break, any move by either party to reopen negotiations might be construed by the other as a sign of weakness. Each side might nevertheless respond to a third-party inquiry by saying, "If the other side is willing to talk, we are too, provided it is clear that we did not initiate the new talks."

A somewhat more active third-party role is that of messenger. Diplomatic relations provide some parallels. A conspicuous one is the way the governments of Great Britain and the Irish Republican Army (IRA) for years would not talk directly. But they did convey messages (feelers) through various unofficial channels. In the 1930s, many managements expressed willingness to talk to their own employees but not to "an organized union," typically referred to as "outside agitators." Although that particular relationship now is seen less often, there are still occasions when parties in conflict feel that they save face by talking through a third party. The messenger can be particularly useful in cases where the responsible leaders are willing to talk but their constituents cannot tolerate direct contact with the "hated enemy." Because the main reasons for not talking directly are those of appearance, the messenger function is mostly tactical.

The Active Mediator

Full-fledged mediation is participation of a third party in the negotiation process, but with the final decision still resting with the principals. The mediator's role can be tactical, strategic, or both. Although the concepts of tactics and strategy are not always clear in the minds of participants, each has its own quite different logic. Hence, they are discussed separately.

The traditional use of bargaining tactics requires one to try to learn the other side's resistance point while hiding one's own. Mediators can be very effective when they identify the resistance points of both sides. For example, if the resistance points overlap (positive contract zone), the mediator's task is only to help the parties find a solution within that range. Thus, the mediator's job is one of assisting communications and perhaps offering alternatives. To discover resistance points, the mediator must have the almost absolute trust of both sides. Not only must they trust him or her to be discreet about what they say and to avoid even subtle hints about it, each side must also trust the mediator not to use such confidences to its disadvantage. To illustrate the many possible complications, let us assume that the mediator proposes terms of a settlement on the basis of superior knowledge gained from the parties, that the terms proposed lie somewhere close to the midpoint of the perceived overlap, and that the proposal has a high probability of being accepted. In these circumstances, a party may have as much to gain by understating its resistance point to the mediator as by understating it to the opponent. Hence, before either side will reveal its true position, it must also have sufficient confidence in the mediator to believe that he or she will not be misled by the other party. Negotiators for either side can destroy their own reputations and hurt their constituents if confidence in a mediator is misplaced. Experienced negotiators are likely to be wary of honestly disclosing information to a third party. Hence, obtaining tactical information is a difficult assignment for mediators.

The strategic role of mediation is less demanding, though it requires particular skills. It does not necessarily require high trust from the negotiating parties, as the mediator does not need confidential information from them to perform the strategic function of altering resistance points. The mediator may "just happen to mention" to the union the case of a firm that had to lay off 20 percent of its work force following a wage settlement that made it noncompetitive. The mediator may also tell management about the employer who lost most of his business during a long strike because his customers switched suppliers. In such instances, the parties must trust that the mediator's stories are not invented for the occasion. But doing so involves a lesser confidence than does telling the mediator one's true resistance point. In any case, the mediator's hints of impending doom may be independently verifiable by the parties. Thus, for the mediator to determine ways to "scare" the negotiators is perhaps a matter more of ingenuity than of trust.

The strategic function is not only easier than the tactical, it is also less risky. Although a mediator may call attention to a certain factor that will change a resistance point, that change remains a voluntary act of the party. Hence, a mediator does not incur "blame" as he or she would by misjudging a position on the basis of confidential statements and then making misguided proposals based on that misjudgment. Also, in a pure strategic function, a mediator is not in a position to violate a confidence that he or she did not receive.

The Federal Mediation and Conciliation Service (FMCS)

Historically, the Federal Mediation and Conciliation Service (FMCS)[13] has provided mediation services to parties in the private, federal, and nonfederal public sectors. The FMCS was established as an independent agency in 1947 under the Taft-Hartley Act. Sections 201(b) and 203 of the act state that governmental facilities for mediation and conciliation should be made available to the parties "in order to prevent or minimize interruptions of the free flow of commerce growing out of labor disputes, to assist parties to labor disputes, [and] . . . to settle such disputes through conciliation and mediation."[14]

The FMCS has a strong commitment to a viable collective bargaining system, which it considers "as a foundation for society's well-being and economic growth."[15] The following mission statement summarizes the role of the FMCS in addressing various aspects of labor-management relations:

MISSION

- Promoting the development of sound and stable labor-management relationships,
- Preventing or minimizing work stoppages by assisting labor and management to settle their disputes through mediation,
- Advocating collective bargaining, mediation and voluntary arbitration as the preferred process for settling issues between employers and representatives of employees,
- Developing the art, science and practice of conflict resolution,
- And fostering the establishment and maintenance of constructive joint processes to improve labor-management relationships, employment security and organizational effectiveness.[16]

In the last 10 years, major changes have been taking place in labor-management relations. Competitive factors have affected the conduct of collective bargaining. In view of the many new developments in the labor relations arena, the director of the FMCS announced the formation of a task force on December 2, 1993. Its purpose was to prepare the agency for the future. Portions of the executive summary of the task force report are included in Appendix A to this chapter.

Fact Finding

Fact finding is a process in which an outsider (or a panel of outsiders) assists the parties in achieving an agreement, but with the settlement itself still subject to voluntary and mutual approval by the parties. Fact finding is frequently utilized in the public sector. (This topic is covered further in Chapter 16, on public-sector collective bargaining.) In some cases, fact finding is requested by the parties in other situations; when public welfare or the public sector is affected, the parties are legally required to utilize this process. Fact finding, referred to as board of inquiry, under section 206 of the Labor Management Relations Act (Taft-Hartley) may be mandated in cases of national emergencies, when "a threatened or actual strike or lockout" affects an "entire industry or a substantial part thereof."[17] A typical fact-finding report traces the background of a particular dispute, identifies the issues, and states the positions of both parties on each issue, possibly summarizing the arguments with which they support their positions. Depending on their charge, the fact finders may or may not recommend terms of settlement, and they may or may not report on all issues.

The fact-finding procedure has several goals. First, if the process is tied to mandatory postponement of a strike until fact finding is completed, there is always the possibility that a strike postponed may be a strike avoided. Second, if the "facts" are made public and reveal unreasonable demands, public opinion may encourage the parties to revise their positions; this in turn may increase the likelihood of a settlement. Third, fact finding may uncover some options that the parties had not previously thought of and that would make it easier for them to settle. Fourth, fact finding may justify a concession for which a union or a management negotiator could not obtain prior approval. Finally, a fact-finding report could serve as a necessary face-saving device for negotiators and help them move away from particular bargaining positions without losing credibility.

Arbitration

Let us now look at some circumstances in which contract arbitration might be feasible. Assume that two parties have gone through a long sequence of negotiations and possibly a strike, mediation, and so on; the parties have failed to reach agreement; and neither party has contemplated arbitration as a possible solution. If arbitration is then suggested "out of the blue," if it is reasonable to assume that an arbitrator would not award anything surpassing the demands and offers already on the record, and if neither party feels that it would be disastrous to be awarded what the other had already offered, arbitration might be a feasible solution. (Under these conditions, it is also highly probable that the parties would reach a settlement on their own!)

By contrast, however, if the parties anticipate from early in negotiations that arbitration will be the last step, their behavior will change from the outset. The urge to understate one's resistance point to the arbitrator is virtually the same as the urge to understate it to the opponent. And whereas an arbitrator in a grievance dispute over rights may find that the "right answer" clearly falls on one side or the other, where there is no law or contract to constrain the arbitrator's judgment, there is a strong tendency to split the difference. Because any prearbitration concession by one party shifts the midpoint of the (negative) overlap in favor of the other party, and the "last offers" of the parties made before the arbitrator will probably be split, an expectation of arbitration makes both parties unwilling to make preliminary concessions. This attitude reduces the incentive for either party to make a negotiating concession. This outcome is referred to as the chilling effect of arbitration on negotiations. There is also a feeling, not wholly unfounded, that when many minor issues come to arbitrators, they tend to award approximately half to each party. Instead of settling minor issues, or "washing them out" of negotiations at an early stage, parties headed for interest arbitration tend to refuse to settle even issues on which their positions and their interests are weak, in the hope that for every such issue the arbitrator denies them, he or she will grant them another to compensate. For both reasons, the anticipation of arbitration can weaken the process of free bargaining.

Furthermore, once a new contract case is assigned to an arbitrator, both parties lose all control over the outcome. And whereas in grievance arbitration, the nature of each case limits the amount of damage that can be done by an arbitrator's decision, the arbitrator's ability to inflict costs on the parties is much greater in interest arbitration. Though one may hope that he or she would not abuse it, the arbitrator has the power to bankrupt the company or disrupt the union. For all these reasons, most private-sector unions and managements in the United States persistently avoid interest arbitration and adamantly oppose its imposition by law. It is sometimes suggested that parties could place upper and lower limits on an arbitrator's award and thereby make arbitration more acceptable. But by the time the parties could agree on those limits, they could probably also agree on a settlement. Besides, contract negotiations often involve issues for which "limits" in that sense have no clear meaning, as in a dispute between plant-wide and departmental seniority.

In some interest arbitration, the decision is made by majority vote of a tripartite board rather than by one or more neutral arbitrators. Such a board includes one or more neutrals and one or more representatives of union and management. With their own representatives helping to formulate the final judgment, the negotiating parties remain informed of progress and of the direction of the neutral arbitrator's sentiment. The negotiation process actually continues into the arbitration decision, and a representative of one party may make concessions at that stage in the hope of influencing the neutral's decision. The neutral arbitrator may also do some negotiating because he or she must elicit a signature from either the union or the management member(s) of the board before the decision is final. If they care to use it, neutral arbitrators have unusually persuasive mediative powers because the parties know they have the reserve power to make the final decision. Despite these mitigating conditions, interest arbitration still delegates more power to outsiders than the parties are usually willing to allow.

A relatively recent addition to public-sector dispute resolution procedures is final-offer arbitration, which is a modification of conventional interest arbitration. This approach is designed to reduce the chilling effect of arbitration on negotiations and is intended to give the parties an incentive to make concessions. Although, in this procedure, arbitrators are given authority to make final and binding awards, their discretion is limited to choosing either the union's or the company's final offer. The expectation is that each party will be motivated to make concessions in the fear that if it holds out for unreasonable terms, the arbitrator will select the more sensible offer. A variant of final-offer arbitration gives the arbitrator the option of selecting the recommendations of a fact finder, if one is appointed to the dispute. Final-offer arbitration can be based on the entire package of each side's proposals, or it can permit the arbitrator to make decisions on an issue-by-issue basis.

Final-offer arbitration has been used in some states in public-sector negotiations, especially in those affecting employees in public-safety jobs such as police and firefighters. As might be anticipated, the success of the process depends much on the parties and the circumstances. A remaining question is whether the parties should be permitted to continue to modify their "final offers" until the arbitrator has made the award, or is close to making it, as contrasted to binding each party to the offer it made at some relatively early stage.[18] Some experts have concluded that arbitration, with all its problems, has been a useful substitute for the strike in public-sector collective bargaining. The private sector, with some exceptions, has refrained from using it as a method for impasse resolution.

ALTERNATIVE IMPASSE RESOLUTION METHODS

Labor-management conflict can be resolved through various dispute resolution systems. Some systems are based on power, some on rights, and some on interests and reconciliation. The strike is an example of a power system at work. Arbitration is a system based on rights. The first two systems are expensive and time-consuming. In the last 10 years, a new system has emerged that stresses reconciliation and the interests of each side; the approach is referred to as win-win or mutual gains-bargaining (MGB).

The MGB process was reviewed at some length in Chapter 9, on the negotiation process. The MGB approach attempts to reconcile the interests of the parties in terms of their needs, desires, concerns, and fears.[19] As compared with traditional approaches, under MGB, disputes are resolved with "lower transaction costs, greater satisfaction with outcomes, less strain on the relationship, and less recurrence of disputes."[20] In contrast to other dispute resolution methods, which focus on the parties' positions, this process emphasizes interests, mutual gains, and win-win strategies.

Utilizing the mutual gains approach changes the negotiation process, affects the resolution of negotiation impasses, and introduces the concept of interest mediation. Such mediation can help the parties in applying the win-win approach to negotiations. Figure 14.5 illustrates the differences between traditional and interest mediation. Traditional mediators identify and challenge positions and concentrate on settlements and closures. In interest mediation, the focus is on interests and mutual gains and not on positions. Also, the emphasis is on more lasting solutions.[21]

Following is an example of mutual gains bargaining. During a particular negotia-

Traditional Mediation	Interest Mediation
Nurture and follow well-established rituals	Advocate and orchestrate a new process
Identify positions, and challenge them	Focus on interests, not positions
Mysterious, closed, vague about process	Open and direct about process
Backward-looking	Future-looking
Content expert	Process expert
Control damage	Manage change
Focus on downside risks	Emphasize potential for mutual gain
Leverage deadlines to force movement on important issues	Allocate time in proportion to importance of issues
Focus on settlement, quick fix, and closure	Focus on lasting solutions
Allocation of wealth	Creation and allocation of wealth

FIGURE 14.5 Contrast of the Two Approaches to Mediation

Source: John Stepp and Jerome Barett. "New Theories on Negotiations and the Changing Role of Mediation" in *Collective Bargaining Negotiations and Contracts.* Reprinted with permission from *Collective Bargaining Negotiations and Contracts.* Table A, p. 14:69. Published by The Bureau of National Affairs, Inc. (800-372-1033).

tion, the union may demand that certain machines be tended by two people at all times. Management counters that the union demand would lead to overstaffing and featherbedding, would make the firm noncompetitive, and may force it out of business. Resolving such a dispute through a strike would not benefit either side. In such a case, interest mediation, with the mediator acting as a facilitator, may help both parties. An examination of each side's interests may reveal new ways for each party to improve its position and still be satisfied with the outcome. The union leaders may be concerned about staff reductions, increased workloads, layoffs, and difficulties for laid-off members of finding work elsewhere. Management's concerns may be to stay competitive, to retain its managerial prerogative to cut unit labor costs, and to have the necessary funds for new capital investment.

Focusing on these interests rather than on the parties' positions opens the door for mutual gains and for arriving at creative solutions. Jointly, the parties may develop new options. Possibly, the change in staffing could be accomplished over time, perhaps through attrition. Work guarantees, job retraining, or recall rights could be given to any potentially displaced worker. Job-sharing possibilities could be explored. Levels of compensation for employees with increased workloads could be adjusted.

In this example, the mutual gains bargaining approach may help the parties avoid an impasse. The outcome could be a mutually acceptable solution instead of a potentially costly confrontation. Initially, to resolve such an impasse, the parties may need the assistance of a facilitator or an interest mediator. Eventually, after both sides acquire sufficient understanding of and experience with the win-win process, outside facilitators may be of less significance for the resolution of such disputes.

THE PUBLIC INTEREST IN IMPASSE

If PDQ VCR Repair on East 72nd Street is struck for six months, the president, the governor, and the mayor will not lose sleep over it. The only parties affected are the firm's management and employees, some customers whose VCRs go unrepaired, and perhaps some creditors of employees or management. But if a strike of truckers, steelworkers, or firefighters causes grocery shelves to go bare, factories to shut down, or houses to burn, the concern is intense. The general logic of a strike is that it puts pressure on the parties until concessions settle the strike. But sometimes the pressure on others is much greater than on the parties to the dispute. Impasse then ceases to be a matter of merely private concern and induces government to act. The problem is that of public emergency strikes; how to prevent them or soften their impact is a matter of serious concern.

Section 8(d) of the Wagner Act, as amended by the Taft-Hartley Act, requires a 60-day written notice to the other party by either party intending to terminate a contract when it expires. The parties must also be willing to meet with each other and confer about negotiating a new contract. The Federal Mediation and Conciliation Service (FMCS) must also be notified within 30 days of the notice to the other party. Because of the essential nature of health care, hospitals and their unions must give each other 90 instead of 60 days' notice and the FMCS 60 instead of 30 days' notice. In this manner, the FMCS is forewarned of a possible approaching dispute that might involve the public welfare—though it is unlikely that any major contract termination would fail to attract advance notice in the media or from the Department of Labor. It also seems unlikely that the parties' notice to each other would tell them anything they did not already know.

Whether a particular strike causes an "emergency" is a matter of both intensity and scope. As to intensity, a strike in a single small hospital is an emergency if only a few lives are endangered or in a fire department if a single dwelling burns for lack of firefighters. By contrast, if 50 million people cannot work for several days for lack of coal, steel, transportation, or power, the loss is not intense at the same level because few lives will be significantly changed in consequence. But the overall effect may be considered an emergency because the total loss runs to billions of dollars and public indignation is high. For many years, it was felt that strikes in private employment were tolerable but that strikes by public employees were not. But in the last three decades, the severity of impact has been more the center of focus: It is realized that public park maintenance employees might strike for weeks with little consequence, whereas private employees of utility, power, or transportation facilities might create an emergency within hours. Moreover, the inconvenience to the public from a transit strike is the same whether the lines are privately or publicly owned; much the same is true for trash collection. The key question in emergency strikes is this: How can we get agreement in a case where the pressure on those who are not parties to the dispute becomes unacceptable before the pressure induces settlement by the parties themselves?

It is not difficult to identify possible alternative ways to handle such a situation. The question is whether they will work. The most obvious alternative is to prohibit strikes in public emergency situations and substitute arbitrated settlements. A modified version of that alternative is to postpone the strike in the hope that a settlement will be reached in the meantime. Enforced mediation might help. Changing the payoffs to the parties through fines, imprisonment, cancellation of government contracts, adverse publicity, tax incentives, or other means could also help. So could softening the effects of the strike (removing the emergency), as by having the parties meet the real emergency needs of the public while nevertheless continuing the pressure on each other. For example, power or fuel could be supplied to hospitals while being cut off elsewhere, or critical military supplies could be hauled while trucks were otherwise stopped. In transit, the "no-strike strike" has been used occasionally. Buses and trains continue to run, but no wages are paid and no fares are collected. However, members of the riding public tend to "tip" the operators the equivalent of fares, in which case the operators get much enlarged incomes. Meanwhile, the employer receives no income while continuing to pay the costs of fuel and upkeep. In this situation, the pressure on the parties is hardly even, and management objects.

Can Strikes Be Prohibited?

Let us look at the other alternatives. Prohibiting strikes is easy to talk about but not to do. The basic logic of the situation is intractable, particularly in private employment. Assuming that the old contract has expired, to prohibit a strike is to require employees to work against their will, at a wage they have not agreed to, for the profit of their private employer. Employers as well as workers may be wary of a precedent in which government requires a seller to deliver something of value for a price he or she considers unacceptable. To have free collective bargaining, the parties must be able to resort to their economic weapons in support of their positions.[22]

The problem of enforcement is even more difficult. The law could state that an employer may discharge any striker who fails to come to work. But employers are already free to get rid of "economic strikers" if they can find permanent replacements. In any case, the problem is to get workers into the plant, not out of it, and if penalties are placed on strikers, they may individually and collectively say, "We quit." They are then no longer "strikers," and neither the government nor the employer has any claim on their services unless we accept something close to slavery. Even without anyone's quitting, penalties on a union or its officers may induce the leadership to call off the strike. An order from the union to go back to work, however, may simply be ignored by the workers. A final difficulty is that, even after the parties agree on all substantive issues, the union must insist as a condition of terminating the strike that all strikers be reinstated with full seniority. These conditions are not entirely the same for government employees as for private ones (see Chapter 16, on public-sector collective bargaining), but even in the public sector the waiving of penalties against illegal strikers may be crucial to final settlement. This statement of underlying logic is also a reasonably accurate summary of actual experience in numerous cases, both public and private, over many decades.

This is not to say that attempts to prohibit strikes will always be ineffective. Some employees and unions are not as militant or self-confident as others, and some may harbor internal or external weaknesses that prevent them from ignoring a legal prohibition. Nevertheless, it seems unwise to incorporate into public policy an assumption that a prohibition of strikes can be enforced, except in unusual circumstances. And as the late George Taylor used to put it, the government should avoid revealing itself to be impotent. All that can be accomplished by an unenforceable prohibition is confusion, frustration, and anger on all sides.

We noted earlier that although the strike is typically seen as a union weapon, it is actually mutual. It is not only a union pressure on management, but also a management pressure on the union and the employees. Hence, to prohibit strikes not only deprives the union of a weapon; it also prohibits management from forcing some sobering second thoughts on the union, as by making it face the consequences to itself of a possible strike. Given the role of the strike, it is hardly an exaggeration to say that to prohibit strikes (if it could be done successfully) would be to destroy the parties' main motive for concession, and hence to destroy bargaining itself. As the experiences of Australia and New Zealand since about 1900 demonstrate, prohibition of strikes and substitution of interest arbitration ends by increasing the number of strikes and by making government the chief determinant of wages.

Except during World War II, when the War Labor Board made binding decisions, we have not had compulsory interest arbitration imposed by the federal government on the private sector in the United States. Even that exception was semivoluntary in a broad sense because representatives of organized labor and of management had agreed that there should be no strikes or lockouts for the war's duration and that both sides would voluntarily accept the decisions of the War Labor Board. And even that arrangement, coupled with the fact that any strike at all seemed unpatriotically to impede the war effort, by no means eliminated strikes, though it clearly reduced them.

The Compulsory Waiting Period

Compulsory postponement of strikes, in the hope of achieving settlement during the waiting period, is partly similar to and partly different from a flat prohibition. The similarity is that even a temporary prohibition is no more enforceable than a permanent one if the employees are firmly resolved to strike. The difference is that the resolve of the parties to strike immediately is likely to be weakened because the parties themselves retain full control of the ultimate outcome and can still put their differences to a test of economic strength after the waiting period if they so desire. The main difficulties are two. One is that circumstances may change during the waiting period in ways that substantially shift bargaining power. If so, the side disadvantaged by the shift quite sensibly sees the mandated postponement as unfair. Which way power shifts depends on the circumstances, and postponement presumably contains no inherent bias in itself. True, employers in some industries might be able to strengthen their positions by accumulating inventory during the waiting period, but workers may be able to use that time to augment their personal savings accounts.

Imposition of a compulsory waiting period in emergency situations, despite its problems, is the course our society has taken. The Taft-Hartley Act incorporates provisions for the handling of national emergency labor disputes (see Sections 206–209). Action under the law is initiated by the president when "a threatened or actual strike or lockout affecting an entire industry or a substantial part thereof . . . will, if permitted to occur or to continue, imperil the national health or safety."[23] Note that public inconvenience and economic loss are not mentioned, nor is intensity of the loss, or even health and safety, if the dispute is local. The law provides no further criteria, making it unclear when it is appropriate for the president to invoke the procedures. For example, is a near-total shutdown of basic steel an emergency, or a threatened emergency, at the moment a strike starts? Or does it become an emergency only after inventories are depleted? What is the "national health or safety," and when is it "imperiled"?

These matters must be decided as each case arises. When the president thinks an actual or potential strike merits attention, he appoints a board of inquiry, to report back at a predetermined time with a statement of the facts but without recommendation. If the president then thinks the action justified, he asks the attorney general to petition a district court to enjoin the strike or lockout. Under Section 209 of the law, it is "the duty of the parties . . . to make every effort to adjust and settle their differences."[24] The Federal Mediation and Conciliation Service is to assist the parties, but neither party is obligated to accept any recommendations. After 60 days the board reconvenes, reporting to the president the current status of negotiations and the positions of the parties. The employer's last offer is also to be reported, and within 15 days the National Labor Relations Board is to take a secret ballot on that offer among the affected employees. The union's last offer is not similarly reported, nor are the affected employers (if there are multiple ones) polled on that offer. After the results of the ballot are reported, the injunction is discharged, and the board of inquiry reports the status of the dispute to Congress, along with possible recommendations. In total, the injunction may run for no more than 80 days.

The Railway Labor Act also stipulates emergency procedures that involve mandatory mediation and a compulsory waiting period in a case where a strike interrupts "interstate commerce to such a degree as to deprive any section of the country of essential transportation."[25] An emergency board appointed by the president has 30 days to report on the threatened or actual stoppage. For those 30 days and an additional 30 after the report is filed, the status quo must be maintained; thus, any strike, lockout, or change in contractual provisions is prohibited. In contrast to the Taft-Hartley procedures, these boards can and do make recommendations for settlement.

Evaluation of the Emergency Procedures

The origin of the Taft-Hartley emergency procedures can be directly traced to the post–World War II strike wave.[26] Use of these procedures has decreased dramatically over time. The act has been invoked 34 times (by the calling of a board of inquiry): ten times by President Truman, seven by Eisenhower, six by Kennedy, five by Johnson, five by Nixon, and once by Carter.[27] The single case under President Carter concerned the extraordinarily long 110-day strike in coal, for which a temporary restraining order was issued. As anticipated, the miners did not return to work. When a full injunction was sought, the court denied it on the ground that the national health or safety was not involved.

There are various reasons why the use of the national emergency dispute procedures has declined so dramatically in the last 20 years. Product market competition has increased through internationalization, and domestic non-union-produced goods provide alternative sources of supply for struck operations. There has been a decrease in industry-wide and multiemployer bargaining. More employers are willing to use strike breakers to operate during strikes.[28] Also, there has been significant decline in the level of unionization in various sectors of the economy.

Full evaluation of exisiting law governing emergency strikes would require information that is essentially not knowable, such as how long a given strike would have lasted if no injunction had been issued or whether the likelihood of the initial strike was increased or decreased because the parties expected government intervention.

Some biases in the current emergency procedures may be noted. One is that injunction is traditionally conceived as directed against the union, plant seizure being the parallel "weapon" against employers. The law is one-sided in providing for injunctions against strikes but not for seizure in case of lockout. Whether these biases "in principle" have disadvantaged unions or employers in the terms of eventual settlements is probably not knowable.

If there is any one reasonably standard observation about impasse settlement machinery, it is that once the parties become familiar with it, they can use it to prosecute, postpone, or settle their dispute, depending on their inclination. Almost any reasonable machinery will probably work fairly well if the parties feel generally obligated to subordinate their own interests to the public good. All things considered, perhaps it is surprising that we have so few emergencies, not that we have so many.

SUMMARY

This chapter focused on the aspect of labor-management relations that is most visible to the public—various types of interest disputes and strikes. We examined the pattern of strike activity over time and discussed various explanations of the reasons for strikes. We reviewed a set of new tactics, including corporate campaigns, being used by organized labor to supplement or replace the strike. We observed that recent years have seen a downward trend in strike activity; there was however, an increase in strikes in 1994. Work stoppage data should be monitored to determine whether declining strike activity may lead to an increase in other forms of conflict.

The chapter also evaluated various impasse procedures. We noted that traditional methods of mediation, fact finding, and arbitration can assist parties in resolving impasses.

Some attention was also focused on mutual gains bargaining or win-win negotiations as a method for reconciling the parties' interests and assisting them in averting impasses.

The impact of strikes on the public and what can be done about it was the final topic of this chapter. Although strike prohibitions may sound like an attractive solution, in the private sector they are not workable. Strikes are costly to the parties and to the general public. It is in everyone's interest to reduce strikes. We should note, however, that there is a tendency to overstate strike costs in the news media. Thus, the public at times may be getting a distorted picture of the costs of strike activity.

Notes

1. Thomas A. Kochan and Harry C. Katz, *Collective Bargaining and Industrial Relations,* 2nd ed. (Homewood, IL: Richard D. Irwin, 1988), p. 242.

2. *Source: News,* United States Department of Labor, Bureau of Labor Statistics, USDL 96–59, Washington, DC, Feb. 21, 1996. Annual work stoppage data are reported in a news release after the end of each year. Monthly work stoppage data appear in the BLS periodicals, *Monthly Labor Review* and *Compensation and Working Conditions.*

3. Orley Ashenfelter and George E. Johnson, "Bargaining Theory, Trade Unions and Industrial Strike Activity," *American Economic Review* 59 (March 1969), pp. 35–49; Bruce E. Kaufman, "The Determinants of Strikes in the United States, 1900–1977," *Industrial and Labor Relations Review* 35 (July 1982), pp. 473–90.

4. Bruce E. Kaufman, "The Determinants of Strikes over Time and across Industries," *Journal of Labor Research* (Spring 1983), pp. 159–75.

5. Michele I. Naples, "An Analysis of Defensive Strikes," *Industrial Relations* 26 (1987), pp. 96–105.

6. Bruce Kaufman, 1982, op. cit.

7. Cynthia L. Gramm, "The Determinants of Strike Incidence and Severity: A Micro-Level Study," *Industrial and Labor Relations Review* (April 1986), pp. 374–75.

8. John F. Schnell and Cynthia L. Gramm, "Learning by Striking: Estimates of the Teetotaler Effect," *Journal of Labor Economics* 5 (1987), pp. 221–41.

9. James E. Martin, "Predictors of Individual Propensity to Strike," *Industrial and Labor Relations Review* 39 (January 1986), pp. 214–27.

10. Sean Flaherty, "Strike Activity, Worker Militancy, and Productivity Change in Manufacturing, 1961–1981," *Industrial and Labor Relations Review* 40 (January 1987), pp. 585–600.

11. Paul Jarley and Cheryl L. Maranto, "Union Corporate Campaigns: An Assessment," *Industrial and Labor Relations Review* 43 (July 1990), pp. 505–7.

12. Ibid., pp. 505–24.

13. Report of the Mediator Task Force on the Future of FMCS, Washington, DC, July 15, 1994.

14. Ibid., p. 23.

15. Ibid., p. 21.

16. Ibid., p. 21.

17. Labor Management Relations Act, Section 206.

18. For an excellent discussion of this topic see Peter Feuille, "Final Offer Arbitration and Negotiating Incentives," *Arbitration Journal* (September 1988), pp. 203–20.

19. William L. Ury, Jeanne M. Brett, and Stephen B. Goldberg, *Getting Disputes Resolved: Designing Systems to Cut the Cost of Conflict* (San Francisco; Jossey-Bass, 1988).

20. Ibid., p. 15.

21. John Stepp and Jerome Barett, "New Theories on Negotiations and the Changing Role of Mediation" in *Collective Bargaining Negotiations and Contracts,* (Washington, DC: Bureau of National Affairs, 1990), pp. 14:61–14:69.

22. Harold Datz, "Economic Warfare in the 1980's, Strikes, Lockouts, Boycotts and Corporate Campaigns," *Industrial Relations Law Journal* 9 (1987), p. 82.

23. Labor Management Relations Act, Sections 206–209.

24. Ibid.

25. Railway Labor Act, Section 10.

26. Charles M. Rehmus, "Emergency Strikes Revisited," *Industrial and Labor Relations Review* 43 (January 1990), p. 176.

27. Ibid., pp. 176–77.

28. Ibid., pp. 177–78.

APPENDIX A

Excerpts from the Task Force Report of the Federal Mediation and Conciliation Service*

On December 2, 1993, the director of the Federal Mediation and Conciliation Service (FMCS) announced the formation of a Task Force whose purpose was to prepare the agency for the future. Excerpts from the executive summary of the Task Force report follow.

EXECUTIVE SUMMARY

The foundation for our strategic vision for the future of FMCS is existing FMCS capabilities. We looked at who the agency's customers are today and what services it is providing to them pursuant to legal mandates and other non-mandated, historical arrangements or practices.

Pursuant to the 1947 Taft-Hartley Act, which established FMCS, the Agency has provided mediation, conciliation and arbitration services in the private sector. From its inception, it has also provided preventive mediation services. Its charter in this arena was significantly enlarged by the 1978 Labor-Management Cooperation Act.

FMCS has also been authorized by statute and Executive Order to provide mediation services for federal sector labor and management parties. Most recently, Executive Order 12871, issued October 1, 1993, directed the formation of labor-management partnerships in the federal sector and named FMCS as a resource provider for training and related assistance.

By historical arrangement and practice, FMCS has from its inception also provided services in non-federal public sectors. It engages in public information activities to promote awareness of collective bargaining and peaceful conflict resolution. It also works with the international labor-management community and governments.

Outside of the labor-management arena, FMCS has been involved in alternative dispute resolution (ADR) activities for federal government agencies pursuant to several

---

*Report of the Mediator Task Force on the Future of the Federal Mediation and Conciliation Service (FMCS), Executive Summary, FMCS, Washington, DC, July 15, 1994, pp. 1–5.

statutes. On an ad hoc basis, FMCS entered into agreements with states to provide ADR services. The Agency is reimbursed by the contract agencies for mediator time and expenses in these activities.

Examining caseload trends, we learned that approximately 80 per cent of FMCS's caseload consists of dispute mediation, down from about 90 per cent in the early 1980s. Concurrently, preventive mediation has gone from about 10 per cent to 20 per cent since the early 1980s. In the federal sector, requests for partnership training have grown steadily since the Executive Order issued last October.

Mediators' jobs are changing. They are more than the "firefighters" who come in to assist parties in resolving a deadline crisis. Increasingly, mediators are called in earlier to train both sides in collaborative dealings and more effective bargaining, and to assist them in forming and maintaining labor management committees. The caseload also reflects increased ADR work, with an exploding demand for these services by federal government agencies, already challenging FMCS's ability to deliver them.

However, caseload trends may not reflect existing capabilities of the Agency as a whole, for there is a perception that there is not sufficient diffusion of skills and experience within the Agency to deliver in a systematic and effective fashion the variety of services being sought from the Agency today. It is perceived that the Agency culture does not provide enough incentive for the "full service" mediator through either an evaluation system or through adequate training opportunities. The question of FMCS's future is complicated by the fact that it now has a broad range of competitors—both private and public—who provide many of the same services FMCS offers. Finally, we looked at what is currently being done to ensure professionalism and service, and concluded that there is no uniform or precise answer. Today, there is no specific or objective measure of service. This question is of highest priority to be answered.

> The Task Force then addressed "Future Needs." What does FMCS need to do to ensure vitality to the year 2000 as a valued added contributor to the nation's labor relations and conflict resolutions systems, particularly given:
>
> - the declining unionized proportion of the workforce
> - the declining number of strikes
> - the expanding expectations of the parties as they experiment with new processes
> - the increasing number of competitors with FMCS, and
> - declining federal budgets and staffing?

We then considered who the Agency's external customers are likely to be into the year 2000: legally mandated (the labor-management community in the private and federal sectors; federal agencies requesting assistance in ADR work, or pursuant to other interagency agreements) and non-mandated (the labor-management community in those state and local governments where FMCS assistance is by joint request of the parties or other arrangement; the international community; and governmental or other organizations seeking non-mandated conflict resolution assistance). Legally mandated customers should be given priority by the Agency as a whole if choices have to be made because of limited resources.

FMCS may have to respond to new legislative mandates, either labor-management or alternative dispute resolution. It will also have to adapt its services to evolving trends and customer needs in an environment where today's strengths may be less often employed and its ingenuity challenged. It must develop a systematic method to continuously assess its customers' changing needs and ensure that it can respond with quality service.

The trends indicate that traditional dispute mediation work may continue to decline.

Clearly, one emergent trend is toward more collaborative processes and higher worker involvement in decision-making. There is an exploding demand for ADR services. Many of these activities, such as working with the parties to restructure both work processes and labor-management relations, require substantial commitment of time and resources. So, the question is, how much of this work can FMCS credibly handle, given the likelihood of declining budget and staffing?

Fundamental questions for the future include:

1. should FMCS branch out into dispute mediation or conflict resolution in a whole variety of fields,
2. should it deepen its involvement in labor-management relations to ensure constructive dispute resolution, cooperative efforts, work reorganization, etc., or
3. should, or can, it do both, given limited resources and staff?

The Task Force wrestled with these questions. A definitive answer is difficult. However, to best prepare for the future, FMCS as an agency should acquire the knowledge, skills and abilities to remain a major contributor to both the labor relations and conflict resolution systems.

The Task Force articulated an expanded role which FMCS should play in providing an institutional framework or imperative to encourage the transformation of work and labor-management relations. Its mandate under the 1978 Labor-Management Cooperation Act clearly provides an avenue for it to support the workplace innovations seen as necessary for American industrial competitiveness.

Through education, advocacy and outreach, FMCS should help to create a climate of trust conducive to harmonious labor-management relationships. Labor-management partnership strengthens trust and teamwork, leading to improved products and customer service, and thus to competitive advantage, profitability and enhanced employment security.

Many of the speakers who addressed the Task Force said that FMCS has a critical role to play as a catalytic agent for workplace innovation. It can serve as a valuable source of information about successful models of change. To play these roles, FMCS will need a strategy for managing its own resources and upgrading or acquiring necessary staff skills. The nature of the work may change significantly.

This report does not begin to address every new initiative or role which FMCS could pursue in the future. Nor does it do justice to every idea suggested by the speakers we heard. What the report hopefully does is generate discussion and focus the attention of the Agency on the need for an ongoing process of learning, improvement, and adaptation to changing needs and evolving trends.

As a centerpiece of the future strategic vision for FMCS, the Task Force identified eight core competencies which the Agency should achieve by the year 2000. The collective ability of mediators, with support from Agency leadership and national office staff, to perform professionally in these eight competencies will position the Agency to meet customer demands in the year 2000 and beyond with responsive, high quality service.

CORE COMPETENCIES

1. Expertise in Collective Bargaining and Labor-Management Relations
2. Assistance to the Parties in the Negotiation of Collective Bargaining Agreements
3. Processes to Improve Labor-Management Relationships
4. Facilitation and Problem-Solving Skills
5. Processes to Improve Organizational Effectiveness
6. Design and Implementation of Conflict Resolution Systems

7. Education, Advocacy and Outreach
8. Knowledge, Skill and Ability in Information Systems

The Task Force made recommendations which hopefully will enable FMCS to "work better and cost less," and meet the future successfully. Its recommendations encompass the following subjects:

- work design
- organizational structure
- systems: "leadership," delivery and support
- staffing
- selection
- training and professional development
- evaluation and rewards
- internal communications and external relationships
- union-management relations

Each aspect of these recommendations should contribute to furthering the Agency's Mission and Values and achieving the core competencies by the year 2000, thereby enabling the Agency to serve its customers better by delivering effective and improved services based on these core competencies.

CHAPTER 15

Contract Administration

After reading this chapter, you should be able to

- Outline and explain the elements of a typical grievance procedure.

- Explain what a grievance is and why charges are almost always filed by workers or unions and rarely by management.

- Explain the role of arbitration of grievances and the process for selecting arbitrators.

- Explain the use of grievance procedures in a nonunion setting.

THE IMPACT OF COLLECTIVE BARGAINING ON EMPLOYEES AND SUPERVISORS

In this chapter, we will focus on the daily impact of collective bargaining on workers and supervisors and on the relations between unions and managements. Contract administration is a continuous process throughout a contract's duration. Given the fact that in unionized organizations, rules of conduct are negotiated in collective bargaining, how are those rules translated into the daily behavior of employer and employee? If disputes arise over the interpretation or application of those rules, how are the disputes to be resolved? We will address these questions and others.

ORGANIZATIONAL GOVERNMENT AND CONTRACT ADMINISTRATION

The Nature and Meaning of Organizational Government

In the private sector, management's chief objective is to be financially successful, and employees are only one means to that end. Viewed as the government of the organization, management does not and cannot govern primarily in the interests of "the governed." The presence of a union, however, prevents management from disregarding the interests of its "subjects" and governing solely in the interests of the rulers.[1]

As viewed by employees, management in most organizations is autocratic, in the sense that power comes from above and the managed cannot replace the managers. Enlightened management policies, a counterforce in the form of a union, or both can protect important human values in the firm. Some companies are operated by authoritarian methods; others are not. It is the purpose of this chapter to describe how a functioning union-management relationship can protect human values and to inquire whether management alone can do the same. In the last 10 years, some employers in both unionized and nonunionized operations have adopted more democratic structures to govern their relationships with their employees. The trends toward teamwork, employee empowerment, employee involvement and participation in decision making, and mutual gains bargaining all seem to have contributed to greater democracy in the workplace. Some of these developments are covered in Chapter 9, on the negotiation process, as well as in the last chapter of the text.

The Concept of Industrial or Organizational Jurisprudence

The term *industrial jurisprudence* was first applied by Sumner Slichter to a functioning plant government in 1941.[2] The concept is analogous to that of public government in a democracy in that it is "a government of laws, not of men." Under the laws, each person's rights and duties are known or determinable. No one may be required to do what the rules do not require, nor may one do what the rules forbid, especially if the act adversely affects the rights of others. In particular, in the firm an employee may be punished only for proved violations of known rules or standards, not at the discretion of a supervisor. Such conditions of law can exist in the absence of a union, and where management has established those conditions, the employees' urge to unionize is usually weak.

Although the mere presence of a union does not guarantee that industrial or organizational jurisprudence will prevail, the particular brand of organizational government that we will describe is widespread under unions. It is normally one of the first things a new union seeks to attain, and it will permanently remain one of the most important.

Some managers believe that organizational jurisprudence destroys management security. It is true, of course, that rules restrict all parties who must obey them, just as public law limits the discretion of administrators and police as well as of citizens. But the effect of organizational jurisprudence on management security depends on the particular rules that are written and the kinds of procedures that are established to carry them out; these must be examined in each individual case. We may note in passing that many employers have better systems of organizational jurisprudence for nonsupervisory employees than for members of management. Managers, from first-line supervisor to president, often have little protection against arbitrary treatment.

Traditionally, one of the most significant differences between union and nonunion jobs has been access to organizational jurisprudence. This distinction is important because of a common-law doctrine called employment-at-will. Under this doctrine, the employer can fire any employee (and employees can quit) at any time for any reason—or for no reason at all.[3] This principle does not apply where employees work under a labor contract specifying the right to due process. The employment-at-will doctrine was eroded by legislation prohibiting discrimination (including termination) on the basis of union status, race, religion, sex, color, national origin, age, pregnancy status, and handicap. Some statutes also outlaw termination on such grounds as sexual preference, marital status, and whistle-blowing. Some state courts have identified a number of exceptions to employment-at-will, such as implied contracts, violation of the obligation to act in good faith, and instances where firing contravenes public policy. As more and more states begin to recognize these exceptions and as jury awards to improperly terminated employees grow, nonunion employers are becoming increasingly interested in establishing due-process systems because they believe this will reduce the likelihood that disciplinary actions will be pursued through the legal system.

In the broadest sense, organizational jurisprudence includes both the establishment of workplace regulations (contract negotiation) and their interpretation and application (contract administration). In Chapter 14, the distinction between contract negotiation and administration was identified as the difference between interest disputes and rights disputes. These two processes are sometimes referred to as primary and secondary bargaining, respectively. In this chapter, the focus is mainly on the more narrow notion of jurisprudence, which specifically entails interpreting the law (the contract) and applying it to particular cases.

Contract Administration

A contract consists mainly of things that management commits itself to do for employees, and it may contain rules limiting management's freedom with respect to employees. The employer receives what he or she wants from the relationship not through agreement from the union but through the employment contract in which each individual agrees to accept and fulfill instructions from a supervisor under pain of discipline or discharge. For the most part, if management satisfies the terms of the contract, no further action is required until contract expiration; this fact is an important background element of organizational jurisprudence. The aspect that requires attention comes into focus when an employee and the union claim that the employer has not followed the contract, and they institute action to remedy the situation. Management can use a similar approach to bring the union into line in areas involving commitments from the union.

The Process of Continuous Negotiation

Organizational governance and contract administration can also be viewed as a continuous process in which union and management negotiate throughout the life of the agreement. That is, the parties, as in contract negotiations, explore issues, exchange proposals and counterproposals, and try to renew agreement on points of contention. In some instances, the parties to formal negotiations agree in principle and leave the details of implementation to be negotiated later. In other instances, conditions might change so radically during the life of an agreement that modifications in the application of contract language are necessary. Finally, the period of contract administration between negotiations reveals important topics for the next round of contract bargaining. Sometimes the parties discover that the language they set down at the negotiating table contributes continuously to grievances. This can create an interest to alter the problematic portion of the agreement. All in all, organizational governance plays as significant a role in labor relations as does the more formal periodic negotiation of agreements.

GRIEVANCE PROCEDURES

The Structure of Grievance Procedures

Because the specifics of a grievance procedure are established by the parties when they negotiate their collective bargaining agreement, few procedures are identical. Nearly all, however, have several features in common (see Figure 15.1 for a typical four-step grievance procedure). A study of 400 union grievance procedures in all industries showed that 8 percent of the procedures had one step, 21 percent had two steps, 51 percent had three steps, 19 percent had four steps, and only 1 percent had five steps[4] (see Table 15.1). Of the contracts specifying how the grievance was to be presented (the first step), about half required that it be in writing, with the rest permitting oral presentation. The amount of time allowed for bringing or appealing a grievance varied, as did the time allowed management to respond, but most contracts specified time limits.[5]

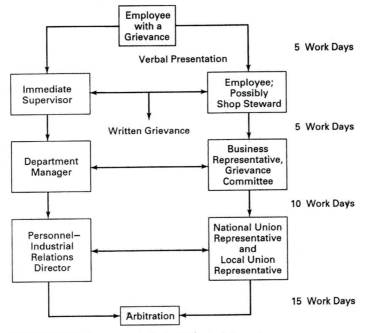

FIGURE 15.1 Structure of a Typical Grievance Procedure

Source: R. E. Allen and T. J. Keaveny, *Contemporary Labor Relations,* 2nd Edition, p. 530. © 1988 by Addison-Wesley Publishing Company, reprinted by permission of publisher.

The Grievance Procedure in Action

A hypothetical case will illustrate how grievance procedures operate. Suppose an employee complains that he or she has been improperly disciplined—a typical grievance. In the first step of the procedure, the employee and/or the shop steward[6] will take the matter to the employee's supervisor. This step usually must be completed within a few working days of the alleged wrongdoing. In many grievance procedures, the supervisor occupies a difficult dual role as defendant and judge. This role requires discretion, wisdom, and self-control. If the supervisor resolves the dispute to the grievant's satisfaction, the matter is closed. The settlement, of course, may not violate the contract—an important reason why

TABLE 15.1 Steps in Grievance Procedures *(Frequency Expressed as Percentage of 396* Contracts Specifying Steps)*

	Number of Steps				
	1	*2*	*3*	*4*	*5*
All Industries	8	21	51	19	1
Manufacturing	4	13	56	26	1
Nonmanufacturing	16	32	43	9	1

*Includes 243 manufacturing and 153 nonmanufacturing provisions.

Source: Basic Patterns in Union Contracts, Fourteenth Edition (Washington, DC: Bureau of National Affairs, 1995), p. 33.

unions insist that union representatives be present at the discussions and why managements want their supervisors to be thoroughly conversant with their contracts. Under the Taft-Hartley Act, the employee has the right to present his or her own case, but the union representative has the right to be present.

If the supervisor's decision is not acceptable, the grievance is put in writing, and the decision can be appealed within a few working days of receipt. In the second step, the grievance goes to the department manager and the grievance committee or to a higher union official. Minutes of the meeting, perhaps initialed by both sides, may become part of the permanent record. If the grievance is denied, it may be appealed—usually within 10 working days—in the third step, which involves local union leadership and perhaps national representation along with the employer's personnel or labor relations director for the particular location. As at previous levels, no settlement may violate or alter the contract. Because this group typically meets regularly and is experienced, it can often settle problems that prove resistant at lower levels. At this step of the procedure, conflict resolution is removed from those directly involved.

If a mutually satisfactory solution cannot be found, the grievant may proceed to the fourth step, involving a request for arbitration by the union. Regardless of the number of prior steps, the last one is usually final and binding arbitration.

Most contracts also specify strict time limits by which management must announce its decision at each step of the grievance procedure. The consequence of inaction at each level is usually quite different for the union and for management. If the union fails to comply with the time limits at any step, the usual consequence is that the grievance is forfeited and no future appeal permitted. Management failure to observe time limits usually is equated with grievance denial at that level, and the grievance can be appealed to the next higher level.

These successive levels within the grievance procedure and the time limits between them serve many functions. First, time limitations require each party to process grievances quickly and efficiently, though enough time must be allotted at each level for a thorough review of the grievance. Second, the successively higher levels necessarily involve individuals with more experience and authority on both sides. The ability to settle difficult cases may rest only with higher levels of management and union governance. Third, the levels of the grievance procedure serve as filters in which, at each step, less worthy grievances are settled. Sometimes the fact that higher levels of authority are involved means that both union and management representatives can look at a case more objectively and see the issues outside the more personal employee-supervisor context.

The final step of the grievance process is arbitration. This process takes several forms, which will be discussed in the next section. In most states, arbitrators' decisions are enforceable in court. Despite occasional exceptions, it is the sense of organizational jurisprudence that no decision may add to, modify, or subtract from the contract. Thus, grievance arbitration interprets the contract or applies it to particular cases. To accomplish this, the arbitrator may have to determine questions of fact or principle concerning the behavior of employee, employer, or union. Although not all grievance procedures work as in this example, the illustration provides a brief look at the grievance procedure in action.

The Scope of Grievance Procedures

What is a grievance? The answer to this question may be less straightforward than one might expect.

As in all other areas of contract negotiation, unions and managements are free, within some legal limits, to fashion any grievance procedure that will satisfy their needs. Thus, it is up to them to decide what issues should be resolved through this process. Most grievance procedures begin with a definition of *grievance.* Although there is no standard meaning for this term, most unions and managements choose to limit the definition in some way. For example, "A grievance is a complaint by an employee or group of employees for whom the Union is the bargaining agent, involving an alleged violation or interpretation of any provision of this Agreement."[7] According to this definition, a worker's complaint about the violation of any right under the agreement is a grievance.

The grievance procedure is used mainly by labor against management and only rarely by management against labor. In fact, only 32 percent of nonmanufacturing and 26 percent of manufacturing contracts allow management even to file grievances, whereas 36 percent of contracts allow unions to file grievances.[8] In virtually all contracts containing grievance procedures, individual employees are the ones who have the right to file grievances. This fact reflects not bias in the system but merely the fact that management is in charge. If management is dissatisfied with an individual, it does not file a grievance; it fires, disciplines, transfers, or retrains him or her. The grievance machinery is a channel of protest. Hence, it is used mainly by the agent of protest, not by the source of authority.

Although the union promises little in the contract, its few obligations may be subject to grievance proceedings initiated by the employer. Strikes authorized by unions in violation of no-strike clauses have been arbitrated, and some penalties have been levied on unions. Complaints that union business is being conducted on company time, that shop stewards are abusing their freedom to investigate cases, or that the union is misusing company bulletin boards would be appropriate subjects for grievance proceedings by management—although management could also handle some such cases by disciplining the individuals involved. Grievance proceedings against the union would normally be initiated at the third step.

Arbitrators have found that only certain types of cases tend to occur frequently. Issues often reaching arbitration are those concerning discipline, seniority rights, drug and alcohol problems, subcontracting, scheduling (particularly of overtime), job classifications, and work methods.

A METHOD OF FINAL RESOLUTION—ARBITRATION

The No-Strike Clause

There is an important relationship among the grievance procedure, the no-strike clause, and arbitration. During the life of a contract, the parties do not want to see each unresolved issue escalate to a strike, nor do they want to encourage the accumulation of many unresolved disputes whose effect on morale and production could be worse than that of a strike. Hence, a no-strike clause is not feasible unless accompanied by a workable grievance procedure. The grievance procedure in turn would be meaningless unless accompanied by a no-strike clause, for otherwise its decisions could be "appealed" to the strike. In the event of deadlock, a workable grievance mechanism must provide a procedure for final resolution of the complaint. Final and binding arbitration fulfills this function. The vast majority of grievances are settled at the early steps of the procedure. When the parties are unable to resolve their differences, they may end up in arbitration.

Development of Arbitration

Ninety-eight percent of all union-management grievance procedures contain arbitration clauses.[9] The logic of using a third party acceptable to both sides to resolve questions of contract interpretation and application seems compelling. Systems of rights arbitration have not, however, always been universally used in this country and are not commonly used in most other countries.

Before World War II, few industries had well-developed systems of rights arbitration. During the war, the War Labor Board was a strong advocate of arbitration systems as part of collective bargaining agreements.[10] A national policy in favor of arbitration was codified in the 1947 Taft-Hartley Act: "Final adjustment by a method agreed upon by the parties is hereby declared to be the desirable method for settlement of grievance disputes arising over the application or interpretation of an existing collective-bargaining agreement."[11]

Despite the current almost universal acceptance of arbitration in this country, most other countries have not adopted similar systems. In most western European countries, for example, the parties are permitted to sue in general courts or special labor courts of law for enforcement and interpretation of labor agreements.[12]

A series of important court cases have strengthened arbitration in the United States. First, in 1957 the Supreme Court decided that labor agreements were binding contracts and agreements to take disputes to arbitration could be enforced.[13] Then in 1960, three Supreme Court decisions, the so-called Steelworkers Trilogy cases, established the circumstances under which courts could compel arbitration. These cases established that, although a court should determine whether an issue is subject to arbitration, it should not judge the merits of the case; that is the job of the arbitrator. Doubts about the arbitrability of a particular issue were to be decided in favor of arbitration. Unless an issue was explicitly excluded from the arbitration clause, the court should assume that the parties meant to arbitrate disputes involving that issue. If a court is asked to review an arbitrator's decision, it is not to examine the merits of the case but only to ascertain that the decision is based on the contract's content.[14] The net effect of these decisions was firmly to establish the arbitration process and to remove the courts from the grievance arena. In practice, the result was the substitution of privately selected judges or arbitrators for the public legal system.

The importance of the arbitration process was amplified further by decisions of the National Labor Relations Board (NLRB). First, if an issue is raised that is both a contract violation and a possible violation of the National Labor Relations Act (NLRA), the NLRB will defer to an existing arbitration award as long as (1) the arbitration proceedings were fair and regular, (2) all of the parties agreed to be bound by the arbitration award, (3) the decision was not clearly repugnant to the NLRA, (4) the contractual issue is factually parallel to the unfair labor practice (ULP), and (5) the arbitrator was presented with the facts relevant for deciding the ULP.[15] Second, not only will the NLRB defer to an existing arbitration award, it will also require workers alleging violations of the NLRA that are also subject to contractual grievance and arbitration procedures to use arbitration.[16]

Arbitrator Selection

The first task facing parties who wish to arbitrate a grievance is selection of an arbitrator. Most contracts initially allow both parties to mutually select an arbitrator they agree to be acceptable. Perhaps they have recently employed an arbitrator that impressed both sides and they agree to check if he or she is available to decide the current grievance. If this selection by mutual agreement fails, most unions and managements use one of two services: the Federal Mediation and Conciliation Service (FMCS) or the American Arbitration Association. These two organizations maintain panels of qualified arbitrators and are the source of most arbitrators in the United States. Upon request of the parties, a list of arbitrators is supplied so they may select one. Arbitrators acquire reputations based on years of experience, past decisions, and expertise in some industries or in certain contractual matters. Most arbitrators are general practitioners who rule and issue opinions on a great variety of issues in various sectors of the economy. Each side is allowed to strike names from the list of arbitrators in order to find a mutually acceptable arbitrator. For example, a union or a management might choose to exclude a particular arbitrator because of specific past experiences or because they believe the arbitrator is hard (or soft) on a particular matter. This process results in the selection of arbitrators satisfactory to both parties.

At the FMCS, the Office of Arbitration Services (OAS) is responsible for administering the arbitration function. The OAS maintains a roster of approximately 1,700 private arbitrators. During fiscal year 1994, the OAS appointed arbitrators in 11,640 cases. In that year, the average elapsed time between hearing and date of award rendered by arbitrator was 76 days.[17]

Some employers and unions, especially those with significant and continuing demands for arbitration services, have found it beneficial to name permanent arbitrators rather than to choose a new one for every case. The advantage in naming either an individual or a small rotating group as permanent arbitrators is their availability and experience. A permanent arbitrator can develop a better understanding of the nature of the work and of the collective bargaining agreement. A permanent arbitrator should be able to give priority to the relationship with a particular firm, and the parties will thus be rewarded with prompt scheduling and quicker resolution of their grievances. Despite these advantages, however, most unions and managements find the permanent system unworkable because of either small or unpredictable caseloads.

The Arbitration Process

Once the arbitrator is chosen, the parties and the arbitrator set a date for a hearing. In many instances, the parties will send prehearing statements of their cases to the arbitrator so that agreed-upon facts might be stipulated at the hearing. Both parties prepare to present their cases at this point. If the parties have performed conscientiously in the earlier steps of the grievance procedure, the nature of the relevant arguments and evidence should be reasonably clear by the time the case gets to arbitration, though exceptions are numerous. Although grievance arbitration is typically less formal than courtroom procedures, the logic of case preparation is not much different. The evidence and the arguments must be marshalled in logical and systematic form. If facts are in dispute, the parties must consider carefully in advance which documents or witnesses will be able to demonstrate the important points. They must also give thought to questions that will elicit the facts from witnesses without seeming to "lead" or "coach" them. Even if one side prefers relatively informal proceedings, it must know how to counter or avoid formal objections the other party may raise to certain testimony or documents. Management will normally provide such documentation as records of payroll, seniority, absences, and vacations because neither the union nor the employee is likely to have such records. Management, of course, will presumably not provide documents helpful to the union's case unless specifically asked for them, with reasonable advance notice.

Arbitration hearings often reflect the relationship prevailing within the firm. In some companies, arbitration is formal and legalistic. Witnesses are sworn, rules of evidence apply as in courts, direct and cross-examinations of witnesses follow the customary pattern, a stenographic record is kept, and formal briefs are often prepared. Such arbitration tends to attract, require, and be dominated by lawyers.

Others prefer informal arbitration. Witnesses may be questioned informally whenever their testimony seems relevant, and they are not sworn. Written notes are confined to those the arbitrator takes. Except for obvious filibustering, any reasonable material is admitted, with the understanding that the arbitrator will separate the relevant from the irrelevant when he or she makes a decision. To "get off the chest" whatever is bothering an employee is considered more important than strict rules of evidence. Some parties want the arbitrator to interpret the contract strictly and apply it rigorously. Some organizations utilize the problem-solving approach; although its adherents would not openly flout a clear contract clause, they prefer a workable decision to one that is formally correct. Usually, formality tends to increase with the numbers of people involved and the importance of the issue. Generally, though, the arbitration process is notable for providing a forum for hearing all sides of the story.

Following the hearing, the arbitrator is charged with rendering an award. Prior to the decision, the parties sometimes prepare posthearing briefs for the arbitrator. These briefs are similar to the prehearing statements in that each party presents its own version of the case. The arbitrator's award, given in writing to the parties, is final and binding unless the parties have made other contractual arrangements.

The Common Law in Organizational Jurisprudence

As case after case is processed within a company, the accumulated decisions can constitute a common law, establishing precedents for the detailed provisions that cannot be spelled out in contract. Two distinct attitudes have arisen toward such common law.

Those who oppose the common law want each grievance processed on its own merits as a unique event, without regard to preceding cases. When cases go to arbitration, those people do not introduce other cases as precedents. They select arbitrators on an ad hoc basis so that a fresh viewpoint is brought to each case. They are interested in the substance of the decision rather than the reasons for it, and they may discourage the writing of supporting opinions by the arbitrators.

Others desire maximum continuity. They note, follow, and possibly codify precedents. They prefer a permanent umpire who handles all cases during his or her tenure of office, and they give great weight to his or her opinions. Some carry the use of precedent beyond the single bargaining unit and, in the extreme case, feel that the whole of American experience should be welded into a single code of labor relations practice. They make their own cases publicly available through reporting services and in turn examine other cases for precedents.

ARBITRAL DECISION MAKING

Arbitrators are primarily called upon to make two kinds of judgments. First, the vast majority of all contracts require that discipline and discharge be for "just cause"; this implies that employees have certain due-process rights. Arbitrators have developed criteria for deciding whether employees' due-process rights have been violated. A second type of arbitration case involves contract interpretation. Here, the arbitrator is called upon to interpret and decide on the meaning of the contract language contained in the labor agreement.

Basic Principles of Due Process

Systems of organizational jurisprudence are designed to provide due process. Due process encompasses the principles of fairness and justice (see Table 15.2); it recognizes employees' right to know the rules and the consequences of violating them. Devising a system for interpreting and enforcing rules presumes the existence of a set of rules. If management devises rules and penalties for their violation without informing workers, then enforcement of those rules might be viewed as unjust. On the other hand, because it is not feasible to specify every potential rule, virtually all contracts permit employers to discipline employees for "just cause." This permits employers to apply generally accepted

TABLE 15.2 Principles of Due Process

1. Employees should know the rules and the consequences for violating them.
2. Employer response to rule violation should be consistent and predictable.
3. Employee discipline should be based on the facts.
4. Employees should be given an opportunity to question the facts and present evidence on their side of the story.
5. Employees should be able to appeal disciplinary decisions.
6. Employees should be given progressive discipline.
7. Each employee should be considered as an individual.

Source: Based on James R. Redeker, *Employee Discipline: Policies and Practices* (Washington, DC: Bureau of National Affairs, 1989), pp. 25–35.

norms of behavior with which all employees are expected to comply. For example, few firms have explicit rules against hitting supervisors. Yet management undoubtedly still has "just cause" to punish such an act.

Selective enforcement can result in charges of discrimination. Enforcement of the rules should be based on what actually occurred, not merely what someone thought might have occurred. The employee needs an opportunity to give his or her version of the facts and to present witnesses and evidence to substantiate those claims.

As in all legal systems, due process in industrial jurisprudence requires the ability to appeal. Thus, mistakes or prejudices at one level of decision making can be corrected by higher levels.

The notion of progressive discipline derives from the proposition that the punishment should fit the crime. Punishment for the first occurrence of a relatively minor offense, such as an unexcused absence, would usually be relatively light, such as a one-day suspension. The next time the same employee has an unexcused absence, the punishment might be a three-day suspension. Repeated occurrences of this same rule violation could eventually lead to discharge. In the case of a more serious violation, like stealing or assaulting a supervisor, the first offense might result in immediate discharge.

Standards for Interpreting Contract Language

Over the years, arbitrators have developed numerous principles to guide them in the interpretation of contract language.[18] In this section we only touch on some of these.

First, the primary function of an arbitrator is to carry out the mutual intent of the parties as expressed in their agreement. Only if the parties disagree on the meaning of contract language is an arbitrator called upon to render a judgment. If mutual intent is not clear from the language, the arbitrator may infer the parties' intent on the basis of bargaining history, discussions during negotiations, and past practice.

If two interpretations of contract language are possible but one of them would make the contract violate the law, the arbitrator will decide on the interpretation that complies with the law. When deciding what meanings to assign specific words, an arbitrator usually relies on the normal or technical uses of those words. If meanings are not specified in the contract itself, they are derived from general and specialized legal dictionaries and decisions of other arbitrators. An arbitrator also interprets any given contract clause in light of the rest of the contract. Again, if two interpretations are possible and one would contradict another part of the contract, the alternate interpretation will generally be preferred. Another guiding principle is the avoidance of harsh or absurd results.

Several arbitration principles are related to contract language. First, it is frequently assumed that if a contract stipulates one point, it excludes another. For example, if an agreement states that employees must work the day before and the day after a holiday to receive holiday pay, then that same rule is not automatically applicable to vacation pay. Where the contract contains both general and specific language, the specific tends to govern. Suppose, for example, one contract clause states that the company will provide the necessary safety equipment to all employees, while another clause states that management will issue hard hats, safety shoes, and protective eyeglasses. Must the company provide earplugs? Because the second clause specifically lists items but does not mention ear protection, an arbitrator may rule that the second clause shall govern with respect to the employer's obligations.

Another arbitration guideline is to consider the principles of reason and equity in contract interpretation. Where contract language leaves room for interpretation and flexibility, arbitrators will take into account reasonableness and fairness in arriving at their decisions. However, if the language is clear and unambiguous, an arbitrator must enforce the mutual intent of the parties even if the results seem unreasonable or inequitable.

ARBITRATION AND EXTERNAL LAW

Arbitrators have been characterized as creatures of the contract: An arbitrator's authority derives from the contract. Arbitrators have been referred to as private judges in a private system of law. Labor and management empower arbitrators and pay them expressly to interpret contract language. Given this system, it is not surprising that most arbitrators do not consider external law in their decisions. They assume that if the parties wanted rulings based on external law, they would take their conflicts to the courts rather than to arbitration.

Given the deference shown by the courts and the NLRB toward the arbitration process, arbitrators may not be able to continue to ignore external law in their arbitration decisions. A landmark 1974 Supreme Court case began to affect some arbitrators' views on the role of external law.[19] In *Alexander v. Gardner-Denver Company,* a minority employee alleged that he had been discharged because of his race. The union contract under which he worked contained a nondiscrimination clause with wording similar to Title VII of the Civil Rights Act of 1964. Under the labor contract, the employee had a right to use either the contractual grievance and arbitration procedure or the court system to seek redress. Alexander opted for arbitration and lost his case, whereupon he filed suit in court. Both the district and appeals courts ruled that, having opted for arbitration, Alexander was precluded from seeking consideration by the courts. The Supreme Court reversed that ruling and decided that Title VII does not permit deferral to arbitration. Although arbitrators are experts in the law of the shop, the Court reasoned, they are not experts in the law of the land. With respect to arbitration, the Court said,

> We adopt no standards as to the weight to be accorded an arbitral decision, since this must be determined in the court's discretion with regard to the facts and circumstances of each case. Relevant factors include the existence of provisions in the collective bargaining agreement that conform substantially with Title VII, the degree of procedural fairness in the arbitral forum, adequacy of the record with respect to the issue of discrimination, and the special competence of particular arbitrators. When an arbitral determination gives full consideration to an employee's Title VII rights, a court may properly accord it great weight. This is especially true when the issue is solely one of fact, specifically addressed by the parties and decided by the arbitrator on the basis of an adequate record. But courts should ever be mindful that Congress, in enacting Title VII, thought it necessary to provide a judicial forum for the ultimate resolution of discriminatory employment claims. It is the duty of courts to assure the full availability of this forum.[20]

When dealing with arbitration decisions involving alleged violations of both the contract and external law, the courts are more likely to support the arbitration award when the arbitrator considers the external law and decides the case in a way consistent with that law. Given this fact and the importance of the final and binding nature of arbitration, some arbitrators have concluded that they must take external law into account when making their decisions.

DUTY OF FAIR REPRESENTATION

In exchange for exclusive recognition, an accompanying duty is imposed upon the union: It must represent all employees in the bargaining unit equally and fairly,[21] whether or not these employees are dues-paying members. This fair representation requirement includes bringing cases to arbitration. The duty of fair representation is violated only if the union acts in an arbitrary, discriminatory, perfunctory, or bad-faith manner. As long as a union does not violate standards of fair representation, it is not legally required to bring every case to arbitration.

As we have noted, an arbitration decision ordinarily is final and binding, and court review is very limited. However, when the union ignores its duty of fair representation, the aggrieved employee can file a lawsuit.[22] In *Bowen v. United States Postal Service,* an employee was unjustly fired by his employer, and the union violated its duty of fair representation by not taking his case to arbitration. The Supreme Court ultimately decided that the employer was liable for back pay from the date of termination until the date when an arbitrator would have reinstated the employee. The union was liable for back pay after the date when the employee would have been reinstated if the union had fulfilled its duty of fair representation.[23] As a result of this decision, unions sometimes knowingly bring grievances without merit to arbitration to avoid not only negative publicity but also the potential liability of violating the duty of fair representation.

GRIEVANCE PROCEDURES IN NONUNION SETTINGS

Grievance procedures also exist in nonunion firms, though they are less common there than in unionized organizations. Despite its potential interference with management's freedom, a functioning grievance procedure can be perceived as a constructive addition to the management of human relations in modern industry. This section reviews the rationale for grievance procedures in nonunion firms.

Is Absence of Grievances a Good Sign?

Business people are sometimes heard to remark, "Before we had a grievance procedure, our people were contented. We practically never had any gripes. Now we have a steady stream of grievances." In evaluating a grievance system, it is important not to equate absence of complaints with worker satisfaction. Grievances may be lacking because there are no complaints—the optimum condition of morale. But they may also be absent because workers are afraid to file them or assume they are fruitless—perhaps the worst condition of morale. Hence, an increase in grievances may mean that dissatisfaction is being "manufactured," or it may mean that discontent is being relieved and its causes corrected.

Grievance Procedures and Channels of Communication

A perpetual difficulty facing top-level executives is getting an honest view of "things at the bottom." Top managers may walk through the floor, but somehow word gets around that they are coming, and therefore they may not witness routine performance. Casual conversations with workers may reveal little, for many workers freeze when talking to executives or feel that criticisms might get back to their supervisors and cause trouble. Reports that go up through channels tend to be overly favorable because they deal with things for which their writers are responsible. Well-run firms have methods for opening the channels of communication, but there is constant danger of clogging, and no method is completely reliable.

A grievance procedure changes things. Now the lowliest worker can carry his or her complaint to the fourth or fifth step, and the worker has direct access to top management. Lower management cannot keep grievances from going to advanced stages by granting all requests, for therein lies a shortcut to chaos. Through grievances, executives can learn many details of day-to-day operation: In the hearing, almost any detail may come forth. With such information, top management can administer more intelligently, and under such scrutiny, lower levels are kept more alert.

Difficulties in Establishing a Nonunion Grievance Procedure

A grievance procedure in which employees have full confidence is difficult to create in the absence of a union. Most grievances allege that management has acted improperly; thus, in a grievance mechanism sponsored by management, the same party is both judge and defendant—not only in the lower step but also in the crucial final step.

Some firms have at the third step a grievance committee consisting of company representatives and representatives elected by the employees. An atmosphere is created in which there need be no hesitation to speak one's piece. There may even be someone to serve as attorney for the grievant.

Nevertheless, this structure embodies several real weaknesses that revolve around the employee's lack of bargaining power in the event of a showdown. First, if the "attorneys" are paid by the company, they are ultimately subject to the company's control, on the assumption that the one who pays the piper calls the tune. If the employees decide to collect contributions to cover this cost, they control the attorneys—but they also have an incipient union. Second, although management may exercise great restraint and gracefully accept unpalatable recommendations from the grievance committee, it is still managerial self-discipline rather than employee bargaining power that brings fair treatment. So long as grievances deal with issues for which there are clear, logical answers or with economic issues of modest proportions, this technique may produce about the same results as a union-management system. But when issues involve such matters as management prerogatives or large amounts of money, they tend to be resolved in favor of management. Even if the grievance is not momentous, the grievant rarely has the protection of binding arbitration if he or she is dissatisfied with management's decision. Relatively few nonunion companies have any arrangements for arbitration. Even short of arbitration, formal grievance procedures in nonunion organizations get relatively little use; employees prefer informal chats in the personnel office. Even this channel may be restricted if the employee fears arousing the supervisor's suspicion.

Some nonunionized employers have developed peer review systems. At Coors Brewing Company,[24] such a system allows employees to bring their grievances before a group that includes their co-workers. It seems that one objective of the Coors system was to deter unionization. An article in *Personnel Journal* describing the system states that "unionization no longer is a threat because it is no longer necessary."[25] Under the Coors system, an employee who questions the application of the employer's policy—but not the policy itself—may within seven days submit an appeal with an employee representative. The representative is charged with appointing an appeal board composed of two randomly selected members of management and three employees from the same classification as the appellant. After a hearing, at which witnesses may testify, the board renders a verdict by a majority vote. The board can uphold the action taken, overturn it completely, or decrease its severity. The board's decisions are final. In 1992, the board decisions upheld supervisors in 58 percent of the 65 appeals heard. Of those decisions, 15 percent were reversed, and 26 percent were modified.[26] During the last few years, Coors has been averaging approximately 60 appeals per year.

A relatively recent workplace trend, which started about 10 years ago, is a requirement that workers sign, as a condition of employment or continued employment, agreements to arbitrate all employment disputes or all employment disputes involving statutory rights. Some arbitrators object to some of these agreements because they permit employers to apply economic leverage that compels employees to sign. The result is a substitution of the arbitration process for statutory remedies. The end effect is a treatment of due process as a mechanism by which the unrepresented worker involuntarily waives statutory procedures.[27]

The American Arbitration Association (AAA) has formulated a Model of Employment Arbitration Procedures, which applies to nonunion arbitration cases. Under those procedures, the AAA is authorized to appoint a neutral arbitrator from its panel of arbitrators. Similar service is provided by the FMCS; however, the FMCS applies a stricter standard when providing arbitrators outside collective bargaining agreements. The FMCS requests that the parties answer the following question in the affirmative before it will provide arbitrators:[28]

1. Is the grievance and arbitration procedure spelled out in a personnel manual or an employee handbook?
2. Do employees have access to the grievance and arbitration procedure as a matter of right?
3. Do employees have a voice in the arbitrator's selection?
4. Do employees have a right to a representative of their choice in the grievance and arbitration process?
5. Is the arbitrator's award binding and enforceable?[29]

There are at least two potential reasons why nonunion employers might willingly establish grievance procedures. First, it may merely be a management tactic to inhibit the desire among workers for union representation. This threat-effect explanation may have had some validity in the past, but, given the decline in union strength over the last few decades, it is less applicable under current conditions. Another reason for nonunion firms' adopting grievance procedures lies in the possibility of improved performance. It is at least theoretically possible that so-called employee voice mechanisms such as grievance procedures may have beneficial impact on the firm's efficiency and productivity.

To conclude, in the typical nonunion organization, the employee with a grievance will probably face some frustrating hazards. And, however generous the management, the grievant without a union is a subject petitioning for redress, not a citizen demanding justice.

GRIEVANCE PROCEDURES AND FIRM PERFORMANCE

The availability or absence of grievance procedures can affect various labor relations outcomes.[30] For example, the turnover rate among registered nurses in hospitals, both union and nonunion, with grievance procedures was significantly lower than in hospitals without such procedures. It is interesting to note that turnover rates were not affected by the inclusion of arbitration as a final step of the grievance procedure.[31]

Existing data indicate that people who file grievances are more likely to leave their employers voluntarily, particularly if they lose their grievances.[32] Although firm conclusions cannot be drawn about grievance use and productivity, grievance procedures can probably improve some aspects of organizational performance.

Performance Criteria for Grievance Arbitration Procedures

Grievance arbitration has several advantages over such alternatives as strikes or litigation in court. Arbitration is much faster, less costly, less legalistic, and more understandable to the parties, and it can provide more flexible remedies.[33] During the last 15 years, because of the increasing influence of external law, some parties and arbitrators have become more legalistic: The parties are employing more lawyers, both as advocates and as arbitrators, they are filing more pre- and posthearing briefs, and requests for hearing transcripts are becoming more common. All these developments increase the expense and lengthen the process of arbitration.

Innovations in Grievance and Arbitration Procedures

Some parties have explored alternatives to the standard grievance-arbitration model, the major motivations being to shorten the time from grievance to eventual resolution and to reduce the cost of the procedure. One such alternative is expedited arbitration. In some expedited procedures, grievance steps are bypassed, and the arbitration hearing is designed to be speedy and informal. In some cases, use of expedited arbitration yields impressive reductions in cost and delay.[34]

Another option being tried is the incorporation of a mediation step into the grievance process prior to arbitration. The most extensive application of grievance mediation has been in the coal mining industry. After the third step of the grievance procedure, the parties can choose to take the case to mediation rather than directly to arbitration. Presentation of the facts is much less formal in mediation than in arbitration. After the facts are presented, the mediator tries to help the parties find mutually acceptable solutions to the problem. If no voluntary agreement is reached, the mediator provides an oral opinion on what an arbitrator would most likely decide if presented with this case. Upon completion of mediation, the parties are free to appeal to arbitration. The mediator is ineligible to be the arbitrator, and nothing said during mediation can be used in any subsequent arbitration hearing.[35]

Although only a relatively small percentage of labor agreements (4 percent) contain a provision for the mediation of grievances, according to a number of reports the participants are satisfied with the results.[36] To illustrate the success of the procedure, in 1992 a formal grievance mediation procedure was agreed upon by the State of Ohio and the Ohio Civil Service Employees Association, representing 37,000 employees. The mediation procedure helped the parties settle 1,700 cases between June 1992 and April 1993.[37] Some arbitrators report a significant momentum toward utilization of the grievance mediation process.[38] The following example illustrates how the grievance mediation procedure works.

MEDIATION COOLS OFF COALFIELDS

An angry coal miner is perhaps the closest thing the nation has to a two-legged nuclear weapon, and, on a recent day, Doc Wellington was one unhappy miner. His rage was forming on one of those sunny, cloudless days that seem to accent the lush and tranquil greens of coal country, but whose peacefulness belies the dirty and often deadly jobs that people perform in the ground below.

After parking a tractor, the bearded Wellington ambled up a driveway and into the office of his employer. He was there strenuously objecting that a less senior miner had leapfrogged him, getting lucrative vacation work that allowed him to work and be paid overtime while the mine was shut down for a period. Sitting three shotgun lengths from a group including Bob Gossman, the labor relations director, Wellington declared, "This was all Gossman's screw-up!"

Was the violence notorious in the coal fields about to erupt at the Wabash mine of Amax Coal Co? Contrary to appearances, no. Both Wellington and Gossman actually were involved in a method of resolving grievances whose guru is Stephen Goldberg, an unminerly Northwestern Law School professor who summers in France, runs marathons and has handled some of major league baseball's controversial salary arbitrations. . . .

In labor relations, as in the legal system, many are convinced that procedures have become too cumbersome and too expensive and have made too many lawyers and arbitrators rich enough to buy their own coal mines.

That's why Goldberg cajoled coal companies, infamous for terrible labor relations, into trying something different. He's doing the same with BellSouth Corp. (the old Southern Bell), the big teachers' union in the state of Washington, a few manufacturing and transportation firms and even a federal judge who farms out cases to him.

The traditional grievance process often results in two sides turning to the binding ruling of an arbitrator. They engage in a formal, courtroom-like process marked by stridency. This nearly always results in great expense and a ruling that may leave both sides unhappy—and leaves unresolved the real employer-employee frustrations underlying the dispute.

Goldberg tries to goad parties into settling the mess themselves. . . .

The accent is on the informal, as evidenced with Doc Wellington. An Amax supervisor had thought only two members of Wellington's day shift would be needed for vacation work. He thus asked Wellington only if he would be interested in vacation work on the two later shifts. Wellington, a proud fellow who prefers his day shift, said no.

Just before the vacation, the company posted a third vacancy for the day shift on a bulletin board, but no one told Wellington about it, and the job was taken by a less senior worker who had previously agreed to work a later shift.

Amax contended that by declining to work the later two shifts, Doc had effectively said he didn't want to work at all. The company admitted it hadn't specifically notified him of its later need for a third worker on the day shift but said Wellington should have read the bulletin board.

Wearing slacks and a sports shirt, Goldberg sat Wellington down at a table with union and company officials and asked everybody to begin explaining their positions. There was no witness box or stenographer. It was all very conversational and loose.

Puffing on a cigarette, Doc Wellington said: "The only gripe I have is why I wasn't asked to work my own shift. Bob Gossman's right, I turned down the second and third shift. But that's because I don't think I should work those."

Goldberg asked management to leave and probed deeper with the union, seeking to learn how one might avoid such a future snafu. He then told the union to leave, brought back management and delicately suggested that he was troubled by the fact that Wellington had never been directly asked about work on his own shift.

"Quite candidly, I think you have a loser if this goes to arbitration," said Goldberg, an experienced arbitrator.

He thus utilized a critical element of his method; the potential pressure in suggesting what end a costly arbitration might bring. It is a pressure point born of labor contracts and thus not really transferrable to nonunion firms without real grievance procedures.

If Amax lost an arbitration, it might have to pay Doc about $1,800 for 17 shifts of pay he arguably missed during the vacation period (including triple time on a Sunday). Gossman reiterated that "I've got a real problem with a guy turning down work and then getting any money."

Goldberg patiently continued and, along the way, got the union to admit that any foul-up was surely inadvertent. He pointed out the union also had a weak point if the case went to arbitration: Wellington's failure to look at the bulletin board.

Over two hours, both sides slowly moved far from rigid stances, and a deal was struck. Doc would get paid for nine shifts, or about $1,000, and procedures would be improved for future vacation openings.

Union official Rick Tygett estimated that by avoiding arbitration, he saved as much as $2,000, including the payment of lost wages for some hearing witnesses. Gossman and mine manager Steve Garcia figured they saved perhaps $1,500. Instead, the two sides split Goldberg's daily fee of $600, which he gets regardless of how many grievances he handles (there were two this day).

But there was something more important than money. "You aren't left with a bad taste in your mouth after mediation," Garcia said. "Arbitration is a semihostile environment, a win-lose situation. This lets a guy blow off steam right in front of you."

"There are a lot of labor-relations people who carry arbitration won-loss records tattooed on their arms," Gossman said, "but maintaining rapport with your people is important." He noted with pride that even with 739 hourly employees, not one grievance had gone to arbitration in three years.

"With mediation, you get a settlement both agree to, not just what a third-party says," Tygett said. "And even after you win arbitrations, bad feelings remain. I'd grade this an A-plus."[39]

There is some opposition to this method of grievance settlement. Some companies and unions are not willing to let third parties in. Moreover, lawyers know that settling grievances early may result in a significant decline in their income.

So far, the experience with grievance mediation appears to have been a success.

SUMMARY

Historically speaking, industrial or organizational jurisprudence is largely a union contribution. Unions brought it about directly by insisting upon it. They also indirectly aided its development because many firms improved their employee relations as a deterrent to unionization.

At its best, organizational jurisprudence is more than a set of techniques; it is a philosophy of organizational life and the application of democratic principles to the workplace. Organizational jurisprudence brings to workers in the economic sphere some of the rights they enjoy in the political sphere. It introduces into the organization a Bill of Rights complete with due process, the equivalent of trial by jury, and increased freedom of speech. It permits workers to deal with their bosses as their approximate equals.

At its worst, the machinery that is supposed to produce organizational jurisprudence can be worse than an arbitrary management. It can disrupt production. Union representatives can be dumb or careless or play favorites, so that processing a grievance through the union system can be more frustrating than even a second-rate management system or none at all—and the worker may have to pay for the union system.

Notes

1. The general line of reasoning here is that of Peter F. Drucker in his *New Society* (New York: Harper, 1949), Chapter 10.
2. Sumner H. Slichter, *Union Policies and Industrial Management* (Washington, DC: The Brookings Institution, 1941), pp. 1–8.

3. Patrick J. Cihon and James O. Castagnera, *Labor and Employment Law* (Boston: PWS-Kent, 1988), p. 557.

4. *Basic Patterns in Union Contracts,* Fourteenth Edition (Washington, DC: Bureau of National Affairs, 1995), p. 33.

5. Ibid., p. 34.

6. The shop steward is an appointed or elected representative of the union within a shop, division, or department of a company. He or she is normally a regular employee of the company but is allowed time away from work to handle grievances. Time thus spent may be paid for by the company, by the union, or by the two jointly, depending on their particular arrangements.

7. Contract between GTE North Inc. and Communication Workers of America.

8. *Basic Patterns in Union Contracts,* op. cit., p. 34.

9. Ibid.

10. Thomas A. Kochan and Harry C. Katz, *Collective Bargaining and Industrial Relations,* 2nd ed. (Homewood, IL: Irwin, 1988), p. 296.

11. Taft-Hartley Act, Section 203(d).

12. John P. Windmuller, "A Comparative Study of Methods and Practice" in *Collective Bargaining in Industrialized Market Economies: A Reappraisal,* Windmuller *et al.,* eds. (Geneva, Switzerland: International Labor Organization, 1987), pp. 133–37.

13. *Textile Workers v. Lincoln Mills,* 353 U.S. 448 (1957).

14. *Steelworkers v. American Manufacturing Co.,* 363 U.S. 564 (1960); *Steelworkers v. Warrior Gulf and Navigation Co.,* 363 U.S. 574 (1960); *Steelworkers v. Enterprise Wheel and Car Corp.,* 363 U.S. 593 (1960).

15. *Spielberg Mfg. Co.,* 112 NLRB 1080 (1955) and *Olin Corporation,* 268 NLRB No. 86 (1984).

16. *Collyer Insulated Wire and Local Union 1098,* 192 NLRB 837 (1971) and *United Technologies,* 268 NLRB No. 83 (1984).

17. Federal Mediation and Conciliation Service, *Annual Reports for Fiscal Years 1993–1994* (Washington, DC: 1995), pp. 27–29.

18. This section relies on Frank Elkouri and Edna Asper Elkouri, *How Arbitration Works,* 4th ed. (Washington, DC: Bureau of National Affairs, 1985), Chapter 9, and Marlin M. Volz and Edward P. Goggin, *Supplement to Elkouri and Elkouri, How Arbitration Works (1985–1987)* (Washington, DC: Bureau of National Affairs, 1988), Chapter 9.

19. *Alexander v. Gardner-Denver Company,* 415 U.S. 147 (1974).

20. Ibid., n. 21.

21. *Steele v. Louisville and Nashville R.R.,* 323 U.S. 192 (1944).

22. *Hines v. Anchor Motor Freight,* 424 U.S. 554 (1976).

23. *Bowen v. United States Postal Service,* 459 U.S. 212 (1983).

24. Dawn Anfuso, "Peer Review Wards off Unions and Lawsuits" in *Personnel Journal,* January 1994, p. 64.

25. Ibid.

26. Ibid.

27. Letter to the author from law professor Alvin Goldman, June 5, 1995.

28. *Arbitration 1990. New Perspectives on Old Issues.* Proceedings of the 43th Annual Meeting, National Academy of Arbitrators, San Diego, California, May 27–June 2, 1990 (Washington, DC: Bureau of National Affairs), pp. 189–90.

29. Ibid.

30. Casey Ichniowski and David Lewin, "Grievance Procedures and Firm Performance" in *Human Resources and the Performance of the Firm,* Morris M. Kleiner, Richard N. Block, Myron Roomkin, and Sidney W. Salsburg, eds. (Madison, WI: Industrial Relations Research Association, 1987), pp. 159–94.

31. Ibid., pp. 177–79.

32. Ibid., pp. 180–82.

33. Robert D. Allen and Timothy J. Keaveny, *Contemporary Labor Relations,* 2nd ed. (Reading, PA: Addison-Wesley, 1988), pp. 565–66.

34. Marcus H. Sandver, Harry R. Blain, and Mark N. Woyar, "Time and Cost Savings through Expedited Arbitration Procedures," *The Arbitration Journal* 36 (December 1981), pp. 11–21.

35. William L. Ury, Jeanne M. Brett, and Stephen B. Goldberg, *Getting Disputes Resolved: Designing Systems to Cut the Costs of Conflict* (San Francisco: Jossey-Bass, 1988), pp. 134–68.

36. *Labor Law Journal,* CCH, April 1995, p. 207.

37. Arthur T. Jacobs, "Use of Grievance Mediation Spreading," *The Chronicle,* National Academy of Arbitrators, January 1994, p. 7.

38. *Arbitration 1993. Arbitration and the Changing World of Work.* Proceedings of the 46th Annual Meeting, National Academy of Arbitrators, Denver, Colorado, May 31–June 6, 1993 (Washington, DC: Bureau of National Affairs), p. 40.

39. J. Warren, "Mediation Cools Off the Coalfields," *Chicago Tribune,* October 8, 1985, sec. 3, p. 1. Copyrighted October 8, 1985, Chicago Tribune Company. All rights reserved. Used with permission. See also Ury et al., op. cit., pp. 153–56.

CHAPTER 16

Public-Sector Collective Bargaining

After reading this chapter, you should be able to

■ Describe the characteristics of the major public-sector unions and the ways they are organized.

■ Compare the sovereignty doctrine with a private-sector management rights clause and explain how this doctrine affects strike activity.

■ Outline some important executive orders that have affected union growth.

■ Outline bargaining unit determination at the federal and state levels.

■ Evaluate the limitations of union security in the public sector and outline the controversy surrounding this issue.

■ Review and evaluate the local, state, and federal regulations surrounding the public employee's right to strike.

THE U.S. SYSTEM OF PUBLIC-SECTOR COLLECTIVE BARGAINING

This chapter will explore similarities, differences, and complexities within the system of public-sector collective bargaining in the United States. The public sector can be divided into the federal, state, and local sectors. The laws governing collective bargaining differ in fundamental ways across these sectors and even within one sector for various occupations.

TRENDS IN PUBLIC-SECTOR EMPLOYMENT AND UNION MEMBERSHIP

In 1995 the proportion of union members in the public sector (37.8 percent) was more than three times as large as in the private sector (10.4 percent).[1] Of 16.4 million union members in the United States, 6.9 million worked for the government.[2] Over 40 percent of all union members, then, are government employees. These numbers reflect the vitality of public-sector col-

---

This chapter was revised by Steven H. Kropp, arbitrator, Boston, Massachusetts.

lective bargaining. With the exception of the early 1980s, there has been relatively constant growth in total public-sector employment since World War II (see Table 16.1). As a percentage of the total work force, however, government employment peaked in the middle of the 1970s. Federal government employment as a percentage of total employment has been dropping almost continuously since 1946. Most of the growth in public-sector jobs occurred within the state and local government sectors. State and local government employment increased by more than 460 percent over this period, whereas federal employment increased a mere 30 percent. Over the same period, the growth rate of total employment was about 260 percent.

The pattern of public-sector employment can be partially explained by general population growth magnified by changes in the demographics of age. The populations over 65 and under 25, those with the largest service needs, grew at a faster rate than the overall population. Another factor responsible for government employment growth was an expanded demand for a wider range of government services in U.S. society. The growth rate slowed in the early 1980s because of U.S. voters' changing view of the role of government.

The Wagner Act (1935) specifically excluded from its definition of *employer* federal, state, and local governments, thus denying public employees the protection afforded by Section 7 and related provisions. The Taft-Hartley Act perpetuated this exclusion. Additionally, Taft-Hartley prescribed mandatory loss of job and civil service status for federal employees who participated in strikes. The 1950s witnessed major clashes between union leaders and the federal government, particularly between the postal union and the Eisenhower administration.

In 1961 President Kennedy appointed the Goldberg-Macy task force, whose main recommendations were incorporated into Executive Order 10988, issued in 1962 and described later in this chapter. This order was hailed by union leaders as the Magna Carta for federal employee unionism. Labor relations in the federal sector came under statutory law with the passage of the Civil Service Reform Act of 1978, Title VII—Federal Service Labor-Management Relations.

Collective bargaining was not widely utilized at the state and local levels until the 1960s. Public-employee legislation passed by state and local governments accelerated noticeably following the 1962 issuance of Executive Order 10988, with most state legislation having been enacted since 1965 and much of it patterned on the private-sector model.

The pattern of relatively low union membership totals during the 1930s, 1940s, and 1950s was followed by sharp membership gains in the 1960s and part of the 1970s. Public-sector union membership was stable, at about 10 percent of the total public-sector work force, during the period from 1933 through 1960 (see Table 16.2). In two years, between 1960 and 1962, unions experienced dramatic growth in the public sector. By 1962 membership had grown by almost 150 percent to 24.3 percent. Initially, most of the growth occurred in the state and local sectors rather than among federal employees. Although the pace of growth slowed after that early dramatic expansion, total public-sector union membership increased steadily until the late 1970s. Since then, membership levels have been relatively stable at about 37 percent of public-sector employment.

FACTORS INFLUENCING THE GROWTH OF PUBLIC-SECTOR COLLECTIVE BARGAINING

The history of public-sector unionization can be divided into three distinct periods. In the pre-1960s "quiescent period," the percentage of organized employees was fairly low at about 10 percent of the labor force. The second period can be described as a major growth stage. This phase began in the early 1960s and ended in 1978, when public-employee union membership peaked at 38.2 percent. The third period, which started in 1980 and

TABLE 16.1 Employment in Federal, State, and Local Government

Year	Total Employment (in thousands)	Total Government		Federal Government		State and Local Government	
		Employment (in thousands)	Percentage of Total Employment	Employment (in thousands)	Percentage of Total Employment	Employment (in thousands)	Percentage of Total Employment
1946	41,652	5,595	13.4%	2,254	5.4%	3,341	8.0%
1950	45,197	6,026	13.3	1,928	4.3	4,098	9.1
1955	50,641	6,914	13.7	2,187	4.3	4,727	9.3
1960	54,189	8,353	15.4	2,270	4.2	6,083	11.2
1965	60,763	10,074	16.6	2,378	3.9	7,696	12.7
1970	70,880	12,554	17.7	2,731	3.9	9,823	13.9
1975	76,945	14,686	19.1	2,748	3.6	11,937	15.5
1980	90,406	16,241	18.0	2,866	3.2	13,375	14.8
1981	91,152	16,031	17.6	2,772	3.0	13,259	14.5
1982	89,544	15,837	17.7	2,739	3.1	13,098	14.6
1983	90,152	15,869	17.6	2,774	3.1	13,096	14.5
1984	94,408	16,024	17.0	2,807	3.0	13,216	14.0
1985	97,387	16,394	16.8	2,875	2.9	13,519	13.9
1986	99,344	16,693	16.8	2,899	2.9	13,794	13.9
1987	101,958	17,010	16.7	2,943	2.9	14,067	13.8
1988	105,210	17,386	16.5	2,971	2.8	14,415	13.7
1989	107,895	17,778	16.5	2,988	2.8	14,791	13.7
1990	109,419	18,304	16.7	3,085	2.8	15,219	13.9
1991	108,256	18,402	17.0	2,966	2.7	15,436	14.3
1992	108,604	18,644	17.1	2,969	2.7	15,675	14.4
1993	110,730	18,816	17.0	2,915	2.6	15,901	14.4
1994	114,034	19,118	16.8	2,870	2.7	16,247	15.0
1995	116,609	19,279	16.5	2,821	2.6	16,457	15.0

Source: Economic Report of the President (Washington, DC: U.S. Government Printing Office, 1996), B–42.

TABLE 16.2   Public-Sector Union Membership

Year	Total Government		Federal Government		State and Local Government	
	Percentage Union Members	Percentage Covered	Percentage Union Members	Percentage Covered	Percentage Union Members	Percentage Covered
1933	9.4					
1939	10.8					
1945	9.8					
1953	11.6					
1958	10.6		23.2			
1960	10.8		23.8			
1962	24.3		26.9		24.3	
1964	26.0		31.0		25.0	
1966	26.1		31.9		24.8	
1968	25.9		37.1		24.9	
1970	25.8		39.6		30.1	
1972	30.1		43.3		33.7	
1974	33.3		40.3		37.1	
1976	36.2		41.5		39.9	
1978	38.2		38.5		35.7	
1980	35.4		36.6		34.1	
1981	35.5		37.2		33.5	
1982	35.8		38.0		33.5	
1983	35.1	46.8	36.8		32.5	
1984	36.0	44.5				
1985	37.1	44.5				
1986	35.9	43.1				
1987	35.8	42.4				
1988	36.7	43.6				
1989	36.7	43.6				
1990	36.5	43.3				
1991	36.9	43.3				
1992	36.7	43.2				
1993	37.7	43.8				
1994	38.7	44.7				
1995	37.8	43.5				

Source: Membership data from 1958 to 1983 are from Leo Troy and Neil Sheflin, *Union Sourcebook: Membership, Structure, Finance, Directory* (West Orange, NJ: Industrial Relations Data and Information Services, 1985), Appendix A. Membership data from 1984 to 1987 and coverage data from 1983 to 1987 are from Michael A. Curme, Barry T. Hirsh, and David A. MacPherson, "Union Membership and Contract Coverage in the United States, 1983–1988," *Industrial and Labor Relations Review* 44 (October 1990), Table 1. Data from 1988 to 1995 are from U.S. Bureau of Labor Statistics, *Employment and Earnings,* various volumes (January issues), January 1996, p. 212.

continues today, can be seen as a consolidation stage.[3] By 1995, union membership, after declining slightly, had rebounded to 37.8 percent of total government employment (see Table 16.2).

The pre-1960 relatively low level of public-sector union membership (compared to that in the private sector) has been explained by a lesser need for unionization due to the greater job security enjoyed by public employees. In the past, government employment was less sensitive to business cycles. Also, the composition of the government employee population was more heavily weighted toward women and white-collar workers, who have traditionally been more difficult for unions to organize. Furthermore, public employees' bargaining power was limited by laws outlawing strikes. Until the 1960s, there were hardly any legal frameworks for certification or recognition of bargaining representatives and no obligation on the part of employers to negotiate with unions. Finally, the presence of the civil service system with its due-process procedures may have reduced the perceived need for unions.[4]

Given all of these factors inhibiting unionization, how can we account for the growth period? First, the professional nature of much of public employment provides a sense of group identity, which has proven to be fertile ground for unionization. That group identity sometimes reflected itself in professional associations, some of which evolved into bargaining representatives. Second, although the fairly low pay offset by stable employment of public-sector jobs may have been attractive during the 1930s, inflation and low private-sector unemployment rates in the 1960s may have changed that view. Third, as public-sector employment grew, younger workers became a larger proportion of the work force. These workers may have had less respect for government authority, and hence more willingness to join unions. Fourth, as public employees became more positive toward unionization, some private-sector unions began to take greater interest in organizing the public sector. Finally, major changes in statutes and federal executive orders provided public employees with bargaining rights.[5]

There is considerable debate among scholars regarding the causal relationship between the new public-sector statutes and union growth. Some argue that the changes in legislation led to increased interest in unionization on the part of public employees.[6] Others believe that the desire of public employees to unionize exerted pressure on policy makers to enact more permissive laws.[7] In summary, we can state that all researchers seem to acknowledge the favorable effect of the new laws on unionization. Some of them, however, have expressed the view that the new statutes were only partially responsible for the accelerated unionization of the public sector between 1962 and 1978 (see Table 16.2). They conclude that some of the factors discussed previously, apart from the new laws, played an important role in the unionization of the public sector.

THE MAJOR UNIONS IN THE PUBLIC SECTOR

This section will outline certain characteristics of major public-sector unions by level of government and employee function, starting at the national level.[8]

Unions of Postal Employees

Two of the oldest trade unions are the National Association of Letter Carriers (NALC) and the American Postal Workers Union (APWU). Currently, the NALC, AFL-CIO, has 210,000 members; the APWU, AFL-CIO, has 261,000 members. These two major unions negotiate jointly.[9] Postal workers are highly unionized, and most of them are covered by collective bargaining agreements.

Postal unions have traditionally been among the most experienced and effective congressional lobbyists. Despite such success, however, postal union leaders sought to replace what they considered "collective begging" with collective bargaining. In 1970 the postal workers, led by the New York City unit, which lacked exclusive recognition at the national level under the bargaining structure created by the executive orders, engaged in a successful, though illegal, strike. They demanded improved economic benefits and a bargaining structure similar to that in the private sector. As a result, the 1970 Postal Reorganization Act was passed, enabling represented workers to avail themselves of traditional NLRB remedies. The scope of bargaining for postal workers now includes wages, hours, and conditions of employment, with the exception of pensions (which remain under congressional jurisdiction) and certain other personnel actions (still controlled by civil service regulations). The act prohibits compulsory union membership and the right to strike, substituting for the latter the right to take bargaining disputes to "interest" arbitration. The Postal Service and its unions have resorted to arbitration on several occasions.

Federal Executive Branch Unions

In 1990 the statistical breakdown of representation by major federal employee unions was as follows: The American Federation of Government Employees (AFGE), AFL-CIO, represented about 642,000 employees, of whom 153,000 were union members. The National Federation of Federal Employees (NFFE), independent, represented 146,000 employees, of whom 52,000 were union members. The National Treasury Employees Union (NTEU), independent, represented 152,000 employees, of whom 140,000 were union members.[10]

The American Federation of Government Employees is the largest union representing federal employees. It continues to face a significant "free rider" problem, evidenced by a large gap between actual membership and representation, which has been only partially explained by the Civil Service Reform Act's prohibition of the compulsory payment of union dues. As a consequence, AFGE in 1987 and 1988 had serious financial difficulties.[11] The union leadership is expected to strive to increase membership.

The National Federation of Federal Employees began in 1917 as a union of federal government employees. In 1962, NFFE condemned the executive order and even instituted litigation, though unsuccessful, challenging its constitutionality. Two years later, after a change in top leadership, the union reversed its position on this issue.

The National Treasury Employees Union originated in 1938 as a union of professionals in the Internal Revenue Service. It now consists primarily of Treasury Department employees, though some members are employed by other federal agencies. The transition from a group of rather specialized, middle-level professionals to an agency-wide, industrial-type union with a considerable representation of clerical workers has not always been smooth. However, the NTEU has emerged as a stronger union, as evidenced by consolidating local agreements into agency-wide collective bargaining agreements. It also gained national recognition rights for all IRS employees and is expected to strengthen further.

State and Local Unions

At the state and local levels, one of the dominant unions is the American Federation of State, County and Municipal Employees (AFSCME), AFL-CIO. With over one million members, this union is one of the few that has continued to grow during the 1980s and 1990s, making it one of the largest affiliates of the AFL-CIO. The AFSCME membership is unusually diverse. As of 1994, this union had 300,000 members in health care, 365,000 white-collar members, 300,000 blue-collar members, and 75,000 members in law enforcement.[12]

The Service Employees International Union (SEIU), AFL-CIO, with about 900,000 members, represents public- and private-sector workers in health care; clerical, technical, and professional employees; and police in New England and on the West Coast. Other major state and local unions are the International Association of Fire Fighters (IAFF), AFL-CIO, which represents most firefighters; the Fraternal Order of Police (FOP), which is the largest police union; and the International Union of Police Associations (IUPA).

The American Nurses Association (ANA) represents private-sector nurses covered by Taft-Hartley and nurses employed by state, county, and city governments.

Representing local transit employees, including bus drivers, are three major unions: the Amalgamated Transit Union (ATU), the Transport Workers Union (TWU), and the United Transportation Union (UTU).

Under Section 13(c) of the Urban Mass Transit Act of 1964, transit companies bought or operated by states and localities with federal assistance are required to continue existing collective bargaining rights, except the right to strike.[13] Transit industry workers are the only nonfederal public employees to bargain under the auspices of federal legislation.

Many unions with origins in the private sector have attracted significant public-employee membership. Unions such as the Communications Workers of America (CWA) and the International Brotherhood of Teamsters (IBT), both AFL-CIO affiliates, have sizable numbers of public employees within their ranks.

National Educational Unions

There are three major unions in education: the National Education Association (NEA), the American Federation of Teachers (AFT), and the American Association of University Professors (AAUP). In contrast to the situation in the federal sector, membership in the educational groups exceeds the extent of collective bargaining coverage because many AAUP chapters still do not engage in collective bargaining.

The NEA is an independent union with over two million members. It is the single largest union in the United States. It originally functioned as a professional organization. Since 1962, however, it has become somewhat similar to the AFT in its bargaining approach. The NEA still differs from the AFT in that it opposes affiliation with the AFL-CIO, allows school administrators a say in its affairs in certain states, and remains comparatively conservative in its policies toward collective bargaining. The AFT is an AFL-CIO affiliate with approximately 600,000 members. It represents teachers in many major cities, including New York, Philadelphia, Detroit, Boston, Pittsburgh, Cleveland, Cincinnati, Minneapolis, Denver, and Baltimore.

These two teacher unions remain very competitive despite several discussions of merger. The AFT has long favored such a merger, but many NEA affiliates have been ambivalent. In 1972 the NEA and the AFT merged in New York State, only to have the merger dissolve in 1976, causing bitter acrimony on the part of the New York NEA, which lost most of its members to the AFT.[14] Recently, merger talks received a boost. The Minnesota Education Association and the Minnesota Federation of Teachers are drafting an agreement to create a single statewide union comprising nearly 80,000 members.[15] Nationally, the AFT and the NEA appointed a joint committee in 1993 to consider a formal merger. The committee's recommendations were expected to be addressed in 1995; however, in December 1994, national merger talks failed again.[16]

The AAUP is an independent organization with about 45,000 active members at the college level. Long an advocate of faculty governance, the AAUP abandoned its opposition to collective bargaining by deciding in 1972 to engage in this process.

THE SOVEREIGNTY DOCTRINE

The sovereignty doctrine derives from the English common law and is expressed in the maxim, "The King can do no wrong." Applied to government employment, the maxim means that only unilateral action by the government employer to establish the terms and conditions of employment is allowed. The sovereignty doctrine is a broader concept than is the management rights concept in the private sector.

Modern legal understanding recognizes that the government can, and often does, "waive" its sovereign immunity in a variety of circumstances. Economist Leo Troy argues that any system of public-sector collective bargaining diminishes the government's sovereignty and is incompatible with the doctrine.[17] Federal legislation and executive orders and state statutes, discussed in the following sections, have been influenced by the sovereignty doctrine. Specifically, these regulations delineate management's rights in unilateral decision making.

The sovereignty doctrine also contributes to another feature of collective bargaining in the public sector—namely, the impropriety of the strike. Thus, the federal and most state and local governments deny their employees the right to strike. The rationale for preventing strikes in the public sector is based also on the essentiality of government services. The right to strike will be discussed in more detail later in this chapter.

EXECUTIVE ORDERS AND FEDERAL LEGISLATION

Executive Order 10988, signed by President Kennedy in 1962, provided the biggest single impetus to the growth of unionization in the federal sector. Among its main features were provisions granting federal employees the right to form and join unions, providing for union recognition, and permitting unions a limited scope of bargaining. Primary responsibility for implementation of the order was placed on each federal agency.

A later executive order, E.O. 11491, articulated the principle of exclusive recognition of employee organizations and established the Federal Labor Relations Council and the Federal Services Impasse Panel. These agencies administer pertinent regulations and provide assistance for resolving disputes. Executive Order 11616 added the requirement that grievance procedures be included in all contracts and stated that interpretation and application of agency regulations could be subject to those grievance procedures. Finally, E.O. 11838 stipulated that all agency regulations dealing with personnel policies were deemed mandatory subjects of bargaining unless the agency could show a "compelling need" not to negotiate.

An important development in the federal sector was the passage of the Civil Service Reform Act of 1978 (CSRA). Together with President Carter's Reorganization Plan No. 2 of 1978, which established a statutory administrative agency, the Federal Labor Relations Authority (FLRA), this law governs labor-management relations in the federal government. The law recognizes that collective bargaining in the federal sector is in the public interest and affords statutory protection of bargaining rights while attempting to ensure fulfillment of certain employee obligations to the public. Coverage of the law extends to most federal executive branch employees, with some exemptions, including persons involved in national security functions and any person who participates in an illegal strike.

The Postal Reorganization Act of 1970 conferred upon postal workers virtually all of the collective bargaining rights, with the exception of the right to strike, enjoyed by employees in the private sector. The act gave the NLRB the responsibility of determining appropriate bargaining units, supervising elections, and hearing unfair labor practice cases involving postal employees. Salaries of postal workers are now set by collective bargaining between the U.S. Postal Service and four unions holding national exclusive recognition: the National Association of Letter Carriers, the American Postal Workers Union, the Rural Letter Carriers Association, and the Mail Handlers Division, Laborer's International Union.

FEDERAL ADMINISTRATIVE AGENCIES AND THEIR FUNCTIONS

Under the CSRA, there has been considerable change in the administration of public-sector labor relations law for federal employees. This statute vests central authority over federal labor-management relations in the Federal Labor Relations Authority (FLRA), an agency composed of three presidential appointees. The General Counsel of the FLRA, also a presidential appointee, is empowered to investigate alleged unfair labor practices and to file and prosecute complaints. The basic function of the FLRA is to provide leadership in establishing policies for the administration of the statute. The structure of the FLRA is modeled largely on that of the National Labor Relations Board.

The Federal Services Impasse Panel (FSIP), an agency within the FLRA, is authorized to review negotiation impasses that may still exist after an unproductive mediation effort by the Federal Mediation and Conciliation Service (FMCS). The FSIP has wide latitude in its approach to impasse resolution. Either party can request its services, or the FSIP can require the parties to accept fact finding with recommendations or arbitration as a means of resolving an impasse.

In 1993, President Clinton appointed a task force, led by Vice President Gore, to review the way the federal government operates. The Gore report, issued in September 1993, sought to change the culture of federal government operations by cutting red tape, putting the customer (the citizen) first, empowering employees to get results, and cutting back to basics—eliminating wasteful spending and unnecessary programs.[18] The Gore report contained a number of recommendations that could affect federal labor-management relations. In October, President Clinton signed Executive Order 12871, establishing a national partnership council to advise the president on labor-management relations in the executive branch. E.O. 12871 also created labor-management partnerships at federal agencies subject to collective bargaining by forming agency-level labor-management committees.

Some scholars have criticized the premises of the Gore task force and report. One writer argues that the Gore report fails to recognize that private-sector management is fundamentally different from public-sector management because the role of the federal government is to implement in a democratic way the laws of the country.[19] According to this view, public-sector management is, at times, necessarily bureaucratic because it requires political accountability, not simply economic efficiency.[20]

STATE AND LOCAL LABOR RELATIONS AND LEGISLATION

The legal status of state and local labor relations has undergone major transformation during the past three decades. By 1993, 43 states and the District of Columbia had laws or executive orders requiring at least some public employers to bargain or meet and confer with public employees (see Table 16.3). Even in the seven states without permissive legislation, collective bargaining is not uncommon.[21] Before the early 1960s, fewer than a handful of states had such legislation.

"There is a . . . lack of any common pattern in current State legislation dealing with public employee bargaining."[22] Nevertheless, almost all statutes provide for exclusive recognition. In most states, an administrative agency is empowered to certify organizations and to conduct representation elections when necessary. At the local level, many governments voluntarily recognize unions, even when they are not statutorily required to do so. Most states currently have criteria for bargaining unit determination. As in the pri-

TABLE 16.3 Coverage of Employees by State Public-Sector Collective Bargaining Laws

State	All or Substantially All Employees Covered	Some Employees Covered
Alabama		*
Alaska	*	
Arizona[1]		*
Arkansas		
California	*	
Colorado	*	
Connecticut	*	
Delaware	*	
District of Columbia	*	
Florida	*	
Georgia		*
Hawaii	*	
Idaho		*
Illinois	*	
Indiana		*
Iowa	*	
Kansas		*
Kentucky		*
Louisiana		
Maine	*	
Maryland		*
Massachusetts	*	
Michigan	*	
Minnesota	*	
Mississippi		
Missouri		*
Montana	*	
Nebraska	*	
Nevada		*
New Hampshire	*	
New Jersey	*	
New Mexico	*	
New York	*	
North Carolina		
North Dakota		*
Ohio	*	
Oklahoma		*
Oregon	*	
Pennsylvania	*	
Rhode Island	*	
South Carolina		
South Dakota	*	
Tennessee		*
Texas		*
Utah[2]		*
Vermont	*	

| | All or Substantially All | |
| TABLE 16.3 (cont.) | | |
State	Employees Covered	Some Employees Covered
Virginia		
Washington	*	
West Virginia		
Wisconsin	*	
Wyoming		*
Total	28	16

[1]City of Phoenix has comprehensive collective bargaining law.

[2]Salt Lake City has comprehensive collective bargaining law.

Source: Public Employees Bargain for Excellence: A Compendium of State Public Sector Labor Relations Laws (Washington, DC: Public Employee Department, AFL-CIO, 1993).

vate sector, the designated administrative agency must, before conducting of a representation election, decide which groups of employees will be represented by the organization and who is thus eligible to vote. A majority of state laws expressly authorize some form of union security, at the very least employer dues deduction. The scope of bargaining differs among and within state and local governments. Grievance procedures also vary considerably, yet many states have kept intact procedures established by civil service commissions. Neither unfair labor practices nor impasse procedures are uniformly specified.

In sum, the variety of state legislation on each of the aforementioned subjects is so broad that only the barest of trends can be identified.

State Agencies

Most of the 43 states that have statutes or executive orders providing legal frameworks for collective bargaining have designated agencies to administer the laws. There is considerable variety among and within states, however. States with designated agencies empower them to establish bargaining units, to develop or comply with established unit determination criteria, and to hear cases involving unfair labor practices stipulated in their statutes (usually similar to those in the private sector). Some states have a two-tiered administrative structure, with one agency for state and the other for local government employees.

DETERMINATION OF THE APPROPRIATE BARGAINING UNIT: FEDERAL AND STATE LEVELS

Bargaining unit determination at the federal level closely resembles the method used in the private sector. The CSRA tests whether an appropriate unit exists by deciding whether the employees have a "clear and identifiable community of interest." Some of the criteria used to verify a "clear and identifiable community of interest" are common skills, similar working conditions, common supervision, common work site, and identical duties. Additionally, the statute stipulates that an appropriate unit must promote effective dealings with the agency involved. The extent to which a particular union has been successful in organizing employees may not be used to define an appropriate unit. Rules pertaining to professionals resemble those in the private sector.

When a federal agency and the union are unable to reach agreement on an appropriate bargaining unit, the dispute is referred to the FLRA. A review of decisions made at this level indicates that large units have generally been found more acceptable than small ones.

The determination of appropriate bargaining units for purposes of collective bargaining is probably no less crucial in terms of outcomes at the state and local levels than at the federal level. Interestingly enough, most state statutes have been much more specific in prescribing criteria for bargaining unit determination than has legislation in the private sector.

In states where "community of interest" is the sole or primary criterion for unit determination, the result is usually "a proliferation of relatively narrow units organized along lines of particular occupational distinctions or organizational components of the employer."[23] Public managers generally seek to avoid proliferation of bargaining units and instead favor large units because small units increase total bargaining time, increase the difficulty of achieving uniform application of wages and benefits, and increase the potential for interunion rivalry. Unions frequently favor whatever unit size will provide them with representation rights and enhance their bargaining power.

Some states have established the appropriateness of type and scope of bargaining units legislatively rather than delegating such authority, on a discretionary basis, to state boards. The rationale for this approach is to discourage unit proliferation that could ensue from petitions for certification of many small units.

An important public-sector bargaining unit issue concerns the status of supervisory and managerial personnel. In the private sector, under Taft-Hartley, supervisors and managers, as representatives of their employers, are denied collective bargaining rights. This restriction seeks to ensure that supervisors and managers give undivided loyalty to their employers. In the nonfederal public sector, however, supervisors and even some managers often are allowed to unionize and engage in collective bargaining. Should supervisors be included in the same units as their subordinates? If not, should the union that represents supervisors in one unit also be allowed to represent their subordinates in a separate unit? Traditionally, middle- and even upper-management employees have been members (and sometimes leaders) of public-sector employee organizations.[24] Some employers and employer organizations argue that the private-sector model of managerial exclusion from bargaining units is also essential for the effective functioning of government.[25] Some writers have made the point that inclusion of supervisors may have a moderating effect on unions, resulting in less militant organizations.[26]

The public-sector bargaining structure is complex and highly fragmented. Its development may be attributed to rigid legislative certification guidelines that have encouraged the emergence of fragmented bargaining structures, composed of many small units, and to the inability of many administrative agencies to modify existing bargaining frameworks. Particularly at the local level, civil service commissions and related agencies have often fragmented the personnel responsibility without substantial benefits to either management or labor. Inappropriate bargaining units may have an adverse effect on labor relations by complicating classification systems, increasing wage inequities, and weakening the processes of bargaining and contract administration.

ELECTIONS, RECOGNITION, AND CERTIFICATION AT THE FEDERAL AND STATE LEVELS

The rights of federal employees to organize and to choose their representatives are set forth in the CSRA of 1978, which closely mirrors the private-sector approach to union recognition. Consent elections may be held to determine the exclusive representatives of bargaining units. The FLRA will investigate whether a question of representation exists if anyone alleges that 30 percent of a bargaining unit believe their exclusive representative no longer represents the majority of the unit or, where there is no exclusive representative, that 30 percent wish to be exclusively represented for the purposes of collective bargaining. Following a hearing, the FLRA will schedule a secret ballot election. Any union that can show that it is the unit's exclusive representative or that it has at least 10 percent support may be placed on the ballot. (As under Taft-Hartley procedures, employees may vote for the choice of no representation.) The union receiving a majority vote is then certified by the FLRA as the exclusive representative.

At the state and local levels, there are procedures for election certification and recognition both in the absence and in the presence of legislation. In the absence of statutory guidelines, the parties resolve these issues among themselves. Under public-sector legislation, many states have established agencies to implement recognition procedures, including unit determination, elections, and certification. Most agency procedures are derived from the NLRB. Most states require a 30-percent show of interest (as evidenced by authorization cards, dues deduction cards, or notarized membership lists). As in the federal and private sectors, the winner must receive a majority of the valid ballots cast. Most statutes allow the certified bargaining agent a period of unchallenged representation, frequently tied to the budget submission date of the employer.[27]

Recognition in the private sector means exclusive representation rights. Under such an arrangement, an employee organization is given the right to represent and bargain for all the employees in the bargaining unit, nonunion as well as union. Nearly all public-sector statutes provide for exclusive bargaining rights. They also provide for the right of individual employees to present their grievances or opinions regardless of whether they belong to unions, often allowing the exclusive bargaining agent to be present at the hearing and/or to be notified of it.

UNFAIR LABOR PRACTICES

Under current federal law governing public employment, agency and union unfair labor practices generally parallel unfair practices as defined under the Taft-Hartley Act. Employer (agency) free speech, other than threats or promises or comments made under coercive conditions, is protected activity during a representational election, as it is in the private sector. Additionally, it is an unfair labor practice for an agency (1) to refuse to consult or negotiate in good faith with a union or (2) to enforce a new regulation that conflicts with an already existing collective bargaining agreement. Unions commit unfair labor practices if they discriminate in membership; if they refuse to cooperate in impasse resolution procedures; or if they engage in slowdowns, strikes, or other than informational picketing against agencies.

There is some variation in what is considered unfair labor practices under state collective bargaining legislation. In general, state statutes on unfair labor practices are also modeled on the provisions of the Wagner and Taft-Hartley Acts.

THE PROCESS OF COLLECTIVE BARGAINING IN THE PUBLIC SECTOR

The goals of public-sector employers are frequently difficult to understand because "they represent a conglomeration of interest pressures more complex than reside in a union."[28] There is a tendency in the public sector for budgetary authority to be fragmented, particularly between the legislative and executive branches.[29] Such fragmentation complicates the collective bargaining process because it may be unclear who has the final decision-making authority. Collective bargaining in the public sector has been described as multilateral, as contrasted with the typical bilateral negotiations occurring in the private sector.[30]

THE SCOPE OF BARGAINING IN THE PUBLIC SECTOR

The range of subjects negotiated between public employee unions and government managers varies considerably among jurisdictions.

Subjects of bargaining in the private sector are classified as mandatory (subjects over which labor and management must bargain), permissive (subjects over which labor and management may bargain), and illegal or prohibited (subjects over which labor and management cannot bargain). In the public sector, there is frequent debate over the appropriateness of utilizing the private-sector analysis, especially in the permissive category. In a few states, there is no permissive category; subjects of bargaining are either mandatory or prohibited. On the question of classifying a subject as mandatory, one author states that

> the main public sector justification for excluding a legal topic from the mandated bargaining process is that the demand involves a significant public policy question which should not be determined in the isolation of the bargaining process in which other vital public interests are not directly represented. If a topic is "too significant" to be classified as a mandatory subject of bargaining, does it make any sense to say it may be bargained about if labor and management agree?[31]

The following distinctions between the public and private sectors are usually advanced by those who argue that the appropriate scope of bargaining in the public sector should be significantly narrower than in the private sector:

1. The common-law doctrine of sovereignty suggests "that the private sector industrial relations model is per se inappropriate for the public sector" because bilateral decision making is thwarted by the employer's sovereignty.
2. The vital public interest that may be present in public-sector bargaining is generally absent in private-sector bargaining.
3. The extent of both regulation and protection is far greater for public- than for private-sector employees.
4. "Market constraints and employer mobility," which may moderate union demands in the private sector, are usually absent in the public sector.
5. "Unions and public employees are able to influence the outcome of political elections that determine the composition of the public management which will be on the other side of the bargaining table. . . . There is little counterpart to these political activities in the private sector."[32]

Increasingly, traditional distinctions are becoming blurred. First, concepts of sovereignty and illegal delegation are no longer serious general impediments to defining the scope of public-sector bargaining in private-sector terms.[33] Second, voters in the 1990s are sensitive to the inevitable trade-offs between tax rates and levels of service, particularly when layoffs are involved. Finally, public-sector bargaining has settled most key scope disputes through litigation, decreasing the prominence of scope issues to the level existing in the private sector.

Under the CSRA of 1978, the scope of bargaining for federal employees is severely constrained. The duty to bargain does not extend to the following facets of an agency's operations: mission, budget, organization, number of employees, and internal security practices. Management's right to hire, assign, direct, lay off, retain, or take disciplinary action against employees is also not subject to negotiation. According to E.O. 12871, however, an agency must bargain with a union on the numbers, types, and grades of employees or positions assigned to any organizational subdivision or work project. It also must agree to bargain on technology, methods, and means of performing work; procedures to be used in the exercising of management authority; and arrangements to be made for employees adversely affected by the exercising of such authority. Wages and benefits are currently controlled by Congress and the president, with actual pay scale determinations governed by the Federal Pay Comparability Act.

Under the Postal Reorganization Act, the scope of bargaining is considerably wider for postal workers than for other federal units because it is governed by relevant provisions of the Taft-Hartley Act to the extent that such are consistent with other provisions of the Reorganization Act. Representatives of postal workers, unlike those who represent federal agency employees, can negotiate "wages, hours and other terms and conditions of employment,"[34] except those expressly reserved to management.

On the state and local levels, a rather different situation exists concerning the scope of bargaining. Most states that have enacted some form of bargaining legislation prescribe a management obligation to bargain over wages, hours, and other terms and conditions of employment. Some states have enacted legislation authorizing negotiation by teachers over a broad list of permissible subjects, including class size, course content, and even textbook selection. The class size issue is an example of a topic that legitimately falls under the traditional "other terms and conditions of employment" but is also central to school district educational policy. This overlap makes it unclear whether the issue should be mandatory or permissive.

Although most state courts and public employee relations boards have relied on the mandatory-permissive-illegal categories, there is an important difference between the private and the public sector in their handling of attempts to draw the line between mandatory and permissive subjects. In the private sector, the controversies are handled on an ad hoc basis by the NLRB and the courts; in the public sector there is, in some cases, much more emphasis on statutory distinction.

UNION SECURITY

In the federal sector, union security clauses that would require either union membership or payment of a service fee as a condition of employment are prohibited by law. Consequently, increasing union membership is a particularly important goal for federal employee unions. One study suggests that "free riders," individuals who are not union members, tend to be women and also seem mostly to be professional, technical, or sales workers. Furthermore, free riders are also apt to receive lower weekly wages.[35] The authors hypothesize that government workers, perceiving greater job security, may be more likely to be free riders than are private-sector workers.[36] In another study examining a small unit of federal employees, the authors conclude that unions, to increase membership, need to maximize participation during election drives or, for established unions, during some other key events.[37]

The most widespread and least controversial form of union security in the public sector is dues checkoff, an agreement between a union and an employer to deduct union dues from employee wages. Most public-sector statutes and agreements stipulate that the dues checkoff must be individually authorized and that it must be revocable either after one year or at the end of the contract.

A significant development that occurred during the 1970s and 1980s was the growing acceptance by state and local government employers of stronger forms of union security. These arrangements included fair-share service fee requirements, agency shops, and, in some cases, union shops.[38]

The form of union security typically found in the public sector is the fair-share provision. This variation of the agency shop requires nonmembers to pay the union a prorated share of bargaining costs as a condition of employment. The fee is calculated to compensate the union for negotiating a contract and processing grievances. Thus, the nonunion member pays only for direct services of the union, not for activities such as political campaigning or lobbying.

Many public-sector statutes do not explicitly state which forms of union security are permitted. There have been conflicting state court decisions as to whether the right to refrain from joining a union authorizes the imposition of compulsory dues payment.[39] In many states, legislation allows agreements that include agency shop provisions. Four states (Connecticut, Hawaii, New York, and Rhode Island) have mandated legislatively the agency shop for at least some classifications of public employees.[40] Under these arrangements, exclusive bargaining representatives automatically receive mandatory dues deductions without having to negotiate union security provisions with employers.

In the public sector, there is considerable controversy regarding union security, which requires actual union membership or the payment of money to a union as a condition of continued employment. Opponents of such requirements contend that they violate (1) individual freedom of speech and association as protected by the U.S. Constitution's First and Fourteenth Amendments, (2) certain merit principles prevalent in much of the public sector, (3) a person's right to work, and (4) teacher tenure laws.

A series of U.S. Supreme Court decisions have addressed the issues of constitutionality and procedures of union security in the public sector.[41] In the *Abood* case, the Court decided that compulsory dues payment does not violate the dissenting employee's freedom of association. The Court did rule, however, that bargaining unit members who object to such payments cannot be required to pay the proportion of dues going to fund activities not related to collective bargaining. After the *Abood* ruling, several states limited legislatively the proportion of dues to be paid by objectors to between 80 and 85 percent of the total.[42]

Next, in the *Hudson* case, the Supreme Court established procedures to be applied for those objecting to the payment of full union dues. First, the burden is on the union to demonstrate the percentage of dues revenue that goes toward collective bargaining and that thus can be legitimately required of all bargaining unit members. Second, those objecting to the union's accounting must have access to a prompt and objective appeals procedure. Third, while that appeal is being pursued, any disputed funds must be held in escrow. This approach effectively excludes objectors' monies from being used, even temporarily, for non–collective bargaining purposes.[43]

The Supreme Court continues to wrestle with union security issues. Most recently, in the *Lehnert* case, the Court sharply divided over precisely what expenses dissenting (nonunion) employees must pay.[44] Public-sector unions can charge dissenters for expenses related to collective bargaining and contract administration, including lobbying activities solely related to legislative ratification of, or fiscal appropriations for, their collective bargaining agreement. Particularly controversial, the Court majority held that unions also may charge dissenters for expenses related to preparation for an illegal strike but not for any expenses incident to engagement in such a job action. Other "chargeable" activities include expenses for conventions, publications, and social activities.

On the other hand, unions are prohibited from charging dissenters for their share of dues related to union organizing, general public relations, political and ideological expenditures, and nearly all lobbying activity. Expenses from litigation conducted outside a dissenter's bargaining unit are also nonchargeable.

THE RIGHT TO STRIKE

Federal employees were prohibited from striking by the executive orders; this prohibition has been perpetuated with stronger sanctions under the CSRA of 1978. Most states prohibit public employees from striking either by statute or by court decisions. Despite these legal obstacles, strikes in government have not been uncommon, nor are they a recent phenomenon. The famous Boston police strike of 1919 brought Governor Calvin Coolidge to national attention with his assertion that there was no right to strike against the public safety for anybody, anywhere, anytime.[45]

Strikes among public employees, particularly at the state and local levels, became increasingly frequent between 1958 and 1979. After reaching its peak in 1979, strike activity decreased significantly, especially in 1981. Because of budget cutbacks effected during the Reagan administration, data on most public-sector strikes are no longer being collected. The significant drop in state and local strike activity occurring during and after 1981 may have been due to President Reagan's firing of striking air traffic controllers in August of that year.

Prohibition of nonfederal public-sector strikes has proved ineffective. Despite stringent potential penalties, many public employees have ignored legal restrictions and have struck their public employers. Significantly, when Ohio and Illinois adopted new public-sector labor legislation in 1984, both states allowed some public employees the right to strike. Currently, 14 states (Alaska, California, Colorado, Hawaii, Idaho, Illinois, Louisiana, Minnesota, Montana, Ohio, Oregon, Pennsylvania, Vermont, and Wisconsin) grant some public employees a limited right to strike.[46]

There are strong arguments for and against legalizing public-sector strikes. First, advocates of legitimizing public employee strikes believe the issue is overblown. They reason that the whole strike issue is detrimental to good labor relations and that it detracts from a positive labor relations atmosphere. Second, those who propose legalizing strikes claim that legitimate group conflict can have a positive or cathartic effect. Credibility of threats requires occasional strikes, and public employees are sometimes prepared to strike regardless of the legal status of their actions. Third, proponents insist that the strike serves as the ultimate test of a union's strength as a bargaining representative. In this light, a potential strike can be used more as a bargaining strategy than as a real weapon. Still another argument for strike legalization centers on achieving comparability with private-sector employees engaged in similar work (e.g., transit, health care, teaching, and the like) who already have the legal right to strike.

Opponents of the right to strike for public employees base their arguments on private-sector analogies. Public-sector management is at a distinct disadvantage because it lacks private-sector constraints governed by profit, competition, and input and output markets. Strike critics argue that economic objectives should be settled at the bargaining table and political objectives in the political arena. Additionally, granting strike rights would lead to a further erosion of government authority. Public employees, unlike their private-sector counterparts, have influence as voters over their public employers. Opponents also argue that legalization of public-employee strikes would contribute significantly to tax increases and inflation. Furthermore, they contend that such strikes are detrimental to public welfare and safety and harm third parties who have no influence on the outcomes. Finally, strike opponents argue that allowing strikes only for nonessential public employees would be unjust and inequitable, thus bolstering their contention that strikes should be prohibited for all public-sector employees.

There are some indications that in the last 15 years attitudes have changed and that the public has become more tolerant and willing to accept the proposition that public employees should have the right to strike. As already mentioned, two industrial states (Ohio and Illinois) recently modified their public-sector bargaining laws, granting some employees the right to strike. In addition, data from Roper polls conducted in 1978, 1985, and 1989 indicate a trend toward increasing support for public employee strike rights.[47] Finally, in 1985, the California Supreme Court found that public employee strikes were not illegal at common law.[48] The Supreme Court of Louisiana followed this approach in 1990.[49] Thus, in those states, where no specific legislation outlaws public-sector strikes, they are permissible.

FACT FINDING AND INTEREST ARBITRATION

Although at some point in the future more legislatures may legalize strikes among public employees, the current trend seems to be toward either fact finding or compulsory arbitration of interest disputes. The vast majority of states (36) employ fact finding as a method of impasse resolution.[50] Fact finding is typically a process in which the fact finder(s) recommend(s) terms of settlement to the disputing parties. These recommendations are nonbinding. Fact finders differ as to the criteria used to reach their recommendations. In addition to determining statutory requirements, many fact finders seek to ascertain what is an acceptable compromise; others consider what the parties would have settled for if they had settled on their own; and some recommend what they deem "fair."[51]

Many states use fact finding in combination with compulsory arbitration (or, in some states, with the strike). In some states fact finding may, however, be the final step in the impasse resolution process. Where that is the case, the union and management may adopt the fact finder's report as a basis for settlement or engage in further bargaining to resolve the impasse.

Twenty-three states provide compulsory arbitration for at least some public employees. All but three of these states require arbitration for police and firefighter disputes.[52]

Considerable research has centered on the effects of the availability of arbitration on the level of strike activity.[53] Although strikes still take place in states mandating arbitration, studies do show a significant decrease in strike activity in those states. When arbitration is available, employers are motivated to provide more generous settlements for fear that the potential arbitration awards may be worse than their settlement offers.

Legislation making arbitration available for public employees is strongly supported by unions and generally opposed by employers. Empirical research indicates that police and firefighter wages are higher (1 to 9 percent) in states with arbitration statutes than in states without such statutes. Furthermore, in arbitration states, nonwage outcomes for police unions are 20 percent more favorable.[54]

Although unions advocate arbitration legislation, research suggests that once states adopt compulsory arbitration, contract terms decided by arbitrators are, on the average, not any more favorable to unions than those reached through negotiation in these same states. This finding is not surprising because an arbitrator typically decides on the size of a fair settlement by examining negotiated settlements of comparable workers.[55] A major study of municipal and provincial collective bargaining in Canada may contain useful lessons for the United States. The authors found that wages decided under compulsory arbitration are about 2 percent higher than wages negotiated under the right to strike, and wages negotiated under the right to strike are about 2 percent higher than wages negotiated in jurisdictions with only duty-to-bargain legislation or no collective bargaining laws.[56] The authors conclude that there is a trade-off between reducing dispute costs and changing settlement outcomes.[57] Compulsory arbitration laws reduce dispute costs but produce the highest wage settlements. Right-to-strike laws raise wages somewhat but raise dispute costs substantially. The authors believe that, for some employers, the savings in dispute costs from compulsory arbitration exceed the concomitant costs in wage increases.

One way in which arbitration may affect the bargaining process is through the so-called "chilling effect." If a party to negotiations expects that an arbitrator will simply "split the difference" between the two parties' final offers, then there is no incentive for either side to make concessions. Under such circumstances, any concession made would just advance an arbitrated settlement closer to the opponent's final offer. Concerns over the chilling effect led to the enactment of legislation containing final-offer arbitration provisions in the following states: Illinois, Iowa, Michigan, New Jersey, Ohio, and Wisconsin. Under this system, the arbitrator must choose either the union's or management's final offer. Each party then has an incentive to make its final offer appear to be the more reasonable, thereby (the party hopes) increasing its chances of being selected by the arbitrator. In many instances, such behavior contributes to successive concessions by each party, a process that ultimately avoids arbitration by facilitating a negotiated settlement. Some final-offer statutes require the arbitrator to choose between a final-offer package presented by the union and one presented by the management. Such packages contain all issues at impasse; this type of final-offer arbitration is designed to provide an incentive for reducing the number of issues brought to arbitration. Other final-offer statutes permit the arbitrator to choose each issue separately from among the union's and management's final offers; thus, the final arbitration award may incorporate some of the issues supported by management and some supported by labor.

Some writers claim that arbitration may have a "narcotic effect," suggesting that if the parties are satisfied with an arbitration outcome in one contract round, this may increase the likelihood that the process will be used again in the future. Research based on arbitration experience in several states indicates that shortly after the enactment of arbitration legislation, parties may have become slightly dependent on this impasse resolution procedure.[58] Although most studies conclude that there are no indications of long-term dependence on this process, a study of arbitration in Ohio did find long-term dependence, particularly among police.[59] In Ohio arbitration is available to safety forces only.

UNION EFFECTS IN THE PUBLIC SECTOR

There have been at least 75 studies of the effects of public-sector unions on wages and several reviews of this literature.[60] The consensus of these studies is that public-sector unions do seem to increase the wages of public employees. The magnitude of this effect, however, tends to be smaller than the effect of unions in the private sector. One review of studies conducted in the 1970s and early 1980s concluded that unions increase public-sector wages by about 10 percent, compared to about 15 percent for the private sector.[61]

Public employers tend to devote a larger proportion of total compensation to employee benefits, compared to the private sector.[62] As in the private sector, unions of public employees tend to raise the levels of employee benefits more than they increase wages.[63]

Public-sector unions have been found to affect levels of employment, municipal budgets, and productivity. Public employee unions seem able to provide increased job security for their members. It appears that unions can use their political power to prevent budget cuts that might have resulted in layoffs.[64] In addition to avoiding layoffs, one study found that public-sector unions, through the political process, were able to increase employment, departmental budgets, and municipal expenditures.[65]

SUMMARY

Public-sector collective bargaining was a fairly isolated phenomenon until the 1960s. During the 1960s and much of the 1970s, public-sector union membership grew rapidly. Since then membership has been fairly stable at about 37 percent of the public-sector labor force (see Table 16.2). It is worth noting that this figure is about triple the union density in the private sector. At present, public-sector employees constitute a significant proportion of the total U.S. labor force.

Parts of this chapter were devoted to comparisons between collective bargaining in the public and the private sectors. To understand these two sectors fully, one must comprehend the particular legal framework within which each operates. In terms of applicable laws and regulations, there are significant differences among the private sector and the federal, state, and local public sectors. Furthermore, there are also major variations among the states themselves, ranging from statutes forbidding collective bargaining (North Carolina) through absence of legislation to laws that are similar to the NLRA.

The final section of this chapter discussed the effects of public-sector unions on a variety of outcomes. Like their private-sector counterparts, public-sector unions raise wages and employee benefits. Unlike unions in the private sector, public employee unions can exert political pressure. The political influence of these unions may explain the research findings that public employee unions are associated with increased public-sector employment as well as with enhanced municipal budgets.

In 1996 the Industrial Relations Research Association published a volume titled *Public Sector Employment in a Time of Transition.*[66] The book covers such topics as public-sector law, employee attitudes, dispute resolution, workplace innovations and systems change, and the public sector in other countries. It is a good supplement to the material in this chapter.

Notes

1. *Employment and Earnings* (Washington, DC: Department of Labor, Bureau of Labor Statistics, January 1996), pp. 210, 212.
2. Ibid.
3. John F. Burton Jr. and Terry Thomason, "The Extent of Collective Bargaining in the Public Sector" in *Public-Sector Bargaining,* 2nd ed., Benjamin Aaron, Joyce M. Najita, and James L. Stern, eds. (Washington, DC: Bureau of National Affairs, 1988), p. 14.
4. Ibid. See also Steven H. Kropp, "Rethinking the Labor and Employment Law Curriculum: Legal Education's Belated Response to the Demise of Collective Bargaining and the Rise of Individual Rights," *University of Cincinnati Law Review* 60 (Fall 1991), pp. 440–43.
5. For a discussion of the enactment of a comprehensive public-sector collective bargaining law in one state, see Berkeley Miller and William Canak, "From 'Porkchoppers' to 'Lambchoppers': The Passage of Florida's Public Employee Relations Act," *Industrial and Labor Relations Review* 44 (January 1991), pp. 349–66.
6. See Casey Ichniowski, "Public Sector Union Growth and Bargaining Laws: A Proportional Hazards Approach with Time-Varying Treatments" in *When Public Sector Workers Unionize,* Richard B. Freeman and Casey Ichniowski, eds. (Chicago: University of Chicago Press, 1988), pp. 19–38; Gregory M. Saltzman, "Public Sector Bargaining Laws Really Matter: Ev-

idence from Ohio and Illinois" in *When Public Sector Workers Unionize,* op. cit., pp. 41–78; Gregory M. Saltzman, "Bargaining Laws as a Cause and Consequence of the Growth of Teacher Unionism" in *Public Sector Labor Relations,* 3rd ed., David Lewin, Peter Feuille, Thomas A. Kochan, and John Thomas Delaney, eds. (Lexington, MA: Lexington Books, 1988), pp. 53–75; and Jeffrey S. Zax and Casey Ichniowski, "Bargaining Laws and Unionization in the Local Public Sector," *Industrial and Labor Relations Review* 43 (April 1990), pp. 447–62.

7. Hugh D. Hindman and David B. Patton, "Unionism in State and Local Governments: Ohio and Illinois, 1982–87," *Industrial Relations* 33 (January 1994), pp. 106–20. Burton and Thomason, op. cit., pp. 17–27.

8. This section relies, in part, on James L. Stern ("Unionism in Public Sector") in Aaron, op. cit., pp. 52–89.

9. C.D. Gifford, *Directory of U.S. Labor Organizations, 1996 Edition* (Washington, DC: Bureau of National Affairs, 1996), pp. 83–84.

10. Representation figures are drawn from William H. Holley and Kenneth M. Jennings, *The Labor Relations Process,* 5th ed. (Fort Worth, TX: Dryden Press, 1994), p. 515. Membership figures are also drawn from Raymond L. Hogler, *Labor and Employment Relations* (St. Paul, MN: West, 1995), p. 297 and from Gifford, ibid.

11. Sar A. Levitan and Frank Gallo, "Can Employee Associations Negotiate New Growth?" *Monthly Labor Review* (July 1989), p. 11.

12. Figures supplied by Jackie Ponton, AFSCME Research Department (Washington, DC, 1995).

13. Matthew M. Bodah, "Twenty-Five Years of Collective Bargaining under the Urban Mass Transit Act of 1964," *Labor Studies Journal* 15, no. 3 (Fall 1990), pp. 36–37.

14. "Teachers' Unions See Strength in Mergers," *Chronicle of Higher Education,* November 16, 1994, p. A26.

15. Ibid.

16. Ibid., p. A25; see also "A Merger Misfires," *Chronicle of Higher Education,* February 17, 1995, p. A17.

17. Leo Troy, *The New Unionism in the New Society: Public Sector Unions in the Redistributive State* (Fairfax, VA: George Mason University Press, 1994), pp. 70–72.

18. Executive Office of the President, National Performance Review, Executive Summary, *From Red Tape to Results: Creating a Government That Works Better and Costs Less* (Washington, DC: U.S. Government Printing Office, 1993).

19. Ronald C. Moe, "The 'Reinventing Government' Exercise: Misinterpreting the Problem, Misjudging the Consequences," *Public Administration Review* 54 (March/April 1994), pp. 112–14, 119.

20. Ibid.

21. B. V. H. Schneider, "Public-Sector Labor Legislation–An Evolutionary Analysis" in *Public-Sector Bargaining,* 2nd ed., Benjamin Aaron, Joyce M. Najita, and James L. Stern, eds. (Washington, DC: Bureau of National Affairs, 1988), pp. 190–92. Roger G. Brown and Terrel L. Rhodes, "Public Employee Bargaining under Prohibitive Legislation: Some Unanticipated Consequences," *Journal of Collective Negotiations* 10, no. 1 (1991), pp. 23–30.

22. Russell A. Smith, Harry T. Edwards, and R. Theodore Clark Jr., *Labor Relations in the Public Sector* (Indianapolis: Bobbs-Merrill, 1974), p. 73.

23. Government Employee Relations Report, "Statewide Bargaining Units in State Governments," *Labor Management Relations Survey,* Vol. 61 (Washington, DC: Bureau of National Affairs, 1977), pp. 41–42.

24. Milton Derber, "Management Organization for Collective Bargaining in the Public Sector," in *Public-Sector Bargaining,* 2nd ed., Benjamin Aaron, Joyce M. Najita, and James L. Stern, eds. (Washington, DC: Bureau of National Affairs, 1988), p. 96.

25. Ibid., pp. 96–97, and Stephen L. Hayford and Anthony V. Sinicropi, "Bargaining Rights Status of Public Sector Supervisors" in *Public Sector Labor Relations,* op. cit., p. 143.

26. T. Gilroy and A. Russo, *Bargaining Unit Issues: Problems, Criteria, Tactics* (Chicago: International Personnel Management Association, 1973), p. 33.

27. Harry H. Wellington and Ralph K. Winter Jr., *The Unions and the Cities* (Washington, DC: Brookings Institution, 1971), pp. 87–88.

28. Ibid.

29. Derber, op. cit., pp. 90–92.

30. Thomas A. Kochan, "A Theory of Multilateral Collective Bargaining in City Governments" in *Public Sector Labor Relations,* op. cit., pp. 195–216.

31. June Miller Weisberger, "The Appropriate Scope of Bargaining in the Public Sector: The Continuing Controversy and the Wisconsin Experience," *Wisconsin Law Review* 1977, no. 3, pp. 688–89.

32. Ibid., pp. 694–98.

33. Ibid., pp. 707–9.

34. Postal Reorganization Act, Title 39, *United States Code,* August 12, 1970; the National Labor Relations Act; and the Labor Management Relations Act.

35. Gary N. Chaison and Dileep G. Dhavale, "The Choice between Union Membership and Free-Rider Status," *Journal of Labor Research* 13 (Fall 1992), pp. 347–58.

36. Ibid., p. 363.

37. Hugh D. Hindman and Charles G. Smith, "Correlates of Union Membership and Joining Intentions in a Unit of Federal Employees," *Journal of Labor Research* 14 (Fall 1993), p. 451.

38. Schneider, op. cit., p. 220.

39. Ibid., p. 221.

40. Ibid., p. 224.

41. *Abood v. Detroit Board of Education,* 431 U.S. 209, 95 LRRM 2411 (1977) and *Chicago Teachers Union v. Hudson,* 106 S.Ct. 1066, 121 LRRM 2793 (1986).

42. Schneider, op. cit., p. 223.

43. David P. Twomey, *Labor & Employment Law, Text and Cases,* 8th ed. (Cincinnati: South-Western, 1989), p. 511. Richard Briffault, "The New York Agency Shop Fee and the Constitution after Ellis and Hudson," *Industrial and Labor Relations Review* 41 (January 1988), pp. 279–93.

44. *Lehnert v. Ferris Faculty Association,* 111 S.Ct. 1950 (1991).

45. Richard J. Murphy, "The Federal Experience in Employee Relations" in *The Crisis in Public Employee Relations in the Decade of the Seventies,* Richard J. Murphy and Morris Sackman, eds. (Washington, DC: Bureau of National Affairs, 1970), p. 71.

46. Donald H. Wollett, Joseph R. Grodin, and June M. Weisberger, *Collective Bargaining in Public Employment,* 4th ed. (St. Paul, MN: West, 1993), pp. 10, 282–87; *Martin v. Montezuma-Cortez School District Re-1,* 841 P. 2d 237 (Colo. 1992).

47. *AFL-CIO News* 35, no. 1 (January 8, 1990), p. 9.

48. *County Sanitation District v. SEIU Local 660,* 38 Cal.3d 564, 119 LRRM 2433, cert. denied 106 S.Ct. 408 (1985).

49. *Davis v. Henry,* 555 So.2nd 457 (La. 1990).

50. Harry T. Edwards, R. Theodore Clark Jr., and Charles B. Craver, *Labor Relations Law in the Public Sector,* 4th ed. (Charlottesville, VA: Michie, 1991), p. 738.

51. Wollett et al., op. cit., pp. 326–29.

52. Schneider, op. cit., p. 205.

53. For reviews of this literature see Craig A. Olson, "Dispute Resolution in the Public Sector" in *Public-Sector Bargaining,* 2nd ed., Benjamin Aaron, Joyce M. Najita, and James L. Stern, eds. (Washington, DC: Bureau of National Affairs, 1988), pp. 160–88, and Lewin et al., op. cit., pp. 340–43.

54. Lewin et al., op. cit., p. 341.

55. Ibid., pp. 341–42.

56. Janet Currie and Sheena McConnell, "Collective Bargaining in the Public Sector: The Effect of Legal Structure on Dispute Costs and Wages," *American Economic Review* 81 (September 1991), pp. 711–13.

57. Ibid., pp. 713–15.

58. James R. Chelius and Marian M. Extejt, "The Narcotic Effect of Impasse Resolution Procedures," *Industrial and Labor Relations Review* 38 (July 1985), pp. 629–37.

59. Harry Graham and Jeffrey Perry, "Interest Arbitration in Ohio. The Narcotic Effect Revisited," *Journal of Collective Negotiations* 22, no. 4 (1993), pp. 323–26.

60. H. Gregg Lewis, "Union/Nonunion Wage Gaps in the Public Sector" in *When Public Sector Workers Unionize,* op. cit., pp. 169–94. Daniel J. B. Mitchell, "Collective Bargaining and Compensation in the Public Sector" in *Public-Sector Bargaining,* op. cit., pp. 124–59. Richard B. Freeman, "Unionism Comes to the Public Sector," *Journal of Economic Literature* 24 (March 1986), pp. 41–86. Ronald G. Ehrenberg and Joshua L. Schwarz, "Public Sector Labor Markets" in *Handbook of Labor Economics,* Orley Ashenfelter and Richard Layard, eds. (Amsterdam: North-Holland Press, 1986), pp. 1219–68.

61. Lewis, op. cit., p. 187.

62. Mitchell, "Collective Bargaining and Compensation in the Public Sector," op. cit., p. 142.

63. Ibid., p. 147.

64. Steven G. Allen, "Unions and Job Security in the Public Sector" in *When Public Sector Workers Unionize,* op. cit., pp. 271–304.

65. Jeffrey Zax and Casey Ichniowski, "The Effects of Public Sector Unionism on Pay, Employment, Department Budgets, and Municipal Expenditures" in *When Public Sector Workers Unionize,* op. cit., pp. 323–64.

66. Dale Belman, Morley Gunderson, and Douglas Hyatt, eds., *Public Sector Employment in a Time of Transition* (Madison, WI: Industrial Relations Research Association, 1996).

CHAPTER 17

Reports of the Commission on the Future of Worker-Management Relations

Fact-Finding Report, *Issued May 1994;* *and* Final Report and Recommendations, *Issued December 1994* *(referred to as the Dunlop Reports)*[1]

After reading this chapter, you should be able to

■ Describe and evaluate the three questions the Dunlop Commission was charged to address.

■ Identify and review the changes in the American workplace that prompted the appointment of the Commission.

■ Understand and explain how section 8(a)(2) of the National Labor Relations Act and subsequent Supreme Court decisions serve to limit employee participation in labor-management partnership systems.

■ Explain and evaluate the Commission's recommendations regarding the legal status of employee workplace participation.

■ Identify difficulties unions encounter in attempting to secure initial contracts.

■ Explain the recommendations of the Commission for reducing the difficulties labor organizations face in negotiating initial contracts.

■ Describe and evaluate the advantages of using alternate dispute resolution procedures to settle labor disputes.

■ Understand the seven priorities listed in the section headed "Learning from Experience."

PREFACE

On March 24, 1993, Secretary of Labor Robert B. Reich and the late Secretary of Commerce Ronald H. Brown announced the formation of the Commission on the Future of Worker-Management Relations to report on the following questions:

1. What (if any) new methods or institutions should be encouraged, or required, to enhance workplace productivity through labor-management cooperation and employee participation?

2. What (if any) changes should be made in the present legal framework and practices of collective bargaining to enhance cooperative behavior, improve productivity, and reduce conflict and delay?

3. What (if anything) should be done to increase the extent to which workplace problems are directly resolved by the parties themselves rather than through recourse to state and federal courts and government regulatory bodies?

INTRODUCTION: THE WORKPLACE AND SOCIETY

Societal Demands on the Workplace

Because a higher proportion of the population is currently in the workplace, with more and more women entering the work force, it has become the central societal institution in the United States. Today's work force, more than any other institution, reflects the racial and ethnic diversity of the population. Because the United States, unlike many other industrialized countries, does not provide benefits from general taxation, its citizens rely on the private workplace to furnish a range of benefits, most notably health insurance and paid vacations. The American workplace also shoulders the burden of many vital training and formal education programs through apprenticeships, internships, residencies, and executive training. Americans spend more time at the workplace than the citizens of any other advanced country except Japan, and more Americans work than vote.

Given concerns of productivity, quality, and competitiveness, the United States' main national asset must be a skilled and hard-working work force. In an increasingly global economy, national economic growth and productivity performance rely on the quality of the workplace.

New Forms of Work Organization

The constantly changing work composition, work locations, and supervisor-worker relationships make the satisfaction of growing societal demands difficult and more complex. Indeed, the traditional distinctions between worker and supervisor do not often remain in many current workplaces. Today's employee may work at home, have flexible work hours, and/or have global customers. Along with these variables, ambiguity in responsibility for training, health and safety, benefits, and legal obligations only serves to raise more questions regarding the definitions of *employee* and *employer*.

THE NEED FOR COOPERATION

An increasing number of employers and unions have found that the best way to compete in the marketplace, securing profits for the firm and good jobs for workers, is cooperative worker-management relations. The presence of more highly educated workers and the changing nature of work allow American employers to redistribute responsibilities and tasks to employees, who often work in teams, as employees express greater desire to participate in workplace decisions. Although relations range from hostility to openly collaborative partnerships, labor and management share the responsibility for creating value in the workplace. A continuing conflict between employees wanting representation and reluctant employers diminishes the ability of the workplace to fulfill critical social and economic functions. Polarization of these groups during organizing campaigns detracts from rational assessment of problems and implementation of mutually beneficial solutions.

How can workers and management, together, reduce the burden on the economy of excessive litigation and administrative proceedings, without infringing on workers' legislative and social rights? Initially, by developing institutions and practices that will allow employees and firms to cooperate in the workplace, contributing optimally to economic growth, competitive performance, and the fulfillment of social norms.

The interests of workers and management are not identical. As buyers and sellers of labor, they have different perspectives on the terms of the sale. The goal should be to resolve disputes cooperatively, with limited conflict, using expert advice and role models to find efficacious solutions to problems. Improving national economic performance requires modernization of labor-management relations, with the goal of bringing the best practices to more firms and workers.

With those considerations in mind, the Dunlop Report serves as a starting point for adjusting the workplace to the changing social and economic environment. A better future requires making the workplace a more productive place for firms and employees.

GOALS FOR THE TWENTY-FIRST-CENTURY AMERICAN WORKPLACE

The Commission, after much consideration of the views of managers, employees, union leaders, and other experts, developed a set of 10 goals for the workplace of the future. The Commission expected that attainment of these 10 integrated objectives would position the American work force and the economy for the twenty-first century.

1. *Expand coverage of employee participation and labor-management partnerships to more workers, more workplaces, and more issues and decisions.* Because employee participation and labor-management partnerships are essential to improved productivity, enhanced quality, and strong economic performance, sustaining and expanding active participation and partnerships to a larger proportion of American workers will be critical to improving workplace performance and the quality of economic and work life. Varied worker needs will require experimentation with alternative forms of participation and cooperative relations.

2. *Provide workers with a readily accessible opportunity to choose or decline union representation and to engage in collective bargaining.* Workers should be allowed free and accessible choice about union representation so they can exercise their collective bargaining rights.

3. *Improve resolution of disputes about workplace rights.* Dispute resolution processes for possible cases of unjust treatment should be rapid, inexpensive, and fair. They should serve as an effective deterrent to future abuses in employment practices.

4. *Decentralize and internalize responsibility for workplace regulations.* Private resolution of disputes by firms and workers should, whenever possible, replace government involvement.

5. *Improve workplace safety and health.* Workplaces must be encouraged to reduce worker injury, occupational disease, and worker compensation costs by developing (with regulatory body assistance) appropriate systems to improve safety and health.

6. *Enhance growth of productivity in the economy as a whole.* The well-being of Americans depends on productivity growth at a sufficient pace to improve living standards for all.

7. *Increase training and learning in the workplace and in related institutions.* On-the-job learning enhances the performance of enterprises, improves the rate of productivity growth, and permits higher wages and benefits. Service sector workers particularly require this at-

tention because of a slow rate of productivity growth and a large number of young, low-skilled workers with inadequate education or training opportunities.

8. ***Reduce the inequality that has increased in the American labor market over the past 10 to 15 years by raising the earnings and benefits of workers in the lower part of the wage distribution.*** An emphasis on training, employee participation, productivity, and quality, along with the opportunity for representation and collective bargaining, will contribute to a reduction in the growing earning disparities.

9. ***Upgrade the economic position of contingent workers.*** Low-wage workers in temporary or contingent employment relationships who are unable to secure full-time, stable, career-oriented jobs with adequate wages and benefits must receive the protection of labor relations and employment laws.

10. ***Increase dialogue at the national and local levels.*** Continually changing work force problems require leaders of business, labor, civil rights, and women's organizations to work with government to develop strategies and policies for meeting new challenges in the workplace.

EMPLOYEE INVOLVEMENT

Fifty-two percent of employees polled in the Worker Representation and Participation Survey[2] reported some form of employee participation program operating in their workplaces; 31 percent indicated that they participated in such programs. Employee involvement programs range from teams dealing with specific problems for short periods to groups meeting for extended periods.

Many employers and union leaders testified before the Commission that employee participation programs enhance productivity, though their effectiveness surely differs in different settings. Of workers involved in these programs, 87 percent view them as either very effective or somewhat effective; 79 percent report that the programs have given them more voice in the workplace. By a two-to-one majority, employees without employee involvement programs would like them implemented at their workplaces.

On the basis of this information, the Commission recommended expansion of employee participation in a variety of forms to increase productivity and improve working life. However, such participation must not in any way interfere with employee choice of independent labor organization representation.

Employee participation programs may violate section 8(a)(2) of the National Labor Relations Act (NLRA) if they address issues related to working conditions and ways to share gains produced by employee involvement. In addition, some programs blur the traditional distinction between managers and workers, raising questions about NLRA coverage.

LEGAL ISSUES REGARDING WORKPLACE EMPLOYEE PARTICIPATION

Section 8(a)(2) of the NLRA makes it an unfair labor practice for an employer to "dominate or interfere with the formation or administration of any labor organization or to contribute financial or other support to it." In turn, Section 2(5) of the Act defines labor organization as "any organization of any kind, or any agency or employee representation committee or plan, in which employees participate and which exists for the purpose, in whole or in part, of dealing with employers concerning grievances, labor disputes, wages, rates of pay, hours of employment, or conditions of work." The phrases are underlined for emphasis; they indicate how broad and how important Congress intended this legal prohibition to be.

The stated aim of the NLRA is to encourage collective bargaining through representatives of the employees' own choosing. Unions whose activities are limited to employees at single firms are perfectly compatible with this policy as long as they are not created or controlled by management. The law does not allow employees to be exposed to employer-dominated structures that "deal" with "conditions of work." Congress assumed that the presence of such company-dominated unions would unduly influence employees in their judgment about whether they needed and wanted to be represented by independent unions.

In the late 1970s and early 1980s, a closely divided National Labor Relations Board (NLRB) examined the original intent and contemporary relevance of Sections 8(a)(2) and 2(5) of the NLRA and found that employer participation in grievance adjudication committees constituted performance of management functions on behalf of the employer rather than representation of employees in dealing with the employer.[3] That same year, a unanimous NLRB panel concluded that a job enrichment program in which production employees were divided into teams that delegated work and overtime did not constitute illegal "dealing with" the employer regarding conditions of work.[4] Meanwhile, several appeals court panels were giving narrower readings to the key statutory terms *labor organization* and *employer domination.* A common sentiment was that the adversarial conception of the employment relationship that led to the 1935 Wagner Act was incompatible with the cooperative relations necessary in the modern economic and human resource environment.

A prominent case, *Electromation,*[5] emerged in 1992, when management, reacting to employee displeasure with the company's new pay and attendance policies, established five committees to address these and other issues such as pay progression, smoking prohibition, and the communication network. The committees, principally composed of employees selected by management from volunteers and one or two supervisors, began to meet weekly. However, after the Teamsters Union surfaced with a petition to represent the employees, the company campaigned actively against union representation of the workers and announced that it would not continue with the committee format until after the NLRB-conducted election. Shortly before the election, the union filed a Section (8)(a)(2) charge with the NLRB, along with a Section (8)(a)(1) charge alleging unlawful employer interference with the election.

The four-member Board was unanimous in finding a violation of the NLRA in this case, reinforcing the traditional Board interpretation of this feature of the NLRA rather than accepting a narrower view that would exclude most or all employee involvement programs found in many workplaces today. Because of the growing role of employee involvement plans in American industry, the Commission expressed the view that some clarification of Section 8(a)(2) is required. Employee involvement programs dealing with production, quality, safety and health, training, or voluntary dispute resolution should be legal as long as they do not promote or develop company unions. In addition, the increased supervisory and managerial roles of today's employees led the Commission to suggest reducing the exclusion of supervisors and managers from the coverage and protection of the NLRA.

COMMISSION RECOMMENDATIONS

Facilitate the Growth of Employee Involvement

The Commission recommended that nonunion employee participation programs not be unlawful simply because they involve discussion of terms and conditions of work or compensation, where such discussion is incidental to the broad purposes of these programs.

Most of the programs now proliferating in the United States do not violate the basic purposes of Section 8(a)(2), according to the Commission. Thus, Congress should clarify Section 8(a)(2), allowing the NLRB to interpret it in a way that encourages employee participation in nonunion settings without adversely affecting employees' ability to select union representation if they so desire. Employee participation programs, as a means for employees to be involved in some workplace issues, are not a form of independent representation for employees and cannot legally deal with the full scope of issues normally covered by collective bargaining.

Continue to Ban Company Unions

The Commission supported the continued prohibition of company-dominated labor organizations. It further recommended that employees involved in participatory committees have the same legal protections from retaliation for expressions of opinion on workplace issues as do workers involved in union activity.

In the Worker Representation and Participation Survey,[6] 33 percent of unionized employees reported being involved in participation programs, compared with 28 percent of nonunion employees. Testimony revealed that employee participation is most effective in a union setting when union and management work together as partners to extend the scope, coverage, and effectiveness of future employee participation. However, issues normally dealt with in collective bargaining should not be discussed in employee involvement programs without the consent of the elected labor organization. Therefore, the Commission recommended that it be an unfair labor practice under NLRA Section 8(a)(1) for an employer to bypass the union or to introduce or manipulate an employee participation program to subvert the collective bargaining process.

The Commission recommended clarifying Section 8(a)(2), the distinction between employee involvement programs and unions. According to the Commission, the protections afforded workers in participation programs will improve the climate for these programs. The safeguards against company-dominated unions under Section 8(a)(2) and the recommendations for reducing conflict and delay in establishing unions where employees so desire should be mutually reinforcing.

Reduce the Scope of the Supervisory and Managerial Exclusions

The Commission recommended that Congress simplify and restrict the supervisory and managerial employee exclusions of the NLRA to ensure that the vast numbers of professionals and other workers who wish to participate in decision making at work are not stripped of their right to do so through collective bargaining if they so choose. However, employees whose primary function is to carry out the employer's labor relations policy by hiring, firing, and disciplining employees are clearly supervisors and should continue to be excluded from the protection of the Act. In addition, employees near the top of the firm's managerial structure who have substantial individual discretion to set major company policy and whose primary function is to develop such policy are clearly managerial employees and should also continue to be excluded.

Members of work teams and joint committees with managerial and/or personnel decision-making authority or professionals and paraprofessionals who direct less-skilled co-workers should be encouraged and not excluded from coverage. Current labor law has not accommodated this change; it continues to draw rigid distinctions between supervisors and employees covered by the NLRA.

Supreme Court jurisprudence has contributed to this problem by creating the managerial employee exclusion and applying it to senior managers and buyers of parts and materials. The Court, then, expanded the scope of this exclusion (*NLRB v. Yeshiva University*)[7] by holding that professors could not constitute an appropriate bargaining unit because they were all managers, voting on such matters as curriculum, class size, and academic standards. The Court felt that these professors exercised "authority which in any other context unquestionably would be managerial."[8] Indeed, this interpretation stripped union members of their collective bargaining rights because they negotiated an employee participation agreement with their employer.[9]

More recently, the Supreme Court expanded the statute's supervisory exclusion, declaring that all acts within the scope of employment or on the authorized business of the employer are in the interest of the employer. In practice, this could mean that any employee who responsibly directs co-workers is a supervisor and is denied protection of the labor law. This case, *NLRB v. Health Care and Retirement Corporation of America*,[10] adversely affects professionals because most have some supervisory responsibilities in the sense of directing another's work (the lawyer her secretary, the teacher his aide, etc.). In the Supreme Court's view, incidental direction of co-workers appears to make one a "supervisor" who lacks collective bargaining rights, but this view fails to take into account the degree to which supervisory tasks have been diffused throughout today's work force. As a consequence, thousands of rank-and-file employees have lost, or may lose, their collective bargaining rights.

Thus, the Commission suggested that the law accommodate the desires of professionals and other employees to engage in workplace participation, whether they desire to do so via independent representation or otherwise.

The Commission also advocated the relaxing of restrictions on the ability of plant guards to participate in collective bargaining (Section 9(b)(3) precludes guards or a local union of guards from affiliating directly or indirectly with an organization that admits to membership employees other than guards). Although separate bargaining units and locals are appropriate, preventing affiliation with an established international union or federation of unions is an unnecessary limitation.

Authorize Prehire Agreements

The Commission felt that when an employer wants to move or to open a new operation, it should be allowed to negotiate a contract with a union interested in representing those who will work at the new operation, as long as the negotiations are conducted at arm's length. In order to ensure that the employees covered under the new agreement support it, the union should be required to demonstrate majority support by the end of the first year of the new operation or face expiration of representative status. The parties would be allowed to verify the union's majority status either by card check or representative election, but the agreement should not serve as a contract bar.

Section 8(a)(2) continues to serve the vital function of precluding "sweetheart" deals between employers and unions that do not represent majorities of employees. Such deals frustrate employee free choice by taking out of the workers' hands the decision concerning independent representation. The policy of generally disallowing employer recognition and support of nonmajority unions remains valid. However, the Commission was concerned that this policy might preclude employer support of a nonmajority union when the employer intends to move or open new operations. The occasion of new or relocated operations often presents an opportunity for innovative cooperation between employers and unions around issues of work organization, employee compensation, and productivity and efficiency.

Such agreements not only improve labor-management relations but also help facilitate the diffusion of high-performance work techniques. In addition, advance negotiations can increase, rather than decrease, the quality of employee choice about collective bargaining. In effect, a prenegotiated contract gives the employees an opportunity to "try out" the union's representation before voting to accept or reject it.

The Commission recommended that Congress examine the NLRB interpretation of Section 8(a)(2), which prohibits employer recognition of a union as part of prospective bargaining and forbids advance negotiation of contract terms altogether, even without recognition, if the employer and union have no previous relationship.

Douglas A. Fraser, a Commission member, dissented from the recommendation that "Congress clarify Section 8(a)(2)" by somehow providing that employee participation programs not be unlawful simply because they involve discussion of terms and conditions of work compensation where such discussion is incidental to the broad purposes of these programs. Fraser felt that employer-dominated employee representation plans should not be permitted merely because they are limited to dealing with specified subjects such as safety and health. "Employer-dominated representation is undemocratic," he said, "regardless of the particular subjects with which the employer-controlled representative deals." Though not minimizing the value of encouraging employee participation and labor-management cooperation, Fraser felt that encouragement should focus on democratic participation and cooperation among equals.

WORKER REPRESENTATION AND COLLECTIVE BARGAINING

The Role of Unions in Society

The preamble to the National Labor Relations Act declares it to be the policy of the United States to "encourage the practices and procedure of collective bargaining and to protect . . . the exercise by workers of full freedom of association, self-organization and designation of representatives of their own choosing, for the purpose of negotiating the terms and conditions of their employment or other mutual aid or protection." According to Senator Orrin Hatch, unions contribute to the economic health of the nation by "leveling the field between labor and management." Indeed, the President's Council of Economic Advisors concluded that the recent decline in the proportion of workers represented by unions has contributed to the rise of income inequality in the United States. Unions, likewise, contribute to the political health of the nation by providing a legitimate and consistent voice to working people in the broader society.

Established Collective Bargaining Relationships

Not all aspects of collective bargaining are in need of repair. The majority of managers and workers with experience under collective bargaining believe that the process is working well.

The Worker Representation and Participation Survey[11] reports that about 90 percent of union members would vote to retain their memberships if asked. Approximately 70 percent rate their experience with their unions as good or very good. Sixty-four percent of the managers surveyed agreed that the unions in their companies improve the work lives of their members. Managers, when asked how the union relationship affects their companies, expressed views that vary considerably. Twenty-seven percent of managers stated that it helps performance, 38 percent believe it hurts performance, and 29 percent believe it neither helps nor hurts. By a two-to-one margin, managers report that in recent years their relations with unions have become more cooperative rather than confrontational.

In general, collective bargaining appears to be adapting to its changing economic and social setting. Work stoppages have declined significantly, and grievance procedures increasingly are leading to settlement through informal discussion or mediation without resort to arbitration. The AFL-CIO's February 1994 report, *The New American Workplace: A Labor Perspective,* is a significant statement endorsing workplace cooperation and labor-management partnerships.

Areas Requiring Improvement

One area in need of greater focus is the responsiveness of workplace practices to the needs of working women. An October 1994 survey by the Women's Bureau of the Department of Labor found that although most women are breadwinners and many the sole support of their families, they are not receiving pay and benefits commensurate with the work they do, the responsibilities they hold, or the societal contributions they make. Collective bargaining needs to continue to evolve and adapt as the work force grows more diverse in terms of gender, race, ethnic background, education, and location of work.

American society—management, labor, and the general public—supports the principle of workers' right to join unions and to engage in collective bargaining if a majority of workers so desire. However, representation elections as currently constituted are highly conflictual for workers, unions, and firms because many new collective bargaining relationships originate in environments that are highly adversarial. The probability that a worker will be discharged or otherwise unfairly discriminated against for exercising legal rights under the NLRA has increased over time. The bulk of meritorious unfair labor charges concern employer practices, but unions have also engaged in unfair practices.

The Worker Representation and Participation Survey[12] found that 32 percent of unorganized workers would vote to join unions if elections were held at their workplaces. Eighty-two percent of those favoring unionization (and 33 percent of all nonunion workers) believe that a majority of their fellow employees would vote to unionize. Despite this support, approximately a third of employees in workplaces that vote in favor of union representation do not obtain collective bargaining contracts with their employers.

Together, these facts document the need to improve the process through which workers decide whether or not to be represented in the workplace and engage in collective bargaining. The Commission considered a proposal to increase the NLRA's jurisdictional floors in view of the substantial increases in wages and prices since the floors were established by statute in 1959. The Commission raised this issue by letter with each major business organization and with the AFL-CIO. Most of the organizations that responded opposed increasing the jurisdictional amounts.

Commission Recommendations

The Commission recommended the following four improvements to laws governing the representation process. The changes would render employee decisions about whether to engage in collective bargaining simpler, more timely, and less conflictual.

Prompt Certification Elections

The process by which workers decide whether or not to engage in collective bargaining is among the most contentious aspects of American labor relations. In order to have a union certified as their representative, American workers must seek an NLRB election to determine whether a majority of an appropriate bargaining unit wishes to be represented by the union. Before holding an election, the Board must address legal issues raised by the employer and the union; the most important concerns the scope of the bargaining unit and inclusion or exclusion of particular employees therein. Either party has a right to a formal hearing on these matters, which causes substantial delay. The automatic availability of such hearing procedures means that a party seeking delay can safely assume it will be able to push an election back three to six months. In practice, it takes workers an average of seven weeks to secure a vote from the time their petition is filed.

During this time, the union and the employer typically face off in a heated campaign. The government has hesitated to regulate the two sides too closely during these contests in order to preserve the parties' freedom of speech. Often, both sides hurl allegations, distortions, and promises that poison the relationship and, in cases where workers vote to unionize, increase the difficulty of achieving a collective bargaining agreement. In recent decades, charges arising during these campaigns have increased, in terms of both (1) the ratio of unfair labor practice charges filed against employers to the number of elections and (2) the percentage of such charges found to have merit. In particular, discharges of union activists are up, occurring in one of every four elections. Seventy-nine percent of American workers consider it likely that employees who seek union representation will lose their jobs, and 41 percent of nonunion workers say they think they might lose their own jobs if they tried to organize. This fear is one explanation for the persistent unsatisfied demand for union representation on the part of a substantial minority of American workers.

The Commission believed that the NLRB should conduct representation elections as promptly as administratively feasible. A lengthy, political-style election campaign serves no useful purpose in the labor-management context. Shortening the campaign significantly would eliminate much of the conflict that mars the election process, while still giving each side ample time to express its views. Thus, the stage would be set for a more cooperative employer-union relationship if and when collective bargaining begins.

Currently, many preelection NLRB hearings are held despite the absence of significant legal issues simply because one of the parties seeks a tactical advantage. There are two principal tactical reasons why parties demand hearings. The first is to secure an advantage in the election by excluding or including particular employees on the basis of the way they are likely to vote. The number of such hearings could be reduced if the interested parties either won the elections or lost by margins greater than the numbers of disputed voters they had hoped to include.

The second tactical reason a party seeks a hearing is to delay an election in order to increase its chances of a favorable outcome. A system is poorly designed if it provides incentive and opportunity to seek delay for its own sake. Hearings motivated by the desire to delay an election would obviously be eliminated altogether in a system that allowed hearings only after the elections had taken place.

Holding elections promptly would also reduce the need for oversight of the parties' conduct during the election campaign. Moreover, shortening the election process would decrease the amount of time during which hostility and antagonism could build up between the parties.

The Commission encouraged employers and unions desiring cooperative relationships to agree to determine the employees' majority preference via a "card check," particularly when a union already represents a segment of an employer's work force and the parties seek a nonconflictual way to determine if additional employees want that same form of representation. By building trust through the card check method, potential or former adversaries create a win-win situation. The opportunity to gain representation rights via a simple majority sign-up gives the union an incentive to cooperate with the employer to make the workplace more efficient. In return, the employer gains the cooperation of the employee representative as a partner in efforts to improve productivity and flexibility and, often, improve morale and reduce turnover as well.

Timely Injunctive Relief for Discriminatory Action

The NLRB can obtain injunctions against unions (for organizational or secondary boycotts) far more easily and swiftly than it can against employers, particularly for discriminatory discharges of union supporters. In general, the remedies the NLRB may prescribe against employers are remedial and reparative rather than deterrent, and the sanctions against employers for violations of labor law are far weaker than analogous penalties for violations of other federal employment statutes. The Commission suggested expedited injunctive relief—which complements prompt representation elections—as the most effective, least litigious, and least costly path.

Resolution of First-Contract Disputes

Once a majority of workers have voted for independent union representation, the Commission felt, the debate about the bargaining relationship is over. At this point, the parties' energies and the public's resources should turn to creating an effective, ongoing relationship that is suited to the needs of the workplace. Every effort should be made to ensure that a satisfactory agreement is concluded and that the process used to reach that agreement leads to the development of a cooperative relationship.

One-third or more of certified units fail to reach first contracts, and strikes during first-contract negotiations tend to be longer and result in fewer settlements than strikes occurring within established bargaining relationships. Moreover, evidence shows that the probability of achieving a first contract is reduced in a setting where unfair labor practices or other hard bargaining tactics are carried over from the election campaign into the contract negotiation process.

At the same time, parties must maintain incentives to negotiate a realistic agreement, avoiding any chance that unworkable or harmful terms will be imposed on the parties by a misinformed neutral. Negotiations sometimes fail because one side or the other holds out for numerous unrealistic proposals. The process should encourage parties to reach their own agreements, accept the possibility that a strike or a lockout may be the most appropriate way to address unrealistic expectations or demands, and allow for the use of arbitration.

The Commission suggested that an employer and a newly certified union have early access to the services of the Federal Mediation and Conciliation Service or to private mediation. A tripartite First-Contract Advisory Board should be established to review disputes not settled by negotiations or mediation. The advisory board should be empowered to use a wide range of options for resolving disputes, including referring them back to the parties for negotiation with the right to strike or lock out, prescribing further mediation or fact finding, and invoking use of arbitration.

Making arbitration available in first-contract cases is crucial to the overall representation system, but the goal should be to maximize the number of voluntary agreements and the development of enduring and cooperative relationships.

Employee Access to Employer and Union Views on Independent Representation

It is a central tenet of U.S. labor policy that employees should be free to make informed and uncoerced choice of independent representation. The effectiveness of that right, as the Supreme Court has stated, "depends in some measure on the ability of employees to learn the advantages and disadvantages of organization from others."[13]

An imbalance occurs in this area because the ability of employers to present their views to employees is assured at the workplace through daily contact, distribution of written material, and even attendance at "captive audience" meetings. In addition, the employer may devote as much work time as it desires to advising employees about the employer's position.

By contrast, employees have little access to the union at work, the one place where they naturally congregate. Union representatives are typically excluded from the work site. Even nonworking areas accessible to the general public (parking lots or cafeterias) are off limits to the union organizer.

True, the union is given a list of employee names and addresses so it can contact workers at home. But the union receives the names of the constituents it seeks to represent only if it is able to achieve the 30-percent level of support necessary to secure an election, and it receives them only 10 to 20 days before the election (in what is typically a 50-day campaign). Efforts to communicate with workers when they leave the work site and disperse into the community are far more costly and far less likely to be successful. As the law stands, it restricts the practical dissemination of statutory representation rights to employees at the work site.

The Commission suggested, as a first step, that Congress reverse the Supreme Court's decision in *Lechmere v. NLRB*,[14] thus allowing union organizers access in privately owned but publicly used spaces, such as shopping malls. Labor groups and others should have access to this form of "public-private" space, which has taken over the role of main street in so many American communities.

In addition, the Commission encouraged the NLRB to "examine its current practice carefully to determine the extent to which it provides employees a fair opportunity to hear a balanced discussion of the relevant issues."

Conclusion

A labor relations environment marked by prompt, prehearing elections; effective injunctive relief for discriminatory reprisals in the representation process; and flexible dispute resolution in first-contract negotiations will provide American workers greater freedom to choose collective bargaining if that is what they want.

EMPLOYMENT LITIGATION AND DISPUTE RESOLUTION

The expansion of federal and state discrimination laws and the growth in common-law and statutory protection against wrongful discharge give employees a broader array of tools with which to challenge employer behavior in court. However, employment litigation is a costly option for both employers and employees. For every dollar paid to employees through litigation, at least another dollar is paid to attorneys. Moreover, employers often dedicate significant sums to the designing of defensive personnel practices to minimize their litigation exposure, and that investment affects compensation.

Alternative dispute resolution (ADR) facilitates private resolution of disputes primarily in three formats: direct in-house negotiations; mediation systems sponsored by the courts or other government agencies; and arbitration, which can produce binding disposition of cases. The Commission recommended encouraging creative alternatives to standard court litigation while ensuring that the legal needs and priorities of a diverse American work force are fairly satisfied. The Commission supported the expansion and development of alternative workplace dispute resolution mechanisms.

In-House Dispute Resolution

Efforts to resolve disputes early and amicably depend heavily on employee participation in the creation and operation of the dispute resolution mechanism. Employee participation can reduce both the number of formal grievances filed and the proportion of grievances taken to the higher steps of the procedure or to arbitration. Effective procedures for communication and workplace problem solving help to build the trust needed to solve problems before they escalate into complaints. Thus, employee participation and worker representation are essential elements of a successful ADR system.

Most experts agree that it is important to involve a wide cross-section of the work force in the design and administration of workplace dispute resolution systems. There is potential, however, for abuse of ADR created by the imbalance of power between employer and employee and the resulting unfairness to employees who, voluntarily or otherwise, submit their disputes to ADR. These concerns are obvious if the process is controlled unilaterally by employers, through clauses designating mandatory arbitration as a condition of employment. Union representation can help reduce this disparity.

The Commission envisioned the development of private systems for prevention or informal resolution of disputes, tailored appropriately to fit different employment settings and essential to the effectiveness of more formal arbitration procedures. Future innovations in such systems may lead unions, professional associations, and other worker advocacy groups to market their services for representing individuals in these processes and providing technical advice and assistance in the design and oversight of these systems.

Binding Arbitration for Public Law Disputes

When voluntary dispute resolution procedures fail, the parties are forced to rely on the federal and state court systems for final and binding decisions. For employees this is a less than ideal method of resolving public law claims because they must endure long waiting periods as governing agencies and overburdened court systems struggle to find time to investigate and hear complaints properly. Moreover, lower-wage workers may not fare as well as higher-wage professionals because they are less able to afford the time required to pursue complaints, and they are less likely to receive significant monetary relief from juries.

A number of employers have begun to incorporate private arbitration systems into their employment contracts, asking employees to agree to participate in those systems and thereby waive the right to pursue claims in court. A number of lower courts have upheld such arrangements.

According to the Commission, private arbitration systems, even when properly administered, should remain voluntary, not a condition of employment. The Commission suggested that Congress pass legislation leaving the choice of means for enforcing statutory employment rights to the individual who feels wronged, rather than letting it be dictated by an employment contract.

The Commission also felt that employees should be encouraged to consider binding arbitration of claims after they have arisen. Employees who do decide to use private arbitration instead of litigation should be bound by its results. To ensure the acceptability of arbitration, employees should have an independent voice in the design and implementation of arbitration systems.

THE FUTURE OF THE AMERICAN WORK FORCE: NATIONAL AND LOCAL FORUMS

The Commission recommended creating a private-public forum for continuing discourse on issues of national concern related to the future of the American work force and a separate national labor-management committee treating labor-management and workplace issues. The forum would comprise representatives from business, labor organizations, women's groups, civil rights organizations, and the executive and legislative branches of the federal government. Among the issues suggested for the forum were the growing income disparity within the work force, including the status of low-wage workers and their families; the interests of working women; government regulations regarding the workplace; the impact of the global economy; and job creation. The labor-management committee would meet periodically to consider issues of employee involvement, cooperation and performance in the workplace, health and safety, conflict and dispute resolution, training measures, and other issues of mutual concern. The forum and the labor-management committee would be authorized to make recommendations concerning private policies, executive action, and legislative proposals.

LEARNING FROM EXPERIENCE

The Commission's suggestions and recommendations imply a number of changes and new directions. According to the Commission, it is essential to learn more systematically than has been done to date on the ongoing workplace experimentation for future development and formulation of private and public policy. Innovations at the workplace level need to systematically inform policy makers at the national level. Accordingly, the Commission proposed creation of a coordinated public-private research group to report and analyze workplace developments. Numerous nonprofit research institutions provide findings and papers on aspects of the changing workplace. A coordination board with some government funding might well develop more systematic basic data collection and reports on a continuing basis with much greater acceptance of published results, much less duplication, and much more professional competence. Among the priorities for study, research, and evaluation are the following topics:

1. The employment experience of various categories of contingent workers
2. Representation elections and initial contract negotiations
3. The processes and results of various types of employee participation plans and labor-management partnerships
4. The views of workers and supervisors on various issues related to worker representation and participation and their attitudes in the workplace
5. The effects of workplace practices on American families
6. The effects of different types of workplace training
7. The results of various forms of health- and safety-related employee involvement programs in the workplace

IMPACT OF THE DUNLOP REPORT

The Dunlop Commission correctly identified the need for greater labor-management cooperation and the need for increased use of dispute resolution mechanisms as two leading issues facing labor-management relations today. It is indeed ironic, therefore, that Commission members were unable to resolve the disputes facing them in a cooperative manner.

Clearly, a compromise set of unanimous recommendations appeared plausible: Labor wanted an easier path for organizing and for obtaining initial contracts more rapidly; management wanted changes in the NLRA to make legal labor-management committees and cooperative efforts on a broader range of topics. It seems that Chairman Dunlop's strategy was "to structure a deal in which management would accede to lower barriers to labor organizing in non-union shops in exchange for the changes sought."[15]

However, partly because of resistance from unions and management and partly because of changes in the political environment, compromise could not be achieved. Regarding the willingness of both sides to make concessions, Thomas Kochan wrote,

> Neither the organized interests of business nor labor were able or willing to negotiate compromises to improve the performance of the existing system. At the same time, neither the business nor labor representatives . . . were willing to consider seriously any fundamentally new approaches or ideas for structuring worker-management relations.[16]

In addition, the election of a Republican majority in Congress suggested to many employer representatives that there was little need to compromise in arriving at the recommendations to be made by the Commission. The management representatives believed that the new Congress would give them everything they wanted regarding a more pro-management Section 8(a)(2) provision. They felt that the new Congress would be willing to amend section 8(a)(2) without employers, in exchange, having to make it easier for unions to organize. As a result of these developments, in the words of *Industry Week,* the recommendations of the Dunlop Commission were "Dead on Arrival."[17]

Notes

1. Dunlop Reports: This chapter contains material from two reports of The Commission on the Future of Worker-Management Relations, John T. Dunlop, Chair. The first report, *Fact-Finding Report,* was released in May 1994. The second, titled *Report and Recommendations,* was published in December 1994. The Commission was established by the U.S. Department of Labor and the U.S. Department of Commerce. Appointment of the Commission was announced by the Secretaries of Labor and Commerce on March 24, 1993.
2. Ibid.
3. *Mercy–Memorial Hospital,* 231 NLRB 1108 (1977).
4. *General Foods,* 231 NLRB 1232 (1977).
5. *Electromation, Inc.,* 309 NLRB 990 (1992).
6. Dunlop Reports, op. cit.
7. 144 U.S. 672 (1980).
8. 444 U.S. 686.
9. *College of Osteopathic Medicine & Surgery,* 265 NLRB 295 (1982).
10. 114 S. Ct. 1778 (1994).
11. Dunlop Reports, op. cit.
12. Ibid.
13. Dunlop, December 1994, op. cit., p. 22.
14. 112 S. Ct. 841 (1992).
15. *Industry Week* 244, no. 3 (February 6, 1995), p. 56.
16. Proceedings of the 10th World Congress of the IIRA, May 31–June 4, 1995, Washington, DC, Presidential Address, p. 12.
17. *Industry Week,* op. cit.

Labor Arbitration Cases

Havens Steel Company [Kansas City, Mo.] and International Association of Bridge, Structural and Ornamental Iron Workers, Shopmen's Local 520

John R. Thornell, Arbitrator. Award issued May 15, 1993.

ISSUE

Ordering drug test—Suspension—Argument with supervisor.

The parties agreed to this submission agreement: "Did the actions of the Company on August 24, 1992 in requiring Grievant to take a drug test and in suspending him for the balance of the shift violate the contract, and if so, what should be the remedy?"

FACTS

The Company is a fabricator of structural steel products, such as beams, columns, girders and trusses used in the construction industry. It operates a plant in Kansas City, Missouri where this grievance arose.

Grievant is classified as a machine operator 1st class. At the time of this dispute he had worked for the Company approximately sixteen years.

The events giving rise to this grievance occurred on August 24, 1992. At that time Grievant was on the second shift (4:30 P.M. to 1:00 A.M.) where he operated a shot-blast machine used to clean steel units that have been fabricated prior to their being painted. These units are of various sizes. Some of them are massive ranging up to several thousand pounds. They are moved through the plant with overhead cranes and on steel carts. The constant moving of bulky pieces of steel in the fabrication process subjects employees to a high risk of injury. There is exposure to welding, cutting, shearing and punching operations. The Company attempts to keep employees on the alert to the dangers involved in their work.

About 6:00 P.M. on the above date the Plant Manager walked by the shot-blast machine where Grievant was engaged in lifting a steel beam frame assembly from a cart. The unit had just been processed through the machine. The Company claims the beam weighed 350 to 400 pounds. Grievant testified it weighed around 168 pounds. The Plant Manager told Grievant that he had the hoist clamps in an inverted lift position, and that it was unsafe to lift the unit that way.

At the ends of the hoist chains on the crane there are clamps with teeth which are used to grip the unit being lifted. These clamps are referred to as dogs. Company wit-

373

nesses testified that Grievant had the dogs attached to the unit he was lifting in an inverted position. The Company claims that there is danger that the dogs will slip off when they are attached from underneath (inverted). The Company asserts that it is unsafe to invert the dogs, and it has stressed this to all employees in safety meetings.

The Company claims that Grievant responded to the Plant Manager that he knew it was the wrong way to lift but "that's the way we do it," and he had been instructed to do it that way by supervision. When the manager replied that was not the correct way to use the dogs, according to Company witnesses, Grievant became belligerent and a heated argument ensued between Grievant and the Plant Manager. The Company asserts that when Grievant's voice became very loud, almost screaming, the manager felt that something was wrong with Grievant and he ordered him to take a drug test.

The Grievant admits that he got angry with the manager because he thought the Company was singling him out and picking on him. He also claims the manager first told him he should be fired. He testified he got "nose to nose" with the manager because the manager yelled at him and mentioned firing him.

The Company has a published Drug and Alcohol Abuse Policy. It provides that the Company may require an employee to take an alcohol or drug test if the Company has cause to suspect an employee of possession or use of alcohol or illegal drugs on the job, or if the Company has cause to believe an employee is under the influence of alcohol or drugs or is not capable of safely performing his job.

Grievant was given a drug test and suspended for the balance of the shift. The drug test came back later as negative. A grievance was filed and processed through the steps resulting in this arbitration.

POSITIONS OF THE PARTIES

The Company

The Company contends that Grievant was committing an unsafe act when he was stopped by supervision, and at that time Grievant became argumentative and belligerent and shouted at the supervisor, got in his face and spit on him.

The Company argues that because of such behavior the Company sent Grievant to take a drug test in accordance with its drug abuse program. The Company then suspended Grievant for the balance of the shift because of his insubordinate behavior and unsafe act.

According to witnesses for the company . . . Grievant was not following a safe practice in inverting the dogs. It was convincingly demonstrated that lifting the unit that way can be hazardous. Grievant testified that he fastened the dogs underneath because the top was filled with shot from the machine. . . . He is supposed to remove the shot with brush or shovel and then attach the dogs in the proper way.

The Company asks that the grievance be denied.

The Union

The Union contends that the Company has not proved that the manner in which Grievant was using the dogs was unsafe or that such justified a drug test and a suspension without pay.

The Union further contends that the Company did not have probable cause to believe that Grievant was under the influence of illegal drugs just because he became angry and argued with a supervisor. The Union argues that the supervisor provoked Grievant by threatening to fire him.

The Union also argues that the negative result of the drug test shows there was not probable cause for testing Grievant, and the Company was wrong in suspending him. The Union asks that Grievant be made whole.

APPLICABLE CONTRACT LANGUAGE

Section 6—Management Prerogatives—Shop Rules

A) The parties signatory to this agreement recognize and agree that nothing contained in this agreement is intended or shall be construed as a waiver of any of the usual inherent and fundamental rights of the company including the right to manage the operation of its plant(s) and business, (and) direct its working forces. . . . It is specifically understood that all rights and functions belonging either to the Company or the Union which are not specifically limited by the provisions of this agreement shall remain with the Company and the Union respectively.

B) The Company shall have the right . . . to . . . suspend, discipline or discharge for proper cause. . . .

C) The Company shall have the right to establish, maintain and enforce reasonable rules and regulations to assure orderly plant operations, it being understood and agreed that such rules and regulations shall not be inconsistent or in conflict with the provisions of this agreement.

PERTINENT PROVISIONS OF COMPANY DRUG AND ALCOHOL ABUSE PROGRAM

So that you will know in advance how the company proposes to administer a program to control alcohol and drug abuse in our plant, you are advised as follows:

1. If the company has cause to suspect an employee of possession or use of alcohol, illegal drugs or other controlled substances while on the job or on company premises (including parking lots and private roads on Company property), or if the company has cause to believe an employee is under the influence of alcohol or any controlled substance and/or is not capable of safely performing his or her job, the company may require the employee to take an alcohol and/or drug test.

QUESTIONS

1. In your view, "Did the actions of the Company on August 24, 1992 in requiring Grievant to take a drug test and in suspending him for the balance of the shift violate the contract?" Why or why not? If yes, what should be the remedy?

2. In your view, did the company have reasonable cause to require Grievant to be given a drug test?

3. Was it proper for the company to suspend the employee for the balance of the shift because of the drug test?

4. Discuss the issues of plant safety and drug testing.

Source: Reprinted with permission from *Labor Relations Reporter–Labor Arbitration Reports,* 100 LA 1190. Copyright 1993 by The Bureau of National Affairs, Inc. (800-372-1033) <http://www.bna.com>

C & A Wallcoverings, Inc. and United Paperworkers International Union, Local 904

Thomas R. McMillen, Arbitrator. Award issued February 4, 1993.

ISSUES

Discharge—Refusal to take drug/alcohol test.

FACTS

The facts of this case are not in dispute. The grievant (M) was present but did not testify. We find that he appeared for work on March 10, 1992 in what his supervisor observed to be an intoxicated condition. The supervisor, Dwayne Slack, was an experienced and well-trained individual on the recognition of alcohol abuse. He observed the grievant on his reach truck, bobbing and weaving back and forth without operating the truck. His eyes were red and glassy, his speech was slurred, and he walked from the truck in a stumbling manner. After offering various unacceptable excuses for not performing his assigned duties, the grievant was asked to take a drug/alcohol test, and the Union shop steward was summoned.

When the Union steward arrived, she met with the supervisor and the grievant in the supervisor's office, and the grievant admitted that he had been up all night and was still drunk. The Union representative also admits in his brief (second page) that M "did in fact report to work in an intoxicated state." He was thereupon suspended for an investigation and was asked to take a drug/alcohol test. A taxicab was waiting to take him to the testing facility.

After a short private conference with the Union steward, the grievant again refused to be tested. He was then told in the presence of the steward that he would be terminated if he refused to be tested or failed the test and that he would be reinstated if the test came out favorably to him.

After the supervisor checked with the Director of Personnel by telephone, he repeated the alternatives to the grievant and the grievant persisted in his refusal to take the test. The Union steward testified that she did not give him any specific advice on taking or not taking the test. The grievant was therefore terminated in accordance with the letter referred to above, he punched out, and went home.

CONTRACTUAL PROVISIONS

The collective bargaining agreement provides in Section 17(A) on Page 16 as follows:

SECTION 17. DISCHARGE

17(A) No employee shall be discriminated against for any Union activities or in any way so as to violate the letter or spirit of this Agreement. After an employee has completed the trial period, he shall not be discharged except for justifiable cause. Except in cases where immediate disciplinary action is necessary, such as, but not limited to, actions which endanger the health, safety or welfare of other occupants of the shop or violate criminal or civil laws, no employee shall be discharged until after the Company shall have first discussed the matter with the Shop Committee. This shall not preclude the Company from effecting the discharge if, in his [sic] judgment, after such discussion, the discharge is warranted.

A further provision in Section 17 provides as follows:

17(C) Any such dispute shall be adjusted in accordance with the procedure set forth in Section 19 hereunder, and the ultimate decision as to whether the employee has been discriminated against or has been unjustifiably discharged, laid off in violation of the provisions of this paragraph [sic] and the remedy prescribed shall be final and binding on the parties hereto. Any employee unjustifiably discharged, or laid off in violation of the established seniority list shall be compensated for all time lost and shall be immediately reinstated. This paragraph shall not interfere with the necessary reduction of the working force in slack periods.

19(D) Arbitrator's Authority—The Arbitrator shall have no authority to add to, subtract from, modify or amend in any way the terms and conditions of this Agreement.

COMPANY'S POSITION

The employer contends that it discharged M for just cause, relying on two sets of facts: (1) Past practice. An employee named T was terminated because she failed to pass a drug test in June, 1989. She was represented by the Union, had been observed under the influence of marijuana during working hours (but outside of the building), took the drug test and failed it. She was therefore discharged and no grievance was filed.

Another incident occurred in the parking lot when two employees were found with empty beer bottles beside their car. However, they did not appear to the supervisor to be under the influence of alcohol and were not asked to submit to a test. They were given a one and one-half day suspension without pay, and no grievance was filed.

Two other instances of failure to give tests were shown in the record, namely, with respect to the condition of W and O. Neither person was given a test because of lack of probable cause to believe they were under the influence of alcohol, but the Union knew of this policy and practice and at least tolerated it.

(2) The Company also relies upon a notice which had been posted next to the time clock at the Hammond plant since 1988. It read as follows:

The use, sale or possession, or being under the influence, of illegal drugs or alcohol on the job or on Company property is prohibited. Employees who violate this prohibition or who are involved in illegal drug activities, whether on or off the job, shall be subject to disciplinary action up to and including termination.

Similar policy statements are contained in a rule book which is given to every employee upon hiring.

UNION'S POSITION

The Union takes the position that the posted notice is not a binding contractual provision and that it says nothing about drug or alcohol testing. Therefore, the Union contends that there is neither a violation of the rule nor of written Company policy by M's refusal to submit to a drug/alcohol test. It does not challenge the determination that the grievant was drunk.

QUESTIONS

1. Was the employee terminated for just cause? Why or why not?

2. Do you feel the refusal to take a drug and alcohol test violated the contract? Why or why not?

3. Evaluate the company's position of past practice. Does this have any effect on this case?

Source: Reprinted with permission from *Labor Relations Reporter–Labor Arbitration Reports,* 100 LA 816. Copyright 1993 by The Bureau of National Affairs, Inc. (800-372-1033) <http://www.bna.com>

Pioneer Flour Mills [San Antonio, Texas] and International Brotherhood of Teamsters, Local 1110

Ed W. Bankston, Arbitrator. Award issued on October 20, 1993.

ISSUE

Drug and Alcohol Testing—Discharge—Refusal to take test—On-the-job-accident—Reasonable suspicion.

GENERAL BACKGROUND

The Union has grieved the March 29, 1993 termination of P, who at the time of the termination was classified as warehouseman. The grievant was discharged for "refusing to give a urine sample as required by the Drug and Alcohol Policy." The Union immediately protested the grievant's termination and timely filed this grievance on April 6, 1993.

RELEVANT PROVISIONS OF THE AGREEMENT

ARTICLE 2—MANAGEMENT RIGHTS

Section 1. The Union recognizes the inherent right of the Company to conduct its business in all particulars except as expressly modified by this Agreement and any written supplement to this Agreement. This Agreement and the Supplement to it shall be interpreted only according to its written provision and in a reasonable and common sense manner consistent with the efficient operations of the business and the specific contract rights of the employees and without regard to past practices or unwritten matters, except where past practice is expressly referred to in this Agreement. All prior negotiations are incorporated in this Agreement, and no prior negotiations are to be referred to in any arbitration.

ARTICLE 9—DISCHARGE AND DISCIPLINARY ACTION

Section 1. No employee shall be discharged without just cause. Such cause shall include the reasons set forth in Schedule "A". Employees may be disciplined up to and including discharge for any of such reasons on the first occurrence. Factors to be considered in determining the degree of discipline shall include the nature of the incident, the employee's overall employment record and the circumstances surrounding the occurrence in question.

Section 2. No employee shall be discharged or suspended without sufficient cause. Such cause shall include any violation of Company Rules. Four violations may result in disciplinary action up to and including discharge. Factors to be considered in administering such discipline shall include the nature of the incident, the employee's overall employment record and the circumstances surrounding the occurrence in question.

Section 3. Written warnings expire twelve (12) months following date of issue.

Section 4. A Union steward shall be present at disciplinary conferences involving discharge. An employee upon request may have a steward present at conferences pertaining to lesser discipline.

Section 5. Copies of all disciplinary action will be provided to the affected employee, the local Union office, and two copies of each disciplinary action shall be provided to the chief steward. Employees who are discharged will be given a written explanation stating the basis of the discharge.

Section 6. Minor infractions shall be brought to the attention of the employee affected within five (5) working days after their occurrence or within five (5) working days after coming to the attention of the Company, or they shall be deemed waived.

SCHEDULE "A"

1. Gross neglect of duty.
2. Insubordination.
3. Dishonesty, including theft, punching the timecard of another employee, falsifying time records, or falsifying any other document.
4. Violation of the Drug and Alcohol Policy.
5. Incompetence.
6. Failure to report any traffic accident while operating a company vehicle.
7. Carrying unauthorized passengers.
8. Any deliberate interference with, stoppage or slowdown of work.
9. Other conduct of sufficient nature to constitute just cause.
10. Failure to comply with security procedures through willful disregard.
11. Failure to comply with safety rules through willful disregard which could cause serious physical injury to any person.

ARTICLE 21—PHYSICAL REQUIREMENTS

Section 2. No one shall be knowingly permitted by the Company to work on the premises while suffering from any contagious, infectious, or mental disease or have in his body any measurable amount of an illegal substance or a blood alcohol level exceeding 0.10%. The Company reserves the right to require a physical examination, including x-ray, of any employee at any time to ascertain the availability of this employee for continued employment. The Company reserves the right to require a physical examination including Drug and Alcohol Screening under either of the following circumstances:

(a) Return-to-work physical;
(b) DOT physical;
(c) Reasonable suspicion;
(d) Following on-the-job accident resulting in medical treatment or reasonable suspicion;
(e) Anytime with notice of testing. The testing is to be completed within twenty (20) days of notice. No employee shall be tested under this provision for

more than four (4) times in one calendar year. The Company shall not post the first notice of testing for 30 days after this contract goes into effect.

Section 3. Employees testing positive under Article 21 Section 2(e) will be subject to the following:

(a) Suspension for up to sixty (60) days;
(b) Employee can request another test anytime after thirty (30) days;
  (i) If tests positive—termination;
  (ii) If tests negative—return to work and Company has right to test again at any time during the next twelve (12) months. If tests positive—termination.

FACTS

On Thursday, March 18, 1993, the grievant reported for his second shift work assignment promptly at 3:00 p.m. In the absence of supervision, the grievant accessed the work instructions through a computer and determined that a certain inventory of shortening was to be relocated out of the cold storage room. He began moving the palletized shortening with a forklift out of the cold storage area through an opening sealed by an electronically operated door. The door allowed access to the cold storage area of the warehouse. After several trips through the open door, it was inadvertently activated by the grievant's forklift moving toward the cold storage area. Grievant failed to stop the forklift, striking the partially closed door and causing it extensive damage. Hearing the noise of the crash, John Davila, a fellow employee, rushed to the scene as did the grievant's supervisor, Juan Camacho. Upon inspecting the scene, Supervisor Camacho ordered the grievant to take a drug test. The grievant refused and instead punched out and left the plant as instructed by Camacho. By Letter of Termination dated March 29, 1993, the grievant was advised that his employment was terminated because he "refused to give a urine sample as required by the Drug and Alcohol Policy." (Letter of Termination). On April 6, 1993, the Union filed a grievance protesting the discharge which was denied by the Company on the same day. (Grievance Report).

POSITIONS OF THE PARTIES

The Company

It is the position of the Company that termination of the grievant's employment was entirely proper and for cause. According to the Company, the grievant was discharged for refusing to provide a urine sample as required by the Drug and Alcohol Policy and as provided by Article 9 of the Agreement. The Company insists that "reasonable suspicion" existed as associated with the grievant's accident and upon which to base its demand for drug testing of the grievant. Further, the Company argues that the grievant had been properly notified and that the grievant had previously consented to such request for testing, refusal of which subjects him to discharge. The Company insists that the grievant ought to have acceded to the request for testing and later grieve the matter as objectionable. The Company asks that the grievance be denied.

The Union

The position of the Union with respect to this dispute is that the grievance should be sustained largely because of the lack of reasonable suspicion upon which the testing request was grounded. Moreover, the grievant was never informed as to any basis for the reasonable suspicion asserted by the Company. According to the Union, there was, in fact, no basis upon which to assert reasonable suspicion. The Union resists the efforts of the Company to insist upon testing as a matter of policy where an uninjured employee has been involved in an accident. The Union contends that the Company failed in its efforts to negotiate such an arrangement and now attempts to assert unilaterally a "policy" securing the very same advantage. The Union further insists that to require the grievant to "obey now and grieve later" is inappropriate under the circumstances. Furthermore, the grievant was never told that his refusal to be tested would lead to discharge. The Union asks that the grievance be sustained and that the grievant be reinstated to his former employment with the Company and that he be made whole with respect to all wages, benefits and seniority.

QUESTIONS

1. In your view, was the grievant's termination in accordance with the Agreement? Explain why or why not.
2. Under Article 9, the reasons for just cause shall include everything set forth in Schedule "A." As an employer, which reason would you rely on for just cause in this case? Why?
3. Discuss and evaluate each party's position. Which party has a better case concerning "reasonable suspicion"?
4. As an arbitrator, how would you decide the case? Why?

Source: Reprinted with permission from *Labor Relations Reporter–Labor Arbitration Reports,* 101 LA 816. Copyright 1993 by The Bureau of National Affairs, Inc. (800-372-1033) <http://www.bna.com>

Scott Paper Company and United Paperworkers International Union Local No. 423
John F. Caraway, Arbitrator. Award issued June 7, 1993.

ISSUES

Off-duty misconduct—Drug possession.

RELEVANT CONTRACT PROVISIONS

Scott Paper Company, Mobil, Alabama facility management and the United Paperworkers International Union and its Local Unions 423, 1421, 1575 and 1873 agree to the procedures in this policy regarding the use, sale or possession of alcohol and controlled substances. The abuse of drugs and alcohol is recognized as a major contributor to poor job performance and an unsafe work environment. It is also recognized as a disruption of family and social life, and contributes to deterioration in emotional and physical well-being. It is regarded as a disease having many causes both personal and social, but a disease, nevertheless, which can be arrested and successfully treated provided the affected individual is sufficiently motivated and rehabilitation efforts are aided by an understanding family, employer and associates. Mobile management and the local unions are committed to the objective of creating a workplace free of drug and alcohol abuse. Procedures in this policy are intended to accomplish this goal. It is not our intent to mandate morality but to take appropriate action when conduct appears to impact job performance or bring public discredit to the company, unions, or employees.

ARTICLE IV. INVESTIGATION AND DISCIPLINE

Employees who . . .

Engage in the unauthorized use, sale and possession of alcohol or controlled substances while on the job or on company property or are convicted by a court of law of any illegal controlled substance activity must be held responsible for this unacceptable behavior. The extent of discipline imposed will depend on many considerations. We have developed general guidelines, outlined below, that are intended to act as a deterrent to this unacceptable behavior.

Guidelines:

Any employees engaged in the unauthorized use, sale or possession of alcohol or controlled substances while on the job or on company property will subject themselves to disciplinary action, up to and including discharge. Any employee convicted by a court of law of any illegal controlled substance activity will be subject to the most severe disciplinary action up to and including discharge. Although we consider clinical dependency on alcohol or drugs a treatable illness, we will not allow it to permit employees to endanger their own or others' safety or to cause damage to company property. Failure on the part of the employees to correct their performance will be handled through the standard disciplinary procedure. The decision to discipline and the degree of discipline imposed will depend on many considerations. While we do not intend to legislate the degree of discipline through this policy, we do want to clearly communicate to our entire work force that the unauthorized use, sale or possession of alcohol or controlled substances while on the job or on company property will not be tolerated. There should be no misunderstanding by any employee as to the company's and the union's intent of this policy, which is to remove drug and alcohol problems from the workplace. While there is genuine interest in employee rehabilitation, offenders of this policy will be dealt with appropriately.

FACTS

The grievant C was discharged on February 10, 1992 for pleading guilty to the offense of unlawful possession of marijuana in the second degree, a Class "A" misdemeanor. He was sentenced to the Mobile County jail for a term of one year, which sentence was suspended for two years pending his good behavior. He was required to pay a fine of $500.00 plus court cost and a victim's fee, which brought his total payment to $676.00. This was on January 27, 1992. On February 15, 1991 C's house was searched by Deputies of Mobile County Sheriff's Department acting with Agents of the United States Alcohol, Tobacco and Firearms Bureau in a combined task force. The Deputies found 1.75 pounds of marijuana in a corner of C's closet. It had a "street value" of slightly less than $2,500.00. The marijuana was packaged in thirty "quarter" bags [that is, plastic bags containing 4 ounces of marijuana], one larger bag about quart size, and one still larger bag, about gallon size. Also were found a box of rolled marijuana cigarettes, a set of postage scales, cash in a bank bag and two pistols. There also was a tray of marijuana cigarette butts. C was not at his residence when the search was made. He later turned himself in to the Sheriff's Department and was charged with unlawful possession of marijuana in the first degree, a Class "C" felony under the Alabama Criminal Code. He made bond. Upon his return to work, the Company learned of his arrest and he was thereupon suspended.

Mr. Connolly, Manager of Labor Relations, testified that at the third step meeting C admitted that he had sold marijuana to "cover the expenses" of his use. He bought the marijuana for himself and friends. Mr. Connolly stated that the discharge of C was based on the fact that the paper company was a hazardous workplace. The use and possession of controlled substances cannot be tolerated. C admitted that he sold and used marijuana. Under the Company's Drug and Alcohol Policy the Company had the right to discharge C after he was convicted of "illegal controlled substance activity." Mr. Connolly stated that C was an average employee and had not given the Company any problems in the past. The Union presented evidence pertaining to the drafting of the Drug and Alcohol Policy. It stated that the Company and Union negotiated the policy with the objective of having a "drug free workplace." It stated that there was never any intent for the policy to apply to off-site conduct. Regarding the provision permitting discipline to impose where the employee was convicted of illegal drug activity, the intent was that activity be in the plant or related to the employee's job. It also stated that personal use of drugs outside of the plant which had no impact upon the plant or its activities would not be subject to the Drug and Alcohol Policy. Mr. Butler testified that he participated in the negotiations of the Drug and Alcohol Policy. The purpose was to make the plant drug free. The Company, at no time, said that the policy would apply to off-duty conduct. C testified that he did not deal in drugs. He only purchased the marijuana in question for the use of himself and his friends. He would advance the money for the marijuana. He would then distribute the marijuana and collect the cost from friends. It was strictly for personal use. He never brought any of the marijuana on the plant site. Mr. Sharp, Manager of Human Resources for the Company, stated that the question of off-plant use for possession of a controlled substance by an employee was never discussed during the negotiations leading to the Drug and Alcohol Policy.

POSITIONS OF THE PARTIES

The Employer

The Company maintains that it properly discharged C. The Company shows that through negotiations with the Union a formal Drug and Alcohol Policy was adopted and made part of the Collective Bargaining Agreement effective June 1, 1989. C is the first employee discharged under that Policy. The Policy provides at pages 67–68 that an employee who is convicted by a court of law of "any illegal controlled substance activity" will be "subject to the most severe disciplinary action up to and including discharge." C was convicted of unlawful possession of marijuana in the second degree. This clearly falls within the cited language of the Policy. The Company determined that such a conviction warranted his discharge. C admitted to having purchased approximately two (2) pounds of marijuana, part of which he sold to one individual and intended to sell to four (4) or five (5) persons. He admitted engaging in such an activity over the past five (5) to six (6) years. Proof that C engaged in this activity was shown by the presence of thirty (30) "quarter bags" containing marijuana which was to be sold by C. The evidence shows that C works in an area of the "Mill" for hazardous chemicals, [chlorine, chlorine dioxide, and sulfur dioxide] can be released into the atmosphere, thereby endangering the 3,000 employees at the plant and thousands of individuals who live in the adjacent areas. The person who is not fully in control mentally and physically could expose large numbers of persons to injury or possible death.

The Company maintains that the Union arguments are without merit. The Union argues that "off-duty" activity was not covered by the Drug and Alcohol Policy. The reading of the policy does not restrict it to "on-site" activity. The Policy characterizes as "unacceptable behavior" convictions by a court of law of any illegal controlled substance activity. There is no demarcation between an employee engaging in such an activity on the plant site or away from the plant site. The Union argues that C's misconduct did not affect the workplace because he did not use marijuana at the plant nor did he sell this substance to any other employee. The fact that C was caught in possession of drugs away from the plant does not rule out an intent on his part to sell drugs at his place of work. Arbitrators have upheld terminations on analogous facts to that of the C case. The argument is advanced that C should not be discharged because of his conviction of a misdemeanor. The evidence in this case shows that C was initially charged with a felony. This was reduced to a misdemeanor in consideration of C testifying in the prosecution of a high drug distributor. In other words, the prosecutor made a "deal" with C.

The Union

The Union maintains that neither the Labor Agreement nor the Drug and Alcohol Policy provides for termination of an employee for engaging in drug activity which is off-duty. The reading of the Drug and Alcohol Policy demonstrates that it was not the intent of the parties to "mandate morality". The purpose was to make a drug free environment at the plant. This was the testimony of the Union witnesses who are members of the committee who negotiated the Drug and Alcohol Policy. They stated that the intent was never to apply this Policy to off-site conduct. The Union argues that C's off-duty and off-premises conduct has no nexus to the employer and therefore "proper cause" does not exist for his discharge. The evidence fails to show that there was any nexus between C's activities and the Company's business. The grievant's job performance and job safety did not suffer. The employees were not adversely affected as proved by the fact that the Union membership voted unanimously to arbitrate C's termination. The evidence failed to show that there was any safety hazard created by C's conduct. C was found guilty of possessing drugs off-duty so that no safety hazard could possibly exist at the plant. The Company treated C differently than another employee, Mr. Pickett, who was retained on the job even though he was on probation after being convicted of possession of cocaine. It is undisputed that C pled guilty to possession of marijuana in the second degree which is a misdemeanor. Finally, the evidence shows that C's conduct can be easily corrected. He will never again buy or sell marijuana on behalf of his friends nor use it.

QUESTIONS

1. Did the company properly discharge C on the grounds of "engaging in the unauthorized use, sale and possession of marijuana" even though he was not actually engaging in these acts "on-site"? Why or why not?

2. Does the fact that C worked with toxic chemicals have any implications regarding his discharge? Why or why not?

3. Would another form of disciplinary action been more appropriate for C? Why or why not?

4. The union contends that C's conviction fails to show us any "nexus" between C's activities and the company's business. Do you agree? Why or why not?

5. How would you decide this case? Why?

Source: Reprinted with permission from *Labor Relations Reporter–Labor Arbitration Reports,* 100 LA 1113. Copyright 1993 by The Bureau of National Affairs, Inc. (800-372-1033) <http://www.bna.com>

Snyder General Corporation
and Sheet Metal Workers, Local 480

Howard M. Bard, Arbitrator. Award issued October 5, 1992.

ISSUES

Discharge—Falsification of time cards—Intent, prior conduct—Punching in at wrong time clock.

RELEVANT CONTRACT PROVISIONS

Article XVIII, "Plant Rules and Discipline"

Section 1. The Company shall not discipline or discharge any employee except for just cause. It is agreed that the employees covered by this Agreement shall be governed by the Plant Rules agreed upon by the parties effective as of the date of this Agreement.

FACTS

The Grievant, Jay De Mars, has been a coil assembler at the air conditioning plant operated by the Employer in Faribault, Minnesota for approximately four (4) years. On April 6, 1992, and again on April 8, 1992, the Grievant was excused from work early to see his physician. The time punched by the clock on the Grievant's time card for the afternoon of April 6 was "1550" hours. On April 8 the Grievant's time card indicated that the Grievant punched out at "1525" hours. The Employer uses a variation of military time: the clock operates on a twenty four (24) hours basis and each hour is split into increments of one hundredth (1/100) of an hour (an employee who is six minutes late to work has missed one tenth [1/10] of the hour, or .1 hours and would be docked six minutes of pay). "1525" hours therefore translates to three fifteen (3:15) P.M. and "1550" hours translates to three thirty (3:30) P.M. In addition to the primary function of stamping the time at which an employee comes to work and leaves work, the time card serves other functions as well, principally as a mechanism for internal time keeping used to track employee productivity and time spent on various work orders during the course of the work day. According to the Grievant, employees are instructed to fill in the time when they begin a particular work order in the "hour/minute" column on the same horizontal line where the work order number is filled in (also by the employee). This was confirmed by Albert Sempaur, the Grievant's Foreman.

Both Sempaur and the Grievant agreed that the work order numbers are not supposed to be entered on the same horizontal line where the clock times appear showing when employees come to work or punch out. Rather, they are to appear in the lines between those two times. The Grievant testified, however, that sometimes it is difficult to "line up" the card in the time clock when punching out, and that on occasion the time entered on the card representing when a work order is performed might obscure or overlap the clock punch out time. A review of the grievant's time cards indicated that, in fact, this occurred both on April 6 and April 8 when the time that the Grievant actually clocked out of the plant had superimposed upon it (or underneath it) the time spent by the grievant performing a particular work task known as "move time." A review of the Grievant's other time cards submitted to the Arbitrator indicated that similar overlapping occurred on

March 12, March 13 and March 14. It is impossible to tell on any of the cards whether the Grievant wrote over the clocked out number or the clocked out number was stamped over the Grievant's handwriting. No expert on such matters . . . was called upon to testify at the hearing. According to the Grievant, the punch out time was superimposed over the work order time. Because the Grievant left early on April 8th, Albert Sempaur pulled the griev-ant's time card to assist him in filling out another form used by the Company, an "ITR" (Irregular Time Report), by which supervisors keep track and report when employees ar-rive late or leave early from their designated shifts. On reviewing the card, Sempaur no-ticed that the time printed in the "hour/minute" column opposite the "move time" work order number was "1550" which was, in fact, one quarter (1/4) of an hour after the Griev-ant had punched out for the day ("1525"). Sempaur then checked back to the Grievant's time card for April 6 and noticed a similar mistake. There, opposite the work order num-ber for move time, the Grievant had written in "1575" which was fifteen (15) minutes later than the actual time the Grievant clocked out from work ("1550").

According to the Grievant, the practice for calculating work time was to subtract fif-teen (15) (or thirty [30]) minutes from the time when the morning break began and, again, fifteen (15) (or thirty [30]) minutes from the time that an employee ended his shift. For example, in the Grievant's case his shift ordinarily ended at 4:00 P.M., or 1600 hours. Or-dinarily, he would therefore subtract either fifteen (15) minutes or 1/2 hour from the end of his shift, which would result in recorded work time of "1575" and "1550", respectively. The Grievant admitted that he had made mistakes on April 6 and 8 and that the time should have been subtracted from the time he actually left for his doctor's appointment, not from the time his normal shift ended. He testified that he had been in a hurry to make his doctor's appointment, and that he had been acting out of habit. He testified that he ex-plained the mistakes to the Employer. Notwithstanding the Grievant's protestations, the Grievant was again terminated from his employment on April 10, 1992 for violation of Plant Rule 30. Plant Rule 30, which is incorporated into the Collective Bargaining Agree-ment ("Agreement"), provides that the first offense for "intentionally falsifying employ-ment application or other records" is grounds for immediate discharge. At the hearing, the grounds for the discharge were expanded to include Plant Rule 28, which provides for im-mediate discharge of an employee for "intentionally punching in or out on another em-ployee's time card or falsifying one's own or another employee's time card, job card, work slip, or time ticket to misrepresent the fact to defraud the Company."

POSITIONS OF THE PARTIES

The Company

The Company contends that it "is not accusing Mr. De Mars of writing over a time card machine punch with intent that the keypunch operator would use the written time in lieu of the clock punch time. The charge is that he wrote a false time in a manner that would be used by the keypunch operator to apply more time to his credit than actually worked and earned, cumulative, thus defrauding the Company in violation of Plant Rule 28." According to the Company, "the coded numbers following the false (wrong) time written in would tell the keypunch operator that she should 'add' move time to the time written based on a predetermined amount—fifteen (15) minutes if move time is split evenly in A.M./P.M. or thirty (30) minutes if move time is recorded previously that shift."

The Company contends that, in fact, had the mistake not been caught by Sempaur on the 8th, the Grievant would have received more pay than he would otherwise have been en-titled as had allegedly occurred on April 6; however, on the 8th Mr. Sempaur diverted the Grievant's time card before it could reach the EDS timekeeping department. The Company contends that the Grievant's actions were deliberate with the intent to defraud the Company

by receiving full pay for two 8 hour shifts even though he left early for medical appointments. The Company contends that the Grievant's prior time cards indicate that he knew
how to properly fill in time cards; furthermore, the concurrence of two such incidents within
a three (3) day period allegedly further indicates the intentional nature of the Grievant's acts.
The Company also sought to establish that the Grievant had a history of trying to manipulate the time card system by punching in at time clocks other than the one located at his department notwithstanding the fact that, according to Sempaur, all of the employees, including De Mars, were told to comply with established job card procedures which included
punching in their time cards in their own departments. (Apparently, if an employee punches
in at a time clock near the front of the plant, it allegedly may take him several minutes to
reach the back and begin to work, whereas if he punches in at his own department, the
punched in time would be more reflective of the actual time when work is begun.)

The Union

The Union contends that the Grievant mistakenly wrote in the wrong time next to
his move time on his time cards, and that the time that he wrote in would, in fact, have
been correct had he worked his normal shift for the days in question. The Union contends
that "the employer failed to show that Jay or any other employee would be aware that the
keypunch operator would record Jay's time as the Employer asserts she did. On the contrary the arbitrator asked the employer the procedure that keypunch operators are to follow when recording time. The employer stated that keypunch operators are to go by the
clock punched time and that the only time they should not go by the clock punch time
would be if there was some written indication by a supervisor that a written in time should
be used." The Union contends that the ITR report is, in fact, designed in part to resolve
problems such as the ones which occurred on April 6 and 8.

The Union objected to the testimony which claimed that the Grievant may have
punched in at other time clocks as well as the one in his own department, noting the testimony of a fellow employee that this was common practice at the Company. In addition,
the Union objected that the Company did not show that the Grievant had ever been disciplined for being late or for punching in at a different time clock. Rather, the only testimony was that the Grievant had on occasion "cut it close," according to Sempaur, but had
not been late. At the hearing, the Union also requested the Arbitrator to clarify his previous award in regard to the application of the interim (discharge) period of the grievant to
Section three (3) of the Agreement, which states that if an employee keeps his or her
record clear of all violations of Plant Rules for a period of twelve (12) months, such prior
violations will not be considered when administering discipline in the event of a subsequent violation, and that any violations which occurred more than two (2) years prior to a
subsequent violation will not be considered when administering discipline.

QUESTIONS

1. The Employer contends that the "Grievant wrote a false time in a manner that would apply more
   time to his credit than actually worked." Do you agree with the Employer? Why or why not?

2. The Union claims that the ITR report is designed in part to resolve problems such as these.
   Is this important to the case? Why or why not?

3. The Union claims that "Management has failed to prove its case." What do you think?

4. According to the Employer, "the Grievant knew how to fill in a time card correctly." Should
   this be a consideration in the decision of the arbitrator? Why or why not?

5. How would you decide this case? Why?

Wholesale Produce Supply Company and Over-the-Road Storage, Grocery and Market Drivers, Helpers and Inside Employees Union, Teamsters Local 544

Mario L. Traynon, Arbitrator. Award issued November 7, 1993.

ISSUES

Discharge—Dishonesty—Videotape evidence—Burden of proof.

RELEVANT CONTRACT PROVISIONS

ARTICLE 23 DISCHARGE

The Employer shall not discharge any employee without just cause, and shall give at least one warning notice of the complaint against such employee, except that no warning notice need be given to an employee before he is discharged if the cause of such discharge is dishonesty. . . .

FACTS

The Company operates a wholesale produce supply company in the Twin Cities and, until March 3, 1993, employed the Grievant, S, as a Warehouseman. On March 2, 1993, the Grievant was responsible for loading a pallet with invoiced produce that a customer would later pick up. The Grievant completed the task and the customer, G, picked up the produce and left the Company's premises. Company representatives, however, believed that the Grievant provided the customer with additional products, without charge to the customer.

The Company's allegations were based on a supervisor's inventory of the produce on the pallet loaded by the Grievant and on a surveillance videotape. The Company contends that the inventory showed that the Grievant placed additional produce on the G pallet without charging G for these additions. The surveillance videotape, according to the Company, further demonstrates that the Grievant allowed G to place approximately five (5) more items on the pallet without noting the same on the customer's invoice. Despite the Grievant's acceptable work record for approximately 18 years, the Company immediately terminated the Grievant for dishonesty. The Grievant challenged the Company's actions and the matter proceeded to the instant arbitration hearing.

POSITIONS OF THE PARTIES

The Company

The Company initially argues that the Grievant was properly discharged in this case because the Grievant engaged in dishonesty. The Company urges that proven dishonesty should result in the immediate termination of employment. The Company next contends that it has proven its case against the Grievant. The Company notes that it has implemented a system of customer orders/invoices so that customers receive no more or no less than that actually ordered. That system insures customer satisfaction and prevents loss to the Company. The Company next points out that on March 2, 1993, the Grievant was solely responsible for filling the G order and that he had a prepared order to follow. However, supervisor H did not know whether an invoice had been prepared on the G order at the time he conducted his brief inventory of the product compiled by the Grievant. Shortly thereafter he discovered that his handwritten inventory of the product the Grievant had compiled for the G order was significantly different from the compilation of produce items appearing on the customer's order/invoice form. Consequently, the Company next reviewed the surveillance videotape maintained by the Company and determined that the Grievant further allowed the customer to add products to the pallet without noting the same or requesting payment for the same.

The Company's review of the videotape indicates the following important information: (1) the Grievant placed the G pallet at the loading area at approximately 5:39 A.M.; (2) H inventoried the pallet at approximately 5:40 A.M.; (3) the Grievant placed several cartons of tomatoes next to the G pallet at approximately 5:44 A.M.; (4) the Grievant then left the pallet unattended and no one approached the G pallet until approximately 6:15 A.M.; (5) at 6:15 A.M. customer G approached the G pallet and placed a carton on the pallet; (6) customer G repeated this procedure four (4) more times and once in the view of the Grievant; and (7) the Grievant then loaded the invoiced tomatoes onto the G pallet and loaded the pallet of produce onto the customer's truck. The Company further points out that its prior inventory of the G pallet indicated that the Grievant placed four (4) additional items on the pallet: one (1) 50# bag of jumbo yellow onions; one (1) carton of 30 celery; one (1) carton of 12 Cello cauliflower; and one (1) carton of Roma tomatoes.

Based on the record the Company contends that the Grievant was guilty of dishonesty. The Company points out that the Grievant had a prior business relationship with G involving the sale of produce, and that relationship may have motivated the Grievant's actions in this case. Moreover, the Company notes that while the Grievant acknowledged he was sensitive to that relationship vis-à-vis his role as a supplier to the customer, the Grievant failed to check the pallet for accuracy and failed to realize the additional materials placed on the pallet by the customer appeared on the videotape as out and out theft. Next, the Company contends that the Grievant was properly terminated under Article 23 of the parties' Agreement. Article 23, according to the Company, authorizes the Company to immediately discharge an employee for dishonesty. In the opinion of the Company the Grievant intended to deceive his employer in this case. Based on the record the Company requests the undersigned to deny the instant grievance.

The Union

The Union asserts that the Company failed to prove its case against the Grievant. The Union points out that the Company alleges that the Grievant "willingly" added items to customer G's order without indicating said items on the Company's order/invoice form, and that the Grievant "willingly" allowed customer G to add produce items to the pallet without paying for the same. The Union urges that it is these two (2) allegations of dishonesty that the Company must prove against the Grievant.

In that regard the Union notes that no witnesses testified that the Grievant somehow intentionally added the identified products to the pallet as an act of dishonesty. Rather, mistakes occur and the Grievant, according to the Union, simply made a mistake in this case. The Union notes that H's visual inventory of the pallet contained errors—that only one (1), not two (2) 50# bags of jumbo yellow onions was loaded onto G's pallet. Thus, errors do indeed occur. Next, the Union challenges the Company's reliance on the videotape to prove dishonesty on the part of the Grievant. The Union notes that on four (4) occasions when G placed an item on the pallet, the Grievant was not on the surveillance tape and the Company did not prove that the Grievant observed the actions of G. In addition, the Union urges that G merely placed empty boxes on the pallet, along with perhaps 6–8 oranges from the wholesaler's discard area. Thus, according to the Union, the Grievant did not witness any wrongdoing on which to report. The Union urges that the Company failed to prove its case against the Grievant.

After a review of the evidence in this case the Union contends that the Company failed to prove its case. The Union notes that the Company has put forth inconsistent reasons for its actions against the Grievant ranging from willingly loading non-invoiced product onto the G pallet to conspiracy with G in this case. Finally, the Union urges that the Grievant had a good work record for 18 years and that he had never been accused of misconduct or dishonesty in the work place. The Union urges that under all the relevant circumstances the discharge was indeed inappropriate and the undersigned should modify the penalty imposed.

QUESTIONS

1. The union contends that the company "failed to prove its case." Do you agree? Why or why not?

2. The company is claiming intentional deception by the grievant. What do you think?

3. In your view, did the company have just cause to discharge the grievant? Discuss.

4. This grievant, at the time of his discharge, had approximately 18 years of service with the company. Should the arbitrator consider this factor in his decision? Why or why not?

5. How would you decide this case? Why?

Source: Reprinted with permission from *Labor Relations Reporter–Labor Arbitration Reports,* 101 LA 1101. Copyright 1993 by The Bureau of National Affairs, Inc. (800-372-1033) <http://www.bna.com>

Hughes Markets [Irwindale, Calif.] and Teamsters Union Local 630
Donald S. Prayzich, Arbitrator. Award issued on January 19, 1994.

ISSUES

1. Did the Company have the right to summarily dismiss the grievant, H, during the agreed upon probationary period without cause being shown?

2. If the answer to Issue No. 1 is in the negative, then, in that event, did the Company have good cause to terminate the grievant, H, on August 26, 1993 after suspending him on August 11, 1993?

3. If not, what is the appropriate remedy?

APPLICABLE CONTRACT PROVISIONS

The relevant portions of the applicable provisions of the Collective Bargaining Agreement are set forth below:

ARTICLE V—PLANT MANAGEMENT AND DIRECTION OF PERSONNEL

A. The Employer shall have the right to discharge any employee for good cause, such as dishonesty, incompetence, drinking while on duty, intoxication and failure to perform work as normally required. Willful falsification of a material fact on an application shall be cause for immediate discharge.

B. Except for discharge for dishonesty, intoxication, flagrant insubordination, or flagrant disobedience of posted company rules, an employee shall not be discharged or subject to disciplinary layoff unless he has had one (1) previous warning notice in writing with a copy to the Union for an offense committed within 365 days prior to the date of discharge. Failure by the employee or the Union to protest or grieve on a warning notice at the time of issuance shall not, in itself, constitute an agreement or admission of the validity of the warning notice or the gravity of the alleged offense.

ARTICLE XIX—PROBATIONARY PERIOD

A. The first thirty (30) workdays of any employee's employment shall be probationary, but no employee shall be laid off during such probationary period to avoid his classification as a regular employee.

B. During the probationary period, an employee may be terminated for any reason and shall have no recourse concerning such termination to the grievance and arbitration procedures set forth in this Agreement.

BACKGROUND

The Company, Hughes Markets, Inc., owns and operates a large retail chain of food supermarkets in Southern California. The Company's warehousing and distribution facilities are located in Irwindale, California. The grievant, H, was hired on August 8, 1988. He worked as a warehouseman at the time of his suspension on August 11, 1993, and subsequent termination on August 26, 1993.

At the time of his discharge, the grievant had been working under the terms of a settlement agreement negotiated on July 27, 1993; one of the key elements of that agreement was a twenty (20) workday "probationary period." The grievant was discharged before the completion of that 20-day period for failure to comply with the terms and provisions of the July 27, 1993 settlement agreement. Prior to this termination, the grievant had previously been discharged on November 6, 1992; in lieu of arbitration, the parties negotiated a settlement agreement on June 21, 1993 providing for the grievant's reinstatement on July 11, 1993, along with a written warning dated November 6, 1992 for failing to report to work on October 16, 1992 after being released by the physician who treated him for an on-the-job injury.

After returning to work, in accordance with the prior settlement agreement (June 21, 1993), the grievant suffered another on-the-job injury, but was released by his physician to return to work on July 25, 1993. The grievant reported for work on that date but did not bring a copy of the physician's release with him, and therefore, was not allowed to work on July 25; he produced a copy of the release to the company on July 26, 1993 but was placed on suspension for failing to report with a copy of his medical release on July 25.

The parties met on July 27, 1993 and negotiated the settlement agreement under which the grievant was working at the time of his suspension on August 11, 1993 leading to his discharge on August 26, 1993.

The Company maintains that the grievant failed to comply with the overall job performance, attendance and productivity requirements which were conditions of his reinstatement. Further, the Company maintains that since the grievant was in a probationary period at the time of his suspension and subsequent termination, he was subject to discharge without cause being shown, for any reason not prohibited by law. That position notwithstanding, the Company points to the grievant's failure to comply with Engineered Production Standards and incidents of tardiness during his probationary period, as grounds for his termination.

The Union contends that the grievant was improperly discharged and did, in fact, comply with the Company's productivity requirements, was not absent during his probationary period and further, faults the Company for not allowing the grievant to complete the full 20-day probationary period agreed to by the parties. The Union also stresses that there are material, mutual misunderstandings as to what was agreed to by the parties on July 27, 1993 as far as the grievant's productivity requirements.

Accordingly, the Union urges the Arbitrator to reinstate the grievant with all lost wages and benefits and to remand the matter back to the parties for renegotiation of the settlement agreement of July 27, 1993.

POSITIONS OF THE PARTIES

The Company

The Company references the language of the Collective Bargaining Agreement (Article XIX) applicable to probationary employees and stresses that the grievant was, in fact, a probationary employee at the time of his termination. The Company submits that, in accordance with that language, the grievant was subject to discharge without cause being established. In support of this position, the Company cites San Jose Mercury News, 48 LA 143, 145 (1966) and Pullman-Standard, 40 LA 757, 762 (1963). The Company emphasizes that there is no element of discrimination present in the instant dispute and the grievant was properly dismissed as a probationary employee during the period of probation agreed to by the parties.

In the event the Company's position that the grievant was properly dismissed as a probationary employee without cause being shown is rejected by the Arbitrator, the Company points to Joint Exhibit No. 3. This document, stresses the Company, placed the grievant on notice by written warning dated November 6, 1992, that any future incident of failing to report for work after being released by a physician would subject the grievant to "more severe disciplinary action, including termination."

The Company stresses that, after the above referenced written warning of November 6, 1992, the grievant was again injured and failed to present a physician's release upon reporting for work; this scenario, submits the employer, set the stage for the July 27, 1993 meeting regarding the grievant's employment status. As a result of the July 27, 1993 meeting, Joint Exhibit No. 4 was prepared, memorializing the new agreement of the parties. A copy of this agreement was faxed to Business Agent Duncan Anderson who confirmed that the document correctly reflected the agreement reached at the July 27 meeting. The Company stresses that Joint Exhibit No. 4 makes no reference to an 80 percent level of productivity and the grievant had to comply with the "expectancy" for production and he was placed on final written warning for "overall work performance and attendance infractions."

In conclusion, the Company submits that it had the right to terminate the grievant as a probationary employee without cause being shown. Assuming arguendo, that the Company "had to prove a failure on the part of the grievant to comply with the terms of the agreement," it has done so. The Company requests that the grievant's discharge be sustained.

The Union

The Union submits that the Company violated the Settlement Agreement and the Collective Bargaining Agreement when it terminated the grievant; the Union stresses that the grievant was not allowed to complete the probationary period agreed to on July 27, 1993. Further, although not allowed to complete the agreed-upon probationary period, the grievant attained a better than 80 percent productivity level average for the period July 27, 1993 until terminated and thus, was in full compliance with the Agreement.

Reviewing the grievant's employment history, the Union points out that the grievant was terminated on November 6, 1992 and had not worked since July 3, 1992 due to an on-the-job injury. In lieu of submitting the propriety of that discharge to arbitration, the parties entered into a Settlement Agreement dated June 21, 1993; that Agreement provided, among other things, for the grievant to be reinstated as a warehouseman effective July 7, 1993. During the grievant's long period of absence, the Company relocated its warehouse and distribution facilities from Glendale to Irwindale, California and added meat, deli and milk items not previously handled in Glendale. Consistent with the June 21, 1993 Agreement, the grievant returned to work on July 11, 1993; the first time he had worked in more than a year. Accordingly, as a previously qualified warehouseman, the grievant was entitled to a two (2) week period before being fully subject to productivity standards and discipline attendant thereto; this two (2) week period was in addition to the one (1) week period given to all warehousemen who transferred from Glendale to Irwindale.

Addressing the sequence of events prior to the July 27, 1993 meeting, the Union stresses that the grievant was fully aware of his responsibility to report for work upon being released by his physician. Accordingly, the grievant reported on July 25, 1993 (Sunday), was not permitted to work because he did not have his medical release with him, and the following day (his day off) obtained another copy of the physician's release so he could work July 26, 1993 (Monday). Instead of being allowed to work, emphasizes the Union, the grievant was placed on indefinite suspension. On Tuesday, July 27, 1993, the parties met and the reinstatement agreement was reached.

The Union stresses that at the commencement of that July 27, 1993 meeting, the Company could not have properly disciplined the grievant for either productivity or attendance; in short, the Union and the grievant compromised his contractual rights in light of the settlement reached, based upon their understandings of what had been agreed to. Pointing to the twenty (20) day probationary period, the Union emphasizes that the grievant had to only maintain an 80 percent average during that twenty (20) working day period, to avoid discipline. Mr. Duncan Anderson, Business Agent for the Union and the grievant, understood the wording "perform at the expectance [sic]" meant that upon conclusion of the twenty (20) day probationary period, the grievant would be treated as any other employee so far as productivity requirements and discipline attendant thereto. This understanding, stresses the Union, is contrary to what the Company maintains they understood the Agreement of July 27, 1993 to mean; that is, the grievant was subject to immediate termination during the probationary period for not maintaining a 91 percent average of Standard. The Union maintains that Business Agent Anderson and the grievant would not have entered into the Agreement on such terms. Clouding the issue even more, the Union stresses that the twenty (20) day probationary period commenced upon reinstatement after the July 27, 1993 meeting and was not 16 days (an assumption of credit for days worked prior to the July 27, 1993 agreement).

In view of the foregoing, the Union maintains that the parties had a mutual, material misunderstanding as to what was agreed to at the July 27, 1993 meeting; this genuine misunderstanding was compounded by the ambiguous written warning notice memorializing the agreement reached regarding the grievant's reinstatement. The Union submits that both parties stated at the arbitration hearing, that if they had known of the other party's understanding of the Agreement, neither party would have entered into the Agreement. Thus, the Union contends that the Arbitrator should order the parties back to the positions they were in at the start of the July 27, 1993 meeting.

In conclusion, the Union requests that the Arbitrator determine that the Company violated the Collective Bargaining Agreement when it terminated the grievant and order reinstatement with full back pay and benefits. In the alternative, the Union requests that the grievant be reinstated to employment as of July 27, 1993 without prejudice to either party and declare the warning notice "rescinded, null and void."

QUESTIONS

1. In your view, did the employer have the right to discharge the employee under the settlement agreement negotiated on July 27, 1993? Why or why not?

2. As an employer, how would you handle the grievant's not being able to present a return-to-work release form from his doctor?

3. Evaluate the union's argument that "the company violated the Settlement Agreement and the Collective Bargaining Agreement when it terminated the grievant . . . by not allowing him to complete the probationary period."

4. How would you decide the case? Why?

Source: Reprinted with permission from *Labor Relations Reporter–Labor Arbitration Reports,* 102 LA 267. Copyright 1993 by The Bureau of National Affairs, Inc. (800-372-1033) <http://www.bna.com>

Minster Machine Company and United Steelworkers Local 3210

Maurice L. Kelman, Arbitrator. Award issued January 18, 1994.

ISSUES

Discipline—Gross insubordination—Wearing political emblems—Notice of discipline.

FACTS

On September 25, 1992, the Company issued the following policy statement. It was in the form of a memo addressed to supervisors and was read aloud to gatherings of employees on both shifts:

> Wearing buttons and displaying posters which state political preferences has the potential to cause controversy among employees. That controversy sets up the possibilities of interference with production. All employees have plenty of time outside of The Minster Machine Company to state their candidate and political preferences. Minster Machine Company is a place of business and not a political forum for debate. Please convey to the employees in your department that the Company would appreciate their cooperation in complying with the policy of not wearing or displaying buttons and posters which state political preferences.

As might be expected, the new policy was not greeted with universal enthusiasm. At the regular monthly meeting with management on October 1, union officers voiced their objections. Their request for a written copy of the company memo was rebuffed with the comment that the subject was covered by the longstanding no-solicitation rule in the published plant rules. Queried about the specific consequences of violating the ban on political displays, Minster Vice President Ronald Olding answered that he had not yet given thought to that matter, and within a week the Union filed two grievances against the no-political-displays policy.

On October 12, four days after the grievances were launched, Local 3210 President Walter Pohlmann met one-on-one with Mr. Olding to pursue the unanswered question of disciplinary sanctions. Mr. Olding reviewed with him the Company's "Corrective Action Guide," a document posted on the plant bulletin board which classifies job offenses according to seriousness, and spells out the progression of penalties for each category. In the "less serious" grouping, including absenteeism, loafing on the job, poor workmanship, and gambling during work hours, a first violation is dealt with by verbal reprimand; not until the fourth infraction can the employee incur a suspension of 1 to 3 days. At the other extreme, misconduct characterized as "intolerable," such as theft, physical assault, or selling drugs, is dischargeable per se. In the middle range are violations deemed "serious." These will subject first offenders to a written warning plus possible suspension for 3 to 5 days. The Corrective Action Guide does not list all conceivable disciplinary infractions. Rather the guide concludes with this statement:

> The types of infractions shown are examples of the more commonly known [;] however, the listing is not intended to be all-inclusive. Specific infractions which are not listed would be handled the same as similar types of infractions.

Looking through the guide, Mr. Olding expressed his tentative impression to Mr. Pohlmann that disregard of the new policy against political emblems should be equated to "failure to follow safety rules or standard procedure" or "refusal to perform assigned work (insubordination)"—both being offenses found in the intermediate category, "serious." Neither the company vice-president nor the union president discussed specifically the case of a button-wearing employee who did not comply with a supervisor's direct order to remove the political paraphernalia. Later in the day on October 12, Mr. Olding verbally confirmed to Pohlmann that violations indeed would be punishable as a "serious" infraction. The Union still lacked a written copy of the new policy, and at the monthly union-management meeting on November 5 it submitted a formal demand for the document. Eventually, on November 24, at a grievance conference on an unrelated matter the Company furnished the Union with the 9-25-92 memorandum to supervisors.

S is a machine tool builder with 19 years of company seniority. On September 25 he learned about the new company rule from two union committeemen. (S himself was and is the vice-president of Local 3210.) He immediately went to the office of the plant superintendent, Gene Burke, and demanded a written copy of the company's statement. Burke told him that the memo could not be shared with him because it was addressed to supervisors. S was later present at the assembly of second-shift employees at which a foreman read the memo to the workers. Once more the grievant requested and was refused a written copy of the statement. In his capacity as a union officer, S attended the October 1 meeting with management (discussed above), and he was conversant with the October 8th grievances challenging the new policy. Because of illness and car trouble S missed work from October 12 through October 14 and was out of touch with co-workers and union colleagues. Thus he was unaware of Walt Pohlmann's discussion on October 12 with Mr. Olding on the subject of disciplinary penalties.

Since repeated requests for the document had been unproductive, S decided on his own to violate the political display ban in a way that would yield written evidence of the company policy in the form of a disciplinary warning. Accordingly he reported for his October 15/16 shift with a Clinton-for-President button pinned to his cap. Although the shift started at 4:30 in the afternoon, it was not until 1 A.M. that he was approached by a supervisor, John Yinger, and told to remove the campaign button. S instead requested union representation. Kevin Pohlman, steward on the second shift, was called over and they were joined by Marv Monnin, who as night shift superintendent was the ranking management official on the premises. Mr. Monnin asked the grievant what he was "trying to prove" by keeping the button on his cap. Monnin indicated that he would "oblige" with a "written verbal warning" and also remarked that the situation could "accelerate very quickly up the disciplinary chain" to the point of S's being "walked out the door" if he did not comply with Yinger's order. At that point the grievant removed the Clinton button from his cap and completed his work shift without further controversy.

When S came to work the next day he was slapped with the three-plus-day suspension at issue before this arbitrator. The suspension notice stated:

> ACTION TAKEN: Suspension from work without pay from the start of your shift, Friday Oct. 16, 1992 until the start of your shift on Wednesday Oct. 21, 1992.

> REASON: Actions on the morning of October 16th, 1992 were a willful and deliberate violation of a known company policy. In so doing, you are guilty of gross insubordination.

POSITIONS OF THE PARTIES

The Company

As a union officer and longtime employee, the grievant knew very well that the correct way to challenge the company's policy against wearing political emblems was not by defiance but through the grievance procedure. Indeed, as he also knew, grievances were already underway and there was no reason to fear that the employer would not be a cooperative adversary in processing the grievances. There was no need or justification for creating a confrontation at work. While it may be true that S was unaware that the local union president had been told that political display infractions would be treated as a "serious" job offense, "grievant's ignorance is no excuse and provides no defense. An employee who openly defies Company policy does so at his peril." And while a 3 to 5 day suspension in addition to a written warning is not a sanction that management invariably resorts to for first-time violators, in this case "the suspension was clearly warranted because of the willful and totally unnecessary nature of the Grievant's actions." Even if the arbitrator might favor a milder penalty, the labor agreement expressly strips the arbitrator of authority to tamper with a suspension or a discharge that is for just cause.

The Union

S does not object to, nor does the Union grieve, the issuance of a written warning for violating the company policy against wearing political buttons at work. In fact a written warning is exactly what the grievant sought and what Mr. Monnin "obliged" him with. The Union's position is that a written warning was the sum total of disciplinary action meted out by supervisors on the scene and that Mr. Olding's subsequent decision to add on a three day suspension amounts to double jeopardy. The Union also charges management with a lack of even-handedness in administering the new policy, citing the instance of another employee, N, who wore a political button at work on October 12, was told by a supervisor to remove the button or be sent home, and who then acceded without receiving any penalty at all.

QUESTIONS

1. The employer claims that the grievant blatantly violated the company policy. Do you agree? Why or why not?

2. The union claims that "management lacks even-handedness in administering the new policy." What do you think?

3. The employer argues that the grievant knew the correct way to challenge a company policy and therefore his actions were willful and deliberate. Is this important to the case? Why or why not?

4. Did the vice-president's comments to the union president about the gravity of political button infractions constitute a notice to employees? Why or why not?

5. How would you decide this case? Why?

Source: Reprinted with permission from *Labor Relations Reporter–Labor Arbitration Reports,* 102 LA 131. Copyright 1993 by The Bureau of National Affairs, Inc. (800-372-1033) <http://www.bna.com>

Nabisco Brands, Inc. and American Federation of Grain Millers, Local 58

Harry J. Dworkin, Arbitrator. Award issued January 14, 1991.

ISSUES

Discipline—Fighting—Profanity—Suspension.

RELEVANT CONTRACT PROVISIONS

Article 24 of the collective bargaining agreement sets forth the "Principal Company Rules" including the rule against fighting:

132. For the benefit of all employees, we are listing below items which constitute infractions of some existing rules and regulations:

4. Fighting on Company property.

Some employees have been careless in observing these rules, and, in the future, all employees will be required to strictly observe all plant rules. Any employees who deliberately violate any plant rules will be liable for disciplinary action.

FACTS

The Company operates a flour mill in Toledo, Ohio, with a work force that includes approximately 150 bargaining unit employees. An incident occurred on October 4, 1988, which involved two employees, "R", and "B" the grievant, both of whom were assigned to the Maintenance Department. The evidence establishes that employee "R" with some 18 years of service, and an otherwise favorable work record, had attended an apprenticeship meeting, where his work performance was the subject of evaluation. It appears further that "R" had been subject to criticism, and had received a less than favorable evaluation, which caused him to be demonstrably upset, and even angry. Following the meeting, "R" returned to the Maintenance Dept., and approached "B" who was at the time engaged in performing his assigned tasks. The evidence indicates that as "R" entered the area, he addressed grievant "B" but that the latter did not immediately respond. "R" then stated "I've said 'hello' to you twice and you didn't respond." "B" is alleged to have responded to "R" with the following verbiage:

"Well, I didn't hear you, and any way, tough s____ —go f____ yourself."

"R" appeared to be deeply offended, or angered by "B's" response; "R" aggressively approached "B" and directed one or more blows towards "B," knocking him to the floor. One or more punches landed in "B's" face; however, "B" did not actively engage in the physical altercation, nor did he strike back. Upon learning of the altercation in the Maintenance Dept., an investigation was conducted, pursuant to which management determined that both employees, "R" and "B" had engaged in misconduct, in violation of a plant rule that prohibits fighting on Company premises. Inasmuch as "R" was adjudged the aggressor, he was subject to a 60 day suspension, without pay. "B" was assessed a five day disciplinary suspension on the ground that he engaged in misconduct in directing obscenities towards "R" which, under the circumstances, were calculated to further anger "R", and accounted, in part, for "R's" violent response towards "B". Management represented at the arbitration that "R" was not discharged for fighting in violation of the plant rule, inasmuch as he acted under provocation on the part of "B". Management determined that "B" was not entirely blameless, and that, his use of gross obscenities of an inflammatory nature towards "R" was designed to induce violence.

Under all the circumstances, management determined that a five day suspension by reason of "B's" provocation, and failing to avoid the violent behavior of a fellow employee, constituted just cause for discipline. A grievance was filed by "B", which was denied. The answer of the foreman consisted of the following: "disciplinary suspension for fighting on the job was warranted. Grievance denied."

POSITIONS OF THE PARTIES

The Company

The Company maintains that the five day disciplinary suspension meted out to the grievant was warranted, and for just cause; the penalty was corrective in its purpose, and commensurate with "B's" misconduct, including directing obscene language towards a fellow employee "R", and in failing to "retreat" or to act in a prudent manner so as to avoid, or lessen the violent behavior on the part of "R". Pursuant to management's version of the occurrence on October 4, 1988, in the Maintenance Dept., "R" had returned from the apprenticeship meeting, and was engaged in discussing with two other employees concerning his treatment, and evaluation. In the course of the discussion "R" expressed the opinion that he had been unfairly evaluated, and manifested a high degree of disappointment, and even anger. It is represented further that grievant "B" approached "R", and the two other employees, and "butted in", stating to "R" "you are just f____ mad at how they [apprenticeship training committee] evaluated you." In response, "R" approached "B" "breast to breast" and "nose to nose". However, "B" continued to use profane language towards "R". "R" represented to management that he saw "B" flinch, and thought "B" was getting set to strike a blow. "R" thereupon struck "B" in the face, and "B" fell to the floor. Later that afternoon, "R", apparently realizing that he had acted improperly, apologized to "B" and asked him to "forgive him".

"R" acknowledged during the course of the arbitration hearing that he was angry and upset when he returned to the Maintenance Dept. "R" admitted further that the obscene language used by "B" was frequently used throughout the shop, and constituted "shop talk". Pursuant to "R's" testimony he stated to "B" that, "I would appreciate it if you wouldn't speak to me that way", thereby indicating that he objected to "B's" use of profanity, and obscenity towards "R". "R" testified further that "B" had provoked him, and failed to heed his request that he refrain from directing profane remarks towards "R", which request "B" ignored, and continued "cussing" "R" stating: "I don't f____ care what you want", at which point "R" approached and struck "B" in the face one or more times. The use of profane language was contrary to "R's" religious and moral beliefs, as expressed during the arbitration hearing. "R" testified further that "B" must have known of "R's" objection to profane language, which was of long standing, and of which his fellow employees were well aware.

Under the circumstances "B" was considered as having engaged in provocative behavior towards "R", and that, his "misconduct" warranted a measure of corrective discipline. Included in the improper behavior attributed to "B" was, that, he should have refrained from continuing to use obscene language, and should have complied with "R's" request that he discontinue directing offensive remarks toward him. The Company feels that "B's" provocative language, and his over-all behavior under the circumstances, fall under the umbrella of the rule against fighting on Company premises, for which discipline was warranted. The penalties assessed against each were deemed reasonable, and for just cause, notwithstanding that neither employee had previously been disciplined, and both had favorable work records.

The Union

The Union points out that the plant rule is confined to "fighting" on Company premises, there being no rule that prohibits use of obscene language by employees. Accordingly, inasmuch as "B" was not the aggressor, and did not engage in any physical combat with "R", his behavior did not warrant any discipline whatsoever.

The use of profane language is commonplace, and in the nature of "shop talk" for which no discipline is warranted. Moreover, "B" retreated in an effort to avoid "R's" aggressive behavior; he kept backing away from "R" and at no time struck "R". Accordingly, "B" was not subject to any discipline, notwithstanding "R" may have objected to "B's" use of obscene language. By reason of all the circumstances, including the fact that there is no rule that prohibits the use of profane language, and the fact that the grievant "B" was not charged with fighting in violation of the rule, his behavior did not warrant any discipline, by reason of which the suspension should be expunged from his personnel file, together with reimbursement for lost wages.

QUESTIONS

1. On what grounds does B feel that he is being unjustly treated? Discuss.
2. Do you think that B's behavior falls under the umbrella of the rule against fighting on company premises? Explain.
3. Is the disciplinary action taken toward B justified? Why or why not?
4. Do the fact that there is no rule that prohibits the use of obscene language and the fact that this language is commonplace ("shop talk") give any merit to B's case?
5. How would you decide this case? Why?

Source: Reprinted with permission from *Labor Relations Reporter–Labor Arbitration Reports,* 96 LA 139. Copyright 1993 by The Bureau of National Affairs, Inc. (800-372-1033) <http://www.bna.com>

The Jaite Packaging Company, Inc. and The United Flexographic Workers Union, Local No. 1

Roland Strasshofer, Arbitrator. Award issued July 1, 1993.

ISSUE

Discharge—Absenteeism—Participating in illegal strike.

INTRODUCTION

The grievance filed by W on July 6, 1992 reads in part as follows: "I was unjustly terminated on July 2, 1992 for accumulating 18 points under the absentee policy. This is contrary to the agreement between the Company and the Union made on June 29, 1992."

CONTRACT PROVISIONS

The Collective Bargaining Agreement includes a typical provision against any strikes or work stoppages during the agreement. It also includes the following provision, which is at the heart of this dispute:

> Article XII—Term of Agreement
>
> This Agreement shall become effective on the 7th day of January, 1989, and remain in effect until midnight, January 6, 1992, and thereafter for successive yearly periods [unless sixty (60) days] prior to said date and to the expiration date of any yearly period, either party serves notice in writing upon the other of its desire to terminate or modify this Agreement, or to negotiate a new Agreement. This Agreement shall continue as long thereafter as the parties may require to negotiate a new Agreement or until either party terminates negotiations by giving seventy-two (72) working hours written notice beforehand. If the parties fail to negotiate a new Agreement before the specific time has elapsed, all obligations under this Agreement are automatically canceled.

The Collective Bargaining Agreement also includes a no-fault type of attendance policy which permits discharge when 18 points are accumulated in any 12-month period. The Grievant did have 18 points if the final 3, assessed because of his absence during a work stoppage, were valid.

DISCUSSION OF FACTS

The Union objects first to points assessed against the Grievant because of his absences on March 12, 1992 and March 13, 1992 and his failure to present a doctor's excuse upon return. The Union contends that the offenses were not proven. However, the warning issued to him was signed by the Grievant and his Union representative. He testified concerning it and admitted that the warning was never grieved. In his testimony as upon cross-examination he did not deny that the offense occurred.

The parties disagree as to whether Article XII should be construed to mean that the Agreement is to continue, regardless of NLRA notifications, until either party terminates negotiations by giving 72 working hours' written notice.

Lastly, as the grievance indicates, the Union contends that an oral agreement was made with Company representatives that no absenteeism points would be assessed for the work stoppage.

The critical question is whether the final points were properly assessed, which depends upon whether there was a legal strike, which in turn depends upon whether the Collective Bargaining Agreement had been terminated prior to the work stoppage, and even if the strike was illegal, whether the Management nevertheless agreed that no points would be assessed.

I find the significant chronology to be as follows:

1. The Company admits that the Union filed in timely fashion the 60-day and 30-day notices required by Sections 8(d)(1) and 8(d)(3) of the National Labor Relations Act.

2. The filing of the two said notices precludes any subsequent finding of an unfair labor practice under the Act.

3. The Act does not preclude the parties from agreeing upon notice provisions for longer periods and including them in collective bargaining agreements, whereupon they become contractual obligations.

4. Local President Bachman delivered a note on or about October 30, 1991 stating desire to terminate or modify the Collective Bargaining Agreement in accordance with Article XII.

5. By letter dated November 8, 1991, the Union gave notice to the FM & CS.

6. On November 13, 1991 the Company advised all employees that it had received the notice to terminate or modify and that bargaining for a new contract would begin in a few weeks.

7. Letter dated January 8, 1992 confirmed an agreement with the Union that the entire agreement would be extended to accommodate the Federal Mediator's schedule.

8. Unsuccessful negotiations transpired.

9. 06/28/92—Picket line about 9:50 P.M.

10. 06/29/92—Conference at gate with Baker, Harriman, Bachman, and Bailey describing strike as illegal. Union disagreed.

11. 06/29/92—Letter from Executive Vice President and General Manager of the Company to Richard Bachman demanding that a strike which had begun that day be ended because of a violation of the no-strike provisions of the agreement. At 3:00 Union agreed to return at 7:00 A.M.

12. 06/29/92—5:20 P.M. Notation from Jon Baker re discussion with Bachman, telling him to return to work at 11:00 P.M. that night and that: "Those absent will be subject to the Attendance Policy," and also mentioning that Nesbitt had said something about attendance points, but that as far as Baker could recall, nothing had been agreed.

13. 07/06/92—Handwritten note signed by V. M. Skeans concerning a talk he had around 3:45 on that date with David Nesbitt, who was concerned about 8 employees who had been fired. He wanted to know whether any more would be fired.

    A discussion was set up. Skeans was not in it, but when Nesbitt left in the afternoon he said: "After talking with Jon and Harry I am not really sure what was said out at the gate. I don't know if Jon said to me we'd get 3 points or we wouldn't."

14. 09/16/92—Included a "Notice Required to Cancel Our Current Collective Bargaining Agreement." It mentioned the Union's desire to terminate or modify the agreement and further that it was being given in accordance with Article XII.

15. 09/18/92—Letter from Atty. Billick to Atty. Vasco stating, among other things, that when Bachman gave the above notice to Baker, it was not intended as the "written 72-working-hour notice provided for in Article XII of the collective bargaining agreement, and the Union was not breaking off negotiations as a result of the submission of this letter." Billick further stated that the Company would not accept that letter as being appropriate 72-hour notice, and stating that "while this letter raises questions concerning whether the Union believes that the

current collective bargaining agreement was extended for one year from January 7, 1992 to January 7, 1993 for lack of proper notice prior to November 6, 1991, the Company merely wishes, through this correspondence, to confirm Mr. Bachman's statements concerning the Union's stated intention." It further said to answer if not in agreement, and any failure to answer would be treated as establishing that any strike by the employees would be a violation of the no-strike clause.

16. 09/18/92—Handwritten notice from Atty. Vasco to Atty. Billick stating, among other things: "This is intended to comply with all the requirements necessary to terminate said labor agreement."

17. 09/24/92—Letter from Anderson, Executive Vice President, to Bachman, Union President, referring to the note from Atty. Vasco and saying that by virtue of the latter's note and the fact that the Company had met with the Union during the 72-hour notice period without a successful conclusion, the agreement would be considered terminated effective 9:30 A.M. on September 19, 1992. The Company said it would no longer check off dues or initiation fees, but was ready, willing, and able to meet with the Local for further negotiations.

POSITIONS OF THE PARTIES

The Union

The Union contends that in October of 1991 it hand-delivered its 60-day notice to terminate or modify the agreement, and in a letter dated November 8, 1991 it informed the FM & CS of its desire to terminate the agreement. In January, 1992, the Union alleges that the Company requested an extension of the agreement, which was granted. However, no further extensions were granted and the strike then took place at 11:00 P.M. on June 28th, ending on June 29th. The Union also pointed out that as of the date of the arbitration hearing no agreement had yet been reached.

The Union insists it had complied with the NLRA, both Sections 8(d)(1) and (3). It further argues that the language of the contract pertaining to a 72-hour notice is a nullity because it would require termination of negotiations in violation of Section 8(a)(5) of the NLRA.

The Union also contends that its first 60-day notice submitted to Jon Baker on October 31, 1991 included a second paragraph specifying that it was given in accordance with Article XII, and that would encompass any 72-hour notice requirement if there were one.

The Union asserts that the firing of three top officers and two stewards was a violation of the NLRA, and more specifically in connection with this grievance, the firing of the Grievant was a violation of the agreement because no points should have been assessed for his participation in the work stoppage.

The Company

The Company notes that all striking employees were given an unexcused absence under the Attendance Policy. It so happened that the Grievant had 15 points at that stage, and had been given a final warning. The Company argues that the Grievant was properly subject to discharge either by reason of violating the no-fault policy or by reason of having participated in an illegal work stoppage.

The Company argues that although the Union did provide the statutory 60-day notice, there is nothing in the NLRA which prevents parties to an agreement from adding additional notice requirements. The Company cites the report of the Senate Committee on the Taft-Hartley amendments to the NLRA in part as follows:

> It should be noted that this section [Section 8(d)] does not render inoperative the obligation to conform to notice provisions for longer periods, if the collective agreement so provides. Failure to give such notice, however, does not become an unfair labor practice if the 60-day provision is complied with.

The Company offers several plausible explanations of the language in dispute. Also, the Company states that Union actions were not consistent with its arguments. For example, the strike was ended upon demand after 24 hours; the September 16th letter gave notice to cancel the "current" Collective Bargaining Agreement months after the strike; and the Union never disputed the Company's statement that the Collective Bargaining Agreement terminated on September 19, 1992.

As to the Grievant's points, the Company notes that he did report for work and did not call off, and there was no agreement that points would not be assessed.

QUESTIONS

1. In your view, did the company have just cause to discharge the grievant? Why or why not?
2. Discuss the importance of the strike's being legal or illegal.
3. Evaluate the following statement from the Employer: "The grievant did not report for work and did not call off, and there was no agreement that points (attendance policy) would not be assessed."
4. How would you decide the case? Why?

Source: Reprinted with permission from *Labor Relations Reporter–Labor Arbitration Reports,* 101 LA 105. Copyright 1993 by The Bureau of National Affairs, Inc. (800-372-1033) <http://www.bna.com>

Fry's Food and Drug of Arizona and United Food & Commercial Workers, Local 99R

Robert F. Oberstein, Arbitrator. Award issued December 10, 1993.

ISSUE

Absenteeism—Last Chance Agreement.

BACKGROUND

The grievant, E, was terminated from Fry's Food Stores of Arizona on 2/24/93. On June 6, 1993, grievant, union and management, under the auspices of a Special Master Med/Arb procedure, agreed to a "Last Chance Agreement," the relevant section of which is as follows:

> 4. Present discipline for tardiness shall stand at a one-day suspension with future discipline for unexcused tardiness for the twelve month period following her date of return as follows: (a) first unexcused tardy shall result in a three day suspension without recourse through grievance procedure; (b) second unexcused tardy shall result in discharge without recourse through the grievance procedure.

> 5. Special Master, Bob Oberstein, will maintain jurisdiction of fact in this matter.

On 7/21/93, grievant reported for work six (6) minutes late. For this action, grievant received, as per the Last Chance Agreement, Item 4(a), a three day disciplinary suspension administered from 7/22/93 to 7/25/93.

On 10/3/93, grievant had been scheduled to work an 8:00 A.M. to 5:00 P.M. shift, but did not show up until 9:01 A.M. Grievant subsequently admitted that she had misread the time schedule that was posted and that she had made a mistake. As a result of this action and the one stated above, Management felt that the grievant had violated Section 4(a) and (b) of the Last Chance Agreement. On 10/15/93, grievant was terminated for "unexcused tardies".

MANAGEMENT POSITION

Since grievant's return, she has continued to be tardy on numerous occasions, as well as having problems with calling in prior to start of shift, for sick leave, dress code, break periods and overall attitude. The grievant was admittedly tardy on 7/21/93 and 10/3/93 and no issues of fact exist in these cases.

For all of the above reasons, management feels that the tardies on 7/21/93 and 10/3/93 violated the Last Chance Agreement. Management feels it has gone more than just an extra mile in favor of this employee who doesn't seem to be able to alter her behavior enough to show that she has appreciated what management has done. Therefore, the Arbitrator, finding no issues of fact, should find that the grievant did violate the Last Chance Agreement and the discharge should be sustained.

UNION POSITION

The union does not dispute the facts with the exception of the definition of "unexcused tardy." To go further, they do not dispute any of the facts regarding the second incident which occurred on 10/3/93 or its being defined as an "unexcused" tardy. The union feels that this second incident was the result of the employee failing to meet her responsibility to accurately read the work schedule. Although, it needs to be noted that the union does feel it was an honest mistake, and given that it was an honest mistake, the union stresses that the employee was only a minute late. Regardless, the union has stated at the outset that it feels the second disciplinary action of 10/3/93, although legitimate, should have actually been the first.

The union takes this position because, although there is no doubt that grievant was six minutes late on 7/21/93, the union refers back to the Last Chance Agreement which utilizes the term "unexcused tardy". Testimony at the hearing revealed that there is no company-wide tardy or attendance policy. Testimony further revealed that Fry's Store No. 10 has an eight minute policy prior to an employee being considered tardy. The union contends that by the very use of the term "unexcused tardies" within the context of the Last Chance Agreement, it is implied that there are also "excused tardies." The union refers back to Fry's Store No. 10's policy of eight minutes within which period of time a tardy is considered excused. "Excused tardies," according to the union, would not be considered violations of the Last Chance Agreement.

The union refers to testimony given and uncontradicted at the hearing, wherein on 7/21/93, which was the first occurrence, grievant was initially told that she would not be considered tardy because she was only six minutes late and another two minutes would have made it "unexcused" which would have resulted in discipline. After discussing the matter with corporate management, the store nevertheless decided to discipline her according to Item 4(a) of the Last Chance Agreement. The union therefore, seeks to have the termination reduced by having the initial disciplinary action of 7/21/93 changed to an "excused" tardy and thereby thrown out. Thus, leaving all of the parties with the second action of 10/3/93 which would therefore be considered the first violation of the Last Chance Agreement, this grievant should be reinstated and made 100% whole.

QUESTIONS

1. Was the incident of 7/21/93, where the grievant showed up for work six minutes late, a violation of the Last Chance Agreement? Why or why not?

2. What is the difference between an "excused" and an "unexcused" tardy?

3. Management feels that it has gone more than just an extra mile in favor of this employee. Do you agree? Why or why not?

4. In your view, is the grievant's termination justified? Why or why not?

Columbia Aluminum Corporation [The Dalles, Ore.] and United Steelworkers of America Local 8147

Martin Henner, Arbitrator. Awarded on January 20, 1994.

ISSUE

Discharge—Last-chance letter—No-fault attendance policy.

FACTS

Attendance Rules: The Company has what is sometimes called a "no fault" attendance policy. This permits a limited number of absence/tardy occurrences prior to the initiation of a scheme of progressive discipline, leading ultimately to termination. The term "no fault" derives from the fact that the Company does not attempt to differentiate between absences for illness, (which may be supported by a physicians note), or for other good cause, and other absences which do not have such justification. Instead, all employees are held to the same attendance standards, with certain exceptions as noted below.

The plant rules implementing this attendance policy have been in effect since the formation of the company in 1987. Substantially similar attendance rules were in effect prior to then, when the Company was under former ownership. There is no evidence that the Union was ever involved in the formulation or adoption of these rules.

The attendance rules are based on "occurrences". An occurrence is an absence for one or more consecutive days. If an employee is "tardy", (reporting to the assigned work area after the work day has begun), or leaves work prior to the end of the work day, (an "early out"), he receives half an occurrence.

As indicated above, the cause of the occurrence will not usually be considered in the application of this policy. However, some absences which are categorized as "non-chargeable" will not be counted. Non-chargeable absences are for vacations, jury duty, witness, bereavement, union business, and absences that are arranged for and approved by the supervisor in advance on a case by case basis.

In addition, the failure of an employee to call in and report that he will be absent or late is a separate infraction of the plant rules. This may also lead to disciplinary action.

The plant rules for progressive discipline regarding attendance provide that if an employee has 3 occurrences within a six month period, a verbal counseling will be given. Then, if there are more occurrences, the supervisor will count back to see if, in the six month period prior to each of these new occurrences, there have been 3 occurrences. If so, corrective discipline will advance to the next step, written counseling of the employee.

If written counseling is given, then the supervisor will check the next occurrences by looking back to see if there have been 2 occurrences in that preceding 6 month period. If this has occurred, then a final counseling is given the employee.

After the final counseling has been given, if the employee has two occurrences in the following six months, or 4 occurrences in the following year, the employee will then be suspended pending termination, pursuant to Article XII of the parties' Collective Bargaining Agreement.

The progressive discipline scheme regarding attendance rules has been summarized as follows:

> VERBAL = 3 occurrences in last six months
>
> WRITTEN = The next occurrences after the verbal
>
> Check if 3 in last six months = WRITTEN
>
> FINAL = Check the next occurrences after written
>
> If 2 in last six months = FINAL
>
> ARTICLE 12 = 2 in six months or 4 in twelve months following final

Grievant's Record: The grievant had been employed approximately 2 years, 1 month, at the time of the incident which triggered his termination. He began employment January, 1991. His attendance record was:

February 12, 1992 Absent, Personal business

VERBAL COUNSELING
April 22 & 23, 1992 Absent, Illness (Flu)

June 1, 1992 Absent, Personal business (Wife in Hospital)

July 5, 1992 n. Absent (Also, no call in)

WRITTEN COUNSELING
July 26, 1992 Absent, Personal Business (Wife in Hospital)

September 27, 1992 Absent (Also, no call in)

September 29, 1992 Early out (Wife had baby), 1/2 occurrence

FINAL COUNSELING
January 9, 1993 Personal business (took wife & baby to doctor)

January 15, 1993 Tardy, Car accident, 1/2 occurrence (Also, called in late)

January 17, 1993 Personal Business, Car Accident (Also, called in late)

LAST CHANCE LETTER
February 22, 1993 Tardy, Court Appearance, 1/2 occurrence

SUSPENDED PENDING TERMINATION

POSITIONS OF THE PARTIES

The Union

The Union's position is that the Company has violated the "just cause" standard for discipline and discharge set forth in Article XIII of the Collective Bargaining Agreement, Management Rights, and therefore the discharge of the Grievant should be set aside.

The Union notes that the attendance work rules of the Company were adopted unilaterally, without the participation or concurrence of the Union. Accordingly, the Union may now challenge these work rules, when they are applied to disciplinary circumstances as being excessively harsh or otherwise inappropriate. Similarly, the Union notes that it did not agree to the terms or sign the last chance letter given the Grievant. Accordingly, the Union may now also challenge the provisions of that letter.

The Union claims also that employees, including the Grievant, were not given advance notice of the consequences of violating the attendance policy. In addition, the Grievant did not understand that his last chance letter meant that another occurrence would cause his discharge. It is claimed that he believed another occurrence would result in a 3 day suspension, which was actually the discipline required by past practice.

The Union claims that other employees were treated more leniently by the Company for similar violations of the same no fault attendance rules which caused the Grievant's discharge. Such an arbitrary and unequal application of the attendance work rules violates the requirements of just cause. Alternatively, if exceptions to its no fault attendance policy were made by the Company for compassionate or policy reasons, then similar compassionate or policy exceptions should have been considered regarding the specific facts in the Grievant's case. And this was not done.

Specifically, the Union argues that there is insufficient evidence that the alleged absence on July 5, 1992 actually occurred. Some of the Grievant's absences should be excused, because they were caused by his wife's pregnancy. It was stipulated by the parties that it was a problem pregnancy with complications, leading to only a 50-50 chance of survival of the mother and child.

The absence and tardy occurrences which led to the issuance of the last chance letter were the result of car accidents caused by icy roads.

Finally, the tardy occurrence that precipitated the discharge was not the fault of the Grievant. He was arrested, and held in jail over the weekend, because of a domestic violence complaint filed by his wife. By the time of his release on Monday morning after appearing in court, it was so late he could not help being tardy. But the charges were dropped and there is no showing before the arbitrator that he was anything other than an innocent victim of a false accusation that arose from an argument with his wife.

The Company

The Company points to the Collective Bargaining Agreement for its specific authority, agreed to by the Union, to "establish and maintain work rules" without consultation with the Union, as part of its management rights. The attendance rules it adopted were reasonable and necessary for the efficient maintenance of its operations. A lack of adequate personnel on the Cel Line, monitoring the operations and adding additional ore as needed, is necessary to prevent dangerous gasses from building up.

The Grievant, despite his later failure to recollect, was indeed informed of the Company work rules, and received a copy of them at the time of hiring. Additionally, at every step of the way during his counseling steps he was apprised of the importance the company placed on attendance. The counseling letter of July 8, 1992, specifically warns that "continued attendance problems may result in action up to termination". The September

30, 1992, letter states, "another occurrence of this nature may result in termination". Both letters were signed by the Grievant.

There is not sufficient evidence to show that a past practice of giving a three day suspension prior to termination ever existed in the Company. The Company was under no obligation to offer a 3 day suspension in this case.

The Grievant's claim that he understood that another occurrence, after his last chance letter, would only result in a 3 day suspension is refuted by the Grievant's testimony. On cross-examination he admitted that he was told that he would be terminated if he missed any more time in the next 60 days.

The text of the letter speaks of the Grievant's record as justifying suspension pending termination. While elsewhere it just mentions suspension, it is clear that it means suspension pending termination. It gives him another chance, but he is to have no absentee or tardy incident before March 27, 1993.

Thus, most of the other employees with similar or worse attendance records have also been subject to progressive disciplinary action, including last chance letters and termination where appropriate. The Company does recognize that in some cases, a compassionate relaxation of the rules is appropriate and proper, and has exercised its discretion in doing so. In one case, the Company excused a number of absences for an employee who had been through an in-patient substance abuse program, and needed to complete the out-patient aftercare program. Other employees were given some excused absences to deal with lung or back problems.

The other occasions where discipline was not as swift as in the Grievant's case were explained by problems with the Company's supervision of its employees. Thus, in one case, a supervisor was off with lyme disease, and a lack of follow-up occurred. Another employee benefited from missing documentation, whereby the Company had to back down in the face of a Union grievance.

The Company claims that it also exercised discretion in the Grievant's case. Had it followed its policy rigidly, it would have issued its written counseling after the June 1, 1992 absence and final counseling after July 5, 1992. The suspension pending termination would have occurred on September 28, 1992.

Instead, the absence on June 1, 1992, where Grievant's wife went to the hospital, did not prompt discipline. It was the July 5, no call, no show which did. Nor did discipline occur following the absence on July 26, when his wife was in the hospital. It was the no call, no show on September 27, which prompted the final counseling. The Company claims also not to have considered the September 29, early out when his wife was giving birth, for disciplinary computation.

The Company claims that based on the Grievant's record, it was fully justified in terminating him after the January 17, 1993 absence because of the weather related car accident. Of 57 people on that shift, only Grievant and his passenger failed to report to work. The Company claimed to have given the Grievant extra consideration out of respect to the Grievant's father, a long time Company employee, and because of the Grievant's youthfulness. It exercised discretion in the Grievant's favor, and gave him a last chance letter instead. There was no requirement that the Union concur or sign this letter.

The Grievant's tardy occurrence on February 22, resulted in his termination, under the terms of its attendance policy, and the last chance letter.

The Company denies that the Grievant's circumstances merit any special consideration. The Grievant was not a long term employee with an excellent work record. On the contrary. The occurrences leading up to his discharge all occurred during Grievant's second year of employment. During that year he was also disciplined for failing to do his job on 3 occasions. He also had two occasions where he failed to call in and notify the company of his absence. In his first year, Grievant came close to termination when he had been found sleeping on the job.

QUESTIONS

1. In your view, did the company have just cause to discharge the grievant? Why or why not?
2. If there was not just cause for a discharge, should a lesser penalty be imposed? If so, based upon what evidence?
3. Evaluate the following statement by the employer: "Continued attendance problems may result in termination." Did the grievant have reason to believe termination would not happen? Why or why not?
4. How would you decide the case? Why?

Source: Reprinted with permission from *Labor Relations Reporter–Labor Arbitration Reports,* 102 LA 274. Copyright 1993 by The Bureau of National Affairs, Inc. (800-372-1033) <http://www.bna.com>

Hercules Engines, Inc. and United Automobile, Aerospace & Agricultural Implement Workers of America, Local 161
Thomas L. Hewitt, Arbitrator. Award issued October 24, 1992.

ISSUES

Subcontracting—Elimination of department—Realization of sizable economies.

RELEVANT CONTRACT PROVISIONS

II. Rights of Management

Section 2.1. The Company retains all of the rights, powers, functions and authority of management, including, but not limited to, the right to hire, promote, discharge or discipline for just cause, to maintain discipline and efficiency of employees, to determine the products to be manufactured, to direct the personnel, and to determine the methods, processes and means of manufacturing, except as those rights, powers, functions and authority are specifically and expressly limited or modified by this agreement.

. . .

XII. Seniority

Section 12.16. Elimination of Departments and Creation of New Departments.

12.16.1. Combination of Departments. If the Company combines two (2) or more existing departments, or parts of departments, each employee in the old departments (or parts, as the case may be) will be transferred to the combined department, if he wishes, and if the departments being combined are within the same seniority group, each will carry with him his departmental seniority from the old department. The jobs in the combined departments will be assigned to those employees who had corresponding jobs in the old departments who have the greatest departmental seniority, if said departments are within the same seniority group, and to such employees who have the greatest plant seniority, if said departments were not in the same seniority group, provided in each instance they are qualified to perform the work in the combined departments. Those employees who are not thereby assigned the jobs in the combined departments will have the displacement rights provided in Section 12.8 of this Article.

12.16.2. Elimination of Departments. If the Company eliminates any department, or parts of a department, the employees holding jobs thereby eliminated will have the displacement rights provided by Section 12.8 of this Article, but if any such employee exercises displacement rights on the basis of his plant seniority, he will then take with him to the department in which he exercises such rights his departmental seniority in the department which was eliminated.

. . .

XXI. Subcontracting

Section 21.1. The Maintenance Departments carry the responsibility of general maintenance work within the confines of the operating division and their buildings. They will perform work of a maintenance, as distinguished from construction, nature.

Section 21.2. They will perform construction work which it is feasible for the Company to do, consistent with equipment and manpower skills available, with the limitation that outside contractors may be called upon when the volume of work required exceeds the normal work load of the Skilled Trades Maintenance Departments at the time the contract is to be let.

21.3. Contracts will be let to outside contractors under specific conditions warranting same. Such outside assistance will be engaged where peculiar skills are involved, where specialized equipment not available at Hercules Engines is required (or where sizable economies can be realized because certain contractors specialize in a certain thing requiring technical skill). Also, work may be contracted out when the volume of construction work being done or scheduled for the Skilled Trades Maintenance Departments precludes the possibility of the work's completion within certain time limitations.

21.4. It is further agreed that the Company, when it thinks it necessary to contract a job out, will, well in advance, notify the Union of its intention by letter, and by means of discussion, if requested by Union officers, qualify their reasons for desiring to contract the work out. Any differences that are left unresolved shall be settled through the grievance procedure.

21.5. Nothing in the above provision shall apply to the subcontracting of non-skilled work as subcontracted in the past.

21.6. It shall be the general policy of the Company not to subcontract skilled trades work when there are journeymen in the trade in question on layoff, and the Company agrees to make a reasonable effort to utilize existing properly skilled personnel to perform the required day to day work, normally and historically performed by them, unless the volume of work in question exceeds the normal work load, sizable economies can be realized because certain contractors specialize in a certain thing requiring technical skill, or the work is of a nature that the Company does not have the equipment or skills to perform, and in such instances the Union will be notified, in advance, by letter and afforded the opportunity to question and discuss the job in question. Any differences remaining unresolved will be settled through the grievance procedure.

Appendix C—Skilled Trades Agreement

8. Seniority in a classification listed above may not be used to displace an employee in any other classification listed above except that any Skilled Trades Employee displaced as a result of job elimination or job-incurred disability may exercise his seniority in any Skilled Trades Department, provided he has the ability and skill to do the available job.

FACTS

Hercules Engines, Inc. manufactures diesel, gas and alternate fuel engines in the 70 to 240 horsepower range. In addition, the Company manufactured studs until December 1991. Eighty percent of the Company's engine production is purchased by the military. The production and maintenance employees at the Canton, Ohio plant are represented for collective bargaining purposes by International Union, United Automobile, Aerospace & Agricultural Implement Workers of America, Local Union No. 161. In 1989, due to the decline of business, it was necessary for the Company to undergo a financial realignment. The creditors obtained control and restructured the Company.

The Tool Hardener is a skilled trade job under the terms of the labor agreement. The Heat Treat Department was operated on a three (3) shift basis with one (1) Tool Hardener on each shift. Due to a change in Federal regulations, the Company was unable to continue producing studs and the stud business was terminated. This reduced the work in the Heat Treat Department by eighty percent (80%). The Company maintained three (3) shifts in the Heat Treat Department even though production was minimal. The Company reduced the Heat Treat to two (2) shifts and laid off one (1) Tool Hardener in March 1992 in accordance with the agreement.

On May 6, 1992, the Company notified the Union that it intended to close the Heat Treat Department and out source the balance of the work: "This letter is to advise you that the schedules in heat treat have fallen to the point that it is no longer economically feasible to continue production in this area. The Company is soliciting bids from other sources to perform the remaining work. It is our intent to cease heat treating operations once we find a source to cover our needs." The Union objected and a meeting was held. The Union made several proposals to the Company regarding the bringing in of other work in an attempt to delay the closing of the Heat Treat Department. The following grievance was filed on April 29, 1992, and properly processed to arbitration: "On 4/24/92 approximately 140 parts were sent to Bodil Inc. for Heat Treating Bids on further numbers of parts, to be heat treated. This is a direct violation of the Contract because at this time we have a Journeyman Heat Treater on layoff."

The Company response to this grievance reads as follows:

Dated: May 6, 1992. Due to the high cost of running the heat treat department and the reduced need for treated parts, it is the intent of the Company to eliminate the heat treat department and out source the remaining work. We can no longer afford the cost of maintaining our current facility. As our volume of business decreases, we must work together to reduce our cost. The future of the Company depends on us being competitive in a commercial marketplace.

POSITIONS OF THE PARTIES

The Union

The Company violated Article 21.6 of the labor agreement when it contracted out the work of the Tool Hardeners who are skilled personnel covered by this paragraph of the agreement. The work the Company is attempting to subcontract is the required day-to-day work normally and historically performed by the Tool Hardeners. The volume of the work does not exceed the normal work load and the Tool Hardeners are able to perform this work. There is no certain technical skill provided by the contractors that is not available with the Tool Hardeners. The Company has the skills and equipment necessary to perform this work. The Company made the decision to subcontract this work without affording the Union the opportunity to question and discuss the jobs in question.

Sections 12.16.1 and 12.16.2 are provisions in the labor agreement involving the elimination of departments and the seniority rights of those who are affected by the departmental elimination. It was never the intent of these provisions to be applicable to departmental elimination through subcontracting. These provisions were to be utilized when departments were combined or the work of one department was no longer necessary due to production method changes. Appendix C, Paragraph 8, was negotiated for the purpose of protecting seniority in the classification for the skilled trade employees displaced as a result of job elimination. The purpose for this was that if a job was no longer required by the Company, the employees' seniority was protected. The intent of the provision and its application throughout the years was for job elimination due to lack of work on the job, not job elimination due to subcontracting. Subcontracting has been a very important and hard bargained issue between the parties as evidenced by its own Section 26 entitled Subcontracting, and the extensive language contained therein.

The Company

The Company does not believe that the work in question is subcontracting, but is out sourcing due to department elimination. There are only two (2) employees in the department and the volume of work in that department is minimal. On the basis of the production in 1991, the total cost of heat treating the material processed through that department, as bid by an outside contractor, is $39,109. On the basis of the 1991 costs, excluding administrative overhead, the cost for producing this material in-house was $222,889. This shows a projected saving of $183,781. This is a very conservative estimate since the volume of 1992 production in the department will be considerably less than in 1991. The cost of the department will remain virtually the same or increase and the out sourced material will decrease; thus that cost will decrease.

Production in 1992 is projected to be approximately twenty percent less than the preceding year provided that the Company secures a re-issuance of a government order for certain motors. Due to the forced restructuring of the Company in 1989, and considering long range projections, it is unrefuted that the Company must cut costs in order to be competitive and remain in business. Section 21.6 states an exception—that is, the Company may out source work because certain contractors specialize in a certain thing requiring technical skill. The subcontractor in this case has the certain technical skill necessary to perform this work. In addition, and more to the point, is another exception that exists—that is, sizable economies can be realized. The Company has proved and it is not questioned by the Union that sizable economic savings can be obtained through this change. The work in question involves a change in the scope and direction of the Company. The Company does not intend to re-enter the heat treat business. The Company bargained with the Union over its decision to contract out the work. It met with the skilled trades' committee as well as informed the Union on many occasions that the continuation of the Heat Treat Department was just not feasible considering the economic plight of the Company.

QUESTIONS

1. The union contends that the employer violated Article 21.6 of the labor agreement. Do you agree with the union? Why or why not?

2. The employer argues that the work in question is not subcontracting, but outsourcing "due to department elimination." Do you agree with the employer? Why or why not?

3. Did the employer make a "reasonable effort" to utilize existing properly skilled personnel to perform the work? Why or why not?

4. The union claims that the company has the skills and equipment necessary to perform this work. What do you think?

5. How would you decide this case? Why?

Source: Reprinted with permission from *Labor Relations Reporter–Labor Arbitration Reports,* 100 LA 574. Copyright 1993 by The Bureau of National Affairs, Inc. (800-372-1033) <http://www.bna.com>

Electrical Contractors' Association of City of Chicago, [Ill.] Inc. and International Brotherhood of Electrical Workers Local 134

Aaron S. Wolff, Arbitrator. Award issued March 22, 1994.

ISSUE

Holiday Pay—Work scheduled on holiday.

BACKGROUND FACTS

On June 14, 1993, the Union filed a grievance as to one of the Contractors members, Fischbach and Moore (the "Company") concerning holiday pay. The Board deadlocked and the undersigned neutral Arbitrator was appointed to resolve the dispute. The parties stipulated that the "neutral arbitrator shall have the lone vote in deciding whether to grant or deny the grievance."

The grievance, in the form of a letter dated June 14, 1993 from the Union to the Association, states as follows:

Fischbach & Moore was working three (3) shifts at McCormick Place in the "Crate Storage Area." The hours of these shifts were, first shift 7:00 A.M. to 3:30 P.M., second shift 3:30 P.M. to 11:30 P.M., third shift 11:30 P.M. to 7:00 A.M. The days of the shifts were Monday thru Friday.

Memorial Day (May 31st, Monday) is a legal holiday and stipulated in the Principal Agreement as a double time day. On the holiday in question the first shift took the holiday off, the second shift took the holiday off, but the third shift came in at their regularly scheduled starting time, 11:30 P.M. Monday night and worked their shift thru to 7:00 A.M. Tuesday.

While not addressed in the Agreement, it is obvious that on a job working three shifts the third shift is entitled to a holiday, it so happens that since they start at 11:30 P.M. on Monday, their holiday would be starting that time until 7:00 A.M. Tuesday morning. In this circumstance the first and second shifts had 32 hours for the week and the third shift had 40 hours.

I request that these men who worked the Monday 11:30 P.M., Tuesday 7:00 A.M. shift be paid double time for that shift. Inasmuch as double time is the maximum pay rate allowed under the Principal Agreement these men were paid straight time and 15% shift differential for that shift; therefore, the amount due would be the difference.

The Principal Agreement does not cover this happenstance, but it is obvious that under a 24 hour, three shift job the third shift on a holiday should be double time.

The Board's minutes of July 6, 1993 recite:

Business Agent Brennan reviewed a question regarding the proper payment for the third shift which began at 11:30 P.M. on Memorial Day, Monday, May 31, 1993. He stated that the graveyard shift was the first shift scheduled for that week and that that shift worked 40 hours while the day and swing shift worked 32 hours. He stated that it was the Union's contention that the graveyard shift which worked from 11:30 P.M., Memorial Day, Monday, May 31, 1993 to 7:00 A.M. Tuesday, June 1, 1993 should be paid at double time for the entire shift. Messrs. Zelma and O'Connor, representing Fischbach and Moore, stated that in their opinion the Holiday ends at midnight, and they should be paid double time for the one-half hour from 11:30 P.M. to 12:00 A.M. They stated that absent clear contract language regarding this situation the shift was properly paid. Management requested a caucus. Upon returning from the caucus, Mr. Nemshick asked Mr. Cody for time to review the situation as well as obtain guidelines if available from NECA's National office. Mr. Cody agreed and Mr. Nemshick stated he would get back to Mr. Cody with an answer as soon as possible.

Unable to resolve the grievance, the Board agreed on August 10, 1993 to seek a neutral arbitrator to do so.

The material facts, most of which are set forth in the grievance, are not in dispute. Also, during the Memorial Day week, the Company's time sheet for the third shift shows that seven (7) employees worked as follows:

FISCHBACH & MOORE

As noted above, none of the employees who worked from 11:30 P.M. on Monday, May 31, 1993 until 7:00 A.M. on Tuesday, June 1, 1993 received doubletime for any of the time worked. One employee received one (1) hour of overtime (time and one-half) on each day from Monday through Friday. Four employees worked on Saturday from five to eight hours, all of which was paid at overtime rates.

RELEVANT CONTRACT PROVISIONS

The pertinent or cited provisions of the Agreement are as follows:

ARTICLE XII Holidays

Section 1. The following days shall be recognized as legal holidays: New Year's Day, Memorial Day, Fourth of July, Labor Day, Thanksgiving Day and Christmas Day or days celebrated as such.

Section 2. It is distinctly understood that no construction work shall be done on the first Monday of September, commonly known as Labor Day, except in emergency to preserve life and property and to maintain service to the public.

ARTICLE XIII Union and Employer Rights

Section 1. The Union understands the Employer is responsible to perform the work required by the owner. The Employer shall therefore have no restrictions, except those specifically provided for in the collective bargaining agreement in planning, directing and controlling the operation of all his work, in deciding the number and kind of Employees to properly perform the work, in hiring and laying off Employees, in transferring Employees from job to job within the Local Union's geographical jurisdiction, in determining the need and number as well as the person who will act as Foreman, in requiring all Employees to observe the Employer's and/or owners' rules and regulations not inconsistent with this Agreement in requiring all Employees to observe all safety regulations.

. . .

ARTICLE XVII Hours of Work—Overtime

Section 1. The regular working day for general foremen, foremen, journeymen wiremen, and apprentices shall consist of eight (8) hours reckoned between 7:00 A.M. and 4:30 P.M., Monday through Friday, except when a designated holiday intervenes. The Employer has the option of changing the starting time of any job or shift by one hour earlier.

Section 2. All overtime shall be reported to the local union.

Section 3. All work performed outside the regularly scheduled working hours and on Saturdays up to 4:30 P.M. (except as otherwise provided herein) shall be paid for at one and one-half times the regular straight time rate of pay. All work performed after 3:30/4:30 P.M. Saturday to 7:00/8:00 A.M. Monday and on all recognized holidays shall be paid for at double time the regular straight time of pay.

Section 4. Double the regular straight time rate of pay shall be paid for all work performed on the following designated legal holidays, unless definitely stated otherwise on certain specified work: New Year's Day, Decoration Day, Independence Day, Labor Day, Thanksgiving Day, Christmas Day or days celebrated as such.

Section 5. A regular workweek may be established from Tuesday through Saturday save when a designated holiday intervenes whereby on Saturday one man per shop may be regularly employed on a straight time basis eight (8) consecutive hours per day beginning at 7:00 A.M. or 8:00 A.M. and such man may do small jobbing and shop work on the Employer's premises during such hours in order to be available to answer emergency calls.

Section 6. When so elected by the contractor, multiple shifts of at least five (5) days duration may be worked. When two (2) or three (3) shifts are worked: The first shift (day shift) shall be worked between the hours of 8:00 A.M. and 4:30 P.M. Workmen on the day shift shall receive eight (8) hours' pay at the regular hourly rate for eight (8) hours work.

The second shift (swing shift) shall be worked between the hours of 4:30 P.M. and 12:30 A.M. Workmen on the swing shift shall receive eight (8) hours' pay at the regular hourly rate plus 10% for seven and one-half (7 1/2) hours work.

The third shift (graveyard shift) shall be worked between the hours of 12:30 A.M. and 8:00 A.M. Workmen on the graveyard shift shall receive eight (8) hours' pay at the regular hourly rate plus 15% for seven (7) hours work.

A lunch period of thirty (30) minutes shall be allowed on each shift.

All overtime work required after the completion of a regular shift shall be paid at one and one-half times the "shift" hourly rate. There shall be no pyramiding of overtime rates and double the straight time rate shall be the maximum compensation for any hour worked.

There shall be no requirement for a day shift when either the second or third shift is worked.

QUESTIONS

1. In your view, should the grievants receive a holiday premium for working on the holiday? Why or why not?
2. Does the fact that the grievant's shift began at 11:30 P.M. the day of the holiday have any bearing on the decision? Why or why not?
3. How would you decide the case? Why?

Source: Reprinted with permission from *Labor Relations Reporter–Labor Arbitration Reports,* 102 LA 660. Copyright 1993 by The Bureau of National Affairs, Inc. (800-372-1033) <http://www.bna.com>

AS Mid-America, Inc. [Lincoln, Neb.] and Local 221, Graphic Communications International Union
Joe L. Levy, Arbitrator. Award issued December 13, 1993.

ISSUES

Strike replacements—Harassment—'Return to Work Resolution'

FACTS

The Company is a commercial printer. Sixty percent of the Company's business is printing commercial catalogs and promotional brochures with the remaining forty percent printing magazine publications. At Lincoln, Nebraska, the Company employs some 800 employees, the vast majority of whom are represented by three local unions.

There was a change of ownership of the Company in the summer of 1992, and thereafter, management began negotiations for a new collective bargaining agreement, and on April 27, 1993, the Unions went out on strike. The strike lasted a relatively short time, but was with incidents of harassment and vandalism by the strikers both at picket lines and at the homes of replacement workers and management. Throughout the course of the strike, there were incidents of:

1. Yelling and catcalls directed at replacements and management.
2. Throwing rocks, nails, coffee at replacements' and management's cars as they entered the property.

3. Making obscene gestures and yelling racial epithets at replacements and management.
4. Acts of vandalism directed at cars parked on Company property.
5. Graffiti, spray painted at private homes, as well as other damage to private homes.
6. Vandalism to cars at private homes including cutting brake lines.

On May 11, 1993, the Company and Union negotiated an agreement known as the "Return to Work Resolution (RTW)" whereby the Union returned to work. The Company wanted to make clear that the vandalism, intimidation, and harassment that had occurred during the strike would not continue. Accordingly, the very first paragraph of the RTW specifically states that

> There shall be no intimidation, discrimination, or harassment because of any person's participation or non-participation in the strike.

Copies of the RTW were distributed to returning strikers on May 16 and May 17, 1993, when they returned to work. There was also a letter attached from Dennis Hiser, Division Director, which specifically made reference to the Company's commitment to end the intolerable events that occurred during the strike. Subsequently, Hiser spoke to all of the employees and discussed the RTW in his presentation.

Not everything went according to plans, and on June 9, 1993, Hiser again spoke to all employees regarding the harassment, and said that it would not be tolerated, and that any employees conducting acts of intimidation and harassment would be suspended awaiting discharge.

The grievance was precipitated over the employee named O, who was a black replacement worker from a sister plant in Memphis, Tennessee. The specific event occurred on June 14, 1993. O was working long hours, consisting of a shift from 11:00 A.M. until 11:00 P.M. About 7:00 in the evening, a fellow employee, H, working in the area with O contacted his foreman and expressed concern about a rumor that he had heard that O was carrying a gun with him and demanded that O be searched. The foreman contacted Wells Fargo Security personnel who then conducted a search. The search revealed that he did not have a gun, and subsequent to the search, O, who was embarrassed and distraught about the incident, went to his foreman's office to complain about the way he was being treated and requested the rest of the day off. He then returned to his press, collected his bag, and returned to an area near the foreman's office to punch out. At about this time, Wells Fargo Security personnel who had been making a routine round rejoined O and walked out of the plant with him.

As O exited the property, Union employees pointed at him, yelled out catcalls, and gave him the stare treatment. One Union employee began to sing a song over the intercom system known as the "na-na-na-na" song—the refrain ending with "good-bye scab".

M, who worked with R, stated that O had threatened to kill him. R and M tried to get the foreman to call the police, but the foreman said he would not do such a thing, so M and R, the grievant in this case, then called the police themselves. The police arrived and investigated the threat. After the investigation was concluded, the police department chose to do nothing.

Many of the Union employees had developed a system of stare tactics in which they would stare for long periods of time at O, who was the only black employee. The staring tactics were part of M and R's method of showing their admitted dislike for O and other so-called "scabs".

During one of O's trips to and from his press, he admitted that he told M "he better get his fuckin' eyes off him," and O also explained that M and R had spent their entire shift staring at him while he was working. The stares from M and R, along with others, apparently were the catalyst for the catcalls and the song over the intercom system.

After the incident, the grievant, R, was suspended for ten days and other disciplinary action was taken against M and another employee.

RELEVANT WORK RULES

The Return to Work Resolution

The parties have negotiated with respect to return to work issues. The Unions agree to terminate the strike. The Company and Unions will cooperate to return company operations to normal. There shall be no intimidation, discrimination, or harassment because of any person's participation or non-participation in the strike. The new labor contracts agreed to by the parties shall be finalized and executed in an expeditious manner.

COMPANY'S CONTENTIONS

1. The Company properly suspended grievant for his role in the harassment of O.
2. The Company complied with just cause standards in suspending grievant for his violation of the anti-harassment policy.
3. The suspension of the grievant was proper under the circumstances and should not be modified by the arbitrator.

UNION CONTENTIONS

1. Regardless of whether the actions of grievant constituted harassment, he should not have been suspended.
2. The evidence is overwhelming that the actions of the grievant were not harassment.

QUESTIONS

1. Was the suspension of the grievant for just cause? Explain why or why not.
2. What is your definition of intimidation and harassment? In your view, did the grievant engage in intimidation and harassment?
3. Considering all the statements and facts of this case, did the company have sufficient grounds for a suspension? Why or why not?
4. Does the violation of the "Return to Work Resolution" in itself provide sufficient grounds for a suspension? Why or why not?

Source: Reprinted with permission from *Labor Relations Reporter–Labor Arbitration Reports,* 101 LA 1177. Copyright 1993 by The Bureau of National Affairs, Inc. (800-372-1033) <http://www.bna.com>

Klauser Corporation (Megafoods) and United Food and Commercial Workers Local 367
Gregg L. McCurdy, Arbitrator. Award issued on March 2, 1994.

ISSUE

Did Employer violate the Pierce County Grocery/Bakery Master Agreement, or the Variety/Drug Supplemental Agreement, or both, when it demoted Grievant into the position of Store Helper in the video department?

BACKGROUND

The fundamental facts are not in dispute. Ms. Lee Whitley (Grievant) was first employed by Klauser Corporation (Employer) in January, 1986. Her entire tenure with Employer has been at one location consisting of a large combined grocery and variety store. Until 1991, Grievant worked in the general merchandise section of the store, which included a video rental operation.

Under the Variety/Drug supplement to the Grocery/Bakery Master Agreement, an employee was either on a progressive pay scale or classified as a Store Helper at an unchanging wage rate roughly equal to the lowest rate on the progressive pay scale. The progressive pay scale is based on total hours of employment; the top of the scale is roughly 173–175 per cent of the starting wage.

Grievant, who was already at the top of the progressive pay scale, was made the first supervisor of the new video department. She was paid $0.75 over scale, or $8.55 per hour, for acting in that capacity, wherein she supervised about four employees. Management has the right to pay over scale on an individual basis, but not less than scale. All the other employees within the video department were Store Helpers, then paid $4.45 per hour under the supplemental Variety/Drug Agreement.

The corporate general merchandise manager, Gerry Schlagel, considered Grievant's supervisory performance unsatisfactory and she was removed from the position. She was considered for two jobs, one as a night stocker and the other as bakery clerk. Managers did not consider Grievant a "task oriented" person who would do well as a stocker, and therefore transferred her to the bakery effective January 4, 1992. Although the bakery position paid $8.18 per hour (under the Grocery master agreement), Grievant's rate of pay was kept at $8.55 per hour. By June 9, 1992, Grievant had received three personnel warnings, primarily for incompetence and negligence of duty for failure to perform assigned tasks, either timely or at all. The reprimands were apparently the only ones ever issued to Grievant, whose performance reviews have been quite good. Her hours were cut back. The personnel warnings cited suspension or termination as the possible result of future warnings.

Grievant was reassigned back to the video department, which resulted in a grievance based on failure to accommodate a disability arising from a medical condition. That basis for the grievance was later dropped. However, an accommodation was reached whereby Employer agreed to pay Grievant $1.00 over the Store Helper scale, for a total of $5.55, and schedule enough hours to maintain earnings at the same level as when Grievant left the bakery. (The $1.00 premium over scale was not paid, inadvertently, it appears.) Union reinstated the grievance filed when Grievant was removed as the video department supervisor.

As the result of a joint union-management grievance meeting, Employer agreed to permit Grievant to try out for the night stocking job at Grievant's progressive pay scale rate. That position was then held by a twenty-three year old male new hire, Joe, on the job for about a month. Employer had Joe keep track of his production in the form of pieces of stock "thrown" (shelved) per hour during his shifts in January, 1993. Over ten work days, Joe averaged 450 pieces per hour. Employer moved Grievant into the position on January 24, 1993.

The measuring period was not started until March 2, 1993, and ran for a period of five weeks. Employer set a target of 400 pieces per hour as acceptable for Grievant. During the test period Grievant's job requirements were eased. Whereas Joe and other stockers staged their own pallets from warehouse to sales floor, Grievant's pallets were staged by other employees. She was also given overlap hours with another shift.

During the course of the test period, union representatives met with the Grievant and management with some regularity to discuss Grievant's progress. Employer maintains

Union agreed to the test method and performance targets as reasonable. Union maintains no such understanding was reached.

At the end of the test period, Grievant averaged substantially less than the 400 pieces per hour, based on records she submitted. On April 9, 1993, Grievant was removed from the stocking position and demoted to Store Clerk in the video department at the Store Clerk rate of pay, $4.55 per hour. Union reinstated its grievance, giving rise to this arbitration.

EMPLOYER'S CASE [SUMMARIZED]

Employer has the right to demote an employee based on demonstrated inability to perform assigned work at a satisfactory level. Demotion of Grievant was not a disciplinary action and may therefore not be overturned at arbitration unless the demotion was arbitrary, capricious and unreasonable. Further, Union approved of the evaluation method used by company and is estopped from contesting it. Even if Union did not agree or participate in the evaluation and performance testing, Employer's determination of Grievant's ability was reasonable. Finally, Employer has the reserved right and power to demote an employee.

UNION'S CASE [SUMMARIZED]

Employer may not demote an employee into a new classification in the absence of changed circumstances or new procedures, including a substantial change in job content, to justify it. Also, demotion of Grievant was disciplinary in nature and effected without the required just cause. In the course of determining Grievant's ability, Employer failed to give Grievant a fair trial at the night stocking position. Finally, neither the Collective Bargaining Agreement, bargaining history nor past practice support Employer's claim to a right to demote an employee into a lower classification once placed into a higher position.

QUESTIONS

1. In your view, did the company have just cause to demote the grievant from supervisor to store helper? Why or why not?

2. In your view, did the company have just cause to demote the grievant from the night stocker position to store clerk? Why or why not?

3. Evaluate the following statement from the Employer: "Demotion of the Grievant was not a disciplinary action and may therefore not be overturned at arbitration unless the demotion was arbitrary, capricious and unreasonable."

4. How would you decide the case based upon the numerous demotions of the grievant? Does the wage reduction of $8.55 to $4.55 per hour have a significant impact on your decision?

Source: Reprinted with permission from *Labor Relations Reporter–Labor Arbitration Reports,* 102 LA 381. Copyright 1993 by The Bureau of National Affairs, Inc. (800-372-1033) <http://www.bna.com>

Eureka Company and IAMAW Local 1000
Duane L. Traynor, Arbitrator. Award issued November 15, 1993.

ISSUES

Sexual harassment—Discharge—Immoral conduct—Offensive environment.

RELEVANT CONTRACT PROVISIONS

ARTICLE VI—DISCHARGES AND DISCIPLINE

. . .

Section 2. Notification of Action Taken

No employee shall be disciplined, suspended, or discharged without a just and sufficient cause. If a grievance results because an employee was suspended or discharged, it may be referred directly to Step 3 of the grievance procedure for processing. However, such grievance must be filed within five (5) working days after receipt by the General Shop Committee of the reason for the suspension or discharge. . . .

Section 4. Method of Reinstatement

In the event an employee has been unjustly suspended or discharged, or the General Shop Committee has not been informed of said suspension or discharge as defined in ARTICLE VI, Section 3, he shall be given the opportunity to return to work, without loss of seniority, and paid for the time lost. . . .

ARTICLE XXVI—DISCRIMINATION

The Company and the Union agree that there will be no discrimination against any individual or group for any reason and the parties also agree they shall comply with the provisions of Title VII of the Civil Rights Act of 1964 and other applicable government regulations. . . .

ARTICLE XXVIII—MANAGEMENT RESPONSIBILITIES

The Company shall have the right to manage the plant, direct the working forces, plan, direct and control the plant operations, hire, promote and demote, relieve employees from duty because of lack of work and for other legitimate reasons, introduce new and improved production methods or facilities or change existing production methods or facilities, improve quality, reduce costs and establish and attain reasonable work and production standards.

The above stated Company rights shall not be exercised when contrary to or inconsistent with any provision of this Agreement, nor any understandings reached by the parties hereto.

SHOP RULES

11. Disorder, loafing, horse play, or immoral conduct on Company property is prohibited at all times. . . .

22. Failure by an employee to meet the above requirements will result in his being disciplined by reprimand, suspension or discharge, depending upon the seriousness of his shortcomings.

SEXUAL HARASSMENT POLICY

SUBJECT: SEXUAL HARASSMENT

The Eureka Company has made a commitment to provide its employees and business contacts with a non-discriminatory environment. Sexual harassment of any employee or business contact by an employee of The Eureka Company is prohibited. Sexual harassment of another employee or business contact is grounds for immediate termination of employment. Sexual harassment is considered to be unwelcome sexual advances, requests for sexual favors and other verbal or physical conduct of a sexual nature when:

1. submission to such conduct is made either explicitly or implicitly a term or condition of an individual's employment or business relationship;
2. submission to or rejection of such conduct by an individual is used as the basis for employment or business decisions affecting such individual; or
3. such conduct has the purpose or effect of unreasonably interfering with an individual's work performance or business relationship or creating an intimidating, hostile or offensive environment.

Sexually suggestive objects, signs or other materials are likewise prohibited. Employees are required to report any and all incidents of sexual harassment to the Personnel Manager and/or other appropriate persons. Supervisors or managers aware of incidents of sexual harassment that fail to report the information are subject to disciplinary action. All complaints will be thoroughly investigated and the innocent parties to the sexual harassment are assured that there will be no reprisals for making a complaint, reporting an incident or cooperating with an investigation.

FACTS

L, a 43 year old man employed as a Material Handler with 25 years of service, was on May 5, 1993 discharged for violation of Shop Rule #12, immoral conduct, and violation of the Sexual Harassment Policy. On the afternoon of April 30, 1993, Bargaining Unit employee T, and salaried employee, V, were working in their respective offices separated by a distance of about 50 feet. At about 2:40 P.M., T received a telephone call from V returning a call which T had made to her concerning a procedural problem with a computer entry. T had just said "Hello" when she heard the outer door of her office open and she saw Grievant standing in the doorway. He said, "Hi, Boobs, look at this." When she turned to look at him, he was standing in the doorway laughing with himself exposed. She told him, "L, zip up your pants and get the f____ out of here," followed with the statement, "I can't believe he's doing this." and slammed down the receiver. V was shocked, stunned and appalled at the grievant's actions and didn't know what to do. She was very upset and horrified that something like that could happen to her at work. She also said that before the incident she had never given him any reason to believe that it was OK to do something like that. His actions offended her and she felt there was no way she could work with him again. Both she and T received teasing from co-workers as a result of the incident.

The Industrial Relations Manager was not available at the time the grievant's supervisor went to talk to him about the incident. As a result the grievant was allowed to work an overtime shift at a different plant on both Saturday and Sunday (the supervisor was unaware of this). The grievant did not come to work on Monday or Tuesday. It was not until Tuesday that Donald McHugh, the Industrial Relations Manager, was informed. T testified that when McHugh approached her on Tuesday, he asked her what had happened. Her response was: "What are you talking about?" He then asked her if the Grievant had exposed himself to her and since he obviously knew about the incident, she told him what had happened. After completing his investigation, McHugh scheduled on Wednesday a meeting with Grievant and Union representatives. McHugh testified that at that meeting he asked Grievant to explain to him what had happened on the day in question. Grievant gave him certain details of conversations he had had with people having talked with both V and T earlier. According to McHugh, he had a good knowledge, detailed knowledge, of other things that he had done, except he had no recall whatsoever of exposing himself to either of the two people. He explained the charges to the Grievant and told him they were very serious. Asked if he knew of any reasons why he would not have any recollection, his reply was: "The only thing would be mixing pain pills with alcohol." Grievant identified a prescription drug container for medicine prescribed for him for pain due to an arm injury which had occurred before the exposure incident.

He testified that on the Friday, the day of the incident, he took some of this medicine before he left home, again took some before lunch. He went home for lunch that day. His lunch consisted of 3 beers. Since the lunch period is only 30 minutes and it takes 5 minutes to and from his home to the Plant, the Union calculates these 3 beers were drunk in 20 minutes. After his discharge, through Union intervention, Grievant had himself admitted to the In-Patient Substance Abuse Program at the Danville, Illinois Veteran's Administration Medical Center on May 19. He stayed there until June 4 when he completed the program and was discharged. Grievant testified that 9 years prior thereto he had also gone through a substance abuse program and 5 years ago he began drinking again. The testimony was that there has never been a situation similar to this and no Bargaining Unit employee heretofore has been discharged for a violation of the Policy. There had been one case involving a Management person who was discharged for that offense before the Sexual Harassment Policy had been established. Diane Scheel, Chairman of the Shop Committee, testified without identifying paper, times or places that over the years there have been a number of sexual incidents on the factory floor and the people kind of know about it, but it doesn't get any higher up and there isn't any action taken. She knew of one particular case where everybody found out about it after the fact with people testifying to where they had sex in various parts of the factory and everybody was kind of getting a joke out of it. She didn't think exposing oneself was a joking matter.

McHugh testified that in his opinion with the Shop Rules being known as well as the Sexual Harassment Policy, his obligation, under those factors and under the law, gave him no choice in what penalty he could issue. In making his decision to terminate, he considered the legal implication of his actions and its effect upon the Company. He considered Grievant's approximate 25 years of service with the Company. It was the Company's conclusion that what Grievant did was so serious and so wrong that they had to remove him from the workplace and terminate his employment. They had found no mitigating circumstances that would allow them to give Grievant a lesser penalty other than his years of service.

POSITIONS OF THE PARTIES

The Union

Grievant was unjustly discharged. There is no direct evidence that Grievant exposed himself to V and T's actions indicate she had no intention of taking action against the Grievant and would not have mentioned the matter except that McHugh indicated to her that he knew what had occurred. The Company's actions indicate that it was not a serious matter as it took 4 days to notify McHugh who was responsible for the investigation and when he did make an investigation, he made no contact with the Grievant in an attempt to interview him and learn his version of the occurrence. It allowed him to work overtime on Saturday and Sunday, even though under the Collective Bargaining Agreement there is a provision allowing the Company the right to send an employee home in serious cases until an investigation is made. The testimony of T . . . shows that Grievant was very much affected by a combination of prescribed medication and alcohol that he had taken the night before and the day of the alleged incident. Grievant had a drinking problem which the Company failed to take into consideration and treat the Grievant's problem as an illness for which corrective action was needed in the case of a 25-year employee rather than discharge. For these reasons, it seeks his reinstatement.

The Company

There was just cause for discipline. While there is no universal definition of "just cause", a review of published arbitration awards reveals that a "common law" set of criteria which, if met, constitute just cause.

It would be absurd to think that the Company would be required to issue "progressive discipline" to Grievant in this matter. The very thought that the Company might be required to issue a penalty less than discharge and in essence give the Grievant a second chance to humiliate these two women or anyone else would be repugnant to the Company and against public policy. Further, throughout the entire investigation, Grievant and Union failed to produce any extenuating or mitigating circumstances which would have possibly explained or justified Grievant's actions or even made a case for imposition of a lesser penalty than discharge other than his drinking a few beers at lunch. Any claim of intoxication is refuted by the evidence. Any attempt to persuade the Arbitrator that although the incidents of him exposing himself to two female employees had occurred he should be reinstated because he went to a substance abuse program one month after his discharge is nothing more than a smoke screen and has no bearing on the seriousness of his offense.

QUESTIONS

1. The union claims that the grievant was unaware of his actions because of an alcohol problem. Do you agree with this defense? Why or why not?

2. Should the fact the sexual harassment had not been reported in the past be considered by the arbitrator? Why or why not?

3. Should the fact that the grievant had been employed for 25 years be considered by the arbitrator? Why or why not?

4. How would you decide this case? Why?

Source: Reprinted with permission from *Labor Relations Reporter–Labor Arbitration Reports,* 101 LA 1151. Copyright 1993 by The Bureau of National Affairs, Inc. (800-372-1033) <http://www.bna.com>

Lohr Distributing Company and Brewery Drivers and Helpers Local 133

Gerald A. Fowler, Arbitrator. Award issued November 23, 1993.

ISSUE

Sexual harassment—Comments to customer.

RELEVANT CONTRACT PROVISIONS

ARTICLE V DISCHARGE

. . .

Section 4. In assessing disciplinary discharges, disciplinary violations for infractions issued prior to five (5) years from the date of the current violation shall not be considered by the Company for such violations.

ARTICLE XV WORK DESCRIBED

. . .

Section 5. A basement or second floor is a stop where there are more than four steps up or down or platform or ramp that is over forty (40) inches up or down. Any new or modified delivery location in violation of the above restrictions will be reviewed on a case by case basis to determine if beer can be delivered in a safe and efficient manner. The Union will not withhold its consent to such stops unreasonably. Drivers are to rotate beer (when possible), deliver products where the customer requests and be polite and courteous to customers, whenever possible.

COMPANY RULES ALL UNION EMPLOYEES MARCH 2, 1992

. . .

11. Conduct: Insubordination, including refusal to follow orders or perform assigned work, is not permitted. There shall be no unlawful or improper conduct during working or nonworking hours, which adversely affects relationships to customers, fellow employees, supervisors, or the Company's products, property, reputation, or goodwill in the community. Employees will not smoke in prohibited areas. Fighting, threatening, coercing or in any way intimidating customers, supervisors, or fellow employees is strictly forbidden.

BACKGROUND

This arbitration involves the discharge of O, an employee of Lohr Distributing Company (hereinafter the "Company") who was represented for purposes of collective bargaining by Brewery Drivers and Helpers Local Union No. 133 (hereinafter the "Union"). O has been employed by the Company as a beer delivery driver since January 1977. This arbitration arises because of the suspension and subsequent discharge of the Grievant which came about as a result of incidents occurring at Bill Bailey's Bar in St. Louis, Missouri on October 13, 1993.

FACTS

The Grievant was discharged based upon his conduct at Bill Bailey's on Wednesday, October 13, 1993. The Company received a complaint from owners of Bill Bailey's Bar indicating that the Grievant had been discourteous and had engaged in offensive sexually related banter with the female bartender on duty when the Grievant attempted to deliver his product. Jim Henry, Plant Manager, indicated that upon his investigation he was informed by T, the female bartender on duty when the Grievant attempted to make his delivery, concerning the events in question. She indicated that the Grievant made inappropriate comments about her jeans and told several offensive jokes and also made offensive remarks to her mother who was seated at the end of the bar. She also informed Mr. Henry that the Grievant made disparaging remarks about the owners of the bar indicating that they were "a_____" and "that their checks bounced like rubber." Mr. Henry indicated that he was advised that these statements were made in front of approximately seven people who were in the bar at the time. Testimony revealed that Bill Bailey's had been put on a cash only basis by Lohr Distributing because of "refusals" in the past. T indicated that when the Grievant returned the second time he indicated that he would wait until the check was delivered to the Company so that he could make delivery of the beer. He indicated that he would order lunch and accepted the offer of a beer on the house by T. He then ordered a hamburger with lettuce and tomato on the side. T indicated that he said to her "that he could not eat the tomato provided with the hamburger because he had an allergic reaction to tomatoes." According to her testimony, he indicated that whenever he ate tomatoes, he "got very horny." While sitting at the bar, the Grievant ordered a second beer and made comments about T's tight jeans. According to T's testimony, he told her mother to stand up and turn around so that he could see where she got her nice a __ from. T said the Grievant repeatedly used profanity during his stay in the bar and that "every other word was 'f____'." She indicated that she was offended and upset. As a result of this behavior on the part of the Grievant, the witness indicated that she contacted her own attorney. She also informed the manager, Doug Bentlage, and advised him that if he did not do something, she would pursue action on her own. She further testified that no other driver had ever treated her in this way. Mr. Bentlage testified that when he arrived back at the bar at 3:00 P.M., T was very upset. He indicated that one of the customers verified to him the behavior which T had related. Further testimony introduced by the Company indicated that all truck drivers wear uniforms which clearly identify them as employees of Lohr distributing and Anheuser-Busch.

Testimony by the Grievant indicated that he arrived at Bill Bailey's at approximately 11:00 A.M. on the morning of October 13, 1993, intending to deliver eighteen cases of beer. He indicated that since the bar had not been a reliable account in the past, he was instructed not to deliver any beer unless the beer was paid for by money order. The Grievant testified that the manager attempted to pay him with a check. The Grievant indicated he could not take the check without verifying this with the Company. Upon contacting Company personnel, the Grievant indicated that he was informed that he could not deliver the beer without a money order. The Grievant then left the bar and finished making deliveries at two remaining stops. The Grievant returned to Bill Bailey's at approximately 2:00 P.M. and talked with the woman bartender, T. He indicated that he was informed that the money was on the way and that the beer would be paid for. He then indicated that he decided to order a hamburger. He indicated that T asked him if he wanted a drink and said that it would be "on the house." The Grievant had a beer and hamburger while waiting. The Grievant admitted to making statements about the bartender's pants and telling her an off-color joke relating to tight pants. He indicated that she did not seem offended and that he considered them to be engaging in harmless banter. According to testimony by the Grievant, he had some conversation with her mother relating to a recent operation. According to testimony by the Grievant, the mother then stood up and turned around making a statement to the effect of "where do you think she got her figure?" The Grievant denied making derogatory comments about the manager or owner indicating that he did not even know the manager or owner. The Grievant did admit to using profanity and indicated that most people having discussions in the bar were, in fact, using profanity.

POSITIONS OF THE PARTIES

The Company

The Company presented evidence and testimony establishing that they had just cause to discharge the Grievant based upon his conduct at Bill Bailey's on Wednesday, October 13, 1993. In discharging the Grievant, the Company alleged that:

1. The Grievant made disparaging remarks directed toward the owner and/or manager of Bill Bailey's Bar.
2. That he referred to the business as "bullshit" and the manager as a "liar".
3. That he stated before patrons of the bar that the checks issued by management were made of rubber.
4. That he made crude and offensive sexual comments to the female bartender and her mother.

Additional testimony was introduced by the Company indicating that the Grievant had been placed on two weeks suspension from July 9, 1990, through July 20, 1990, for:

1. Initiating extreme profane arguments with a variety of personnel in the city.
2. Failing to operate his truck in a safe and courteous manner.
3. Intentionally tying up traffic and refusing to move his vehicle until instructed to do so by a police officer.

The suspension letter received by the Grievant on this occasion contained the following statement: "Further occurrences of this nature will result in your discharge." The Company maintains that using profane language and embarrassing the Company and casting it in a bad light with the public is similar to the type of behavior engaged in by the Grievant on October 13, 1993. In summary, the Company contends that not only did the Grievant's misconduct at Bill Bailey's constitute sufficient grounds for discharge, but it also was justified because of his prior disciplinary record with concomitant final warning. The Company argues that they should not be forced to suffer another embarrassment by this employee. The Company points to the millions of dollars expended by Anheuser-Busch for advertising and establishment of goodwill on the part of patrons and its customers. Company testimony substantiated the fact that all individuals associated with the brewery operations are expected to do everything possible to enhance the image of the Company and that behavior such as demonstrated by the Grievant simply cannot be tolerated. The Company argues that there is just cause to discharge the Grievant and that there is no basis to mitigate or substitute a lesser penalty.

The Union

Testimony provided by the Union indicated that the Grievant felt that he had not engaged in any behavior which would result in severe disciplinary action. In summary, the Union maintains that the Grievant's testimony should be believed and that he did not knowingly engage in any sexual harassment or deliberately attempt to harm the Company's image. The Union argues that the Grievant merely engaged in flirtatious conversation with the woman bartender and her mother at the bar. The Union elicited testimony from T in cross-examination indicating that she had at no time indicated during her conversation with the Grievant that his comments were offensive to her. Rather she attempted to dismiss his comments in a "light" fashion. The Union argues that there was no evidence presented to demonstrate that the Grievant intended to harass the woman bartender or her mother. The Union acknowledges that the Company has a legitimate concern with regard to customer complaints, however, they maintain that the circumstances of the instant grievance do not demonstrate that the Company's reputation has been harmed nor that it lost any customers because of the behavior of the Grievant. Further, the Union argues that the complaint should be viewed with some skepticism because of the customer's past relationship with the Company resulting in a cash only basis type of transaction. The Union presented testimony indicating that the Grievant was not required to go to the bar a second time in an attempt to deliver the beer since the manager had failed to produce a money order. They argue that the Grievant did this in an attempt to accommodate the needs of the customer and that he had no intention to harass or create poor customer relations. The Union maintains that the Grievant's conduct is simply not as serious as the Company wishes to contend.

In conclusion, the Union maintains that the Company acted without just cause in discharging the Grievant. Therefore, the Union requests that the grievance be sustained and the Grievant be reinstated with full back pay, seniority and benefits. In their argument to the Arbitrator, the Union acknowledges that it would probably be in the best interest of the Company and the Grievant that his reinstatement be conditioned upon his not being permitted to select a route which includes Bill Bailey's bar.

QUESTIONS

1. In your view, did the employer have "just cause" to discharge the grievant? Discuss.
2. The union contends that the grievant did not knowingly engage in any sexual harassment. Do you agree with the union? Why or why not?
3. Should the fact that the Grievant was placed on suspension in 1990 have any merit in this case? Why or why not?
4. The union claims that there is no evidence to demonstrate that the grievant intended to harass the bartender. What do you think?
5. How would you decide this case? Why?

Source: Reprinted with permission from *Labor Relations Reporter–Labor Arbitration Reports,* 101 LA 1217. Copyright 1993 by The Bureau of National Affairs, Inc. (800-372-1033) <http://www.bna.com>

Tynan Lumber Company and International Brotherhood of Teamsters, Local 890

C. Allen Pool, Arbitrator. Award issued January 21, 1992.

ISSUES

Layoff—Reinstatement—Disability—Seniority rights.

RELEVANT CONTRACT PROVISIONS

Section 23—Seniority

Seniority is defined as a length of an employee's continuous service with the Company from the date of his last employment in his classification of employment. Where a company has more than one (1) lumberyard within the jurisdiction of this Agreement, there shall be a separate seniority list for each location. Seniority shall not apply to an employee until he shall have been employed by the Company for a period of One Hundred Twenty (120) days. Once acquired, seniority shall be effective from the date of hire.

In the event of layoff of an employee in a classification covered by this Agreement, subject to qualifications and ability to perform the work required, the last man hired shall be the first man laid off; in the event of a rehire, the last man laid off shall be the first man rehired. This provision shall not apply in the event the layoff is in excess of twelve (12) months.

FACTS

The Company operates two lumberyards in the Central Coast region of California, one in Salinas and the other in Monterey. (The two cities are about 20 miles apart.) This grievance arose out of the Monterey yard. The Yard Manager in Monterey has been an employee of the Company for 41 years. The Assistant Manager there has been a Company employee for approximately ten (10) years. The Grievant was hired by the Company on September 27, 1987 into the classification of Yardman. Employees in this classification perform a variety of jobs. In the yard, at varying times, they will switch between mill work and driving a forklift. In addition, they are frequently called upon to drive a truck on the public roadways.

On October 8, 1990 the Grievant asked to be released from work early to take his dog to be put to sleep. On his way to Carmel Valley, he was involved in a serious auto accident and taken to the hospital. His wife testified that she telephoned the Assistant Manager the next morning at about 8:00 A.M. and told him that her husband was in the hospital and would not be coming to work. She also testified that she told the Assistant Manager that her husband's condition at that time was unknown. The Assistant Manager testified that he learned of the Grievant's accident from another Yardman and does not remember receiving a call from the Grievant's wife. However, he did testify that it is possible that she did make such a call. The Company, at this point, hired a person to replace the Grievant. The Monterey Yard Seniority List does not show the replacement's date of hire. However, [it] is clear that he was hired to replace the Grievant within a few days, perhaps only one day, after the Grievant's accident. The Company stated that the Grievant was in "very dire straits in the hospital and would probably not make it. . . . Based on that information, we replaced" the Grievant. The Yard Manager testified that the decision to replace the Grievant was his. He said he had heard from one of the Yardmen that the Grievant "had a very bad accident and they didn't know whether he was going to pull through or not." He also said that he never received any calls from any member of the Grievant's family. The Yard Manager testified "We were extremely busy. We couldn't get along with less help than we had, so we had to hire somebody else to take his place."

The Grievant spent about six to eight weeks in the hospital in a bodycast and in traction. When he did leave the hospital and went home, he continued to stay in traction and under the care of a private nurse. It was three to four months before he became ambulatory. He continued to progress in his recovery and his physician told him he could eventually return to work. In the middle or latter part of July, 1991, the Grievant telephoned the Assistant Manager to inform him that his physician would soon release him from the medical disability and he would be able to return to work. The Assistant Manager told the Grievant he had been replaced but would be given consideration if there was a future opening. The physician signed the Grievant's medical release on September 4, 1991. It stated: "Peter may return to a trial of full employment in his usual and customary work on 9/4/91." The Grievant took the release to the Company's office in Salinas and presented it to the vice-president, Diane Spencer. She told the Grievant that the Monterey Manager and Assistant Manager considered him as having been replaced and that the matter was being turned over to the Company's attorney. A grievance was filed which proceeded to this Arbitration.

POSITIONS OF THE PARTIES

The Union

The Union contends that the Company's refusal to return the Grievant to work upon release by his physician violated his seniority rights under the Agreement. The language contained in Section 23 entitles employees who are off work for any nonculpable reason, including disability, to return to their jobs within twelve months. The Grievant's absence from work to recover from his injuries constituted a "layoff" within the meaning of Section 23. The Agreement protected his seniority rights to work over junior employees at the point he was physically able to return to his job.

The term "layoff" is unqualified and encompasses periods of no work because of disability as well as lack of work opportunities because of business reasons. The generic meaning of the term is not restricted to an economic layoff. It is all inclusive. The unqualified use of the term in Section 23 is significant in that the agreement does not expressly address disability absences, leaves of absence, or other non-disciplinary periods off the job. The proper interpretation of "layoff" in these circumstances is that it encompasses all of the various kinds of absences from work that do not terminate the employment relationship. The Company has a past practice of permitting employees to return to work after prolonged absences attributable to ill health. This practice has given specific meaning to Section 23 of the Agreement. The Company did nothing to terminate the Grievant. Neither the Grievant nor the Union received any written communication concerning his status. The Company records show no change in his status. Throughout the Grievant's absence, the Company treated him as continuing to have an employment relationship. In contract terms, he was simply "laid off," awaiting a release to return to work. It is respectfully submitted that the Company should be found to have violated the Agreement by not returning the Grievant to work on September 4, to work with full back pay and benefits.

The Company

The Company did not have the duty to protect the Grievant's seniority under the Agreement following his off-the-job accident and injury. Section 23 only refers to a description of seniority and then seniority protection in a layoff situation. Neither an on-the-job injury nor an off-the-job injury is considered a layoff within the meaning of labor relations. Section 23 protects an employee's seniority for twelve months only in the event of a layoff which is in the control of the Company's hands. An accident is not in control of anyone's hands. If the Agreement was meant to provide seniority protection in the event of an accident, it would certainly be mentioned in the Agreement. The two other situations where long-term employees received their jobs back after an illness are distinguishable from the current case. In those cases, it was not necessary to replace them because they had enough people to do the job. In the current case, it was necessary to the business to replace the Grievant. Following the accident, the Company was so busy that they could not get along without additional help. In the absence of clear and convincing language within the four corners of the Agreement, the Company is under no legal requirement to protect the Grievant's seniority to the extent that another employee would have to be laid off and have his seniority violated. It is respectfully submitted that the grievance be denied.

QUESTIONS

1. The employer claims that they have no "duty to protect the Grievant's seniority . . . following his off-the-job accident." Do you agree with this? Why or why not?

2. The union contends that the employer violated Section 23 of the agreement. Do you agree with the union? Why or why not?

3. The union contends that the company has past practice of permitting employees to return to work after prolonged absences attributed to ill health. Is this important to the case? Why or why not?

4. What is the proper interpretation of the term *layoff*?

5. How would you decide this case? Why?

Source: Reprinted with permission from *Labor Relations Reporter–Labor Arbitration Reports,* 98 LA 1103. Copyright 1993 by The Bureau of National Affairs, Inc. (800-372-1033) <http://www.bna.com>

Bargaining Simulation in the Supermarket Industry

The Tower Supermarkets Company (TSC) and the National Food Employees Union (NFEU)

CONTENTS

EVALUATION FORMS

INTRODUCTION

The first question to be asked is, Why did the author choose the supermarket industry for this simulation? There are a number of reasons for this selection:

1. All of us, directly or indirectly, shop at supermarkets; this should help simulation participants to remember collective bargaining and its ramifications long after the conclusion of this exercise.

2. We all have the opportunity to observe and to familiarize ourselves with some aspects of supermarket operations—for example, vendor stocking, compensation of the work force, store hours, and so on. The easy access to supermarkets can help simulation participants to understand, to conceptualize, and to identify some of the problems and issues over which they will have to negotiate.

3. Some of the problems and developments experienced by other industries are also encountered by the supermarket industry and their unions. These are: corporate restructuring, union mergers, union organizing campaigns, and very intense marketplace competitive pressures to which the companies and unions have to respond.

This simulation permits you to "go to the bargaining table" in a key contract negotiation between a large company and a large national union representing a segment of its supermarket employees. Every effort has been made to simulate an actual bargaining situation. However, the names of the company and of the union presented here are fictitious.

The simulation starts in the *midst* of negotiations. A number of items have been tentatively agreed to, and the parties now confine their negotiations to the remaining open issues:

Wages

Vendor Stocking

Union Shop and Checkoff (Union Security)

Management Rights

Technological Change(s)

Evening Premium

Night Shift Premium

Seniority

Store Closing(s)

Grievance and Arbitration Procedure

Union Cooperation

Establishment of a Joint Union-Management Committee

Holidays

Vacations

See the existing contract language on the preceding items. The current contract articles are included in a latter section of this simulation.

As you and your colleagues face off on the above issues, you will set strategy, develop demands or offers, and conduct negotiations, and it is to be hoped that you will reach a settlement. You may assume the role of a particular participant and feel some of his or her pressures and frustrations—some across the table and some in the caucus room. The purpose of this simulation is to acquaint you with tactics, strategies, procedures, attitudes, ideas, pressures, and issues emerging in the bargaining process. You will learn to work with other participants as a bargaining team. You will acquire negotiation experience under "real-world" constraints in terms of budget, time pressures, actual agreement provisions, and current labor statistics from the Bureau of Labor Statistics.

The company bargaining team includes the Director of Human Resources/Employee Relations, the Vice-President of Operations, the Division Controller, and the Administrative Assistant to the Director of Human Resources/Labor Relations. The union bargaining team includes the National Union Representative, the Local Union President, the Local Union Vice-President and Secretary/Treasurer, and the Local Vice-President and Chair of the Grievance Committee. (See role descriptions in a latter section of this simulation.)

Your team is expected to reach an agreement. To be able to attain a settlement, you must understand and study your group's interests, goals, and issues. You must also perceive and anticipate the objectives and interests of the other side. You should be prepared for demands and offers made by your counterparts. You should be ready to respond to these. You must develop tactics and strategies that will assist you in reaching a satisfactory contract.

One of the objectives of this simulation is to try to reach the targets contained in your confidential instructions distributed by your instructor.

Another objective is for the union team to reach a better settlement than any other union group participating in the simulation. The objective for the management team is to reach a better agreement than any other company team.

Team scoring in this simulation will reflect how well you achieve the objectives given your bargaining committee by union or company officials. Postgame self-evaluation is also included to measure how effectively you carried out your particular role assignment and what you learned about the process of negotiation during the course of the simulation.

SIMULATION INSTRUCTIONS

1. Consultation or fraternization with the opposition or with other teams is strictly prohibited during the course of the simulation.

2. Negotiators are not permitted to attend negotiations of other teams.

3. Each team member must be given an opportunity to represent the team in bargaining over specific topics. All team members will participate in negotiation of all issues. Each team will select a spokesperson who will also be responsible for particular subjects.

4. In order to reach an agreement and provide a realistic negotiation environment, each team can compromise positions, trade issues, drop demands, be creative, explore options, offer counterproposals, and so on.

5. During the first negotiation session, each labor-management group will reach agreement on the following procedural issues:

   a. Duration of negotiation sessions and caucuses; both of these issues can be renegotiated later by the parties.

   b. Agenda sequence for the first session and how the agenda sequence will be determined in future sessions. It is recommended that you first start negotiating the least difficult, noneconomic issues.

   c. It is suggested that all agreements arrived at during the negotiations be tentative until a final agreement on all issues and articles is reached.

6. You may caucus as often as necessary.

7. You should notify the opposition who is going to be the spokesperson for your team.

8. Pocket calculators are essential in costing out the contract. Computer spreadsheet software programs are strongly recommended for costing out the agreement.

9. Review the suggested sequence for this simulation.

10. Forms IV–VIII are to be used as a guide in costing out your negotiation positions on wages, cost of living, and benefits.

11. To determine the current wage at TSC, consult the latest available issue of *Employment and Earnings.*[1]

12. For sources of library material, consult this text's bibliography.

13. If the parties do not reach an agreement at the contract deadline set by the instructor, a strike will take place. The contract deadline cannot be extended by mutual agreement of the parties.

14. At the conclusion of bargaining, each team will submit to the instructor completed forms II–IX and Appendix A: Forms A–D and the complete content of the bargaining binder. The binder should include all notes, statistical data, agreed-upon and proposed contract language, evaluation forms, your library research, and other relevant data, including notes of phone inquiries.

15. Form X, *confidential* individual evaluations of your team members and of your opponents, and Form XI are to be submitted to your instructor at the end of the simulation.

The aforementioned material, including all costing computations, must be completed and submitted to the instructor even if a strike takes place.

PERFORMANCE EVALUATION

Your team and individual performance in this simulation will be evaluated according to the following criteria:

TEAM PERFORMANCE CRITERIA

1. Your team's compliance with confidential parameters, limits, and guidelines.

2. The evaluation of your team by your opposition.

3. Your team's bargaining preparations.

4. Your team's bargaining performance as well as the team's application of various tactics and strategies during negotiations as observed by your instructor.

5. The content of your bargaining file submitted to your instructor at the end of the simulation, as per item 14 of your instructions listed above.

6. The achievement of projected contract terms as stated by your team on Form I. Before your team starts to negotiate, this form is to be submitted to your instructor; this is to take place immediately after the conclusion of the first caucus.

7. The final results achieved by your team on contract language changes.

8. The final results achieved by your team on cost of wages and benefits.

INDIVIDUAL PERFORMANCE CRITERIA

1. The confidential evaluation by each of your teammates of your individual contribution and performance.

---

[1]A monthly publication providing statistics on employment, unemployment, hours, and earnings. U.S. Department of Labor, Bureau of Labor Statistics. For further details, see Worksheet A.

2. The confidential evaluation by each of your opponents of your individual contribution and performance.

3. Your individual bargaining preparation.

4. Your contribution to the team's bargaining file submitted to your instructor at the end of the simulation.

5. Your individual performance in negotiations as observed by your instructor.

6. Your completion of Form X for all your teammates and for all the negotiators on the other side, as well as Form XI.

SUGGESTED SEQUENCE

	Instructor	Participant	Suggested Time Increments
Read Simulation.	X	X	Outside preparation
Assign roles.	X		Thirty minutes
Review instructions and suggested sequence.	X		
Announce year in which negotiations take place.	X		
Conduct library research; consult sources listed in section titled "Sources of Information."	X	X	Outside preparation
Distribute company and union packets to the respective teams.	X		
Hold separate caucuses to establish initial demands or offers and team strategy.		X	Decide, jointly with your opponents, length of caucus
Submit Form I to instructor.		X	
Commence bargaining: 1. Establish procedure. 2. Present positions. 3. Caucus to analyze opponents' demands or offers. 4. Caucus as necessary. 5. Establish strike deadline.		X	Length of simulation is approximately three to nine hours (depending upon strike deadline established by the instructor).
At conclusion of bargaining, turn in all forms to instructor.		X	
Compute team scoring.	X		
Complete evaluation questionnaire.		X	

BACKGROUND OF THE COMPANY

The Tower Supermarkets Company (TSC) is a retail grocery chain that has been operating successfully for over 75 years. The company operates about 430 supermarkets and about 320 convenience stores. It also operates food-processing and nonfood manufacturing facilities in which it produces many private-label goods. The company conducts its business in the Midwest. The company has about 70,000 employees. Of these, approximately 1,000 are in this bargaining unit, which covers 10 supermarkets in a midwestern city. These employees are represented by Local 1207 of the National Food Employees Union (NFEU).

The company has more than 70 labor agreements in place. The vast majority of these have been renegotiated without any labor stoppages. Two years ago, however, the company experienced a lengthy strike in one of its divisions. In the company's view, this strike was an aberration. After the strike, the company has made an effort to improve communications with the unions and begun to address key issues prior to negotiations.

In the 1980s, the company was financially restructured, and its long-term debt, issued at a very high interest rate, more than quadrupled. Recently, the company replaced high-cost debt with lower-cost securities; it also redeemed some of its debentures. These developments significantly reduced interest expenses. The highlights of the financial statements are as follows: Common equity (equity of the common stockholders) has been in the minus column for the last five years. Currently it stands at minus $899 million. No dividends have been distributed for the last four years. On the positive side, earnings per share have been improving significantly, from a deficit that took place four years ago to earnings of $.37 per share in the current year (see Tables I through III).

New supercenters pose a competitive threat to the company. Wal-Mart, Kmart, and other retailers are major competitors. Some of these operators combine food stores with general merchandise outlets; others offer groceries in warehouse-type premises. These competitors, with their advanced distribution systems, offer low prices at one-stop shopping locations.

The company's operating strategy is to stress growth and improvements in annual cash flow, which it expects to achieve in the following way:

1. New store construction and remodeling. This should increase net food store square footage by over 3 percent annually.

2. Investment in cost-saving technology in such areas as automation of labor scheduling, store delivery accounting, self-management programs, and installation of a satellite-based system that will link most stores into a real-time communication network.

3. Improved efficiencies in procurement and distribution systems; adoption of "just in time" inventory systems to reduce distribution costs; coordination of product purchasing across retail divisions, which should reduce acquisition costs.

BACKGROUND OF THE UNION

The National Food Employees Union (NFEU), Local 1207 is the exclusive bargaining agent for the 10 midwestern stores of the Tower Supermarkets Company (TSC). This is a large multicity local of 18,000 members. The local represents employees in various companies in the Midwest.

The parent union of the local, the NFEU, represents workers in food retail stores, in food processing, and in the meat-packing industry. The union was formed 10 years ago by a merger of retail market employees together with the meat employees' union. The union has over 300,000 members.

Prior to the merger, the two unions bargained separately with the Tower Supermarkets Company. The merger strengthened the union financially and increased its bargaining power.

The NFEU has negotiated 70 different agreements with the Tower Supermarkets Company at its various locations. Most of these agreements were reached peacefully. The union negotiates agreements with many different employers that range in size from very small to very large national corporations.

The Tower Supermarkets Company has been expanding by building larger supermarkets. This has provided the NFEU with the opportunity to expand its membership base. The NFEU has been successful in organizing many of the new employees.

The big challenge confronting Local 1207 as well as the TSC is new low-price competition from supercenters and warehouse-type retailers who are entering the grocery market. The new supermarket companies are nonunionized and do not provide any fringe benefits to most of their employees. They primarily employ part-time help. These developments are of great concern both to the membership and to the union leadership. The local is working on an organizing campaign directed at the new companies entering the local market.

The issue of the nonunionized supermarkets presents the NFEU with a major challenge at the local as well as at the national level. The NFEU realizes that it is partially responsible for the current developments. In the past, the union neglected organizing the new companies because it was too preoccupied with its own internal restructuring. In the future, the NFEU will devote more resources to organizing, at both national and local levels. This is necessary in order to protect union jobs as well as for the financial strength of the union.

Prior to the start of contract negotiations, the local union officers have worked closely with the membership on initial demands to be submitted to the company. They promised a program of regular and detailed progress reports on the bargaining via the union newspaper and bulletin board announcements. They privately worried, however, about how they could release enough information to neutralize the dissidents inside the union without releasing "too much" and thereby reducing their flexibility at the bargaining table.

FINANCIAL INFORMATION

As a publicly held corporation, TSC is required by law to disclose financial information. The primary device utilized for this purpose is the company's annual report. Copies go to each shareholder and to the media, employees, investment firms, business libraries, financial institutions, and individuals and organizations requesting copies.

Veteran analysts are little influenced by the glossy paper, the multicolor printing, and the photography. They turn immediately to the data on earnings and financial position. They look at income data (see Table I), balance sheet data (see Table II), and per-share data (see Table III).

TABLE I   Tower Supermarkets Company (TSC)
Income Data (Millions), 10-Year Review

Year Ended Dec. 31	Revenues	Operating Income	Capital Expenditures	Depreciation	Interest Expenses	Net Before Taxes	Net Income	Cash Flow
This year	7374	296	82	80	158	58	34	114
Last year	7110	311	75	78	178	56	34	112
3 years ago	6747	304	76	79	188	47	28	107
4 years ago	6362	280	44	79	217	d3	d5	72
5 years ago	6345	229	126	82	70	17	12	88
6 years ago	5881	210	154	73	37	108	61	132
7 years ago	5702	192	164	75	37	32	19	93
8 years ago	5702	205	170	69	36	107	60	130
9 years ago	5302	176	106	64	33	88	52	116
10 years ago	5074	155	131	60	32	71	42	101

TABLE II Tower Supermarkets Company (TSC)
Balance Sheet Data (Millions), 10-Year Review

| Year Ended Dec. 31 | Cash | Current | | | Total Assets | Long-Term Debt | Common Equity (net worth) | Total Capital | % Return on Equity |
		Assets	Liabilities	Ratio					
This year	35	722	724	1.0	1433	1490	d899	683	NM
Last year	1	663	395	1.0	1370	1468	d915	642	NM
3 years ago	18	649	687	0.9	1372	1518	d952	656	NM
4 years ago	38	682	689	1.0	1413	1573	d987	684	NM
5 years ago	70	823	721	1.1	1536	1573	d975	782	NM
6 years ago	38	718	654	1.1	1485	329	336	804	18.0
7 years ago	71	650	590	1.1	1357	252	343	734	4.8
8 years ago	35	666	575	1.2	1391	308	396	809	15.7
9 years ago	54	579	488	1.2	1228	259	383	733	14.0
10 years ago	38	545	432	1.3	1166	292	357	727	10.5

TABLE III Tower Supermarkets Company (TSC)
Per-Share Data ($), 10-Year Review

Year Ended Dec. 31	Cash Flow	Earnings	Dividends
This year	1.25	0.37	NIL
Last year	1.24	0.37	NIL
3 years ago	1.24	0.32	NIL
4 years ago	0.89	d0.08	NIL
5 years ago	1.11	0.08	13.594*
6 years ago	1.65	0.73	0.350
7 years ago	1.07	0.20	0.341
8 years ago	1.47	0.68	0.333
9 years ago	1.29	0.58	0.333
10 years ago	1.11	0.46	0.318

*Special cash dividend

In reviewing these tables, compare the performance of TSC with that of other companies in the industry. Good sources of information are reports published by The Value Line and by the Standard and Poor's Corp. These publications offer a guide that provides a perspective and explains the significance of the financial information. Most libraries subscribe to these two reporting services.

SOURCES OF INFORMATION

Each negotiating team should familiarize itself with recent economic developments and the latest results of major negotiations. The simulation participants should consult the most recent issues of the following publications:

Employment and Earnings. This monthly report provides current statistics on U.S. employment, unemployment, hours, and earnings. *Source:* U.S. Department of Labor, Bureau of Labor Statistics (BLS).

CPI Detailed Report. This monthly periodical features detailed data on consumer price movements. *Source:* U.S. Department of Labor, BLS.

Monthly Labor Review (MLR). One section of the MLR provides current principal statistical labor series data collected and calculated by the BLS. The tables present information on hours and earnings by industry, consumer price indexes, productivity, and labor-management data. *Source:* U.S. Department of Labor, BLS.

Press Releases. The BLS statistical series are made available to the news media through press releases. Many of these releases are also available to the public upon request. Press releases regarding latest "Major Collective Bargaining Settlements" can be very useful for this simulation. *Source:* U.S. Department of Labor, BLS.

Area Wage Surveys. This is a continuing series of reports on BLS surveys covering hourly earnings. *Source:* U.S. Department of Labor, BLS.

Basic Patterns in Union Contracts. Consult the latest edition of *Collective Bargaining Negotiations and Contracts. Source:* Bureau of National Affairs.

Handbook of Labor Statistics. This publication provides in one volume the major series available from the BLS. *Source:* U.S. Department of Labor, BLS.

Compensation and Working Conditions. This monthly publication of the Bureau of Labor Statistics contains current information on wages, employee benefits, labor-management relations, and workplace safety and health. *Source:* U.S. Department of Labor, BLS.

Moody's Industry Review (Grocery Chains—Miscellaneous). *Source:* Moody's Investors Service, Inc.

Personal Consumption Expenditures on Food. *Source:* Department of Commerce, Bureau of Economic Analysis.

Income Statement for Corporations in Retail Trade, Retail Food Stores. *Source: Quarterly Financial Report,* U.S. Department of Commerce.

Standard and Poor's Industry Survey on Supermarkets. *Source:* Standard and Poor's Compustat Services, Inc.

"Supermarket Business." Review articles.

Survey of Current Business. Price indexes for food. *Source:* U.S. Department of Commerce, Bureau of Economic Analysis.

TSC AND NFEU: SOME OF THE PRESENT CONTRACT ARTICLES AND TERMS

Article 1   Vendor Stocking

The present practice of outside vendors stocking shelves shall not be expanded during the term of this Agreement, except that, if a brand of merchandise now being stocked by outside vendors is discontinued and another brand substituted or a new brand is added, representatives of vendors may stock all brands of the same type of merchandise. For example, if a new brand of potato chips is added or substituted, representatives of vendors may stock the new brand.

Article 2   Union Shop and Checkoff (Union Security)

2.1 *Union Shop*—It shall be a condition of employment that all employees of the Employer covered by this Agreement who are members of the Union in good standing on the execution date of this Agreement shall remain members in good standing, and those who are not members on the execution date of this Agreement shall, on the sixty-first (61st) day following the execution date of this Agreement, become and remain members in good standing in the Union. It shall also be a condition of employment that all employees covered by this Agreement and hired on or after its execution date shall, on the sixty-first (61st) day following the beginning of such employment, become and remain members in good standing in the Union. The Employer may secure new employees from any source whatsoever.

During the first sixty (60) calendar days of employment, a new employee shall be on a trial basis and may be discharged at the discretion of the Employer, and such discharge shall not be subject to the Grievance and Arbitration Procedure.

2.2 *Checkoff*—The Employer agrees to deduct weekly Union dues and/or service fees and uniform assessments from the wages of employees in the bargaining unit who individually certify, in writing, authorization for such deduction in a form authorized by law. The Employer agrees, in the case of new Union members, to deduct the Union initiation fee and in the case of a nonmember, an initial service fee from the wages of any new or non-member Union employee who certifies in writing authorization for such deduction in a form authorized by law.

Article 3 Management Rights

The management of the business and the direction of the working forces, including the right to plan, direct and control store and meat plant operations, hire, suspend or discharge for proper cause, transfer or relieve employees from duty because of lack of work or for other legitimate reasons; the right to study or introduce new or improved production methods or facilities subject to the provisions of Article 4; and the right to establish and maintain reasonable rules and regulations covering the operation of the store or meat plant, a violation of which shall be among the causes for discharge, are vested in the Employer; provided, however, that this right shall be exercised with due regard for the rights of the employees, and provided, further, that it will not be used for the purpose of discrimination against any employee or for the purpose of invalidating any contract provision.

Article 4 Technological Changes

In the event that the Employer contemplates the introduction of major technological changes affecting bargaining unit work, advance notice of such change will be given to the Union. If requested to do so, the Employer will meet with the Union to discuss the implementation of such changes before putting such changes into effect.

Article 5 Evening Premium

An evening premium of 3 percent of Current Average Hourly Wage shall be paid for all work after 6:00 P.M. and before 12:00 midnight.

Article 6 Night Shift Premiums

All employees working from 12:00 midnight to 6:00 A.M. will receive an 8 percent premium in addition to their regular rate.

Article 7 Seniority

Application—In layoffs, recalls, transfers, scheduling, and the reduction of hours, the principle of seniority shall apply. In the matter of promotions, the Employer shall have the right to exercise this final judgement after giving due regard to seniority. This shall not preclude the Union from questioning through the Grievance and Arbitration Procedure whether or not the Employer has given due regard to seniority.

Article 8   Store Closings

In the event that the Employer permanently closes or sells a store or stores and/or a fabricating plant, and employees are terminated as a result thereof, separation pay will be paid under the conditions detailed below.

An employee who has averaged at least thirty (30) hours per week for the eight (8) weeks preceding his or her separation due to the sale or closing will qualify for separation pay if:

1. The employee has had two (2) or more years of service;
2. Does not refuse a transfer within the bargaining unit as outlined in the Agreement, or retraining or reassignment in connection therewith;
3. Does not voluntarily terminate employment.

Such employees will be paid at the rate of one (1) week's pay for each year of continuous full-time service, not to exceed six (6) weeks.

Severance pay will equate the average number of hours worked in the eight (8) weeks preceding separation, not to exceed forty (40) hours straight-time pay.

Article 9   Grievance and Arbitration Procedure

Grievance Procedure—Should any "grievance" arise over the interpretation or application of the contents of this Agreement, there shall be an earnest effort on the part of both parties to settle same promptly through the following steps. The term *grievance* includes any complaint, difficulty, disagreement or dispute between the Employer and the Union or any employee covered by this Agreement, and which complaint, difficulty, disagreement or dispute pertains to the interpretation or application of any and all provisions of this Agreement.

Step 1.   By conference between the aggrieved employee, the job steward or both and/or a representative of the Union and the manager of the store or meat plant foreman. If the grievance is not settled, it shall be reduced to writing with copies to the Union and Employer and referred within ten (10) days to Step 2, unless such time period is mutually extended by the Union and the zone manager or meat plant manager.

Step 2.   By conference between the representative of the Union and the zone manager or meat plant manager. If this step does not settle the grievance, it shall be referred within ten (10) days to Step 3, unless such time period is mutually extended by the Union and the zone manager or meat plant manager.

Step 3.   By conference between the business representative and/or the executive officer of the Union, the Human Resource Manager and/or a representative delegated by the Employer. In the event the grievance is not settled in this step, a written response will be exchanged by the parties within twenty (20) days from the Step 3 conference unless otherwise mutually agreed to.

Step 4.   In the event that the last step fails to settle satisfactorily the grievance, and either party wishes to submit it to arbitration, the party desiring arbitration must so advise the other party in writing within forty-five (45) days from the Step 3 written response, or the grievance will be considered settled in Step 3.

Article 10   Union Cooperation

10.1—The Union agrees to uphold the rules and regulations of the Employer in regard to punctual and steady attendance, proper and sufficient notification in case of necessary absence, conduct on the job, and all other reasonable rules and regulations established by the Employer.

10.2—The Union agrees to cooperate with the Employer in maintaining and improving safe working conditions and practices, in improving the cleanliness and good housekeeping of the stores, and in caring for equipment and machinery.

10.3—The Union recognizes the need for improved methods and output in the interest of the employees and the business and agrees to cooperate with the Employer in the installation of such methods, in suggesting improved methods, and in the education of its members in the necessity for such changes and improvements.

10.4—The Union recognizes the need for conservation and the elimination of waste and agrees to cooperate with the Employer in suggesting and practicing methods in the interest of conservation and waste elimination.

Fringe Benefits	
Approximate Percentage of Total Hourly Wage and Fringe Benefit Costs (THWF)[2] Spent on Each Fringe Benefit[3]	
1. Holidays	3% of THWF
2. Vacations	5% of THWF
3. Other Fringe Benefits: Medical insurance Pension Government payments Miscellaneous insurance	25.33% of THWF
	33.33%

Article 11   Holidays

Holidays—Approximate Cost 3 Percent of THWF

11.1 *Legal Holidays*—The following shall be considered holidays: New Year's Day, Memorial Day, Fourth of July, Labor Day, Thanksgiving Day, and Christmas Day. When one of these holidays falls on a Sunday, the holiday shall be celebrated on the Monday immediately following.

11.2 *Personal Holidays*—In addition to the holidays called for in 11.1, an additional paid holiday shall be granted all employees on the same basis as other holidays on the employee's anniversary date of employment.

All employees shall be entitled to the Monday or the first scheduled day within the basic workweek following the employee's first week of vacation as an additional holiday which is not to be construed as part of the employee's vacation.

---

[2]THWF is total base compensation (wages and fringes) for T.S.C., Inc. Wages are 67 percent of THWF and fringes are 33 percent.

[3]Contract articles for each fringe benefit listed on this table are presented below.

Article 12   Vacation

Vacations—Approximate Cost 5 Percent of THWF

Vacations with pay will be granted in each calendar year to hourly rated employees as follows:

Years of Continuous Service	Vacation
1 or more but less than 5 years of service	1 week
5 or more but less than 10 years of service	2 weeks
10 or more but less than 20 years of service	3 weeks
20 or more but less than 25 years of service	4 weeks
Over 25 years of service	5 weeks

Eligibility for vacation shall begin after the completion of twelve (12) months of continuous service following appointment.

Length of Service of Employees in the Bargaining Unit	
Less than one year of service	100
1 or more but less than 3 years of service	50
3 or more but less than 5 years of service	150
5 or more but less than 10 years of service	350
10 or more but less than 15 years of service	100
15 or more but less than 20 years of service	100
20 or more but less than 25 years of service	50
Over 25 years of service	100
	1000

Article 13   Health Care

Medical Care—Approximate Cost 9 Percent of THWF

The employer agrees to make a contribution of 9 percent of THWF toward a medical health care plan. This will apply to all straight-time hours worked by the employees covered by this agreement.

Article 14   Pension

Pension—Approximate Cost 4 Percent of THWF

The employer agrees to make a contribution of 4 percent of THWF toward a pension plan. This will apply to all straight-time hours worked by the employees covered by this Agreement. Effective with employees hired this year, no contribution will be paid for the first twelve (12) months of employment. Contributions shall also be made on hours for which employees receive holiday pay and vacation pay. No contribution shall be made on hours worked in excess of forty (40) per week.

The contributions shall be made to the NFEU Pension Plan, which shall be administered by an equal number of trustees representing the Employer and an equal number of trustees representing the Union. The Pension Trust Fund shall be established pursuant to a Pension Trust Agreement and Pension Plan to be hereafter entered into by the parties hereto for the sole purpose of providing pensions for eligible employees as defined in such Pension Plan.

The present pension plan as described in full in a separate document is hereby made part of this agreement.

Legally Required Payments—Approximate Cost 9.8 percent of THWF

Covers:

Workers' compensation

Unemployment compensation

Social Security (FICA)

Group Term Life Insurance—Approximate Cost .2 percent of THWF

Covers:

Group life insurance

Accidental death and dismemberment insurance

All employees who have completed ninety (90) days of service with the Company shall be eligible for the above coverage. The Company shall assume the full cost of the above coverage.

Additional Miscellaneous Benefits—Approximate Cost 2.33 Percent of THWF

Paid rest periods

Personal clean-up times

Other benefits

Duration of Agreement

This agreement shall remain in full force and effect commencing on the 1st day of the month of _____ 19__ and terminating on the last day of the month of _____ 19__ (2 years later). This Agreement shall automatically renew itself from year to year thereafter unless notice is given in writing by either the Union or the Company to the other party not less than sixty (60) days prior to the expiration date of this Agreement or any anniversary date thereafter, of its desire to modify, amend, or terminate this Agreement.

Cost-of-Living Adjustment

Present contract has no cost-of-living adjustment clause.

CURRENT WAGES AND BENEFITS AT TSC

To determine the current wages and benefits at TSC, each team or the instructor will consult the *latest* available issue of *Employment and Earnings*[4] and determine the average hourly earnings for the retail trade, grocery stores. This amount will be the average hourly earning under the existing contract. For purposes of this simulation, assume that all the employees in the TSC bargaining unit are paid the same wage.

---

[4]Source: Employment and Earnings, Table heading: "Establishment Data, Hours and Earnings, Not Seasonally Adjusted Average Hours and Earnings of production or nonsupervisory workers . . . Subheading: Retail Trade . . . Food Stores, Grocery Stores."

Assume that TSC's average hourly earning is a median[5] for the industry. Assume that the dispersion of earnings in the industry is such that the highest-paid workers in the industry earn 20 percent above TSC's rate and the lowest-paid workers earn 20 percent below TSC's rate.

Employee benefits are assumed to be average for industry. This means that they constitute one-third of the total payroll cost. To calculate the total hourly payroll cost for TSC, simply multiply average hourly wage rate by 150 percent.

To compute the benefit cost, multiply the total hourly payroll cost by 33 percent. For example: (1) If the average hourly wage is $10.00, then the total hourly payroll cost is $15.00 ($10.00 × 150%); (2) benefits represent approximately one-third of $15.00 or $5.00 per hour ($15.00 × 33%) or 50% of $10.00 = $5.00.

To compute the total annual payroll cost of the existing contract, multiply the number of hours worked per year (2080) times the number of employees in the bargaining unit (1000) times the total hourly payroll cost, which consists of wages and fringe benefits (hourly wage rate times 150%).

You can calculate individual benefits by referring to the worksheet for the percentage represented by each. Vacations, in this example, would be 75 cents per hour (5% × $15.00), holidays would be about 45 cents per hour (3% × $15.00), and so on. Consider in your negotiations the roll-up effect.[6]

JOINT PRESS RELEASE

LABOR NEGOTIATIONS BEGIN AT TSC

Management negotiators for TSC and the NFEU representing TSC store employees opened contract negotiations today.

The representatives for both sides agreed to meet as frequently as necessary to reach a peaceful settlement by the expiration date of the current contract.

The company bargaining team includes the Director of Human Resources/Employee Relations, the Vice-President of Operations, the Division Controller, and the Administrative Assistant to the Director of Human Resources/Labor Relations. The union bargaining team includes the National Union Representative, the Local Union President, the Local Union Vice-President, Secretary/Treasurer, and the Local Vice-President and Chair of the Grievance Committee.

The commencement of bargaining between representatives of TSC and the Union began with this short press release.

PRELIMINARY AREAS OF AGREEMENT

The pace and intensity of negotiations have been gradually building. The early get-acquainted meetings of the first several weeks soon moved into more frequent, more intense working sessions in which the parties tackled a number of tough questions.

With tentative agreement slowly reached on many issues, including pensions and a two-year contract, both parties seemed to experience a psychological lift, and they pre-

---

[5]The median may be defined as the middle measure or middle item in a series in which all measures have been arranged in the order of their size.

[6]Roll up measures the impact of wage increases on costs of some wage-related fringe benefits.

pared for the bargaining over wages and benefits with a vigor not seen at the negotiating table for some weeks. A final, no-strike settlement was anticipated, but the more experienced negotiators knew that this momentum could be easily lost in the delicate process of maintaining a balance between arm's-length hard bargaining on purely economic issues, on the one hand, and good-faith efforts to solve mutual problems on the other. Good examples of each had been experienced, however, and the negotiators turned to the final economic issues with guarded optimism.

At the close of the last bargaining session, the company and the union representatives agreed to present their latest proposals at the next meeting. They also agreed not to negotiate over improvements of holidays and vacations for the first year of the contract. They enumerated the following items to be bargained over in future sessions:

Wages

Vendor Stocking

Union Shop and Checkoff (Union Security)

Management Rights

Technological Change(s)

Evening Premium

Night Shift Premium

Seniority

Store Closing(s)

Grievance and Arbitration Procedures

Union Cooperation

Establishment of a Joint Union-Management Committee

Holidays

Vacations

See the existing contract language and articles on the above items.

ROLE PROFILES

You may be expected to assume the role of one of the negotiators profiled below. In effect, what they have already done, you have done. What takes place next is up to you. In some instances, roles may be shared or modified, or new roles may be developed by the instructor.

Union—NFEU

National Union Representative

This role involves coordination of national and local issues. On the one hand, you are responsible to the National Headquarters of the NFEU for carrying out its objectives. In your role, you must consider the potential effect of this settlement on other contracts that the Union has negotiated and will be negotiating with this and with other companies. You must protect union resources from an unnecessary strike and preserve the National's influence on the Local. On the other hand, you must relate to the others on the bargaining team and through them to the membership of the Local. You must know and understand their priorities and respond to them if you can.

You must consider the division between wages and benefits because some in the unit (and even at the bargaining table) will disagree on the proper balance. Differences among your negotiators will require your utmost skill to bring about sufficient consensus to ultimately get the committee to recommend a tentative package to the membership for ratification.

You must constantly appear sufficiently aggressive to satisfy the more militant members of the union without unduly antagonizing the Director of Human Resources/Labor Relations.

Local Union President

This role involves a more specialized interest than that of the National Representative. You are elected by the membership of the Local and must necessarily satisfy that constituency. In cases where the interests of the Local and the national union headquarters are in conflict, your loyalty is to the local. You want a settlement that will satisfy the membership, and if you cannot obtain it, a strike may be acceptable. In that case, as you see it, your Local deserves strike benefits from the national union even if the strike fund is low. You feel your members have paid their dues for many years and have that support coming to them if they will need it. Nonetheless, you are seldom belligerent at the bargaining table and are glad to have the National Rep play the "heavy." You must preserve a decent working relationship with the Director of Human Resources/Labor Relations, with whom you will be dealing almost daily during the term of the new agreement.

You are ultimately responsible for approving all final proposals. You have to determine the Health and Welfare agenda. You also have to coordinate the tactics and strategy of the team.

Local Union Vice-President and Secretary/Treasurer

In this role, you work closely with the President. You are responsible for providing a financial analysis of different wage–fringe benefit packages under consideration. You assist the team in determining priorities and in formulating new and counterproposals.

You supply the team with all the necessary data and information. You are concerned about the financial state of your local. You collaborate with the Local President on bargaining tactics and strategy.

Local Vice-President and Chair of the Grievance Committee

This role involves keeping records of grievances and arbitration decisions. You are familiar with all complaints about the administration as well as about the content of the existing labor contract. You keep a log of employee concerns about working conditions and behavior of supervisors and of the policies of the company.

For bargaining purposes, you maintain a record of offers and counteroffers. You monitor the effectiveness of the current grievance procedure; you review every issue under consideration in terms of its potential for future grievances. You want the contract to be as explicit as possible in order to minimize future problems.

Company—TSC, Inc.

Director of Human Resources/Employee Relations

In this role, you have a responsibility to the company and to the employees. On the one hand, you must see to it that the contract is satisfactory to management in all functional areas, at the store as well as the corporate level. On the other hand, the settlement must be perceived as equitable by a majority of all employees.

You must ensure proper balance between wages and benefits. You must be sensitive to differences among your own negotiators and reconcile those differences. You also must be aware of differences among negotiators on the union side and not allow internal dissent to derail the overall objective of reaching a settlement.

You will be dealing with the union almost daily during the contract term and thus must behave in such a way as to maintain your credibility and retain the respect of the union representatives.

You accept the union's role as agent for the employees, but you bargain as hard as you can to achieve the company's objectives.

Vice-President of Operations

In this role, you are primarily interested in obtaining a settlement that provides you with maximum flexibility to manage the stores efficiently and cost-effectively. You are concerned with the following issues: tighter control over jobs and costs, amount of overtime, and level of discipline within the stores.

You are frustrated by the bargaining process and would like to conclude negotiations as quickly as possible, so you can get back to doing what you like best—managing stores.

Division Controller

In this role, you provide financial data and analyses to the Director of Human Resources/Labor Relations regarding different wage-benefit proposals considered by the parties. You are in charge of all costing calculations during negotiations. You consider the effect of economic data on as many issues as possible.

You are responsible for the allocation of funds for different expenditures within your division. For you the financial considerations are of primary importance; everything else is secondary. Keeping the cost structure in line with other divisions of the company is very important for you. Your expertise in administering cost control methods is highly respected by your colleagues.

Administrative Assistant to the Director of Human Resources/Labor Relations

In this role, you provide supportive data to the Director of Human Resources/Labor Relations. You maintain a record of offers and counteroffers. You collect, integrate, and distribute data required for formulation of tactics and strategies. You gather for the team information on wage rates, on current practices in the industry, and on recent economic developments. You also compare and contrast labor contracts in the industry and evaluate their significance for the current negotiations.

FORM I (CONFIDENTIAL)   Initial Demands, Offers, Priorities, and Expectations

(Provide copy to instructor before you start to negotiate.)

Priorities	Demands or Offers	Expectations	*Final Acceptable Contract Terms (your resistance points)*

List all team members: _____

Group: _____

PLEASE FILL OUT THIS FORM. To complete this form you can use additional pages. On this form you do not have to include proposed contract language. Agreed-upon and proposed contract language must be included with all your data submitted to your instructor at the end of your simulation.

FORM II Demands and/or Offers and Arguments Justifying Party's Positions	
Demands or Offers	*Arguments*

List all team members: _____

Group: _____

PLEASE COMPLETE THIS FORM.

FORM III   Opposition Demands and/or Offers and Arguments Justifying Opponent's Positions

Opposition Demands or Offers	*Revision of Demands*	*Arguments by Opposition*

List all team members: _____

Group: _____

PLEASE COMPLETE THIS FORM.

FORM IV (CONFIDENTIAL) Demands, Offers, Priorities, and Expectations

(Provide copy to instructor before your last session.)

Priorities	Demands or Offers	Expectations	Final Acceptable Contract Terms (your resistance points)

List all team members: _____

Group: _____

PLEASE COMPLETE THIS FORM.

INSTRUCTIONS FOR WORKSHEET A

1. Compute the hourly cost of each benefit.
2. Compute the total hourly wage and benefit costs (THWF).
3. Compute total annual cost of wages and benefits under the present contract.
   You can calculate total annual cost by multiplying total hourly compensation by 2080 hours by 1000 employees.
   Each 1 cent per hour equals $20,800 per year plus roll-up.

WORKSHEET A   Wages and Benefits

This worksheet is to be completed by each team. List all team members:

Current Average Hourly Wage $CAHW^1$ = Current Average Hourly Wage $ _____ /hour	CAHW _____ /×150% = THWF _____ CAHW = Current Average Hourly Wage THWF = Total Hourly Wage and Benefit Costs or Total Hourly Payroll Costs THWF _____ − CAHW _____ = _____ [2]

	A. Percentage of total base compensation spent on each fringe benefit		B. Total Hourly Payroll Cost (THWF or CAHW × 150%)[3]			C. Dollar cost, per hour, of various benefits[3]
	A	×	*B*	=		*C*
Holidays	3%	×	$ _____ /hr	=		$ _____
Vacations	5%	×	$ _____ /hr	=		$ _____
Other benefits: Medical insurance Pension Government payments Miscellaneous insurance	25.33%	×	$ _____ /hr	=		$ _____
TOTAL	33.33%	×	$ _____ /hr		TOTAL $ _____

The sum of this column equals 33.33% of the total hourly payroll cost.

Total Annual Cost (wages and benefits under current contract) =
THWF $ _____ /×2080 hours × 1000 workers = $[4] _____ /.

---

[1]The current hourly wage rate of TSC is the latest monthly average hourly earnings for food store nonsupervisory workers, published in the most recent available issues of *Employment and Earnings* (E&E); see E&E table heading: "Establishment Data Hours and Earnings. . . . Not seasonally adjusted average hours and earnings of production or nonsupervisory workers. . . ." Subheading: Retail Trade . . . Food Stores Grocery Stores. U.S. Department of Labor, Bureau of Labor Statistics. The current hourly wage at TSC represents approximately 67 percent of the total payroll dollar.

[2]Hourly cost of fringe benefits.

[3]See the preceding section titled "Current Wages and Benefits at TSC, Inc."; for example, if total hourly payroll cost is $15.00 ($10.00 × 150%), then holiday cost is $15.00 × 3%, or approximately 45 cents.

[4]This total does not include overtime, Sunday, holiday, evening and night shift premiums, and jury duty.

INSTRUCTIONS FOR FORMS V–XI

1. Summarize newly negotiated provisions, if any, of the ten contract clauses listed on Form IX.

2. Compute the hourly cost of *each* old benefit under the newly negotiated average hourly rate. (Form V, Worksheets 1 and 2 indicate higher costs of old fringes under the newly negotiated wage rate. The forms reflect the roll-up effect, which measures the impact of wage increases on cost of some wage-related fringe benefits. Form V, Worksheet 2 does not reflect costs of newly negotiated improvements in holidays and vacations, if any.)

3. Calculate hourly wage, cost-of-living, and fringe benefit increases for each year of the newly negotiated contract.

4. Calculate the average hourly cost-of-wage, cost-of-living, and fringe benefit increases over the life of the contract.

5. Compute the average annual total cost of your new contract.

6. Compute the annual cost-of-wage, cost-of-living, and fringe benefit increases. Do it for each year of your newly negotiated contract.

7. Calculate the total percentage increases of wages, cost of living, and fringe benefits for each year of your contract.

8. Complete Forms V through XI.

FORM V, WORKSHEET I Wages and Benefits

This worksheet is to be completed by each team. List all team members:

Wages
1st Year of Contract
NNAHW = Newly Negotiated
Average Hourly Wage
$ _____ /hour

NNAHW _____ /× 150% = THWF _____
NNAHW = Newly Negotiated Average Hourly Wage at TSC
THWF = Total Hourly Wage and Fringe Benefit Costs or
Total Hourly Payroll Cost

THWF $ _____ − NNAHW $ _____ = _____ = [1]
Hourly Cost of Fringe Benefits

	A. Percentage of total base compensation (under old contract) spent on each fringe benefit	B. Total Hourly Payroll Cost (THWF or NNAHW × 150%[2])	C. Hourly dollar cost of various existing fringe benefits under the newly negotiated wage rate[3]	D. Hourly dollar cost of various existing fringe benefits under the old contract (from Worksheet A)	E. Increased hourly dollar cost of various existing fringe benefits under the newly negotiated wage rate $C − D = E.$
	A	B	C	D	E
Holidays	3%	× _____ = $ _____ /hr	= $ _____	_____	_____
Vacations	5%	× _____ = $ _____ /hr	= $ _____	_____	_____
Other fringe benefits: Medical insurance Pension Government payments Miscellaneous insurance	25.33%	× _____ = $ _____ /hr	= $ _____	_____	_____
TOTAL	33.33%	× _____ = $ _____ /hr	= $ _____	_____	_____

Total annual cost (wages and existing fringes 1st year of contract) =
THWF $ _____ /× 2080 hours × 1000 workers = $ _____ /.

[1] THWF − NNAHW = Hourly cost of fringe benefits, first year of contract. For example, if NNAHW were $10.00 and THWF were $15.00 ($10.00 × 150%), hourly cost of fringe benefits would be $5.00 ($15.00 − $10.00 = $5.00).

[2] See the section titled "Current Wages and Benefits at TSC, Inc."

[3] The dollar cost covers only the cost of old fringes under the newly negotiated wage rate. The parties agreed not to negotiate over improvements of holidays and vacations for the first year of the contract. The sum of this column equals 33.33% of the total hourly payroll cost.

FORM V, WORKSHEET 2 Wages and Benefits

This worksheet is to be completed by each team. List all team members:

Wages
Second Year of Contract
NNAHW = Newly Negotiated Average Hourly Wage
$ _____ /hour

NNAHW _____ / × 150% = THWF _____
NNAHW = Newly Negotiated Average Hourly Wage at TSC
THWF = Total Hourly Wage and Fringe Benefit Costs or Total Hourly Payroll Cost

THWF $ _____ − NNAHW $ _____ = _____ [1]
Hourly Cost of Fringe Benefits

	A. Percentage of total base compensation (under old contract) spent on each fringe benefit		B. Total Hourly Payroll Cost (THWF or NNAHW × 150%[2])		C. Hourly dollar cost of various existing fringe benefits under the newly negotiated wage rate[3]		D. Hourly dollar cost of various existing fringe benefits under the first year of the contract (from Form V, Worksheet 1)	E. Increased hourly dollar cost of various existing fringe benefits under the newly negotiated wage rate $C - D = E$
	A		B		C		D	E
Holidays	3%	×	$ _____ /hr	=	$ _____	=	_____	_____
Vacations	5%	×	$ _____ /hr	=	$ _____	=	_____	_____
Other fringe benefits:	25.33%	×	$ _____ /hr	=	$ _____	=	_____	_____
Medical insurance								
Pension								
Government payments								
Miscellaneous insurance								
TOTAL	33.33%	×	$ _____ /hr	=	$ _____			

Total annual cost (wages and existing fringes) under second year of contract =
THWF $ _____ /× 2080 hours × 1000 workers = $ _____ /.

---

[1] THWF − NNAHW = Hourly cost of fringe benefits. For example, if NNAHW were $10.00 and THWF were $15.00 ($10.00 × 150%), hourly cost of fringe benefits would be $5.00 ($15.00 − $10.00 = $5.00).

[2] See the section titled "Current Wages and Benefits at TSC, Inc."

[3] Improvements in fringe benefits negotiated under the new contract (if any) are not included in this particular calculation. The dollar cost covers only the higher cost of old fringes under the newly negotiated wage rate. This is the roll-up effect.

FORM V, WORKSHEET 3 Computation of Newly Negotiated Hourly Holiday Costs, If Any

This worksheet is to be completed by each team. List all team members:

_____

The parties agreed not to negotiate over improvements of holidays for the first year of the contract. Increased costs of holidays for the first year of the contract as shown on Form V, Worksheet 1 and on Form V, Worksheet 2 for the second year of the contract are entirely the result of the roll-up effect.[1]

Indicate number of newly negotiated additional holiday hours if any _____ .

Total Annual Cost (TAC[2])

Number of Employees[3]	$\times$	NNAHW[4] as per Form V, Worksheet 2	$\times$	Newly[5] Negotiated Holiday Hours	=	Total Annual Cost for All Employees (TAC[2])
_____	$\times$	_____	$\times$	_____	=	_____

Example

1000 employees[3]	$\times$	\$10.00[4]	$\times$	16[5]	=	\$160,000 (TAC[2])

Average Annual Hourly Cost of Newly Negotiated Holiday Hours, in Cents per Hour (HCNNH[5])

$$\frac{TAC^2}{Hours^7 \times Employees^3} = HCNNH^6 \underline{\hspace{3cm}}$$

Example

$$\frac{160{,}000^2}{2080^7 \times 1000^3} = 0.077^6$$

---

[1]Roll-up measures the impact of wage increases on costs of some wage-related fringe benefits.

[2]Total annual cost of newly negotiated holidays for all employees (TAC).

[3]Assume that there are 1000 employees.

[4]Newly Negotiated Average Hourly Wage (NNAHW), as per Form V, Worksheet 2; for purposes of example assume \$10.00. Although in our examples we used NNAHW totals, an argument can be made for using Total Hourly Wage and Fringe Benefits Costs (THWF) since cost of holiday pay includes cost of fringe benefits. Both sides will compute the cost of any new holidays, if any, on the basis of any agreed-upon method. Your team must negotiate whether to apply to holiday costing the NNAHW or the THWF method.

[5]Newly negotiated paid holiday hours; for purposes of example assume 16 hours.

[6]Average annual hourly cost of newly negotiated holiday hours, in cents per hour (HCNNH).

[7]Assume that each employee works 2080 hours per year.

FORM V, WORKSHEET 4   Computation of Newly Negotiated Hourly Vacation Costs, If Any[1]

This worksheet is to be completed by each team. List all team members:

_____

The parties agreed not to negotiate over improvements of vacations for the first year of the contract. Increased costs of vacations for the first year of the contract as shown on Form V, Worksheet 1 and on Form V, Worksheet 2 for the second year of the contract are entirely the result of the roll-up effect.[2]

100 employees with less than 1 year of service	Newly negotiated vacation days	8 hours per day	NNAHW	Increased annual cost of vacation for employees with less than 1 year of service.
_____ ×	_____ ×	_____ ×	_____ =	_____
50 employees with 1–3 years of service	Newly negotiated vacation days	8 hours per day	NNAHW	Increased annual cost of vacation for employees with 1–3 years of service.
_____ ×	_____ ×	_____ ×	_____ =	_____
150 employees with 3–5 years of service	Newly negotiated vacation days	8 hours per day	NNAHW	Increased annual cost of vacation for employees with 3–5 years of service.
_____ ×	_____ ×	_____ ×	_____ =	_____
350 employees with 5–10 years of service	Newly negotiated vacation days	8 hours per day	NNAHW	Increased annual cost of vacation for employees with 5–10 years of service.
_____ ×	_____ ×	_____ ×	_____ =	_____
100 employees with 10–15 years of service	Newly negotiated vacation days	8 hours per day	NNAHW	Increased annual cost of vacation for employees with 10–15 years of service.
_____ ×	_____ ×	_____ ×	_____ =	_____
100 employees with 15–20 years of service	Newly negotiated vacation days	8 hours per day	NNAHW	Increased annual cost of vacation for employees with 15–20 years of service.
_____ ×	_____ ×	_____ ×	_____ =	_____
50 employees with 20–25 years of service	Newly negotiated vacation days	8 hours per day	NNAHW	Increased annual cost of vacation for employees with 20–25 years of service.
_____ ×	_____ ×	_____ ×	_____ =	_____
100 employees with over 25 years of service	Newly negotiated vacation days	8 hours per day	NNAHW	Increased annual cost of vacation for employees with over 25 years of service.
_____ ×	_____ ×	_____ ×	_____ =	_____

FORM V, WORKSHEET 4 Computation of Newly Negotiated Hourly Vacation Costs, If Any[1] (Cont.)

This worksheet is to be completed by each team. List all team members:

Total Annual Cost of newly negotiated vacations (TACV)[3] = _____

$$\frac{\text{TACV}}{2080^{[4]} \times 1000^{[5]}} = \underline{\hspace{3cm}} = \text{Average Annual Hourly Cost of Newly Negotiated Vacations per Employee, in Cents per Hour (HCNNV}^{[6]})$$

For example,

350 employees[7]	×	5[8]	×	8[9]	×	$10.00[10]	=	$140,000
100 employees[7]	×	5[8]	×	8[9]	×	$10.00[10]	=	$ 40,000

Total annual cost of newly negotiated vacations for employees with 5 to 10 years and those with 15 to 20 years of service $180,000[11]

$$\frac{\text{(TACV) }\$180,000^{[5]}}{2080^{[4]} \times 1000^{[5]}} = 0.086^{[6]} \text{ (HCNNV}^{[6]})$$

[1]You can calculate additional vacation days by computing additional negotiated vacation days for each group of employees classified by years of continuing service. Multiply the number of employees in the group given the additional vacation days by the number of such additional days. Number of additional days for all groups are to be totalled; e.g., if employees with 20 to 25 years of service get an additional 5 days of vacation per year, and there are 250 employees in this group and those over 25 years of service get an additional 5 days per year and there are 200 employees in this group, and the other groups do not get any improvements in vacation, then the total number of additional vacation days is 2250 [(250 × 5) + (200 × 5)]. 2250 vacation days × 8 hours = 18,000 Newly Negotiated Vacation Hours (NNVH). To obtain total cost of NNVH, multiply hours times NNAHW[10] Although in our examples we used NNAHW totals, an argument can be made for using Total Hourly Wage and Fringe Benefits Costs (THWF) since cost of vacation pay includes cost of fringe benefits. Whether to apply to vacation costing the NNAHW or the THWF method is subject to negotiations. Both sides will compute the costs of any new vacation days, if any, on the basis of any agreed-upon method.

[2]Roll-up measures the impact of wage increases on costs of some wage-related fringe benefits.

[3]Total Annual Cost of Newly Negotiated Vacations (TACV).

[4]Assume that each employee works 2080 hours per year.

[5]Assume 1000 employees in the bargaining unit.

[6]Average Annual Hourly Cost of Newly Negotiated Vacations in cents per hour (HCNNV).

[7]Number of employees affected, according to years of continuing service.

[8]Newly Negotiated Vacation Days; assume 5 days

[9]Assume each vacation day is equal to 8 hours.

[10]Newly Negotiated Average Hourly Wage (NNAHW); assume $10.00

[11]Total Annual Cost of Newly Negotiated Vacations for two groups of affected employees.

FORM V, WORKSHEET 5

This worksheet is to be completed by each team. List all team members:

	A^1		B^2		C^3		D^4
	Hourly Increases First Year of Contract		Cost of First-Year Increases over a Two-Year Contract $A^1 + A^1 = B^2$		Hourly Increases Second Year of Contract		Total Hourly Increases for Full Term of Contract (THIFTC) $B^2 + C^3 = D^4$
Hourly wage increases[5]	$_____	$\times 2^6=$ $_____		+ _____		= _____
Hourly cost increases of all existing fringe benefits under the newly negotiated wage rate from Form V, Worksheets 1 and 2	$_____	$\times 2^6=$ $_____		+ _____		= _____
Hourly cost of cost-of-living adjustments, if any	$_____	$\times 2^6=$ $_____		+ _____		= _____
Hourly cost of newly negotiated improvements in holidays, if any; see Form V, Worksheet 3	(na)		(na)		_____		= _____
Hourly cost of newly negotiated improvements in vacations, if any; see Form V, Worksheet 4	(na)		(na)		_____		= _____
Total hourly wage, cost-of-living and fringe benefit increases	$_____	$\times 2^6=$ $_____		+ $ _____		= THIFTC $ _____

[1]Hourly increases first year of contract (A^1).

[2]Cost of first-year increases over a two-year contract (B^2).

[3]Hourly increases second year of contract (C^3).

[4]Total hourly increases for full term of contract (THIFTC) $B + C = D$.

[5]To calculate the negotiated hourly wage increase of the 1st year of your contract, subtract the originally hourly wage (as per Worksheet A) from the newly negotiated hourly wage of your 1st-year contract (as per Form V, Worksheet 1). To calculate the negotiated hourly wage increase of the 2nd year of your contract, subtract the 1st-year negotiated hourly wage (as per Form V, Worksheet 1) from the negotiated hourly wage of your 2nd-year contract (as per Form V, Worksheet 2).

[6]First-year increases over a two-year contract. If a two-year contract provides for the following increases: $0.71 per hour 1st year, $1.32 per hour 2nd year, then the cost for the first year is $0.71 per hour, and for the 2nd year it is $2.03 ($1.32 + 0.71), and the total hourly increase for the two-year contract is $2.74 = (0.71 + 0.71 + $1.32) = ($A^1 + A^1 + C^3 = D^4$) or ($B^2 + C^3 = D^4$). The total hourly increases for the two-year contract are: $D^4 = \$2.74$ (cost of first-year increases over a two-year contract, $1.42, B^2) plus (hourly increases of second year of contract, $1.32, C^3) = $B^2 + C^3 = D^4 = \$1.42 + \$1.32 = \$2.74$. (The above example does not include any new fringe benefit increases, if any, of a two-year contract.)

FORM VI

This worksheet is to be completed by each team. List all team members:

_____

Calculate the average hourly cost of a wage, cost-of-living, and fringe benefit increase over the life of this contract.

To compute the average hourly cost of a wage, cost-of-living, and fringe benefit increase of a multiyear contract, arrive at the total hourly increase over the life of the new contract and then divide this sum by the length of the contract. *Source:* Form V, Worksheet 5.

If per-hour wage, cost-of-living, and fringe benefit increase of two-year contract is THIFTC* and the contract is in effect for *n* years, then the average annual hourly cost of wage, cost-of-living and benefit increase per year is THIFTC/*n*.

THIFTC* from Worksheet 5 $ _____ ÷2 = _____ = AC**

For example, assume a per-hour wage, COLA, and fringe benefit increase of $2.74 over a two-year contract.

$$\frac{\$2.74}{2 \text{ years}} = \$1.37 = \text{average annual hourly cost of wage, COLA, and fringe benefit increase} = AC**$$

To compute the average annual total cost increase of your new contract, multiply number of hours by number of employees by average hourly cost of wage, cost-of-living, and fringe benefit increase over the life of a two-year contract.

For example, number of hours worked per year (2080) × number of employees (1000) × average hourly cost of wage, cost-of-living, and benefit increase over life of two-year contract (assume for purposes of example $1.37):

2080 × 1000 × $1.37 = $2,849,600 = annual total cost of a new contract.

Compute the average annual total cost of your new contract.

D Number of hours worked per year		*E* Number of employees		*F* Average annual hourly cost of wage, cost-of-living, and benefit increase over life of a two-year contract		*G* Annual total cost increase of the new contract $(D) \times (E) \times (F) = G$
2080	×	1000	×	_____	=	_____

*THIFTC (see Worksheet 5) = total hourly increases for the full term of the contract.

**Average hourly cost of wage, cost-of-living, and benefit increase per year (AC).

FORM VII

This form is to be completed by each team. List all team members:

_____

Compute your cost increases for first and second years of contract.

_____

First year contract[1]

H		I		J		K[2]
Total hourly wage,[2] cost-of-living, and fringe benefit increases		Number of hours worked per year		Number of employees		Annual cost increases $H \times I \times J = K$
_____	×	2080	×	1000	=	_____

Second year of contract[3]

L		M		N		O
Total hourly wage,[2] cost-of-living, and fringe benefit increases		Number of hours worked per year		Number of employees		Annual cost increase $L \times M \times N = O$
_____	×	2080	×	1000	=	_____

Calculate your annual percentage increases for each year of the newly negotiated contract.

For example: If annual cost increase is $2 million and the old total annual cost was $40 million, then the percentage increase is 5 percent.

$$\frac{2 \text{ million}}{40 \text{ million}} \times 100 = 5\%$$

We multiply by 100 in order to express the result as a percentage.

$$\frac{\text{1st - year annual cost increase}[1](\qquad)}{\text{Annual cost of old contract}[4](\qquad)} \times 100 = \text{Annual percentage increase of 1st-year contract}$$

$$\frac{\text{2nd - year annual cost increase}[3](\qquad)}{\text{Total annual cost of 1st - year contract}[5](\qquad)} \times 100 = \text{Annual percentage increase of 2nd-year contract}$$

X		Y		Z		
Annual percentage increase of 1st-year contract		Annual percentage increase of 2nd-year contract		Total percentage increase of a two-year contract		Average percentage increase of a two-year contract
_____	+	_____	=	_____	÷ 2 =	_____

[1]First year of contract, annual cost increase, $H \times I \times J = K$.

[2]*Source:* Form V, Worksheet 5.

[3]Second year of contract, annual cost increase, $L \times M \times N = O$.

[4]*Source:* Worksheet A. To compute the total annual payroll cost of the existing contract, multiply the number of hours worked per year (2080) times the number of employees in the bargaining unit (1000) times the total hourly payroll cost, which consists of wages and fringe benefits (hourly wage rate times 150%).

[5]*Source:* Worksheet 1.

FORM VIII   Summary of Forms V–VII

This form is to be completed by each team. List all team members:

_____

First Year of Contract; Source: Form V, Worksheet 1

Newly negotiated average hourly wage _____

Increased hourly cost of all existing fringe benefits under the newly negotiated wage rate _____

Total annual cost of the first year of contract _____

Second Year of Contract: Source: Form V, Worksheet 2

Newly negotiated average hourly wage _____

Increased hourly cost of all *existing* fringe benefits under the newly negotiated wage rate _____

Annual cost of second year of contract (wages and *existing* fringes): does not include cost of any newly negotiated fringes _____

Holiday Data, Source: Form V, Worksheet 3

Number of newly negotiated holidays, if any _____

Total annual cost of newly negotiated holidays, if any _____

Vacation Data: Source: Form V, Worksheet 4

Increased annual cost of vacations for all employees, if any _____

Number of newly negotiated vacation days, and weeks if any:

Vacation weeks: _____

Vacation days: _____

Form V, Worksheet 5, Column D

Total hourly wage increases for the full term of the contract _____

Total hourly increases of all *existing* fringe benefits for the full term of the contract _____

Total hourly cost of newly negotiated improvements in holidays, if any _____

Total hourly cost-of-living adjustments, if any _____

Total hourly cost of newly negotiated improvements in vacations, if any _____

Total hourly wage, COLA, and fringe benefit increases for the full term of the contract _____

From Form VII

Annual percentage increase of first year of contract _____

Annual percentage increase of second year of contract _____

At the conclusion of negotiations, this form is to be completed by each team. Indicate with an "X" your opinion of the final contract terms for the following: coverage vendor stocking, union security, management rights, technological change, evening premium, night shift premium, seniority, store closing, grievance and arbitration procedure, labor-management committee.

List all team members:

FORM IX Final Contract Terms						
	Coverage Vendor Stocking	*Union Security*	*Management Rights*	*Technological Change*	*Evening Premium*	*Night Shift Premium*
No Change of Existing Clause						
Existing Clause Has Been Revised; Explain						
New Clause Favors Management						
New Clause Strongly Favors Management						
New Clause Favors Union						
New Clause Strongly Favors Union						

	Seniority	*Store Closing*	*Grievance and Arbitration Procedure*	*Labor-Management Committee*
No Change of Existing Clause				
Existing Clause Has Been Revised; Explain				
New Clause Favors Management				
New Clause Strongly Favors Management				
New Clause Favors Union				
New Clause Strongly Favors Union				

On a separate page you are required to provide a rationale for your rating of any of the above contract clauses as either favorable to the union or to the management side; also provide the text of the above newly negotiated clauses, if any.

FORM X (CONFIDENTIAL) Individual Evaluation Form

Name _____

A confidential evaluation of your team members and your opponents is to be provided to your instructor at the end of the simulation.

Please use a separate sheet to evaluate each member of the management and the union teams. In your evaluation, apply the criteria and use the format shown below. To each criterion, respond in a very brief separate paragraph, consisting of one or more short sentences. Also assign for each criterion a letter grade on a scale of A through F. No grade is necessary for evaluating weaknesses and strengths.

Individual Evaluation Form—Confidential

Name of person being evaluated: _____

Team no. _____

Union or Management _____

Criterion	Letter Grade	Comment
Effectiveness	_____	_____
Contributions/ preparations	_____	_____
Weaknesses	Describe	_____
Strengths	Describe	_____
Cooperation	_____	_____
Leadership	_____	_____
Initiative	_____	_____
Grasp of issues	_____	_____
Overall evaluations	_____	_____

FORM XI   Individual Evaluation of This Simulation

An individual evaluation is to be submitted to your instructor at the end of the simulation.

Please evaluate the following elements of the simulation:

Content of contract articles over which you had to negotiate

Confidential simulation instructions

Costing forms

Amount of time allocated for negotiations

Final debriefing

Please comment on the following:

Weaknesses of the simulation

Strengths of the simulation

Any suggestions for change

Any other comments

STATEMENT OF CONTRIBUTIONS

Each Union and Management team must provide a very brief, jointly prepared statement listing *specific* contributions of each team member (e.g., Worksheet IV was prepared by Mr./Ms. X; library research on the following topics was compiled by Mr./Ms. Y). The statement of contributions should be inserted in the front part of the final binder to be submitted to your instructor.

FINAL INSTRUCTIONS

At the conclusion of negotiations, your team is to provide your instructor with all the materials and forms as per the "Simulation Instructions" provided at the beginning of this exercise.

DEBRIEFING

At the conclusion of the simulation, all teams will meet in class for a debriefing session. Following are the questions to be addressed.

1. How did the negotiations start?
2. How did the beginning of the negotiations affect later stages?
3. How were the tone and climate of the negotiations affected by your statements and the other side's statements?
4. How successful were you in achieving your original goals?
5. What worked well and why? What appeared to be effective?
6. What might you do differently next time?
7. How did the personalities of your teammates influence the negotiations?
8. How did the personalities and behavior of your opponents influence the negotiations?
9. What comments do you have about working jointly as a team?
10. Describe any intraorganizational bargaining.
11. What were some of the tactics and strategies, if any, used by your team?
12. How successful were your tactics and strategies?
13. If you had to conduct these negotiations again, would you change your tactics and strategies? How?
14. Did the other side apply any tactics? If yes, did you see through their tactics? How did you respond?
15. Which contract terms were most difficult to negotiate? Why?
16. Evaluate the strengths and weaknesses of your team and of your opponents' team.
17. Discuss mistakes made by your team and by your opposition.
18. How did the magnitude and frequency of concessions by your opposition—from their initial position—influence your bargaining behavior?
19. Was communication clear?
20. Was there any miscommunication?
21. How much did you disclose? Comment on openness versus disclosure.
22. Evaluate the impact of time pressures and deadlines on your team members and on your opponents' behavior, particularly during the last 30 minutes of negotiations.
23. What, if anything, surprised you? Did you appear surprised?
24. Were you satisfied with the outcome?

Evaluation Forms

To be completed by each participant
Group _____
Your name _____
Role _____

1. How effectively do you think your group functioned in this simulation?
   - ☐ very effectively
   - ☐ effectively
   - ☐ not very effectively
   - ☐ ineffectively

   Why?

2. What contributed most toward the effectiveness of your group?

3. What most inhibited the effectiveness of your group?

4. How would you evaluate your overall contribution to the effectiveness of your group?
   - ☐ substantial
   - ☐ above average
   - ☐ average
   - ☐ below average

5. How could you have made a greater contribution?

6. How effectively did you carry out your assigned role:
   (a) during the process when your group was establishing its initial demands/offer?
   - ☐ very effectively
   - ☐ effectively
   - ☐ not very effectively
   - ☐ ineffectively

   Why?

   (b) during the process of negotiations?
   - ☐ very effectively
   - ☐ effectively
   - ☐ not very effectively
   - ☐ ineffectively

   Why?

(c) during the process of concluding a settlement?

      ☐ very effectively
      ☐ effectively
      ☐ not very effectively
      ☐ ineffectively

Why?

7. How satisfied were you with the final outcome?

      ☐ very satisfied
      ☐ satisfied
      ☐ not very satisfied
      ☐ dissatisfied

Why?

FORM B Evaluating the Process of Negotiations: Rate Your Group

To be completed by each participant

Group _____

Your name _____

Role _____

Rate your group as it functioned during the three major elements of negotiations. In each case, mark the line at the point that you feel best describes the group.

I. Process of Establishing Initial Demands/Offer

Cooperativeness within group

5	4	3	2	1
high degree	above average	average	below average	low degree

Tolerance of individual roles and views

5	4	3	2	1
high degree	above average	average	below average	low degree

General agreement on strategy

5	4	3	2	1
high degree	above average	average	below average	low degree

General agreement on demands/offer

5	4	3	2	1
high degree	above average	average	below average	low degree

General willingness to accept leadership

5	4	3	2	1
high degree	above average	average	below average	low degree

II. Process of Negotiations

Outside preparation by individuals constituting the group

5	4	3	2	1
high degree	above average	average	below average	low degree

Persuasiveness in presenting positions

5	4	3	2	1
high degree	above average	average	below average	low degree

Effectiveness of counterarguments to opposition arguments

5	4	3	2	1
high degree	above average	average	below average	low degree

Grasp of the issues

5	4	3	2	1
high degree	above average	average	below average	low degree

Group's utilization of original strategy

5	4	3	2	1
high degree	above average	average	below average	low degree

Group's ability to adapt strategy to changing situation

5	4	3	2	1
high degree	above average	average	below average	low degree

Group's internal cohesiveness

5	4	3	2	1
high degree	above average	average	below average	low degree

Group's willingness to accept leadership

5	4	3	2	1
high degree	above average	average	below average	low degree

Group's inclination to compromise individual roles to advance the total group

5	4	3	2	1
high degree	above average	average	below average	low degree

III. Process of Concluding Negotiations

Final willingness of group to compromise individual goals for group goals

5	4	3	2	1
high degree	above average	average	below average	low degree

Final willingness of group to compromise group goals to obtain a settlement

5	4	3	2	1
high degree	above average	average	below average	low degree

Group's agreement on terms of the settlement

5	4	3	2	1
high degree	above average	average	below average	low degree

Group's satisfaction with final settlement

5	4	3	2	1
high degree	above average	average	below average	low degree

General satisfaction of individuals with final settlement

5	4	3	2	1
high degree	above average	average	below average	low degree

FORM C Evaluating Opponent's Group Behavior and Effectiveness

To be completed by each participant

Group _____

Your name _____

Role _____

1. How effectively do you think your opponent's group functioned in this simulation?

☐ very effectively
☐ effectively
☐ not very effectively
☐ ineffectively

Why?

2. In your view, what contributed most toward the effectiveness of your opponent's group?

3. In your view, what most inhibited the effectiveness of your opponent's group?

FORM D Evaluating the Process of Negotiations: Rate Your Opponent's Group

To be completed by each participant
Group _____
Your name _____
Role _____

Rate your opponent's group as it functioned during negotiations. In each case, mark the line at the point that you feel best describes the group.

I. Process of Negotiations

Cooperativeness within group

5	4	3	2	1
high degree	above average	average	below average	low degree

Tolerance of individual roles and views

5	4	3	2	1
high degree	above average	average	below average	low degree

Persuasiveness in presenting positions

5	4	3	2	1
high degree	above average	average	below average	low degree

Effectiveness of counterarguments to your group's arguments

5	4	3	2	1
high degree	above average	average	below average	low degree

Grasp of the issues

5	4	3	2	1
high degree	above average	average	below average	low degree

Group's ability to adapt strategy to changing situations

5	4	3	2	1
high degree	above average	average	below average	low degree

Group's internal cohesiveness

5	4	3	2	1
high degree	above average	average	below average	low degree

Group's willingness to accept leadership

5 high degree	4 above average	3 average	2 below average	1 low degree

Group's inclination to compromise individual roles to advance the total group

5 high degree	4 above average	3 average	2 below average	1 low degree

Group's agreement on terms of the settlement

5 high degree	4 above average	3 average	2 below average	1 low degree

Team Composition Forms

Team I	
Company	*Union*
Director of Human Resources/Employee Relations	National Union Representative
_____	_____
Vice-President of Operations	Local Union President
_____	_____
Division Controller	Local Vice-President and Secretary/Treasurer
_____	_____
Administrative Assistant to the Director of Human Resources/Labor Relations	Local Vice-President and Chair of the Grievance Committee
_____	_____

Team II	
Company	*Union*
Director of Human Resources/Employee Relations	National Union Representative
_____	_____
Vice-President of Operations	Local Union President
_____	_____
Division Controller	Local Vice-President and Secretary/Treasurer
_____	_____
Administrative Assistant to the Director of Human Resources/Labor Relations	Local Vice-President and Chair of the Grievance Committee
_____	_____

Team III	
Company	*Union*
Director of Human Resources/Employee Relations	National Union Representative
_____	_____
Vice-President of Operations	Local Union President
_____	_____
Division Controller	Local Vice-President and Secretary/Treasurer
_____	_____
Administrative Assistant to the Director of Human Resources/Labor Relations	Local Vice-President and Chair of the Grievance Committee
_____	_____

*In some instances, roles may be shared or modified, or new roles may be developed by the instructor.

Texts of Statutes

NATIONAL LABOR RELATIONS ACT

Also cited NLRA or the Act; 29 U.S.C. §§151–169

[Title 29, Chapter 7, Subchapter II, United States Code]

FINDINGS AND POLICIES

Section 1. [§151.] The denial by some employers of the right of employees to organize and the refusal by some employers to accept the procedure of collective bargaining lead to strikes and other forms of industrial strife or unrest, which have the intent or the necessary effect of burdening or obstructing commerce by (a) impairing the efficiency, safety, or operation of the instrumentalities of commerce; (b) occurring in the current of commerce; (c) materially affecting, restraining, or controlling the flow of raw materials or manufactured or processed goods from or into the channels of commerce, or the prices of such materials or goods in commerce; or (d) causing diminution of employment and wages in such volume as substantially to impair or disrupt the market for goods flowing from or into the channels of commerce.

The inequality of bargaining power between employees who do not possess full freedom of association or actual liberty of contract and employers who are organized in the corporate or other forms of ownership association substantially burdens and affects the flow of commerce, and tends to aggravate recurrent business depressions, by depressing wage rates and the purchasing power of wage earners in industry and by preventing the stabilization of competitive wage rates and working conditions within and between industries.

Experience has proved that protection by law of the right of employees to organize and bargain collectively safeguards commerce from injury, impairment, or interruption, and promotes the flow of commerce by removing certain recognized sources of industrial strife and unrest, by encouraging practices fundamental to the friendly adjustment of industrial disputes arising out of differences as to wages, hours, or other working conditions, and by restoring equality of bargaining power between employers and employees.

Experience has further demonstrated that certain practices by some labor organizations, their officers, and members have the intent or the necessary effect of burdening or obstructing commerce by preventing the free flow of goods in such commerce through strikes and other forms of industrial unrest or through concerted activities which impair the interest of the public in the free flow of such commerce. The elimination of such practices is a necessary condition to the assurance of the rights herein guaranteed.

It is declared to be the policy of the United States to eliminate the causes of certain substantial obstructions to the free flow of commerce and to mitigate and eliminate these obstructions when they have occurred by encouraging the practice and procedure of collective bargaining and by protecting the exercise by workers of full freedom of association, self-organization, and designation of representatives of their own choosing, for the purpose of negotiating the terms and conditions of their employment or other mutual aid or protection.

DEFINITIONS

Sec. 2. [§152.] When used in this Act [subchapter]—

(1) The term "person" includes one or more individuals, labor organizations, partnerships, associations, corporations, legal representatives, trustees, trustees in cases under title 11 of the United States Code [under title 11], or receivers.

(2) The term "employer" includes any person acting as an agent of an employer, directly or indirectly, but shall not include the United States or any wholly owned Government corporation, or any Federal Reserve Bank, or any State or political subdivision thereof, or any person subject to the Railway Labor Act [45 U.S.C. §151 et seq.], as amended from time to time, or any labor organization (other than when acting as an employer), or anyone acting in the capacity of officer or agent of such labor organization.

[Pub. L. 93–360, §1(a), July 26, 1974, 88 Stat. 395, deleted the phrase "or any corporation or association operating a hospital, if no part of the net earnings inures to the benefit of any private shareholder or individual" from the definition of "employer."]

(3) The term "employee" shall include any employee, and shall not be limited to the employees of a particular employer, unless the Act [this subchapter] explicitly states otherwise, and shall include any individual whose work has ceased as a consequence of, or in connection with, any current labor dispute or because of any unfair labor practice, and who has not obtained any other regular and substantially equivalent employment, but shall not include any individual employed as an agricultural laborer, or in the domestic service of any family or person at his home, or any individual employed by his parent or spouse, or any individual having the status of an independent contractor, or any individual employed as a supervisor, or any individual employed by an employer subject to the Railway Labor Act [45 U.S.C. §151 et seq.], as amended from time to time, or by any other person who is not an employer as herein defined.

(4) The term "representatives" includes any individual or labor organization.

(5) The term "labor organization" means any organization of any kind, or any agency or employee representation committee or plan, in which employees participate and which exists for the purpose, in whole or in part, of dealing with employers concerning grievances, labor disputes, wages, rates of pay, hours of employment, or conditions of work.

(6) The term "commerce" means trade, traffic, commerce, transportation or communication among the several States, or between the District of Columbia or any Territory of the United States and any State or other Territory, or between any foreign country and any State, Territory, or the District of Columbia, or within the District of Columbia or any Territory, or between points in the same State but through any other State or any Territory or the District of Columbia or any foreign country.

(7) The term "affecting commerce" means in commerce, or burdening or obstructing commerce or the free flow of commerce, or having led or tending to lead to a labor dispute burdening or obstructing commerce or the free flow of commerce.

(8) The term "unfair labor practice" means any unfair labor practice listed in section 8 [section 158 of this title].

(9) The term "labor dispute" includes any controversy concerning term, tenure or conditions of employment, or concerning the association or representation of persons in negotiating, fixing, maintaining, changing, or seeking to arrange terms or conditions of employment, regardless of whether the disputants stand in the proximate relation of employer and employee.

(10) The term "National Labor Relations Board" means the National Labor Relations Board provided for in section 3 of this Act [section 153 of this title].

(11) The term "supervisor" means any individual having authority, in the interest of the employer, to hire, transfer, suspend, lay off, recall, promote, discharge, assign, reward, or discipline other employees, or responsibly to direct them, or to adjust their grievances, or effectively to recommend such action, if in connection with the foregoing the exercise of such authority is not of a merely routine or clerical nature, but requires the use of independent judgment.

(12) The term "professional employee" means—

(a) any employee engaged in work (i) predominantly intellectual and varied in character as opposed to routine mental, manual, mechanical, or physical work; (ii) involving the consistent exercise of discretion and judgment in its performance; (iii) of such a character that the output produced or the result accomplished cannot be standardized in relation to a given period of time; (iv) requiring knowledge of an advanced type in a field of science or learning customarily acquired by a prolonged course of specialized intellectual instruction and study in an institution of higher learning or a hospital, as distinguished from a general academic education or from an apprenticeship or from training in the performance of routine mental, manual, or physical processes; or

(b) any employee, who (i) has completed the courses of specialized intellectual instruction and study described in clause (iv) of paragraph (a), and (ii) is performing related work under the supervision of a professional person to qualify himself to become a professional employee as defined in paragraph (a).

(13) In determining whether any person is acting as an "agent" of another person so as to make such other person responsible for his acts, the question of whether the specific acts performed were actually authorized or subsequently ratified shall not be controlling.

(14) The term "health care institution" shall include any hospital, convalescent hospital, health maintenance organization, health clinic, nursing home, extended care facility, or other institution devoted to the care of sick, infirm, or aged person.

[Pub. L. 93–360, §1(b), July 26, 1974, 88 Stat. 395, added par. (14).]

NATIONAL LABOR RELATIONS BOARD

Sec. 3. [§153.] (a) [Creation, composition, appointment, and tenure; Chairman; removal of members] The National Labor Relations Board (hereinafter called the "Board") created by this Act [subchapter] prior to its amendment by the Labor Management Relations Act, 1947 [29 U.S.C. §141 et seq.], is continued as an agency of the United States, except that the Board shall consist of five instead of three members, appointed by the President by and with the advice and consent of the Senate. Of the two additional members so provided for, one shall be appointed for a term of five years and the other for a term of two years. Their successors, and the successors of the other members, shall be appointed for terms of five years each, excepting that any individual chosen to fill a vacancy shall be appointed only for the unexpired term of the member whom he shall succeed. The President shall designate one member to serve as Chairman of the Board. Any member of the Board may be removed by the President, upon notice and hearing, for neglect of duty or malfeasance in office, but for no other cause.

(b) [Delegation of powers to members and regional directors; review and stay of actions of regional directors; quorum; seal] The Board is authorized to delegate to any group of three or more members any or all of the powers which it may itself exercise. The Board is also authorized to delegate to its regional directors its powers under section 9 [section 159 of this title] to determine the unit appropriate for the purpose of collective bargaining, to investigate and provide for hearings, and determine whether a question of representation exists, and to direct an election or take a secret ballot under subsection (c) or (e) of section 9 [section 159 of this title] and certify the results thereof, except that upon the filling of a request therefor with the Board by any interested person, the Board may review any action of a regional director delegated to him under this paragraph, but such a review shall not, unless specifically ordered by the Board, operate as a stay of any action taken by the regional director. A vacancy in the Board shall not impair the right of the remaining members to exercise all of the powers of the Board, and three members of the Board shall, at all times, constitute a quorum of the Board, except that two members shall constitute a quorum of any group designated pursuant to the first sentence hereof. The Board shall have an official seal which shall be judicially noticed.

(c) [Annual reports to Congress and the President] The Board shall at the close of each fiscal year make a report in writing to Congress and to the President summarizing significant case activities and operations for that fiscal year.

(d) [General Counsel; appointment and tenure; powers and duties; vacancy] There shall be a General Counsel of the Board who shall be appointed by the President, by and with the advice and consent of the Senate, for a term of four years. The General Counsel of the Board shall exercise general supervision over all attorneys employed by the Board (other than administrative law judges and legal assistants to Board members) and over the officers and employees in the regional offices. He shall have final authority, on behalf of the Board, in respect of the investigation of charges and issuance of complaints under section 10 [section 160 of this title], and in respect of the prosecution of such complaints before the Board, and shall have such other duties as the Board may prescribe or as may be provided by law. In case of vacancy in the office of the General Counsel the President is authorized to designate the officer or employee who shall act as General Counsel during such vacancy, but no person or persons so designated shall so act (1) for more than forty days when the Congress is in session unless a nomination to fill such vacancy shall have been submitted to the Senate, or (2) after the adjournment sine die of the session of the Senate in which such nomination was submitted.

[The title "administrative law judge" was adopted in 5 U.S.C. §3105.]

Sec. 4. [§154. Eligibility for reappointment; officers and employees; payment of expenses] (a) Each member of the Board and the General Counsel of the Board shall be eligible for reappointment, and shall not engage in any other business, vocation, or employment. The Board shall appoint an executive secretary, and such attorneys, examiners, and regional directors, and such other employees as it may from time to time find necessary for the proper performance of its duties. The Board may not employ any attorneys for the purpose of reviewing transcripts of hearings or preparing drafts of opinions except that any attorney employed for assignment as a legal assistant to any Board member may for such Board member review such transcripts and prepare such drafts. No administrative law judge's report shall be reviewed, either before or after its publication, by any person other than a member of the Board or his legal assistant, and no administrative law judge shall advise or consult with the Board with respect to exceptions taken to his findings, rulings, or recommendations. The Board may establish or utilize such regional, local, or other agencies, and utilize such voluntary and uncompensated services, as may from time to time be needed. Attorneys appointed under this section may, at the direction of the Board, appear for and represent the Board in any case in court. Nothing in this Act [subchapter] shall be construed to authorize the Board to appoint individuals for the purpose of conciliation or mediation, or for economic analysis.

[The title "administrative law judge" was adopted in 5 U.S.C. §3105.]

(b) All of the expenses of the Board, including all necessary traveling and subsistence expenses outside the District of Columbia incurred by the members or employees of the Board under its orders, shall be allowed and paid on the presentation of itemized vouchers therefor approved by the Board or by any individual it designates for that purpose.

Sec. 5. [§155. Principal office, conducting inquiries throughout country; participation in decisions or inquiries conducted by member] The principal office of the Board shall be in the District of Columbia, but it may meet and exercise any or all of its powers at any other place. The Board may, by one or more of its members or by such agents or agencies as it may designate, prosecute any inquiry necessary to its functions in any part of the United States. A member who participates in such an inquiry shall not be disqualified from subsequently participating in a decision of the Board in the same case.

Sec. 6. [§156. Rules and regulations] The Board shall have authority from time to time to make, amend, and rescind, in the manner prescribed by the Administrative Procedure Act [by subchapter II of chapter 5 of title 5], such rules and regulations as may be necessary to carry out the provisions of this Act [subchapter].

RIGHTS OF EMPLOYEES

Sec. 7. [§157.] Employees shall have the right to self-organization, to form, join, or assist labor organizations, to bargain collectively through representatives of their own choosing, and to engage in other concerted activities for the purpose of collective bargaining or other mutual aid or protection, and shall also have the right to refrain from any or all such activities except to the extent that such right may be affected by an agreement requiring membership in a labor organization as a condition of employment as authorized in section 8(a)(3) [section 158(a)(3) of this title].

UNFAIR LABOR PRACTICES

Sec. 8. [§158.] (a) [Unfair labor practices by employer] It shall be an unfair labor practice for an employer—

(1) to interfere with, restrain, or coerce employees in the exercise of the rights guaranteed in section 7 [section 157 of this title];

(2) to dominate or interfere with the formation or administration of any labor organization or contribute financial or other support to it: *Provided,* That subject to rules and regulations made and published by the Board pursuant to section 6 [section 156 of this title], an employer shall not be prohibited from permitting employees to confer with him during working hours without loss of time or pay;

(3) by discrimination in regard to hire or tenure of employment or any term or condition of employment to encourage or discourage membership in any labor organization: *Provided,* That nothing in this Act [subchapter], or in any other statute of the United States, shall preclude an employer from making an agreement with a labor organization (not established, maintained, or assisted by any action defined in section 8(a) of this Act [in this subsection] as an unfair labor practice) to require as a condition of employment membership therein on or after the thirtieth day following the beginning of such employment or the effective date of such agreement, whichever is the later, (i) if such labor organization is the representative of the employees as provided in section 9(a) [section 159(a) of this title], in the appropriate collective-bargaining unit covered by such agreement when made, and (ii) unless following an election held as provided in section 9(e) [section 159(e) of this title] within one year preceding the effective date of such agreement, the Board shall have certified that at least a majority of the employees eligible to vote in such election have voted to rescind the authority of such labor organization to make such an agreement: *Provided further,* That no employer shall justify any discrimination against an employee for nonmembership in a labor organization (A) if he has reasonable grounds for

believing that such membership was not available to the employee on the same terms and conditions generally applicable to other members, or (B) if he has reasonable grounds for believing that membership was denied or terminated for reasons other than the failure of the employee to tender the periodic dues and the initiation fees uniformly required as a condition of acquiring or retaining membership;

(4) to discharge or otherwise discriminate against an employee because he has filed charges or given testimony under this Act [subchapter];

(5) to refuse to bargain collectively with the representatives of his employees, subject to the provisions of section 9(a) [section 159(a) of this title].

(b) [Unfair labor practices by labor organization] It shall be an unfair labor practice for a labor organization or its agents—

(1) to restrain or coerce (A) employees in the exercise of the rights guaranteed in section 7 [section 157 of this title]: *Provided,* That this paragraph shall not impair the right of a labor organization to prescribe its own rules with respect to the acquisition or retention of membership therein; or (B) an employer in the selection of his representatives for the purposes of collective bargaining or the adjustment of grievances;

(2) to cause or attempt to cause an employer to discriminate against an employee in violation of subsection (a)(3) [of subsection (a)(3) of this section] or to discriminate against an employee with respect to whom membership in such organization has been denied or terminated on some ground other than his failure to tender the periodic dues and the initiation fees uniformly required as a condition of acquiring or retaining membership;

(3) to refuse to bargain collectively with an employer, provided it is the representative of his employees subject to the provisions of section 9(a) [section 159(a) of this title];

(4)(i) to engage in, or to induce or encourage any individual employed by any person engaged in commerce or in an industry affecting commerce to engage in, a strike or a refusal in the course of his employment to use, manufacture, process, transport, or otherwise handle or work on any goods, articles, materials, or commodities or to perform any services; or (ii) to threaten, coerce, or restrain any person engaged in commerce or in an industry affecting commerce, where in either case an object thereof is—

(A) forcing or requiring any employer or self-employed person to join any labor or employer organization or to enter into any agreement which is prohibited by section 8(e) [subsection (e) of this section];

(B) forcing or requiring any person to cease using, selling, handling, transporting, or otherwise dealing in the products of any other producer, processor, or manufacturer, or to cease doing business with any other person, or forcing or requiring any other employer to recognize or bargain with a labor organization as the representative of his employees unless such labor organization has been certified as the representative of such employees under the provisions of section 9 [section 159 of this title]: *Provided,* That nothing contained in this clause (B) shall be construed to make unlawful, where not otherwise unlawful, any primary strike or primary picketing;

(C) forcing or requiring any employer to recognize or bargain with a particular labor organization as the representative of his employees if another labor organization has been certified as the representative of such employees under the provisions of section 9 [section 159 of this title];

(D) forcing or requiring any employer to assign particular work to employees in a particular labor organization or in a particular trade, craft, or class rather than to employees in another labor organization or in another trade, craft, or class, unless such employer is failing to conform to an order or certification of the Board determining the bargaining representative for employees performing such work:

Provided, That nothing contained in this subsection (b) [this subsection] shall be construed to make unlawful a refusal by any person to enter upon the premises of any employer (other than his own employer), if the employees of such employer are engaged in a strike ratified or approved by a representative of such employees whom such employer is required to recognize under this Act [subchapter]: *Provided further,* That for the purposes of this paragraph (4) only, nothing contained in such paragraph shall be construed to prohibit publicity, other than picketing, for the purpose of truthfully advising the public, including consumers and members of a labor organization, that a product or products are produced by an employer with whom the labor organization has a primary dispute and are distributed by another employer, as long as such publicity does not have an effect of inducing any individual employed by any person other than the primary employer in the course of his employment to refuse to pick up, deliver, or transport any goods, or not to perform any services, at the establishment of the employer engaged in such distribution;

(5) to require of employees covered by an agreement authorized under subsection (a)(3) [of this section] the payment, as a condition precedent to becoming a member of such organization, of a fee in an amount which the Board finds excessive or discriminatory under all the circumstances. In making such a finding, the Board shall consider, among other relevant factors, the practices and customs of labor organizations in the particular industry, and the wages currently paid to the employees affected;

(6) to cause or attempt to cause an employer to pay or deliver or agree to pay or deliver any money or other thing of value, in the nature of an exaction, for services which are not performed or not to be performed; and

(7) to picket or cause to be picketed, or threaten to picket or cause to be picketed, any employer where an object thereof is forcing or requiring an employer to recognize or bargain with a labor organization as the representative of his employees, or forcing or requiring the employees of an employer to accept or select such labor organization as their collective-bargaining representative, unless such labor organization is currently certified as the representative of such employees:

(A) where the employer has lawfully recognized in accordance with this Act [subchapter] any other labor organization and a question concerning representation may not appropriately be raised under section 9(c) of this Act [section 159(c) of this title],

(B) where within the preceding twelve months a valid election under section 9(c) of this Act [section 159(c) of this title] has been conducted, or

(C) where such picketing has been conducted without a petition under section 9(c) [section 159(c) of this title] being filed within a reasonable period of time not to exceed thirty days from the commencement of such picketing: *Provided,* That when such a petition has been filed the Board shall forthwith, without regard to the provisions of section 9(c)(1) [section 159(c)(1) of this title] or the absence of a showing of a substantial interest on the part of the labor organization, direct an election in such unit as the Board finds to be appropriate and shall certify the results thereof: *Provided further,* That nothing in this subparagraph (C) shall be construed to prohibit any picketing or other publicity for the purpose of truthfully advising the public (including consumers) that an employer does not employ members of, or have a contract with, a labor organization, unless an effect of such picketing is to induce any individual employed by any other person in the course of his employment, not to pick up, deliver or transport any goods or not to perform any services.

Nothing in this paragraph (7) shall be construed to permit any act which would otherwise be an unfair labor practice under this section 8(b) [this subsection].

(c) [Expression of views without threat of reprisal or force or promise of benefit] The expressing of any views, argument, or opinion, or the dissemination thereof, whether in written, printed, graphic, or visual form, shall not constitute or be evidence of an unfair labor practice under any of the provisions of this Act [subchapter], if such expression contains no threat of reprisal or force or promise of benefit.

(d) [Obligation to bargain collectively] For the purposes of this section, to bargain collectively is the performance of the mutual obligation of the employer and the representative of the employees to meet at reasonable times and confer in good faith with respect to wages, hours, and other terms and conditions of employment, or the negotiation of an agreement or any question arising thereunder, and the execution of a written contract incorporating any agreement reached if requested by either party, but such obligation does not compel either party to agree to a proposal or require the making of a concession: *Provided,* That where there is in effect a collective-bargaining contract covering employees in an industry affecting commerce, the duty to bargain collectively shall also mean that no party to such contract shall terminate or modify such contract, unless the party desiring such termination or modification—

(1) serves a written notice upon the other party to the contract of the proposed termination or modification sixty days prior to the expiration date thereof, or in the event such contract contains no expiration date, sixty days prior to the time it is proposed to make such termination or modification;

(2) offers to meet and confer with the other party for the purpose of negotiating a new contract or a contract containing the proposed modifications;

(3) notifies the Federal Mediation and Conciliation Service within thirty days after such notice of the existence of a dispute, and simultaneously therewith notifies any State or Territorial agency established to mediate and conciliate disputes within the State or Territory where the dispute occurred, provided no agreement has been reached by that time; and

(4) continues in full force and effect, without resorting to strike or lockout, all the terms and conditions of the existing contract for a period of sixty days after such notice is given or until the expiration date of such contract, whichever occurs later:

The duties imposed upon employers, employees, and labor organizations by paragraphs (2), (3), and (4) [paragraphs (2) to (4) of this subsection] shall become inapplicable upon an intervening certification of the Board, under which the labor organization or individual, which is a party to the contract, has been superseded as or ceased to be the representative of the employees subject to the provisions of section 9(a) [section 159(a) of this title], and the duties so imposed shall not be construed as requiring either party to discuss or agree to any modification of the terms and conditions contained in a contract for a fixed period, if such modification is to become effective before such terms and conditions can be reopened under the provisions of the contract. Any employee who engages in a strike within any notice period specified in this subsection, or who engages in any strike within the appropriate period specified in subsection (g) of this section, shall lose his status as an employee of the employer engaged in the particular labor dispute, for the purposes of sections 8, 9, and 10 of this Act [sections 158, 159, and 160 of this title], but such loss of status for such employee shall terminate if and when he is reemployed by such employer. Whenever the collective bargaining involves employees of a health care institution, the provisions of this section 8(d) [this subsection] shall be modified as follows:

(A) The notice of section 8(d)(1) [paragraph (1) of this subsection] shall be ninety days; the notice of section 8(d)(3) [paragraph (3) of this subsection] shall be sixty days; and the contract period of section 8(d)(4) [paragraph (4) of this subsection] shall be ninety days.

(B) Where the bargaining is for an initial agreement following certification or recognition, at least thirty days' notice of the existence of a dispute shall be given by the labor organization to the agencies set forth in section 8(d)(3) [in paragraph (3) of this subsection].

(C) After notice is given to the Federal Mediation and Conciliation Service under either clause (A) or (B) of this sentence, the Service shall promptly communicate with the parties and use its best efforts, by mediation and conciliation, to bring them to agreement. The parties shall participate fully and promptly in such meetings as may be undertaken by the Service for the purpose of aiding in a settlement of the dispute.

[Pub. L. 93–360, July 26, 1974, 88 Stat. 395, amended the last sentence of Sec. 8(d) by striking the words "the sixty-day" and inserting the words "any notice" and by inserting before the words "shall lose" the phrase ", or who engages in any strike within the appropriate period specified in subsection (g) of this section." It also amended the end of paragraph Sec. 8(d) by adding a new sentence "Whenever the collective bargaining . . . aiding in a settlement of the dispute."]

(e) [Enforceability of contract or agreement to boycott any other employer; exception] It shall be an unfair labor practice for any labor organization and any employer to enter into any contract or agreement, express or implied, whereby such employer ceases or refrains or agrees to cease or refrain from handling, using, selling, transporting or otherwise dealing in any of the products of any other employer, or cease doing business with any other person, and any contract or agreement entered into heretofore or hereafter containing such an agreement shall be to such extent unenforceable and void: *Provided,* That nothing in this subsection (e) [this subsection] shall apply to an agreement between a labor organization and an employer in the construction industry relating to the contracting or subcontracting of work to be done at the site of the construction, alteration, painting, or repair of a building, structure, or other work: *Provided further,* That for the purposes of this subsection (e) and section 8(b)(4)(B) [this subsection and subsection (b)(4)(B) of this section] the terms "any employer," "any person engaged in commerce or an industry affecting commerce," and "any person" when used in relation to the terms "any other producer, processor, or manufacturer," "any other employer," or "any other person" shall not include persons in the relation of a jobber, manufacturer, contractor, or subcontractor working on the goods or premises of the jobber or manufacturer or performing parts of an integrated process of production in the apparel and clothing industry: *Provided further,* That nothing in this Act [subchapter] shall prohibit the enforcement of any agreement which is within the foregoing exception.

(f) [Agreements covering employees in the building and construction industry] It shall not be an unfair labor practice under subsections (a) and (b) of this section for an employer engaged primarily in the building and construction industry to make an agreement covering employees engaged (or who, upon their employment, will be engaged) in the building and construction industry with a labor organization of which building and construction employees are members (not established, maintained, or assisted by any action defined in section 8(a) of this Act [subsection (a) of this section] as an unfair labor practice) because (1) the majority status of such labor organization has not been established under the provisions of section 9 of this Act [section 159 of this title] prior to the making of such agreement, or (2) such agreement requires as a condition of employment, membership in such labor organization after the seventh day following the beginning of such employment or the effective date of the agreement, whichever is later, or (3) such agreement requires the employer to notify such labor organization of opportunities for employment with such employer, or gives such labor organization an opportunity to refer qualified applicants for such employment, or (4) such agreement specifies minimum training or experience qualifications for employment or provides for priority in opportunities for employment based upon length of service with such employer, in the industry or in the particular geographical area: *Provided,* That nothing in this subsection shall set aside the final proviso to section 8(a)(3) of this Act [subsection (a)(3) of this section]: *Provided further,* That any agreement which would be invalid, but for clause (1) of this subsection, shall not be a bar to a petition filed pursuant to section 9(c) or 9(e) [section 159(c) or 159(e) of this title].

(g) [Notification of intention to strike or picket at any health care institution] A labor organization before engaging in any strike, picketing, or other concerted refusal to work at any health care institution shall, not less than ten days prior to such action, notify the institution in writing and the Federal Mediation and Conciliation Service of that intention, except that in the case of bargaining for an initial agreement following certification or recognition the notice required by this subsection shall not be given until the expiration of the period specified in clause (B) of the last sentence of section 8(d) of this Act [subsection (d) of this section]. The notice shall state the date and time that such action will commence. The notice, once given, may be extended by the written agreement of both parties.

[Pub. L. 93–360, July 26, 1974, 88 Stat. 396, added subsec. (g).]

REPRESENTATIVES AND ELECTIONS

Sec. 9 [§159.] (a) [Exclusive representatives; employees' adjustment of grievances directly with employer] Representatives designated or selected for the purposes of collective bargaining by the majority of the employees in a unit appropriate for such purposes, shall be the exclusive representatives of all the employees in such unit for the purposes of collective bargaining in respect to rates of pay, wages, hours of employment, or other conditions of employment: *Provided,* That any individual employee or a group of employees shall have the right at any time to present grievances to their employer and to have such grievances adjusted, without the intervention of the bargaining representative, as long as the adjustment is not inconsistent with the terms of a collective-bargaining contract or agreement then in effect: *Provided further,* That the bargaining representative has been given opportunity to be present at such adjustment.

(b) [Determination of bargaining unit by Board] The Board shall decide in each case whether, in order to assure to employees the fullest freedom in exercising the rights guaranteed by this Act [subchapter], the unit appropriate for the purposes of collective bargaining shall be the employer unit, craft unit, plant unit, or subdivision thereof: *Provided,* That the Board shall not (1) decide that any unit is appropriate for such purposes if such unit includes both professional employees and employees who are not professional employees unless a majority of such professional employees vote for inclusion in such unit; or (2) decide that any craft unit is inappropriate for such purposes on the ground that a different unit has been established by a prior Board determination, unless a majority of the employees in the proposed craft unit votes against separate representation or (3) decide that any unit is appropriate for such purposes if it includes, together with other employees, any individual employed as a guard to enforce against employees and other persons rules to protect property of the employer or to protect the safety of persons on the employer's premises; but no labor organization shall be certified as the representative of employees in a bargaining unit of guards if such organization admits to membership, or is affiliated directly or indirectly with an organization which admits to membership, employees other than guards.

(c) [Hearing on questions affecting commerce; rules and regulations] (1) Whenever a petition shall have been filed, in accordance with such regulations as may be prescribed by the Board—

(A) by an employee or group of employees or any individual or labor organization acting in their behalf alleging that a substantial number of employees (i) wish to be represented for collective bargaining and that their employer declines to recognize their representative as the representative defined in section 9(a) [subsection (a) of this section], or (ii) assert that the individual or labor organization, which has been certified or is being currently recognized by their employer as the bargaining representative, is no longer a representative as defined in section 9(a) [subsection (a) of this section]; or

(B) by an employer, alleging that one or more individuals or labor organizations have presented to him a claim to be recognized as the representative defined in section 9(a) [subsection (a) of this section]; the Board shall investigate such petition and if it has reasonable cause to believe that a question of representation affecting commerce exists shall provide for an appropriate hearing upon due notice. Such hearing may be conducted by an officer or employee of the regional office, who shall not make any recommendations with respect thereto. If the Board finds upon the record of such hearing that such a question of representation exists, it shall direct an election by secret ballot and shall certify the results thereof.

(2) In determining whether or not a question of representation affecting commerce exists, the same regulations and rules of decision shall apply irrespective of the identity of the persons filing the petition or the kind of relief sought and in no case shall the Board deny a labor organization a place on the ballot by reason of an order with respect to such labor organization or its predecessor not issued in conformity with section 10(c) [section 160(c) of this title].

(3) No election shall be directed in any bargaining unit or any subdivision within which, in the preceding twelve-month period, a valid election shall have been held. Employees engaged in an economic strike who are not entitled to reinstatement shall be eligible to vote under such regulations as the Board shall find are consistent with the purposes and provisions of this Act [subchapter] in any election conducted within twelve months after the commencement of the strike. In any election where none of the choices on the ballot receives a majority, a run-off shall be conducted, the ballot providing for a selection between the two choices receiving the largest and second largest number of valid votes cast in the election.

(4) Nothing in this section shall be construed to prohibit the waiving of hearings by stipulation for the purpose of a consent election in conformity with regulations and rules of decision of the Board.

(5) In determining whether a unit is appropriate for the purposes specified in subsection (b) [of this section] the extent to which the employees have organized shall not be controlling.

(d) [Petition for enforcement or review; transcript] Whenever an order of the Board made pursuant to section 10(c) [section 160(c) of this title] is based in whole or in part upon facts certified following an investigation pursuant to subsection (c) of this section and there is a petition for the enforcement or review of such order, such certification and the record of such investigation shall be included in the transcript of the entire record required to be filed under section 10(e) or 10(f) [subsection (e) or (f) of section 160 of this title], and thereupon the decree of the court enforcing, modifying, or setting aside in whole or in part the order of the Board shall be made and entered upon the pleadings, testimony, and proceedings set forth in such transcript.

(e) [Secret ballot; limitation of elections] (1) Upon the filing with the Board, by 30 per centum or more of the employees in a bargaining unit covered by an agreement between their employer and labor organization made pursuant to section 8(a)(3) [section 158(a)(3) of this title], of a petition alleging they desire that such authorization be rescinded, the Board shall take a secret ballot of the employees in such unit and certify the results thereof to such labor organization and to the employer.

(2) No election shall be conducted pursuant to this subsection in any bargaining unit or any subdivision within which, in the preceding twelve-month period, a valid election shall have been held.

PREVENTION OF UNFAIR LABOR PRACTICES

Sec. 10. [§160.] (a) [Powers of Board generally] The Board is empowered, as here-inafter provided, to prevent any person from engaging in any unfair labor practice (listed in section 8 [section 158 of this title]) affecting commerce. This power shall not be affected by any other means of adjustment or prevention that has been or may be established by agreement, law or otherwise: *Provided,* That the Board is empowered by agreement with any agency of any State or Territory to cede to such agency jurisdiction over any cases in any industry (other than mining, manufacturing, communications, and transportation except where predominately local in character) even though such cases may involve labor disputes affecting commerce, unless the provision of the State or Territorial statute applicable to the determination of such cases by such agency is inconsistent with the corresponding provision of this Act [subchapter] or has received a construction inconsistent therewith.

(b) [Complaint and notice of hearing; six-month limitation; answer; court rules of evidence inapplicable] Whenever it is charged that any person has engaged in or is engaging in any such unfair labor practice, the Board, or any agent or agency designated by the Board for such purposes, shall have power to issue and cause to be served upon such person a complaint stating the charges in that respect, and containing a notice of hearing before the Board or a member thereof, or before a designated agent or agency, at a place therein fixed, not less than five days after the serving of said complaint: *Provided,* That no complaint shall issue based upon any unfair labor practice occurring more than six months prior to the filing of the charge with the Board and the service of a copy thereof upon the person against whom such charge is made, unless the person aggrieved thereby was prevented from filing such charge by reason of service in the armed forces, in which event the six-month period shall be computed from the day of his discharge. Any such complaint may be amended by the member, agent, or agency conducting the hearing or the Board in its discretion at any time prior to the issuance of an order based thereon. The person so complained of shall have the right to file an answer to the original or amended complaint and to appear in person or otherwise and give testimony at the place and time fixed in the complaint. In the discretion of the member, agent, or agency conducting the hearing or the Board, any other person may be allowed to intervene in the said proceeding and to present testimony. Any such proceeding shall, so far as practicable, be conducted in accordance with the rules of evidence applicable in the district courts of the United States under the rules of civil procedure for the district courts of the United States, adopted by the Supreme Court of the United States pursuant to section 2072 of title 28, United States Code [section 2072 of title 28].

(c) [Reduction of testimony to writing; findings and orders of Board] The testimony taken by such member, agent, or agency or the Board shall be reduced to writing and filed with the Board. Thereafter, in its discretion, the Board upon notice may take further testimony or hear argument. If upon the preponderance of the testimony taken the Board shall be of the opinion that any person named in the complaint has engaged in or is engaging in any such unfair labor practice, then the Board shall state its findings of fact and shall issue and cause to be served on such person an order requiring such person to cease and desist from such unfair labor practice, and to take such affirmative action including reinstatement of employees with or without back pay, as will effectuate the policies of this Act [subchapter]: *Provided,* That where an order directs reinstatement of an employee, back pay may be required of the employer or labor organization, as the case may be, responsible for the discrimination suffered by him: *And provided further,* That in determining whether a complaint shall issue alleging a violation of section 8(a)(1) or section 8(a)(2) [subsection (a)(1) or (a)(2) of section 158 of this title], and in deciding such cases, the same regulations and rules of decision shall apply irrespective of whether or not the labor organization affected is affiliated with a labor organization national or international in scope. Such order may further require such person to make reports from time to time showing the extent to which it has complied with the order. If upon the preponderance of the testimony taken the Board shall not be of the opinion that the person named in the complaint has engaged in or is engaging in any such unfair labor practice, then the Board shall state its findings of fact and shall issue an order dismissing the said complaint. No order of the Board shall require the reinstatement of any individual as an employee who has been suspended or discharged, or the payment to him of any back pay, if such individual was suspended or discharged for cause. In case the evidence is presented before a member of the Board, or before an administrative law judge or judges thereof, such member, or such judge or judges, as the case may be, shall issue and cause to be served on the parties to the proceeding a proposed report, together with a recommended order, which shall be filed with the Board, and if no exceptions are filed within twenty days after service thereof upon such parties, or within such further period as the Board may authorize, such recommended order shall become the order of the Board and become affective as therein prescribed.

[The title "administrative law judge" was adopted in 5 U.S.C. §3105.]

(d) [Modification of findings or orders prior to filing record in court] Until the record in a case shall have been filed in a court, as hereinafter provided, the Board may at any time, upon reasonable notice and in such manner as it shall deem proper, modify or set aside, in whole or in part, any finding or order made or issued by it.

(e) [Petition to court for enforcement of order; proceedings; review of judgment] The Board shall have power to petition any court of appeals of the United States, or if all the courts of appeals to which application may be made are in vacation, any district court of the United States, within any circuit or district, respectively, wherein the unfair labor practice in question occurred or wherein such person resides or transacts business, for the enforcement of such order and for appropriate temporary relief or restraining order, and shall file in the court the record in the proceeding, as provided in section 2112 of title 28, United States Code [section 2112 of title 28]. Upon the filing of such petition, the court shall cause notice thereof to be served upon such person, and thereupon shall have jurisdiction of the proceeding and of the question determined therein, and shall have power to grant such temporary relief or restraining order as it deems just and proper, and to make and enter a decree enforcing, modifying and enforcing as so modified, or setting aside in whole or in part the order of the Board. No objection that has not been urged before the Board, its member, agent, or agency, shall be considered by the court, unless the failure or neglect to urge such objection shall be excused because of extraordinary circumstances. The findings of the Board with respect to questions of fact if supported by substantial evidence on the record considered as a whole shall be conclusive. If either party shall apply to the court for leave to adduce additional evidence and shall show to the satisfaction of the court that such additional evidence is material and that there were reasonable grounds for the failure to adduce such evidence in the hearing before the Board, its member, agent, or agency, the court may order such additional evidence to be taken before the Board, its member, agent, or agency, and to be made a part of the record. The Board may modify its findings as to the facts, or make new findings, by reason of additional evidence so taken and filed, and it shall file such modified or new findings, which findings with respect to question of fact if supported by substantial evidence on the record considered as a whole shall be conclusive, and shall file its recommendations, if any, for the modification or setting aside of its original order. Upon the filing of the record with it the jurisdiction of the court shall be exclusive and its judgment and decree shall be final, except that the same shall be subject to review by the appropriate United States court of appeals if application was made to the district court as hereinabove provided, and by the Supreme Court of the United States upon writ of certiorari or certification as provided in section 1254 of title 28.

(f) [Review of final order of Board on petition to court] Any person aggrieved by a final order of the Board granting or denying in whole or in part the relief sought may obtain a review of such order in any United States court of appeals in the circuit wherein the unfair labor practice in question was alleged to have been engaged in or wherein such person resides or transacts business, or in the United States Court of Appeals for the District of Columbia, by filing in such court a written petition praying that the order of the Board be modified or set aside. A copy of such petition shall be forthwith transmitted by the clerk of the court to the Board, and thereupon the aggrieved party shall file in the court the record in the proceeding, certified by the Board, as provided in section 2112 of title 28, United States Code [section 2112 of title 28]. Upon the filing of such petition, the court shall proceed in the same manner as in the case of an application by the Board under subsection (e) of this section, and shall have the same jurisdiction to grant to the Board such temporary relief or restraining order as it deems just and proper, and in like manner to make and enter a decree enforcing, modifying and enforcing as so modified, or setting aside in whole or in part the order of the Board; the findings of the Board with respect to questions of fact if supported by substantial evidence on the record considered as a whole shall in like manner be conclusive.

(g) [Institution of court proceedings as stay of Board's order] The commencement of proceedings under subsection (e) or (f) of this section shall not, unless specifically ordered by the court, operate as a stay of the Board's order.

(h) [Jurisdiction of courts unaffected by limitations prescribed in chapter 6 of this title] When granting appropriate temporary relief or a restraining order, or making and entering a decree enforcing, modifying and enforcing as so modified, or setting aside in whole or in part an order of the Board, as provided in this section, the jurisdiction of courts sitting in equity shall not be limited by sections 101 to 115 of title 29, United States Code [chapter 6 of this title] [known as the "Norris-LaGuardia Act"].

(i) Repealed.

(j) [Injunctions] The Board shall have power, upon issuance of a complaint as provided in subsection (b) [of this section] charging that any person has engaged in or is engaging in an unfair labor practice, to petition any United States district court, within any district wherein the unfair labor practice in question is alleged to have occurred or wherein such person resides or transacts business, for appropriate temporary relief or restraining order. Upon the filing of any such petition the court shall cause notice thereof to be served upon such person, and thereupon shall have jurisdiction to grant to the Board such temporary relief or restraining order as it deems just and proper.

(k) [Hearings on jurisdictional strikes] Whenever it is charged that any person has engaged in an unfair labor practice within the meaning of paragraph (4)(D) of section 8(b) [section 158(b) of this title], the Board is empowered and directed to hear and determine the dispute out of which such unfair labor practice shall have arisen, unless, within ten days after notice that such charge has been filed, the parties to such dispute submit to the Board satisfactory evidence that they have adjusted, or agreed upon methods for the voluntary adjustment of, the dispute. Upon compliance by the parties to the dispute with the decision of the Board or upon such voluntary adjustment of the dispute, such charge shall be dismissed.

(l) [Boycotts and strikes to force recognition of uncertified labor organizations; injunctions; notice; service of process] Whenever it is charged that any person has engaged in an unfair labor practice within the meaning of paragraph (4)(A), (B), or (C) of section 8(b) [section 158(b) of this title], or section 8(e) [section 158(e) of this title] or section 8(b)(7) [section 158(b)(7) of this title], the preliminary investigation of such charge shall be made forthwith and given priority over all other cases except cases of like character in the office where it is filed or to which it is referred. If, after such investigation, the officer or regional attorney to whom the matter may be referred has reasonable cause to believe such charge is true and that a complaint should issue, he shall, on behalf of the Board, petition any United States district court within any district where the unfair labor practice in question has occurred, is alleged to have occurred, or wherein such person resides or transacts business, for appropriate injunctive relief pending the final adjudication of the Board with respect to such matter. Upon the filing of any such petition the district court shall have jurisdiction to grant such injunctive relief or temporary restraining order as it deems just and proper, notwithstanding any other provision of law: *Provided further,* That no temporary restraining order shall be issued without notice unless a petition alleges that substantial and irreparable injury to the charging party will be unavoidable and such temporary restraining order shall be effective for no longer than five days and will become void at the expiration of such period: *Provided further,* That such officer or regional attorney shall not apply for any restraining order under section 8(b)(7) [section 158(b)(7) of this title] if a charge against the employer under section 8(a)(2) [section 158(a)(2) of this title] has been filed and after the preliminary investigation, he has reasonable cause to believe that such charge is true and that a complaint should issue. Upon filing of any such petition the courts shall cause notice thereof to be served upon any person involved in the charge and such person, including the charging party, shall be given an opportunity to appear by counsel and present any relevant testimony: *Provided further,* That for the purposes of this subsection district courts shall be deemed to have jurisdiction of a labor organization (1) in the district in which such organization maintains its principal office, or (2) in any district in which its duly authorized officers or agents are engaged in promoting or protecting the interests of employee members. The service of legal process upon such officer or agent shall constitute service upon the labor organization and make such organization a party to the suit. In situations where such relief is appropriate the procedure specified herein shall apply to charges with respect to section 8(b)(4)(D) [section 158(b)(4)(D) of this title].

(m) [Priority of cases] Whenever it is charged that any person has engaged in an unfair labor practice within the meaning of subsection (a)(3) or (b)(2) of section 8 [section 158 of this title], such charge shall be given priority over all other cases except cases of like character in the office where it is filed or to which it is referred and cases given priority under subsection (1) [of this section].

INVESTIGATORY POWERS

Sec. 11. [§161.] For the purpose of all hearings and investigations, which, in the opinion of the Board, are necessary and proper for the exercise of the powers vested in it by section 9 and section 10 [sections 159 and 160 of this title]—

(1) [Documentary evidence; summoning witnesses and taking testimony] The Board, or its duly authorized agents or agencies, shall at all reasonable times have access to, for the purpose of examination, and the right to copy any evidence of any person being investigated or proceeded against that relates to any matter under investigation or in question. The Board, or any member thereof, shall upon application of any party to such proceedings, forthwith issue to such party subpoenas requiring the attendance and testimony of witnesses or the production of any evidence in such proceeding or investigation requested in such application. Within five days after the service of a subpoena on any person requiring the production of any evidence in his possession or under his control, such person may petition the Board to revoke, and the Board shall revoke, such subpoena if in its opinion the evidence whose production is required does not relate to any matter under investigation, or any matter in question in such proceedings, or if in its opinion such subpoena does not describe with sufficient particularity the evidence whose production is required. Any member of the Board, or any agent or agency designated by the Board for such purposes, may administer oaths and affirmations, examine witnesses, and receive evidence. Such attendance of witnesses and the production of such evidence may be required from any place in the United States or any Territory or possession thereof, at any designated place of hearing.

(2) [Court aid in compelling production of evidence and attendance of witnesses] In case on contumacy or refusal to obey a subpoena issued to any person, any United States district court or the United States courts of any Territory or possession, within the jurisdiction of which the inquiry is carried on or within the jurisdiction of which said person guilty of contumacy or refusal to obey is found or resides or transacts business, upon application by the Board shall have jurisdiction to issue to such person an order requiring such person to appear before the Board, its member, agent, or agency, there to produce evidence if so ordered, or there to give testimony touching the matter under investigation or in question; and any failure to obey such order of the court may be punished by said court as a contempt thereof.

(3) Repealed

[Immunity of witnesses. See 18 U.S.C. §6001 et seq.]

(4) [Process, service and return; fees of witnesses] Complaints, orders and other process and papers of the Board, its member, agent, or agency, may be served either personally or by registered or certified mail or by telegraph or by leaving a copy thereof at the principal office or place of business of the person required to be served. The verified return by the individual so serving the same setting forth the manner of such service shall be proof of the same, and the return post office receipt or telegraph receipt therefor when registered or certified and mailed or when telegraphed as aforesaid shall be proof of service of the same. Witnesses summoned before the Board, its member, agent, or agency, shall be paid the same fees and mileage that are paid witnesses in the courts of the United States, and witnesses whose depositions are taken and the persons taking the same shall severally be entitled to the same fees as are paid for like services in the courts of the United States.

(5) [Process, where served] All process of any court to which application may be made under this Act [subchapter] may be served in the judicial district wherein the defendant or other person required to be served resides or may be found.

(6) [Information and assistance from departments] The several departments and agencies of the Government, when directed by the President, shall furnish the Board, upon its request, all records, papers, and information in their possession relating to any matter before the Board.

Sec. 12. [§162. Offenses and penalties] Any person who shall willfully resist, prevent, impede, or interfere with any member of the Board or any of its agents or agencies in the performance of duties pursuant to this Act [subchapter] shall be punished by a fine of not more than $5,000 or by imprisonment for not more than one year, or both.

LIMITATIONS

Sec. 13. [§163. Right to strike preserved] Nothing in this Act [subchapter], except as specifically provided for herein, shall be construed so as either to interfere with or impede or diminish in any way the right to strike, or to affect the limitations or qualifications on that right.

Sec. 14. [§164. Construction of provisions] (a) [Supervisors as union members] Nothing herein shall prohibit any individual employed as a supervisor from becoming or remaining a member of a labor organization, but no employer subject to this Act [subchapter] shall be compelled to deem individuals defined herein as supervisors as employees for the purpose of any law, either national or local, relating to collective bargaining.

(b) [Agreements requiring union membership in violation of State law] Nothing in this Act [subchapter] shall be construed as authorizing the execution or application of agreements requiring membership in a labor organization as a condition of employment in any State or Territory in which such execution or application is prohibited by State or Territorial law.

(c) [Power of Board to decline jurisdiction of labor disputes; assertion of jurisdiction by State and Territorial courts] (1) The Board, in its discretion, may, by rule of decision or by published rules adopted pursuant to the Administrative Procedure Act [to subchapter II of chapter 5 of title 5], decline to assert jurisdiction over any labor dispute involving any class or category of employers, where, in the opinion of the Board, the effect of such labor dispute on commerce is not sufficiently substantial to warrant the exercise of its jurisdiction: *Provided,* That the Board shall not decline to assert jurisdiction over any labor dispute over which it would assert jurisdiction under the standards prevailing upon August 1, 1959.

(2) Nothing in this Act [subchapter] shall be deemed to prevent or bar any agency or the courts of any State or Territory (including the Commonwealth of Puerto Rico, Guam, and the Virgin Islands), from assuming and asserting jurisdiction over labor disputes over which the Board declines, pursuant to paragraph (1) of this subsection, to assert jurisdiction.

Sec. 15. [§165.] Omitted.

[Reference to repealed provisions of bankruptcy statute.]

Sec. 16. [§166. Separability of provisions] If any provision of this Act [subchapter], or the application of such provision to any person or circumstances, shall be held invalid, the remainder of this Act [subchapter], or the application of such provision to persons or circumstances other than those as to which it is held invalid, shall not be affected thereby.

Sec. 17. [§167. Short title] This Act [subchapter] may be cited as the "National Labor Relations Act."

Sec. 18. [§168.] Omitted.

[Reference to former sec. 9(f), (g), and (h).]

INDIVIDUALS WITH RELIGIOUS CONVICTIONS

Sec. 19. [§169.] Any employee who is a member of and adheres to established and traditional tenets or teachings of a bona fide religion, body, or sect which has historically held conscientious objections to joining or financially supporting labor organizations shall not be required to join or financially support any labor organization as a condition of employment; except that such employee may be required in a contract between such employee's employer and a labor organization in lieu of periodic dues and initiation fees, to pay sums equal to such dues and initiation fees to a nonreligious, nonlabor organization charitable fund exempt from taxation under section 501(c)(3) of title 26 of the Internal Revenue Code [section 501(c)(3) of title 26], chosen by such employee from a list of at least three such funds, designated in such contract or if the contract fails to designate such funds, then to any such fund chosen by the employee. If such employee who holds conscientious objections pursuant to this section requests the labor organization to use the grievance-arbitration procedure on the employee's behalf, the labor organization is authorized to charge the employee for the reasonable cost of using such procedure.

[Sec. added, Pub. L. 93–360, July 26, 1974, 88 Stat. 397, and amended, Pub. L. 96–593, Dec. 24, 1980, 94 Stat. 3452.]

LABOR MANAGEMENT RELATIONS ACT

Also cited LMRA; 29 U.S.C. §§141–197

[Title 29, Chapter 7, United States Code]

Section 1.   [§141.]   (a) This Act [chapter] may be cited as the "Labor Management Relations Act, 1947." [Also known as the "Taft-Hartley Act."]

(b) Industrial strife which interferes with the normal flow of commerce and with the full production of articles and commodities for commerce, can be avoided or substantially minimized if employers, employees, and labor organizations each recognize under law one another's legitimate rights in their relations with each other, and above all recognize under law that neither party has any right in its relations with any other to engage in acts or practices which jeopardize the public health, safety, or interest.

It is the purpose and policy of this Act [chapter], in order to promote the full flow of commerce, to prescribe the legitimate rights of both employees and employers in their relations affecting commerce, to provide orderly and peaceful procedures for preventing the interference by either with the legitimate rights of the other, to protect the rights of individual employees in their relations with labor organizations whose activities affect commerce, to define and proscribe practices on the part of labor and management which affect commerce and are inimical to the general welfare, and to protect the rights of the public in connection with labor disputes affecting commerce.

TITLE I, Amendments to

NATIONAL LABOR RELATIONS ACT

29 U.S.C. §§151–169 (printed above)

TITLE II

[Title 29, Chapter 7, Subchapter III, United States Code]

Sec. 201. [§171. Declaration of purpose and policy]   It is the policy of the United States that—

(a) sound and stable industrial peace and the advancement of the general welfare, health, and safety of the Nation and of the best interest of employers and employees can most satisfactorily be secured by the settlement of issues between employers and employees through the processes of conference and collective bargaining between employers and the representatives of their employees;

(b) the settlement of issues between employers and employees through collective bargaining may be advanced by making available full and adequate governmental facilities for conciliation, mediation, and voluntary arbitration to aid and encourage employers and the representatives of their employees to reach and maintain agreements concerning rates of pay, hours, and working conditions, and to make all reasonable efforts to settle their differences by mutual agreement reached through conferences and collective bargaining or by such methods as may be provided for in any applicable agreement for the settlement of disputes; and

(c) certain controversies which arise between parties to collective-bargaining agreements may be avoided or minimized by making available full and adequate governmental facilities for furnishing assistance to employers and the representatives of their employees in formulating for inclusion within such agreements provision for adequate notice of any proposed changes in the terms of such agreements, for the final adjustment of grievances or questions regarding the application or interpretation of such agreements, and other provisions designed to prevent the subsequent arising of such controversies.

Sec. 202.   [§172.   Federal Mediation and Conciliation Service]

(a) [Creation; appointment of Director] There is created an independent agency to be known as the Federal Mediation and Conciliation Service (herein referred to as the "Service," except that for sixty days after June 23, 1947, such term shall refer to the Conciliation Service of the Department of Labor). The Service shall be under the direction of a Federal Mediation and Conciliation Director (hereinafter referred to as the "Director"), who shall be appointed by the President by and with the advice and consent of the Senate. The Director shall not engage in any other business, vocation, or employment.

(b) [Appointment of officers and employees; expenditures for supplies, facilities, and services] The Director is authorized, subject to the civil service laws, to appoint such clerical and other personnel as may be necessary for the execution of the functions of the Service, and shall fix their compensation in accordance with sections 5101 to 5115 and sections 5331 to 5338 of title 5, United States Code [chapter 51 and subchapter III of chapter 53 of title 5], and may, without regard to the provisions of the civil service laws, appoint such conciliators and mediators as may be necessary to carry out the functions of the Service. The Director is authorized to make such expenditures for supplies, facilities, and services as he deems necessary. Such expenditures shall be allowed and paid upon presentation of itemized vouchers therefor approved by the Director or by any employee designated by him for that purpose.

(c) [Principal and regional offices; delegation of authority by Director; annual report to Congress] The principal office of the Service shall be in the District of Columbia, but the Director may establish regional offices convenient to localities in which labor controversies are likely to arise. The Director may by order, subject to revocation at any time, delegate any authority and discretion conferred upon him by this Act [chapter] to any regional director, or other officer or employee of the Service. The Director may establish suitable procedures for cooperation with State and local mediation agencies. The Director shall make an annual report in writing to Congress at the end of the fiscal year.

(d) [Transfer of all mediation and conciliation services to Service; effective date; pending proceedings unaffected] All mediation and conciliation functions of the Secretary of Labor or the United States Conciliation Service under section 51 [repealed] of title 29, United States Code [this title], and all functions of the United States Conciliation Service under any other law are transferred to the Federal Mediation and Conciliation Service, together with the personnel and records of the United States Conciliation Service. Such transfer shall take effect upon the sixtieth day after June 23, 1947. Such transfer shall not affect any proceedings pending before the United States Conciliation Service or any certification, order, rule, or regulation theretofore made by it or by the Secretary of Labor. The Director and the Service shall not be subject in any way to the jurisdiction or authority of the Secretary of Labor or any official or division of the Department of Labor.

FUNCTIONS OF THE SERVICE

Sec. 203.   [§173.   Functions of Service]   (a) [Settlement of disputes through conciliation and mediation] It shall be the duty of the Service, in order to prevent or minimize interruptions of the free flow of commerce growing out of labor disputes, to assist parties to labor disputes in industries affecting commerce to settle such disputes through conciliation and mediation.

(b) [Intervention on motion of Service or request of parties; avoidance of mediation of minor disputes] The Service may proffer its services in any labor dispute in any industry affecting commerce, either upon its own motion or upon the request of one or more of the parties to the dispute, whenever in its judgment such dispute threatens to cause a substantial interruption of commerce. The Director and the Service are directed to avoid attempting to mediate disputes which would have only a minor effect on interstate commerce if State or other conciliation services are available to the parties. Whenever the Service does proffer its services in any dispute, it shall be the duty of the Service promptly to put itself in communication with the parties and to use its best efforts, by mediation and conciliation, to bring them to agreement.

(c) [Settlement of disputes by other means upon failure of conciliation] If the Director is not able to bring the parties to agreement by conciliation within a reasonable time, he shall seek to induce the parties voluntarily to seek other means of settling the dispute without resort to strike, lockout, or other coercion, including submission to the employees in the bargaining unit of the employer's last offer of settlement for approval or rejection in a secret ballot. The failure or refusal of either party to agree to any procedure suggested by the Director shall not be deemed a violation of any duty or obligation imposed by this Act [chapter].

(d) [Use of conciliation and mediation services as last resort] Final adjustment by a method agreed upon by the parties is declared to be the desirable method for settlement of grievance disputes arising over the application or interpretation of an existing collective-bargaining agreement. The Service is directed to make its conciliation and mediation services available in the settlement of such grievance disputes only as a last resort and in exceptional cases.

(e) [Encouragement and support of establishment and operation of joint labor management activities conducted by committees] The Service is authorized and directed to encourage and support the establishment and operation of joint labor management activities conducted by plant, area, and industrywide committees designed to improve labor management relationships, job security and organizational effectiveness, in accordance with the provisions of section 205A [section 175a of this title].

[Pub. L. 95-524, §6(c)(1), Oct. 27, 1978, 92 Stat. 2020, added subsec. (e).]

Sec. 204.   [§174. Co-equal obligations of employees, their representatives, and management to minimize labor disputes]

(a) In order to prevent or minimize interruptions of the free flow of commerce growing out of labor disputes, employers and employees and their representatives, in any industry affecting commerce, shall—

(1) exert every reasonable effort to make and maintain agreements concerning rates of pay, hours, and working conditions, including provision for adequate notice of any proposed change in the terms of such agreements;

(2) whenever a dispute arises over the terms or application of a collective-bargaining agreement and a conference is requested by a party or prospective party thereto, arrange promptly for such a conference to be held and endeavor in such conference to settle such dispute expeditiously; and

(3) in case such dispute is not settled by conference, participate fully and promptly in such meetings as may be undertaken by the Service under this Act [chapter] for the purpose of aiding in a settlement of the dispute.

Sec. 205. [§175. National Labor-Management Panel; creation and composition; appointment, tenure, and compensation; duties] (a) There is created a National Labor-Management Panel which shall be composed of twelve members appointed by the President, six of whom shall be selected from among persons outstanding in the field of management and six of whom shall be selected from among persons outstanding in the field of labor. Each member shall hold office for a term of three years, except that any member appointed to fill a vacancy occurring prior to the expiration of the term for which his predecessor was appointed shall be appointed for the remainder of such term, and the terms of office of the members first taking office shall expire, as designated by the President at the time of appointment, four at the end of the first year, four at the end of the second year, and four at the end of the third year after the date of appointment. Members of the panel, when serving on business of the panel, shall be paid compensation at the rate of $25 per day, and shall also be entitled to receive an allowance for actual and necessary travel and subsistence expenses while so serving away from their places of residence.

(b) It shall be the duty of the panel, at the request of the Director, to advise in the avoidance of industrial controversies and the manner in which mediation and voluntary adjustment shall be administered, particularly with reference to controversies affecting the general welfare of the country.

Sec. 205A. [§175a. Assistance to plant, area, and industrywide labor management committees]

(a) [Establishment and operation of plant, area, and industrywide committees] (1) The Service is authorized and directed to provide assistance in the establishment and operation of plant, area and industrywide labor management committees which—

(A) have been organized jointly by employers and labor organizations representing employees in that plant, area, or industry; and

(B) are established for the purpose of improving labor management relationships, job security, organizational effectiveness, enhancing economic development or involving workers in decisions affecting their jobs including improving communication with respect to subjects of mutual interest and concern.

(2) The Service is authorized and directed to enter into contracts and to make grants, where necessary or appropriate, to fulfill its responsibilities under this section.

(b) [Restrictions on grants, contracts, or other assistance] (1) No grant may be made, no contract may be entered into and no other assistance may be provided under the provisions of this section to a plant labor management committee unless the employees in that plant are represented by a labor organization and there is in effect at that plant a collective bargaining agreement.

(2) No grant may be made, no contract may be entered into and no other assistance may be provided under the provisions of this section to an area or industrywide labor management committee unless its participants include any labor organizations certified or recognized as the representative of the employees of an employer participating in such committee. Nothing in this clause shall prohibit participation in an area or industrywide committee by an employer whose employees are not represented by a labor organization.

(3) No grant may be made under the provisions of this section to any labor management committee which the Service finds to have as one of its purposes the discouragement of the exercise of rights contained in section 7 of the National Labor Relations Act (29 U.S.C. §157) [section 157 of this title], or the interference with collective bargaining in any plant, or industry.

(c) **[Establishment of office]** The Service shall carry out the provisions of this section through an office established for that purpose.

(d) **[Authorization of appropriations]** There are authorized to be appropriated to carry out the provisions of this section $10,000,000 for the fiscal year 1979, and such sums as may be necessary thereafter.

[Pub. L. 95-524, §6(c)(2), Oct. 27, 1978, 92 Stat. 2020, added Sec. 205A.]

NATIONAL EMERGENCIES

Sec. 206. **[§176. Appointment of board of inquiry by President; report; contents; filing with Service]** Whenever in the opinion of the President of the United States, a threatened or actual strike or lockout affecting an entire industry or a substantial part thereof engaged in trade, commerce, transportation, transmission, or communication among the several States or with foreign nations, or engaged in the production of goods for commerce, will, if permitted to occur or to continue, imperil the national health or safety, he may appoint a board of inquiry to inquire into the issues involved in the dispute and to make a written report to him within such time as he shall prescribe. Such report shall include a statement of the facts with respect to the dispute, including each party's statement of its position but shall not contain any recommendations. The President shall file a copy of such report with the Service and shall make its contents available to the public.

Sec. 207. **[§177. Board of inquiry]** (a) **[Composition]** A board of inquiry shall be composed of a chairman and such other members as the President shall determine, and shall have power to sit and act in any place within the United States and to conduct such hearings either in public or in private, as it may deem necessary or proper, to ascertain the facts with respect to the causes and circumstances of the dispute.

(b) **[Compensation]** Members of a board of inquiry shall receive compensation at the rate of $50 for each day actually spent by them in the work of the board, together with necessary travel and subsistence expenses.

(c) **[Powers of discovery]** For the purpose of any hearing or inquiry conducted by any board appointed under this title, the provisions of sections 49 and 50 of title 15, United States Code [sections 49 and 50 of title 15] (relating to the attendance of witnesses and the production of books, papers, and documents) are made applicable to the powers and duties of such board.

Sec. 208. **[§178. Injunctions during national emergency]**

(a) **[Petition to district court by Attorney General on direction of President]** Upon receiving a report from a board of inquiry the President may direct the Attorney General to petition any district court of the United States having jurisdiction of the parties to enjoin such strike or lockout or the continuing thereof, and if the court finds that such threatened or actual strike or lockout—

(i) affects an entire industry or a substantial part thereof engaged in trade, commerce, transportation, transmission, or communication among the several States or with foreign nations, or engaged in the production of goods for commerce; and

(ii) if permitted to occur or to continue, will imperil the national health or safety, it shall have jurisdiction to enjoin any such strike or lockout, or the continuing thereof, and to make such other orders as may be appropriate.

(b) **[Inapplicability of chapter 6]** In any case, the provisions of sections 101 to 115 of title 29, United States Code [chapter 6 of this title] [known as the "Norris-LaGuardia Act"] shall not be applicable.

(c) **[Review of orders]** The order or orders of the court shall be subject to review by the appropriate United States court of appeals and by the Supreme Court upon writ of certiorari or certification as provided in section 1254 of title 28, United States Code [section 1254 of title 28].

Sec. 209. [§179. Injunctions during national emergency; adjustment efforts by parties during injunction period]

(a) [Assistance of Service; acceptance of Service's proposed settlement] Whenever a district court has issued an order under section 208 [section 178 of this title] enjoining acts or practices which imperil or threaten to imperil the national health or safety, it shall be the duty of the parties to the labor dispute giving rise to such order to make every effort to adjust and settle their differences, with the assistance of the Service created by this Act [chapter]. Neither party shall be under any duty to accept, in whole or in part, any proposal of settlement made by the Service.

(b) [Reconvening of board of inquiry; report by board; contents; secret ballot of employees by National Labor Relations Board; certification of results to Attorney General] Upon the issuance of such order, the President shall reconvene the board of inquiry which has previously reported with respect to the dispute. At the end of a sixty-day period (unless the dispute has been settled by that time), the board of inquiry shall report to the President the current position of the parties and the efforts which have been made for settlement, and shall include a statement by each party of its position and a statement of the employer's last offer of settlement. The President shall make such report available to the public. The National Labor Relations Board, within the succeeding fifteen days, shall take a secret ballot of the employees of each employer involved in the dispute on the question of whether they wish to accept the final offer of settlement made by their employer as stated by him and shall certify the results thereof to the Attorney General within five days thereafter.

Sec. 210. [§180. Discharge of injunction upon certification of results of election or settlement; report to Congress] Upon the certification of the results of such ballot or upon a settlement being reached, whichever happens sooner, the Attorney General shall move the court to discharge the injunction, which motion shall then be granted and the injunction discharged. When such motion is granted, the President shall submit to the Congress a full and comprehensive report of the proceedings, including the findings of the board of inquiry and the ballot taken by the National Labor Relations Board, together with such recommendations as he may see fit to make for consideration and appropriate action.

COMPILATION OF COLLECTIVE-BARGAINING AGREEMENTS, ETC.

Sec. 211. [§181.] (a) For the guidance and information of interested representatives of employers, employees and the general public, the Bureau of Labor Statistics of the Department of Labor shall maintain a file of copies of all available collective bargaining agreements and other available agreements and actions thereunder settling or adjusting labor disputes. Such file shall be open to inspection under appropriate conditions prescribed by the Secretary of Labor, except that no specific information submitted in confidence shall be disclosed.

(b) The Bureau of Labor Statistics in the Department of Labor is authorized to furnish upon request of the Service, or employers, employees, or their representatives, all available data and factual information which may aid in the settlement of any labor dispute, except that no specific information submitted in confidence shall be disclosed.

EXEMPTION OF RAILWAY LABOR ACT

Sec. 212. [§182.] The provisions of this title [subchapter] shall not be applicable with respect to any matter which is subject to the provisions of the Railway Labor Act [45 U.S.C. §151 et seq.], as amended from time to time.

CONCILIATION OF LABOR DISPUTES IN THE HEALTH CARE INDUSTRY

Sec. 213. [§183.] (a) [Establishment of Boards of Inquiry; membership] If, in the opinion of the Director of the Federal Mediation and Conciliation Service, a threatened or actual strike or lockout affecting a health care institution will, if permitted to occur or to continue, substantially interrupt the delivery of health care in the locality concerned, the Director may further assist in the resolution of the impasse by establishing within 30 days after the notice to the Federal Mediation and Conciliation Service under clause (A) of the last sentence of section 8(d) [section 158(d) of this title] (which is required by clause (3) of such section 8(d) [section 158(d) of this title]), or within 10 days after the notice under clause (B), an impartial Board of Inquiry to investigate the issues involved in the dispute and to make a written report thereon to the parties within fifteen (15) days after the establishment of such a Board. The written report shall contain the findings of fact together with the Board's recommendations for settling the dispute, with the objective of achieving a prompt, peaceful and just settlement of the dispute. Each such Board shall be composed of such number of individuals as the Director may deem desirable. No member appointed under this section shall have any interest or involvement in the health care institutions or the employee organizations involved in the dispute.

(b) [Compensation of members of Boards of Inquiry] (1) Members of any board established under this section who are otherwise employed by the Federal Government shall serve without compensation but shall be reimbursed for travel, subsistence, and other necessary expenses incurred by them in carrying out its duties under this section.

(2) Members of any board established under this section who are not subject to paragraph (1) shall receive compensation at a rate prescribed by the Director but not to exceed the daily rate prescribed for GS-18 of the General Schedule under section 5332 of title 5, United States Code [section 5332 of title 5], including travel for each day they are engaged in the performance of their duties under this section and shall be entitled to reimbursement for travel, subsistence, and other necessary expenses incurred by them in carrying out their duties under this section.

(c) [Maintenance of status quo] After the establishment of a board under subsection (a) of this section and for 15 days after any such board has issued its report, no change in the status quo in effect prior to the expiration of the contract in the case of negotiations for a contract renewal, or in effect prior to the time of the impasse in the case of an initial bargaining negotiation, except by agreement, shall be made by the parties to the controversy.

(d) [Authorization of appropriations] There are authorized to be appropriated such sums as may be necessary to carry out the provisions of this section.

TITLE III

[Title 29, Chapter 7, Subchapter IV, United States Code]

SUITS BY AND AGAINST LABOR ORGANIZATIONS

Sec. 301. [§185.] (a) [Venue, amount, and citizenship] Suits for violation of contracts between an employer and a labor organization representing employees in an industry affecting commerce as defined in this Act [chapter], or between any such labor organization, may be brought in any district court of the United States having jurisdiction of the parties, without respect to the amount in controversy or without regard to the citizenship of the parties.

(b) [Responsibility for acts of agent; entity for purposes of suit; enforcement of money judgments] Any labor organization which represents employees in an industry affecting commerce as defined in this Act [chapter] and any employer whose activities affect commerce as defined in this Act [chapter] shall be bound by the acts of its agents. Any such labor organization may sue or be sued as an entity and in behalf of the employees whom it represents in the courts of the United States. Any money judgment against a labor organization in a district court of the United States shall be enforceable only against the organization as an entity and against its assets, and shall not be enforceable against any individual member or his assets.

(c) [Jurisdiction] For the purposes of actions and proceedings by or against labor organizations in the district courts of the United States, district courts shall be deemed to have jurisdiction of a labor organization (1) in the district in which such organization maintains its principal offices, or (2) in any district in which its duly authorized officers or agents are engaged in representing or acting for employee members.

(d) [Service of process] The service of summons, subpoena, or other legal process of any court of the United States upon an officer or agent of a labor organization, in his capacity as such, shall constitute service upon the labor organization.

(e) [Determination of question of agency] For the purposes of this section, in determining whether any person is acting as an "agent" of another person so as to make such other person responsible for his acts, the question of whether the specific acts performed were actually authorized or subsequently ratified shall not be controlling.

RESTRICTIONS ON PAYMENTS TO EMPLOYEE REPRESENTATIVES

Sec. 302. [§186.] **(a) [Payment or lending, etc., of money by employer or agent to employees, representatives, or labor organizations]** It shall be unlawful for any employer or association of employers or any person who acts as a labor relations expert, adviser, or consultant to an employer or who acts in the interest of an employer to pay, lend, or deliver, or agree to pay, lend, or deliver, any money or other thing of value—

(1) to any representative of any of his employees who are employed in an industry affecting commerce; or

(2) to any labor organization, or any officer or employee thereof, which represents, seeks to represent, or would admit to membership, any of the employees of such employer who are employed in an industry affecting commerce;

(3) to any employee or group or committee of employees of such employer employed in an industry affecting commerce in excess of their normal compensation for the purpose of causing such employee or group or committee directly or indirectly to influence any other employees in the exercise of the right to organize and bargain collectively through representatives of their own choosing; or

(4) to any officer or employee of a labor organization engaged in an industry affecting commerce with intent to influence him in respect to any of his actions, decisions, or duties as a representative of employees or as such officer or employee of such labor organization.

(b) [Request, demand, etc., for money or other thing of value] (1) It shall be unlawful for any person to request, demand, receive, or accept, or agree to receive or accept, any payment, loan, or delivery of any money or other thing of value prohibited by subsection (a) [of this section].

(2) It shall be unlawful for any labor organization, or for any person acting as an officer, agent, representative, or employee of such labor organization, to demand or accept from the operator of any motor vehicle (as defined in part II of the Interstate Commerce Act [49 U.S.C. §301 et seq.]) employed in the transportation of property in commerce, or the employer of any such operator, any money or other thing of value payable to such organization or to an officer, agent, representative or employee thereof as a fee or charge for

the unloading, or in connection with the unloading, of the cargo of such vehicle: *Provided,* That nothing in this paragraph shall be construed to make unlawful any payment by an employer to any of his employees as compensation for their services as employees.

(c) [Exceptions] The provisions of this section shall not be applicable (1) in respect to any money or other thing of value payable by an employer to any of his employees whose established duties include acting openly for such employer in matters of labor relations or personnel administration or to any representative of his employees, or to any officer or employee of a labor organization, who is also an employee or former employee of such employer, as compensation for, or by reason of, his service as an employee of such employer; (2) with respect to the payment or delivery of any money or other thing of value in satisfaction of a judgment of any court or a decision or award of an arbitrator or impartial chairman or in compromise, adjustment, settlement, or release of any claim, complaint, grievance, or dispute in the absence of fraud or duress; (3) with respect to the sale or purchase of an article or commodity at the prevailing market price in the regular course of business; (4) with respect to money deducted from the wages of employees in payment of membership dues in a labor organization: *Provided,* That the employer has received from each employee, on whose account such deductions are made, a written assignment which shall not be irrevocable for a period of more than one year, or beyond the termination date of the applicable collective agreement, whichever occurs sooner; (5) with respect to money or other thing of value paid to a trust fund established by such representative, for the sole and exclusive benefit of the employees of such employer, and their families and dependents (or of such employees, families, and dependents jointly with the employees of other employers making similar payments, and their families and dependents): *Provided,* That (A) such payments are held in trust for the purpose of paying, either from principal or income or both, for the benefit of employees, their families and dependents, for medical or hospital care, pensions on retirement or death of employees, compensation for injuries or illness resulting from occupational activity or insurance to provide any of the foregoing, or unemployment benefits or life insurance, disability and sickness insurance, or accident insurance; (B) the detailed basis on which such payments are to be made is specified in a written agreement with the employer, and employees and employers are equally represented in the administration of such fund, together with such neutral persons as the representatives of the employers and the representatives of employees may agree upon and in the event the employer and employee groups deadlock on the administration of such fund and there are no neutral persons empowered to break such deadlock, such agreement provides that the two groups shall agree on an impartial umpire to decide such dispute, or in event of their failure to agree within a reasonable length of time, an impartial umpire to decide such dispute shall, on petition of either group, be appointed by the district court of the United States for the district where the trust fund has its principal office, and shall also contain provisions for an annual audit of the trust fund, a statement of the results of which shall be available for inspection by interested persons at the principal office of the trust fund and at such other places as may be designated in such written agreement; and (C) such payments as are intended to be used for the purpose of providing pensions or annuities for employees are made to a separate trust which provides that the funds held therein cannot be used for any purpose other than paying such pensions or annuities; (6) with respect to money or other thing of value paid by any employer to a trust fund established by such representative for the purpose of pooled vacation, holiday, severance or similar benefits, or defraying costs of apprenticeship or other training programs: *Provided,* That the requirements of clause (B) of the proviso to clause (5) of this subsection shall apply to such trust funds; (7) with respect to money or other thing of value paid by any employer to a pooled or individual trust fund established by such representative for the purpose of (A) scholarships for the benefit of employees, their families, and dependents for study at educational institutions, or (B) child care centers for preschool and school age dependents of employees: *Provided,* That no labor organization or employer shall be required to bargain on the establishment of any such trust fund, and refusal to do so shall not constitute an unfair labor practice: *Provided further,* That the requirements of clause (B) of the proviso to clause (5) of this subsection shall apply to such trust funds; (8) with respect to money or any other thing of value paid by any employer to a trust fund established by such representative for the purpose of defraying the costs of legal services for employees, their families, and dependents for counsel or plan of their choice: *Provided,* That the requirements of clause (B) of the proviso to clause (5) of this subsection shall apply to such trust funds: *Provided further,* That no such legal services shall be furnished: (A) to initiate any proceeding directed (i) against any such employer or its officers or agents except in workman's compensation cases; or (ii) against such labor organization, or its parent or subordinate bodies, or their officers or agents, or (iii) against any other employer or labor organization, or their officers or agents, in any matter arising under the National Labor Relations Act, or this Act [under subchapter II of this chapter or this chapter]; and (B) in any proceeding where a labor organization would be prohibited from defraying the costs of legal services by the provisions of the Labor-Management Reporting and Disclosure Act of 1959 [29 U.S.C. §401 et seq.]; or (9) with respect to money or other things of value paid by an employer to a plant, area or industrywide labor management committee established for one or more of the purposes set forth in section 5(b) of the Labor Management Cooperation Act of 1978.

[Sec. 302(c)(7) was added by Pub. L. 91-86, Oct. 14, 1969, 83 Stat. 133; Sec. 302(c)(8) by Pub. L. 93-95, Aug. 15, 1973, 87 Stat. 314; and Sec. 302(c)(9) by Pub. L. 95-524, Oct. 27, 1978, 92 Stat. 2021.]

(d) [Penalty for violations] Any person who willfully violates any of the provisions of this section shall, upon conviction thereof, be guilty of a misdemeanor and be subject to a fine of not more than $10,000 or to imprisonment for not more than one year, or both.

(e) [Jurisdiction of courts] The district courts of the United States and the United States courts of the Territories and possessions shall have jurisdiction, for cause shown, and subject to the provisions of rule 65 of the Federal Rules of Civil Procedure [section 381 (repealed) of title 28] (relating to notice to opposite party) to restrain violations of this section, without regard to the provisions of section 17 of title 15 and section 52 of title 29, United States Code [of this title] [known as the "Clayton Act"], and the provisions of sections 101 to 115 of title 29, United States Code [chapter 6 of this title] [known as the "Norris-LaGuardia Act"].

(f) [Effective date of provisions] This section shall not apply to any contract in force on June 23, 1947, until the expiration of such contract, or until July 1, 1948, whichever first occurs.

(g) [Contributions to trust funds] Compliance with the restrictions contained in subsection (c)(5)(B) [of this section] upon contributions to trust funds, otherwise lawful, shall not be applicable to contributions to such trust funds established by collective agreement prior to January 1, 1946, nor shall subsection (c)(5)(A) [of this section] be construed as prohibiting contributions to such trust funds if prior to January 1, 1947, such funds contained provisions for pooled vacation benefits.

BOYCOTTS AND OTHER UNLAWFUL COMBINATIONS

Sec. 303. **[§187.]** (a) It shall be unlawful, for the purpose of this section only, in an industry or activity affecting commerce, for any labor organization to engage in any activity or conduct defined as an unfair labor practice in section 8(b)(4) of the National Labor Relations Act [section 158(b)(4) of this title].

(b) Whoever shall be injured in his business or property by reason of any violation of subsection (a) [of this section] may sue therefor in any district court of the United States subject to the limitation and provisions of section 301 hereof [section 185 of this title] without respect to the amount in controversy, or in any other court having jurisdiction of the parties, and shall recover the damages by him sustained and the cost of the suit.

RESTRICTION ON POLITICAL CONTRIBUTIONS

Sec. 304.   Repealed.

[See sec. 316 of the Federal Election Campaign Act of 1972, 2 U.S.C. §441b.]

Sec. 305.   [§188.]   Strikes by Government employees. Repealed.

[See 5 U.S.C. §7311 and 18 U.S.C. §1918.]

TITLE IV

[Title 29, Chapter 7, Subchapter V, United States Code]

CREATION OF JOINT COMMITTEE TO STUDY AND REPORT ON BASIC PROBLEMS
AFFECTING FRIENDLY LABOR RELATIONS AND PRODUCTIVITY

Secs. 401–407.   [§§191–197.]   Omitted.

TITLE V

[Title 29, Chapter 7, Subchapter I, United States Code]

DEFINITIONS

Sec. 501.   [§142.]   When used in this Act [chapter]—

(1) The term "industry affecting commerce" means any industry or activity in commerce or in which a labor dispute would burden or obstruct commerce or tend to burden or obstruct commerce or the free flow of commerce.

(2) The term "strike" includes any strike or other concerted stoppage of work by employees (including a stoppage by reason of the expiration of a collective-bargaining agreement) and any concerted slowdown or other concerted interruption of operations by employees.

(3) The terms "commerce", "labor disputes", "employer", "employee", "labor organization", "representative", "person", and "supervisor" shall have the same meaning as when used in the National Labor Relations Act as amended by this Act [in subchapter II of this chapter].

SAVING PROVISION

Sec. 502.   [§143.] [Abnormally dangerous conditions]   Nothing in this Act [chapter] shall be construed to require an individual employee to render labor or service without his consent, nor shall anything in this Act [chapter] be construed to make the quitting of his labor by an individual employee an illegal act; nor shall any court issue any process to compel the performance by an individual employee of such labor or service, without his consent; nor shall the quitting of labor by an employee or employees in good faith because of abnormally dangerous conditions for work at the place of employment of such employee or employees be deemed a strike under this Act [chapter].

SEPARABILITY

Sec. 503. **[§144.]** If any provision of this Act [chapter], or the application of such provision to any person or circumstance, shall be held invalid, the remainder of this Act [chapter], or the application of such provision to persons or circumstances other than those as to which it is held invalid, shall not be affected thereby.

Bibliography

BIBLIOGRAPHIES AND DICTIONARIES

Coleman, Charles J., and Theodora T. Haynes, eds., *Arbitration: An Annotated Bibliography* (Cornell Industrial and Labor Relations Bibliography Series, no. 17). Ithaca, NY: ILR Press, 1994. 271 pp.

Cornell University, Libraries, Industrial and Labor Relations Library, *Library Catalog of the New York State School of Industrial and Labor Relations.* Boston: G.K. Hall, 1967–1981. 12 vols. with supplements.

Doherty, Robert E., *Industrial and Labor Relations Terms: A Glossary* (ILR Bulletin, no. 44), 5th ed. rev. Ithaca, NY: New York State School of Industrial and Labor Relations, Cornell University, 1989. 36 pp.

Herman, Georgianna, and Gwendolyn Lloyd, "PAIR Literature: Keeping Up to Date." In *ASPA Handbook of Industrial Relations,* Vol. 8: *Professional PAIR.* Dale Yoder and Herbert G. Henemen, Jr., eds. Washington, DC: Bureau of National Affairs, 1979, pp. 8-113–8-248.

McBrearty, James C., *American Labor History and Comparative Labor Movements: A Selected Bibliography.* Tucson: University of Arizona Press, 1973. 262 pp.

Neufeld, Maurice F., Daniel J. Leab, and Dorothy Swanson, *American Working Class History: A Representative Bibliography,* rev. ed. New York: Bowker, 1983. 356 pp.

Roberts, Harold S., *Roberts' Dictionary of Industrial Relations,* 4th ed. Washington, DC: Bureau of National Affairs, 1994. 874 pp.

Seide, Katharine, ed., *The Paul Felix Warburg Union Catalog of Arbitration: A Selective Bibliography and Subject Index of Peaceful Dispute Settlement Procedures.* Totowa, NJ: Published for Rowman and Littlefield (published for the Eastman Library of the American Arbitration Association), 1974. 3 vols.

Selected References. Princeton, NJ: Princeton University, Industrial Relations Section, 1945 [irregular].

Shafritz, Jay M., *Facts on File Dictionary of Personnel Management and Labor Relations,* 2nd ed., rev. and expanded. New York: Facts on File, Inc., 1985. 534 pp.

Soltow, Martha Jane, and Jo Ann S. Sokkar, *Industrial Relations and Personnel Management: Selected Information Sources.* Metuchen, NJ: Scarecrow Press, 1979. 286 pp.

Soltow, Martha Jane, and Mary K. Wery, *American Women and the Labor Movement, 1825–1974: An Annotated Bibliography,* 2nd ed. Metuchen, NJ: Scarecrow Press, 1976. 247 pp.

Vocino, Michael C., and Lucille W. Cameron, comps., *Labor and Industrial Relations Journals and Serials: An Analytical Guide.* New York: Greenwood Press, 1989. 214 pp.

*This bibliography was compiled by Philip R. Dankert, Collection Development Librarian, Martin P. Catherwood Library, New York State School of Industrial and Labor Relations, Cornell University, Ithaca, NY: 14853-3901.

Space limitations prevented a more complete listing. (Thus, it is to be hoped that omissions were intentional.) Certain subject areas are excluded—for example, organizational behavior and personnel management.

We wish to express our great appreciation to Helen Hamilton for her tireless efforts in typing and checking the accuracy of the various entries in this bibliography.

Wilson, Joseph, *Black Labor in America, 1865–1983: A Selected Annotated Bibliography.* New York: Greenwood Press, 1986. 118 pp.

BIOGRAPHIES

Directory of Labor Arbitrators. Fort Washington, PA: Labor Relations Press, 1982– [loose-leaf].

Dubofsky, Melvyn, and Warren Van Tine, eds., *Labor Leaders in America.* Urbana: University of Illinois Press, 1987. 396 pp.

Fink, Gary M., ed., *Biographical Dictionary of American Labor,* 2nd ed. Westport, CT: Greenwood Press, 1984. 767 pp.

Industrial Relations Research Association, *Membership Directory Handbook.* Madison, WI: 1949– [irregular].

National Academy of Arbitrators, *Membership Directory.* Washington, DC: 1947– [annual].

Who's Who in Labor. New York: Dryden Press, 1946. 480 pp.

JOURNALS/SERIALS

Advances in Industrial and Labor Relations. Greenwich, CT: JAI Press, 1983– [annual].

British Journal of Industrial Relations. London: London School of Economics and Political Science, 1963– [triannual].

Compensation & Benefits Management. Greenvale, NY: Panel Publishers, 1984– [quarterly].

Directory of U.S. Labor Organizations. Washington, DC: Bureau of National Affairs, 1982/1983– [biennial].

Dispute Resolution Journal. New York: American Arbitration Association, 1993– [quarterly].

Economic and Industrial Democracy. London: Sage Publications, Ltd., 1980– [quarterly].

Employee Benefit Plan Review. Chicago: Charles D. Spencer and Associates, 1946– [monthly].

Employee Relations Law Journal. New York: Executive Enterprises Publications, 1975– [quarterly].

Employee Responsibilities and Rights Journal. New York: Plenum, 1988– [quarterly].

European Journal of Industrial Relations. London: Sage, 1995. [triannual].

Hofstra Labor Law Journal. Hempstead, NY: Hofstra University School of Law, 1984– [semiannual].

Industrial and Labor Relations Review. Ithaca: New York State School of Industrial and Labor Relations, Cornell University, 1947– [quarterly].

Industrial Relations: A Journal of Political Economy. Berkeley: Institute of Industrial Relations, University of California, 1961– [triannual].

Industrial Relations Journal. London: Business Publications Ltd., 1970– [quarterly].

Industrial Relations Law Journal. Berkeley: School of Law, University of California, 1976– [quarterly].

International Journal of Comparative Labour Law and Industrial Relations. Leicester, England: 1985– [quarterly].

International Journal of Conflict Management. Bowling Green, KY: Center for Advanced Studies in Management, 1990– [quarterly].

International Labour Review. Geneva, Switzerland: International Labour Office, 1921– [bimonthly].

Journal of Collective Negotiations in the Public Sector. Farmingdale, NY: Baywood Publishing Co., 1972– [quarterly].

Journal of Individual Employment Rights. Amityville, NY: Baywood Publishing Co., 1992– [quarterly].

Journal of Labor Research. Fairfax, VA: Department of Economics, George Mason University, 1980– [quarterly].

Labor History. New York: Tamiment Institute, New York University, 1960– [quarterly].

Labor Law Journal. Chicago: Commerce Clearing House, 1949– [monthly].

Labor Studies Journal. New Brunswick, NJ: Transaction Periodicals Consortium, Rutgers University, 1973– [triannual].

Monthly Labor Review. Washington, DC: U.S. Government Printing Office, 1915– [monthly].

New Technology, Work and Employment. Oxford, England: Blackwell, 1986– [biannual].

N.L.R.B. Election Report. U.S. National Labor Relations Board, Washington, DC, 1962– [monthly].

Relations Industrielles. Industrial Relations. Quebec, Canada: Department of Industrial Relations, Laval University, 1950– [quarterly].

Research on Negotiation in Organizations. Greenwich, CT: JAI Press, 1986– [biennial].

ELECTRONIC RESOURCES

CD/ROMs

ABI/INFORM. Contains abstracts to articles appearing in approximately 1,000 international periodicals covering business and management and related functional areas including labor, industrial relations, and human resource studies. Coverage is from 1971. The full text version of ABI/INFORM contains the complete text of 550 periodicals from 1988 (SilverPlatter or UMI; $17,550.00/year).

EconLit. Citations to and selected abstracts of international literature in the field of economics since 1969. Topics include economic theory and history, labor economics, international and urban economics, and other related subjects (SilverPlatter; $1,595.00/year).

LABORDOC. Records of documents processed in the ILO Central Library and Documentation Branch including books, reports, ILO publications, and selected publications of other international organizations from 1965. Covers labor and employment issues worldwide including labor relations, labor law, occupational safety and health, vocational training, and technological change (SilverPlatter; $850.00/year).

OSHROM. Brings together four complete bibliographic databases covering international occupational safety and health information. Coverage is from 1960 and contains citations to journals, books, and technical reports. It includes the following:

1. NIOSHTIC—National Institute for Occupational Safety and Health

2. HSELINE—Health and Safety Executive (UK)

3. CISDOC—International Occupational Safety and Health Information Centre of the ILO

(SilverPlatter; $1,078.00/year)

PAIS International. Selective bibliographic index to the public and social policy literature of business, economics, government, law, political science, and other social sciences. Dating from 1972, it contains references to journal articles, books, government documents, conference proceedings, pamphlets, reports, and microfiche from all over the world (SilverPlatter; $1,995.00/year).

Statistical Abstracts from A Matter of Fact Database. Contains statements reflecting current social, economic, political, and health public policy issues. The abstracts do not display raw numbers in tables and charts; rather they present the data selected by writers and speakers to influence others. Approximately 25 percent of the abstracts are derived from congressional hearings, another 15 percent from the *Congressional Record,* and the remaining from both general interest and specialized periodicals, newsletters, and newspapers. Coverage is from 1984 (SilverPlatter; $495.00/year).

List Servers

H–Labor—Labor History. To subscribe send an e-mail message to: listserv@msu.edu.

Within the message, include the following one-line command: subscribe H–Labor firstname lastname.

HRNET—Human Resource Management. To subscribe send an e-mail message to the following address: listserv@cornell.edu.

Within the message, include only the following one-line command, precisely using the following format: sub hrnet firstname lastname.

IERN–L—International Employee Relations Network. To subscribe send an e-mail message to: listserv@ube.ubalt.edu.

Within the message, include the following one-line command: subscribe IERN–L firstname lastname.

IRRA—Industrial Relations and Human Resources. To subscribe send an e-mail message to: listserv@relay.doit.wisc.edu.

Within the message, include the following one-line command: subscribe irra firstname lastname.

Web Sites

Bureau of Labor Statistics (http://www.bls.gov). Includes BLS information (mission statement, other statistical sites); publications information; a listing of published and unpublished BLS research papers and an annotated bibliography of statistical papers; and surveys and programs dealing with employment and unemployment, employment projections, compensation and working conditions, productivity and technology, etc.

WorkNet@ILR (http://www.ilr.cornell.edu). Includes general information about the ILR School at Cornell University; an Electronic Bookshelf of collections, databases, and archives of government documents such as the *Glass Ceiling* reports; and the *Industrial and Labor Relations Virtual Library,* a guide to other internet resources including Gopher, Web FTP, and mailing lists in related fields. (Other ILR Schools have web sites—e.g., UC Berkeley, University of Illinois at Urbana-Champaign, and Princeton–Library.)

LaborWeb: The ALF-CIO's Home Page (http://www.aflcio.org). Includes union organizations on the web; other labor-related web sites; policy statements, press releases, and issue papers; and the *AFL-CIO News* on-line.

Occupational Safety and Health Administration (http://www.osha.gov). Includes information about OSHA, publications, media releases, programs and services, statistics (e.g., occupational injury and illness incidence rates), standards, and safety and health Internet sites.

Other Electronic Resources

LEXIS-NEXIS. One of the world's largest full-text electronic libraries, it includes extensive libraries on law, legislation, the news media, as well as databases covering the social sciences.

PROCEEDINGS OF PROFESSIONAL ORGANIZATIONS

Conference on Labor, New York University, *Proceedings, 1st–*. New York: Matthew Bender, 1948– [annual].

Industrial Relations Research Association (IRRA), *Proceedings of the Annual Spring Meeting, 1st–*. Madison, WI, 1958–.

Industrial Relations Research Association (IRRA), *Proceedings of the Annual Winter Meeting, 1st–*. Madison, WI, 1948–.

National Academy of Arbitrators, *Proceedings of the Annual Meeting, 1st–*. Washington, DC: Bureau of National Affairs, 1955–.

Society of Professionals in Dispute Resolution (SPIDR), *Proceedings of the Annual Convention*. Washington, DC, 1973–.

Southwestern Legal Foundation, Institute of Labor Law, *Proceedings, 1st–*. New York: Matthew Bender, 1949– [annual].

SELECTED LOOSE-LEAF REPORTING SERVICES AND RELATED PUBLICATIONS

BNA Policy and Practice Series. Washington, DC: Bureau of National Affairs, 1950– [loose-leaf].

BNA's Employee Relations Weekly. Washington, DC: Bureau of National Affairs, 1983–.

Collective Bargaining Negotiations and Contracts. Washington, DC: Bureau of National Affairs, 1951– [loose-leaf].

Compensation and Benefits Guide. Washington, DC: Bureau of National Affairs, 1993– [loose-leaf].

Daily Labor Report. Washington, DC: Bureau of National Affairs, 1941–.

Employment Practices Guide. Chicago: Commerce Clearing House, 1965– [loose-leaf].

Federal Labor Relations Reporter. Fort Washington, PA: Labor Relations Press, 1970– [loose-leaf].

Federal Merit Systems Reporter. Fort Washington, PA: Labor Relations Press, 1981– [loose-leaf].

Government Employee Relations Report. Washington, DC: Bureau of National Affairs, 1963– [loose-leaf].

Hebert, L. Camille, *Employee Privacy Law.* Deerfield, IL: Clark Boardman Callaghan, 1993– [loose-leaf].

Kheel, Theodore W., *Labor Law.* New York: Matthew Bender, 1972– [loose-leaf. 10 vols. plus Consolidated Table of Cases and Index].

Labor and Employment Arbitration. New York: Matthew Bender, 1988– [loose-leaf].

Labor Arbitration Awards. Chicago: Commerce Clearing House, 1961– [loose-leaf].

Labor Arbitration Information System. Fort Washington, PA: Labor Relations Press, 1981– [loose-leaf].

Labor Law Reporter. Chicago: Commerce Clearing House, 1960– [loose-leaf].

Labor Relations Reporter. Washington, DC: Bureau of National Affairs, 1947– [loose-leaf].

Labor Relations Week. Washington, DC: Bureau of National Affairs, 1987–.

Larson, Arthur, *Employment Discrimination.* New York: Matthew Bender, 1975– [loose-leaf].

National Public Employment Reporter. Fort Washington, PA: Labor Relations Press, 1979– [loose-leaf].

NLRB Advice Memorandum Reporter. Fort Washington, PA: Labor Relations Press, 1976– [loose-leaf].

Pennsylvania Public Employee Reporter. Fort Washington, PA: Labor Relations Press, 1971– (Labor Relations Press also publishes state reporters for California, Florida, Indiana, New Jersey, New York, and Ohio.) [loose-leaf].

Stessin, Lawrence, and Len Smedresman, *Encyclopedia of Collective Bargaining Contract Clauses.* New York: Business Research Publications, 1984– [loose-leaf].

Union Labor Report. Washington, DC: Bureau of National Affairs, 1954– [loose-leaf].

U.S. National Labor Relations Board. *Decisions and Orders, Vol. 1–.* Washington, DC: U.S. Government Printing Office, 1935/36–.

ARBITRATION/MEDIATION

Bernstein, Irving, *Arbitration of Wages.* Berkeley: University of California Press, Institute of Industrial Relations, 1954. 125 pp.

Bognanno, Mario F., and Charles J. Coleman, eds., *Labor Arbitration in America: The Profession and Practice.* New York: Praeger, 1992. 186 pp.

Ewing, David W., *Justice on the Job: Resolving Grievances in the Nonunion Workplace.* Boston: Harvard Business School Press, 1989. 337 pp.

Grenig, Jay E., and R. Wayne Estes, *Labor Arbitration Advocacy: Effective Tactics and Techniques.* Stoneham, MA: Butterworth, 1989. 319 pp.

Grossman, Mark M., *The Question of Arbitrability: Challenges to the Arbitrator's Jurisdiction and Authority.* Ithaca: ILR Press, New York State School of Industrial and Labor Relations, Cornell University, 1984. 122 pp.

Hill, Marvin F., and Anthony V. Sinicropi, *Evidence in Arbitration,* 2nd ed. Washington, DC: Bureau of National Affairs, 1987. 465 pp.

———, *Remedies in Arbitration,* 2nd ed. Washington, DC: Bureau of National Affairs, 1991. 575 pp.

Kolb, Deborah M., *The Mediators.* Cambridge, MA: MIT Press, Series on Organization Studies, 1983. 230 pp.

Kressel, Kenneth, et al., *Mediation Research: The Process and Effectiveness of Third-Party Intervention.* San Francisco; Jossey-Bass, 1989. 457 pp.

McKelvey, Jean T., ed., *The Changing Law of Fair Representation.* Ithaca: ILR Press, New York State School of Industrial and Labor Relations, Cornell University, 1985. 298 pp.

Loughran, Charles S., *How to Prepare and Present a Labor Arbitration Case: Strategy and Tactics for Advocates.* Washington, DC: Bureau of National Affairs, 1996. 551 pp.

Oehmke, Thomas H., *Employment, Labor & Pension Arbitration.* Rochester, NY: Lawyers Cooperative Pub. Co.; San Francisco: Bancroft-Whitney, 1989. 786 pp.

Pops, Gerald M., *Emergence of the Public Sector Arbitrator.* Lexington, MA: Lexington Books, 1976. 136 pp.

Prasow, Paul, and Edward Peters, *Arbitration and Collective Bargaining: Conflict Resolution in Labor Relations,* 2nd ed. New York: McGraw-Hill, 1983. 536 pp.

Simkin, William E., and Nicholas A. Fidandis, *Mediation and the Dynamics of Collective Bargaining,* 2nd ed. Washington, DC: Bureau of National Affairs, 1986. 300 pp.

Volz, Marlin M., and Edward P. Goggin, eds., *How Arbitration Works,* 5th ed. Washington, DC: Bureau of National Affairs, 1997. 1233 pp.

Zack, Arnold M., ed., *Arbitration in Practice.* Ithaca, NY: ILR Press, New York State School of Industrial and Labor Relations, Cornell University, 1984. 256 pp.

COLLECTIVE BARGAINING/NEGOTIATION

Aaron, Benjamin, Joyce M. Nijita, and James L. Stern, *Public-Sector Bargaining,* 2nd ed. Washington, DC: Bureau of National Affairs, 1988. 334 pp.

Atherton, Wallace N., *Theory of Union Bargaining Goals.* Princeton, NJ: Princeton University Press, 1973. 168 pp.

Bacharach, Samuel B., and Edward J. Lawler, *Bargaining, Tactics, and Outcomes.* San Francisco: Jossey-Bass, 1981. 234 pp.

Bartos, Otomar J., *Process and Outcome of Negotiations.* New York: Columbia University Press, 1974. 451 pp.

Begin, James P., and Edwin F. Beal, *The Practice of Collective Bargaining,* 8th ed. Homewood, IL: R. D. Irwin, 1989. 638 pp.

Berendt, Gerald E., *Collective Bargaining.* Charlottesville, VA: Contemporary Litigation Series, Michie, 1984. 340 pp.

Breslin, J. William, and Jeffrey Z. Rubin, eds., *Negotiation Theory and Practice.* Cambridge, MA: Program on Negotiation at Harvard Law School, 1993. 458 pp.

Chamberlain, Neil W., and James W. Kuhn, *Collective Bargaining,* 3rd ed. New York: McGraw-Hill, 1986. 493 pp.

Chernish, William N., *Coalition Bargaining: A Study of Union Tactics and Public Policy* (Pennsylvania University Wharton School of Finance and Commerce, Industrial Research Unit, Research Studies, no. 45). Philadelphia: University of Pennsylvania Press, 1969. 286 pp.

Cross, John G., *The Economics of Bargaining.* New York: Basic Books, 1969. 247 pp.

Cutcher-Gershenfeld, Joel, Robert B. McKersie, and Richard E. Walton, *Pathways to Change: Case Studies of Strategic Negotiation.* Kalamazoo, MI: W.E. Upjohn Institute for Employment Research, 1995. 257 pp.

Davey, Harold W., Mario F. Bognono, and David L. Estenson, *Contemporary Collective Bargaining,* 4th ed. Englewood Cliffs, NJ: Prentice Hall, 1982. 472 pp.

De Menil, George, *Bargaining: Monopoly Power versus Union Power.* Cambridge, MA: MIT Press, 1971. 123 pp.

Dunlop, John T., *Dispute Resolution: Negotiation and Consensus Building.* Dover, MA: Auburn House, 1984. 296 pp.

Fisher, Roger, and William Ury, *Getting to Yes: Negotiating Agreement without Giving In,* 2nd ed. New York: Penguin Books, 1991. 200 pp.

Friedman, Raymond A., *Front Stage, Backstage: The Dramatic Structure of Labor Negotiations* (MIT Press Series on Organization Studies, 10). Cambridge, MA: MIT Press, 1994. 257 pp.

Gibbons, Muriel K., et al., *Portrait of a Process: Collective Negotiations in Public Employment.* Fort Washington, PA: Labor Relations Press, 1979. 463 pp.

Granof, Michael H., *How to Cost Your Labor Contract.* Washington, DC: Bureau of National Affairs, 1973. 147 pp.

Holoviak, Stephen J., *Costing Labor Contracts and Judging Their Financial Impact.* New York: Praeger, 1984. 194 pp.

Jandt, Fred E., *Win-Win, Negotiating: Turning Conflict into Agreement,* New York: Wiley, 1985. 300 pp.

Karrass, Chester L., *Give and Take: The Complete Guide to Negotiating Strategies and Tactics.* New York: Crowell, 1974. 280 pp.

Katz, Harry C., and Thomas A. Kochan, *An Introduction to Collective Bargaining and Industrial Relations.* New York: McGraw-Hill, 1992. 538 pp.

Kniveton, Bromley, *The Psychology of Bargaining.* Brookfield, VT: Avebury, 1989. 169 pp.

Kochan, Thomas A., *Collective Bargaining and Industrial Relations: From Theory to Policy and Practice,* 2nd ed. Homewood, Ill: R. D. Irwin, 1988. 496 pp.

Kramer, Roderick M., and David M. Messick, eds., *Negotiation as a Social Process.* Thousand Oaks, CA: Sage Publications, 1995. 348 pp.

Lebow, Richard N., *The Art of Bargaining.* Baltimore, MD: Johns Hopkins University Press, 1996. 193 pp.

Lipsky, David B., and Clifford B. Donn, eds., *Collective Bargaining in American Industry: Contemporary Perspectives and Future Directions.* Lexington, MA: Lexington Books, 1987. 351 pp.

Loughran, Charles S., *Negotiating a Labor Contract: A Management Handbook,* 2nd ed. Washington, DC: Bureau of National Affairs, 1992. 559 pp.

Mastenbroek, Willem F. G., *Negotiate.* New York: Blackwell, 1989. 170 pp.

Morley, Ian E., and Geoffrey M. Stephenson, *The Social Psychology of Bargaining.* London: G. Allen and Unwin, 1977. 317 pp.

Morse, Bruce, *How to Negotiate the Labor Agreement: An Outline Summary of Tested Bargaining Practice Expanded from Earlier Editions,* 10th ed. Southfield, MI.: Trends Publishing Co., 1984. 83 pp.

Moskow, Michael H., J. Joseph Loewenberg, and Edward C. Koziara, *Collective Bargaining in Public Employment.* New York: Random House, 1970. 336 pp.

Nierenberg, Gerald I., *The Art of Negotiating: Psychological Strategies for Gaining Advantageous Bargains.* New York: Hawthorne Books, 1968. 195 pp.

Richardson, Reed C., *Collective Bargaining by Objectives: A Positive Approach,* 2nd ed. Englewood Cliffs, NJ: Prentice Hall, 1985. 326 pp.

Roth, Alvin E., ed., *Game-Theoretic Models of Bargaining.* New York: Cambridge University Press, 1985. 390 pp.

Rubin, Jeffrey Z., and Bert R. Brown, *The Social Psychology of Bargaining and Negotiation.* New York: Academic Press, 1975. 359 pp.

Siegel, Abraham J., ed., *The Impact of Computers on Collective Bargaining.* Cambridge, MA: MIT Press, 1969. 294 pp.

Slichter, Sumner H., James J. Healy, and E. Robert Livernash, *The Impact of Collective Bargaining on Management.* Washington, DC: Brookings Institution, 1960. 982 pp.

Strauss, Anselm L., *Negotiations: Varieties, Contexts, Processes, and Social Order.* San Francisco: Jossey-Bass, 1978. 275 pp.

Voos, Paula B., ed., *Contemporary Collective Bargaining in the Private Sector* (Industrial Relations Research Association Series). Madison, WI: Industrial Relations Research Association, 1994. 548 pp.

Walton, Richard E., and Robert B. McKersie, *A Behavioral Theory of Labor Negotiations: An Analysis of a Social Interaction System,* 2nd ed. Ithaca, NY: ILR Press, 1991. 437 pp.

Weber, Arnold R., ed., *The Structure of Collective Bargaining* (Chicago University Graduate School of Business Publications, Third Series: Studies in Business). New York: Free Press, 1961, 380 pp.

Weitzman, Joan P., *The Scope of Bargaining in Public Employment.* New York: Praeger, 1975. 384 pp.

Young, Oran R., ed., *Bargaining: Formal Theories of Negotiation.* Urbana: University of Illinois Press, 1975. 412 pp.

Zack, Arnold, *Public Sector Mediation.* Washington, DC: Bureau of National Affairs, 1985. 200 pp.

EMPLOYEE BENEFITS

Beam, Burton T., and John J. McFadden, *Employee Benefits,* 3rd ed. Chicago: Dearborn Financial Pub., 1992. 576 pp.

DeCenzo, David A., and Stephen J. Holoviak, *Employee Benefits.* Englewood Cliffs, NJ: Prentice Hall, 1989. 223 pp.

Gomez-Mejia, Luis R., ed. *Compensation and Benefits.* Washington, DC: Bureau of National Affairs, 1989. 288 pp.

Griffes, Ernest J. E., *Employee Benefits Programs: Management, Planning, and Control,* 2nd ed. Homewood, IL: Dow Jones–Irwin, 1990. 392 pp.

Mamorsky, Jeffrey D., ed., *Employee Benefits Handbook,* rev. ed. Boston: Warren, Gorham & Lamont, 1987. 1 vol.

Milkovich, George T., and Jerry M. Newman, *Compensation,* 5th ed. Chicago: Irwin, 1996. 716 pp.

Rosenbloom, Jerry S., ed., *The Handbook of Employee Benefits: Design, Funding, and Administration,* 2nd ed. Homewood, IL: Dow Jones–Irwin, 1988. 1170 pp.

INDUSTRIAL RELATIONS

Aaron, Benjamin, et al., *The Next Twenty-Five Years of Industrial Relations,* Gerald G. Somers, ed. (Industrial Relations Research Association Series). Madison, WI: Industrial Relations Research Association, 1973. 207 pp.

Adams, Roy J., *Industrial Relations under Liberal Democracy: North America in Comparative Perspective* (Studies in Industrial Relations). Columbia: University of South Carolina Press, 1995. 219 pp.

Adams, Roy J., and Noah M. Meltz, eds., *Industrial Relations Theory: Its Nature, Scope, and Pedagogy* (Institute of Management and Labor Relations Series, no. 4). Metuchen, NJ: Scarecrow Press, 1993. 403 pp.

Barocci, Thomas, et al., *Industrial Relations Research in the 1970's: A Review and Appraisal.* Madison, WI: Industrial Relations Research Association, 1982. 314 pp.

Bina, Cyrus, Laurie Clements, and Chuck Davis, eds., *Beyond Survival: Wage Labor in the Late Twentieth Century.* Armonk, NY: M.E. Sharpe, 1996. 261 pp.

Block, Richard, et al., *U.S. Industrial Relations, 1950–1980: A Critical Assessment.* Madison, WI: Industrial Relations Research Association, 1981. 361 pp.

Bluestone, Barry, and Irving Bluestone, *Negotiating the Future: Labor Perspective on American Business.* New York: Basic Books, 1992. 335 pp.

Blum, Albert A., ed., *International Handbook of Industrial Relations: Contemporary Developments and Research.* Westport, CT: Greenwood Press, 1981. 698 pp.

Clark, Gordon L., *Unions and Communities under Siege: American Communities and the Crisis of Organized Labor.* New York: Cambridge University Press, 1989. 309 pp.

Cohen-Rosenthal, Edward, and Cynthia E. Burton, *Mutual Gains: Guide to Union-Management Cooperation,* 2nd ed., rev. and updated. Ithaca, NY: ILR Press, 1993. 344 pp.

Commission on the Future of Worker-Management Relations, *Fact-Finding Report.* Washington, DC: U.S. Department of Labor, 1994. 163 pp.

———, *Report and Recommendations.* Washington, DC: U.S. Department of Labor, 1994. 70 pp.

Derber, Milton, *The American Idea of Industrial Democracy, 1865–1965.* Urbana: University of Illinois Press, 1970. 553 pp.

Dilts, David A., and Clarence R. Deitsch, *Labor Relations.* New York: Macmillan, 1983. 476 pp.

Doeringer, Peter B., *Industrial Relations in International Perspective: Essays on Research and Policy.* New York: Holmes and Meier, 1981. 425 pp.

Dunlop, John T., *Industrial Relations Systems,* rev. ed. Boston: Harvard Business School Press, 1993. 331 pp.

Edwards, Paul K., *Conflict at Work: A Materialist Analysis of Workplace Relations.* New York: B. Blackwell, 1986. 357 pp.

Edwards, Richard, *Rights at Work: Employment Relations in the Post-Union Era.* Washington, DC: Brookings Institution, 1993. 265 pp.

Flanagan, Robert J., et al., *Economics of the Employment Relationship.* Glenview, IL: Scott, Foresman, 1989. 677 pp.

Flood, Lawrence G., ed., *Unions and Public Policy: The New Economy, Law, and Democratic Politics* (Contributions in Political Science, no. 364). Westport, CT: Greenwood Press, 1995. 208 pp.

Fossum, John A., *Labor Relations: Development, Structure, Process,* 6th ed. Homewood, IL: Irwin, 1995. 576 pp.

Gamst, Frederick C., ed., *Meanings of Work: Considerations for the Twenty-First Century.* Albany: State University of New York Press, 1995. 277 pp.

Gross, James A., *Broken Promise: The Subversion of U.S. Labor Policy, 1947–1994.* Philadelphia: Temple University Press, 1995. 404 pp.

Harris, Howell J., *The Right to Manage: Industrial Relations Policies of American Business in the 1940s.* Madison, WI: University of Wisconsin Press, 1982. 290 pp.

Heckscher, Charles, *The New Unionism: Employee Involvement in the Changing Corporation.* New York: Basic Books, 1988. 302 pp.

Hills, Stephen M., *Employment Relations and the Social Sciences.* Columbia: University of South Carolina Press, 1995. 167 pp.

Hirsch, Barry T., and John T. Addison, *The Economic Analysis of Unions: New Approaches and Evidence.* Boston: Allen & Unwin, 1986. 337 pp.

Jacoby, Sanford M., ed., *The Workers of Nations: Industrial Relations in a Global Economy.* New York: Oxford University Press, 1995. 231 pp.

Juris, Hervey A., and Myron Roomkin, eds., *The Shrinking Perimeter: Unionism and Labor Relations in the Manufacturing Sector.* Lexington, MA: Lexington Books, 1980. 223 pp.

Kaufman, Bruce E., *The Origins & Evolution of the Field of Industrial Relations in the United States* (Cornell Studies in Industrial and Labor Relations, no. 25). Ithaca, NY: ILR Press, 1993. 286 pp.

Kerr, Clark, and Paul D. Staudohar, eds., *Industrial Relations in a New Age.* San Francisco: Jossey-Bass, 1986. 419 pp.

———, *Labor Economics and Industrial Relations: Markets and Institutions* (Wertheim Publications in Industrial Relations). Cambridge, MA: Harvard University Press, 1994. 704 pp.

Kilgour, John G., *Preventive Labor Relations.* New York: AMACOM, 1981. 338 pp.

Kochan, Thomas A., ed., *Challenges and Choices Facing American Labor.* Cambridge, MA: MIT Press, 1985. 356 pp.

Kochan, Thomas A., Harry C. Katz, and Robert B. McKersie, *The Transformation of American Industrial Relations,* 1st ILR Press ed. (new preface) Ithaca, NY: ILR Press, 1994. 287 pp.

Kochan, Thomas A., and Paul Osterman, *The Mutual Gains Enterprise: Forging a Winning Partnership among Labor, Management, and Government.* Boston: Harvard Business School Press, 1994. 260 pp.

Lewin, David, Olivia S. Mitchell, and Peter D. Sherer, eds., *Research Frontiers in Industrial Relations and Human Resources* (Industrial Relations Research Association Series). Madison, WI: Industrial Relations Research Association, 1992. 625 pp.

Locke, Richard, Thomas Kochan, and Michael Piore, eds., *Employment Relations in a Changing World Economy.* Cambridge, MA: MIT Press, 1995. 395 pp.

Mills, Daniel Q., *Labor-Management Relations,* 4th ed. New York: McGraw-Hill, 1989. 670 pp.

Reynolds, Lloyd G., Stanley H. Masters, and Colletta H. Moser, *Labor Economics and Labor Relations,* 10th ed. Englewood Cliffs, NJ: Prentice Hall, 1991. 610 pp.

Schuster, Michael H., *Union-Management Cooperation: Structure, Process, Impact.* Kalamazoo, MI: W. E. Upjohn Institute for Employment Research, 1984. 235 pp.

Siegel, Irving H., and Edgar Weinberg, *Labor-Management Cooperation: The American Experience.* Kalamazoo, MI.: W. E. Upjohn Institute for Employment Research, 1982. 316 pp.

Sloane, Arthur A., and Fred Witney, *Labor Relations,* 8th ed. Englewood Cliffs, NJ: Prentice Hall, 1994. 596 pp.

Somers, Gerald G., ed. *Essays in Industrial Relations Theory.* Ames: Iowa State University Press, 1969. 200 pp.

————, *Labor, Management, and Social Policy: Essays in the John R. Commons Tradition.* Madison: University of Wisconsin Press, 1963. 303 pp.

Thurley, Keith, and Stephen Wood, eds., *Industrial Relations and Management Strategy* (Management and Industrial Relations Series, 4). New York: Cambridge University Press, 1983. 242 pp.

Walton, Richard E., Joel Cutcher-Gershenfeld, and Robert B. McKersie, *Strategic Negotiations: A Theory of Change in Labor-Management Relations.* Boston: Harvard Business School Press, 1994. 376 pp.

Wever, Kirsten, and Lowell Turner, eds., *The Comparative Political Economy of Industrial Relations.* Madison, WI: Industrial Relations Research Association, 1995. 192 pp.

Wheeler, Hoyt N., *Industrial Conflict: An Integrative Theory.* Columbia: University of South Carolina Press, 1985. 293 pp.

LABOR LAW

Block, Richard N., John Beck, and Daniel H. Kruger, *Labor Law, Industrial Relations and Employee Choice: The State of the Workplace in the 1990s: Hearings of the Commission on the Future of Worker-Management Relations.* Kalamazoo, MI: W.E. Upjohn Institute for Employment Research, 1996. 115 pp.

Cox, Archibald, et al., *Cases and Materials on Labor Law,* 11th ed. (University Casebook Series). Mineola, NY: Foundation Press, 1991. 1249 pp. (Kept up to date by statutory supplements.)

The Developing Labor Law: The Board, the Courts, and the National Labor Relations Act, 3rd ed. Editor-in-chief, Patrick Hardin. Washington, DC: Bureau of National Affairs, 1992. 2 vols.

Edwards, Harry T. R., Theodore Clark Jr., and Charles B. Craver, *Labor Relations Law in the Public Sector: Cases and Materials,* 4th ed. (Contemporary Legal Education Series). Charlottesville, VA: Michie, 1991. 1168 pp. (Kept up to date by supplements.)

Ernst, Daniel R., *Lawyers against Labor: From Individual Rights to Corporate Liberalism.* Urbana: University of Illinois Press, 1995. 334 pp.

Flanagan, Robert J., *Labor Relations and the Litigation Explosion.* Washington, DC: Brookings Institution, 1987. 122 pp.

Freedman, Warren, *The Employment Contract: Rights and Duties of Employers and Employees.* New York: Quorum Books, 1989. 190 pp.

Friedman, Sheldon, et al., *Restoring the Promise of American Labor Law.* Ithaca, NY: ILR Press, 1994. 366 pp.

Getman, Julius G., and Bertrand B. Pogrebin, *Labor Relations: The Basic Processes, Law and Practice.* Westbury, NY: The Foundation Press, Inc., 1988. 396 pp.

Getman, Julius G., Stephen B. Goldberg, and Jeanne B. Herman, *Union Representative Elections: Law and Reality.* New York: Russell Sage Foundation, 1976. 218 pp.

Goldman, Alvin L., *Labor Law and Industrial Relations in the United States of America,* 2nd ed. Washington, DC: Bureau of National Affairs, 1984. 373 pp.

———, *The Supreme Court and Labor-Management Relations Law.* Lexington, MA: Lexington Books, 1976. 191 pp.

Gould, William B., *A Primer on American Labor Law,* 3rd ed. Cambridge, MA: MIT Press, 1993. 326 pp.

———, *Agenda for Reform: The Future of Employment Relationships and the Law.* Cambridge, MA.: MIT Press, 1993. 313 pp.

Justice, Betty W., *Unions, Workers and the Law.* Washington, DC: Bureau of National Affairs, 1983. 291 pp.

Lehrer, Susan, *Origins of Protective Labor Legislation for Women, 1905–1925* (SUNY Series on Women in Work). Albany, NY: State University of New York Press, 1987. 318 pp.

Levitan, Sar A., Peter E. Carlson, and Isaac Shapiro, *Protecting American Workers: An Assessment of Government Programs.* Washington, DC: Bureau of National Affairs, 1986. 280 pp.

Malin, Martin H., and Lorraine A. Schmall, *Individual Rights within the Union.* Washington, DC: Bureau of National Affairs, 1988. 734 pp.

McLaughlin, Doris B., and Anita W. Schoomaker, *The Landrum-Griffin Act and Union Democracy.* Ann Arbor: University of Michigan Press, 1979. 288 pp.

Merrifield, Leroy S., Theodore J. St. Antoine, and Charles B. Craver, *Labor Relations Law: Cases and Materials,* 8th ed. (Contemporary Legal Education Series). Charlottesville, VA: Michie, 1989. 982 pp.

———, *Labor Relations Law: Cases and Materials: Statutory Appendix,* 8th ed. (Contemporary Legal Education Series). Charlottesville, VA: Michie, 1989. 189 pp.

Mills, Harry A., and Emily C. Brown, *From the Wagner Act to Taft-Hartley: A Study of National Labor Policy and Labor Relations.* Chicago: University of Chicago Press, 1950. 723 pp.

Morris, Charles J., ed., *American Labor Policy: A Critical Appraisal of the National Labor Relations Act.* Washington, DC: Bureau of National Affairs, 1987. 431 pp.

Oberer, Walter E., Kurt L. Hanslow, and Timothy J. Heinsz, *Cases and Materials on Labor Law: Collective Bargaining in a Free Society,* 4th ed. St. Paul, MN: West Publishing Co., 1994. 866 pp. (Kept up to date by supplements.)

Player, Mack A., Elaine W. Shoben, and Risa Lieberwitz, *Employment Discrimination Law,* 3rd ed. St. Paul, MN: West Publishing Co., 1990. 827 pp. (Kept up to date by supplements.)

Schlossberg, Stephen I., and Judith A. Scott, *Organizing and the Law,* 4th ed. Washington, DC: Bureau of National Affairs, 1991. 467 pp.

Smith, Arthur B., Charles B. Craver, and Leroy D. Clark, *Employment Discrimination Law: Cases and Materials,* 4th ed. (Contemporary Legal Education Series). Charlottesville, VA: Michie, 1994. 1012 pp.

Specter, Howard, and Matthew W. Finkin, *Individual Employment Law and Litigation.* Charlottesville, VA: Michie, 1989. 2 vols. (Kept up to date by pocket parts.)

Taylor, Benjamin J., and Fred Witney, *Labor Relations Law.* 7th ed. Englewood Cliffs, NJ: Prentice Hall, 1996. 518 pp.

———, *U.S. Labor Relations Law: Historical Development,* Englewood Cliffs, NJ: Prentice Hall, 1992. 240 pp.

Townley, Barbara, *Labor Law Reform in U.S. Industrial Relations.* Brookfield, VT: Gower, 1986. 263 pp.

Twomey, David P., *Labor and Employment Law, Text and Cases,* 9th ed. Cincinnati: South Western Publishing Co., 1994. 751 pp.

Wellington, Harry H., *Labor and the Legal Process.* New Haven, CT: Yale University Press, 1968. 409 pp.

LABOR/LABOR UNIONS—HISTORY

Beard, Mary R., *A Short History of the American Labor Movement.* New York: George H. Doran Co., 1924. Reprint, Westport, CT: Greenwood Press, 1968. 206 pp.

Bernstein, Irving, *The Lean Years: A History of the American Worker, 1920–1933.* New York: Da Capo Press, 1983. 577, 16 pp.

———, *Turbulent Years: A History of the American Worker, 1933–1941.* Boston: Houghton Mifflin, 1969. 873 pp.

Bognanno, Mario F., and Morris M. Kleiner, eds., *Labor Market Institutions and the Future Role of Unions.* Cambridge, MA: Blackwell, 1992. 228 pp.

Buhle, Paul, and Alan Dawley, eds., *Working for Democracy: American Workers from the Revolution to the Present.* Urbana: University of Illinois Press, 1985. 148 pp.

Cobble, Dorothy S., ed., *Women and Unions: Forging a Partnership.* Ithaca, NY: ILR Press, 1993. 452 pp.

Commons, John R., *History of Labor in the United States,* The Macmillan Co., 1926–35, p. 785 (Reprints of Economic Classics, 1918, reprint). Fairfield, NJ: Kelley, 1966. 4 vols.

Commons, John R., et al., *A Documentary History of American Industrial Society* (1909–1911, Reprint). New York: Russell and Russell, 1958. 10 vols.

Craver, Charles B., *Can Unions Survive?: The Rejuvenation of the American Labor Movement.* New York: New York University Press, 1993. 213 pp.

Dubofsky, Melvyn, *Industrialism and the American Worker, 1865–1920,* 2nd ed. Arlington Heights, IL: Harlan Davidson, 1985. 167 pp.

Dubofsky, Melvyn, and Warren Van Tyne, *John L. Lewis: A Biography.* New York: New York Times Book Co., 1977. 619 pp.

Dulles, Foster R., and Melvyn Dubofsky, *Labor in America: A History,* 5th ed. Arlington Heights, IL: Harlan Davidson, 1993. 434 pp.

Dunlop, John T., *The Management of Labor Unions: Decision Making with Historical Constraints.* Lexington, MA: Lexington Books, 1990. 163 pp.

Filippelli, Ronald L., *Labor in America: A History.* New York: Alfred A. Knopf, 1984. 315 pp.

Foner, Philip S., *History of the Labor Movement in the United States.* New York: International Publishing Co., 1947–1980. 5 vols.

Freeman, Richard B., and James L. Medoff, *What Do Unions Do?* New York: Basic Books, 1984. 239 pp.

Galenson, Walter, *The American Labor Movement, 1955–1995* (Contributions in Labor Studies, no. 47). Westport, CT: Greenwood Press, 1996. 171 pp.

Gompers, Samuel, *Seventy Years of Life and Labour: An Autobiography* (Library of American Labor History Reprints of Economic Classics, 1953, reprint). New York: Dutton, 1967. 2 vols.

Goulden, Joseph C., *Meany.* New York: Atheneum, 1972. 504 pp.

Green, Max, *Epitaph for American Labor: How Union Leaders Lost Touch with America.* Washington, DC: AEI Press, 1996. 207 pp.

Green, William C., and Ernest J. Yanarella, eds., *North American Auto Unions in Crisis: Lean Production as Contested Terrain* (SUNY Studies in the Sociology of Work). Albany: State University of New York Press, 1996. 246 pp.

Gutman, Herbert G., and Ira Berlin, eds., *Power & Culture: Essays on the American Working Class.* New York: Pantheon Books, 1987. 452 pp.

Huang, Wei-Chiao, ed., *Organized Labor at the Crossroads.* Kalamazoo, MI: W. E. Upjohn Institute for Employment Research, 1989. 162 pp.

Kaufman, Stuart B., ed., *The Samuel Gompers Papers.* Urbana: University of Illinois Press, 1986. 3 vols.

Labor Unions. Gary M. Fink, editor-in chief (The Greenwood Encyclopedia of American Institutions). Westport, CT: Greenwood Press, 1977. 520 pp.

Larson, Simeon, and Bruce Nissen, eds., *Theories of the Labor Movement.* Detroit: Wayne State University Press, 1987. 395 pp.

Laslett, John H. M., ed., *The United Mine Workers of America: A Model of Industrial Solidarity?* University Park: Pennsylvania State University Press, 1996. 576 pp.

Lipset, Seymour M., ed., *Unions in Transition: Entering the Second Century.* San Francisco: ICS Press, 1986. 506 pp.

Millis, Harry A., and Royal E. Montgomery, *Organized Labor* (The Labor Movement in Fiction and Nonfiction, 1945, reprint). New York: AMS Press, 1976. 930 pp.

Montgomery, David, *The Fall of the House of Labor: The Workplace, the State, and American Labor Activism, 1865–1925.* New York: Cambridge University Press, 1987. 494 pp.

Moody, J. Carroll, and Alice Kessler-Harris, *Perspectives on American Labor History: The Problems of Synthesis.* DeKalb: Northern Illinois University Press, 1989. 236 pp.

Morris, Richard B., *The U.S. Department of Labor Bicentennial History of the American Worker.* Washington, DC: U.S. Government Printing Office, 1976. 327 pp.

Pelling, Henry, *American Labor.* Chicago: University of Chicago Press, 1960. 247 pp.

Perlman, Selig, *A History of Trade Unionism in the United States,* New York: Macmillan, 1922. Reprint, Fairfield, NJ: Kelley, 1950. 313 pp.

Phelan, Craig, *William Green: A Biography of a Labor Leader.* Albany: State University of New York Press, 1989. 223 pp.

Rees, Albert, *The Economics of Trade Unions,* 3rd ed. Chicago: University of Chicago Press, 1989. 204 pp.

Reuther, Victor G., *The Brothers Reuther and the Story of the UAW: A Memoir.* Boston: Houghton Mifflin, 1976. 523 pp.

Robinson, Archie, *George Meany and His Times. A Biography.* New York: Simon and Schuster, 1961. 445 pp.

Spomer, Cynthia R., ed., *American Directory of Organized Labor: Unions, Locals, Agreements, and Employers.* Detroit: Gale Research Inc., 1992. 1638 pp.

Stephenson, Charles, and Robert Asher, eds., *Life and Labor: Dimensions of American Working-Class History* (American Labor History Series). Albany: State University of New York Press, 1986. 343 pp.

Strauss, George, Daniel G. Gallagher, and Jack Fiorito, eds., *The State of the Unions* (Industrial Relations Research Association Series). Madison, WI: Industrial Relations Research Association, 1991. 426 pp.

Taft, Philip, *Organized Labor in American History.* New York: Harper and Row, 1964. 818 pp.

Ulman, Lloyd, *The Rise of the National Trade Union: The Development and Significance of Its Structure, Governing Institutions, and Economic Policies,* 2nd ed. (Wertheim Publications in Industrial Relations). Cambridge, MA: Harvard University Press, 1966. 639 pp.

Wilson, Joseph F., *Tearing Down the Color Bar: A Documentary History of the Brotherhood of Sleeping Car Porters.* New York: Columbia University Press, 1989. 396 pp.

Zieger, Robert H., *American Workers, American Unions, 1920–1985.* Baltimore: Johns Hopkins University Press, 1986. 233 pp.

Glossary

Administrative Law Judge—An employee of the *National Labor Relations Board* who issues decisions in cases in which an *unfair labor practice* has been charged. Once a *field examiner* has conducted a preliminary investigation of the charge, the administrative law judge hears the case. The administrative law judge's opinion may be appealed by either party to the NLRB. Formerly called "trial examiner."

Agency Shop—A bargaining unit covered by a union security clause in the collective bargaining agreement which states that all employees in the unit must pay the union a sum equal to union fees and dues as a condition of continuing employment. Nonunion employees, however, are not required to join the union as a condition of employment.

Apprenticeship—A method of perpetuating the skills of a trade as well as of regulating the entrance of craftsmen into the trade. It is designed to maintain standards of workmanship and skill.

Arbitration—A method of settling a dispute which involves having an impartial third party, known as an arbitrator, render a decision that is binding on both the union and the employer.

Areawide Bargaining—A type of *multiemployer bargaining* in which bargaining takes place between union and employer representatives on a local or city level. This is the usual form of bargaining for construction, bakery, and laundry industries. Not to be confused with *regional bargaining*.

Authorization Card—A statement obtained from each employee by a union during an organization drive. The statement authorizes the union to represent the employee for purposes of collective bargaining.

Back-Loaded—Providing a greater wage increase during the later part of a multiyear agreement. Used to describe a contract. See *front-loaded*.

Back Pay—Wages due an employee because of (1) employer violation of the overtime or minimum wage provisions of the *Fair Labor Standards Act* or of *Title VII, Civil Rights Act of 1964;* (2) suspension or discharge in violation of the *collective bargaining agreement;* or (3) adjustment of piece rate following a *grievance*. To be distinguished from *retroactive pay*.

Back-to-Work Movement—A return of strikers to their jobs before their union has declared an end to the strike. Some back-to-work movements are induced by management in an attempt to get workers to abandon a strike. Others are brought about by the workers themselves, either as a protest against the stand of their union leaders or because economic pressures force them to go back to work.

---

*This glossary was compiled by Philip R. Dankert, Collection Development Librarian, Martin P. Catherwood Library, New York State School of Industrial and Labor Relations, Cornell University, Ithaca, New York 14853-3901.

The compiler gratefully acknowledges his reliance on *Industrial and Labor Relations: A Glossary* by Robert E. Doherty (ILR Press, 1979, 1989), from which many of these definitions were drawn.

Bargaining Agent—A union that is the exclusive representative to the employer of all workers, both union and nonunion, in a *bargaining unit.* An employer may voluntarily recognize a particular union as a bargaining agent for his or her workers, or the question of representation may be settled by a secret-ballot election, conducted by the *National Labor Relations Board* or the appropriate state agency. See *certification, exclusivity,* and *representation election.*

Bargaining Power—The relative power positions of management and labor during the negotiating process.

Bargaining Unit—A group of employees (or jobs) in a plant or industry with sufficient commonality to constitute the unit represented in collective bargaining by a particular bargaining agent.

Blacklist—A list of workers circulated among employers containing the names of "undesirable" employees. Workers whose names are listed are often fired from their jobs or not hired in new ones. It was declared an unfair labor practice by the *National Labor Relations Act* in 1935.

Blue Flu—A job action in which large numbers of uniformed workers of a law enforcement agency call in sick. The purpose of the blue flu is to win concessions from the employer without resorting to an illegal strike.

Boulwarism—A collective bargaining approach in which the employer attempts to persuade his employees that his or her initial offer is in their best interests, thus bypassing the union, and changes this offer only if new information or persuasive arguments are received from the union. It was originally named after Lemuel Boulware, a former vice-president for employee and public relations at the General Electric Company.

Boycott—An organized refusal by employees and their union to deal with an employer, used to win concessions. Primary boycotts usually take the form of putting pressure on consumers not to buy the goods of an employer who is directly involved in a dispute. In the dress industry, for example, the International Ladies' Garment Workers' Union frequently boycotts the sale of nonunion-made dresses. Secondary boycotts are those in which pressure is exerted on employers who are not directly involved in a dispute; for instance, workers of company A refuse to use or handle goods of company B, which is engaged in a labor dispute. Workers in the two companies are often but not always members of the same union. The *Taft-Hartley Act* outlawed certain types of secondary boycotts, and the *Landrum-Griffin Act* placed additional restrictions on such activities.

Bumping—A practice allowing a worker laid off from a job for lack of work to displace some other worker with less *seniority* in the same plant. Often provided for in *collective bargaining agreements,* bumping is designed to protect job rights of workers with the greatest seniority.

Business Agent—A full-time local union officer who handles the union's financial, administrative, and labor-relations problems.

Certification—Official recognition by the *National Labor Relations Board,* or an appropriate state agency, that a particular union is the majority choice and thus the exclusive bargaining agent of all employees in a particular bargaining unit.

Checkoff—A procedure under which the employer deducts from the pay of all employees who are union members union dues, assessments, and initiation fees and turns these funds over to the union.

Closed Shop—A union security arrangement under which the employer is required to hire only employees who are members of the union. Membership in the union is also a condition of continued employment. The closed shop was declared illegal by the *Taft-Hartley Act* in 1947.

Coalition Bargaining—A form of collective bargaining in which several different unions representing several different categories of employees of a single employer attempt to coordinate their bargaining.

Collective Bargaining—A method of determining terms and conditions of employment by negotiation between representatives of the employer and union representatives of the employee.

Collective Negotiations—A method for determining the terms and conditions of employment for public-sector employees. Collective negotiations or professional negotiations have come to resemble collective bargaining in most respects, the chief distinction being that in most instances public-sector employee organizations cannot use the bargaining leverage of a strike or threat thereof.

Collusion—A conspiracy engaged in by an employer and the certified representative of his or her employees to defraud the employees represented while providing the semblance of a genuine bargaining relationship.

Common-Situs Picketing—A form of *picketing* in which employees of a struck employer who work at a common site with employees of at least one neutral employer may picket only at their entrance to the work site. The employees of the neutral employers must enter the work site through other gates. Picketing is restricted to the entrance of the struck employer so as not to encourage a secondary *boycott* on the part of the employees of the neutral employers. Common-situs picketing is found most often in the construction industry.

Company Union—An organization of employees, usually of a single company, that is either dominated or strongly influenced by management. The *National Labor Relations Act* of 1935 declared that such management interference is an unfair labor practice.

Comparable Worth—The notion that wages and benefits should be based on the worth of the job to the employer rather than on circumstances dictated by the vagaries of the labor market. Worth is measured by such qualities as effort, skill, and responsibility. Many argue that wage and salary disparity is due to sex discrimination and therefore in violation of *Title VII, Civil Rights Act of 1964.*

Concession Bargaining—Sometimes called employee or union givebacks, concession bargaining usually describes those instances when unions agree to modify terms in the existing contract in exchange for other benefits. During the 1980s, for example, many unions agreed to modify such issues as *work rules* and *seniority* provisions in exchange for greater *job security.*

Conciliation—A process under which a third party acts as the intermediary in bringing together the parties to an industrial dispute but does not take an active part in the settlement process.

Cost-of-Living Adjustment (COLA)—A provision found in collective bargaining agreements that ties wage increases to the cost of living during the term of the agreement. Sometimes referred to as an "escalator clause."

Craft Union—A union that limits its membership to workers in a particular craft. Many craft unions have enlarged their jurisdictions to include as members many occupations and skills not closely related to the originally designated crafts.

Decertification—The procedure for removing a union as the certified bargaining representative of employees in a bargaining unit. This is done after petition alleging that the union no longer represents the majority of the employees.

Discouraged Worker—An individual who does not look for employment because he or she believes that jobs are not available or that no jobs are available for which he or she could qualify.

Double-Breasting—A practice, usually confined to the construction industry, wherein a single employer operates two subsidiaries, one unionized and the other nonunion. Employers believe that under this arrangement they can better compete with *open shop* (and nonunion) firms.

Duty of Fair Representation—A union's obligation to represent fairly all individuals in the *bargaining unit*. The Supreme Court has held that the power of a majority representative to speak for all *bargaining unit* employees gives rise to a duty to represent those employees fairly and in good faith. A bargaining representative has a duty both in *collective bargaining* negotiations and in the enforcement of the *collective bargaining agreement* to serve the interests of all members of the bargaining unit without hostility, discrimination, or arbitrary conduct—whether or not members of the bargaining unit are members of the union or voted for the union and whether or not they are members of some racial or ethnic minority group.

Economic Strike—A work stoppage that results from a dispute over wages, hours, and other terms of employment. Economic strikers retain employee status, but they may be permanently replaced and are not entitled to bump their replacements when the strike has been terminated.

Emergency Dispute—A labor-management dispute believed to endanger the public's health or safety.

Employment-at-Will—The doctrine that employment may be terminated by either the employee or the employer without cause. Under this concept, all employees whose *job security* is not protected by a *collective bargaining agreement, tenure,* or civil service law are subject to employment-at-will discharge. In recent years, the employment-at-will doctrine has been challenged in the courts, where the plaintiffs have argued in the main that there is an implicit employment contract between employee and employer that cannot be abrogated by the employer absent due-process proceedings. In some cases, employees who believed they had been unjustly discharged have successfully sued employers for damages.

Fact-Finding—The investigation of a labor-management dispute by a board or panel or an individual usually appointed by the head of a government agency that administers a labor relations law. These boards or, in the case of an individual, fact finders issue reports that describe the issues in a dispute and frequently make recommendations for their solution.

Featherbedding—Labor practices on the part of some unions to make work for their members that is inefficient or unprofitable for the employer. This includes payment for work not performed and the creation of nonessential jobs.

Field Examiner—An employee of the *National Labor Relations Board* whose primary duties are to conduct certification elections and to carry out preliminary investigations of *unfair labor practice* charges. To be distinguished from *administrative law judge.*

Final Offer Arbitration—A type of *interest arbitration* in which the arbitrator selects either the union's or the employer's final proposal. In some instances, the arbitrator selects one side's entire "package," in other cases the final proposal of either party on each issue in dispute. Also known as "last best offer arbitration."

Flexitime—A work scheduling system that allows workers to vary their arrival and departure times but does not change the number of hours they must work. Most flexitime schedules are based on a flexible workday rather than week or month. They require employees to be present for a specified period known as "core time" but allow them to complete the remainder of the required hours at their discretion.

Free Rider—A worker in a *bargaining unit* who is eligible for union membership but does not join the union. Union members maintain that free riders receive all the benefits of the union contract, yet do not pay the dues or fees that make these benefits possible. Opponents of compulsory unionism argue, on the other hand, that no worker should be forced to join a union as a condition of employment. See *agency shop, maintenance-of-membership clause, right-to-work laws,* and *union security.*

Fringe Benefits—Nonwage items and payments received by or credited to workers in addition to wages, often not in exchange for time worked: for instance, *supplemental unemployment benefits,* pensions, vacation and holiday pay, and health insurance. Although fringe benefits antedate World War II, their growth was greatly stimulated in the war years because wage rates were frozen. Since many fringe benefits were not immediately inflationary (some benefits like pensions involved deferred expenditure), they were authorized by the National War Labor Board. In recent years, fringe benefits have accounted for an increasing percentage of worker income and labor costs.

Front-Loaded—Providing a greater wage increase in the early period of a multiyear *collective bargaining agreement* than in the later period—for instance, an 8-percent wage increase in the first year of a three-year agreement and a 7-percent increase in the two years following. See *back-loaded.*

General Strike—A strike by all or most organized workers in a given community or nation. Such strikes usually are politically motivated rather than attempts to improve conditions of work and are rare in the United States.

Good-Faith Bargaining—Negotiations in which two parties meet and confer at reasonable times, minds open to persuasion, with a view to reaching agreement on new contract terms. Good-faith bargaining does not imply that either party is required to make concessions or reach agreement on any proposal. Lack of good-faith bargaining is an *unfair labor practice.*

Grandfather Clause—A contract provision stipulating that employees on the payroll before a specified time will not be subject to certain terms of a new contract. Thus, if all current employees were working under a noncontributory pension plan and the new agreement called for contributions by new hires, current employees would be "grandfathered"—they would still be beneficiaries of the noncontributory plan.

Grievance—Any complaint, usually by an employee but sometimes by the union or management, concerning any aspect of the employment relationship.

Grievance Arbitration—A method of adjudicating a grievance, in which the grievance is submitted to an arbitrator for a final and binding decision, usually the last step of the *grievance procedure.* The arbitrator's task is to determine whether the contract or longstanding work practice, which frequently has the force of a contract provision, has been misinterpreted or misapplied. Sometimes referred to as "rights arbitration."

Grievance Procedure—The steps spelled out in a *collective bargaining agreement* for the handling of *grievances.* The intent of the process is to settle a complaint, customarily an allegation that the contract has been misinterpreted or misapplied, as soon as possible without interrupting the employer's operations. The first step usually occurs at the shop level, where most grievances are settled. If an agreement is not reached at this level, the grievance may be appealed in successive steps. The number and types of these steps vary among contracts. Most procedures call for *arbitration* of grievances as a final step.

Guaranteed Annual Wage (GAW) Plan—An arrangement in which an employer agrees to provide his employees a guaranteed minimum of employment or income for a year. Not widely practiced, GAW has, nonetheless, been an important bargaining issue in recent years. Unions argue that GAW plans add significantly to income and employment stability. Management argues, on the other hand, that GAW does not take into account the fluctuating demand for goods and would add significantly to the risk of investment because wages would have to be paid even if the investment proved unprofitable.

Hiring Hall—A type of employment office, established to meet the needs of workers in the casual trades—for instance, the construction trades, maritime trades, or food services. When the *closed shop* existed, hiring halls were operated exclusively by the unions for the benefit of their members. Since 1947, when the *Taft-Hartley Act* outlawed the closed shop, hiring halls have commonly come to be operated jointly by labor and management, often with state assistance or supervision. A characteristic practice of many hiring halls is the assignment of workers in strict order of their registration for jobs, thus preventing discrimination in job assignments.

Hot Cargo Provisions—Contract provisions that allow workers to refuse to handle or process "hot cargo" goods coming from a plant where there is a labor dispute.

Impasse—In negotiation, a situation in which no further progress in reaching agreement can be made. Either party may determine when an impasse has been reached.

Independent Union—A union that is not affiliated with the AFL-CIO. Not to be confused with *company union.*

Industrial Union—A union representing all workers, both skilled and unskilled, in a plant or industry.

Industrywide Bargaining—A form of *multiemployer bargaining* that results in a *master agreement* negotiated for all employees in an industry by one or more unions representing their workers throughout an entire industry.

Initiation Fees—Payment to a union required of a worker when he or she joins the union, the amount usually being set forth in the union's constitution. The *Taft-Hartley Act* prohibits excessive or discriminatory fees in *union shops,* where workers are required to join the union to remain employed.

Injunction—A court order that restrains an individual or a group from committing acts that the court has determined will do irreparable harm. There are two types of injunctions: temporary restraining orders and permanent injunctions.

Interest Arbitration—Adjudication to resolve an impasse in contract negotiations. Infrequently used in the private sector, interest arbitration has, since the early 1970s, become widespread in the resolution of disputes in the public sector, particularly for police and fire fighters. To be distinguished from *grievance arbitration.* See *final offer arbitration.*

International Representative—A staff officer of an *international union* who is appointed by the union's executive board or president or regional vice-president to serve as liaison between the national or international level of the union and the locals. The international representative usually comes from the ranks of union members, and his or her duties include aiding in the negotiating of contracts, assisting local unions in the handling of *grievances* and other matters, and organizing unorganized shops in the union's *jurisdiction.*

International Union—The national organization of a labor union, so called because many unions have affiliates in Canada. Financially supported by a per capita tax of all its members, its chief functions are extending union organization; chartering *local unions;* setting jurisdictional boundaries; conducting educational programs; doing research in areas related to trade union objectives; engaging in lobbying; aiding local unions in bargaining; and, where *multiemployer bargaining* is used, negotiating directly with industry representatives.

Job Action—A concerted activity by employees on the job designed to put pressure on an employer without resorting to a strike. *Work-to-rule* and *slowdown* are job actions.

Job Security—Generally, the quest to retain one's job. Many union contracts contain provisions that protect jobs for bargaining unit members and provide for fair dismissal or just cause procedures for individuals subjected to discharge.

Jurisdictional Dispute—A conflict between two or more unions over the right of their memberships to perform certain types of work. If the conflict develops into a work stoppage, it is called a *jurisdictional strike.* The term may also refer to conflict between two or more unions over organizing or representing groups of workers. Such conflicts can usually be resolved by a representation election conducted by the *National Labor Relations Board.*

Jurisdictional Strike—A strike resulting from a dispute over representation rights by two rival unions.

Just Cause—Provocation found by an arbitrator to be sufficient to substantiate an employer's disciplinary action. In making the determination, an arbitrator looks at the *collective bargaining agreement,* the customs and standards of the workplace and the community, standards of justice and equity, and the facts of the particular case.

Layoff—Temporary and indefinite separation from work, due usually to slack season, shortage of materials, temporary decline in the market, or other factors over which the worker has no control. To be distinguished from discharge or firing, whereby the worker is permanently separated from his or her job for such reasons as insubordination, absenteeism, or poor job performance, and from termination, in which the job is eliminated.

Lockout—A suspension of work initiated by the employer as the result of a labor dispute. A lockout is the employer counterpart of a strike, which is initiated by the workers. Used primarily to avert a threatened strike.

Maintenance of Membership—A provision in a collective bargaining agreement stating that no worker must join the union as a condition of employment, but all workers who voluntarily join must maintain their membership for the duration of the contract in order to keep their jobs. Most include an escape clause setting aside an interval, usually 10 days or two weeks, during which members may withdraw from the union without penalty.

Management Prerogatives—Rights that management believes are exclusively its own and thus are not subject to collective bargaining. Such rights may include production, scheduling, determining process of manufacture, and so forth.

Mandatory Issue—A bargaining issue upon which the union and management are free to bargain to impasse and are required to bargain in good faith.

Mediation—An attempt by a third party, usually a government official, to bring together the parties in an industrial dispute. The mediator does not have the power to force a settlement. Although often used interchangeably with "conciliation," there is a distinction. Whereas conciliation merely attempts to bring the two sides together, mediation may involve the suggesting of compromise solutions by the third party.

Multiemployer Bargaining—Collective bargaining that involves more than one company in a given industry. It takes such forms as areawide bargaining and industrywide bargaining.

Multiplant Bargaining—Collective bargaining in which the employer negotiates and bargains with more than one plant.

National Emergency Strike—A strike not specifically forbidden by the *Taft-Hartley Act* but that may be enjoined for up to 80 days if, in the opinion of the President of the United States and the appropriate court of competent jurisdiction, it threatens the nation's health or safety.

National Labor Relations Board—A body created by the *National Labor Relations Act* of 1935. The Board's primary duties are to hold elections to determine representation and to interpret and apply the law concerning *unfair labor practices*. The courts may review the Board's decisions on unfair labor practices, but the Board's decisions on representation elections are final.

Negotiation—The process by which representatives of labor and management bargain to set terms and conditions of work, that is, wages, hours, and benefits.

No-Raiding Agreement—A compact among individual *international unions* in which they promise not to persuade workers to leave one union and join another when the first union has established a bargaining relationship. AFL-CIO-affiliated unions in good standing are signators to a general no-raiding pact. In addition, several unions have signed bilateral agreements covering the organization of unorganized workers.

Open Shop—A factory or business establishment in which there is no union. The term is also sometimes applied to places of work in which there is no union or where union membership is not a condition of employment.

Paper Local—Local unions which frequently obtain charters or are self-chartered for the purpose primarily of obtaining payoffs from employers. Such organizations are opposed by legitimate trade unions.

Parity—Equivalence established between the wage schedules of certain categories of employees. Used commonly in the public sector to describe the ratio maintained between the salaries of police and firefighters.

Past Practice—A mutually recognized and consistent employer response to a given set of workplace circumstances over an extended period of time. Wash-up time before the completion of a shift could be an example; allowing employees to leave work early on the day before a holiday could be another.

Pattern Bargaining—A procedure in collective bargaining under which key terms reached in a settlement in one company are closely followed by other companies.

Permissive Issue—A bargaining issue that may be placed on the table by either party, but the other party is not required to bargain over the issue.

Picketing—The actual patrolling at or near the employer's place of business during a strike or other dispute to give notice of the existence of a labor dispute, to publicize it, or to persuade workers to join the union and to discourage or prevent persons from entering or going to work. *Informational picketing* occurs when off-duty employees picket to inform the public of the union's position in a dispute. *Organizational* or *recognition picketing* is an attempt on the part of a union to force the employer to recognize the union.

Preferential Hiring—A form of union security (that may be considered illegal) in which the employer agrees that, in the hiring of new workers, preference will be given to union members.

Premium Pay—An amount greater than the regular rate of pay paid because of inconvenience or unpleasantness. Employees often receive premium pay for working overtime, in late shifts, on holidays, or in hazardous working conditions.

Productivity—A measurement of the efficiency of production; a ratio of output to input.

Productivity Bargaining—A *collective bargaining* arrangement that provides for wage increases based upon the increased *productivity* of the operation. In many instances, wage increases are the quid pro quo for *profit sharing*.

Profit Sharing—A form of compensation to employees based upon the profits of the company and paid in addition to wages. Usually, profit-sharing plans take one of two forms: (1) a cash plan, giving employees a share of profits on a cash basis quarterly, semiannually, or annually; or (2) a deferred plan, in which a trust fund is established and payments are made to workers at the time of their retirement, death, or disability.

Ratification—The process of approval of a newly negotiated collective bargaining agreement by the union membership.

Recognition—Acknowledgment by an employer that the majority of his or her employees in a given bargaining unit want a specific union to represent them in collective bargaining.

Reopening Clause—A provision in a collective bargaining agreement that permits either side to reopen the contract during its term, generally under specific circumstances, to reconsider economic and other issues. Often called a "reopener."

Representation Election—A referendum held among employees in a *bargaining unit* to determine what *bargaining agent,* if any, will represent them for *collective bargaining* purposes.

Retroactive Pay—(1) A delayed wage payment for work done previously at a lower rate. (2) Income due to workers when a new contract provides for a wage increase for work completed prior to the time the contract goes into effect, often dating back to the expiration of the previous contract. A contract signed in June, for instance, may call for a 10-cent-an-hour increase beginning the first day of the previous January, the beginning of the new contract. To be distinguished from *back pay.*

Rights Dispute—A controversy over the interpretation or application of the terms of a *collective bargaining agreement.* Such a dispute is usually dealt with through the *grievance procedures,* sometimes ending up in a grievance arbitration.

Right-to-Work Laws—Provisions in state laws that prohibit the union shop, maintenance of membership, preferential hiring, or any other union-security provisions calling for compulsary union membership.

Roll-up, Impact, Creep, Add-On—Terms commonly used to describe the costs of nonwage contractual items linked to wage rates that must be added to the total cost of a negotiated wage-and-benefit settlement in order to reflect accurately the ultimate labor cost for a given contract term.

Runaway Shop—A unionized business concern that moves to another state or area to escape the union. For many enterprises, however, a decision to move may be prompted by factors other than a desire to employ nonunion labor, such as tax inducements from other communities and the desire to be nearer sources of raw materials or markets.

Scab—An individual who continues to work while a strike is in progress. Also, a worker who is hired to replace one who is on strike.

Secondary Boycott—Pressure exerted on employers who are not directly involved in a dispute. It may involve the refusal to handle or work on products of a company that is dealing with an employer with whom a union has a dispute.

Seniority—The length of continuous employment an employee has in the plant.

Shop Steward—A representative of the union who carries out union duties in the plant or shop. Included here are handling grievances, collecting dues, and recruiting new members. He or she can be either elected by other union members in the plant or appointed by higher union officials.

Slowdown—A concerted and deliberate effort by workers to reduce output and efficiency in order to obtain concessions from an employer.

Speedup—An increase in production without a compensating increase in wages to workers: For example, an assembly line is speeded up, thus increasing production, but there is no increase in wages.

Strike Benefits—Union payments, usually a small proportion of regular income, to workers during a strike. Many unions do not supply monetary aid but distribute groceries and other types of aid to needy striking families.

Strikebreaker—An outsider brought in by an employer to fill a job vacated by a striker. Often an employer attempts to break a strike by hiring outsiders so as to lower the strikers' morale and to maintain production. See *scab.*

Strike Fund—Money put aside, generally by the international union, to defray the expenses of a strike. Strike expenses cover strike benefits to individual members, legal fees, publicity, and other miscellaneous expenses.

Strike Notice—A notice filed with the *Federal Mediation and Conciliation Service* or appropriate state agency that the union has rejected the company's latest offer and a strike is impending. The *National Labor Relations Act* requires that, if a *collective bargaining agreement* exists between the union and the employer, the union may not call a strike until 60 days after it has notified the employer of its desire to modify or terminate the existing agreement. The union must also notify the Federal Mediation and Conciliation Service within 30 days of notifying the employer. If the union strikes without observing these rules, the strikers lose the rights granted to them by the act.

Struck Work—A situation where work done is for an employer or company whose employees are on strike.

Sweetheart Contract—A *collective bargaining agreement,* usually between a racketeer head of a *paper local* (but sometimes a legitimate union) and a corrupt employer. The employer's advantages in such an arrangement are that legitimate unions then have difficulty in organizing the shop, the employer pays less in wages and in other benefits, and he or she has to contend with few restrictions. The union racketeer benefits from the payoff received from the grateful employer or the dues collected from employees or both. Sweetheart contracts were denounced by the AFL-CIO in its *Code of Ethical Practices.*

Sympathy Strike—A strike by workers not directly involved in a labor dispute; an attempt to demonstrate labor solidarity.

Tenure—A form of *job security,* customarily confined to educational employees, although civil service employees also have a form of tenure protection. Tenure is achieved after a specified probationary period has been served, in academic institutions usually from three to six years. An individual with tenure has assurance of continuous employment and can be terminated only because of unusual financial exigencies, or for *just cause.* In the latter instance, a terminated employee often has the protection of a due-process procedure.

Trusteeship—Assumption of control over a *local union* by an *international union,* which suspends the normal governmental process of a local union and takes over management of the local's assets and the administration of its internal affairs. The constitutions of many international unions authorize international officers to establish trusteeships over local unions in order to prevent corruption, mismanagement, and other abuses. The *Landrum-Griffin Act* of 1959 established controls over the establishment and administration of trusteeships.

Two-Tier Wages—An arrangement whereby compensation of new hires is substantially below that of current employees doing the same work. Two-tier wage structures became widespread in the airline industry during the late 1970s and early 1980s in part because of the intense competition that resulted from the deregulation of that industry. Unions have objected strongly to this practice.

Unfair Labor Practice—An action of either union or management that violates provisions of national or state labor relations acts. Failing to bargain in good faith is an example of an unfair labor practice on the part of either management or a union.

Union Dues—Periodic payments, usually on a monthly basis, paid by members to the union in order to defray the costs of the organization. Their amount is set by either the constitution or the by-laws and is subject to revision by the membership.

Union Label—An imprint attached to a manufactured product (e.g., clothing, printing) indicating that work on the article was done by union workers. Unions often encourage their members and the public at large to buy only products bearing this label to enhance the economic positions of those unions using the label.

Union Organizer—Member of a staff of a *local union* or *international union* whose main function is to recruit new members.

Union Security Clauses—Provisions in collective bargaining agreements designed to protect the union against employers, nonunion employees, and/or raids by competing unions. For more complete information on the significance of this clause, see Chapter 6, "Management and Union Security."

Union Shop—A form of union security that allows the employer to hire whomever he or she pleases but requires all new employees to become members of the union within a specified period of time after being hired and to retain membership as a condition of continuing employment.

Unit Determination—The process of establishing a unit of appropriate job titles for the purpose of *collective bargaining*. The *National Labor Relations Board* and state labor relations agencies frequently use the following criteria when determining a *bargaining unit:* the desire of the employees, similarity of skills or occupations, collective bargaining history, and the organizational structure of the employer organization. Membership in a bargaining unit determines whether an employee may vote in a *representation election;* members of a bargaining unit are covered by the terms of subsequently negotiated collective bargaining elections. See *certification.*

Wildcat Strike—A work stoppage that violates the contract and is not authorized by the union.

Work Rules—Regulations stipulating on-the-job conditions of work, usually incorporated in the *collective bargaining agreement.* Examples include (1) limiting production work of supervisory personnel, (2) limiting the assignment of work outside an employee's classification, (3) requiring a minimum number of workers on a job, and (4) limiting the use of labor-saving methods and equipment. Work rules are also imposed by the employer (see *management prerogatives*), and in some cases, unions may seek to impose their own work rules without incorporating them in the agreement. The purpose of work rules from the union point of view is to maximize employment opportunities, ensure decent working conditions and health standards, and protect workers from arbitrary employer action. Employers complain that work rules are frequently responsible for waste and inefficiency and that they are merely a form of *featherbedding* and encroach on management prerogatives. The issue of work rules has assumed increasing importance in recent years in the negotiation of collective bargaining agreements.

Work-to-Rule—A type of job action whereby employees perform only the minimum tasks required of them by official rules or regulations. Employees sometimes use the work-to-rule technique in attempts to win concessions in circumstances where a strike is illegal.

Yellow-Dog Contract—An agreement between an employer and a worker that provides as a condition of employment that the worker will refrain from joining a union or, if a member, will leave the organization. The *Norris-Laguardia Act* of 1932 nullified the yellow-dog contract by declaring it unenforceable in the courts.

Zipper Clause—A standard provision in a negotiated contract that attempts to preclude any negotiations of employment conditions during the life of the contract. The clause asserts that the agreement is the sole and complete instrument between the parties.

Index